THE COMPLETE HISTORY OF
CROSS-COUNTRY
RUNNING

FROM THE NINETEENTH CENTURY TO THE PRESENT DAY

Andrew Boyd Hutchinson
Foreword by Craig Virgin

CARREL BOOKS

Dedicated to all runners who possess imagination, and to those who have ever been curious as to the origin of things . . . and to my parents.

"Thank you for this fascinating well-researched story of cross-country racing through the ages. While narrating the evolution of this most basic and inclusive of sports, you have given the reader opportunity to feel the allure of the never-ending challenges and adventures that come with the preparation and competition over hills and barriers, across fields and streams—frequently in harsh weather—at the World Cross-Country Championships. To paraphrase Paula Radcliffe, who has expressed my sentiments so well, winning such a championship is as rewarding as an Olympic medal, for all the best of the world's runners are there together in one race. And all know the journey to be equally rewarding, as is the privilege of competing for one's country and with teammates."

—Doris Brown Heritage, five-time International Cross-Country Champion, five-time US National Cross-Country Champion, and first female member of the Cross-Country and Road Running Committee of the IAAF.

"I have only praise for *The Complete History of Cross-Country Running*. Our most powerful connection with our atavistic nature is running over the land. Out of the African savannahs, through European pastures, over western mountain trails and golf courses, this is what formed and perpetuated our hunter ancestors—the long chase. This wonderful history is absolutely crucial to understanding how we have incorporated our running into society for millennia. Well, well done."

—Kenny Moore, author of Bowerman and the Men of Oregon, US National Cross-Country Champion (1967) and founding member, US Olympic Committee's Athletes Advisory Council.

"Cross-country running has always represented the 'soul' of running, which after all is supposed to launch human athletes into the natural environment. Andrew Hutchinson's *Complete History* is just that—a complete and entertaining account of cross-country's long and colorful past. You can't read these pages without reflecting on your own best cross-country days, or maybe plotting for the next one."

—Amby Burfoot, 1968 Boston Marathon Winner, *Runner's World* Editor at Large.

"Andrew Hutchinson's engaging history calls us to take to the trails, brush off the dust of civilization and enjoy the thrill and challenge of cross-country running. From its origins in British schoolboy races to shopgirls in France, he dives into a largely unknown corner of history and illuminates the colorful ancestry of a sport I love."

—Mina Samuels, author of *Run Like a Girl: How Strong Women Make Happy Lives.*

"Cross-country is what made me love running from the very beginning, and it gets far too little attention within the world of racing today. Hutchinson does an excellent job connecting the past with the present in this detailed description of harrier history. If you are not a cross-country runner or fan, you will be after this book."

—Ryan Vail, five-time All-American at Oklahoma State University, five-time member of Team USA at the World Cross-Country Championships (earning team silver in 2013), 2:10 marathoner, Brooks Athlete.

"Andrew Boyd Hutchinson's *Complete History of Cross-Country* is an ambitious examination of cross-country running and the special past that makes it one of the world's purest sports."

—Liam Fayle, HAWI Management.

"Cross-country has always been my favorite discipline and Andrew's book reminds me why it is such a great sport. The simplicity and history of the sport is difficult to put into words and Andrew has done an amazing job chronicling the important historical points and describing the feel of racing off through fields and over fencerows. The amount of effort Andrew puts into researching the past is one of the great aspects of this book. He also passionately recounts the events and characters of modern cross-country that have continued to raise the bar on American cross-country and it's impact around the world."

—Max King, four-time World Cross-Country member for Team USA.

"Andrew Hutchinson's *Complete History of Cross-Country Running* is a detailed look at the history of cross-country running. The book drives into a detailed account of the sport including all the sweat, mud, and drama. Hutchinson doesn't miss a beat in this book telling the fascinating history of cross-country running."

—Margaret Schlachter, author of *Obstacle Race Training* and founder of the award-winning website Dirt in Your Skirt.

"I really liked *The Complete History of Cross-Country Running*. It was detailed and well-written. I found that I was forced to focus on learning about the sport, and that is a positive for both the educated runner and the casual fan. What I really enjoyed was the first chapter. Andrew pulled information from a span of history that I had never known, and here I am in my 17th year of running. I think that really shows how important it is for a book to come out that points out the foundation of our sport instead of the countless we already have that just talk about the present. *The Complete History of Cross-Country* is a genius account of how this seemingly crazy spectacle grew its roots into a healthy and heavily participated sport across the world."

—Craig Lutz, 2016 US National Cross-Country Champion.

"A fantastic read, for coaches and young cross-country runners across America who are involved in this brilliant, competitive, high-level sport!"

—Bill Rodgers, World Cross-Country Championship medalist.

"For anyone who came up running as a kid our memories are flooded with crisp fall mornings running and racing through the forest during cross-country. Even after competing in a couple of Olympics in the marathon and spending most of my time on the roads, still, whenever fall rolls around I find myself reminiscing about cross-country. Yet, rarely are the war stories of cross-country told. Andrew does a brilliant job compiling a complete history of cross-country running. I've never seen such a thorough celebration and telling of the beautiful sport that cross-country is."

—Ryan Hall, Olympic marathoner.

The Athenian Greek was the most perfect natural man that history records; certainly the most consummate physical being the world has known, and in his education the care and development of his body came first. In the Palestra, the Gymnasium . . . the Greek youth was taught to make his body a perfect habitation for his mind.

—Colonel Charles W. Larned, United States Military Academy

When you experience the run, you relive the hunt. Running is about 30 miles of chasing prey that can outrun you in a sprint, and tracking it down and bringing life back to your village. It's a beautiful thing.

—Shawn Found, Olympic Trials Competitor and University of Colorado Graduate

The start, the sprint,
The spikes that flail.
The biting, frosty air inhale.
Across the plough,
Up hill and down dale,
The field, the ditch, the paper trail.
The end in sight, the last half-mile;
The race is lost, but the run's worth while.

—Lawrence N. Richardson, *Jubilee History of the International Cross-Country Union 1903–1953*

Never stop at the top, never dally in the valley—Oh,
Do not shilly-shally when you hear the shout of Tally-ho.
Up, down, chase around, obey the master's call—
Till hares are caught, no hunter ought, to take a rest at all.

—Reputed Winner of the 1998 Trevelyan Lake Hunt Sing-Song

Contents

Foreword

Long before there were tracks or roads, man ran over the natural landscape, either away from danger or after a food source. Running was a skill, key to survival. But, I'm sure that many youth back then also ran for the fun of it or in competitive games—for the esteemed honor of being deemed one of the "fastest" in their tribe, a title that still appeals to young people today.

Fast-forward centuries, and we have three disciplines of organized competitive running: track and field, road racing, and cross-country. Of the three, cross-country was, and still is, my first love! I first experienced it as a freshman in high school and was smitten from the first meet on. It was the perfect sport for an Illinois farm boy like me. Maybe that's why the Kenyans and Ethiopians are also so good at it—as much of their economy remains agrarian-based and many of their best runners grow up on farms—with the requisite hard work that raising crops and livestock entails. Running after animals in a pasture or from a tractor in the field back to the homestead is just part of the job. Doing so at altitude makes one even tougher, as the East Africans have shown on a yearly basis.

Growing up in Southwestern Illinois I had a farm life experience, like my East African competitors, which fostered an appreciation for both the soil and the terrain, as well as the weather. Running on grass or dirt, up and down hills, in all weather conditions is what this sport is all about. Cross-country is the most "organic and all-natural" of all running sports today . . . maybe even of all sports, period.

Being from the United States, my cross-country experience initially revolved around my school years, first in high school and then at university. Like my prior sports of baseball and basketball, cross-country is a team sport. Unlike those sports, cross-country also features an individual aspect of measured competition as well. One's satisfaction can be derived from the team accomplishment, from individual results, or both. This dual team and individual aspect is very much part of the charm of cross-country.

The worldwide aspect of cross-country cannot be overlooked. Almost all countries participate in the World Championships. In America, cross-country is organized as competition between school teams, while the rest of the world organizes competitions between non-school clubs of young and old alike. In much of the world, distance runners of all ages prepare for their track seasons by competing in cross-country. It fosters the development of endurance and stamina that presents a perfect base for any distance runner to build before the athlete transitions back to the track. In America, most cross-country competitions are staged from August to November. In Europe, they are staged from November to March.

Even current International Association of Athletics Federations (IAAF) president and former world record middle-distance runner, Sebastian Coe, has gone on record stating that cross-country is the perfect preparation for all track mid- and long-distance competitors. While based on his own personal athletic career and "old school," his praise is important because the survival of the IAAF World Cross-Country Championships may hang in the balance over the next few years. Cross-country will soon need "friends in high places" if the IAAF is to rebrand and reorganize the World Championships in order to survive and thrive in the future.

Cross-country is cost-effective. The fact that the same shoes and apparel can double back for track in the spring makes it very attractive to schools, clubs, families, and individuals. Entry fees are usually reasonable. It is also gender-equal, as both men and women have the same opportunities to compete even if their distances might be different. Finally, cross-country courses do not cost millions of dollars to build, but access to land is imperative—usually involving school property, parks, or other public lands. The best courses are laid out to be participant- and spectator-friendly while still challenging to the competitors. Today's technology even allows intermediate team scores to be calculated and screened digitally, which makes cross-country more exciting for the fan, and friendly to the media. "Lowest score wins" is an easy concept to grasp to stay informed during the race. In short, the sport is affordable, easy to organize and watch, not hard to understand, and offers equal opportunity gender-wise. And, it makes its participants generally healthier. What's not to like about any of that?

If you ever ran cross-country, you may have wondered just how and where the sport got started. This book tells you all that and more. The author, Andrew Boyd Hutchinson, has taken the time and energy to intensively research the sport like nothing I have ever seen. This is an incredible compilation of sport-specific history. The fact that he traces cross-country back to its infant days in the early to mid-1800s in England is fascinating. This book details the growth and development of cross-country as well as the people, teams, places, and events that shaped the sport as the decades went by. You can find out everything significant you ever wanted to know about the sport as you read this book, and I know it will occupy a special place of honor on my reference bookshelf. To better understand the past makes for a deeper appreciation of the present, and a wiser plan for the future of the sport as well. So, grab a comfortable chair and settle back in for a long enjoyable read to learn almost everything possible about the sport we call cross-country.

—Craig Virgin, three-time Olympian, two-time World Cross-Country champion

Preface

On Monday, December 9, 2013, Sebastian Coe welcomed more than one hundred association participants and cross-country champions to the Serbian capital of Belgrade for the International Association of Athletics Federations (IAAF) Global Seminar on Cross-Country Running. Featured guests included cross-country gold medalists Annette Sergent of France and Craig Virgin of the United States and recent champions Benjamin Limo of Kenya, Sonia O'Sullivan of Ireland, and Paula Radcliffe of Great Britain. These athletes spoke on the importance of cross-country and how it has helped them to succeed in their track and road careers.

"Doing well at the World Cross-Country Championships was a catalyst for all my other successes," reflected Virgin, whose thoughts were echoed by the other attendees. A roundtable panel represented by various stakeholders in athletics (and cross-country running specifically) answered questions on issues ranging from the international calendar and structure, to the possibility of cross-country running returning to the Olympic Games.

Coe, who moderated the event, stated, "We have a challenge to maintain a global perspective on this aspect of the sport, which not only has great tradition, but tremendous potential, not only as a unique discipline, but as a bedrock of endurance running."

The purpose of this meeting was aimed at resuscitation. Paula Radcliffe, an English National Cross-Country champion and five-time medalist at World Cross, believed the worldwide appeal of cross-country captured the essence of distance running. "It's relentless. There's nothing like it," she said. "I keep saying it's as good as winning the Olympics, or better, because all the top runners are there, in the one race." A long-distance footrace featuring the world's best, against nature's toughest terrain and weather, deserved to be a sought-after event.

Many believed that the governance of the IAAF was responsible for the downplaying of cross-country running, as they oversaw all major athletics competitions. But changes had been a long time coming. Exactly one hundred years earlier, at a board meeting for the International Cross-Country Union, a resolution was adopted to standardize the course layout for the sport. "The country promoting the International should provide as natural a cross-country course as possible," the resolution stated, "and the course should include some hill, natural or other obstacles such as ditches, gates, or hedges and a little road."

That course credence was no longer recognizable. In one hundred years the distance had shortened for the men: first from 14.5 kilometers to 12 kilometers (in 1963), and finally to 10 kilometers (in 2017). In 2011, only one city, Bydgoszcz, in Poland, sent in a request to host the event. "I can say that at the moment, we are only having one bid from Bydgoszcz," IAAF secretary general Pierre Weiss was quoted as saying. "Bahrain had a good running course, but it has been worked on and it is not the same. So they are out." Having only two bids for a World Championship was startling.

Even recent participants expressed complaints. "Cross-country racing comes from a background of running through plowed fields, going down dirt trails and maybe even hopping over a couple of fences. Somehow we've gotten away from that. It's become more of a grass track meet," claimed 2008 World Cross participant Max King.

Dathan Ritzenhein, a three-time US champion and 2001 World Cross medalist, shared, "I loved it before, but it's lost its luster. It's held every other year now and the locations are not as good. If the crowd's not into it, and the athletes aren't going, then that's just the way it's going to go."

How could a sport with such a vibrant participation level see such demise? In 2012, the *Wall Street Journal* reported that participation was on the rise at the National Collegiate Athletic Association (NCAA) Division I level: up 19 percent over the ten preceding years. The National Federation of State High School Associations determined that over half a million high school boys and girls had participated in cross-country annually over the last decade. So where was the disconnect? One problem, among many, was that the cumulative history of the sport lay dormant; forgotten, unassembled, unrecognized . . . lost.

Unlike track and field and road running, which had easy-to-manage lists of top athletes and times (along with historical venues with great traditions), similar attention had not been paid to cross-country. "Track and field is spectacular, but you can't help knowing 'What's his split?' the eternal refrain of the track coach," said Dennis Young of the US Track & Field and Cross-Country Coaches Association. "No one cares about splits in cross-country. In a sport that's been mostly bleached of any messy subjectivity, cross-country remains wonderfully untamed and unknowable." Untamed running was a wonderful opportunity for athletes looking to escape the track, but "unknowable" revealed a different problem. There was nowhere an athlete could go to learn about the stories, legacies, and processes in developing the sport. That had to change.

The interest in the sport remains. The participation numbers speak for themselves, and the experts agree. As Sebastian Coe stated when he oversaw the Global Seminar on Cross-Country Running, "Cross-country should be a standard part of preparation for middle- and long-distance athletes. Until we get back to recognizing that cross-country is an important part of the conditioning process then we will not see standards of European distance running rise." It's time to raise the standards, and instill the importance of this fascinating sport.

The Arrow

All sports have special abbreviations and insignia, cross-country running included. Additionally, the association between cross-country running and track and field has often been inexorably linked. Both fall under the umbrella of athletics, and each has a unique history and appeal: distance runners yearning for the outdoors in the autumn will leave the track as summer wanes and head for the trails—only to return again in the spring.

This book seeks to separate these unique sports. Cross-country, while connected to track and field, has a history steeped in tradition away from the athletics stadium. Yet as distance running's greatest names often compete in both disciplines in their careers, an isolated examination of cross-country on its own is impossible. Later decades will clarify why both are important. In fact, the association of track and cross-country can even be found in their respective logos.

The origin of the cross-country logo bears explaining. Simple and straightforward, it consists of an arrow superimposed on a CC or XC abbreviation. But why an arrow?

Explanations range from convenient misconceptions to the wholly inaccurate. One myth suggests the logo represents Native Americans firing arrows during a hunt and retrieving the arrows that missed their target (commonly translated as "running to the point where the arrow has struck"). Another misconception was that the arrow was used as a convenience: a practical design element pointing the direction to run.

Of the two, the directionally inspired arrow is closest to the truth, and history gives clues as to where it originated. The game "Chalk the Corner" (a forebearer to modern cross-country running) gained popularity along the East Coast and the Midwest in the mid-nineteenth century. Leaders often used chalk to mark a freely designed path. Occasionally at intersections, forerunning youth would chalk an arrow to indicate the direction they ran. Those in pursuit would have to check off the arrows as they followed, ensuring they marked the correct path. As the sport changed, it was accepted that the arrow design was kept as a nod to this older game.

Unsurprisingly, some of the earliest recorded evidence of the cross-country logo appears in the urban Midwest. The 1921 Michigan State University cross-country team gives early photographic evidence of the insignia, worn on their team sweater. And as early as 1911, Eastern High School in Detroit ran an invitational race in which the first five to finish were awarded an orange "ECCC" (Eastern Cross-Country Championship) script monogram with a black arrow extending through it. However, there exists a more ancient connection that forms the best argument of all.

The Greek god Apollo, a solar deity known for being fleet of foot, was depicted with winged sandals, necessary as he carried the sun across the horizon. According to Greek mythology, Apollo gave his half-brother Hermes the winged sandals as a prize for being the fleetest of foot of all the gods. Hermes remained the patron god of the gymnastic games for the Greeks, and from the first Olympic contests was connected to athletics. Even in modern day, the winged foot, or winged shoe, is commonly associated with the track and field logo and abbreviation.

Apollo had a twin sister, Artemis, who was described by Homer as "Artemis of the wildland, Mistress of Animals." The Hellenistic goddess of the wilderness, Artemis was most known for having hunting dogs and a sacred connection to deer. But she also had a golden bow and arrows, given to her by Zeus and fashioned by the Cyclops.

As Apollo's winged sandals are associated with track and field, his twin sister Artemis's golden arrows appear for cross-country running: a symbol of strength, and a reminder of the connection between these twin disciplines within athletics.

Glossary of Important Terms

SISU: A uniquely Finnish ideal that literally translates to "having courage against the odds," this quality enables athletes from Finland to resolve difficult situations whether in war or sport. *Sisu* is Finland's capacity—their willpower—to make superhuman efforts at the spur of the moment.

PACK: For runners, this term originated with the game "Hare-and-Hounds," the precursor to modern cross-country. The "pack" represented the group of runners who chased down the "hares" or leading trail-layers. Today, pack running remains a common goal within teams both for training and racing, and for scoring purposes.

SCRATCH: This term describes a runner who starts without a time handicap. Popularized in the late nineteenth century, runners of varying abilities were given a set amount of time to start ahead of the field (or in some cases, the field was given a head start ahead of the best runner), so that even with varying ability, all runners would be heading to the finish line at the same time. The phrase "to start from scratch" (to begin something without prior preparation) originated with handicap footraces. The term "scratch" has been applied since the eighteenth century to describe a starting line that was scratched on the ground, and has usages in cricket, boxing, and golf, among other sports.

HANDICAP: This term refers to an amount of time allotted for slower runners to start ahead of the field. The term originated with a wagering game as early as 1653, and the term appeared 101 years later in horse racing, where superior horses carried extra weight to equalize the field. Over time, the word "handicap" came to refer to any specific action that worked to make a contest more equitable. In running, it means to give runners of different abilities the opportunity to finish a race at the same time.

CRACK: A "crack" distance runner refers to a top talent. In the late 1800s and early 1900s, the term appeared in many contexts where both quickness and accuracy were involved, such as "crack shot" or "crackerjack wit." In French, the term *craquer* signifies "to boast."

PEDESTRIANISM: This is a nineteenth-century term for any wager opportunity dependent on the legs (including running and racewalking). During the late eighteenth and nineteenth centuries, "pedestrianism," like horse racing (equestrianism), was a popular spectator sport and became a fixture at fairs—developing from wagers on footraces, rambling, and seventeenth-century footman wagering. As early as the seventeenth century, sources in England tell of aristocrats pitting their carriage footmen, constrained to walk by the speed of their masters' carriages, against one another. By the end of the eighteenth century, feats of foot travel over great distances gained attention, and were labeled "pedestrianism." As the sport of cross-country running grew in England, it fell under this category in the public eye.

CHECKS: Referred to as "the usual checks and falses," a "check" in Hare-and-Hounds concerned a false paper-chase trail. The intention of the hares leading the pack was to devise a route with the most difficult terrain possible. Frequently, this also meant laying multiple paper trails that faded out, or ended abruptly, to keep the pack off the right path. These dead-end trails were called "checks," as the trailing runners had to check to make sure that the path they were following was valid. A term popularized in chess matches, checks helped to prolong the game as the following group had to investigate all possible routes to finish.

LAW: This term refers to the time between forerunning hares setting a trail and the hounds following in pursuit. In timed versions of Hare-and-Hounds, "law" would be set before the pack could pursue the hares laying the trail. The word applied to the control and regulation of the game, with the only "law" being that the hares had an advantage to lay the paper trail.

Chapter 1

That night, everyone studied the map and flicked through the old log books detailing past catches. I gleaned all I could about the game. Hounds were described as "grey, unrecognizable figures, with cruel, animal, nightmare faces advancing along by silent leaps." They were involved in "stalking, bravading, cliff-scaling and scientific circumnavigations—resulting in the desperate chase and slaughter of the more injured hare." The most devious would drop prone on rocks, pretending to be injured, so the hare would feel obliged to come to the rescue. But the hares, the "vermin," could be equally terrifying. There were legends of some hares defending themselves with iron-shod beams.

—Alice Thomson

YEARS 1800–1850: THE HUNT BEGINS

The call of the hunt permeated over the still earth. All that could be heard were the sounds of footsteps and shallow breathing, eyes stinging in the early autumn air, nostrils bleeding with moisture, muscles burning as the ground swept underfoot. Cross-country running was born in the hearts of the young men of Shrewsbury School, yearning to escape the confines of society; it was simple, principled, and universally adaptable. Well before modern conveniences, the hunt originated prior to society as we know it now.

The first recorded evidence of cross-country running as a sport appeared at the dawn of the Victorian Age. In the northwest Midlands of England, rolling fields, and wet, marshy grassland cultured a schoolboy's game that would transform from a rebellious, spirited undertaking into one of the world's most accessible pastimes. In the quiet mornings and cool evenings of Shrewsbury—an academy proud of its rigorous academics and development of men with character—the soul of cross-country running was forged from a restless fire. The Shrewsbury schoolboys harnessed their adolescent adrenaline, answered the call of the outdoors, and aligned with their comrades to escape the rigor and discipline of the classroom. These were the seeds that allowed the sport to grow on a global scale.

As a sport, cross-country running did not initially appear in the form that we know it today. In fact, it "simplified" over time. Originally, a variety of games accounted for cross-country, but they all followed the same principles. Shrewsbury School called their game "The Hounds" as early as 1819. Rugby School, one hundred miles to the southeast, established "Big Side Hare-and-Hounds" by

1837. Eton College's "Steeplechase" appeared before 1846. In fact, a game called "Hunt the Fox" or "Hunt the Hare" had been referenced in English schoolboy literature as early as the Elizabethan Age. For example, in a poem titled "The Longer Thou Livest the More Foul Thou Art," first published in 1568, the following is part of a speech made by an idle schoolboy: "And also when we play and hunt the fox, I outrun all the boys at the schoole." Other variations of the game appeared during the nineteenth century, and they adopted a recognizable nickname, the "Paper-Chase" (also referenced as "paper-chasing"), in addition to Hare-and-Hounds.

In every instantiation, cross-country running began out of imitation. An earlier organized sport, fox hunting on horseback, predates the earliest "Hunt the Fox" footrace reference by more than one hundred years. In addition, horseback steeplechases came into fashion in Ireland and England in the late 1700s—as an analogue to cross-country horse races, which went from church steeple to church steeple. In both cases, young men were imitating the privileged class's ability to partake in these events. The allure of the outdoors, the excitement of the chase, the social benefit, and the following in the footsteps of the more adventurous elite inspired the practice of hare-and-hound runs and foot-steeplechases in the early nineteenth century.

Hare-and-Hounds was a simple game. Hares (sometimes called foxes) were pre-delegated runners who laid a trail for others to follow. With a grace period known as "law," they dropped pieces of paper on a random course. In pursuit came two groups: the hounds (usually younger runners who followed any leads for the course) and the pack, sometimes called the field (the most experienced runners at the back poised to run in at the sight of the hares).

The Elizabethan variation of "Hunt the Fox" more closely resembled hide-and-seek, with an undetermined chase route. Formally, the game of Hare-and-Hounds involved an agreed-upon time for law, and a route or set boundary for direction. All manner of obstacles was encouraged—and deviations from the course were expected (the hounds would cover any "checks" where the paper trail was lost). Those in pursuit were expected to cover many false trails, as well as incur the delay for water-crossings, bogs, hedges, fences, hills, ditches, logs, and other barriers in the way.

Once the hares ran out of paper, the paper sack was laid in a line, and in some cases the end point for the paper trail was predetermined. In either case, the run-in would occur when all parties gathered at this mark and then the true race would start. Hounds would be timed in the sprint home, with victory awarded to the first finisher. Overall time was also recorded in most cases, for the length of the hunt and for the fastest and slowest runners. Those who completed the runs in top form became legends, and were sometimes awarded prizes: goblets, plates, cups, trophies, or medals.

Measured courses and foot-grinds also gained popularity along with paper-chasing in England. Modeled after true steeplechases, the trails were riddled with all manner of fences and hedges to obscure and complicate the footrace. While less common than Hare-and-Hounds until the middle of the nineteenth century, they were also a notable forebearer to modern cross-country running.

Did You Know?

There were common variations on Hare-and-Hounds. Occasionally hares resisted capture by outsmarting their pursuers in daylong marathon hunts. More often, timekeeping was ignored. Some alternatives were to use flour or ribbon to mark the course, while in urban climates participants used chalk. More traditional hunts sounded horns when a hare was sighted. Other forms of the game insisted the purpose was to punish the hares upon capture, and stories in the 1800s abound with ugly consequences for more precarious chases.

While references to "Hunt the Fox" exist prior to the dates recorded at Shrewsbury School, the weathered books kept for the Royal Shrewsbury School Hunt contain the earliest accounts written by students themselves. In sketchy black ink, the records adjust annually with each new secretary. The oldest is dated 1831, and references indicate the sport was established at Shrewsbury by 1819—almost twenty years before Thomas Hughes ran "Big Side Hare-and-Hounds" at Rugby (Hughes was often misattributed to having recorded the first account of Hare-and-Hounds).

The detail within the Shrewsbury *Hound Books* is staggering. Every run has a report (twice a week between September and Christmas) with the route, participants, distance, time, and any adventures worthy of note. The runs acquired names ("The Tucks and The Long," "The Benjies," "The Bog," "The Drayton"), as did the students who took part. Hounds rebelled against social constructs, and inside jokes and stories united the group.

Runners enjoyed sharing three great passions apart from running: eating, drinking, and trespassing. They liked to "refresh themselves" during runs and occasionally they would stop to "imbibe punch at the farm of N. Lloyd Esq." or rehydrate, as one entry states, when they "washed the hounds' mouths out with some beer" and "regaled our pack with punch." While running "The Long," students drank beer and sherry at the inn at Atcham. On special occasions, they feasted ("were regaled with a substantial repast").

The books tell of the "Huntsman" who would appear dressed in a black cap, scarlet jersey, and stockings, and would set the pace. The "Gentlemen of the Run" would follow the first group in the pack, running without coats and carrying bludgeons to ward off the stone-throwing town "toughs" who would harass the runners. The final group would be a second division of runners, clad in mortarboard hats and gowns. By the end, participants often had a few cuts and bruises to show for their efforts, but all who took part seemed to enjoy the excitement.

The Shrewsbury headmaster, Dr. Benjamin Kennedy, a reputable Latin scholar, attempted to constrain the students. But, the *Hound Books* record, "as stolen fruit is always the sweetest, we determined to revive the good old custom of running out of bounds." Stories recounted vaulting hedges, enraging a nearby miller, defying farmers, chasing off neighboring dogs, and taking off down a secluded road known as Fornicators Lane. Dr. Kennedy attempted to make runners wear mortarboards, locked their dormitories, and stood out in the cold to take the names of those breaking the rules (they whooped by on the other side of the hedge). Once, students reported, "Ben nabbed the scent bag." For revenge they shredded copies of his recently published *Kennedy's Latin Primer* textbook to use for the paper trail. "Frantic but fruitless" was how they described his efforts to undo the damage.

Not surprisingly, relations with local farmers and other school authorities were not always harmonious. The *Hound Books* recorded "altercations" with local farmers, "threats," and "burning execrations." The boys apparently bore no grudges. After one infuriated old man threatened "a summunds" against them, the runners responded, "saying good for the old fellow we struck into the lane."

But while the *Hound Books* gave great first-person detail, one of the most fascinating misconceptions of cross-country running had to do with its true origin. *Tom Brown's Schooldays*, a Victorian novel written by Thomas Hughes in 1857, focused on the life of a schoolboy at Rugby School. Not only was this work frequently cited as being the impetus for future organizations to start their own harrier clubs, but it was often misattributed as being the earliest record of hare-and-hound running as well. Hughes intended the book to be well-referenced and included many personal diatribes from his own experiences in sports and scholarship. And despite overtones of his own moral and religious convictions, Hughes's story was largely historically accurate. *Tom Brown's Schooldays* received mass distribution, was widely read and accepted, and saw exposure in a way Shrewsbury's *Hound Books*, merely record entries kept at the school, could not.

In the opening chapters, set in Tom Brown's home area in the English countryside, Hughes showed that the growth of organized sports in the nineteenth century had roots in age-old rural festivals with games, fights, and races. Any new education, he claimed, would need "some equivalent for the games of the old country 'veast' [feast or festival]; something to put in place of the backswording and wrestling and racing." Furthermore, Rugby's account of "Big Side Hare-and-Hounds" was one of the most valuable influences on cross-country running. Hughes stated that Big Side Hare-and-Hounds was an actual institution at Rugby, so it wasn't just written in the story—it gave first-person detail to the manner of experience needed on the paper trail.

The effect of *Tom Brown's Schooldays* was not just idealistic; Big Side Hare-and-Hounds provided a model for others to follow. *Schooldays* inspired the first adult harrier club, Thames Hare and Hounds, founded near London in 1868. Thames's first president, Walter Rye, was also cross-country running's first historian. The club's history, *The Annals of Thames Hare and Hounds*, affirmed "Walter Rye always said that the idea of paper-chasing came to him from *Tom Brown's Schooldays*," and Thomas Hughes was an invited judge in the second event that Thames hosted, the Thames Handicap Steeplechase Number 2. Beyond England, Pierre de Coubertin, the founder of the modern Olympics, kept the Rugby myth alive. He read *Schooldays* at the age of twelve and developed his Olympic ideals during a visit to England's schools in 1883. He praised Rugby School's principal, Thomas Arnold, as the first to support athletics in education.

Rugby School kept their own version of the *Hound Books* from as early as 1837. Aptly titled *The Big Side Books* for Big Side Hare-and-Hounds, these books recorded runs, times, places, and participants that rivaled the intricacies found in any other. *The Big Side Books* also had an appointed secretary since 1837. Known as "The Holder of Big Side Books," this secretary would delegate four years in succession and then pass the title down the line for the next four years (the first name recorded was S. F. Craddock).

The earliest records showed at least five runs being a fixture at Rugby School: "Barby Hill," "Bilton," "Lawford," "Lilbourne and Catthorpe," and "Thurlaston." In 1838, the "Crick Run" first appears with several others. The Barby Hill Run was run over an eight-mile distance, roughly 13 kilometers. Rugby's Crick Run was over 14 miles. Walter Lea was the first recorded winner of the Crick; and the first recorded winner of the Barby Hill was Arthur Hugh Clough, the poet. At this early stage the routes used weren't always fixed, and, as a result, a comparison of the times is nearly impossible.

* * *

The scandalous and enjoyable qualities found in the early hare-and-hound chases at locations like Shrewsbury and Rugby ended up spreading to other academies in the United Kingdom, and eventually evolved into club races embraced by adult harrier teams. But these earliest examples of the sport were far from refined. What British distance runner Chris Chataway would one day call "a convivial affair," cross-country remained appealing to the youth through the early years of the nineteenth century and would eventually become more standardized and accepted by runners of all ages. Despite the dangerous and "rough and tumble" nature of the accounts of the Crick and Barby Hill, the soul of cross-country, its openness and accessibility included, would be celebrated by schoolboys for years to come.

EVENT SPOTLIGHT: THE CRICK RUN (1838) AND THE BARBY HILL RUN (1837)

LOCATION: RUGBY COLLEGE

The Crick Run

Adapted from an excerpt written by George Melly (1854)

It was to be the "Crick Run" to a little village eight miles from Rugby, passing the village back to within a mile or two of the school, where the great "come in" (run-in) was to take place. At three o'clock half the house was assembled in the hall, in a uniform of white trousers supported by a black belt and white jerseys, with caps of various shape, and wide-awakes of every hue. Coats, jackets, and outer garments were discarded, a very fast run being anticipated from the well-known pluck of the hares. Here they come, with two long canvas bags full of torn-up paper, to throw along their way for "scent." They have been in deep consultation with the leader of the hounds as to the particular line of country to take. We give them a partial cheer as they go off, and they scatter a handful of "scent" as they jump through the hall window, and by this maneuver gain two minutes more for the race.

Time is up; the leader of the hounds is determined to catch the hares before they arrive at the terminus, and to do the run quicker than it has ever been done before. He puts up his watch, vaults through the window, and walks down to the road, to give everyone time to catch him. He begins quietly; a six-mile-an-hour trot brings us all together to the end of the first mile. Here the younger ones begin to pant; then the pace quickens, till, at the end of the second mile, a few of the smaller boys are missed. The third mile has rid us of all who push on at a slower pace for the "come-in." We are reduced to a gallant little band of 10 or 15 only, and the next five miles find us an unchanged pack.

Crick is passed, and the pace becomes more severe while the scent is less frequent; were it not for the continual checks, no one would last till the end. The leader and his four or five rivals are racing now, and a field or two separates them and the courageous few behind, while one or two are at the Crick Inn, almost at their last gasp.

"Only a mile more," the leader whispers to the classmate that has been neck and neck for the last 10 minutes; he understands the challenge, and the pace becomes terrific. They think they are safe to be first and second, but they forget the undaunted pluck of Smyth, who is immediately behind them, and who intends to be the winner today.

They reach the brow of the hill above the river; the hares are in sight. The leader cheers, and as he pulls out his watch, he gives Smyth a chance for the victory; he is "in waiting" as jockeys say, about 50 yards behind. As for me, I am in "extremis," and am in great doubt if I shall ever reach that mound, now in full view, though the dusky winter's evening casts a shadow over all the country. But even if I arrive the last, the "Crick Run" in 90 minutes would have been a feather in my cap forever.

The two hares are lying down a few yards apart dreadfully out of breath, with a pencil, notebook, and watch, ready to mark down the winner and the time. Smyth passes the leader at a rapid pace, and wins by two yards; and even I put on an extra spurt, and come in next to last.

We throw ourselves on the grass, and feel as if nothing would ever rouse us again. We walk quickly home; after the run we have had, so sober a pace as walking seems a rest. We burst into the hall, where all the house are at tea, and announce in hoarse tones: "The Crick Run, 14 miles in 80 minutes; beat the hares by seven minutes; Smyth first, leader second; 24 started, nine in."

And I lean over my friend and say, "I was only six minutes behind them, and was last but one. I am so ill, do come up and undress me."

He jumps up, and puts me to bed in no time, saying, "What a fool you were to try the great Crick Run!"

The Barby Hill Run

Adapted from an excerpt written by Thomas Hughes (1857)

The only incident worth recording here was his first run at Hare-and-Hounds. On the last Tuesday, Tom was passing through the hall after dinner, when he was hailed with shouts from Tadpole and several others seated at one of the long tables, who all said, "Come and help us tear up paper for scent."

Tom approached the table, obedient to the command and always ready to help, and found the party engaged in tearing up old newspapers, copybooks, and magazines into small pieces, as they filled four large canvas bags. "It's the turn of our house to create the scent for Big Side Hare-and-Hounds," explained Tadpole. "Tear away, there's no time to lose before calling-over."

"I think it's a great shame," said another small boy, "to have such a hard run for the last day."

"Which run is it?" asked Tadpole.

"Oh, the Barby Run I hear," answered the other. "Nine miles at least, and hard ground; no chance of getting in at the finish, unless you're a first-rate runner."

"Well, I'm going to have a try," said Tadpole. "It's the last run of the half, and if a fellow gets in at the end, Big Side serves ale and bread and cheese, and a bowl of punch."

After calling-over there were two boys at the door, proclaiming "Big Side Hare-and-Hounds meet at White Hall!" and Tom, having put his belt on, left all superfluous clothing behind and set off. With Tom came the boy they called East, and at the meet they found some 40 or 50 boys, and Tom felt sure—from having seen many of them run playing football—that he and East were more likely to get in than they. After a few minutes of waiting, two well-known runners, chosen as the hares, buckled on the four bags filled with scent, compared their watches, and started off at a fast pace across the fields in the direction of Barby.

Then the hounds clustered around Thorne, who explained, "They're to have six minutes law. We run into the Cock Tavern, and everyone who arrives within 15 minutes of the hares will be counted, as long as they have gone around Barby Church." Then came a minute's pause, the watches were pocketed, and the pack was led through the gateway into the field the hares had first crossed.

Here they broke into a trot, scattering over the field to find the first traces of the scent. The older, more experienced, hounds made straight for the likely points, and in a minute a cry of "Forward" came from one of them, with the whole pack quickening their pace for the spot. The boy who hit the scent first, and the two or three nearest to him, were over the first fence, and made a play along the hedgerow in the long grass-field beyond.

The rest of the pack rushed the gap and scrambled through, jostling one another. "Forward" again, before they were half through. The pace quickened into a sharp run, the tailing hounds all straining to get up with the leaders. The hares were talented, and the scent lay thick across another meadow and into a ploughed field, where the pace began to slow, then over a good fence with a ditch on the other side, and down a large pasture studded with old thorns, which sloped down to the first brook, the grazing sheep charging away across the field as the pack came racing down.

The brook was a small one, and the scent lay up the opposite slope, as thick as ever, not a turn or a check to favor the tailing hounds, now trailing in a long line. Many a youngster began to drag his legs and feel his heartbeat like a hammer, and the ones most tired thought that after all it wasn't worthwhile to keep it up.

Tom, East, and Tadpole had a good start, and were doing well for such young hands. After rising the slope and crossing the next field, they found themselves up with the leading hounds who had overrun the scent and were trying back; they had come a mile and a half in about 11

minutes. About 25 of the original starters showed here, the rest having already given up; the leaders were busy searching for the scent in the fields on the left and right, and the others were catching their second wind.

Then came the cry of "Forward" again from the extreme left, and the pack settled down to work steadily, keeping pretty well together. The scent, though still good, was not thick—but there was no need of that, for in this part of the run everyone knew the line that had to be taken, with good downright running and fence-jumping to be done. All up front intended coming in, and they came to the foot of Barby Hill without losing more than two or three more of the pack. This last straight two and a half miles was always a vantage ground for the hounds, and the hares knew it well. But not a sign of them appeared, so now there was hard work for the hounds, and there was nothing to do but search for the scent, for it was now the hares' turn, and they intended to baffle the pack in the next two miles.

At this stage of the run, when the evening was closing in, no one remarked about running outside the path, sticking to those crafty hounds who kept edging away to the right, not following someone reckless like young Brooke, whose legs were twice as long.

Now came a brook, with stiff clay banks, and they heard faint cries for help from Tadpole, who had gotten stuck. But they had too little energy left to pull up. Three fields more, and another check, and then "Forward" called to the extreme right. For Tom and East, their souls died within them; they wouldn't make it. Young Brooke agreed, and said kindly, "You'll cross a lane after the next field, keep down it, and you'll hit Dunchurch road," and then steamed away for the run-in, in which he'd surely be first, as if he were just starting. They struggled on across the next field, the "Forwards" getting fainter and fainter, and then ceasing. The whole hunt was out of earshot, and all hope of coming in was over.

Chapter 2

Cross-country running, and, above all, hare-and-hound running, is fun while you are doing it. The farther you go the better you feel—it is an increasing joy as long as it lasts—you are free as a bird almost. Clothes, sidewalks, ridiculous stiff boxes called hats, ridiculous narrow grooves called streets, trolley cars, L-trains, and other artificial means of locomotion are thrown aside; you're yourself and the world's your own. Are there ten miles or so of rough country between you and home—ten miles of thickets and meadow-land and brooks and rugged hillsides? You've got your legs and you've got your lungs, and you know them and know what they can do. And so it's up the hills and through the thickets and over the meadows—hit up the pace and the devil take the hindmost! In all the list of athletic sports there is none that will do more to brush away from you the dust of overcivilization, that will do more to set you on your feet and give you a grip on the world than the run across country.
—Arthur Brown Ruhl

YEARS 1850–70: THE SPORT TAKES HOLD IN ENGLAND

It was nearly 5:00 p.m. on a chilly December night, and unbeknownst to the dozen men present on the starting line, a popular movement was taking root. As darkness loomed they joked about their circumstance, gathered on the edge of Wimbledon Common—a wild, ragged, untamed tract of bog and field—parkland purchased and protected by the Lord Earl Spencer in 1864.

These 12 on December 7, 1867 were no wiser to their pioneer status than the average Englishman—but they were, in fact, literal trailblazers. Prior to this race, known as the Thames Handicap Steeplechase Number 1, there were other, less organized attempts in expansion, and England saw an increased enthusiasm regarding paper-chases, steeplechases, and other off-road pedestrian adventures through the decades of the 1850s, '60s, and '70s. But the 1867 event was counted as the first official start by an independent club in England. And by the end of the 1870s the game would even find relevancy in a new market: across the Atlantic Ocean in America.

By 1850, the appeal of both hare-and-hound running and foot-steeplechases had expanded throughout the English public and private school systems. Running across country found its place in secondary schools, trade schools, and universities. Traditions were shared and passed down to each inaugurated class of students—and were still very much of a rebellious nature, bending the rules of the formal structures in place to govern boys' sports. By 1850 nearly two dozen schools across England

had organized some form of hunt, paper-chase, or foot-grind across open land.

Harriers in England played Hare-and-Hounds throughout the fall and winter. Subsequently, the game reached American shores via oceanic influence, and "Chalk the Corner" games were played (along with a host of others) in port cities like New York and Boston as early as the 1850s. The allure of the outdoors and the social camaraderie was irresistible, and the sport would continue to thrive at this grassroots level among the youth well into the next century.

Oxford University introduced its first interschool cross-country race in 1850. On the night following the College Horse-Riding Steeplechase (known commonly as the "College Grind"), which had been run on a course near campus, a group of Oxford students recounted the event from the previous afternoon. R. F. Bowles, James Aitken, George Russell, Marcus Southwell, and Halifax Wyatt were exhausted from the ordeal, despite the enjoyable camaraderie. "Sooner than ride such a brute again," said Wyatt, whose horse had landed on his head instead of his legs, "I'd run across two miles of country on foot."

"Well, why not?" said the others. "Let's have a college foot-grind." The Oxford Steeplechase was born.

With stakes drawn up, a course agreed upon, and officials appointed, the first meeting for "athletic sports" was inaugurated. The afternoon featured a "chase" two miles across country with 24 jumps. Stewards included students and supportive faculty—some new to the idea, and some present from the original meeting. Notice of the event was posted on a blackboard in the porter's lodge.

Entries for the steeplechase were plentiful. Bowles, Aitken, Russell, Southwell, and Wyatt were all present, as were about 19 others. The course was laid on a flat marshy farm at Binsey, near the Seven Bridge Road—some fields "swimming" in water, with the starting area waterlogged as well. Despite this, many of the 24 starters ran in cricket shoes and flannels. Plenty of supporters, on horse and foot, came to see this new event (for men were always on the lookout for "some new thing"), and in this instance, judging from the excitement and the encouragement given to the competitors, the novelty was much appreciated.

At the gun, about half of the starters sprinted from the starting post and were soon tired and done with. Aitken advanced through the fading pack and found himself in the lead with one field to go, when Wyatt and Scott, who had been gradually creeping up, made it to Aitken. They all jumped the last fence together. Wyatt landed on firmer ground and was quickest on his legs; he came in a comparatively easy winner. But there was a tremendous struggle for second place, which was barely obtained by Aitken. The finishing time was slow, the ground was deep, the fences big, and all the competitors were heavily restricted by the wet flannels on their legs.

Further holdings of the event saw Oxford University adopt a two-mile (3.2-kilometer) cross-country steeplechase that became a part of the "University of Oxford Sports" (an athletics meeting where many of the modern track and field events were founded). The cross-country variation was replaced in 1865 by a steeplechase event over barriers on a flat field; later it was configured for the cinder track. By then, Oxford was also using Wimbledon Common to run cross-country.

The school adoption of games like Hare-and-Hounds and other pastimes complemented a growing market for texts devoted to the physical improvement of the body in the mid-nineteenth century. From Sir John Sinclair's early work on training and emetics, to Donald Walker's *Manly Exercises*, an embryonic "science" developed around the role of athletic activity that sought to build a public preoccupation with healthy exercise. And yet, the exploits and accomplishments of athletes who came before this sports literature were never officially recognized. Tracing a lineage of formalized sport in England outside of preparatory schools and universities reveals some important clues—especially about distance running and record-keeping.

A FORGOTTEN ERA

It was on May 9, 1770 that James Parrott, a costermonger, completed a measured mile in just less than four minutes, becoming the first human on record to break this elite barrier. From Charterhouse Wall on Goswell Road, Parrott crossed the road, turned right, and ran the length of Old Street for a wager of 15 guineas to five. Parrott's bet was that he would finish just above four minutes, but the men who cleared the road did such a good job, and the conditions were so near perfect, that as he sped along Old Street it was clear he would be well inside the target time.

James Parrott appears in no history of athletics and he has never received any official recognition for his feat. The truth is that it remains unbelievable. In 1770, runners were seen as being third-rate—and those who measured the distance, timed the event, recorded it, and reported it to the newspapers were perceptibly seen as being incompetent in doing their jobs, too.

Skepticism about these performances was understandable. Far too little was known about them, and it was more common to doubt them than to believe what was reported without question. Nevertheless, it should not be assumed that distances could not be measured accurately in the eighteenth century. In 1770, when Parrott was reported to have run a mile in four minutes, distances were routinely measured using agricultural chains that were accurate to a centimeter or so, and any reader of Dava Sobel's *Longitude* knew that they could measure time accurately. The technology existed to measure Parrott's distance and time well enough to hold true.

But even with this evidence, it was still a surprise. Part of the problem lay in the understanding that time records from the Victorian era rose phenomenally, and that most performances before then were so poor and inconsistent they had to be dismissed. Also, the Victorians, who first controlled the new sport of athletics (along with rowing), were ideologically driven to exclude large sections of society. It was morally correct to exclude anyone who wasn't an *amateur*, and so all those who ran or rowed for money were eliminated.

But before the Amateur Athletic Association in England began to control athletics in 1880, men and women of all social classes ran for money on the streets and on the moors and greens of England. Later, athletics was policed to eliminate any monetary gain from running, a consequence that tainted athletes and rendered them *professionals*. They also excluded women. Betting and wagering was contentious throughout the nineteenth century, and was a major issue relative to cross-country running.

More of these reasons will be explored later, but in early examples of cross-country, records were not preserved due to the wagering present. A few existed (for many Victorian record-keepers, athletic marks truly begin at Exeter College, Oxford in 1850, untainted by the professional element present throughout the previous two hundred years), but not many, and evidence for the expansion of the sport in England became refocused on cross-country's purity.

For many years two sets of records were maintained (professional and amateur), and these can still be seen and compared in the 1888 work *British Rural Sports* by J. H. Walsh, who wrote under the pseudonym "Stonehenge." They confirm that one of the motivating forces behind the new amateur ideal was that there were many middle-class men who wanted to take part but were "far from being good enough to hold their own in professional company."

One of the earliest steeplechases was reported in the *Sporting Press* in 1838, when 12 gentlemen raced over four miles of difficult country near Glastonbury for a silver goblet valued at 32 guineas "with a purse of 10 guineas," and other similar events were advertised, such as the Exeter College Steeplechase of 1850. But it's difficult to trace a pattern for these events cohesively.

What *can* be determined by research was that off-road running was not sanctioned in an organized fashion, and it would take the assembly of a more reputable body to put the sport on the map for good.

THAMES CHANGES THE COURSE OF HISTORY

By the 1860s there was an increased interest in athletics of all kinds, including cricket, bicycling, and rowing, and both the London Athletic Club (1863) and the Amateur Athletic Club (1866) were founded to cater exclusively to athletes. The Thames Rowing Club (1860), "more a plea-sure boat club than anything else," was also beginning to train seriously. In 1866 they won the Junior Eights divi-sion at the Metropolitan Regatta, and held their first sports meeting featuring a plethora of water events. "The Sports" became an annual tradition, and the Thames Rowing Club built a legacy.

Walter Rye, twenty-four years old, helped pioneer the English athletic movement. Athlete, manager, journalist, writer, and one of the great figures of cross-country run-ning lore, Rye was secretary for the London Athletic Club and was active in the Thames Rowing Club. In 1867 it was Rye and a few other dedicated members who conceived of holding the first "open" steeplechase—an event intended to keep the group together and training during the off-sea-son. On December 7, 1867, the Thames Handicap Steeple-chase Number 1 was held.

The appeal of the inaugural Thames Handicap Stee-plechase could not be ignored: attendance grew with each race and more than 17 cross-country events were held by the Thames group through the end of the decade.

The efforts by the Thames Rowing Club stood out because organized cross-country running for privileged gentlemen was nearly unheard of. Predictably, the inaugu-ration of a series of races was difficult. First was the chal-lenge in advertising the event; word of mouth and internal prodding within the London Athletic Club were all that attracted participants. Second was the legitimacy of the club itself—there were no other harrier clubs in existence, so to convince men to run was a process that took time.

October 1868 was the first paper-chase of the newly re-branded Thames Hare and Hounds after two "experi-mental" runs. Club headquarters, an inn located in Roe-hampton called the King's Head, gave Thames the luxury of using Wimbledon Common. Thames got permission directly from the Lord of the Common, Earl Spencer, to run and drop paper—a singular right that persisted even after the Richmond Park authorities took control of the land in 1871. Conservators of other open spaces, like Epping For-est, prohibited the laying of trails.

It was with a notice in *The Sportsman* on October 3, 1868, that the Thames Hare and Hounds inaugurated. The notice also advertised their "official" paper-chase

event, formally called a "handicap paper hunt." While the announcement was simple enough, the credence that participants "must be introduced by some member of the Thames Rowing Club or belong to an athletic club, row-ing club, or school" certainly deterred a few interested. "A pewter given to the hound first to reach each hare," was included in the posting to add incentive.

This official paper-chase under the new "Thames Hare and Hounds" banner went off promptly at 4:48 p.m. with 22 runners. Walter Rye and E. G. Boor were the hares for the event, and started "at a furious pace" up the hill near Kingston Road. After five minutes of law, timekeeper H. F. Wilkinson dispatched the hounds on minute intervals. After a vigorous beginning, the hounds lost the trail and were forced to rely on a gentleman from Marlborough to pick up the scent again.

Eventually, E. G. Boor, who had lost a shoe (and was wearing his scent bag wrapped around his foot for protec-tion), was caught. Walter Rye, however, kept his lead, and he ran over a series of marshy grass fields, surmounted gates, and clambered up a steep rise by Pettiwade Wood. By the time he made it back to Wimbledon Common, Rye's lead was so narrow that he threw away his scent bag and came home 100 yards ahead of pursuer Chenery. Rye's time for nearly eight miles was 61:27, with Chenery cov-ering about 6.5 miles (and starting nine minutes later) fin-ishing in 52:45.

These pioneering cross-country runners had to do more than simply traverse the common; they had to chal-lenge nature and the elements. *The Annals* teems with sto-ries of cross-country runners who finished races muddied and bloodied. The first meeting in 1867 included bogs, briars, hills, and Beverley Brook, which was also known as the Watersplash: "They splashed their way to the side of Beverley Brook, through the Dismal Swamp to Coombe Bridge, and up the hill as straight as they could make it to the Windmill."

In order to market these events, Thames had to expand their offering and develop a team scoring system that would satisfy all parties. It wasn't long before the club offered pack runs, squadron runs, and individual handi-cap runs interspersed with paper-chases. It was with these events that the practice of adding the top finishing places for each team was perfected, and teams from six runners through eight or more became the standard for scoring.

However, Thames also used a scoring method that penalized clubs who finished all but one of their team in the top 10. A team could still lose if the last counter was so far back that other squads could get all their runners in. To compensate both systems, Thames experimented with an aggregate time method to count runners. This approach put considerable strain on timekeepers and left clubs open to accusations of malpractice (it was only temporarily used).

Other traditions remained. Banquets following the occasion were a feature of cross-country races from day one. "Tea is always on the table within a half hour of the run, a wonderful sight and the best part of the program," claimed *The Annals.* "There seemed to be a couple of chops and four eggs to each man, and when disposed of, what a wonderful account each gave of his performance."

The post-race tea often progressed to elaborate dinners with singing, spelling bees, and story swapping. There was also plenty of ale, though it was Walter Rye who believed that "ginger beer and gin is the favorite drink, having been found by long experience to best carry off the extra heat of the body caused by a long run."

Notably, the first cross-country runners navigated the terrain in the dark—as most events began after 5:00 p.m. *The Field* claimed it was because park space was used for rifle shooting in daylight, and *Bell's Life* claimed that it was to suit the city men, who had to catch the 3:45 p.m. train. No wonder they had accidents. One evening, a Thames runner didn't reappear until 10:00 p.m., four hours after everyone else. He looked so cold, bedraggled, and exhausted that he was judged to be "in a dying condition." Other examples included a runner who "came back wrapped in a corn sack" and another who "was found roaming about disconsolately quite lost three miles away."

Even Walter Rye was quoted in *The Athletic Field and Swimming World* with adventures:

The country was taken very much as it came, rivers and all. I remember going hare with G. P. Rodgers, and, thinking to shake the hounds off at the back of the paper mills, took the scent [paper] over the deep part of the stream on a bitter cold, snowy day. Determining to have dry things to run home in, I stripped off jersey and knickerbockers and, packing them in my scent-bag which I weighted with a brickbat, flung them over the river. But it fell about a foot short, and I had the pleasure of having to re-dress in very wet garments. I have often been cold before and since, but never so cold as I was when I ran home that day. The worst of it was that the hounds found a plank bridge further up and never wet a shoe, and very nearly caught us, entering the courtyard just as we crept up the ladder.

Notwithstanding these tribulations, Walter Rye judged cross-country running to be supremely healthy: "From an experience covering twenty years, we can positively say that we know of no man who has been injured in distance running, and the rate of mortality among running men is singularly small." Its benefits to the character were even greater: "To be a good runner over country," claimed Rye, "a man must be abstemious, patient, and good-tempered. A sprinter might indulge both in smoke and drink, but woe betide the long-distance runner who takes too much of either before a hard race." The game soon spread, and paper-chases became comparatively common around London, especially at Hampstead and Hornsey. To that point, it was Thames Hare and Hounds who were the only club paper-chasing, amidst other, more spontaneous affairs put on by different cricket or football clubs.

And despite Thames's success, it was the ability to lay paper trails that restricted the growth of other cross-country clubs in the early days in England. Several other metropolitan clubs tried prior to 1870, including the Hornsey Harriers and the Mars Harriers, who conducted weekly hunts at the Lea Bridge District; the Peckham Amateur Athletic Club (soon known as the Blackheath Harriers); and the South London Harriers, the Lea Harriers, and the Spartan Harriers.

Thames Hare and Hounds also had races against the Gentlemen of Hampstead (not a club, but a collection of invitees) in November 1870. And in the Midlands of England it was not long before the Birchfield Harriers and Coventry Godiva Harriers started runs in 1876, following the founding of the Moseley Harriers. By this time other clubs were coming into existence in various parts of the country, often temporarily. These and several other packs were confined to gentlemen, but there were also tradesmen's runs fortnightly, which took place at Hampstead Heath and elsewhere.

Surprisingly, beyond the burgeoning harrier clubs throughout England, the sport was also taking root (similar to the schoolboy/grassroots movement seen at Shrewsbury and Rugby) nearly 3,300 miles to the west. While many European families were transitioning to America to begin a new life, cross-country running was carried by the privileged class's assimilation into Ivy League universities.

TOM BROWN AND THE PAPER-CHASE ARRIVE IN AMERICA

Within three years of the 1857 publication of *Tom Brown's Schooldays*, the Rugby novel had made an impact on running and other sports in America, especially in the country's universities. According to the *Amherst College University Quarterly II* in July 1860, William Blaikie, an athlete and Harvard graduate of 1866, believed that the influence on American college sport by Thomas Hughes was "greater, perhaps, than that of any other Englishman." At Andover Theological Seminary in Massachusetts, the imported Rugby School game of Hare-and-Hounds was the "rage" in 1860. But at Andover and other institutions, interest in paper-chasing was periodic at best until organized track meets spread in the 1870s. Yale students tried Hare-and-Hounds in 1870, but it died out almost as soon as it was introduced.

Harvard experimented with the sport in 1876, just one week before the inaugural Thanksgiving Day championship football game. Harvard hares were given 15-minutes law, trailing paper scent over a seven-mile course around Cambridge. All manner of jumping fences, running through backyards, and evading irritated property owners was enjoyed. Whether it was because of angered landowners or exhausted runners, no more chases were had for three years, until the Harvard Athletic Association tried again. Harvard's popular football captain, Robert Bacon, gave the sport a new boost when he participated in a 10-mile paper-chase which included 40 hounds and two hares in 1879. (Bacon had close ties with future US President Theodore Roosevelt. Whether Roosevelt took part in this particular chase remains unknown.)

While the game of Hare-and-Hounds was featured on American soil at the collegiate level only sporadically, it proved to be the first evidence of the sport being organized outside of England. And it would continue to grow as the game took root on the East Coast in the United States.

* * *

Conclusively, the boldness of the Thames Hare and Hounds in bringing the game to the adult ranks in England became the catalyst for further expansion and standard-ization. In the span of the twenty years between 1850 and 1870, more opportunities emerged to participate in the sport beyond the college and university level.

But while cross-country running was already becoming a staple at the preparatory and collegiate level in England (and limitedly in the United States), challenges that were nonexistent for schools became nearly insurmountable for athletic clubs. A steady stream of able bodies walked the halls at every academic institution, ensuring there would always be candidates to partake in the game. But for teams like Thames, the pressure to maintain adequate membership in keeping this activity alive would be a major threat in the years to come.

EVENT SPOTLIGHT: THE THAMES HANDICAP STEEPLECHASE NUMBER 1 (DECEMBER 7, 1867)

LOCATION: WIMBLEDON COMMON

London

Adapted from an excerpt written by James Ryan

The event was the first of its kind. Open to run by anyone associated with Thames Rowing Club, the race saw 21 men sign up, with a dozen physically present for the affair. In the chill and dusk of the London night, 12 men started a race near 5:00 p.m.—each at different intervals. The handicap was a delay of about 10 seconds between each runner.

The course was laid out at Wimbledon Common, through the thickets and brush and single-track trails. The ground was hard going since the common had not been drained. Despite this, the distance "carefully measured on the ordinance map one inch to the mile, was as nearly as possible 2.75 miles." Rye, in the *Badminton Library*, declared it 2.25 miles. A fairer estimate would be 3.5 miles—with doubt as to whether a good runner could cover this distance over rough ground in the dark—in 21:54.

John Shearman wrote of this first race sixty-six years later, and his words provide a personal report as it were from the actual winner: "I did not see the race, but Cross told me a good deal about it. The runners dressed anywhere they could near the starting place. They put their clothes in a cart which met them at the finish."

No doubt the 12 participants were helped by the bright moonlight as they splashed their way by the side of Beverley Brook through the Dismal Swamp to Coombe Bridge, where E. C. Rye checked their names and directed them sharply left up the hill, as straight as they could make it to the Windmill. Meanwhile, the carriage with clothes and the officials was driven back by a cutting to the Windmill, which they reached five minutes before the winner.

Many were the misadventures in the race, and those who had previously gone over the course had a much better time. E. G. Boor deviated on his own, which took him to Wimbledon Village, and he was naturally last. In a happy phrase, "all appeared in time to take part in the dinner in the club room at Putney," where prizes were distributed.

1. W. C. Cross	(20 sec. start)	21:34
2. C. E. Rainsford	(36 sec. start)	21:50
3. J. G. Webster	(30 sec. start)	21:56
4. W. F. Woods	(90 sec. start)	22:00

Walter Rye (scratch) was fifth, having been delayed by a temporary sojourn in a morass at the bottom of a ravine.

Chapter 3

I doubt whether any man ever feels more thoroughly satisfied with his physical condition, or more keenly anticipates the pleasures which such condition has fitted him to enjoy, than a well-trained cross-country runner who follows the sport for the sport's sake. He is strong in legs and heart and lungs, the red blood leaps through his veins, and as he starts away over the hills on his errand of health he is the personification of freedom.
—Ernest Harold Baynes

THE DECADE OF THE 1870s: HELPING TO TRANSFORM OUTDOOR SPORT

The 1870s saw drastic cross-country running expansion. By 1870, the Peckham Amateur Athletic Club had incorporated in South London, becoming the first opponent to the Thames Hare and Hounds, which had 40 members. Both clubs not only organized races—runners also competed consistently, which fostered growth and attracted participants. A quick name change by the Peckham Club to the Blackheath Harriers ensured their rivalry in London was a serious one. By the end of the decade, runners in Ireland, Scotland, and the United States had also formed their own local paper-chase clubs.

Cross-country running embodied transitional characteristics that were beginning to get attention. Not only was there demand for the sport and interest—cultured workers in cities began to see the countryside as a place for consumption. Instead of regarding rural land uncivilized and backward, society—especially during the 1870s—began to view nature as an ideal component of a well-rounded gentleman. The growing popularity of cross-country and the rapid growth of independent clubs brought more attention to the pleasures of the outdoors. Other sports, such as cycling, walking, mountaineering, and sailing also imparted benefits, and all encouraged interaction between social classes.

Cross-country running celebrated these healthy, new, outdoor virtues. It advocated freedom in a setting without boundaries, as a counter to the structure of urban life. It also helped to develop the health in mind and body for gentlemen in ways that other activities could not. It retained the values of a *new* middle class, and it was an opportunity for all men to participate, regardless of occupation or background.

ENGLAND EMBRACES ITS NEW SPORT

Many of London's emerging running clubs supported the notion of the "Gentleman Amateur," a man of good family, breeding, or social position that committed to sports without pay—and Thames Hare and Hounds advocated this position most intensely.

At first, acceptance wasn't universal: in November 1872 the London Athletic Club decided to accept membership from tradesmen, and 60 members of Thames Hare and Hounds signed a letter of protest penned by Walter Rye, who led the opposition. The objectors thought that tradesmen should form their own clubs and stick to them, and that gentlemen should not compete against them (a gentleman would not, for instance, compete in an open event at "Marshall and Snellgrove's Sports" as this was a tradesman's meeting). Despite this adamant stance about membership, the Thames Hare and Hounds did, at an earlier date, entertain the idea that a cross-country championship should be open to all.

Early in the decade, organizing matches between teams was difficult. But in October 1876, Thames Hare and Hounds invited the South London Harriers, Spartan Harriers, and Birmingham Athletic Club to run a cross-country championship in North London on November 18. The chosen course, Epping Forest, had been a venue Thames had selected for a run the previous season that had never materialized. This 1876 event might have been the first real "national" championship, but unfortunately all 32 competitors went off course and the race was declared void. A storm swamped the paper trail, and competitors were left paddling haplessly for hours.

The year 1877 saw another attempt at an annual championship, this one in Thames's own backyard over Wimbledon Common. Thames's own Percy Stenning became the first individual champion (he would win four championship races in a row), and Thames also won the first team championship. The South London Harriers, Spartan Harriers, and Birmingham Beagles also took part.

Prior to the first championship, the main business of the Thames Hare and Hounds was paper-chasing; although other races, such as steeplechases, also took place. And in 1874, there was a fundamental development: "Challenge Cup Races," based on a format run by the London Athletic Club. Early that year two silver trophy cups were purchased using club funds. The existing steeplechase courses of 4.75 miles and eight miles were selected for the short- and long-distance cups, respectively, and the first races at each distance were both narrowly won by runner Walter Slade.

Runs took place fortnightly, which made it easier for members to socialize. This benefit, coupled with a sanctioned schedule, membership growth, and an established championship on the calendar, allowed Thames to secure their spot among the more prominent harrier clubs.

THE FORMATION OF A PARTICULAR MIDLANDS CROSS-COUNTRY CLUB

The South of England was not the only area to see growth in the sport. When Victoria became Queen in 1837 most of her subjects were country dwellers. When she died sixty-four years later, a majority were townspeople and the number of large towns in England had doubled. This was one of history's great social and economic transformations.

England had become the world's first urbanized nation, and the city of Birmingham, about 140 miles to the northwest of Roehampton and the Thames Club, was in the vanguard of provincial growth. Within a generation during the nineteenth century the population had risen threefold to 522,204, and, in that time, Birmingham exploded with athletic promise. Working men from all backgrounds embraced opportunities for exercise, and as a result, Midlands athletics clubs in cross-country found success.

Of note was a dispute that arose over a cross-country race promoted by the Excelsior Football Club in 1876. A faulty trail led to a protest, and the dissatisfied competitors decided to call a meeting to form a separate cross-country club. It was here that the Birchfield Harriers were born.

In the Midlands, the center of sporting activity was the Aston Lower Grounds. It had been part of the grounds of Aston Hall, an impressive sixteenth-century building and home to the Holte family. Birmingham City Council purchased the Hall and the surrounding park in 1864, opening it to the public in 1872. Sporting activities took place on the meadow, and it was here that Birchfield began running cross-country.

By February 1879, Birchfield was good enough to challenge the Moseley Harriers for the Midland Championship. The race ended with a lost paper trail in Sutton Park with H. M. Oliver (Moseley) and C. Beesley (Birchfield) being the only two to finish the course.

The following season was notable for the administration of W. W. Alexander. His leadership of the club, and that of his family for generations to follow, was eventually commemorated in the name of Birmingham's primary athletics stadium. But his arrival also coincided with the club's first real progress: that season Birchfield made history by beating the Moseley Harriers in the Midland Cross-Country Championship. Joey Law beat the renowned Walter George for the individual title and the team was victorious, 36 points to 77 (the top six finishers scored). The Birchfield heroes on the day included G. Hibberd in fifth place; F. Lockyer in sixth; A. H. Hill in seventh; T. Lawrence in eighth; and J. Ogden in ninth.

This performance encouraged Birchfield to enter the English "National" Cross-Country Championship at Roehampton, where they went on to became the first provincial club to win the event. The significance of Birchfield's first national title cannot be overstated. As Thames was the inaugurator of the championship, it was accepted that they would always be in contention for the title—or at the very least, among the leaders in the event based on their proximity to its origin. Teams from the Southern Counties were expected to be the best—as they had the most practice and saw the highest concentration of clubs. When Birchfield won in 1880, they changed the precedent for what it meant to be a successful cross-country club in England.

Did You Know?

In England, there was a high level of concern over gambling during this period, which led to the establishment of governing bodies. Once various regional cross-country associations came together, the National Cross-Country Union was formed in 1884. Surprisingly, the Thames Hare and Hounds were unsupportive; Walter Rye claimed the new union could not control professionalism, betting, and "roping." Truthfully, these were problems everywhere cross-country was popular.

INTERNATIONAL PROGRESS OCCURS

There were also many "great strides" in the decade made outside of England. In July 1873, the first Irish National Track and Field Championships were held in Dublin. Three years later, the London Athletic Club visited Ireland for a track and field meet, the first multinational athletics event on record.

By December 1875, the Intercollegiate Association of Amateur Athletes of America (IC4A) was formed in the United States. The following autumn saw the first American Track and Field Championship, held at the Mott Haven track in New York. Cross-country running was also beginning to gain popularity in the United States. The first regular Hare-and-Hounds club—the Westchester Hare and Hounds—was organized in New York in 1878.

In Scotland, paper-chasing became popular during the 1870s. Despite an ancient tradition of running and field events in Scotland, running across country took longer to penetrate the Scottish school system than it did in England. It emerged from a blanket of professional activity both associated with pedestrianism and other official games.

Initially, there was little room for physical activity in Scottish schools in the nineteenth century. Education for children was a singular chore that obligated them to apply themselves to a narrow curriculum, and ignored the role of a healthy and active body. Physical contentment started and ended with the idea of getting through daily chores. It was only in the 1870s that some of the Scottish schools broke with this tradition and used sports as a means of engaging students. Until then, students played in the meadows of Edinburgh, where Scottish sports historian John Paterson recalled they played scratch games of "Hatty, Bulls, Tops and Pieries, 'kick the can', King, and 'sixty a side soccer with a three-penny rubber ball' . . . and 'Hare-and-Hounds through the Grassmarket.'"

While Scottish acceptance of cross-country running within its preparatory school system took time to develop, its proliferation throughout the country thereafter was quite swift. It would be in the following decade that the sport became viewed as a pastime alongside their English neighbors. Meanwhile, as track and field gained an established role in Ireland and the United States, cross-country running benefitted via association. Before long, sanctioned practices in schools and universities for exploits on the track would bring legitimacy for cross-country as well.

COLLEGIATE TRACK AND FIELD IN THE UNITED STATES: AN ADDENDUM

Track and field is not always separated in the public's mind from cross-country running, but they were viewed as different sports in nineteenth-century Britain. Because the English kept the distinction, it was logical for Americans to do the same. Although it's not clear when knowledge of track contests first arrived at American colleges, the first track and field event in the United States was held at Princeton University.

Princeton was a logical site for the development of college track because of its strong Scottish background. Scotland had a long tradition of running and field events, in organized contests known as the Caledonian Games. First recorded in America in Boston in 1853, it was at Scottish Princeton that a Caledonian-inspired track and field meet was held in 1859, where S. J. Humphries won a traditional Caledonian contest, the hop-step-jump (today called the triple jump), with a distance of over 40 feet. Annual contests, though, did not appear until Scottish immigrant and Caledonian performer George Goldie was hired as director of Princeton's new gymnasium in 1869. Soon, the Caledonian Games were a major attraction for Princeton students.

Princeton was not the only college experiencing the growth of track around 1870, nor were the Caledonian Games the sole model for the growth of track and field.

In 1874, the growth of collegiate track and field was spurred by *New York Herald* owner James Gordon Bennett Jr., who hosted the second annual intercollegiate track meet his paper called the "New York Herald Olympic Games" in Saratoga, New York. Thirty students from eight colleges participated in five events: the 100-yard dash, one-mile run, three-mile run, 120-yard hurdles, and seven-mile walk, with winners receiving trophies that Bennett had financed.

This intercollegiate track meet, held alongside the annual intercollegiate rowing regatta, motivated colleges to form track associations and to hold regular meets on individual campuses. Only Columbia, Yale, Princeton, and Cornell had track clubs before the 1873 event sponsored by Bennett, and within a year, Williams College, the University of Pennsylvania, Amherst, Stevens, Rutgers, and Harvard also began to sponsor "athletics" championships for track athletes. A Harvard man, proud that his college had joined others, wrote, "At last we have the various foot contests so well known in the British universities."

With colleges showing interest in forming athletic associations to promote track, the regatta-associated track meet sponsored by Bennett was set to grow. Even Southern colleges, notably Virginia and William & Mary, were invited. In 1875, the regatta event doubled the number of track contests featured as part of its promotion.

Incidentally, the intercollegiate track meet was growing at exactly the same time that the Intercollegiate Rowing Association was about to disintegrate. When Yale and Harvard could not win in the large crew meet, they decided to withdraw to compete only against each other. As the rowing association fell apart, the track athletes decided to form their own organization.

THE IC4A IS BORN

Wanting a greater identity and more freedom, the trackmen took direct control of their annual meet, requisitioning it from the regatta committee. Following an invitation from the presidents of the Harvard and Yale athletic associations, ten colleges met in December 1875 to form a track and field association. The result of the meeting (held in Springfield, Massachusetts) was the creation of the Intercollegiate Association of Amateur Athletes of America (IC4A), with Creighton Webb of Yale at the helm. A constitution was quickly adopted, and it gave track and field management to a committee of students directly involved in the sport.

One of the early decisions of the IC4A has remained for over a century. The group decided "not to invite the Englishmen or foreigners of any description to compete." This mirrored the decision of the Intercollegiate Rowing Association not to compete against foreign universities. Track competition between American collegians and English collegians would not occur for another two decades, and by then it was outside of IC4A control.

A second decision of the IC4A was to ensure that all prizes were of equal worth. Previously, one silver cup for winning the three-mile walk might be worth double that of the three-mile run. Earlier silverware prizes might not come from the same sponsor, and the values varied widely. With this decision, prize value became fixed.

Without the intercollegiate regatta at Saratoga, the IC4A looked for another site for its annual games. A solution materialized in 1876 when Daniel M. Stern was chosen as meet referee. Stern was a member of the New York Athletic Club (NYAC), the leader in American track and field. The NYAC facility at Mott Haven became the IC4A site for the next six years. Separated from rowing, the IC4A was able to develop its own way, holding meets at three sites in New York City until the early 1900s.

In a short time, both the IC4A organization and the area of Mott Haven in New York would be significant for the development of cross-country running in the United States. Through a variety of factors, running in the fall months over hill and dale would become tied intrinsically with the success of both the IC4A and the NYAC—but in the 1870s in the United States, cross-country club running was starting off inauspiciously.

CROSS-COUNTRY RUNNING LANDS IN THE UNITED STATES

The earliest record of a US cross-country team is an account by the Harlem Athletic Club in 1878. Loosely organized paper-chase games had been played in American colleges since the 1850s, but these were treated in America as they were in England—without real organization. Spurred by the desire to stay in shape during the winter months in New York, the Westchester Hare and Hounds formed when Walter S. Vosburgh wrote to C. D. Evitt of the South London Harriers and obtained a rulebook to officiate proceedings.

Despite two straight days of rain, Westchester Hare and Hounds held their inaugural run on Thanksgiving Day in 1878. With ankle-deep mud and all pathways flooded,

about a dozen or so members of the club chased after hares for three hours. The hares were determined to make it as challenging as possible. Frank Banham finished first at the run-in, and Walter Vosburgh, who was pacing the hounds for much of the affair, finished second. The group ended the day with a grand feast, speeches, and songs—and became temporary heroes in the press when newspapers devoted entire columns to the chase the following day.

The next club to take up Hare-and-Hounds was the American Athletic Club, whose members organized the American Athletic Club Harriers and held their first run on Washington's Birthday in 1879. But meetings occurred only three times: once on Thanksgiving, once on Christmas, and the aforementioned Washington's Birthday. The Westchester Hare and Hounds flourished for two seasons and, by 1881, the New York Hare-and-Hounds had replaced the Westchester group with many of the same members. In a suitable conclusion, Charles Brandt, a member of the New York Hare-and-Hounds Club (of which Colonel De Lancy Kane, who participated in the 1878 Thanksgiving Day run, became president) formally organized the sport at Harvard University in 1880 while he was a student there.

* * *

As teams such as the Thames Hare and Hounds and Birchfield Harriers began to legitimize the sport in England, it was still viewed as a pedestrian obscurity elsewhere in the world. However, the 1870s were recognized for bringing organizational structure to the sport, and, as a result, athletic clubs both inside and outside the university system held meetings. The Westchester Hare and Hounds became the first independent cross-country club in America as a tribute to improved organization, and growth slowly crept in the Scottish, Irish, and American school systems as well. Before long, it would be clear as to whether the sport would flourish outside England, or simply remain a niche pastime.

EVENT SPOTLIGHT: THE FIRST ENGLISH NATIONAL CROSS-COUNTRY CHAMPIONSHIP (NOVEMBER 18, 1876)

LOCATION: EPPING FOREST

Bald-Faced Stag, Buckhurst Hill

In January 1876, the Thames Hare and Hounds were invited to an interclub paper-chase with Birmingham Athletic Club. However, with only one athlete competing (and winning) from Thames there was not much fanfare involved. That following October, a consensus was formed within the Thames club to invite the South London Harriers, Spartan Harriers, and Birmingham Athletic Club to run a cross-country "championship match" in North London on November 18. Prior to 1876, there had been matches between various teams, but a real championship race had not yet taken place. Discussion included opening this event to any cross-country club that cared to compete, but in the end only the three London clubs reported.

On the day of the event, 32 competitors showed up: South London started 14 men, Thames 13, and Spartans five. The venue was the Bald-Faced Stag, Buckhurst Hill, which Thames had selected for a run the previous season, and the format was a paper-chase through the Epping Forest grounds. However, the championship race proved to be disastrous. As Walter Rye recounted: "The attempt to bring it off in the wilds of Epping Forest proved a great failure, everyone losing his way separately on his own account."

More detail was given in a letter by H. Y. Groombridge, who joined Thames in 1873 and was an active member for many years: "I well remember preparation for the first cross-country championship in 1876. It was a bitterly cold day and most of us were in a frozen condition when we finally did get back. The officials thought it necessary to restore circulation by rubbing with spirit. Personally, I thought internal application would be better and snatched the glass and imbibed a considerable quantity. The next thing I remember is waking up in the Old Pavilion Music Hall."

Stormy conditions turned the park into a swamp, and the competitors were lost for hours. The rain fell in sheets for the duration of the run, and the paper laid for the trail eventually ran out. So few competitors finished in an adequate time that the race was declared null and void on the championship record, and it was agreed that the first "official" national championship would have to be rerun at a later date. According to the Thames *Annals*, "The rain poured down, the paper ran out, the runners wandered about frozen and lost, no race was declared and it was agreed to re-run at Roehampton."

WIMBLEDON COMMON: THE FIRST OFFICIAL NATIONAL CHAMPIONSHIP

The most difficult country near Roehampton had long been recognized to be around Cannon Hill, with its heavy grass fields and slushy turf; Thames Hare and Hounds only ventured in this direction when feeling extra energetic. This was the obvious choice for fighting out a championship, and a long course over 12 miles in length was worked out, circling the whole of the common first (via Putney Pound), over the railway by the footbridge to Morden Park, and back via New Malden Station and the outward half of the long steeplechase course. Several runs over this course were open to members of all three clubs to test its quality, and it was decided to be suitable.

The run-in was also changed to be the inward half of the long course, which made the distance 11.75 miles exactly. It was described as including 24 jumps and comprising "8 miles 320 yards turf and field and 3 miles 1,000 yards of path and road."

As reported, "The first race for the championship of the metropolitan paper-chase clubs" came off on February 24, 1877. Walter Rye took no chances with the paper, and along with H. Moresby, laid the trail himself "using up six scent-bags in the process." Punctually at 3:55 p.m. the race began, along with viewers of the event who had heeded Rye's advice that "nearly all the racing can be witnessed by anyone having a fast-trotting horse and a light trap."

Walter Rye had expected South London to win, with J. Gibb as the first individual. Gibb, in fact, built up a big lead, and was well ahead at seven miles, but he lost ground quickly, and after taking advice from "a party in a waggonette," went astray in Malden Lane. When he retraced his steps, he was 20 yards behind Percy Stenning, who drew away to win comfortably from the second finisher Fuller, with Gibb falling back to eighth position.

The championship statistics are as follows:

Date: February 24, 1877			
Starters: 3 teams, 34 runners			
Distance: 11.75 miles			
Individual Results:			
1.	P. H. Stenning	01:15:40	Thames Hare and Hounds
2.	W. E. Fuller	01:16:50	Thames Hare and Hounds
3.	C. H. Mason	01:17:45	Thames Hare and Hounds
4.	C. H. Larette	01:18:20	South London Harriers
5.	W. A. Tyler	01:18:35	Spartan Harriers
6.	A. E. Duncan	01:18:52	Thames Hare and Hounds

In the final position, in 27th place, was W. H. Eyre for Thames Hare and Hounds.

Team Results:		
1.	Thames Hare and Hounds	35 points
2.	South London Harriers	58 points
3.	Spartan Harriers	94 points

Another run of all three clubs was held at Roehampton in the December following the first race, and it was agreed to make the championship an annual event on a fixed date and to throw it open "to all bona-fide cross-country clubs in England." It was correctly urged that unless this were done it could not be a "championship." It has been held every subsequent March since.

Chapter 4

Cross-country running is the most pleasurable form of distance work. If possible it is best to get a number to run together. For three or four days in the week the whole pack can go together, led by a man who has sense enough not to get them racing. Then, about a mile or a mile and a half from home, on the return, the men can be lined up and allowed to race the remainder of the distance. If one wishes to try out the men, it is best to do so by handicaps, or by dividing the men into two or more packs, according to their speed. A very great deal of the pleasure in this work will depend upon the leader, and it is an essential that this position should be given to a man who will watch his pack and run at such a speed that, although there is no loafing, the run will not be a race.

—George Orton

THE DECADE OF THE 1880s: ALLIANCES, ASSOCIATIONS, INTERNATIONAL EXPANSION, AND VICE

The 1880s saw cross-country expand on a massive scale. Harrier clubs embraced the practice of both steeplechases and hare-and-hound paper-chases, and participation surged during this period. This decade celebrated the status of the gentleman amateur in athletics—working individuals who would organize together for the love of the game—and saw the emergence of official governing bodies to manage and legitimize these activities. Internationally, cross-country began to take hold in America, Scotland, Ireland, Canada, and Australia. It also flourished in England. Colleges and universities on both sides of the Atlantic adopted rules and organized meets. And while the threat of gambling on races and other illicit activities shadowed the sport, it was clear the momentum of cross-country would carry it far.

The New York Athletic Club (NYAC) was one of the first North American clubs to seek club-based organization that would change the practice of relying on newspapers to schedule meets and seek challenges. Organized in 1866, the NYAC found early success with impromptu steeplechase meetings and flourished in the 1870s, sponsoring closed athletic meetings for its members as well as "open" cross-country races anyone could enter.

Coincidently, there was an abundance of harrier clubs along the East Coast of the United States by the 1880s, and the sport of cross-country (as well as athletic clubs generally) had spread to Philadelphia, New Jersey, Buffalo, Chicago, and St. Louis. But despite acknowledgement of the value of the "gentleman amateur," there remained a dark underside to many "open" running events. Gambling was still prevalent, and prizes, many times in the form of cash or higher-valued artifacts, were awarded to champions at these meets, which further interfered with the status of amateur competitors.

At the time, organizations relied on the English definition of "gentleman amateur" popularized in rowing circles. Defined as "any person who has never competed in an open competition or for public money, or for admission money, or with professionals, for a prize, public money or admission money or at any period of his life taught or assisted in the pursuit of athletic exercises as a means of livelihood; or is a mechanic, artisan, or laborer . . ." it was often students and civil servants who met these requirements.

Wanting to prevent negative influences, many athletic clubs in America enforced strict guidelines about amateurism in their cross-country meets. For example, individuals could no longer compete under a false name or have a history of running for public or admission money. Colleges and universities, meanwhile, were aligning with these institutions, allowing students who were still in college to compete as amateurs in independently run events.

In Canada, pedestrian clubs had been popular since 1840, and by 1865 the Montreal Pedestrian Club was a leading force in Canadian athletics. The Montreal Pedestrian Club modeled their organization on prominent English clubs, namely the London Athletic Club and the Amateur Athletic Club, and both Canadian– and United States–based organizations borrowed much of their by-laws and practices from these English groups.

Canada also felt an especially strong influence from the English author Thomas Hughes and his book *Tom Brown's Schooldays*. Similar to how it was adopted at the Ivy League schools, Hughes's notions of sportsmanship and moral education provided a model to follow and had a powerful influence on the Canadian sport community. Runners were introduced to the hare-and-hound form of cross-country running and were also concerned with the integrity of the game. When East Coast American athletic clubs sought to organize to protect the rules of the sport, Canadian clubs were on board from the beginning and saw an opportunity to standardize North American sanctity in distance running.

Meanwhile, concerns over upholding the amateur ethos prompted the first meeting of athletic clubs in the United States in the winter of 1878–79. The New York Athletic Club, Manhattan Athletic Club, Staten Island Athletic Club, Plainfield Athletic Club, Scottish-American Athletic Club, Short Hills Athletic Club, Union Athletic Club (of Boston), and New Jersey Athletic Club all agreed to form the National Association of Amateur Athletes of America (NAAAA). As in England, organization helped legitimize cross-country running and prevent mishaps related to gambling.

ENGLAND: WALTER GEORGE, A RARE MIDLANDS TALENT

In England, amidst concerns over gambling and the formation of the National Cross-Country Union, cross-country running was quickly spreading from the South to the North. Clubs in the Midlands had been motivated to organize their own "Midlands" association after the establishment of the Moseley Harriers, who, like the Birchfield Harriers, were from the neighborhood of Birmingham. Led by a former Spartan Harriers member named H. M. Oliver, the Moseley Harriers helped inaugurate the Midland Athletic Association in September 1879.

The second championship race for the Midlands, the first under association jurisdiction, took place on February 14, 1880, over a course from Moseley to Coleshill. After defeating the Moseley Harriers, Holte Harriers, and Sparkbrook Harriers, the Birchfield Harriers went on to win their first English National Cross-Country title, defeating the Thames Hare and Hounds. In the Midland race it was Joey Law, a new Birchfield addition, who finished first, with Moseley Harriers's Walter George second. But despite Law's victory, it was Walter George who gained notoriety during the decade.

Born on September 9, 1858, Walter George spent most of his youth in Calne, about one hundred miles south of Birmingham. At the age of sixteen, George became an apprentice to a chemist (pharmacist) and began working long hours. Accordingly, he entered cycling and then walking races on weekends for exercise. Before turning twenty in 1878, he trained for three months and boasted, to his friends' amusement, that he would one day run a

mile in 4:12. This was at a time when the amateur mile record was 4:24 and the professional mile record was 4:17. He wrote in a notebook then the quarter-mile splits required to achieve such a time: 0:59, 2:02, and 3:08, and focused on these goals. George's unorthodox training techniques, necessitated by his apprenticeship, included what he called "100-up," which involved running in place with high knee lifts, and baths in brine. He found quick success, winning the 1879 Amateur Championships of England in the mile (4:29) and in the four miles.

In 1884, George's best year, he set amateur bests for the mile (4:18), two miles (9:17), three miles (14:39), six miles (30:21), and 10 miles (51:20). He also ran 18,555 meters in one hour, the longest amateur mark for the hour run. His greatest opponent was sprinter Lon Myers from the United States. Out of nine clashes at agreed-upon middle distances, the American won six, and George three.

Walter George was also a standout in cross-country. Despite coming up short against Joey Law in the 1879–80 Midlands Championship, he led the Moseley Harriers to four successive English National Cross-Country team titles from 1881–84. He also won individual national titles in cross-country in 1882 and 1884. In the Midlands, George was individual champion in 1879, 1882, and 1884, and led Moseley to two team victories as well. Following the 1884 season, seeking better competition and higher monetary gain, George left his amateur standing and turned professional. Moseley has not won a cross-country national team title since.

ENGLISH REPRESENTATION

On April 24, 1880, the English Amateur Athletic Association (AAA) was founded in Oxford, with four delegates representing cross-country. Determined to be the official national governing body for English sports, the AAA eventually allied with the Scottish and Irish Amateur Associations and with the British Swimming and Cycling Associations.

Meanwhile, as some teams were prospering, the Thames Hare and Hounds witnessed an end to their meteoric rise to the top of cross-country running. In 1881, the club was in serious contention for the championship, but bad course conditions saw them slip to sixth place. In 1882, they fell to seventh, and in 1883, unable to raise a team, the official program recorded "Thames Hare and Hounds have scratched"—a result of not recruiting a sufficient amount of new members.

In 1881, Thames had relied on the performances of longtime members Percy Stenning and J. A. Voelcker to carry the club, but these two could not do it alone. With a one-time membership high of 74, it was down to 54 by 1884. Meanwhile, other clubs were growing rapidly: both Blackheath and the South London Harriers each boasted more than 200 members in 1883. While there may have been several reasons for Thames's decline, Walter Rye had little doubt that card playing and betting were to blame.

The reality was that betting and gambling was just as much a distraction for the English harrier teams as it was in America. Arthur Ball, secretary of the Thames Hare and Hounds from November 1878 to October 1880, wrote to Percy Stenning: "I am very glad that you have hopes of resuscitating the Thames Hare and Hounds, but I fear that you will have very little chance of success, as with what has already done more than anything else toward spoiling the club (card playing and gambling), be utterly abolished." Wagering while playing cards was inexorably linked with gambling in other venues, and both were frowned upon in a group whose sole purpose was to run cross-country for the love of the game. With these distractions crippling the once powerful Thames club, it was no wonder Walter Rye had his doubts.

The cross-country delegates who were part of the English Amateur Athletic Association decided that they would have more success operating independently, and so a meeting was called in May 1883, in London, to discuss the formation of a National Cross-Country Union. Thames was against its formation (as mentioned before, Rye did not think an association of harrier clubs who could not control their own betting practices would be able to curb the activity as a union), with the resolution passing sixteen votes to four (the only four "against" being from Thames). It would be no surprise when Thames was "conspicuous by their absence" once the Southern Counties Cross-Country Association was formed to represent South London clubs one month later.

On August 18, 1883, delegates from the Northern, Southern, and Midland Associations met at Birmingham to constitute the first meeting of the National Cross-Country Union. Walter Rye was unanimously selected as president (despite showing no support) and W. M. Colson was deputed to obtain his consent (Rye did not consent). T. Shore, of the Spartan Harriers was therefore elected president soon after.

In addition to being absent from the newly formed union, Thames also lost hosting duties for the national championship. In 1884, the championship moved away from Roehampton because it was no longer considered suitable; large crowds of spectators could not be controlled, and after scenes in 1883 (when runners had difficulty finishing) the *Sportsman* reported, "In the future it would be better to select another course." Despite Thames's shift out of the spotlight, the sport in England was more popular than ever.

ENGLISH YOUTH MOVEMENT

Oxford University and Cambridge University first raced cross-country in 1880. Known as the "Inter-Varsity Cross-Country Meeting" this dual meet has persisted in December (barring the war years) until the present day. Oxford hosted and won the first race, defeating Cambridge 22 points to 33. However, it was an unsatisfactory result as "malicious boys tampered with the trail," causing two Cambridge runners to finish well behind the field.

At first, the universities took turns hosting the race. But unsurprisingly, the method of marking the trail was not always consistent, and the competitors, particularly those from the visiting side, often got lost. The most infamous occurrence of this happened in 1886, when a 9.5-mile Oxford course was laid from the University Arms to Shotover Hill. In that event, Frederick Philpot (St. John's, Cambridge) was possibly denied victory when he lost the trail, and William West (Christ Church)—one of Oxford's top runners—also trailed in 20 minutes behind the pack.

After Oxford's controversial initial win, Cambridge won seven races in a row up to 1887. Their dominance stemmed not only from a wealth of talent at their disposal, but also from Oxford's recruitment problems. At the time, Oxford University Hare and Hounds was a part of Oxford University Athletic Club (OUAC), which supported the prejudice that training for cross-country made a man slow for the track. As a result, OUAC's top milers and three-milers were discouraged from running cross-country. Oxford might have been slow to embrace the opportunity, but finally did so in the late 1880s due to the efforts of William Pollock Hill—Oxford's first real star, and cross-country champion in 1886, 1888, and 1889.

By the middle of the decade, club teams like the Thames Hare and Hounds were actively running with the universities to garner support for their own purposes. In November 1885 Thames suffered a defeat in its first match against Cambridge, but by February 1888, had scored a one-point victory in their first match against Oxford.

Thames was not the first harrier club to run against Oxford and Cambridge (Cambridge beat Blackheath 38 to 40 on March 15, 1882), but when the universities decided to seek a neutral venue for their own match in 1890, they looked to Thames and Wimbledon Common, who accepted the responsibility as hosts.

An influx of younger runners was also seen in the Midlands with the formation of a Midland Junior Association. This division of junior and senior runners was significant at the time, but would eventually be replaced by age-group qualifications later in the twentieth century. Yet with the notion that the junior ranks could "feed" the senior teams successfully, an important step had been taken to prevent the recruitment problems plaguing teams like the Thames Hare and Hounds and others.

Outside of England, the interest in cross-country running by younger, college-aged athletes remained strong. While organizations formed to remove the professional element from the sport, school teams maintained stability and grew steadily, which provided the foundation for cross-country to remain current and popular in Ireland and beyond.

CROSS-COUNTRY GROWS IN IRELAND

In the 1860s and '70s, Ireland had quietly built a steady following for amateur athletics. When the Amateur Athletic Club held the first track and field championship in England in 1866, a similar trend followed in Ireland. The

Irish Sportsman of January 18, 1873, reported the establishment of the Irish Champions Athletics Club (ICAC)—the first of its kind—with 18 members named.

The first ICAC track and field championship was held at College Park in Dublin in July 1873. In December of that same year, the club purchased 8.25 acres at Lansdowne Road in Dublin and laid a cinder running track (578 yards in circumference). Notable uses of the track included an international meet with England in 1876 and the national championship in May 1880.

But despite interest in amateur athletics in Ireland, and seven successful championship races held between 1873 and 1880, crisis overtook the ICAC and the organization disbanded in November 1880. Ireland was able to organize a temporary governing body (with adopted English rules), and in 1881 the City and Suburban Harriers Club was founded, along with the Irish Cross-Country Association.

On November 1, 1884, the Gaelic Athletic Association was founded in Ireland, and its panel included some members of the Irish Cross-Country Association. But three months later, the Irish Amateur Athletic Association (IAAA) was established. While certain members of the Gaelic Athletic Association gave a backlash to what would be a larger, more egalitarian-structured body, the Irish Amateur Athletic Association received the support from, and had representation from, all of the harrier clubs.

Although there had been a club at Trinity since the early 1870s, the Dublin University Harriers and Athletic Club officially formed in December 1886 and were promptly elected to the Irish Cross-Country Association (which brought the strength of that body to seven clubs). Harrier clubs in Ireland were developing gradually, and throughout the 1880s and '90s the measure of growth was comparable to that of other cross-country teams elsewhere in the world. The Clonliffe Harriers, Donore Harriers, Haddington Harriers, and Galway City Harriers all appeared during this period.

As a result of this growth and stability brought by the IAAA, the 1886 Championships at Baldoyle attracted 79 runners and six club teams. C. C. Carter of County Dublin won the 10-mile race in 35:14 (he would win a second title the following year), while Haddington won the team title. The Irish Cross-Country Association continued to run in alliance with the Irish Amateur Athletic Association until 1922.

CROSS-COUNTRY TAKES HOLD IN SCOTLAND

The earliest harriers clubs of Scotland were formed in 1885 and 1886, and the evolution of the sport in Scotland was unique. Public school influence was at play, but not to the same degree as in England. Adults and students developed cross-country running alongside the formation of harrier clubs, with support coming from governing bodies like the Scottish Amateur Athletics Association (SAAA) in 1883, and the Scottish Cross-Country Union (SCCU). Participation within the universities was limited to informal runs by students as training for other sports, although intervarsity competition between the four major universities of Scotland started to take off at about the same time as clubs started developing.

In Scotland's Edinburgh University Athletic Club, David Scott Duncan influenced both the formation of cross-country clubs and the eventual governing body of cross-country running. In 1883 Duncan competed in the Scottish Track Championships, winning the mile while representing Edinburgh University in a time of 4:35, and in 1885 he was instrumental in the formation of Edinburgh Harriers. He and other Edinburgh University men also served on the new governing body of athletics, the Scottish Amateur Athletics Association.

The period of 1885–88 was particularly important as the sport started to move from its hare-and-hounds approach to the more familiar individual contest seen in cross-country today. While there was a slow, increasing interest in this form of running in England, Scotland appeared to make the transition from pack to individual running relatively quickly.

The first cross-country running club to form outside Scottish schools and universities was the Clydesdale Harriers, based in Glasgow. Formed on May 4, 1885, their first run—from the Black Bull Inn at Milngavie—did not take place until October. Formed, in part, because of the McNeill brothers of the Glasgow Rangers Football Club, this connection to football (soccer) was unique to cross-country club development in nineteenth-century Scotland and also explained the partial decline of the sport in the twentieth century, as cross-country found difficulty competing with more exciting sports. Without ownership of their own clubrooms and grounds, cross-country clubs in Scotland were very much dependent on the success of soccer during this period.

The Clydesdale club was followed by the Edinburgh Harriers, the first club to form in the east of Scotland. The Edinburgh Harriers was a different club in social composition and founding principle. Among its members were former schoolboys of the Edinburgh merchant schools, including writers, surgeons, doctors, bricklayers, gardeners, iron molders, and retail stationers. David Scott Duncan, generally accepted as the "Father of Scottish Athletics" and one of the leading officials of the fledgling SAAA, was a key founding member. Forming clubs for athletic purposes outside the "old boys" clubs of the public schools was still new, since most sports were conducted through the older methods or through the large cricket and football clubs being established. The Edinburgh Harriers was a test to see whether the sport could exist in its own right rather than as an offshoot of the more powerful clubs.

Scotland's first interclub cross-country meet took place between Clydesdale and Edinburgh on November 28, 1885, at Corstorphine, in Edinburgh. A total of 34 runners were present: 26 representing Edinburgh and eight from Clydesdale. A second interclub meet took place in January 1886, with 32 runners once again present—14 from Clydesdale, 13 from the Edinburgh club, and five from the Lanarkshire Bicycle Club Harriers Section.

The third club to emerge during this period was the West of Scotland Harriers, a Glasgow-based club founded on September 14, 1886. This club would become a healthy rival to the Clydesdale Harriers, and they provided an alternative to the single-club (multi-section) format that Clydesdale used. This club structure (and their approach) became appealing as a training medium for other sports, and not just as a new sport in its own right—but it wasn't long before participants in other sports began running for the West of Scotland Harriers as their principal activity. Membership continued to increase, and in 1887 Clydesdale had 420 members, Edinburgh Harriers had 300, and the West of Scotland Harriers had 111.

The increase in membership did not directly result in an increase in participation in the newly inaugurated Scottish national cross-country championships, as each club selected only its best runners to participate. The 1887 championship, as an example, played a testament to this. Held at Hampden Park, Glasgow, an innovative course included laps within the stadium as well as a path set across the open country around the venue. Runners would appear between the laps of the country for a lap of the stadium before setting out again; four laps in total were covered. Meanwhile, the fans, who paid admission, were treated to a soccer game between the non-competing athletes during the race.

Teams, growing larger, saw the national championships expand, which increased the prestige of winning. In this process, however, the harrier clubs missed one key opportunity. Despite the sport's popularity, none of the cross-country clubs legitimized a stable headquarters from which to run. The sport was migratory, and the attitude of taking cross-country meets out to various venues to "spread the word" and to seek recruits meant that it lacked the stability of a recognized venue. While various clubs had particular locations they would revisit in Scotland, particularly in the villages surrounding the expanding urban sprawl of Glasgow, Edinburgh, and Dundee, the venues were limited by accessibility and, ultimately, facility. Changing at inns and hotels was fine while numbers were relatively low but as numbers grew, so did the need for better facilities.

Did You Know?

The diversity found in Scottish cross-country club membership in the 1880s was due to recruiting from other sports (like soccer), with running matches between harriers and football clubs seen frequently. For teams like the Clydesdale Harriers, the Rangers Football Club actively promoted the club, and granted access to Ibrox Park Stadium in order to train on the track. This connection would provide teams like Clydesdale with a unique way of developing and expanding their ranks during this period.

By 1887–88 the clubs felt confident enough to break away from the governance of the Scottish Amateur Athletic Association to form their own cross-country association. On December 11, 1887, the Scottish Cross-Country Association (SCCA) was formed. Internal representation wasn't possible for all the Scottish harrier clubs, and Clydesdale struggled to select members for the Scottish championships. As a result of loyalty to the old system, the club made a decision that was to split the sport. Clydesdale refused to join the SCCA—although they did participate in the 1888 championships, winning the individual and team titles.

The first championships under the new Scottish Cross-Country Association were entrusted to a subcommittee of just three people, who were given only five weeks to prepare. Meanwhile, the Clydesdale Harriers became the first Scottish team to compete in the English National Cross-Country Championships held in Manchester on March 2 that same year. The club finished a creditable sixth as a team behind the harrier clubs of Birchfield, Salford, Worcester, South London, and Burton.

The disapproval of the new association by the Clydesdale club acted as a catalyst for the formation of the Scottish Harriers Union (SHU), which also decided to hold a junior competition in December 1889. A "junior" in Scottish cross-country competition didn't indicate a competitor's age, but instead meant an athlete hadn't placed on a team competing in any previous championship. Despite the separation of the harrier associations in Scotland, and even with the addition of a junior championship, cross-country running as a sport was universally accepted in Scotland throughout the decade.

ELSEWHERE IN THE WORLD

Elsewhere, the sport was taking root in Australia, New Zealand, and Canada, and was being formalized by athletic clubs and increasing in popularity collegiately in the United States.

As in Scotland, the year 1887 was pivotal for the sport in Australia. It was then that a man by the name of Richard Coombes established the New South Wales Amateur Athletic Association. Coombes was the forebearer of bringing cross-country running to Sydney (along with other amateur sports like competitive walking), via the Sydney Amateur Walkers' Club, and in 1888, he founded the Sydney Harriers—where the first paper trail was laid.

Richard Coombes was also influential outside of cross-country running. Born and raised in Hampton Court, Middlesex, England, Coombes attended Hampton Grammar School and eventually became captain of the Harefield Hare and Hounds. He then immigrated to Sydney in 1886 as a journalist, becoming a contributor to the *Referee*. As a team manager later in life, Coombes took an Australian track team to New Zealand in 1889, the first of twenty visits.

In 1891 Coombes was interested by a proposal in the *London Greater Britain* that a "Pan Brittanic and Anglo-Saxon Olympiad" be held and, with help, he arranged the first Australasian championships in Melbourne a year later. Contenders from New South Wales, Victoria, and New Zealand competed (they were intended to produce competitors for the Olympics, but the plan fell apart). In 1895 Coombes took a team to Queensland and helped to set up the Queensland Amateur Athletic Association. By the next year he had founded the Amateur Athletic Union of Australia.

Outside of Australia and the home countries of the United Kingdom, Canada was also experiencing a formalization of athletics. The governing body for track and field in Canada, which today is called Athletics Canada, was established in 1884, and remains one of the oldest affiliated bodies of the International Association of Athletics Federations (IAAF). Following preliminary meetings on April 11, 1884, where the athletics associations of Quebec and Ontario sent some 50 representatives to meet at the Toronto Fencing Clubhouse, the association eventually ratified a constitution for the newly formed Canadian Amateur Athletics Association. Only seventeen years had passed since Sir John A. MacDonald and the Fathers of Confederation had established the political entity of the Dominion of Canada, but these athletics planners already had a considerable tradition upon which to draw—with pedestrian and snowshoe clubs leading the way. The first track and field championships were held in Montreal on September 27, 1884, with many amateur athletic clubs organizing hare-and-hound chases on a smaller level until the 1900s.

The decade of the 1880s saw a blossoming of cross-country running in Canada. In Montreal, on October 24, 1885, J. W. Moffatt, the Canadian Amateur champion at the half-mile and mile runs, won a six-mile Canadian cross-country championship in 38:47. The following year, S. D. Jones took the title, which was contested in Toronto. By 1889 an Amateur Cross-Country Team Championship of Canada was won by the Toronto Athletic Club.

Athletic clubs in North America were supported by the strong college and university system, which maintained the international influence introduced from England. In the United States, Harvard became a beacon for Hare-and-Hounds in 1881, when a Harvard paper-chasing club was founded.

Cambridge University in Massachusetts also adopted "that Rugby sport" in 1881. The University of Pennsylvania, Cornell, the College of the City of New York, Yale, and Brown soon followed suit (Columbia first started paper-chasing after the 1878 Thanksgiving Day race sponsored by the Westchester Hare and Hounds). Princeton formed a Hare and Hounds Club in 1880, and sought to challenge Columbia in a 12-mile cross-country run in the spring of 1881, but Columbia declined the invitation. Three years after the National Cross-Country Association in America held its first championship, the University of Pennsylvania beat Cornell in the first American intercollegiate race. It was clear the international fixation with cross-country running outside of England was not going anywhere.

THE REORGANIZATION OF AMERICAN GOVERNING BODIES

By 1880, North America was making great steps forward in legitimizing cross-country running and amateur athletics.

The National Association of Amateur Athletes of America held championships in a variety of sports, and even Canadian clubs were eager to become members. At a dinner honoring visiting Englishmen, the Honorary Secretary of the English Amateur Athletic Association expressed his hopes that the AAA and the NAAAA would eventually combine to form an international body.

Unfortunately, it was not to be. At a meeting held on May 11, 1886, the Board of Governors of the New York Athletic Club (NYAC) decided to withdraw from the National Association of Amateur Athletes of America. Their decision was reached in the aftermath of a boxing championship held that February, in which a NYAC member was questioned over his amateur status. The NAAAA was also under scrutiny for protecting gate money instead of promoting athletics, failing to disqualify professionals under amateur circumstances, and inconsistent college competition against certain member teams. With the loss of the NYAC, the National Association of Amateur Athletes of America was reduced to six active member clubs.

The Manhattan Athletic Club, a NAAAA member that had organized in November 1877, was the only other challenger that could match the athletic and financial strength of the New York Athletic Club. As such, an intense rivalry existed between these two. The bitterness was intensified when the NYAC withdrew from the NAAAA, because the Manhattan Athletic Club was left without an equal on the board. In a predictable turn of events, the New York Athletic Club soon reorganized with new clubs. On January 21, 1888, the Amateur Athletic Union (AAU) of the United States was formed.

Over 14 athletic clubs agreed to form the AAU, including many outside the East Coast. The Detroit Athletic Club, Chicago Athletic Club, Columbia Athletic Club of Washington, D.C., and Warren Athletic Club of Delaware all joined 10 other clubs representing New Jersey and New York, including the New York Athletic Club. In August 1888, it was determined that any athlete who competed at an event not under the rules of the AAU would no longer be eligible. The board also concluded that the rules of the National Association of Amateur Athletes of America were not approved by the AAU, deliberately ostracizing themselves from the NAAAA.

On August 1, 1889, the National Association of Amateur Athletes of America officially disbanded, though a few executive officers were allowed onto the board of managers for the Amateur Athletic Union. While seemingly a sidenote to the greater expansion of cross-country running at the time, the political dealings between the New York and Manhattan Athletic Clubs would have far-reaching consequences in the development of the sport, specifically concerning the American national championship.

Despite this political tumultuousness, the development of harrier clubs along the East Coast (including New York) was a major accomplishment during the 1880s. The New York Hare and Hound Club, which carried many members of the inaugural Westchester Hare and Hounds from the previous decade, flourished in regular meetings.

As the number of clubs increased, members pursued inter-club races and East Coast clubs dropped the old-fashioned paper-chase and instead offered prizes for runs over measured courses.

The first race of any importance was held in 1883, when the New York Athletic Club instituted an individual championship. The course was in the vicinity of its own grounds—Mott Haven, New York—and was open to all amateurs. Won by T. F. Delaney of Williamsburg Athletic Club, the reigning five-mile champion of America, the first American cross-country championship was such a success that a second one was held the following year. In that event a team of Canadians competed, and the winner proved to be D. D. McTaggart, the two-mile champion of Canada and member of the Montreal Athletic Association. The distance of the championship was about five miles.

Back in England, fans were cheering for E. C. Carter, a young distance runner who had suddenly arrived at the fore. Better known as "the little boy in pink" for his youthful appearance and the color of his running suit, Carter was a victor at the Southern Counties Cross-Country Championship and runner-up to Walter George at the English National. Having demonstrated his ability in England, he sailed for America and competed in the American individual cross-country championship in 1885. He won that race after a close battle with J. T. Macmahon, of Connecticut, and successfully defended his title the following year.

In the meantime, club rivalry had been growing and momentum was building for a team championship. Delegates from all the leading clubs around New York held a meeting in March 1887 and organized the National Cross-Country Association. Later that spring, the first team championship was held, open to teams between six and 12 members strong.

One of the stronger teams at that time, the Prospect Harriers, had formed in October 1886 (named after the park that was to be the scene of many of their club races) and built their ranks with members of the Nassau Athletic Club and the Polytechnic Athletic Association. In one season, 1887–88, they held 55 club runs and covered 290 miles.

A second strong club, the Suburban Harriers, became multiple-time champions. First organized out of the Knickerbocker Cottage in New York on March 21, 1887, the club was proud to run many of the fleetest distance runners in America. E. C. Carter himself was a member of the club and was the team's first captain. An added incentive, the "Kilpatrick Bronze," named after its donor (the second president of the club), was issued to the winner of the club championship—and became the permanent property of the man who won it three times. Unsurprisingly, E. C. Carter was one of the first individuals to take ownership of it.

In fact, it was Carter who wrote a column in the *New York Herald* describing the rivalry between the two clubs in 1890:

> The organization of the Prospect Harriers was, I believe, the means of rescuing cross-country running from a state of lethargy and has led to its

present popularity. The Prospect Harriers, since its organization, has held its runs no matter what kind of weather, and I have seen them turn out in a club handicap, clad in their running suits, and with bare calves, when the thermometer registered two degrees below zero. In the spring of 1887 the Prospect Harriers sent invitations to meet for the purpose of forming a national cross-country association, and to give a team championship. It was this invitation that led to the formation of the Suburban Harriers, which formed with the idea of sending a team to the proposed championship.

This first team championship involved three teams: the Manhattan Athletic Club, the Prospect Harriers, and the Suburban Harriers. The course was laid out at High Bridge—over entirely natural country, with plenty of hills and fences to test the participants. E. C. Carter won the individual title in magnificent style, leading for the entirety, and then, without pausing to rest, ran back along the course to encourage his men. Responding bravely to their captain's call, five of the Suburban Harriers came in near the front and won the team championship. The victorious harriers carried off an elaborate banner, presented by Mr. G. M. L. Sachs, and E. C. Carter, G. Y. Gilbert, P. D. Skillman, E. W. Hjertberg, W. F. Thompson, and T. O'Day each received a gold medal.

In the fall Carter again captured the individual championship held by the New York Athletic Club, and the following spring each of the three clubs were poised for another chance at victory. The Manhattan Athletic Club was favored, bolstered by the arrival of T. P. Conneff, the long-distance champion of Ireland. Fleetwood Park was selected for the course, and the spectators in attendance saw a great contest. Conneff was an old rival of Carter's and had defeated him in an exciting four-mile race in England. Both were thoroughly determined to win the individual title, and as they neared the finish, cries of "Conneff wins" and "Carter wins" broke alternately from the crowd. A few hundred yards from the tape, however, the Irish champion succumbed to the pace and fainted (never finishing), while Carter won the individual championship for the fourth race in succession. The club cry of the Suburbans rang as Carter passed the winning-post and brought courage to his weary teammates—they were once again victorious. With the exception of T. Avery Collett, who filled Skillman's place, the finishers were the same that won the year before.

With fear that interest in the event would fall if the Suburban Harriers won again, its members decided to disband and build up other teams. Collett went to the Pastime Athletic Club, Hjertberg went to the New Jersey Athletic Club, and Carter, Gilbert, and Skillman went to the New York Athletic Club.

As a result, in the spring of 1889, veteran returners were in for a surprise. Several of them, knowing that Carter would not compete in the team championship, imagined that they were going to win the title, but on the day of the race an upstart team from the New Jersey Athletic Club had other plans. At Fleetwood Park, slightly-built nineteen-year-old (and New Jersey Athletic Club member) William D. Day ran away from everyone, and gave the first evidence of becoming one of the greatest cross-country runners ever born in America. With his entrance to the scene in 1889, American cross-country would never be the same.

* * *

With a strong push to standardize the sport due to unwanted elements like gambling, cross-country running became a much more recognizable fixture in America and beyond. Individual performers, including Walter George, E. C. Carter, and Willie Day aided in establishing the sport's identity. And thankfully, largely due to its novelty, cross-country was rising in popularity both with independent athletic clubs and their fans, and within schools and colleges. But there was still work to be done to keep it popular among other pastimes. Competitive runners from every corner of the globe would come to define the sport as the twentieth century approached—and with a more significant influence, cross-country would eventually bridge isolated groups of people as they began to participate.

EVENT SPOTLIGHT: THE FIRST AMATEUR INDIVIDUAL CROSS-COUNTRY CHAMPIONSHIP IN AMERICA (NOVEMBER 6, 1883)

LOCATION: MOTT HAVEN, NEW YORK

Tenth Avenue

On November 6, 1883, the New York Athletic Club hosted the very first cross-country championship conducted on American soil. In the vicinity of Carmansville and Fort Washington, residents were surprised to see two stage-coaches each being drawn by four horses. Fifty men total—leading the parade and within the carriages—arrived as the officials and participants of the event. Trailing behind came a number of street boys eager to witness what was happening, as women and girls along the side of the road waved handkerchiefs. The start of the race was at the end of Tenth Avenue, and as the carriages pulled up, the plains of Inwood, the proposed site for the World's Fair, lay before the party.

The weather was clear and pleasant, with almost no wind. The course, starting from the north end of Tenth Avenue, led down a steep hill; across a meadow to the Kingsbridge Road; up to and across Kingsbridge; up Ford-ham Hill; through field, farm, and garden to Fordham Heights; down the hill; across the new Harlem footbridge; and through the fields to the finish flag on the Dyckman Farm. The scene was reported to be a beautiful one. To the west were the heights of Inwood with beautiful villas and mansions, and behind them the Hudson River shone a silver streak, beyond which the bluffs of Fort Lee rose blue in the mist of the morning. To the north were the church steeples of Yonkers and Kingsbridge glinting in the sunlight. The wooded heights of Fordham and Tremont appeared in the east while below, the placid Harlem, with its tortuous windings, reflected the tints of the blue and gold foliage of the autumn-touched trees.

Nineteen men were registered for the event. Among them were Lon Myers of Manhattan Athletic Club, Thomas Delaney of Williamsburg Athletic Club, P. Golden of West Side Athletic Club (WSAC), and C. A. J. Queck-berner of the New York Athletic Club (who was a massive weight thrower and duly uncharacteristic of the general build of those participating in the event). The start was to have been 11:00 a.m., but it was not until 11:25 a.m. that the 19 "men who itch for honors to be gained by leaping field and ditch" were sent away.

The course was said to be five miles in length, but a subsequent investigation showed only four and a quarter were traveled. It was flagged its entire length by red flags, and men were stationed along the route to guide the runners when necessary. When starter B. C. Williams fired the pistol,

Queckberner dashed in front and led the way down the hill and over a ditch. Myers and Delaney started together a short distance behind, and the others strung out in single file.

They took off in style, and the spectators, who by that time numbered 1,000 (on foot, horse, and in carriages), cheered them lustily. Turning from Barne's field into the Kingsbridge flats, Myers and Delaney passed Queckber-ner, who dropped like a rock and in quick succession was passed by all the other runners. For a time Roedel headed the second division, but when taking to the road he gave way to Ryan and the others until he became Queckbern-er's companion in distress.

In the meantime, Myers and Delaney were having an exciting race. The pace was forced by Delaney, with Myers flitting along behind him like a shadow. Up the road to Kingsbridge and over a bridge spanning Spuyten Duyvil Creek went the pair, and then down to Fordham Heights. Fences, stone walls, and ditches were taken flying and poor jumpers fell into the mud and mire, much to the amusement of the spectators. The hill to Fordham Heights was a difficult one for Myers, who began to tire; turning into the Kilpatrick estate, Delaney started to pad his lead. Mr. Frank Kilpatrick, his wife, and a party of ladies were on the lawn in front of the mansion, and clapped their hands and urged the racers on.

Down a hill to the end of the estate the men met a six-bar fence. Delaney climbed over it and Myers tried to crawl through, but slender as he was he was caught between the bars and Delaney increased his lead. When the others undertook to cross the same fence nearly all met with mishaps, and "Spider" Phillips tore the skin from his hands and arms.

The race from that point was without interest, except that before the Fordham Bridge had been crossed and the hill on Dyckman's farm, where the race finished, was reached, six men passed Myers, who was thoroughly exhausted. One runner managed to lose his trousers during the race and came in covered with "confusion and a horse blanket," but all enjoyed the spectacle. The Individual Cross-Country Championship of America statistics are as follows:

Date: November 6, 1883			
Starters: 19 runners			
Distance: 4.25 miles			
Individual Results:			
1.	T. F. Delaney	26:30	Williamsburg Athletic Club
2.	P. Golden	28:00	West Side Athletic Club
3.	J. A. Collett	28:15	Pastime Athletic Club
4.	G. D. Phillips	28:45	New York Athletic Club
5.	J. Kerns	29:00	Greater Athletic Club

6.	E. J. Ryan	29:15	Williamsburg Athletic Club
7.	L. E. Myers	Time Not Reported*	Manhattan Athletic Club
8.	F. Girand	Time Not Reported	American Athletic Club
9.	P. J. McCarthy	Time Not Reported	Greater Athletic Club
10.	J. Newnham	Time Not Reported	North Side Athletic Club

J. J. Collins, Kingsbridge; T. D. Day, Bridgeport Athletic Club; and H. S. Whitaker, New York Athletic Club, did not complete the distance and were disqualified.

*Archival sources failed to publicly report the finishing times for the seventh, eighth, ninth, and tenth places. Team scores were also not recorded for this championship.

Chapter 5

Now the sport is entirely changed. "Hare-and-Hounds" or paper-chasing, is almost a thing of the past in this country; it has given way to cross-country racing, a more severe, though less enjoyable, form of the game. That the latter is popular with athletes however, is shown by the fact that while there was only one pack in the United States in 1877, there are a thousand in the country today.

—*The* New York Times, *February 1893*

THE DECADE OF THE 1890s

In a decade filled with change, the 1890s saw more citizens move to urban centers than lived in the rural countryside. Commercial expansion created a new middle class: the category of the consumer. For the sport of cross-country, participation grew worldwide, and other activities also became commonplace during leisure time. However, the decade was not without its drawbacks: gradual economic decline in the middle years impacted the formation of new harrier clubs and saw inconsistencies with the number of championships offered.

While the decade of the 1890s was centered on the expansion of cross-country running (and its variations) in new markets, it was its transition from hare-and-hound running into the more traditional format seen today that led to its appeal at both the American university level and in new countries. Legitimization consequently followed. Cross-country was finally booming for a range of age levels in a way that was cohesively understood.

AMERICAN UNIVERSITIES CARRY THE MANTLE

By 1890, organized club teams existed at the university level in American institutions from the Ivy League to New York City. Promoted by students who had connections to harrier clubs along the East Coast, cross-country was formally addressing the need to train for distance running during the off-months of track and field. Standardized adaptations saw the presentation of the sport change—set courses were agreed upon and participants were given equal opportunity to run against each other at the same time. This is not to say that handicap races or paper-chasing disappeared overnight, but the championship format

featured at the club level was carried over to the college and university scene, and a pronounced shift took place away from older racing formats—although obstacles and natural elements were still very much in favor.

As one example, Cornell University divided up weekends in the fall to run both hare-and-hound and "traditional" cross-country races for a time. And in the winter of 1890, the University of Pennsylvania defeated Cornell in the first intercollegiate cross-country race—an experimental affair that gave students from both sites a chance to compete against outside competition. Meanwhile, the College of the City of New York also held its first "championship" over a course near Fort George in 1890. By the end of the decade these achievements would result in an association constituted entirely by university teams.

The "championship" held by the College of the City of New York in March of 1890 was an inter-squad handicap cross-country meet billed as the finale for the end of the season. E. H. Baynes, a member of the Suburban Harriers and a student at the college, was the runner from scratch and the first home. While many universities held hare-and-hound meetings and had formal teams, the implicit notion of holding a championship at the end of the season for a collection of schools was still a work in progress.

On the West Coast of the United States, Stanford University also listed the occasional "casual" meeting for campus cross-country runs or hare-and-hound chases in their on-campus publication *The Stanford Daily* as early as May 1894. Despite this, track and field, baseball, tennis, swimming, and football remained the only varsity sports on campus for the student body.

Back at Cornell, records indicated that captain E. H. Brown organized one of the school's first cross-country clubs in 1891, running hare-and-hound races between 3.5 and five miles, five-mile handicap races, and intercollegiate races with the University of Pennsylvania in 1894, '95, '96, and '98. By 1898, Cornell captain Arthur J. Sweet, with inspiration from the previous year's captain Walter Yeatman, perpetuated the idea of a cross-country association for the colleges. With the help of the Cornell athletic government and support from the student body, Sweet wrote to Pennsylvania, Yale, Princeton, Columbia, Brown, and Harvard, suggesting a conference in New York where these institutions could form an official intercollegiate cross-country association. In April 1899, the Intercollegiate Cross-Country Association of Amateur Athletics of America was formed, with representatives from every university except Harvard and Brown. On Saturday November 18, 1899, the first Intercollegiate Cross-Country Championship was held.

Princeton's top runner and team captain, J. F. Cregan was the first individual champion at the inaugural Intercollegiate Cross-Country Championship, covering the 6.125-mile course at Morris Park in 34:05. Despite this victory, Princeton as a team finished in last place. Scoring the top four finishers for each school, Cornell was the victor with 24 points, Yale second with 32, University of Pennsylvania third with 50 points, Columbia fourth, and Princeton fifth. Cornell's leading runner, A. J. Sweet, finished behind Cregan in third position and led his teammates home, as Cornell claimed the third, fifth, sixth, and 10th places overall.

CONTROVERSY STRIKES THE NATIONAL CROSS-COUNTRY ASSOCIATION OF AMERICA

By the end of 1889, with the disbandment of the National Association of Amateur Athletes of America (NAAAA), amateur athletics officially came under the control of the Amateur Athletic Union (AAU). In addition, the National Cross-Country Association, which had formed as a response to the New York Athletic Club's individual cross-country championship in the fall, continued to manage the team championship in the spring. While this was a result of the efforts of individuals in the Manhattan Athletic Club and the Prospect Harriers, the National Cross-Country Association came under scrutiny at the very moment the NAAAA and AAU were trying to merge.

Charles Hughes, a prominent administrator for amateur athletics in England (including the Amateur Athletic Association), had been secretary of the Manhattan Athletic Club for seven years—and was named the first president of the National Cross-Country Association of America when the body formed in 1887. And when the NAAAA and Amateur Athletic Union merged in 1889, Hughes became a delegate-at-large for the AAU. With vested interest in keeping power over the National Cross-Country Association, Hughes nominated fellow Manhattan Athletic Club member Fredrick Ware to act as president for the remainder of the decade.

But controversy followed. In March 1889, Otto Ruhl, acting president of the New York Athletic Club (as well

as the first-elected treasurer of the AAU), filed a lawsuit against Frederick Ware over the right to use the National Cross-Country Association name. Ruhl had nominated William Halpin, member of the Olympic Athletic Club, as his vice president. The suit attempted to prevent anyone but Ruhl's organization from constituting a meet or championship with the National Cross-Country Association.

As outlined in an April 1889 *New York Times* article, the Ware-supported national team championship that was initially planned to run on April 27 had to move to October in order to have the athletes "be in better condition after their summer training." Conversely, Otto Ruhl (listed in the article as president of the Association) sanctioned the April 27 championship under AAU rules and kept it on the calendar as the "official" championship.

With the confusing matter of who was in charge of the National Cross-Country Association away from the public eye, the championship in April was more popular than ever: 57 runners started the event, and events such as a 100-yard dash, a 220-yard hurdle challenge, and a three-mile bicycle race all coincided with the meet and drew an impressive number of spectators. As mentioned earlier, the Prospect Harriers won the team championship, and it proved to be the first individual title for William "Willie" D. Day, who was not previously known. With the disbandment of the Suburban Harriers, this particular championship was heralded as the coming of a brand-new champion. Day was overlooked on the starting line—representing the New Jersey Athletic Club and listed at only five foot five and 106 pounds—but wouldn't remain anonymous for long.

THE LEGACY OF WILLIAM D. DAY

Willie Day's career was short-lived, but his legacy was never forgotten. Slim, pale, and small-limbed, Day had a flat chest and a long body. With no coach, Day would usually embark on long runs on his own, and his training complemented time spent swimming or rowing. He didn't take great care of himself in his personal time, but he put up a remarkable string of races in the later part of the nineteenth century. In October 1889, Day lined up to run a 10-mile race on the track against the English cross-country champion Sidney Thomas. Day was victorious and set an American record of 52:38. The following month Day again beat Thomas when he won a cross-country race held by the Mohican Athletic Club in Newark, New Jersey, running 6.5 miles in 40:58. Day gave Thomas a 10-second head start and defeated him easily. Thomas's friends claimed that Sidney was not in the best condition, and the stage was set for a follow-up meeting.

On March 16, 1890, the first cross-country handicap was featured at the newly opened Morris Park horse racing track in New York, and was set to be a rematch between Day and Sidney Thomas. The New York Jockey Club was responsible for Morris Park—having taken an interest in distance running as a means to build publicity for the site—and use of the racetrack and grandstand was granted with valuable prizes prepared. As part of the four-mile course, large sections of ground were ploughed up, fences and hurdles were erected, and a large water jump was featured in front of the grandstand.

The distance of this first handicap race was eight miles, so the entire course had to be covered twice. Day (who was only 19 years old at the time) was on scratch, and conceded handicaps to his opponents ranging from 30 seconds (given to Thomas) to seven and a half minutes. Conditions were terrible: a rain that had begun early Friday continued until Saturday morning, along with a few hours of damp, sticky snow, followed by a raw, cutting wind from the north. Nevertheless, more than 200 brave souls showed up to run. Despite ankle-deep mud on the plowed sections paired with a combined hedge and ditch (recently added), Day was not afraid of the field or the man-made challenges. Catching Thomas at 2.5 miles, Day worked his way through the pack, but staggered as he neared the finish. Crossing the line completely exasperated, covered with mud and bruised from falls, Day finished the race victorious in 53:34.

Two months later, over the same eight-mile course at Morris Park, Day won the US National Cross-Country Championship with ease. He joked with the judges at each flag, and jumped the hurdles that his pursuers struggled over. Finishing "as if he had been out for an easy jog," Day vaulted the finisher's fence and ran up the hill to the dressing room, where he took a shower and was having a rub down, as the second-place runner was just finishing the race. Running the eight-mile course in 47:41, "although the ground was very heavy," Day was more than three minutes faster than his nearest opponent.

However, in one of the stranger and more mysterious storylines in the history of cross-country running, Day was arrested four years later, in August 1894, for an outstanding debt of $112 that he owed the Manhattan Laundry, where he worked. Owner of two individual cross-country championship titles and American distance records from two to 10 miles, Day was overwhelmingly embarrassed by this event. The following morning, having been bailed out by a friend, Day was sighted running through Bergen Point, a wooded trail near where he set many of his records. This was the last anyone would see of him alive. Day's body was found hanging some days later from a wild cherry tree overlooking the track at Bergen Point. Officially ruled a suicide, newspapers hinted at information they weren't willing to print.

Regardless, Day was not a thief: in a letter to the *New York Times* accompanying his obituary, the manager of the laundry admitted that a "grave error" had been made and that Day had never taken any money from the firm.

THE UPS AND DOWNS OF THE NATIONAL CROSS-COUNTRY CHAMPIONSHIP

The US National Cross-Country Championship held in 1891 was run without Day's presence, but was significant nonetheless. The Prospect Harriers made history when they became the first team at the championship to finish with a perfect score, having six athletes cross the line before anyone else. The individual winner, M. Kennedy, covered the eight-mile course at Morris Park in 46:30, and he led home J. D. Lloyd, F. H. Kuhlke, W. W. Kuhlke, S. T. Freeth, and R. H. Collins.

The National Cross-Country Association, which had suffered financial troubles and seen remarkable turnover since the lawsuit filed in 1889, officially disbanded as a governing body in 1893. As a result, the US National Cross-Country Championship disappeared from 1892 to 1897, pushing the sport out of the limelight for a short period.

But after a five-year hiatus, the Amateur Athletic Union reinstated the championship in April 1897. Held at Morris Park, the course was just over six miles and contained 43 jumps in all, four of which were water jumps. Fifty-seven runners started the event, and eight teams participated.

At this time, from 1891 through 1902, no athlete in North America won more amateur long-distance running championships than George Orton. Born in Ontario, Canada, in 1873, Orton graduated from Toronto University in 1893 and enrolled at the University of Pennsylvania as a graduate student. He was only five foot six and 125 pounds, but was praised for his gifted running ability and mental toughness. In the early part of the 1890s, Orton made his name on the track, winning titles in the mile and the 3,000-meter steeplechase. His victory in the 1897 US National Cross-Country Championship was particularly significant, as not only did he cross the line 100 yards in front of the second-place finisher, but it was also this event that sparked his love for cross-country running. Later in life, Orton wrote about the sport in his book *Distance and Cross-Country Running*, which he published in 1903: "Cross-country is the basis for all distance success," Orton begins.

In April 1898, 71 men competed in the US National Cross-Country Championship run at Morris Park over a distance of nearly seven miles and covering 44 jumps. Orton was again the winner, and the Knickerbocker Athletic Club repeated as team champion. Cornell University also entered a team in this event, with A. J. Sweet being their top finisher. With the inclusion of a college team, it was clear that the AAU was looking for the successful younger generation to reinvigorate support for the championship. It wouldn't be the first time—at the annual New York Athletic Club cross-country run in November 1989, Yale and Cornell participated but were unable to beat the NYAC over their home turf.

One of the bright spots for the National Cross-Country Championships was the integration of a junior division, which produced terrific storylines. The inaugural race occurred in the spring of 1890. The Prospect Harriers were able to enter two complete teams, and won the first championship with ease. A rival group, the Acorn Athletic Association from Bay Ridge, disputed the legality of the Prospect team entering two squads and demanded a rematch—thus the junior championship was rerun on November 4 later that year. In this second event, the Prospect Harriers beat Acorn Athletic Association handily, 41 points to 76 (Acorn was conspicuously absent at the award ceremony).

With similar methods used in the home countries of the United Kingdom, the prerequisite for running in the American junior event was not an age restriction, but a clean prior record. As a result, the interest generated by having both junior and senior divisions compete for a championship ensured that this format would carry well into the future.

ELSEWHERE IN AMERICA

In addition to a junior division, the end of the decade saw the emergence of high school competitors in the United States. The New York Interscholastic Athletic Association, or "Interscholastic League," pioneered the formation of high school sports leagues. This league was exclusively composed of private schools in the New York metropolitan area. Notable members included Berkeley, Cutler, Barnard, Columbia Grammar School, Trinity, and Dwight. These were the first secondary schools in the country to conduct cross-country meets when in the late 1890s Trinity school sponsored an annual "Interscholastic League" meet.

Sports organizations for high schools in the United States began with a bang in the 1890s. But public education was conservative, and high school sports did not receive popular enthusiasm until after the turn of the century. In the *Proceedings* of the Physical Training Conference of 1889, "mention was made of athletic sports only twice, once by Hartwell of John Hopkins, and once by Hitchcock of Amherst." This was not a surprise; sports for youth were not a priority from an administrative standpoint. Moreover, in the decade that followed, it was students, rather than teachers, who began taking their playground activities off school grounds and scheduling games with nearby rivals, either teams of other schools, "town" teams, or, more often still, "school and community" teams.

Faculty attitude in American high schools followed the pattern set by the universities: in the beginning, opposition; next, tolerance; finally, encouragement and control. By the turn of the century, high school executives began forming local leagues, which, limited by poor transportation, could only include nearby schools. Institutions were still in the horse-and-buggy age, when a sudden mud hole might isolate a community for weeks. Because of this, urban high schools in the oldest parts of the country were the first to organize interscholastic athletics. Several attempts in the 1890s are of record. According to Cozens and Stumpf in their book *Sports in American Life*, the New York Public School Athletic League was organized in 1903 and "served as a pattern for the formation of other city school athletic organizations. Seventeen cities are reported to have formed similar leagues."

> **Did You Know?**
>
> It was in the Bay Area in California that the Olympic Athletic Club (the oldest athletic club in the United States) pioneered cross-country meets. Evidenced by results printed in the *S. F. Newsletter* and *Outing Magazine* as early as 1890, the Olympic Athletic Club held meets in Sausalito, with 28 men running a seven-mile race to Lime Point, while other races started in Sausalito and ran three miles out to Fog Station and back. Additional meets were held further south on the peninsula in Millbrae and San Mateo, where trophies were issued to the top winners as well as a leather medal for the final-place finisher.

A DIVIDE IN SCOTLAND NATIONAL CROSS-COUNTRY

On Saturday, December 8, 1888, at the Bath Hotel in Glasgow, the Clydesdale Harriers—Scotland's most prestigious and well-recognized cross-country club—formed a new association known as the Scottish Harriers Union (SHU). This body separated the Clydesdale club from the Scottish Cross-Country Association (SCCA), which had formed a year earlier. In a similar fashion to what transpired across the Atlantic between the New York Athletic Club and the Manhattan Athletic Club, the Clydesdale Harriers had minor disagreements with the SCCA and voiced their displeasure.

As a result, by 1890, the Scottish Harriers Union had formed links with other sporting bodies and opened correspondence with the English National Cross-Country Union, seeking to affiliate and hold championships in Scotland. This was clearly designed to lead to a confrontation with the SCCA, as arrangements had been made by both organizations to hold their respective versions of the Scottish cross-country championships within a two-week window of each other.

There was one benefit to the schism between these two associations, however, and that was the interest generated in the public by having two national championships. The championships of the Scottish Harrier Union were a resounding success. Andrew Hannah, Clydesdale's leading distance runner was victorious, and would go on to win five titles in seven years.

The championships of the SCCA were disastrous. In the 1890 edition, the field followed the wrong trail, voiding the results. While this was not unusual, it glared in the wake of the successful SHU event two weeks before. Only the Hamilton Harriers had followed the correct trail, while no other club finished a full team.

With continual pressure from both the SCCA and the SHU to end their dispute, a SHU "Junior Championship" took place at Ibrox Park in December 1889. With 11 teams and more than 100 athletes, the event boasted the largest gathering of athletes at a championship event in Scotland to date. It was an outstanding success.

A resolution occurred a few months later. At a meeting on February 1, 1890, the two organizations negotiated a merge, forming the Scottish Cross-Country Union (SCCU). Upon agreement of terms, the following statement was issued by the newly formed body: "It is important to realize that both the SCCA and the SHU were dissolved to allow the formation of the Scottish Cross-Country Union. This did not represent a takeover by either organization."

The energies of the Clydesdale club in building the base of running in Scotland was bearing fruit, especially with the junior race and in the high quality of organization of their championships. The sport was now able to focus on the rising numbers of clubs and the success of runner Andrew Hannah, who finished a creditable ninth in the English Cross-Country Championships that same year.

THE JUNIOR MOVEMENT IN SCOTLAND

With the previous schism resolved, the new Scottish Cross-Country Union next had to direct its attention to the issue of "junior" clubs. As the sport grew rapidly and the six established senior clubs had regular attendance, new, inexperienced "junior" clubs were finding difficulty in accessing the sport at the championship level. The previous "junior championship" held by the Scottish Harriers Union in 1889 was not renewed, and this meant the junior clubs (which soon numbered over 50 registered), were left without a championship, as only members from the established senior teams were eligible to run.

This issue grew in importance as it began to diminish the junior ranks, since the only way a talented runner in one of the junior clubs could compete in the championship was to join one of the senior clubs. And as new clubs formed, a lack of access to the senior championship became a major problem.

A junior championship eventually came to fruition when clubs in the west of Scotland formed a Western District Junior Cross-Country Association (the use of the word "Association" was important, given the differences previously within the senior clubs). The roots of this body were sown as early as February 1893, just a mere three years after the inception of the new Scottish Cross-Country Union.

With a slow but inevitable rise in club membership for the junior association by the middle years of the 1890s, it wasn't long before more junior teams were competing in the Western District Junior Championship than the Senior National Championship. And by 1898, the re-branded Scottish Cross-Country Association (Western District) had more members than the SCCU. But despite repeated requests by the junior clubs that the SCCU oversee their growing championship, a refusal was always issued. The SCCU either saw itself as elitist, or had no funds to support further competition.

However, with their change in title and growing numbers the junior association could not be ignored; they became a direct threat to the authority of the SCCU. The Scottish Cross-Country Association (Western District) next

made a request to affiliate with the Scottish Amateur Athletic Association in September 1897, which circumvented the SCCU and entitled the SCCA to a seat on the committee. While this outcome was not achieved, the challenge was real. Another resolution was inevitable.

While a period of relative calm existed for about two years, meetings were arranged behind the scenes. An agreement was reached at a conference in December 1901, resulting in the eventual disbandment of the SCCU. Clubs in affiliation were asked to vote on a committee motion for amalgamation with the Scottish Cross-Country Association (Western District) in order to finally, and conclusively, agree on a Scottish governing body for cross-country.

SCOTLAND'S DISTANCE PRODIGY OF THE DECADE

Meanwhile, Andrew Hannah, who competed for the Clydesdale Harriers during the 1890s, was one of Scotland's premier record holders and received remarkable praise for his achievements. National champion in distance track events ranging from one mile to 10 miles (many marks set during the early part of the decade), Hannah traveled between Scotland and England lowering his nation-leading times. On the cross-country course Hannah was nearly unstoppable. At the final Scottish Harrier Union Championships held in February 1890, Hannah was the champion by a wide margin. Upon the merging of the SCCA and the SHU into the SCCU that same year, Hannah won four of the next six championships.

Hannah's string of victories, which occurred in 1890, '91, '93, '94, and '96, were the most titles accumulated until Nathaniel Muir won eight between 1979 and 1987, nearly 90 years later. The Hannah Cup, which is the oldest trophy in the Clydesdale Harrier club, dates back to 1900, when Andrew Hannah himself donated it. It is still coveted today as part of Clydesdale's club cross-country season. Hannah's top 10 performances at the English Cross-Country Championships during this time were also a harbinger for an international movement that was gaining steam in Northern Europe.

IRELAND CONTINUES TO FLOURISH

While Scotland saw limited success and a lot of association volatility, the 1890s in Ireland saw cross-country consistency—a rarity among clubs in Europe (there were no schisms, divides, or merging of organizations). During the decade, the Irish Cross-Country Association not only introduced a junior championship over six miles, but they also adjusted the senior championship, creating a Northern Branch (Ulster) Championship and a Southern Branch (Connacht, Munster and Leinster) Championship.

And as Ireland did not make any drastic adjustment to the way they conducted cross-country within the decade, it was refreshing to note that their governance of the sport remained stable. Because of their close proximity to Scotland, England, and Wales, Ireland's involvement became a more relevant theme in the years following the turn of the century. Their stability mattered too, because outside the home nations of the United Kingdom, other European nations were beginning to adapt the sport as well—and opportunities for international competition were coming.

BELGIUM'S FIRST NATIONAL CHAMPIONSHIP

In 1896—prompted by other athletic organizations taking shape, notably track and field and football—Belgium introduced its first National Cross-Country Championship, with Charles Van der Beeken as the first winner.

For the next five editions, however, one Belgian athlete would rule them all. Born in 1880, Jules Lesage became one of Belgium's first distance running prodigies. From 1897 to 1903, Lesage was victorious six times in seven years and lost only one cross-country national championship. In the early years of the twentieth century, Lesage turned his focus to marathon running, winning the Belgian national marathon-running championship in 1903, '04, and '05.

For Belgium, the cross-country national earned steady notoriety with the public, despite there being only three different champions in its first 10 years. It would take another generation, however, for Belgium to develop an administration to match the English enthusiasm with the sport.

BACK TO ENGLAND

During the 1890s England continued to manage the growth of its harrier clubs. A Northern Counties Association and Southern Counties Association soon joined the Midlands Association, all three of which conducted their own championship just prior to the English National on the calendar. Powerful teams like the Salford Harriers, Manchester Harriers, and Bolton Wanderers were represented in the Northern Counties, while teams like the Moseley Harriers, Birchfield Harriers, and Worcester Harriers found success in the Midlands. In the Southern Counties, teams like the Finchley Harriers, Ranelagh Harriers, and Essex Beagles were in close proximity to each other competitively, while teams like the Thames Hare and Hounds remained absent from the record books due to their own concerns about betting and roping.

In 1898, an article published in *The Badminton Magazine of Sports and Pastimes* offered a unique glimpse of the sport from the English perspective during this period:

Cross-country running is essentially the sport of the masses. The classes either pass it contemptuously by on the other side, or judge its votaries by the attenuated and lightly clad specimens of humanity who may be seen scampering round suburban roads in the gathering darkness of a winter Saturday afternoon. But we cannot help regarding it as a most important branch of athletics. Nearly all our best distance runners train regularly across country

in the off season, and while our sprinters go down before the flying Americans, and our jumpers are outdone by the nimble Gael, we can still claim an undisputed supremacy at the longer distances, and it is across country that the majority of such contests are decided. When we consider the sport itself, the reason of its popularity, especially in the metropolitan district, is not hard to find. The cost is trifling, the outfit of the simplest, and it can be pursued at an hour which would render any other outdoor sports impossible. Much senseless rubbish has been talked about the dangers of cross-country running; but these are incurred only by the foolish. There is no more delightful sensation than that of a good stretch over a sporting course, when wind and limb alike are in good condition, and one can stride out right through from end to end.

Other English news featured more familiar names with the Thames Hare and Hounds. Despite running strongly as late as 1890, club and national champion Percy Stenning passed away unexpectedly in June 1892. Further, despite lowering the minimum age for membership, Thames experienced a great drop-off in attendance; in 1894 only nine members showed up for runs regularly.

But this was the darkest hour before the dawn; within two months of the 1895 General Meeting, 11 new members had been elected to join Thames. Runs also resumed most Saturdays, matches against both Oxford and Cambridge (after a lapse of five years) were again arranged, and the secretary at the next Annual General Meeting could refer to "the very satisfactory progress" that had been made, and that ". . . thanks to the generous support of certain of the older members, the Club had slowly but surely made up its lost ground." The presence of Edwin Flack (an Australian who had been trained by former Thames member E. M. Wilson—himself a 4:44-miler) at the opening run had a lot to do with the transformation within the Thames club.

Around the same time in England, ties were developing with the traditional form of the sport of cross-country and fell running. One example, initiated by George Macaulay Trevelyan (an undergraduate at Trinity College in Cambridge) was to create the Trevelyan Lake Hunt—a hare-and-hound game of notorious difficulty. He and two other students pored over maps until they found the bleakest spot in Britain—10 miles wide, with scant cover, freezing lakes, and vertiginous cliffs. They divided into two camps: the chased and the chasers. The sport became so vicious that for a time the hares, then known as "cavalier couriers," had to double "as security for their own nerves and necks." The game was only stopped during the two World Wars when numbers were depleted. But as soon as peace broke out, the manhunt reconvened.

When the Trevelyan Lake Hunt first started, the men would run all day and find shelter in a hut at night. Future runs saw the field return to a guesthouse for lukewarm baths and teas. The only noticeable change over time was in the dress. Members were chosen by word of mouth.

Fathers passed their lineage on to their sons. They needed to be sharp enough to spot a broken branch, fast enough to chase for several hours, and hardy enough to keep going with swollen ankles and broken fingers—a list of qualifications that seemed to produce a bizarre mixture of PhDs, distance runners, rugby players, members of parliament, and eccentric aristocrats.

Elsewhere in England, the Birchfield Harriers in the Midlands overcame serious financial trouble (due to expenses related to hosting meets) and low attendance (by 1887 there were only 10 runners left in the club) to find success in the 1890s. At the time, it was a remarkable feat for this squad to travel around England and be competitive. The end of the 1880s saw Birchfield with a two-time National Cross-Country champion (J. E. Hickman, from Godiva), and a record of being national team champions four times overall (winning three straight from 1886 to 1888).

By the start of the 1890s, further trends justified the progress expressed previously. The 1891–92 season saw the introduction of a Novice Championship by the Midlands Cross-Country Association. Although many competitors were recognized as "juniors," the entrance criteria, like in other places at the time, was based on experience rather than age. The dichotomy experienced by the Birchfield Harriers (financial struggles in the background of all their team success) was not rare. Other teams experienced similar financial trouble—as did the governing bodies themselves, exemplified by the inconsistent holding of the Midlands County Cross-Country Championship. This was a reflection of difficult economic times everywhere—similar situations also hit in Canada and the United States. But despite crumbling teams in some areas, the achievements of individual athletes left a lasting mark on the sport.

OUTSIDE DEALINGS DURING THE 1890s

When England became interested in a first-ever international cross-country meeting, it was because other nations had enthusiastically begun organizing the sport internally. Australia was notable in the decade—quickly followed by France—two such nations that constructed formats to explore the sport on a national level.

In Australia, 1890 marked the first year that the New South Wales (NSW) Annual Cross-Country Championship took place. For every year up until 1908, the NSW Athletic Association put on a club championship for any harrier teams in the area. The 1906 event was held at Kensington Racecourse, while the 1907 event took place at Eastwood Park. Teams such as the East Brisbane Harriers, Thompson Estate Harriers, and the New South Wales Harriers competed annually for the championship until a national meet was developed in 1908, electing teams to be represented by statehood instead of by club.

In April 1889, France held their first National Cross-Country Championship, with Mat Bersin winning the inaugural event, which was held in Meudon. On April 20, 1890, Frantz Reichel won the second annual French Cross-Country Championship. Held in Chaville, Reichel took the title from Bersin. Reichel was the first famous multi-sport athlete in France and in 1889 he won the support from the "Congress for the Propagation of Physical Exercise in Education" founded by Pierre de Coubertin, whose eclectic program included events in running, horseback riding, gymnastics, fencing, boxing, swimming, and rowing. Reichel also played rugby at Racing Club de France and the Sporting Club University of France (SCUF), and won a National Boxing Championship. He won his second title in the third running of the French National Cross-Country Championship in April 1891.

The French National was held primarily in Ville-d'Avray, with a course ranging from 14 kilometers to 16.5 kilometers. Michel Soalhat won back-to-back titles in 1896 and 1897 before Englishman Alfred Tunmer won the event on March 6, 1898. Two weeks later British journalist Harry Hardwick led the top eight finishers of the English National Cross-Country Championship against a French team composed of their eight best runners.

* * *

With the sport growing exponentially in Europe, and with the increasing support of junior and collegiate runners across the globe, the future for cross-country remained bright. Even with the challenges faced by associations and the economic hardships of providing for a sport with limited spectator visibility, a legion of devoted competitors was pushing the pace forward.

EVENT SPOTLIGHT: THE FIRST INTERNATIONAL CROSS-COUNTRY MEETING—CROSS DES NATIONS (MARCH 20, 1898)

LOCATION: VILLE-D'AVRAY, FRANCE

Early Preparations: London

British journalist Harry Hardwick was the official handicapper for the English Cross-Country Association and was also an expert businessman. In 1890, Hardwick organized the first overseas voyage of an athletics club—the Salford Harriers—and was responsible for the first international meeting between England and America on the track. Eight years later it was Hardwick who led a group of British cross-country specialists in a pioneering expedition, directed at introducing Europe to the practice of cross-country. France had no real tradition in the sport (having only started their own national meet eight years prior) and this initial match with the British was seen as largely unequal. Correspondence with France had brought up the issue of cost for the meet, but one of the primary motivations in accepting the French invitation was when the French offered to cover expenses.

In the end, the top eight finishers at the 1898 English National Cross-Country Championship were chosen to represent England and were sent to France to compete in a cross-country meet against a French national team. The Cross des Nations in Paris took place on March 20, 1898. The race was held over a course of nine miles, 20 yards (14.5 kilometers), from Ville-d'Avray, near Sevres, and finished on the Versailles road. The weather was bad leading up to the race, but the French Athletic Federation insisted the meet take place despite the poor conditions of the course.

On the day of the race, conditions cleared, and a large number of cyclists, racing fans, and journalists gathered well before the 10:00 a.m. start to witness the momentous occasion. Although French experts knew better than to believe their own competitors would defeat the strong British team, they still expected that the French runners would recover well on the flat stretches and make up lost ground on the uphill portions.

Seventeen runners started the event, with eight from France and nine from England. The English, headed by champion Sid Robinson, started at once uphill at a sharp pace, drawing ahead of the French immediately. At the halfway mark, despite the fact that the terrain was unknown and not in the best condition, the eight Englishmen were in a bunch, leading the first Frenchman by 38 seconds.

The finish line was reached in the following order and time:

England		
1	S. J. Robinson (Northampton Cycling & Athletic Club)	56:36
2	H. Harrison (Manchester Harriers)	56:36.4
3	C. Bennett (Finchley Harriers)	57:14
4	T. Bartlett (Essex Beagles)	57:22
5	J. D. Marsh (Salford Harriers)	57:48
6	G. Barlow (Manchester Harriers)	57:51
	(21 Points)	
7	J. Cook (Salford Harriers)	58:44
8	A. H. Meacham (Birchfield Harriers)	58:44

France		
9	A. Touquet	59:08
10	H. Freeman (England)	61:33
11	E. Pican	61:42
12	A. Genet	62:51
13	I. Cennetin	63:10
14	M. Dupre	63:18
	(69 points)	
15	A. Marchais	64:11
16	A. Aubert	64:18

Robinson, the winner, came in slow and smiling, and in fact assisted Harrison, who showed signs of weakness after crossing the line in second place. The next six for England appeared just as fresh as the winner (although when Touquet, the first Frenchman, crossed the line, he dropped down in an insensible heap and, hurting his head in the fall, had to be carried away). Robinson expressed himself "greatly satisfied" at the result of the race. He owned that "the ground was heavy" but declared that "the other conditions were perfect, for there was not a breath of wind, no sun shining, and the air was keen and invigorating."

The teams and officials were entertained to a banquet in Paris that evening, and Viscount de Janze, who presided over the race, said he hoped the event would lead to other meetings between the two countries. All were impressed by the way the French team conducted themselves, and respect was paid to Touquet in particular. Six English cross-country officials from various clubs accompanied the team and were honored at the banquet. It is also interesting to note that the English runners wore uniforms identical to the ones they would wear in future international championships through the Second World War: white shorts and vests with the red rose badge.

During this period, émigrés played a significant role in the global expansion of cross-country running. In particular, the British Empire and its dominions benefited from the social and economic traffic of runners as they moved throughout the world for business and pleasure. The sport was therefore an export with its rules and regulations, and often its social and organizational structures, which explained its rapid growth and even assisted in the formation of governing bodies. The records of the International Athletics Federation show that the development of cross-country legitimization took place mainly in Britain and its Empire. For example, the governing bodies of sport for athletics and cross-country were constituted in Australia, New Zealand, Canada, and South Africa before such European countries as Germany, Finland, Sweden, and Belgium. Cross-country, internationally, had a strong British perspective in its development and form—and this was no different to the expansion of other sports in the late nineteenth century.

Chapter 6

Of all forms of pedestrianism and, indeed, of all branches of athletics there can be nothing superior to cross-country running for either pleasure or health. The sport itself is ideal, whether a race be contested in fine or muddy weather. Track or road running is apt to grow monotonous, however exciting it may be; but there is nothing monotonous in an open country run. Even the training itself is almost as enjoyable as the race, and from first to last I defy anybody to find a single point to cavil at.

—*Alfred Shrubb*

THE 1900s

During the 1900s, cross-country took root in the public consciousness as an expected form of sport during the fall, winter, and spring months. No longer seen as a mere pastime or leisure activity, the sport had instilled itself in the athletics culture throughout Europe, and was making a significant rise across North America. The biggest names in distance running became regular participants, and the sport stabilized—or gained momentum—in previously unpopular areas. In many major cities, cross-country running was grabbing headlines.

NORTH AMERICAN RISE

While the official cross-country championship in America experienced a down period between 1898 and 1905—running only twice—grassroots iterations of the sport were flourishing. Amateur and collegiate teams were running in the "modern" interpretation of competition, and hare-and-hound variations began to disappear. A number of colleges along the East Coast, including the Ivy League, fielded teams by the start of the decade and met at the championship hosted by the Intercollegiate Cross-Country Association. Cornell won three of the first four team titles contested, and top runner W. E. Schutt won the individual championship in 1903 in a record-breaking 33:15.

Three primary factors led to the success at the collegiate level: the first was the physical benefit, coupled with the intercollegiate rivalry between universities; second was incorporation of like-minded colleges; and third was the success of the Intercollegiate Cross-Country Association, which continued to hold annual championships along the East Coast and saw the inclusion of more teams into the fold throughout the decade.

> **Did You Know?**
>
> In 1905, Missouri University started its first cross-country club team, where small "squad" races were held. Cross-country at Michigan State University (then Michigan Agricultural College) dated to 1907, when a large, split-squad, intra-college competition was held on campus. By the end of the decade, Southern schools in the Southern Intercollegiate Athletic Association (established at Vanderbilt by chemistry professor Dr. William Dudley in 1894) and others in the Midwest, like those in the Western Conference (Big Ten Conference—established in 1896—which first held a cross-country championship in 1910), were also fielding cross-country teams.

Prior to 1908, the Collegiate Cross-Country Championship was held by this association, which was nearing its 10th anniversary. Cornell remained the leading university for the sport, and other charter members from East Coast schools, such as Princeton, Yale, University of Pennsylvania, and Columbia remained heavily involved. But by 1908, the meet had doubled in size and a new governing body took over: the Intercollegiate Association of Amateur Athletes of America (IC4A). IC4A governance contained universities in the New England and mid-Atlantic States, north and inclusive of Maryland and Delaware. This body, which had first aligned in 1876 for track and field, had also maintained success through this period, and it was fitting that they would govern the Collegiate Cross-Country Championship.

Despite the change in authority, Cornell remained dominant, winning nine team titles in 10 years. Individual success also followed: after H. C. Young won at Princeton in 1908, Young's teammate T. S. Berna was victorious over six miles in Brookline Massachusetts the following year. Defeated teams expanded to include Massachusetts Institute of Technology (MIT), University of Michigan, Yale, Dartmouth, Syracuse, Harvard, University of Pennsylvania, Columbia, and Princeton.

For high schools, the first major interscholastic cross-country meet in the country was the "American Interscholastic," first conducted by the University of Pennsylvania in the fall of 1903. This meet was novel in its scope: invitations were mailed up and down the Eastern seaboard urging schoolboys to converge in Philadelphia on the first Saturday in December to compete for what was called a "national" prep championship.

Thus began a close association between colleges and high schools within the sport; soon, other universities in America began conducting their own interscholastics, notably Princeton, Yale, and Columbia. Elsewhere, one of the earliest high school cross-country runs was started in Canada, at St. Andrew's College in Aurora, Ontario. A member of the Little Big Four (LBF) independent school league from 1899 to 1968, St. Andrew's held their run annually and included all levels of students and faculty.

Did You Know?

Princeton's first interscholastic (high school invitational) occurred in November 1906. Run on Brokaw field—a three-mile course which featured hurdles meant to mimic Morris Park in New York—the race hosted 14 high schools where 49 runners finished. Mercersburg Academy won with 39 points, while teams attended from Philadelphia, New York, Pittsburgh, and New Jersey. The top four finishers from each team (out of seven) were scored.

Meanwhile, although a few Chicago-area institutions had taken up cross-country, Oak Park High School became the first to sponsor interscholastic competition in the fall of 1904, when a 3.5-mile race was held that December. The *Chicago Tribune* reported, "The first event met with such success that the event seems sure to be a fixture at the suburban school. The distance was shortened to three and one-half miles so that it would not be too hard on the boys . . ." Next came a Cook County League meet in 1908, which awarded team and individual championships. The event, held in a blinding snowstorm, was witnessed by 5,000 spectators, but only attracted three schools: Oak Park, Englewood, and Crane. The Amateur Athletic Union then held a meet for high schools at Sherman Park in 1909, which marked the final time the sport would appear at the high school level in Chicago until the mid-1920s.

While the early years in the 1900s saw only sporadic glimmers of what was to come, the later years of the decade reaffirmed the stature of cross-country running in North America. Predominantly well-known on the East Coast before the turn of the century, cross-country running's acceptance in the American West and South gave a bold prediction as to where the next great achievements would be found within the sport.

THE DIPSEA

One summer day in 1904, several members of San Francisco's Olympic Athletic Club set off for the newly opened Dipsea Inn, which overlooked the Pacific Ocean. They took the ferry to Sausalito and the train to their starting point: the depot in Mill Valley, a small town north of San Francisco. A wager was made to see who could make it to the inn first. After mapping out the route and setting out across the countryside, the challenge proved so exciting that club members decided to make an annual race of it. Race committees were established, the adventurous group identified themselves as the Dipsea Indians, and San Francisco judge Timothy Fitzpatrick was chosen as the Grand Chief.

Prior to inviting the public, the Dipsea Indians settled on two of the enduring foundations that were to forever make the Dipsea special. First, although a suggested route was marked, runners were free to choose their own way from downtown Mill Valley to Willow Camp. The second was the idea of giving head starts (thereby handicapping the field). It has been a tradition that has persisted to the present day.

The first Dipsea captured the public's imagination as no other footrace had done before. All major San Francisco newspapers gave the race feature coverage (and would continue to do so for decades). The *Chronicle* splashed a bold headline across the front sports page proclaiming, "Great Cross-Country Run from Mill Valley to Dipsea." Below a picture of the contestants was the caption, "The contest proved to be the greatest athletic event ever held in the history of the Olympic Club." The *Morning Call* said, "The success of the contest, both in its record entry [111 runners—double the estimates and high by the standards of the era] and in its outcome, is expected to have a strong influence on athletics on this coast." The *Examiner* proclaimed the race, "The greatest cross-country run that was ever held in this or any country."

Over the years the course has shortened slightly and has seen more structure. Head starts became based on age in the 1960s. Women were officially admitted in 1971, although they had been running the race since 1950 and all-women's Dipseas held from 1918 through 1922 actually outdrew the "men's" editions (and were startlingly egalitarian for the time). And while the event itself is perhaps best categorized as a distance trail run for numerous factors, its soul was born at an age where the Olympic Club's exploits with Hare-and-Hounds and West Coast cross-country affairs made headlines.

AUSTRALASIAN DEVELOPMENTS

Meanwhile, further west, in 1903, Christchurch hosted the first New Zealand National Cross-Country Championship at Lancaster Park, which saw P. Malthus win in a time of 28:55 for five miles. In 1908, the very first unofficial Australian National Cross-Country Championship took place when an interstate meet was held with teams from New South Wales, Victoria, Queensland, and Tasmania. The run was contested over a five-mile route at Victoria Park Racecourse in Sydney on September 12.

Born out of the New South Wales Annual Cross-Country Championship started in 1890, this particular event marked the first time that different regions of Australia were represented (prior to this, only club teams from the Sydney area would compete). The Australian National Cross-Country Championship appeared again in 1910, and was contested biannually until 1973.

INTERNATIONAL STATUS ARRIVES FOR CROSS-COUNTRY

Did You Know?

European nations adapted and organized the sport at the turn of the century, and this was partly due to the growth and development of athletic clubs in England, Scotland, Ireland, Wales, and France. European governing bodies, impressed by the success of other spectator sports, adopted the rules of cross-country for clubs prior to many schools and colleges playing the game. It was a quick transition between Europe having little to no activity with cross-country to seeing national championships appear. Here is a general list of European nations and their sanction of the sport during the decade:

- In March 1900 Jean Bongard became the first Swiss National Cross-Country champion, winning over a long course in Geneva. The event would not be contested again until 1904, when Gustav Gurwang became the second champion. André Alberganti became the first repeat Swiss National Cross-Country champion when he won his second title in two years in 1908 in Lausanne. Alberganti would eventually win four titles in five years.
- In September 1907 Josef Jahnzon became the first Swedish National Cross-Country champion. Running the eight-kilometer course in 50:03, Jahnzon, who was more widely known for being a national-caliber speed skater, impressed the crowd. The following year Gösta Ljungström won the second championship in Göteborg, running 55:49 for eight kilometers.

1909 and 1910 saw Sweden's first repeat National Cross-Country champion, when Georg Pettersson won the event, first in Norrköping and then in Stockholm.
- For the first five years of the decade, Austria ran a National Cross-Country Championship. Leopold Sax won the first two titles, both held in Vienna, in 1900 and 1901. On July 9, 1905, Felix Kwieton won his second championship, following a victory in June 1902. Kwieton was one of Austria's first distance running stars; he had tremendous range, going on to run the 1,500 meters on the track in 4:16 at the 1906 Summer Olympic Games, and then the marathon in the 1912 Summer Olympic Games. After Kwieton's victory in 1905, the Austrian National Cross-Country Championship was not contested again until 1921.
- The first Danish National Cross-Country Championship, contested in 1901, lists Axel Poulsen the winner of the 15-kilometer race, which he won in 1:10:29. Poulsen repeated as champion the following year, winning in a time of 1:07:03. Amazingly, for the first ten editions of the Denmark National, only six different individual winners appeared: Carl Jörgensen (1903 and 1904), Kjeld Nielsen (1906 and 1907), and Viggo Pedersen (1909 and 1910) were repeat winners. Pedersen went on to be a national champion in the 10,000-meter run.
- Hungary began their National Cross-Country Championship in 1908, with Jozsef Nagy winning back-to-back titles in 1909 and 1910. Born in 1881, Nagy gained popularity when he became a member of the bronze-medal Hungarian medley relay team, which competed at the 1908 Summer Olympics in London. As an Olympian, Nagy brought an air of legitimacy to the sport, and large crowds were present for both of his victories.
- In June 1908, Pericle Pagliani became the winner of the first National Cross-Country Championship in Italy, which was run over the l'Acqua Acetosa ei Parioli in Rome on a 14-kilometer course. Pagliani then repeated in 1909, when 20 athletes competed on a 10-kilometer paper trail course. The Messenger in June 1909 reported, "The competitors set out in a group led by Pagliani of Lazio, which stuck together for the first two kilometers. Opening up ground on the other competitors the strong Roman champion managed to take the lead and kept it throughout the race. He commanded the field, arriving first at the finish with a great advantage, taking the 10-kilometer race in 33 minutes."

Expectedly at the turn of the century, the English cross-country scene was booming. Coming off their 1898 domination in their first international meeting with France, England felt superior to every other nation when it came to distance running, and they had the top performances to prove it. Meanwhile, the strength of the other home nations of the United Kingdom was variable.

While English cross-country was undeniably strong due to its long tradition and more developed club infrastructure, both the Irish and Scots had competed against the English at their championships and interclub contests. And though arrangements had been made between England and Ireland in 1902 for an international match at the Cork Exhibition, it never materialized. England insisted that their National Championships were the appropriate place for an "International Championship," and this attempt to elevate the race to a defacto United Kingdom Championships was not well received by the other home nations.

Scotland's involvement through the Clydesdale Harriers and the success of Andrew Hannah at the English Championship gave a rousing case for support for international competition, as they had proved it wasn't just English breeding that produced champions.

Ireland too had runners of note but the structure and strength of the sport there was still relatively unknown internationally. Their strongest athletes came from the University of Dublin while the oldest Irish club, Haddington Harriers, as well as the Clonliffe Harriers, were represented well throughout the decade.

Meanwhile, the situation in Wales was clearer. The Welsh Cross-Country Association was formed in 1896 making it the youngest of the governing bodies of the home nations. The strength of Welsh cross-country centered on the industrial cities of Newport, Cardiff, and Swansea. The Newport Harriers had operated similarly to the Clydesdale Harriers, and had won the Welsh Championship five consecutive times through 1903.

But the development of meaningful international competition could not be considered without the presence of England. And with the arrival of Alfred Shrubb to the national scene, the English cross-country movement was about to witness its first superstar.

THE LITTLE WONDER

Born on December 12, 1879—the fifth child to William Shrubb, a farmer in West Sussex, and his wife Harriet—Alfred Shrubb arrived into the world at a time when England was in a major agricultural depression. Shrubb was small and thin, barely over five feet, but he loved the outdoor life and his lack of height and weight disguised a surprising level of fitness and stamina.

Training mostly for fun, by the spring of 1900, Shrubb's few but successful track exploits had caught the attention of Thomas Sinnott, a well-known official (and club president) of the South London Harriers (SLH). Equally excited about Shrubb's emergence was Harry Andrews, a running

Did You Know?

As a young boy, Alfred Shrubb was naturally fit and found running across the countryside an exhilarating experience. Shrubb would go on boyhood fox hunts on foot by himself. *C. B. Fry's Magazine* would later eulogize, "On he plods, never varying his pace, occasionally glancing around—from curiosity, not apprehension—on, on, at the same gait to the end. He is happy even over ploughland. While his opponents have toiled through the holding earth, Shrubb runs so lightly that he travels over it, skimming it like a bird, and with such grace and ease . . ."

coach and well-known figure in athletics circles. With their guidance, Shrubb joined the South London Harriers that summer. Soon, Sinnott had issued Shrubb the nickname "The Little Wonder," which would resurface many times in the press.

On November 3, 1900, Shrubb got his first taste at competitive paper-chasing in South Croyden, and he did not disappoint, capturing South London's Gibb Cup over a five-mile course. After winning the Gibb Cup, Shrubb then lined up against Oxford University's cross-country team three weeks later in a challenge match. He showed the elitist students his heels, leading South London to an emphatic victory.

With the South London Harriers's Gibb and Norton trophies under his belt by the end of the year, Shrubb now focused on becoming cross-country's first superstar. SLH craved the prestige of having a National Cross-Country champion and they had a serious candidate in Shrubb. In early 1901 the club sent Coach Andrews to Horsham for three weeks to prepare Shrubb for the cross-country championship season that spring. But Shrubb was delayed before he ever started, as the Southern Cross-Country Championships at Wembley Park was rescheduled. In the interim, the athletics press reported that Shrubb, the young contender for the crown, was attracting much attention in the buildup. "Shrubb is held in the highest esteem despite his lack of experience. No man has carried off the Southern in his first try, much less in his first season! If he can do it, he's a veritable wonder," claimed one correspondent.

Around 200 runners representing Southern England's top 17 clubs lined up at Wembley Park where the 10-mile course was in good condition. The race was off at 3:33 p.m. and Shrubb, anxious not to get trapped, tried to blast his way to the front. Eventually an opening presented itself, and he emerged alongside early leader George Pearce of the Essex Beagles. After running together, they both arrived at a long stretch of ploughed terrain, and a delighted Shrubb knew that was his moment. "I had been resting a little till then, preparing for a good scamper," he recalled. "Much to Pearce's surprise, as he admitted afterwards, I ran that field almost as if it had been a grass path." From that point, there was only one winner.

Alfred Shrubb was champion of the South. The next task, seven days away, was to try and become champion of England. Meanwhile *Athletic News* said that for Shrubb to win both the Southern and National titles in his first season would be "an achievement without parallel."

The 25th English National Cross-Country Championship was staged at Leicester Racecourse, just outside the town at Oadby. A total of 113 participants representing 12 clubs turned out, creating a spectacular stampede at the start. After a mile, Shrubb was in the leading pack, with a Northampton runner just in front, and after four miles Shrubb had forged a lead of 200 yards. There was no sign of the mighty Olympic gold medalist George Rimmer (who was anticipated to give Shrubb trouble). In fact, Shrubb was so far in front that some observers thought he was about to be lapped. He was running like a deer, simply striding out, while the rest were traveling with considerable trouble over the heavy, cloying mud. Andrews recalled with pride: "At the end of the second lap we were waiting looking up the racecourse and then a little speck came into sight all alone. He had dropped Rimmer by nearly a minute on the plough and run him off his legs."

Leading into the summer, Alfred Shrubb won his local county meet (also winning the team prize), and then captured the South London Harriers's Thornton Challenge Cup over a 10-mile course on the Surrey-London border. Toward the end of the nineteenth century the practice of counties staging their own cross-country championships had begun to die out, but Sussex—encouraged by Shrubb's emergence—had been one bidding to revive the event. Shrubb then saw continued success, beating English rival (and former cross-country champion) Sid Robinson over many distances on the track. In his debut campaign, Shrubb had won every contest he'd entered—immediately catapulting himself into the pantheon of cross-country running greats.

After a season filled with more victories, Shrubb returned to cross-country for the 1902–03 campaign. This was a particularly significant season, as plans were announced for a prototype world championship in Scotland—and the organizers would have their work cut out finding a date convenient for Shrubb, the sport's star performer.

After England, Scotland, Wales, and Ireland established their own organizing bodies in the latter years of the nineteenth century, they formed the International Cross-Country Union (ICCU) in early 1903, and began promoting the first "International Championship" at Hamilton in Scotland. When the English officials heard that the event would be on March 21, 1903, they were horrified to discover their top runner, Shrubb, was already committed to an event in Paris. England was so desperate to win the first staging of the new event they applied for a postponement. The ICCU agreed without fuss, and so it came to pass that the sport's first "World Championship" was rearranged to suit the schedule of one special competitor.

With victories once again in the Southern and National Cross-Country Championships, Shrubb was hailed as one of the best ever, especially by the magazine *Sport and Play*: "The relative value of performances in these cross-country races is difficult to gauge for many reasons; but tested any way and every way, the South London star stands out with conspicuous brilliancy and is undoubtedly looked upon by the best of good judges as the equal of any of his predecessors and by many as the best of them all."

Then, shortly after the 1903 National, England announced their team of 12 runners—three regional champions plus the next nine best placed from the National—to face the other home countries in the new International Cross-Country Championship. But prior to this Shrubb had two more races to contend with: the annual cross-country title in his home county Sussex, plus an interclub race in Paris featuring four European clubs.

The Paris event was the first of its kind. With the South London Harriers represented, it marked the first time that French and English cross-country teams had met on French soil since the 1898 Cross des Nations. It also marked the first international appearance in cross-country of any team representing Switzerland or Belgium.

The meet got underway in the wooded Parisian district of Bois de Saint-Cloud. SLH were up against hosts Racing Club de Paris, plus two club teams from Belgium and Switzerland. Shrubb overcame a couple of worrying moments when he inadvertently wandered off course after losing sight of the trail, but recovered to win by almost a mile in 62:29, with the French club's Chastini second in 67:42. The course exceeded the stated 10 miles, and included a four-mile stretch of road, which didn't endear the event to runners who were wearing spikes.

But after his successful trip home, Shrubb put his unbeaten record at cross-country on the line the following week at the inaugural "International Championship." His performance did not disappoint and the streak remained intact. Going into his fourth summer as a competitive athlete, 23-year-old Shrubb was unbeaten in three seasons and had more than enough titles to lay claim to the title of world's best cross-country runner.

In 1904, Shrubb was intent on making history by winning the Southern and English National Cross-Country titles for a fourth year in a row. Ominously, a record entry of 21 clubs appeared at the Southern Championship, but Shrubb was not phased, winning his fourth successive title by 300 yards. The *West Sussex County Times* concluded that Shrubb "was now demonstrating, race after race, that he is pretty well the finest runner the world has ever seen."

The spring of 1904 would be Shrubb's last on the amateur cross-country circuit—a year that proved to be his most successful as a distance runner—when he finished as the holder of 15 amateur distance track records, from 2,000 yards to the one-hour continuous run.

At Christmas Shrubb left for a five-month tour of Australia with American sprinter Arthur Duffy, effectively nullifying any chance of competing in the winter and spring for cross-country. His record of county, national, and international cross-country victories would eventually end, despite a triumphant conclusion to Shrubb's cross-country career, which featured a dozen straight victories. By the winter of 1905, the English Amateur Athletic Association determined that payouts made to Shrubb on his behalf violated his amateur status. As a result, in January 1906, Alfred Shrubb was banned from competing in amateur competition, but he found more prosperous and lucrative opportunities continuing to compete on the track as a professional.

Stories like the one of Alfred Shrubb became more common as cross-country gained prominence around the world. Expectedly, both individual superstardom and international expansion would come to define the rise of cross-country running in the twentieth century.

But also of note within the decade was the 1907 International Cross-Country Championship—a 16-kilometer run in Glasgow, Scotland—that included a French national team among the four home nations of the United Kingdom for the first time. England took the first four places and the team championship while the first French runner crossed the line in 11th place overall (exhibiting quite the improvement since the 1898 Cross des Nations). This sporting contribution to the "Entente Cordiale" was appreciated, and Paris was chosen as the venue for the 1908 International Championship.

Clearly the sport was more popular than ever before in England, and it was due in large part to the momentum created by having an international championship to vie for.

Once France was accepted as a participating member, the glory of national pride was on the line and those interested found themselves more invested in cross-country running performances. Outside of England, the same type of craze was about to land in the greater parts of Europe, as other nations saw an opportunity to take part in the action.

* * *

While the European expansion of cross-country running increased its reach globally, it was the development of the International Cross-Country Championship that was a truly new vanguard for the sport. Once England accepted that it was a necessity and not just an extension of their own national format, a larger audience became intrigued by the notion of national pride—and that gave the sport new legitimacy. Cross-country running became a worldwide phenomenon, not just a local game played by schoolchildren. Distance runners like Alfred Shrubb, who trained seriously and broke world records, gave credence to this new identity for the sport. The sport was also expanding in such places as the United States and Australia while embracing a new international format outside of England. By the twentieth century, cross-country had emerged as a unique and fascinating entity among the other major sports—with its own traditions, characters, and storylines.

EVENT SPOTLIGHT: THE INAUGURAL HOLDING OF THE INTERNATIONAL CROSS-COUNTRY CHAMPIONSHIP (MARCH 28, 1903)

LOCATION: HAMILTON PARK, SCOTLAND

The Home Nations of the United Kingdom

In 1903, Scotland, Wales, Ireland, and a reluctant England formed the International Cross-Country Union (ICCU) and promoted the first International Championship in Hamilton, Scotland. England had been reluctant to join because they maintained that their English National Cross-Country Championship was open to all amateur teams and could be used as a medium for settling international rivalry. Eventually the English conceded after the potential financial gains were discussed as well as the potential for true international representation from French and Belgian teams.

The distance at Hamilton Park was eight miles total over a two-mile lap of the course, covered four times. Alfred Shrubb, who had just returned from Paris in an international club meeting with the South London Harriers, had an impeccable unbeaten record at cross-country, and as such went into the inaugural International Championship as the favorite. The cream of English, Scottish, Welsh, and Irish runners competed against each other as a team for the first time, and each fielded its strongest side. The first six finishers for each nation were elected to score.

In miserable weather the day of the race, the going became increasingly difficult. England—represented by Shrubb, Hosker, Smith, Robinson, Mercer, Lawson, Edwards, Silsby, Pearce, Aldridge, Thomas, and Randles—packed seven runners into the first 10 to justify their status as favorites. Although Shrubb got to the front early on, it was not until three miles that he was able to open a significant gap. He won by 200 yards in 46:22, leading teammate Tom Edwards (Manchester), and Irishman John Daly third. England scored 25 points; Ireland 78; Scotland 107; and Wales 140.

The top 25 finishers appear below:

1	Alfred Shrubb	England	46:22
2	Tom Edwards	England	46:56
3	John Daly	Ireland	47:10
4	Albert Aldridge	England	47:10
5	Sid Robinson	England	47:21
6	W. A. Mercer	England	47:37
7	Harry Lawson	England	47:50
8	Tom Hynes	Ireland	47:58
9	J. Thomas	England	48:10
10	James Crosbie	Scotland	48:47
11	George Smith	England	48:51
12	Jack Marsh	Wales	48:54
13	J. Creedon	Ireland	49:00
14	John Ranken	Scotland	49:08
15	Charlie Silsby	England	49:14
16	Pat Whyte	Ireland	49:18
17	James Ure	Scotland	49:25
18	Frank Curtis	Ircland	49:26
19	D. G. Harris	Wales	49:40
20	P. J. McCafferty	Ireland	49:41
21	T. C. Hughes	Scotland	49:51
22	James Reston	Scotland	49:59
23	Thomas Mulrine	Scotland	50:02
24	James Hosker	England	50:22
25	Arthur Turner	Wales	50:25

In total, 41 athletes finished the event out of 45 starters. At the dinner that followed the race, Scottish sportsman Mr. Fred A. Lumley of Edinburgh offered to present a trophy for annual competition, and thus the Lumley Shield came into being. The race was so successful, and the friendships formed so attractive, that it was at once realized the race had come to stay. Discussions on the train journey between Hamilton Park and Glasgow led to an understanding of promoting a similar race the following year at Haydock Park, near Warrington, in Lancashire.

CULTURAL SPOTLIGHT:
THE OLYMPIC MOVEMENT

Today, the Olympic Games are the world's largest pageant of athletic skill and competitive spirit—in addition to being one of the best displays of nationalism, commerce, and politics. With worldwide recognition, they have been used to promote understanding and friendship among nations, but have also been a hotbed of political disputes and boycotts. The modern iteration of the games was introduced just prior to the twentieth century, and from the outset was meant to bridge multicultural attitudes about sport. Cross-country running, which had also started to gain acceptance internationally during this period, found itself associated with the Games early on.

Strong ties existed between the origin of the Olympic Games and a city well known for cross-country running success. Birmingham in England, the home to the Birchfield Harriers cross-country club, was the center for both amateur ideals and cross-country participation as early as the 1850s. While Frenchman Baron Pierre de Coubertin is credited with establishing the modern Olympics, it was England that revived the initiative, and it was in the Midlands where de Coubertin was introduced to it.

As early as 1612, Robert Dover established an English athletics contest known as "The Olympicks" at Chipping Camden, Gloucestershire, which involved running, jumping, throwing the hammer, and pitching the bar. That event continued until 1852. However, even more significant was an annual festival at Much Wenlock, Shropshire, started in 1850 by Dr. William Penny Brookes, which held events that were more similar to the athletic offerings seen today. In 1860 Brookes separated the group from the festival and called it the Wenlock Olympian Society.

During this period, de Coubertin was interested in England and its development of sports in public schools. He, like the Thames Hare and Hounds before him, found inspiration in Thomas Hughes's book *Tom Brown's Schooldays*, and in 1886 visited Rugby, the school where Hughes's novel had been set. A rower, fencer, and boxer himself, de Coubertin devoted his time to the study of physical education. He believed that if France were to adopt the British sporting culture, the French population would be revived into action: raising national athletic awareness, and motivated to lead France as a world power in sport. In 1889 he organized the Congress of Physical Education in Paris and in the next year he made his visit to Much Wenlock to meet Brooke and observe the Olympian Society.

Brookes's original aim was also to create an international Olympics, primarily to promote physical education in participating countries. He fell short of that goal but was very helpful to de Coubertin over dinner 25 years later, where they shared their mutual interest in physical education and their dreams of global expansion.

The *Wellington Journal* noted in 1890: "A special autumn festival in connection with Wenlock Olympian Society was held [to] enlighten Baron Pierre de Coubertin, a French gentleman, who desires to introduce athletics more largely among his own countrymen, upon the methods adopted for the training of athletes in England. Dr. Brookes, who is an untiring advocate of physical education among the young, was on this occasion largely instrumental in bringing about this meeting."

The idea of reviving the ancient Olympic Games as a true international festival came from this meeting. And, despite a few difficulties, on June 23, 1894, de Coubertin presided over an assembly of 79 delegates representing 12 countries who voted unanimously for the plan. At first, de Coubertin gave credit to Brookes, saying, "If the Olympic Games, which modern Greece had not been able to revive, still survive today, it is not to a Greek that we are indebted, but rather to Dr. W. P. Brookes."

However, once the Games had been organized as an international event and Brookes had passed away, de Coubertin began taking the credit for himself. As *The Times* noted: "If rip-offs had been in the Olympics, this one would have carried off the gold." Even the opening and closing ceremonies followed the Wenlock model. In 1896, under the patronage of the King of Greece, the Games of the first Olympiad of the modern cycle were held. Back in Birmingham, the Birchfield Harriers were quietly building a cross-country legacy of their own.

Historian Lawrence Richardson commented: "For a runner to secure his cross-country colors is considered as great an achievement as gaining Olympic honors." The modern Olympic movement was still in its infancy, and it was not until London hosted the Games of 1908 that the Olympics resonated with the British public. While Richardson might have been correct, the Olympic movement helped foster a sense of internationalism within sport by promoting athletics as an extension of a physical ideal. This emerging credo of "Olympism" also agreed with the strong amateur principles of the athletic "gentleman," which prevailed in cross-country running.

But for many of the top names in cross-country running, the Olympics were an afterthought. For example, five Olympic Games came and went during Alfred Shrubb's time as a top runner. He was absent from the Paris 1900, St. Louis 1904, Athens 1906, London 1908, and Stockholm 1912 Games. Coincidently, Shrubb's appearance might have furthered the case to include the sport of cross-country. As the sport's greatest champion, his participation would have held weight.

Yet with a strong Franco-Anglo influence within the International Olympic Committee it was inevitable that cross-country running would find its way into the program. Aspects of the sport were first introduced at the 1900 Games in Paris as a 5,000-meter team race won by a joint British-Australian team, and at the 1904 Games held in St. Louis, Missouri, a team competition consisting of a four-mile run was pitched as the "Four-Mile International Team Race" where finishing place dictated the team scores.

Finally, in October 1910, at a meeting of the Amateur Athletic Association, Percy Fischer—a member of the Olympic track committee—announced that "thanks to the good offices of the British representatives in the International Olympic Committee, the 800 meters, the 10,000-meter run, and a cross-country race of five miles were added to the program of the Games of Stockholm 1912." The British, who were trying to give particular importance to the discipline of cross-country, would have also liked to include a steeplechase of two miles, but the International Olympic Committee was opposed.

At the time of this decision many strong Nordic nations, such as Finland and Sweden, were absent from the International Cross-Country Championship—either by calculated design or invitation oversight. It was guaranteed then, that the sport of cross-country would be forever changed by this fortuitous addition to the Olympic program in the coming two decades.

Chapter 7

The development of cross-country running in our preparatory schools, colleges, and clubs has been the most important factor in raising the standard of distance runners in this country. It was not until the United States began to foster cross-country running that we began to develop good distance runners. Cross-country running, if properly indulged in, is one of the most healthful recreations I know of, even if one does not follow it in the hope of becoming a champion distance runner. If indulged in moderately it strengthens every part of the body, and I have seen many a boy who was almost made over by the sport. Not only is it good for distance runners, but in a modified form is invaluable for footballers, oarsmen, and those who merely want some good conditioning exercise.

—*Michael C. Murphy*

THE DECADE OF THE 1910s

The second decade of the twentieth century welcomed new champions and expansion across Europe and North America. Developments in technology made communicating and traveling easier, and this impacted the rise of international meetings between countries. Nationalism also rose, as runners felt a new sense of pride in their heritage and a desire to prove themselves against competition from other countries. Cross-country appeared in the Summer Olympics for the first time, and the International Cross-Country Championship ingrained itself on the athletics calendar. If not for the interference of the Great War, which halted the growing momentum of the sport beginning in 1915, this decade might have been even more impactful.

A growing number of European nations embraced the sport of cross-country in the 1910s, and with good reason: the sport's relative simplicity garnered encouragement from governing bodies that were exposed to the sport through the first meeting of the International Association of Athletics Federations (IAAF), which officially convened in Sweden in 1912. This push for nations to take part in the sport, raised by the legislating bodies themselves, explained this rapid spread. The reality was, in order to affiliate officially with the IAAF, member countries had to standardize their athletics calendar and their practices—which meant that nations first had to practice cross-country.

> **Did You Know?**
>
> The decade of the 1910s saw further expansion among sovereign nations in Europe and elsewhere who began to host their own national championships:
>
> - In May 1910 Luxembourg held their inaugural National Cross-Country Championship, continuing the tradition in 1911, 1912, and 1913. Jean-Paul Völker won the first championship, which was contested in Luxembourg City (where it was held for the entire decade). René Faber won two of the next three events. Interesting to note is that Luxembourg did not hold a national track and field championship until much later, preferring to promote distance races in cross-country, which saw large crowds.
> - In September 1910 the first official Australasian Cross-Country Championship in Hobart, Tasmania took place. Andrew Wood won the 10-mile race in 60:15, beating Charles Weyman, runner-up in the 1908 event, by three seconds. While the first three places went to the squad from New South Wales, the team score was relatively close between them and Victoria. The event continued to run every two years prior to 1921, when it was put on hiatus during the Great War, and was reinstated after the 1920s.

- In 1911, 1912, and 1913, Portugal held a National Cross-Country Championship, and each year saw a different winner: Francisco Lázaro, Matias Carvalho, and Germano Garcês. Despite its popularity, the event was not held again until 1922.
- In 1912, Tunisia became the first African country to hold an official National Cross-Country Championship. Antoine Renda was the winner, and in reporting the event, the daily La Depeche Tunisian indicated that the race was organized by the Alumni Association of the College Alaoui and had nearly 4,000 spectators in attendance. The team championship was won by a Pommier (of the third military company) over teams from Vendôme and Paris. After two more editions there would not be another championship until 1921.
- The first German National Cross-Country Championship was contested in 1913, with Fritz Blankenburg (a 34:45 10,000-meter runner) the winner. The cross-country championship would not be held again officially until 1919.
- Norway held their first National Cross-Country Championship in 1913, in Oslo. Thorstein Larsen won the first three editions, and Eugen Borchgrevink and Alf Halstvedt each won two titles within the decade.
- Romania held its first National Championship in April 1916, and Constantin Dumitrescu was the winner over an eight-kilometer course in Bucuresti. Fittingly, in the second championship run four years later, Dumitrescu was again champion.
- The Netherlands held their first National Championship in August 1919. Jan Postma won the first three editions of the event.

SPAIN REWRITES THE SCRIPT

While the cross-country origin story for many European nations came from the need to organize athletics internationally, Spain adapted the sport in a different way. Because of this, their attachment to the sport saw a national passion for distance running that was unmatched in the decades following its inception. First run in February 1916, the Spanish National Cross-Country Championship ran annually until 1936. Pedro Prat won the first two events, and in the inaugural championship, held over a course of 15 kilometers in Madrid, Prat won in 59:02.

This inaugural event was born out of a challenge made by Pedro Prat to runner Emilio Gonzalez (who was also nationally known). Prat, who had no real competition in his hometown of Catalonia, issued his challenge to Gonzalez in the weekly Spanish sporting magazine *Espana Sportiva*. The November 1915 edition of the paper published all the details. Aptly titled "El Gran Premio Nacional,

Campeonato de España" (The First Big National Championship of Spain), the race was run in Salamanca, in the center of Madrid, starting and finishing at the Plaza de Colón. The rules allowed for both individuals and teams from various regions (represented with no less than five runners) to compete.

The day of the race was cold and sunny and there were only a few spectators in attendance. At the sound of the gun, the runners completed a lap of the track, disappeared behind a section known as Nuevos Ministerios, took the Cuatro Caminos (road) to Dehesa de la Villa, and finished back in the Plaza de Colón. Pedro Prat won the 15-kilometer event, with a surprise second-place by José Erra, also of Catalonia. Emilio González finished in third, two minutes behind Erra and three minutes behind Prat. Catalonia won the team title, followed by Sociedad Cultural Deportiva in second, and Sociedad Deportiva Obrera in third. With the success of this event, the *Espana Sportiva* elected to hold the second edition the following year.

Did You Know?

While the inaugural Spanish National Cross-Country Championship in 1916 was initiated by runners from Catalonia, there was no money to send their athletes to Madrid. When they were finally able to finance the trip, the team could only afford a third-class carriage, and arrived nearly starving, having traveled almost 24 hours straight to arrive at the event without proper rations, like food.

THE INTERNATIONAL CROSS-COUNTRY CHAMPIONSHIP PROVIDES EXCITEMENT

Beyond European national fervor, international cross-country dominance was demonstrated by England at the International Cross-Country Championship—despite their hesitancy to join the other home nations in perpetuating the event only 10 years prior. Meanwhile, the advancement of France in their commitment to become better at cross-country running spurred a fierce rivalry with England, which continued for the greater part of the twentieth century.

This rivalry intensified in the 1910 edition of the International. With England beating Ireland for the team title for the second year in a row, it was the French national champion, Jean Bouin, who appeared to be the biggest threat to English hegemony. But according to a line printed in the *Glasgow Herald*, Bouin "met with a mishap and dropped out in the course of the second lap." As France had only started six men, they were uncounted in the team score.

By the culmination of the 1913 event, however, Jean Bouin had become the first runner to win the International three times in a row. France had also improved nationally, finishing second in the team race to England, with a score of 61 points to England's 38. Considering that they had entered the event for the first time just six years prior, France's performance on the day was remarkable.

On August 4, 1914, the First World War began. For five years, European National Championships and the International were interrupted (without competition in 1915, 1916, 1917, 1918, or 1919). Unfortunately, one of the early victims of the war was cross-country champion Jean Bouin, who was killed in action. The "Jean Bouin Stadium" in Paris was constructed as a permanent reminder of his legacy.

JEAN BOUIN OF FRANCE

Born in December 1888, Bouin made his debut early, winning a cross-country race in France in February 1904 at the age of 15. He claimed his first French National Cross-Country title in 1909, and went on to win four straight titles through 1912. To prepare, he indulged in gymnastic exercises, and after years of intense physical training Bouin earned the nickname "Hercule de Marseille."

Bouin famously faced Finnish distance runner Hannes Kolehmainen in the 1912 Summer Olympics, but it would be one of his last rivalries. After enrolling in the French infantry as *instructeur de sport des Armees*, Bouin fell victim to a tragic error of the French artillery, and a howitzer put a premature end to his life. He was not yet 26. *L'Auto* described Bouin as "the most amazing pedestrian France has ever had."

SCOTLAND'S PREMIER TALENT

Another remarkable story from the decade concerned one of Scotland's finest runners. George Wallach represented the Bolton United Harriers and Greenock Glenpark Harriers at different points in his career, and became the first Scottish International medalist when he finished third in 1911 (he would later cross second in 1914), and represented Scotland on nine occasions from 1910 to 1924. But more astonishing was the fact that Wallach first represented Scotland at the age of 28 in 1910 and lost time when the championship was suspended for the First World War.

Wallach's career in the International had an eventful start. Having achieved third in the English National in 1910, he was selected by Scotland to run in Belfast in his first appearance at the International. Approaching the final stages of the race in the lead, Wallach was forcibly removed from the competition by the police. Police officers had noticed that his shorts had torn substantially from one of the barbed wire fence obstacles on the course, and on grounds of public decency, took him out.

Wallach's next greatest achievement, a second-place finish in the International of 1914, was also dramatic. Despite leading for most of the race, Wallach fell at the final water jump and could not catch Nicholls of England who had overtaken him. Yet despite these setbacks, Wallach's achievements spoke for themselves, with one silver, one bronze, two fourth places, and two more top-10 finishes spanning his nine appearances at the International Cross-Country Championship over 14 years.

Wallach's success enabled him to represent Great Britain in the 10,000 meters at the 1912 Stockholm Olympics, although he was never selected for the cross-country event. Instead, despite the domination of English, French, and Scottish runners, a new breed of distance runner was about to earn Olympic cross-country notoriety. The unsuspecting nation of Finland was perfectly set to culture future champions. A temperate climate in the spring and summer months, along with geographic elevation changes and numerous wooded trails, allowed Finnish runners nearly unlimited access to fine cross-country training grounds, enabling their athletes to become among the best in the world.

THE ARRIVAL OF FINLAND

By the year 1910, Finland, with a population of three million, was under Russian czardom, and had been for over a century. While Finland had been attempting to develop in many areas, competitive distance running had not been one of them (their first national track championships appeared in 1908). During this period, even serious athletes trained on public roads without the proper equipment or attire.

In the early twentieth century, it was only possible to prepare for a sports contest in Finland through trial and error. A lack of reliable training knowledge, few coaches, and even fewer formal venues to compete in all contributed to this. On the other hand, there was plenty of speculation as to what made other European nations great, and athletes had plenty of freedom to experiment with methods they determined necessary.

In Kuopio, by Kallavesi Lake in the southeastern part of Finland, the Kolehmainen brothers found their path to the top ranks of distance running almost by accident. In 1906, news from the Interim Olympic Games in Athens was carried to Finnish shores. Remarkably, Finland had won two gold medals with wrestler Verner Weckman and discus thrower Verner Jarvinen. Inspired by these stories, the first marathon race was organized in Finland in August that year. And the young Kolehmainen brothers at the foot of Puijo Hill were unable to resist the temptation.

Hannes Kolehmainen ran his first two marathons when he was only 17. That was in 1907, and within two years he had logged eight in total. "Work, healthy life, good sleep, fresh air, suitable nourishment, regular sauna baths, gymnastic exercises, massage, lots of moving about in open air, and running based on theoretical and empirical research—those were the magic tricks that carried Hannes Kolehmainen to Olympic glory," *Suomen Urheilulehti* (the leading Finnish sports magazine of the time) suggested as the Stockholm Olympics drew near.

Quietly, after years spent cross-country skiing (making many trips to the town of Iisalmi, 100 kilometers away) and swimming with his three brothers, Kolehmainen began preparing seriously for distance running. Hannes had moved to Helsinki and joined the well-known sports club Helsingin KisaVeikot in 1909, but by the winter of 1912 he transferred to the racing colors of Helsingin Jyry—a workers' association. By that point, Kolehmainen had broken several Finnish track records. The year prior, he'd won all his 22 races, including the British four-mile title in London, which was the first big international achievement for Finnish distance running.

Regular letters from brother Wiljami—now an experienced professional runner in the United States and Scotland—had been the difference. "Do lots of walking and exercises," Wiljami wrote in early 1912, "but remember track training, too. Do not neglect speed!" With two national victories in the 5,000 meters and one in the 10,000 meters, "Smiling" Hannes Kolehmainen was just becoming well known.

OLYMPIC GLORY

Oppressive heat had been plaguing Stockholm in the days leading up to the fifth iteration of the Summer Olympics, but it didn't change the high expectations for the Games. In the 16 years since Baron Pierre de Coubertin had first organized them, momentum had finally caught on. At first, few nations understood the need to participate, but by the 1912 Games, the Frenchman had reason to rejoice. Twenty-eight nations and 2,408 competitors, including 48 women, competed in 102 events in 14 sports. It was the last Olympics to issue solid gold medals and, with Japan's debut, the first time an Asian nation participated.

The 1912 edition of the Summer Olympiad not only featured cross-country running for the first time, but also produced a stellar showdown between Kolehmainen and France's Jean Bouin, who had won his two International Cross-Country titles in succession in 1911 and 1912. And despite the tremendous pressure facing him in his first Olympics, Kolehmainen secured three gold medals, including the 10,000-meter and 5,000-meter runs. When it came to cross-country, however, even more pride was on the line—it turned out to be a worthy finale, and entire teams never before seen in the International Cross-Country Championship were ready to stake their claim in the sport. This drama made it possible for Sweden to conduct an edition of the games that efficiently outdid all previous iterations, and left the Frenchman Bouin hungry in his final showdown with the Flying Finn Kolehmainen.

THE BIRTH OF THE IAAF

While cross-country experienced an important debut that summer, a less-publicized development also occurred during the 1912 Olympics in Stockholm: a group of dedicated officials, spearheaded by members of Svenska Idrottsforbundet (the Swedish Athletics Federation), conceived the idea of founding the International Amateur Athletics Federation (IAAF), which became the governing body of the sport on a worldwide scale. Today it remains the international standard for athletics (in 2001 the name was changed to the "International Association of Athletics Federations").

The first congress of the IAAF was held three days after the conclusion of the Olympics in the Parliament building (Riksdagshuset), with delegates from 17 countries. The first president was Johannes Sigfrid Edström of Sweden, who would govern the body until 1946 and become the fourth elected president of the International Olympic Committee in 1942.

The official constitution passed to the congress of Berlin in 1913, with the declared aims of the newly-formed body as follows: 1) To draw up and agree to the rules and regulations for international athletics competition; 2) To register all World, Olympic, and National Records and maintain a register of these at a central office; and 3) To define "amateur" for international competition purposes. The beginning stages were not easy and were further complicated by the Great War. And with various national-level bodies out of step with the new international standards, several years went by before many of the IAAF goals were achieved.

THE LEGACY OF THE FLYING FINNS

But not only did the 1912 Olympics result in the establishment of the IAAF, they also inspired Finland to formalize cross-county competition. On May 25, 1913, the country held its first National Cross-Country Championship in Turku. Arvi Kokkonen was the event's first champion and also won the second meeting the following year. Then, national stalwart Albin Stenroos became the champion of the next three.

Oskar Albinus ("Albin") Stenroos would go on to win the marathon at the 1924 Summer Olympics, but first became famous for winning the 10,000 meters at the Finnish nationals in 1910. Without the presence of Hannes Kolehmainen, Stenroos won the Finnish National Championships in 5,000 and 10,000 meters from 1912 to 1916. He also won the national cross-country title from 1915 to 1917. At the 1912 Summer Olympics, Stenroos won the bronze medal in the 10,000 meters behind Kolehmainen.

But for Finland, the decade of the 1910s was meant to celebrate the three-time Olympic gold medalist Kolehmainen—and yet he was mysteriously absent from the nation's cross-country championship. It just so happened that he was thousands of miles away, across the Atlantic, in the United States.

NORTH AMERICA EXPANDS AND CONTINUES THE CHARGE

At the time, the United States was a haven for elite distance runners from abroad and was seeing domestic growth as well. By the end of the first decade of the 1900s, cross-country at the high school and collegiate level was widespread. The state of Massachusetts became the site of the first non-collegiate-organized high school invitational on record (with the Mystic Valley Cross-Country Run for Schools in 1911), while Wisconsin held its first cross-country state tournament for high schools in 1913.

Milwaukee Normal School (now University of Wisconsin–Milwaukee) conducted this first "state meet."

Columbia University perpetuated the bond between colleges and high schools by inaugurating an interscholastic cross-country run in 1911 that was won by Morris High School. That same year Princeton also hosted its sixth annual fall Interscholastic.

But the Columbia University Interscholastic was not the only meet where Morris High School found success. Reported in 1912, the first cross-country race in Van Cortlandt Park, New York, occurred when the New York Interscholastic Championship was held there on December 7, and Morris High was the winning team, front and center.

THE ORIGIN OF THE MECCA: VAN CORTLANDT PARK

In the first description of Van Cortlandt Park in New York being used for cross-country running, thousands of spectators were in attendance to view the high school cross-country championship in December 1912. It was there that Bronx Parks Commissioner Thomas J. Higgins acted as the honorary referee, instructing two mounted policemen to lead the runners on the course, something he also reportedly did the following year.

The race started on the polo fields, and *The Tribune* wrote of the current "Tortoise and Hare" trail landmarks in its coverage, including "the old aqueduct," "the golf links," and the "bridge over the lake."

Named a New York City park in 1888, it was the Van Cortlandt family that sold the land to the city—and while impossible to verify, it's suspected that more people have run a cross-country race at Van Cortlandt Park than at any other venue in the United States. Along with its early opening, the park's cross-country course was in high demand from the very beginning: used throughout

the fall by high schools, colleges, and outside competitors ranging from novice to elite. Today it even has its own hall of fame.

In terms of layout, the traditional start occurs at the "Parade Ground" (also known as "The Flats"), a flat and open area whose first inhabitants were the Wiechquaeskeck tribe of the Lenape nation. From there, the course heads into a wooded area via the "cow path" (also known as "the chute"). Next, bisected by highways built mid-century, a unique feature is a cross-country-specific bridge that joins two sections of the park together. Leading to that bridge is the short, steep "freshman hill." Once across the bridge, the runners negotiate the "back hills" before returning across the bridge. Longer races—typically eight kilometers or more—run the dreaded "Cemetery Hill," named only partly for its location next to a burial plot. But whether coming straight off the bridge or negotiating Cemetery Hill, the finish is always back in the flats. Various combinations of this setup can be made for distances ranging anywhere from four to 15 kilometers.

And while it might have had humble beginnings in 1912, Van Cortlandt has been the site of more US National Cross-Country Championships than any other venue (25 total, with the next nearest, Chicago's Washington Park, at a paltry 10). The Manhattan College Invitational, the largest single-day high school cross-country invitational in the nation, sees nearly 20,000 runners in the span of 12 hours, rain or shine—and the biggest names in American distance running have all come through Van Cortlandt (from Lindgren, to Prefontaine, to Cheserek). As the mecca of cross-country in the United States, running at this hallowed course is certainly a rite of passage—one shared with a multitude of cross-country running legends.

FURTHER EAST COAST EXPLOITS

Van Cortlandt was not alone in providing a central location for cross-country meets along the East Coast. By 1914, in preparation for the New England Interscholastic Athletic Association (NEIAA) Cross-Country Championships, a new 4.8-mile cross-country course was established in Boston's Franklin Park.

Franklin Park, the largest park in Boston's "Emerald Necklace" of interconnected parks, was designed by Frederick Law Olmsted in the 1880s to offer the outdoor comforts of the country to city dwellers. It was here that a cross-country course was designed to loop around or across fairways on the park's golf course.

Later on, the course was adjusted to start and end in the wide-open "playstead" area, with races generally comprised of three sections: the Stadium Loop, which circled the park's White Stadium; the Bear Cage Hill Loop, a path up a hill where the Franklin Park Zoo used to house its bears; and the Wilderness Loop, which went into a wooded area before coming back into the open playstead.

It was at this point that preparatory schools such as Arlington, Somerville, and Medford found success in the appropriately named "Mystic Valley League" for Massachusetts cross-country running.

NORTH AMERICA EMBRACES THE SPORT

New recognition followed the sport as it was established in universities and high schools throughout the country, and the possibility of stardom further enticed individual and team champions. Michigan State University (then Michigan Agricultural College) became one of the first Midwest universities to make cross-country a varsity sport in 1910. By the end of the decade Michigan Agricultural College was winning intercollegiate meets, while teams at Notre Dame and other Great Lakes schools took up the sport. North of Michigan, the Canadian Intercollegiate AU Cross-Country Championship of the 1913–14 season was held in Montreal. By 1913, many of the heartland colleges were also running cross-country, fielded with men from their track teams.

And while the colleges were flourishing, the amateur teams were doing just as well. The Amateur Athletic Union held the US Cross-Country Championships in New York's Van Cortlandt Park almost exclusively throughout the 1910s. The popularity of club teams, aside from those composed of collegiate or high school athletes, had transformed by this point from harrier clubs solely composed of young men in major cities to more dedicated athletes who specialized in competition on the track, on the roads, and over trails.

In 1914, two years after his Olympic cross-country debut, Hannes Kolehmainen won the US National Cross-Country title running for the Irish-American Athletic Club. The following year, Kolehmainen finished second to a Greek runner by the name of Nick Gianakopoulos, each covering the six-mile course in less than 33 minutes.

Kolehmainen, who had run 32:53 two weeks prior at the Metropolitan Cross-Country Championship (winning the race), finished in the national meet a second faster (32:52), but lost to Gianakopoulos who ran 32:46. The race, which included Cemetery Hill, had rocky hillsides, stretches of ice, fallen logs, and thick brush. Gianakopoulos's team, the Millrose Athletic Association, lost the team battle to the Irish-American club 25 to 30. Kolehmainen had been previously unbeaten in cross-country races.

In 1916 Hannes Kolehmainen once again finished second at the National Cross-Country Championship, this time to Willie Kyronen, another Finnish runner competing for the Millrose Athletic Association. Kolehmainen was in the lead with about a half mile to go when he suffered severe back pain after crossing the water jump for the second time. Johnny Overton of Yale, twice the winner of the Intercollegiate Cross-Country Championship, finished third in the race.

The 1917 National Championship, held at Boston's Franklin Park, had the closest finish to date, with the previous year's winner Willie Kyronen losing the lead by less than a second to James Henigan of Massachusetts's Dorchester Club.

* * *

Cross-country running, like many events this decade, was impacted by the onset of the First World War, which greatly altered the ability and willingness of sporting organizers to hold meets. It also played a part in the livelihood of some of cross-country's finest athletes. Despite this, the 1910s was buoyed by the arrival of cross-country in the Summer Olympic program, and further celebrated when sites were chosen as primary grounds for the sport, such as Van Cortlandt Park in New York and Franklin Park in Boston. Overall, this decade witnessed the attraction of international celebrity and top competition in cross-country running, which pushed the sport to new heights and introduced an entirely new subset of distance runners from Sweden and Finland. Soon, these new storylines would result in even more compelling tales of achievement and conquest.

EVENT SPOTLIGHT: HANNES KOLEHMAINEN AND THE FIRST CROSS-COUNTRY EVENT AT THE STOCKHOLM OLYMPICS (JULY 15, 1912)

LOCATION: OLYMPIASTADION

Stockholm, Sweden

The first Cross-Country Individual and Team Championship was run in the Summer Olympics on Monday, July 15, 1912. The 12-kilometer course encompassed an area that ran in a wide curve north of the stadium in Stockholm. Starting on the track, athletes ran one quarter-mile lap, then branched out into the surrounding countryside where steep hills, a deep forested section, and obstacles including small fences and a rock wall awaited them. The British and American runners were not used to these kinds of conditions for cross-country, and the Swedes and Finns dominated the race. Surprisingly, this was the first International Cross-Country "Championship" that included any nations outside of France and the four home nations of the United Kingdom.

The International Cross-Country Championship had been won in 1911 and 1912 by the French runner Jean Bouin (who would also win in 1913). But Hannes Kolehmainen had already won the 5,000 and 10,000 meters at Stockholm, so when he elected to run the cross-country race, he was the overwhelming favorite.

The backgrounds of the two titans were quite different. Hannes Kolehmainen had competed on the Stockholm track five times prior to the cross-country event. In the 10,000 meters he took the gold medal 250 meters ahead of Lewis Tewanima, a Hopi Indian from the United States, to win in 31:20. Next came an easy victory for Kolehmainen in his 5,000-meter heat. But there was danger looming: Jean Bouin of France had won *his* heat in 15:05—a half minute faster. In spite of being the world-record holder for the 10,000 meters (30:58 in Paris in 1911), Bouin had skipped the longer distance. There was no doubt why: he was wary of the young Finn.

Six days before the inaugural cross-country event, Bouin and Kolehmainen gave one of the most epic distance running performances of all time when they raced head-to-head in the 5,000-meter final on the track. Kolehmainen tucked in right behind Bouin for most of the race, and then each man ran neck and neck to the tape with Kolehmainen victorious by two steps. Their time of 14:36 was 25 seconds faster than the previous world record. With this in mind, the rematch between the two rivals over the Swedish countryside was eagerly anticipated.

The cross-country course was not revealed to the competitors before the race started, but it was marked clearly with red ribbons and red paper on the path. It included two loops of about six kilometers each, starting and ending in the Olympic Stadium and including a half a lap on the track in the middle.

Out of 45 starters, only 28 were able to finish, with the first three home for each nation counting toward the team score. After the gun fired for the start, competitor Axel Lindahl, representing Sweden, came in the stadium after the first loop of the course in second place, only about 200 meters behind the leader Kolehmainen. However, on the way out of the stadium entering the second loop, Lindahl took an elbow from one of the slower runners entering, and it was so powerful that Lindahl was knocked to the ground and forced to retire. Hjalmar Andersson, a fellow Swede, was gaining on Kolehmainen as the race neared an end, but ultimately lost to the Flying Finn by 30 seconds. Meanwhile another Swedish runner, John Eke, won the bronze. Bouin, who had been highly touted, started the race but did not finish. Sweden beat Finland by one point for the team title, and Great Britain, favored at the start, finished third.

This event also marked the first time that the United States had entered an international cross-country race, with the top American, Harry Hellawell, finishing 12th overall in 48:12. Only two individuals out of five were able to finish the race for the American team, Harry Hellawell and Louis Scott. Scott finished in 24th place but would later compete and help the United States win gold in the 3,000-meter team race on the track. Hellawell, a member of the New York Athletic Club, placed second in the US National Cross-Country Championship in 1912.

Eight years later, after many phases of his life, Hannes Kolehmainen sealed his Olympic career in an unforgettable way. But even in 1912—although he wouldn't return to his homeland until two years later—Kolehmainen had ignited something unique in Finnish distance running. The fire of inspiration would burn for many decades to come.

Chapter 8

Fifty yards from the finish, he was vaguely aware of the patter of footsteps behind him. The steps came nearer, he heard the agonized breathing of another runner at his shoulder. He knew then that the time had come to call upon the last resources of his stamina, to make use of that splendid reserve of strength which had never yet failed him.

He wanted to look around, to find out definitely whether it was Benton or Webb who was giving him battle. But his athletic instinct forbade his turning; the only thing he could do was to fight his way to the finish, to kill off all opposition in that last fifty yards.

He had been sure, but an instant before, that he had reached the limit of his endurance, of his speed. But now, with the necessity of greater speed urging him on, he somehow increased his pace. With every step of the way an agony, with his whole body crying out for relief, he called upon his weary muscles for additional effort—and forged slowly ahead. The heavy breathing at his shoulder grew indistinct, lost itself in the thunder of cheers which struck into his ears as from a great distance. And then, the tape loomed up almost over him; he threw himself forward, arms upraised. The tape snapped quietly across his chest. With a wheezing sigh of relief, he let himself go for a moment; then opened his eyes and smiled happily . . .

—*David Stone*, Yank Brown, Cross-Country Runner, 1922

THE DECADE OF THE 1920s

The 1920s reaffirmed humanism and progress. After the horrors of the Great War, the world was ready to come together and recommit to practiced recreation. For cross-country runners, the continuance of the sport in the Summer Olympics and the momentum gained by the International Championship fed a passion that had started years prior and only became stronger. Colonization was also an important culprit. England's reach as an imperial power set the standard for the sport and led the way in organizing it abroad. North American and European nations had been exposed to cross-country in year's prior, but during the 1920s less developed nations in South America, Asia, and Africa were first introduced to the sport. Consequences from this expansion would transform cross-country running significantly.

COLONIZATION IN EAST AFRICA BRINGS A CROSS-COUNTRY TRANSFORMATION

The introduction of cross-country to the East African territories of Kenya, Uganda, Ethiopia, Tanzania, and Somalia occurred almost single-handedly because of Western European colonization during the turn of the century. In the late–nineteenth-century "Scramble for Africa," Ethiopia was the only African country to defeat a European colonial power and retain its sovereignty as an independent country. In Kenya and Uganda, British colonial influence introduced distance running, among other sports, in the early stages of the 1900s.

Cash crops such as coffee and tea, the use of a railroad (financed by the British), and the development of the Western Highlands by settlers made Eastern Africa a valuable location during the first two decades of the new century. This inevitably fed the warring imperial powers in Europe. For instance, Britain was concerned with its communications with India and with the safety of the railway as Germany rose to power during the Great War.

By 1920 the British East Africa Protectorate was turned into a colony and renamed Kenya, for its highest mountain. Soon after, the colonial government refocused on the plight of African peoples, and education for Africans became the first improvement. Previously, missionaries had provided nearly all African schooling, but as more Africans worked on European farms and in urban areas such as Nairobi, they began to imitate political techniques used by Europeans and attempted to gain more representation in colonial politics. By the mid-1920s Kenya's economy had wholly revived from the pressures of the First World War.

The first schools built for the Kenyan population accomplished two things: they taught Western educational models to the Kenyan youth with varying levels of success, and they brought sport to Kenya for the governing classes, specifically golf, tennis, horse racing, and polo. The British also encouraged the Africans to play football (soccer)—still regarded as Kenya's most popular sport—to box, and to run.

Despite the introduction of sport, cross-country running did not develop quickly in Kenya. Primarily a winter sport in Britain, the colonial influence found difficulty organizing a sport in a section of Africa where the weather was temperate and where there was not a clearly defined winter season. There was the issue of environment too—the African countryside had steeper hills, bumpier pathways, and thornier bushes. Without much developed land devoted to recreation, a park space large enough to hold a meet was difficult to find. Additionally, the institution and financing of club teams did not happen for many years. New schools gave some Kenyans a sense of cohesion, but the scattered livelihoods of many native Kenyans made it difficult to fund a group that could train distance runners adequately.

It would take another thirty years before Kenya would send its first distance runner to Europe to compete in the Empire Games (Lazaro Chepkwony in July 1954)—and another ten years beyond that before British expat Derek Erskine would take control of the Kenyan Amateur Athletics Association (in 1963). Despite obstacles and early setbacks, the sport of cross-country was introduced in Kenya at the grassroots level in the early 1920s in the British colonial schools and was developed independently by the Kenyan army, the police, and the few athletes who practiced the sport for recreational purposes. At the time, few could have predicted Africa's future domination.

CROSS-COUNTRY DEVELOPMENTS IN ENGLAND DURING THE 1920s

Back in England, a youth movement was being felt. In 1925, the Berkshire Schools Athletic Association was founded in Reading, and representatives for nearly 100 schools in the county attended the meeting. This would become the precursor to the English Schools Athletic Association.

Furthering this development, the first county track and field championships were held at Palmer Park, and events for boys included the 100 yards, 220 yards, 440-yard relay, 75-yard hurdles, high jump, long jump, and tug-of-war. For girls, there were an equal number of events (minus the tug-of-war), the only difference being a 150-yard race instead of 220. While cross-country (and athletics generally) had been unequal within gender, there was more acceptance given to equality at the preparatory school level, which was a significant milestone.

Elsewhere in England in 1925, a meeting held in the offices of the Amateur Athletic Association proposed that County Associations promote an Inter-County Championship. This was largely in response to increasing participation in the specific counties (Northern, Midland, and Southern), and the desire to screen faster qualifiers for

the English National. Thus the Counties Athletic Union (CAU) was formed in February 1926, with the first staging of the Inter-County Cross-Country Championship in Beaconsfield in April that same year.

Did You Know?

Poland and Estonia joined their European neighbors in the decade of the 1920s to institute their own cross-country national championships, along with the sport appearing in South America for the first time:

- Poland's first cross-country championship was instituted in 1921. Alfred Freyer, winner of the 1926 and 1927 Polish National Cross-Country Championships, had English ancestry—his family had moved to Poland from England when he was a young boy. Growing up Freyer enjoyed equestrianism and loved to play football (soccer). But it wasn't until he won a bet racing a horse-drawn carriage on foot that he took up distance running seriously. Tragically, Freyer lost his life at the age of 26 in December 1927 when a library collapsed due to a fire. With two victories in the Polish National Cross-Country Championships (winning the 1926 10-kilometer event in 35:25, and the 1927 event in 31:29), there is no telling how many more titles he would have won. Later, Poland's national distance running champion and future 10,000-meter Olympic gold medal winner Janusz Kusociński would win three cross-country national titles.

- In 1922, the small Latvian country of Estonia held its first national cross-country event, and well-known athlete Heinrich Paal was the victor of the initial race as well as the first four events. Paal was captain of the Estonian national soccer team and competed in the 1924 Summer Olympics for the Estonian team against the United States. A man of inexhaustible stamina, he was also ranked nationally in the marathon (with a time 2:54:00 in 1918), competed in the decathlon, and held the Estonian national record for five and 20 kilometers on the track. After his four cross-country titles, Paal lost his life fighting for Estonia in the Second World War, passing away in a Soviet prison camp in December 1941.

- On April 21, 1924, Manuel Plaza from Chile won the 15-Kilometer Cross-Country Event, the first time that cross-country was officially included in the South American Championships in Athletics. Held in Buenos Aires, the event brought together athletes from Argentina, Chile, and Uruguay. Finishing first in 58:17, Plaza led Chilean athletes in second and third place for the event as well.

NURMI CARRIES THE OLYMPIC TORCH FOR FINLAND

With Kolehmainen and Kyronen in the United States, it was time for another champion to come to the fore in Finland. It had been a longtime dream for the young Paavo Nurmi to be a successful distance runner. As early as 1908, he had run a 1,500-meter time trial and had been clocked by Fabian Liesinen, a member of the club Turun Urheiluliitto, in 5:02. For an 11-year-old boy it was an exceptional time; in fact, it was almost unbelievable. Nurmi knew he had the talent—he just had to make his dream a reality.

Antwerp, Belgium, in 1920, saw resuscitation to the Olympic ideal after the horrors of the First World War. It had been eight years since the previous Olympic Games but only one and a half since unloading the guns. Wounds were still fresh and Germany and the Soviet Union, the two countries blamed for the war, were not invited to the games.

Paavo Nurmi had run his first competitive race at age seventeen in 1914 (3,000 meters in 10:06), but had been disappointed by the result. For training, Nurmi had been running briskly on a course ranging from two to six kilometers three or four times a week, and racing regularly, inspired to break the 16-minute barrier for 5,000 meters. That was the first time that revered sports coach Lauri Pihkala heard about "a boy who trains seriously and somehow resembles Hannes." Nurmi intimately knew of the performances of Hannes Kolehmainen, who was said to "have run Finland onto the map of the world" at the 1912 Olympics. But with limited coaching advice, Nurmi improved his 5,000-meter time by only 10 seconds in the next three years.

Everything changed in 1919. Nurmi started his 18-month national military service and was given free reign when it came to training. Nurmi quickly impressed in athletic competitions: while others marched, he ran complete distances with a rifle on his shoulder and a backpack full of sand. But Nurmi was not alone in representing his country for distance glory. Another big name in the cross-country circuit was also vying for Olympic gold.

JOSEPH GUILLEMOT, FRANCE'S CHAMPION OF THE 1920s

Born in Le Dorat in October 1899, Joseph Guillemot was frequently touted for a rare birth condition—that his heart was on the right side of his chest—which was never confirmed by French doctors. Robert Pariente, a French track historian, simply shared that Guillemot had an extraordinary lung capacity and a low heart rate, which allowed for a quick recovery. Others touted Guillemot for his personality, which was flamboyant: equal parts generosity and embellishment.

After serving for France in the later stages of World War I, Guillemot became a good runner and was at home in cross-country races. His claim to fame occurred when he won his regiment's cross-country championship in 1919. The next year, he won his first French National

Cross-Country title over a course at Bry sur Marne, and then went on to win the English National—the two championships not thirty days apart. In 1922 he repeated the feat—winning both national championships again—en route to his first International Cross-Country title, which he won in Glasgow, Scotland on April 1 of the same year. France was also able to claim the gold medal for their team finish in the 1922 event (their first team title ever).

Four years later, Guillemot once again returned to the top—winning the French National for the third time and second at the International—with France once again winning the team title. After that, his performances began to fade, and by 1927 he had all but disappeared. "Guigui," as the French called him, was remembered as a runner whose true potential was untapped, chiefly if not entirely due to his casual approach to training.

GUILLEMOT AND NURMI FACE OFF

In August 1920, Paavo Nurmi toed the starting line of an Olympic final for the first time (he had recovered from a bout of seasickness in solitude). It was the 5,000-meter final, where the heavy footsteps of Joseph Guillemot shadowed Nurmi like a hawk. The Finn was not afraid of the soft track. He crossed the halfway point in 7:12—then fatigue set in.

Guillemot, age 20, passed Nurmi with 100 meters to go, breaking the tape as an Olympic champion in 14:55. It was the most illustrious moment of his short career. Nurmi would exact revenge three days later, winning the 10,000-meter race, with Guillemot an exhausted second place. The rivalry was even heading into the cross-country event.

Six days after their harrowing 10,000 meters, cross-country running was featured for the second time in the Summer Olympics. Forty-seven runners from 12 nations competed over an eight-kilometer course. While touted as an epic showdown between Paavo Nurmi and Joseph Guillemot, the Frenchman sprained an ankle just after the 5,000-meter mark and had to drop out. Paavo Nurmi and Eric Backman of Sweden remained to pull away, with Nurmi winning in a sprint. Teams had been allowed six runners each with the top three finishers counting—and eight of the 12 nations were able to field complete teams. Led by Nurmi, with help from third-place finisher Heikki Liimatainen, Finland claimed the gold with 10 points; Great Britain was second with 21; Sweden, third with 23. The United States finished fourth with 36 points after Pat Flynn—a steeplechaser and member of the Paulist Athletic Club of New York—crossed in ninth overall.

THE PHANTOM FINN CHALLENGES NEW COMPETITION

From May 1920 to May 1922 Nurmi won three Finnish cross-country titles. Two years after his second Olympic gold medal in the cross-country event, Nurmi returned to the Finnish National Cross-Country Championship and was champion once again. His victory in Helsinki on May 9, 1926, was 28:52, a truly remarkable pace considering the nine-kilometer distance. Nurmi won again in 1928, 1930, and 1932—earning seven national cross-country titles in 12 years.

And while it may have seemed as though Nurmi was running alone, his closest rivals were not far behind. Countryman Väinö Sipilä won three straight Finnish cross-country titles while Nurmi toured the world between 1923 and 1925 and set records on the track. Edvin Wide was the third-best long-distance runner in the world. An elementary school teacher from Sweden, Wide was a five-time Swedish cross-country champion, winning his titles from Örebro to Stockholm to Uppsala all in succession. But one man shadowed Nurmi more than anyone: Finland's Ville Ritola.

Ritola began training seriously in the Olympic spring of 1920. Together with Hannes Kolehmainen, he was doing long walks—"frighteningly long," he later claimed. It was marathon training: speed, pace, rhythm, and tempo—all new to Ritola. Ritola was in fantastic shape, but, consumed with work and marriage plans, he did not participate in the Antwerp Olympics. Inspired by the gold medals won by Guillemot and Nurmi, Ritola went on training hard, running to work and back on the asphalt streets in New York wearing heavy steel-heeled shoes. And Ritola was progressing, he soon finished second at the 1922 Boston Marathon, losing only to the legendary Clarence de Mar.

By the Olympic spring of 1924, Paavo Nurmi was stepping through the front door of his home in Turku for a training session three times a day. He was feeling unbelievably fit—and then disaster struck. In a club cross-country race on a serene Sunday in April—on a course he had himself designed—Nurmi fell badly on an icy patch, seriously injuring his knee. For two weeks Nurmi was unable to run a step. By the third week Nurmi was able to sneak onto the Turku Sports Park track late one evening and run 800 meters flat out. The time was a pedestrian 2:12. "That was the gloomiest day of my life," Nurmi confessed years later.

It was at this point that Finnish fans saw Ville Ritola run for the first time. Ritola began by winning the Olympic trials 5,000 meters in 14:47, and then, on the second day, with copious amounts of rain and mud, he went on to break Nurmi's 10,000-meter world record. Having returned to his home country in December, Ritola trained like an animal through the winter. Given ample assistance by the Finnish Olympic committee, his performance was the sensation of the trials. There were many experts who thought Nurmi's era was over.

Paavo Nurmi was able to silence the doubters quickly, running not one, but two, world records less than a month later. First was the 1,500-meter world record in a time of 3:52, where he ran the first lap in 57.3 seconds. Nurmi then attacked the 5,000 meters just 55 minutes later in a world-record time of 14:28.

The 1924 Summer Olympics, held in Paris, France, marked the showdown between Nurmi and Ritola. It was also the third and final time that cross-country was contested as its own event at the Olympic level, both for team and individual honors.

In the early stages of the Games, it was Ritola who earned gold, running the 10,000 meters on the track in a new world record of 30:23, which was the fastest 10,000-meter run of his career, with Edvin Wide of Sweden clocking 30:55 for second. Within three days Ritola had won his steeplechase heat and his 5,000-meter heat and was toeing the line of the 3,000-meter steeplechase final. Shadowed by his young teammate Elias Katz, Ritola won gold medal number two. Four days after Ritola's record time in the 10,000 meters, Nurmi and Ritola were set to face off. First, in the morning, Paavo Nurmi won the 1,500 meters in an Olympic record time of 3:53. Then, with less than an hour between the 1,500- and 5,000-meter finals, Nurmi and Ritola lined up for the 5,000 meters.

Edvin Wide of Sweden took the field out quickly, but he gradually had to leave the Finnish twosome alone. Lapping in front in shifts, Nurmi and Ritola crossed the line with one stride separating them at the finish: 14:31.2 and 14:31.4—then Wide followed, some half a minute behind. For Nurmi and Ritola, the score was now even at two gold medals apiece. But both men needed to preserve their energy, as each would be facing a heat of the 3,000-meter team race and, the day after, a punishing furnace of fire: the 10,650-meter cross-country race.

The 1924 Olympic cross-country event has become the story of legend—earning hundreds of columns that detailed the horrifying conditions—and it still hasn't lost any of its impact. The course, which started directly outside the Stade de Colombes and ran along the banks of the river Seine was reasonably flat, but the temperature was unbearable: 97 degrees Fahrenheit in the shade, more than 120 degrees in the sun. As far as is known, there was never a hotter day in Olympic history, before or since. With a nearby factory spewing toxic fumes into the air along the course, only 15 runners were able to finish out of a field of 39 starters.

Well before modern practice, the lack of proper hydration played a part, and the combination of conditions produced bouts of sunstroke, unconsciousness, disorientation, vomiting, and exhaustion for a majority of the athletes. Eight athletes were taken away on stretchers and two were pronounced dead from heat exhaustion (both runners eventually recovered).

The course was marked by flags and used the surrounding countryside of rough grass, dirt roads, and a few measurable obstacles. Competitors had to negotiate the entire 10,650 meters combating heavy dust, thick weeds, and noxious fumes.

Edvin Wide began the contest with a fast start, but after 4.5 kilometers Nurmi and Ritola left Wide behind—and the Swede never made it to the finish. A couple of kilometers later Nurmi made his move, and toward the end his lead only increased. With others fainting into the weeds along the Seine, and ambulances howling on the streets of Paris, Nurmi's face remained stoic, almost unstrained.

He sped round the course hundreds of meters ahead of his rivals, crossing the finish line a minute and a half ahead of Ritola and appearing only slightly tired.

Edwin James, columnist for the *New York Times*, picked up the story: "Behind Nurmi and Ritola, there came into the stadium a big American boy, R. Earl Johnson of Pittsburgh. Entering about a minute behind Ritola, he slowly but steadily edged his way round the half circle of the stadium toward the tape. He was still running, but his run was fast becoming an amble. Ten yards behind Johnson came an Englishman, Harper, who struggled even more painfully. His legs moved as if each had a ten-pound weight attached to it. For a moment it seemed doubtful if he could reach the tape. He did, but he stood groping blindly with his hands, seeking support, and was caught fainting in the arms of his countrymen." Only three teams got three men home: Finland won with 11 points, the USA was second with 14, and France was third with 20. Paavo Nurmi's time was 32:54, Ville Ritola came second in 34:19, and Earl Johnson came third in 35:21.

Ambulances were out on the path for two hours accounting for all of the runners. Journalists Kieran and Daley wrote in 1948: "A few [runners] staggered into the stadium and fell in utter exhaustion with the finish line in sight. One runner entered the stadium gates in a daze, turned in the wrong direction and ran head-on into a concrete wall, splitting his scalp badly and falling to the ground covered with blood. Andia Aguilar of Spain suffered sunstroke out on the course and was carried to a hospital where, for some days, his life was despaired of." Because of these disastrous results, the individual and team cross-country running event was removed from the Olympic program thereafter.

As for Finland's champions, the Olympic pressure had been tremendous for the two: Nurmi, seven races in six days; Ritola, eight races in eight days. They had no rest days at all, and many years later, Nurmi and Ritola revealed they had sleeping troubles toward the end of the Olympic week; each had gone through the night in a stupor, restlessly staring at the ceiling of their rooms. But it was worth the cost. In Finland, both Nurmi and Ritola were certified heroes.

ON THE NORTH AMERICAN SHORES

In November 1921, the Amateur Athletic Union (AAU) US National Cross-Country Championship was contested in Schenley Park in Pittsburgh. The race was important for two reasons: it marked the first time the championship was run anywhere outside of Boston or New York; and R. Earl Johnson, the winner of the race and a local favorite, had faced Fred Faller, the winner of the event the two previous years.

Faller, fresh off the 1920 Summer Olympic cross-country event where he had finished 15th overall, competed for the Dorchester Athletic Club out of Boston. Earl Johnson was the first nationally prominent African American distance runner. A member of the Thompson Steelworks Athletic Association near Pittsburgh, Johnson was also an Olympian, making his debut in 1920 when he was eliminated in a heat of the 10,000 meters. In cross-country, Johnson later became the best American finisher ever in the Olympic event when he won the bronze medal in 1924. In the 1921 AAU US National Cross-Country Championship, it was Johnson who beat Faller and every other entrant by running the five-mile course in 24:23—defeating even Finland's Ville Ritola, who came in second.

In American colleges and universities during this period there were no Finnish superstars to challenge, but there was a fleet of homegrown talent. By the early 1920s, universities within the Midwest and up and down the East Coast were watching the sport thrive—and the connection between universities and high schools was also improving. The University of Iowa hosted its first interscholastic high school championship in 1922, attracting between 25 and 30 schools to participate for the better part of the decade. In addition to championships at other major universities east of the Mississippi, dual meets, like those between Michigan State College and the University of Michigan, were also popular.

Conference championships were the mark of record, however. The Southwest Conference (organized in 1914), included Texas, Texas A&M, Oklahoma A&M, and Rice University, and started competition for conference cross-country honors as early as 1920. The first championship was held in College Station (home of Texas A&M), and the University of Texas was the first conference champion.

In 1929, Missouri became part of the Big Six Conference with Iowa State, Kansas State, Kansas, Missouri, Nebraska, and Oklahoma as charter members. Oklahoma A&M (Oklahoma State), Grinnell, Drake, and Washington University were left to make their own conference—and Drake has remained in the Missouri Valley to this day. Similarly, in 1926 the Central Intercollegiate Conference was born when four universities—Marquette, Michigan State, Butler, and Notre Dame—agreed to align their varsity sports into a new athletic conference.

The Intercollegiate Association of Amateur Athletics of America (IC4A) Cross-Country Championship, which had initially featured colleges in the Ivy League and along the East Coast, was being held annually at New York's Van Cortlandt Park throughout the 1920s. This meet represented, at least for the eastern United States, the de facto national championship prior to inception of the National Collegiate Athletic Association (NCAA) meet, and lent an air of credibility to the fledgling championship's chosen venue.

Of note was a strong 1929 Michigan State team that represented the first real Midwestern college to challenge the best teams in the IC4A Cross-Country Championship. The *New York Times* reported, "The surprising total [of 23 varsity teams] exceeds by five the number of teams entered for the classic chase in 1928, and indicates widespread interest this year in the strenuous sport of galloping six long miles over hill and dale. Constituting the first intersectional threat in the history of cross-country,

Michigan State College entered a team of nine men headed by Captain Theodore Willmarth and Lauren P. Brown."

The trailblazing Spartans clearly acquitted themselves well. Entering the 1929 IC4A, the Spartans had won every dual meet during the season, as well as the Central Intercollegiate Championship. When Brown and Chamberlain finished third and fourth, respectively, Michigan State finished second as a team. The University of Maine runners—who were accustomed to the hilly conditions—nosed out the Spartans for first place.

Meanwhile, at the prep level in California, the oldest contemporary records showed high school cross-country started section championships in 1925 (which included San Diego County schools). However, there were few multi-team invitationals due to the lack of high schools offering cross-country as an interscholastic sport. Most races were dual meets, oftentimes scheduled to start and conclude on tracks during halftimes of football games.

With entry into the Olympic cross-country event and the experimentation of the sport in a host of new locations, cross-country solidified its standing in America.

THE INTERNATIONAL GAINS STEAM

In 1920, the International Cross-Country Championship was held for the first time since 1914, and was run in Belfast Belvoir Park in Ireland. Running for the Greenock Glenpark Harriers, Jim Wilson of Scotland won the individual title, becoming the first Scottish winner of the event. Wales was unable to send a team due to illness, and England won the team title over Ireland, who came second. This event was still confined to France and the four home nations of the United Kingdom, however, without inclusion of the European runners so dominant at the previous two Olympics.

By 1922, it had been fifteen years since France first entered the International, and in that time they had taken second place in 1908 and 1913 and had provided the individual winner three times. Victory was savored when, at Hampden Park, near Glasgow, over an ideal course, France recorded a double victory in winning the team race with a score of 53 points and winning the individual event with Joseph Guillemot. The English, despite winning 14 team championships leading to the event, suffered their first defeat. For years to come, the race for supremacy was destined to be a struggle between England and France.

The first appearance of Belgium in the International occurred in 1923. This race, held at the Paris Maison-Laffitte course in France, saw Belgium finish third overall with 112 points, beating Scotland by one point. France won their second straight team title. Joe Blewitt, a great steeplechaser from England (representing the Birchfield Harriers) won the individual title, running the 16-kilometer course in 58:11. England finished second as a team.

1924 was notable for an English resurgence. About 400 yards from home, J. J. Ryan, a well-known Irish champion, looked like he had the race won when he suddenly collapsed with a cramp in his legs, allowing England's William Cotterell to secure the individual title. Not only did Cotterell snatch victory from the jaws of defeat, but England scored 21 points—a perfect score—the lowest possible with six athletes.

The years 1925–28 saw an increased attention paid to pack running, of which the French team gained the most notoriety. And in 1928, arrangements were made to host the International in a European continental country every third year, after France and Belgium both had difficulty in transporting teams to venues in England.

In the spring of 1929, after a decade where France and Belgian teams came and went from the event, a multitude of European nations finally committed to the International Cross-Country Championship. Run at the Paris Hippodrome de Vincennes on March 23, 1929, a total of 10 teams competed for world supremacy in cross-country, the largest field the championship had seen. The entries ranged from the expected to the obscure: France won the team competition for the fourth year in a row. England was 43 points behind and came in second, with Spain, Belgium, and Scotland following close on their heels. Italy was sixth, Ireland seventh, and Switzerland eighth. Wales came in ninth place, and Luxemburg rounded out the scoring in 10th place. Individual honors went to William Cotterell of England (his second title of the decade), who beat Henri Dartigues of France by two seconds (the 14-kilometer race was won in a time of 42:46). Once again France predominated, but the surprise of the race was the performance of Spain, who finished third.

* * *

The 1920s can be reviewed as "experimental" times—or perhaps even "transitory" times. These terms apply to the proliferation and expansion the sport saw in the United States at various levels, the extent to which cross-country appeared on the Olympic program—twice, with unfortunate consequences in 1924—and the brief but bright International Championship event that featured 10 European teams (but only lasted for a single incarnation). These experiments would provide lasting consequences, many positive—such as the American attraction to the sport—but some with a darker future, as with cross-country running's place (or lack thereof) on the Olympic agenda. Regardless, there were more intricate connections among locations featuring the sport, more impactful rivalries, and more exciting races. The decade of the '20s was roaring on many levels, and the sport's transitory nature would yield to permanency in the coming years.

EVENT SPOTLIGHT: CORNELL UNIVERSITY VERSUS OXFORD/CAMBRIDGE TEAM IN ENGLAND (DECEMBER 30, 1920)

LOCATION: WIMBLEDON COMMON

Ithaca, New York (Home of Cornell University)

On December 30, 1920, Cornell University's cross-country team traveled to England to face a combined cross-country team featuring the best Oxford and Cambridge University students. Coach Jack Moakley, who had been in charge of the track and cross-country teams at Cornell for more than twenty-five years, organized the affair and claimed that it was one of the greatest races he had ever witnessed.

The course, which was the same Roehampton cross-country course used by the Thames Hare and Hounds, encompassed over seven miles of difficult terrain comprised of more than two miles of dirt road, one mile of ploughed land, four miles of rough grass fields, and a finish on Wimbledon Common. It also contained two hills of low elevation and two water jumps, which were just wide enough to ensure the runners got properly wet. The weather prior to the event was especially bad, with heavy rains soaking the course the day before the race. Undeterred, Moakley, Cornell's head coach, was put on the record stating that though his team lacked the stars featured by the English universities, he had faith in Cornell's "pack"—believing his team, by united effort, would be able to win.

The race included seven runners for each team, with five to score. The British team had both the Oxford and Cambridge team captains competing, with the last names of Montague and Seagrove, respectively. Cornell, who had won the IC4A Cross-Country Championship earlier in 1920, was led by seniors Carter and McDermott.

For the first half-mile of the race all of the men were bunched together. This lasted until mile two, when Montague, Seagrove, Carter, McDermott, and Oxford's McInnes separated from the pack. When McInnes drew away, Cornell's Carter went with him, and they set a blistering pace to the finish. At the two-mile mark it seemed an apparent American victory, but after the first water jump and the ploughed fields, James Dickinson, the Cornell University captain, began to fall back, crushing any hopes of Cornell finishing as a pack. Coming into Wimbledon Common for the mile-and-a-half finish, McInnes and Carter were stride for stride, while McDermott and Montague were battling for third place. McInnes began his kick early, separating himself with a mile to go, and finished 100 yards ahead of Carter. McDermott beat Montague for third, and finished only 50 yards behind his teammate Carter. Final tally put the score close, but Britain's mettle proved to be too strong. Montague, the Oxford captain who finished fourth, collapsed at the line, having run the entire race with an injured foot.

The course record for the 7.5-mile Roehampton run was a blazing 41:55, set in favorable conditions. Yet on this day McInnes finished in 42:00 flat, a full minute faster than the winning time from the Oxford-Cambridge dual meet three weeks prior. The closeness of the contest (only three points separated the two teams, Oxford/Cambridge winning 26 to Cornell's 29), despite the rain, saw the final man home finish only 2:03 behind McInnes. A special correspondent to the *New York Times* wrote from London: "Because of the sporting spirit in which the Americans came and tackled us in our own backyard at a sport we know best, and because of the desperately close nature of the struggle, one of the closest in the age-long story of this ancient sport, today's affair will go down in the annuals of athletics as a classic."

Did You Know?

Storylines proliferated from the combined Cornell-Oxford/Cambridge University Championship in 1920. Oxford's E. A. Montague had been well known to American runners, as he had traveled to the Penn Relays with an Oxford/Cambridge team the previous year and had finished as the runner-up in a dramatic three-mile run on the track. He had also been a two-time winner of the Oxford-Cambridge dual meet run over the same course at Roehampton. Cambridge's captain, W. R. Seagrove, would go on to win the Oxford-Cambridge dual in 1921, with N. A. McInnes the winner once again in 1922. With the graduation of Carter and McDermott, Cornell's own Robert Brown would go on to win the IC4A Intercollegiate Cross-Country title the following season, with teammate Norman Brown (who finished sixth in this event) the second-place finisher just behind.

CULTURAL SPOTLIGHT: WOMEN IN CROSS-COUNTRY RUNNING

Historically, there were many examples of women participating in running competitions prior to the twentieth century. Footracing (petticoat races) and boxing booths for women were present at country fairs, while wagers aimed exclusively at female participation in pedestrianism could be traced back to the eighteenth century. By the early twentieth century, cross-country running was much more accessible to the general population, and this period saw the establishment of area organizations to monitor the sport. Women were not excluded from this; in Paris in 1903, a 12-kilometer race to Nanterre on dirt roads attracted 2,500 shop girls. By the 1920s, the development of athletics in schools also laid a firm foundation for female participation. Certain sports for women became popular, producing many significant performances. For instance, 53,000 spectators watched a women's football (soccer) match on Boxing Day 1920.

Yet even while this was happening, a social backlash was brewing. The International Olympic Committee rejected the newly formed Federation Feminine Sportive de France's pleas for women's events in the Olympics in 1919. In 1921 the (English) Football Association banned women from playing on their grounds, effectively wiping out the women's game until 1971 when the ban was rescinded. The Amateur Athletic Association in Britain told the Women's Amateur Athletic Association that they would be better off on their own when the women applied for affiliation in 1923.

As a sport, running formed the backbone for this narrative. The first women's track and field meet was held in 1885 in Poughkeepsie, New York, and within thirty years, the appeal for women's track and field was so great the International Olympic Committee (IOC) was forced to take action, leading to their rejection of women's events in the Olympics.

As a response, in 1921, French rower Alice Milliat founded the Federation Sportive Feminine Internationale (FSFI). And in 1922, the FSFI staged the first world games: the Women's Olympics, which was open only to female participants and hosted a dozen events. In short order, "Olympics" was dropped from the title in exchange for limited inclusion (five events) in the IOC's program, but the FSFI continued to hold their own Women's World Games every four years until 1934.

Yet even when five women's events appeared in the Amsterdam Olympic Games in 1928 (the 100 meters, 800 meters, 4 × 100–meter relay, high jump, and discus), prejudices followed. After the 800-meter run, women were banned from competing in any event further than 200 meters because several competitors appeared to "collapse" (a common occurrence for members of both sexes after running 800 meters, before this event and since).

Organizationally, it wouldn't be until 1936 that the FSFI merged with the International Amateur Athletics Federation (IAAF)—and there would be no female representation on the council until 1995 (the Women's Amateur Athletic Association [WAAA] gained representation in the Amateur Athletic Association [AAA] in 1991). In 1937 the British Amateur Athletic Board was formed, and the WAAA was allowed representation. Twenty-three years later, the women's 400-meter and 800-meter races were finally reinstated to the Olympic program.

But despite the difficulty in gaining recognition, progress did take place, and it was in France where the movement for women in athletics began. France was able to provide a model that was easily adaptable in Europe: representation and organization. French women were organizing cycling races as early as 1869 in Bordeaux. And the first 19 women to compete in the modern Olympics Games did so in Paris in 1900, where they played tennis, golf, and croquet. Margaret Abbott, an art student in Paris, became the first American woman to win an Olympic gold medal, winning the nine-hole golf tournament by shooting a 47.

Momentum was built in France after the formation of the first women's gymnastics club in 1900—where running events were also practiced. This led to the first all-female interclub contest in track and field in 1915 at Brancion Stadium, where "Femina Sport" (founded in 1912 by Pierre Paysse) and "Academia" (founded by Gustave de Lafrete 1915) faced off. This event led to many more; the end result being the formation of the first Women's Athletics Championships in July 1917, which crowned Therese Brule and Suzanne Liebrard the first champions. Both displayed incredible versatility, setting a new female world record an average of every four events. The resulting public enthusiasm allowed organizers Paysse Pierre and Albert Pelan to establish la Federation des Societes Feminines Sportives de France (the Federation of Societies for Feminine Sports of France [FSFSF]).

Hostility from the athletics community remained strong, and Alice Milliat, the then-treasurer of the FSFSF, knew that time was of the essence. With colleagues, Milliat organized the first cross-country championship for women in April 1918. With help from *L'Echo des Sports* and *L'Auto* (two major French sports newspapers of the time) 42 participants with their associated clubs took part. Conducted with what many at the time considered indecent dress—shorts and jerseys—the race followed a course through 2,400 meters of wooded trails, and was won by Anne Tinguy in 9:58.

Beyond 1918, the French Women's Cross-Country Championship ran annually without interruption, and remains the longest standing (and most consistent) female cross-country race on the planet. During the early years, Lucie Bréard won two of the first four events (in 1920 and 1921). In 1921, both the Fédération des Sociétés Françaises de Sport Féminin and the Fédération Française Féminines du Sport Athlètique held championships. The rivalry was intended to destabilize the efforts of Alice Milliat, and would only last until 1925. By then, France was not the only place where female cross-county runners could take up the sport.

Harrier clubs in England, such as the Birchfield Harriers, were offering female participation in cross-country as early as 1922. By that point international track competition was available for women in England, and English female track runners used cross-country runs for winter training (a photo from that era shows three women in shorts and long-sleeved jerseys vigorously leaping over a muddy ditch). In 1924, Birchfield listed Miss Woodwooley as the winner of the first ladies' cross-country race held at Percy Barr.

In 1927, a senior Women's Cross-Country Championship was held in England for the first time, over a course in Luton. Anne M. Williams, representing the Littlehampton Ladies Athletic Club was the individual winner. Lilian Styles, also representing the Littlehampton Ladies AC, won the following year, when the competition moved to Chigwell Row in February. Also in 1927, Birchfield Harriers's Gladys Lunn debuted her talents on the track, winning the 440 yards and 880 yards, and finishing second in the long jump for the Nottingham Cup.

Meanwhile, the Middlesex Ladies Athletic Club won three women's senior team cross-country titles in a row (from 1927 to 1930). But it wasn't until the 1931 event that Gladys Lunn and the Birchfield women entered the competition. Lunn took home first place in her debut, while the Birchfield team finished sixth as a squad. In 1932, at Coventry, Lunn again won the individual prize. This time, the Birchfield Harriers ladies team finished first as well.

On March 22, 1931, the first international women's cross-country race was staged in Douai, France. Alice Milliat, now a well-known athletic advocate for women, used her connections within the Federation Sportive Feminine Internationale (FSFI) to host the meet. Gladys Lunn was the victor, representing England, with countrymate Lilian Styles hot on her heels. The women raced a course of just under two miles (3,000 meters) with Lunn clocking 11:12 and Styles clocking 11:25. Suzanne Lenoir—the French national champion two weeks previous—finished third in this event. England won first place as a team with 15 points, France second with 21, and Belgium third with 42.

The following year the second edition of the event was held in Croydon, England. Again Lunn was declared champion, and again the course was run over the 3,000-meter distance. This time, however, the team battle was much closer, with Lunn finishing the course in 12:56 and Suzanne Hedouin of France coming in second in 13:06. Lilian Styles finished in third for England and Ruth Christmas of England in fourth. Suzanne Lenoir of France made the competition close by finishing in fifth, but the next two English finishers sealed the deal for the British team. Final score: England 14, France 22.

A women's international event was not contested again until 1935. In that race only England and Scotland competed. And while these women's events in the early 1930s were considered unofficial, great effort was made by individual organizers, like Milliat, to ensure a unique day and venue were available for the event, with expenses covered for traveling teams.

The unofficial women's international championship appeared for the final time in the 1930s in Lille, France, in March 1938. This time 18 participants, once again representing France, England, and Belgium, competed over a 3,000-meter course. Winning in 12:40, Evelyne Forster of England finished well ahead of the competition, securing an English team victory. From there, it was a long hiatus before another "Women's International" appeared in Birmingham in 1954, where England reconfirmed, with the success of Diane Leather, the strength of its tradition among women.

The individuals who took great steps to popularize the sport for women gained international notoriety. Alice Milliat of France, who was paramount in organizing the French National Women's Cross-Country Championship and the International Women's Cross-Country Championship in the 1920s and '30s, helped the IAAF gain control over women's sports. Gladys Lunn, whose performances made headlines, remained an ambassador and cultivated the sport for women in England through the 1940s. Dale Greig became one of 10 founders of the inaugural Scottish Women's Cross-Country Association and formed her own local club, the Tannahill Harriers. And yet the challenges for these pioneers remained. It was not until the late 1950s and early 1960s that any real recognition would be given to women competing in cross-country—and by then, there would be new names to advance the sport.

Chapter 9

The art of running consists, in essence, of reaching the threshold of unconsciousness at the instant of breasting the tape. It is not an easy process for the body rebels against such agonizing usage and must be disciplined by the spirit and the mind. Few events in sport offer so ultimate a test of human courage and human will and human ability to dare and endure for the simple sake of struggle.

—Paul O'Neil, in the first issue of Sports Illustrated

THE DECADE OF THE 1930s

Some aspects of cross-country competition mirrored society-at-large during the 1930s; notably, when the growth seen in the early stages of the twentieth century began to slow. For example, for the first time in a decade, cross-country was absent from the Olympic agenda. In addition, the true international smattering seen in attendance for a brief year in 1929 in the International Cross-Country Championship fell away; Belgium and France were left as the only two countries outside the home nations of the United Kingdom to compete in regular attendance during the decade.

But despite this stagnation, cross-country was marked by great achievement, dramatic competition, and new champions in other forms during the 1930s. In America, the sport witnessed the rise of a cohesive National Collegiate Athletic Association (NCAA) Championship. State-level championships and the support for more junior competition—not to mention the further competition of female cross-country runners—also expanded the sport. New world champions and new world records in distance running added to the appeal of competition and kept participation levels steady. Globally, cross-country running stabilized after a decade of change and growth, and old barriers were broken by a new fleet of well-trained athletes.

DOMESTIC STABILIZATION

By 1930, four states in the United States had officially sanctioned the sport of cross-country running at the high school level for state competition: Wisconsin, Iowa, New Jersey, and Ohio. Motivated by associations that were assembling on a state-by-state basis, other sports like football, basketball, baseball, and track and field were seeing large numbers in participation by students, and regional tournaments and "state championship tournaments" were all the rage. Cross-country was seeing growth in national participation informally as more schools included it in their fall programming, but only a few made a point to recognize it on the same scale as other sports.

Illinois, Michigan, and New Hampshire were also offering statewide interscholastic "championship" competition, although with limited finances much of it was independent or inconsistent. Other interscholastic meets, hosted by state colleges and universities, were flourishing. By the middle of the decade, the New England Interscholastic Championships were giving high school students a reason to celebrate, as Vermont, Maine, Massachusetts, and New Hampshire all agreed to participate in team and individual competition for a "New England Champion" cross-country title. By the end of the decade Pennsylvania, Connecticut, Rhode Island, and Oklahoma were also sponsoring state-sanctioned state competition.

THE STRENGTH OF THE UNITED STATES'S MIDWESTERN UNIVERSITIES

Lauren Brown took over as head cross-country coach of Michigan State College (MSC) in 1931, inheriting a team captained by his former teammate Clark Chamberlain. And despite the moderate success that MSC had achieved in the years with Brown as an athlete, within two years it was the *Wolverine*, the on-campus newspaper at Michigan State, that celebrated Brown's prowess at the helm as coach: "If it is true that great cross-country runners are made and not born then Coach Lauren P. Brown, head mentor of Michigan State's distance harriers, has made a stack of them in his three years here. Brown had picked up many inside tricks of the trade during his years of competition and imparted that information to his pupils. He pursued an ambitious policy that was soon to raise Spartan cross-country to new peaks."

The primary accomplishment for the Spartans was an undefeated 1933 season and their dominance at the Intercollegiate Association of Amateur Athletics of America (IC4A) meet in New York's Van Cortland Park. Michigan State finished in front of Manhattan with 54 points and became the first "Western" school to win the coveted title. The remainder of the "Eastern" field all finished with 100 points or more.

"It was the first time in history that Michigan State had garnered a national crown in any sport and much praise was heaped on the squad that turned the trick. Behind it all was the reclining figure of Lauren Brown," wrote the *Wolverine*.

This was the first of five straight IC4A championships for Michigan State, and Brown's Spartans won in a variety of ways. For example, in the 1933 and 1934 IC4A Michigan State was led by dominating performances by captain Tom Ottey.

The 1935 race presented a different story. Captain Eddie Bechtold's surprise victory buoyed the Spartans, but a blue-collar team effort caught opponents off guard right from the start. Michigan State continued to dominate the IC4A race with Brown replacing athletes as seniors graduated and freshmen arrived. In 1937 MSC, Cornell, and Syracuse, each with four all-time victories apiece, raced with a chance to "retire" the IC4A trophy permanently.

The *New York Times* reported the outcome from the perspective of Syracuse's coach, whose top runners dominated much of the race:

As the veteran Tom Keane, coaching maestro of the Orange, peered down the home stretch to see his up-starters romping in, he could find only Southard, Cavileer, Harry Sentiff, and Stanley Romanowski up with the leaders—all within the first thirteen. And as the wearied athletes flashed by him, he searched in vain for his fifth man and victory. The odd part about it was that Keane had been the most insistent man in the IC4A that Michigan State be admitted to membership some years back. That was as a personal gesture to Ralph Young, then the Spartan coach and now athletic director who brought into prominence Lauren Brown, the present mentor.

Michigan State pulled out the upset that day, and the victory led to national legitimacy for Lauren Brown and the Michigan State cross-country program.

At nearby Indiana University, in Bloomington, Indiana, another blue-collar attempt was being made to build a cross-country program. Coach Earle C. "Billy" Hayes fostered his talented athletes and transformed the distance running culture of the school on the credence of hard work. Hayes became the cross-country coach in 1924,

> **Did You Know?**
>
> When Michigan State competed in the IC4A Cross-Country Championship, they endured a multi-hour trip, all to defeat the powerful East Coast universities—but Coach Lauren Brown still yearned for an event that was consummate and undisputable. In 1926, Michigan State's Ralph H. Young (also head track coach), along with Knute Rockne of Notre Dame (famous as a football coach), and Conrad M. Jennings of Marquette (athletic director and track coach), founded the Central Collegiate Conference to promote track and field and cross-country among colleges in the Midwest. Michigan State then won the inaugural Central Collegiate Conference Cross-Country Championship. But by the 1930s it was Brown who saw the potential in transforming the Central Collegiate Conference Cross-Country Championship into something greater. It was here the NCAA Cross-Country Championship was born.

transferring from Mississippi A&M where he had coached football, basketball, and track. At that time, Indiana was lackluster in the department of distance running, finishing last in the Big Ten Conference for many of the early years of the 1920s. Coach Hayes didn't waste any time in turning the team around. In 1928, three years after his first season as coach, Indiana won their first Big Ten Conference title outright in cross-country, and they kept their number one position for the next five runnings (the streak might have been 11, had it not been for the depression-pinched conference temporarily dropping cross-country from 1933 to 1937).

Part of the reason for Indiana's success was Hayes's acquisition of Sid Robinson as assistant coach, who, in 1930, was already receiving world-renowned eminence as a physiologist (no relation to the aforementioned Sid Robinson, the top distance runner in England at the turn of the century). Hayes had coached Robinson while at Mississippi A&M, and Robinson had made the 1928 Olympic team for the United States in the 1,500 meters.

The lack of a conference title to defend between the years 1933–37 was no obstacle, and Coach Hayes led the Hoosiers to victory at the inaugural NCAA Championship meet in 1938 and 1940, and tied for first in 1942. He was also responsible for dual meet wins against rival Michigan State in 1935, 1936, 1937, 1939, and 1940. In fact, these victories proved to be the only season-losses for Coach Lauren Brown and the Spartans. Indiana came up short in 1934 and 1938, although the margin of error was small: in 1934, Michigan State beat Indiana 26 to 29, and in 1938, the Spartans won 27 to 28.

The 1934 dual meet, where Michigan State came out victorious against Indiana, proved to be the start for a special name in distance running: Don Lash. Part of the appeal of that cross-country dual meet loss to Michigan State for Indiana's coach Billy Hayes was not that Indiana made such a close event of it—but that Lash, in his sophomore debut for Indiana, finished first overall. Lash had begun his career in cross-country with a third-place finish. It would be the only cross-country race he ever lost.

THE REMARKABLE DON LASH: THE IRON MAN FROM INDIANA

Don Lash, who attended Indiana University from the fall of 1933 to the spring of 1938, made his greatest strides in distance running during this time. This was especially true in cross-country. Years later, *Sports Illustrated* would call Lash "the first great American distance runner" and "possibly the best US cross-country runner ever."

Lash was the golden child on a golden team at Indiana University, but that wasn't always his modus operandi. As the middle child of five children, and with ample exposure to farm life, hard work, and the great outdoors growing up, Don Lash developed as a dependable provider for the family and put his ingenuity to good use. Instead of following his older brother into football and basketball at Auburn High School, Don avoided contact sports and focused solely on running.

Auburn High School did not have a track. Outdoors, Lash and the other athletes ran in a pasture for workouts, and in bad weather would train in the school building. As Lash recounted in his autobiography: "Since our school was a two-story building with an attic, our coach, Zeke Young, would have us start in the gym, run upstairs to the second floor, run up another set of stairs to the attic, down both flights of stairs and into the gym again. We ran this course until Zeke thought we had had a good workout. Of course, this was done after school."

By the time Lash entered Indiana University the college had already won five straight Big Ten Conference titles in cross-country (from 1928 to 1932), as well as the team title at the US National Cross-Country Championship in 1931. And under the guidance of Hayes and Robinson, Lash became one of the world's best.

In his time at Indiana, Lash led the Hoosiers to a four-year dual meet winning record, which was unmatched. But more remarkable, without a college conference meet to contend for, and with the NCAA Championship coming the fall after Lash's graduation, the US National Cross-Country Championship would become his proving ground. Beginning in 1934 and ending in 1940, Lash would win seven consecutive national cross-country titles. The highlight came in the fall of 1936, when, running at Branch Brook Park in Newark New Jersey, the Indiana University Hoosiers won the team title with a perfect score, with Lash placing first. Because of his hard training and ability to run fast in multiple events on the track, the *New York Sports Writers* dubbed Lash, "The Iron Man from Indiana."

THE ORIGIN OF THE NCAA

Back at the university, word was getting around that the conference schools were planning on inaugurating an "official" collegiate cross-country championship—one governed by the NCAA. But it was necessary to understand the trajectory of events that led to the first National Collegiate Athletic Association Cross-Country National Championship.

The NCAA dated its formation to two White House conferences, convened by US President Theodore Roosevelt to "encourage reforms" to college football in the early twentieth century. The American form of football had resulted in repeated injuries and deaths and "prompted many colleges and universities to discontinue the sport." Following the White House meetings, Chancellor Henry MacCracken of New York University invited 13 colleges and universities to make changes to football playing rules; and at a follow-up meeting in New York on December 28, 1905, 62 higher-education institutions became charter members of the Intercollegiate Athletic Association of the United States (IAAUS). The IAAUS was officially established on March 31, 1906, and took its present name, the NCAA, in 1910.

However, the organization that became the nation's principal regulatory body for intercollegiate athletics did not start out that way. Nearly fifty years passed before the NCAA claimed a significant regulatory role. Although regulation was set forth as an objective (and regulatory language appeared) in the Association's founding documents, the real authority was vested in the member institutions. The athletics activities of American colleges and universities were to be "maintained on an ethical plane in keeping with the dignity and high purpose of education." The founders expected that "a high standard of personal honor, eligibility and fair play" would be preserved and any abuses remedied.

The foundation of the first constitution was amateurism, but the Association was not responsible for enforcing these rules. As noted earlier, this was the province of the member institutions, and later of the college conferences as well. Those entities were to be the guardians of amateurism, because the NCAA was intended to be an educational "body" with agreed upon legislation binding membership.

When early national championships were legitimized using the NCAA organization as a regulatory cover-all (since there were member institutions large and small who agreed with the principles), regulation soon became necessary for all sports. In 1921 the first NCAA Track and Field Championship was held at Stagg Field in Chicago, where the University of Illinois won the team championship. Soon, other sports were holding their own championships (1924, men's swimming and diving; 1928, men's wrestling; 1932, boxing; 1938, men's gymnastics; 1939, men's golf; and in 1939, men's basketball). Along with these others, the first NCAA Cross-Country Championship occurred in November 1938.

Many of these early championships were held in the Midwest in an attempt to attract schools beyond the traditional East Coast conferences. And in the beginning stages, due to low numbers in attendance, few other major universities took part (and the NCAA Championships remained open to any affiliated school). For cross-country it was a plan by three Midwestern track coaches (including Michigan State's Lauren Brown) that led to the idea of the collegiate national championship being affiliated with the NCAA.

THE BIRTH OF THE NCAA CROSS-COUNTRY CHAMPIONSHIP

The establishment of an NCAA Cross-Country Championship was a significant step forward as it brought together every conference and every school under one mighty banner. While the IC4A had a rich tradition, the NCAA would ensure every institution was following the same standards and could accommodate any university—regardless of where they were located. The IC4A simply did not have the reach of the NCAA outside of track and field events. But in order to legislate, there first needed to be a coaches' association to sanction the new championship.

The National Collegiate Cross-Country Coaches Association (NCCCCA) emerged from a coaches' banquet on November 20, 1938, the evening prior to the inaugural NCAA Cross-Country Championship. The formation of this organization was not pre-ordained but rather evolved from informal discussion. Chaired by Michigan State's Ralph H. Young, it was he who "suggested that this eve of the first NCAA cross-country meet might be an appropriate time to consider organizing a cross-country coaches association, perhaps with aims similar to those of the National Collegiate Track Coaches Association." The first officer slate was put in place for the subsequent year and included Charles Werner of Pennsylvania State University as president, Indiana's Billy Hayes as vice-president, Lauren Brown of Michigan State (secretary), and Franklin Johnson of Drake University (treasurer).

Initial business included securing the location for the second NCAA Championship (decided to be held again at Michigan State), and the scheduling of the NCAA Championship in conjunction with conference championships (with the suggestion that the weekend prior to Thanksgiving be reserved for the NCAA meet). The decision to use Michigan State twice as a host venue was consistent with other major championships of the time, including the IC4A, but it was a leap of faith, considering the location of the second event was chosen site unseen. Discretion was left to individual conferences as to whether their championships would precede or succeed the NCAAs, and it was heard that the Northern schools would likely run theirs earlier and the Southern schools later, both in deference to local weather. Precedent was established regarding the location, format, and content of NCCCCA meetings that remained virtually unchanged for over a quarter century.

Eighteen colleges were represented on the official 1938 NCAA Cross-Country Championship meet entry records, including 15 full teams of at least five men, but only 12 colleges ran, with six fielding complete teams. Greg Rice of Notre Dame took top honors in a time of 20:12 for four

miles. The team title went to Indiana, while the rebuilding Michigan State Spartans took fourth behind Notre Dame and Drake.

Surprisingly, the NCAA Cross-Country Championship wasn't the only large-scale event orchestrated in the decade, nor was Michigan State's the sole cross-country course that saw substantial action. In 1937, the Oklahoma Territorial Agricultural and Mechanical (A&M) College (now known as Oklahoma State University) started an inaugural cross-country invitational at a golf course in Stillwater. Dubbed the "Cowboy Jamboree" it lays claim to being the longest-running collegiate invitational in the United States.

Now run on a manicured course designed specifically for cross-country, the original race had creek crossings and a fence partition on the campus golf course, which were seen as challenges for the runners. Save for a four-year period during World War II, this invitational has run uninterrupted since its inception without postponement or cancellation. Now a massive all-day affair including high schools, community colleges, and four-year schools, the original edition only featured a smattering of four-year heartland colleges.

EUROPEAN CROSS-COUNTRY DOMINANCE IN THE 1930s

While new stars were rising and new cross-country events were being advocated in the United States, 1932 marked the end of the Paavo Nurmi era in Europe. That year, Polish distance star Janusz Kusocinski broke Nurmi's record for 3,000 meters on the track. Kusocinski had won his first Polish National Cross-Country title in 1928 and went on to claim back-to-back titles in 1930 and 1931. While proficient in cross-country, Kusocinski also won a national title in the 800 meters (1:56) and won Olympic gold in the 10,000 meters. Recurring injuries dampened his hopes for further records in the decade.

Furthering Finnish dominance in the sport, Lauri Lehtinen also broke a Nurmi record in 1932 when he ran 14:16 in the 5,000 meters (he would win an Olympic gold in that event the same year). Lehtinen won his only Finnish National Cross-Country title in May 1937 when he ran 33:58 for 11 kilometers. By that time another good runner was gathering momentum. Taisto Mäki would be the last of Finland's premier distance runners for this age. He gained national recognition in 1934 and worldwide notoriety in 1936, but his real breakthrough came in 1938, when he ran a world record in the 5,000 meters. On May 22 of that same year he ran 25:13 for an eight-kilometer course to win his one and only Finnish national title in cross-country. He would go on to set world records in two miles and 10,000 meters as well.

In Portugal, 2,500 miles to the south, Manuel Dias, a dominant runner with exceptional range, was also coming to the forefront. Not only was he able to win eight national titles in the outdoor 5,000 meters from 1926 to 1934, but he also placed 17th in the 1936 Summer Olympics in the marathon. In 1937 he set a personal best for that distance, covering it in 2:30:38. But in cross-country, Dias was nearly unstoppable. Starting in 1928, Dias won the Portuguese National Cross-Country Championship eight times in a 10-year span, winning five straight between 1930 and 1934, and again in 1936 and 1937. It would be forty-five years before Carlos Lopes, one of cross-country's most decorated heroes, would break Dias's record.

ITALY'S LEGENDARY "FIVE MILLS"

On January 21, 1933, in the small town of San Vittore Olona, Italy—which lies about twenty-five kilometers northwest of Milan—a snowstorm blanketed the countryside. Normally this would not pose an issue for the small, unassuming town of less than 7,500 inhabitants. However, on this occasion there was reason to be alarmed. Giovanni Malerba, the event organizer of the first annual cross-country race—which would come to be known as the Cinque Mulini—had to convince his friends to clear snow-covered paths to allow runners to compete the following day.

The local sporting club started the event in 1933 as a direct response to a neighboring town's organization of a race that unfolded between seven clock towers. Luckily, the town of San Vittore Olona approved Giovanni Malerba's vision to hold a cross-country race on a combination of dirt roads, grass, and private property (he mapped the course over five grueling 2,000-meter laps). Athletes, while accustomed to races that ran over banks and through ditches, were surprised to find that the main attraction was that the route itself passed through the town's watermills, right next to the river Olona. With Mario Fiocchi winning the inaugural event, and Luigi Pellin (future Italian National Cross-Country Championship winner) victorious the next three, the event gained notoriety and Malerba expanded the race distance to 12 kilometers to include all five of the town's watermills.

Remarkably, the race has run uninterrupted since 1933, despite the Second World War (the race was run with local and regional runners), and a 1939 mandate from the Federazione Italiana di Atletica Leggera (FIDAL) that ordered all cross-country competitions be postponed. Since 1933, some 23 Olympic gold medalists have made the journey to San Vittore Olona for the quirky, downright odd, race that has become as much a part of local folklore as the five watermills that gave the race its name.

England's Brendan Foster, a one-time world 3,000-meter record holder and Olympic 10,000-meter bronze medalist, described the race in his autobiography:

> You go across some fields, then alongside the smelliest river you have ever known in your life, jumping over holes in the canal bank. Then you run into the mills themselves. You have to enter through someone's backyard and into their kitchen, then up about six steps onto the mill, which is next to the kitchen because the flour used to come straight into it from the mill. Then you go across a bridge, where wheels are turning and water is being thrown all over the place, and you get barked at by yelping dogs, while trying to keep your feet on the slippery cobblestones. The course goes through a chicken yard . . . and then back (to the finish area) before heading out for the next circuit.

Journalist Simon Taylor also described the occasion:

> By day, and night, the streets are largely quiet. Even the day before the event the only visible signs that a big cross-country race is looming are one or two posters, a couple of banners strung limply across the street, and the occasional direction arrow to guide spectators and competitors to the venue. On race day, however, the town is transformed. The locals flock to the course, filling the small grandstand and vying for vantage points around the circuit. The mill areas are particularly popular. With runners having to plunge in and out of the darkened buildings while taking sharp hairpin corners at five-minute-mile pace, the occasional tumble is inevitable. The course lies close to the town center, in and around the Centro Sportivo Comunale Giovanni Malerba, named after the founder himself. After the snowstorm at the initial holding, the event was moved in later years to the spring.

As for the race's history, it would be twenty years after the inaugural event before international runners were invited to compete. Tunisian runner Ahmed Labidi was the first foreign winner, and Yugoslavia's Olympic marathon silver medalist Franjo Mihalic won three times in five years in the early 1960s. In terms of its international appeal, the turning point for the race came in 1965 when the USA's Olympic 10,000-meter champion Billy Mills triumphed.

Since then, the reports of past participants reads like a who's who of international distance running: Olympic champions Steve Ovett, Pekka Vasala, John Walker, Filbert Bayi, and Kip Keino have all taken part. As have legends like Lasse Viren, Frank Shorter, Grete Waitz, Paul Tergat, Haile Gebrselassie, Kenenisa Bekele, John Ngugi, and Khalid Skah. Even the legendary John Akii-Bua, the 1972 Ugandan Olympic champion in the 400-meter hurdles, has run the event. He finished last, apparently, after being in the leading group on the first lap. Great Britain's David Bedford is the only man to win both the junior and senior races, achieving the feat in 1969 and 1972.

ENGLAND DOMINATES THE INTERNATIONAL

While Italy had not yet submitted a formal application for admission into the International Cross-Country Union, other action was taking place at the International. In 1930, on a rough and hilly course, England ended the four-year string of French team titles when they placed six men in the first eight. Tom Evenson, representing Salford Harriers, led the English in his first International. Thirty thousand people saw the race over a course of nine miles, and the finish between Evenson and R. R. Sutherland (Garscube Harriers) was close, both runners finishing within a second of each other. Surprisingly, Spain entered a team, but finished only five men in the affair and were unable to count toward the team score.

The following year, Spain was accepted as a member nation, while individual winner Tim Smythe became the first Irishman to win the International. More astounding than the conditions—snow and sleet had fallen since early in the morning and continued up to the start of the race—Smythe had only been introduced to the sport four years previously. England was again a dominant team, with six finishers in the first nine.

Other oddities marked the decade within the International. England was nearly unstoppable, and in addition to earning a perfect team score in 1932 (with the first through sixth positions), France was able to record six consecutive finishers as well (ninth, 10th, 11th, 12th, 13th, and 14th places overall). Summer weather prevailed in 1933, and impatient spectators rushed the barriers at Caerleon Racecourse in Wales (depriving the event of gate money). The heat was so extreme that a member of the English team, George Bailey, flung off his running singlet before climbing up the steep, 250-foot-long Lodge Hill, known to cross-country runners as "Heartbreak Hill." This climb, after running six miles on flat terrain, resulted in scenes of complete exhaustion: some runners collapsed, many fell off the side, and a few returned to the staging area by way of paramedics.

The individual winner in 1933 was Jack Holden of the Tipton Harriers, who achieved greatness by winning the event four times in the decade. After three Holden victories in a row between 1933 and 1935, and a runner-up in 1936, the 1937 individual champion proved to be the Scottish national champion J. C. Flockhart from the Shettleston Harriers. Flockhart avoided the minor moves made by his continental counterparts and instead focused on a major move with a mile and a half to go. Holden, despite his previous run of success, had to be helped off the course at the midway point after an injury.

Yet despite an English revival at the International, by 1939 war clouds were gathering over Europe and it was doubtful that continental teams would be allowed to leave their respective countries. Fortunately, nothing transpired to interfere with the full complement of seven countries competing. At the race, England lost the team title, although Jack Holden set a record by winning the event for the fourth time. France won the team race with a score of 36 points to England's second with 95 points; Belgium came in third with 115 points. Of note was that on the morning of the race, the International Cross-Country Union met to discuss the consideration for cross-country running to be given Olympic status in the Winter Games. The subject was voted upon by all of the member countries, which favored the idea. The secretary of the International Cross-Country Union was asked to deliver the decision to the secretary of the International Amateur Athletic Federation. Then the world was at war.

JACK HOLDEN: THE FIRST FOUR-TIME WINNER OF THE INTERNATIONAL CROSS-COUNTRY CHAMPIONSHIP

According to Jim Peters, who broke one of Holden's road records in 1953, Jack Holden was "a ruthless runner, starting with the absolute determination to kill the opposition right from the off." And between 1933 and 1939 Holden did just that: smashing the opposition, winning the International Cross-Country Championships four times. Despite a lengthy career as a marathon runner later in his career, Holden's first major successes came as a cross-country runner, with his first English representation in the International in 1929. Holden then won the Inter-Counties Championship in 1931, 1932, and 1933; the National in 1938 and 1939; and the International in 1933, 1934, 1935, and 1939.

In the evenings, Holden ran the roads of Wolverhampton, Bilston, and beyond, laying a strong foundation. "I was the first to run 100 miles a week in training," he reflected. "All at night, after I'd finished work. Jim Peters wrote to me asking for help, and I told him he had to do more and more miles. They all copied me."

But just as Holden was hitting his peak years, he had to serve for the Royal Air Force. Surprisingly, he decided to return to athletics after the war, despite being thirty-nine years old. His return proved to be an instant success and he won the English National in 1946, which gave him the opportunity to compete again in the International Cross-Country Championship, where he finished sixth. The following year, bad snow made it impossible for him to attend the English National and he was excluded from the team for the International. Holden was furious, as he had been the country's best cross-country runner for more than a decade; he vowed never to do a cross-country race again. This would prove to be a huge loss for the English team.

* * *

While the decade of the 1930s proved to be challenging economically and socially for the developed world, there were a few bright spots in the sport of cross-country running. Domestic growth in the United States saw the beginning of a new, official collegiate cross-country championship, while strong English runners brought team success back to the home country in the International. Individual superstars like Lash in the United States, Holden in England, Wylie in Scotland, Smythe in Ireland, Weightman in Australia, Dias in Portugal, and Maki in Finland maintained prestige in their respective nations—and notable events like the Cinque Mulini appeared to support the sport. There was even discussion regarding the admission of the sport to the Winter Olympic program. If not for the onset of the Second World War, perhaps even greater progress could have been made for cross-country running during this time.

EVENT SPOTLIGHT: THE 1935 ENGLISH CROSS-COUNTRY NATIONAL—BELGRAVE VERSUS BIRCHFIELD (MARCH 9, 1935)

LOCATION: BEACONSFIELD, BUCKINGHAMSHIRE, ENGLAND

Birmingham

The Birchfield Harriers were synonymous with dominance in the 1930s in England. Heading into the 1935 season, Birchfield had won not only the previous seven English National Cross-Country titles, dating back to 1927, but also they had lost the team title only once since 1920. The Birchfield team was again strong in 1935, with A. Bourton leading the charge—he had won the 1935 Warwickshire County Championship—and with names like J. T. Richards (future Warwickshire County champion), R. Sutherland (1934 top finisher for Birchfield on the National Cross-Country winning team), D. A. Currie (Everill Cup, Novice, and Midland champion), and J. Beman (who ran two marathons in 10 days at one point, winning both) also attached, they were the clear favorite to win.

But competition on the starting line for the 1935 English National was fierce. With the recent International dominance of the English team (winners of five straight national team titles over France), the amount of talent representing different clubs within England itself guaranteed a more competitive contest than might be found internationally. The previous week, Jack Holden of the Tipton Harriers had lost the Midlands senior title to Currie of Birchfield by mere inches. Later in 1935, Holden would go on to win his third International. In this race he finished ninth.

With 28 teams represented and 295 runners, it was anyone's guess what score would be needed to win. The previous three years had seen Birchfield challenged by the Salford Harriers, who were hot on their heels. In 1932, Birchfield had beaten Salford 66 to 79. In 1933 the margin grew, with Birchfield winning 80 to 101. In 1934, Birchfield beat Salford 88 to 112. Fans were beginning to notice the trend.

The racecourse at Beaconsfield was waterlogged and a biting wind lashed the runners so that even the leaders took more than an hour to cover the 10 miles. But with the crack of the gun, George Bailey went hard from the start and employed the tactics that had gained him his second Northern Championship. He tried to break up the leaders with a long-sustained forcing effort, which—while admirably done—did not work as he had anticipated. At his shoulder was Frank Close, a 21-year-old Reading athlete, who in 1935 was largely inexperienced but spurred by adrenaline.

Close, a millworker from Newbury, was a virtual unknown in the cross-country world before the season started. However, during the year he had became the most talked about man in the sport. A member of Reading Athletic Club, Close had burst onto the scene by winning the Southern Counties Championships in his first 10-mile race (two weeks prior to the National). Later, in his first International in Paris, he finished fourth.

In the 1935 National, between Close and Baily at the front, came J. C. Flockhart of the Shettleston Harriers. Scottish by birth, Flockhart would help Scotland finish second in the International two weeks later. Missing from the front ranks was anyone wearing a Birchfield jersey—or for that matter, one from Belgrave. Belgrave, a team from Wimbledon, ended up striving for the victory using an age-old strategy. Despite not having any individuals in the top 10, and despite losing to Surrey in the Southern Counties Championship, they garnered victory at the English National by having an awesome pack of runners. Their top six of Footer, Patience, Ginty, Taylor, Carter, and Shields scored in 11th, 14th, 15th, 18th, 19th and 20th positions, respectively.

Entering the championship, Belgrave had talent but had yet to put it all together—and 1935 was looking daunting even prior to the event. At the start of the decade a runner by the name of Arthur "Nutty" Penny had joined Belgrave full-time. With unquestioned desire and experience in running, he was one of the most talented runners to toe the line for the Wimbledon club. In 1929, Penny won an individual bronze and helped Belgrave to a team gold in the Surrey Cross-Country Championships, the club's first major cross-country victory of note.

And no one was more important to that team than legendary captain Bert Footer. Footer was a strict disciplinarian who coached his pack meticulously, and the arrival of Penny gave him further impetus. A strong rivalry developed between these two—they were inseparable and soon became known as "the twins." They were amongst the first to take up daily training when running only on Tuesdays, Thursdays, and weekends was the norm.

Leading to the 1935 spring cross-country season, Penny and Footer were in full swing and looked dominant—then disaster struck. Penny fractured his foot, ending his 1935 campaign.

However, Footer did not let that stop Belgrave from showing their true mettle. Footer and Patience, the Belgrave number two runner, were locked together for the second half of the 1935 English National and gave each other no quarter. They moved up several places and passed Jack Holden near the end (Holden was able to exact his revenge right before the finish). Footer secured 11th place overall for his team; Patience finished in 14th. They were both selected to travel with the English national team, which then achieved victory in the International.

Birchfield, while powerful on paper and in reputation, could only muster a fourth-place finish behind Belgrave, Salford, and Surrey. For Belgrave it was their first English

National Cross-Country title. Belgrave's total, 97 points, was well ahead of Birchfield's 186.

Three months later, at the British Games on Whit Monday, Belgrave and Birchfield ran a three-mile grudge-match on the track—with eight runners per side and six scoring for team honors. Birchfield exacted revenge in this contest, with an outstanding performance from Eddie Webster. However, on this day of the cross-country national in March, Belgrave surprised everyone with a staunch pack mentality and more fortitude than anyone else.

Date: Saturday, March 9, 1935	
Starters: 295	
Finishers: 248	
Teams: 28 Teams Completed	
Distance: 10 miles	
Location: Beaconsfield, Buckinghamshire	

Top 15 Individual Finishers	
1. F. Close	Reading Athletic Club
2. J. C. Flockhart	Shettleston Harriers
3. G. Bailey	Salford Harriers
4. R. Walker	Wakefield Trinity Harriers
5. W. Eaton	Salford Harriers
6. J. H. Potts	Saltwell Harriers
7. T. Evenson	Manchester Cross-Country Club
8. F. Marsland	Manchester Harriers
9. J. Holden	Tipton Harriers
10. J. A. Burns	Elswick Harriers
11. R. Sutherland	Birchfield Harriers
12. J. Noble	Hallamshire Harriers
13. G. Forryan	Birchfield Harriers
14. H. Footer	Belgrave Harriers
15. S. Scarsbrook	Surrey Athletic Club

Team Results			
1.	Belgrave Harriers	(South County)	97 Points
	H. Footer (11)	D. Patience (14)	J. Ginty (15)
	A. Taylor (18)	C. Carter (19)	W. Shields (20)
2.	Salford Harriers	(North County)	154 Points
	G. Bailey (02)	W. Eaton (04)	H. Platt (28)
	F. Partington (36)	J. Sadler (39)	A. Partington (45)
3.	Surrey A.C.	(South County)	156 Points
	S. Scarsbrook (12)	E. Agate (16)	S. Belton (23)
	G. Ward (31)	C. Nichols (33)	R. Nichols (41)
4.	Birchfield Harriers	(Midlands County)	186 Points
	R. Sutherland (08)	G. Forryan (10)	A. Robinson (29)
	J. Richards (35)	J. Beman (44)	C. Whitehouse (60)
5.	Sheffield United	(North County)	217 Points
	F. Darby (21)	W. Hibberd (24)	J. Meeke (27)
	W. Simpson (34)	H. Wright (40)	I. Badderley (71)

Chapter 10

Sizeable numbers of disenchanted city-dwellers—and not just the radical young—have migrated to the country to live a simpler sort of life. Others, stuck in the city, split for the country at every opportunity to back-pack, mountain-climb, hike and run—away from the noise, pavement and fumes of the crowded, car-oriented metropolitan areas. The more urbanized and mechanized a person's daily life becomes, the more he wants and needs to reestablish non-mechanical contact with the natural elements. The more he enjoys the feel of the unpaved earth under his feet and the taste of unpolluted air. What does this have to do with cross-country? Everything. Even the runner gets somewhat separated from the earth, and from running in its purest and simplest form.

—Bob Anderson and Joe Henderson

THE 1940s USHERS IN A NEW ERA FOR CROSS-COUNTRY

Internationally, much of the 1940s were consumed by the horrors of the Second World War. Momentum for the sport, which grew after the Great War throughout the 1920s and 1930s, seemingly disappeared overnight. However, while war reduced opportunities for competition, the training techniques developed and knowledge gained from previous generations did not disappear. And, as the world stabilized in the second half of the decade, athletes and coaches worldwide refocused on training and racing. The emergence of powerful cross-country runners from countries like Belgium, Sweden, and Czechoslovakia reaffirmed this point.

In the United States, there was a widespread push for higher physical fitness standards following the Second World War, and the practice of cross-country running in high schools increased rapidly. This resulted in events like the Mount San Antonio College "Mt. SAC" Invitational becoming one of the largest cross-country meets in the nation.

Overseas, stars like Emil Zátopek were just beginning to gain notoriety, while other names from lesser-known pockets within Europe would begin challenging for International Cross-Country supremacy—although the French and English teams were still fighting to defend their well-established legacies.

BELGIUM RISES TO THE TOP OF INTERNATIONAL WATERS

The sound of gunfire and shelling had hardly died away before the committee of the National Cross-Country Union of Scotland announced they were prepared to stage the International at Ayr, Scotland, in March 1946. And although the transportation systems on the European continent and in England were disorganized, the Belgian and French teams overcame the inconvenience of their long journeys by sea and rail to compete in the championship. At the council meeting, the delegates from the two countries were warmly thanked for their great sacrifice in attending.

With a team victory, France picked up right where they left off, scoring 43 points. France's national champion, Raphael Pujazon, finished first to win the Maisons-Laffitte trophy (awarded to the top individual finisher), beating Belgium's Marcel VandeWattyne by 33 seconds. Remarkably, Belgium finished second as a team and displaced England, scoring 77 points to England's 96, with young Belgian stars Henri Ost and Frans Feremans in eighth and ninth place, respectively, and Belgium's national cross-country champion, Jean Chapelle, finishing 29th.

The following year Raphaël Puzajon won again, this time in front of his home crowd at the Hippodrome de St. Cloud in Paris, beating runner-up Jean Chapelle by 25 seconds and leading the French team to victory. Belgium's second place team finish, which they earned even with the absence of Gaston Reiff (who dropped out halfway due to neuritis), was encouraging and indicated that the previous year was not a fluke.

By March 1948, many elite athletes were focused on training for the Summer Olympics and were absent from the International Cross-Country Championship. Despite this, with summer-like conditions and 15,200 spectators in attendance, it was the surprising Belgian team that was focused on a team victory. With a lap to go in the race, Belgium's two leaders, steeplechase specialist John Doms and cross-country veteran Emile Renson, fought to stay ahead of France's Mohamed Lahoucine and Charles Cérou. Doms crossed the line first in 54:05, with Renson next, 20 seconds later. And with a spectacular finish by Belgian Frans Wauters in fifth, the victory was sealed: Belgium defeated France 46 points to 47 for the team championship. The members of the Belgian team were overwhelmed with emotion.

Edouard Hermes, President of the Ligue Royale Belge d'Athletisme, shared the result:

> News was given on the radio in Brussels with astounding rapidity, and papers giving the results were on sale half-an-hour after the finish. Telegrams were flowing into Maidenhead (the team's headquarters) and to Reading Town Hall (during the banquet). The [train] platform of the Gare du Nord (in Brussels) was packed with hundreds of friends and admirers. The Bourgomaster of Brussels was there, but when the train stopped there was such enthusiasm that he was swept away by the crowd and we never saw him. On the platform we were kissed by everybody, and many were crying with joy. The affection continued increasingly, and Clemme organized a small party at the Hotel Cosmopolite, which was full immediately with an exuberant crowd. I tried everything possible to join my wife and children who were waiting for me somewhere. We had telegrams from M. Spaak, other ministers, and from all corners of the country.

Included in the rise of Belgian stardom in cross-country was the inauguration of the Cross International de Hannut. Held in the small town of Hannut Belgium, the event was started by brothers Lucien and Roger Gustin. The race was originally intended to provide entertainment for the town during the German occupation, with the first edition taking place on March 9, 1941. In fact, profits from the event were used to send care-packages to help Belgian prisoners of war in Germany. Gaston Reiff and Eduard Schroeven (Schroeven finished sixth in the 1937 International and was a three-time Belgian National Cross-Country champion) traded victories in the 1942, 1943, 1944, and 1947 editions.

Gaston Reiff was one of Belgium's first real distance running stars. His claim to fame began in 1939 when he won two major cross-country races in the span of eight days. Reiff went on to win Belgian National Cross-Country titles in 1943, 1944, and 1947.

Jean Chapelle was another big name. He was a Belgian National Cross-Country champion in 1939, 1940, 1945, and 1946, and ran for Belgium in the International Cross-Country Championship seven times. He finished second overall in 1938 and 1947 and 11th or better five times.

Final Belgian highlights included Marcel VandeWattyne and the Cross der Vlaanderen. Held in Ronse, Belgium, and started in 1943, the Cross der Vlaanderen remains the oldest athletics contest in Ronse (and uses the same loops of the course today). Marcel VandeWattyne, who competed on 20 different occasions at the International (where he was runner-up three times in three different decades), won the Cross der Vlaanderen 11 times between 1946 and 1964. He was also the Belgian National Cross-Country champion six times leading into the 1950s.

FRANCE REMAINS DOMINANT IN THE 1940s

Yet despite Belgium's rise to prominence during the 1940s, France remained the team to beat for the better part of the decade. And one man came before all others in French distance running: Raphaël Puzajon. From 1944 to 1950, Puzajon was a member of the Racing Club de France and it was there that he built his reputation, winning his first French National Cross-Country title in 1944 (he went on to win five more in succession). A European champion in the 3,000-meter steeplechase in 1946, Puzajon gained the most notoriety in cross-country, helping France to team victory in the International Cross-Country Championship in 1946, 1947, 1949, and 1950. In 1946 and 1947 he was the individual champion, and finished second overall in 1949. In 1946 Puzajon also won the Cross International de Saint-Cloud, and was second overall in the Cross International Dublin in 1949.

Another French athlete who made big strides during the 1940s was Alain Mimoun. Mimoun, an Algerian by birth, represented France at a time when its colonies were accepted as part of the host nation. After joining the French army (where he almost had a foot blasted off in the battle for Monte Cassino), Mimoun discovered a talent for running by happenstance, joining in a race as he was passing a suburban track with some friends after his recuperation. Soon after, the 21-year-old Mimoun won the 1942 North African Cross-Country Championship. He then joined the Racing Club de France in Paris and worked as a waiter in a restaurant on the edge of the Bois de Boulogne, where he trained.

Mimoun finished second in the 1946 French National Championships in the 10,000 meters, despite losing a shoe in the effort. However, cross-country remained Mimoun's favorite discipline—Mimoun called himself a "runner who loved wild nature"—and he appeared in the International 11 times over three decades. Mimoun won his first individual title in 1949, and went on to be international champion four times, runner-up twice, and French National Cross-Country champion six times.

ENGLAND EXPERIENCES THE HORRORS FIRSTHAND

Unlike in France and Belgium, where not a single National Cross-Country Championship was canceled, consequences of the war in England were more immediate. Cross-country clubs throughout the nation were affected, with loss of club property (clubhouses and training grounds alike), shortages of members, and overnight blackouts impacting the sport.

Both the Birchfield Harriers and the Thames Hare and Hounds were impacted by the war directly. Soon after the outbreak of war in 1939, Birchfield's Alexander Stadium was requisitioned by the government for use by the Home

Guard. For Thames, several bombs fell on Roehampton Lane and Wimbledon Common, and an unexploded bomb at the head of Medfield Road barred running in that direction until it was detonated. All championships were suspended for the duration of the war. Birchfield's Bob Reid had been prominent in many of England's cross-country races and the war robbed him of his best years as an athlete. The same could be said of many athletes in England and elsewhere.

Still, small pockets of success were seen for various English cross-country clubs during the decade. For Birchfield, the cross-country men won the Warwickshire and Midland Championships and placed second in the National at Leamington in 1946. The Birchfield women were able to celebrate an English National Cross-Country Championship victory when Pat Sandall led them home first in 1946. The London Olympics were a major event in 1948, but Birchfield's big news was the victory of the ladies in the National at Sutton Park, their third win in succession (they also won a fourth the following year). The highlight for the Birchfield men was their convincing victory at the 1948 Midlands race.

For Thames Hare and Hounds, the club saw 23 members attend the first postwar General Meeting in September 1945. A university race between Cambridge and Oxford later in the fall returned to Roehampton for the first time since 1925. And the Southern Counties Championship was held on Wimbledon Common, where Thames finished 18th out of 22 teams.

New members slowly began to rebuild the Thames squad. Strong runners from London University helped bolster results from T. P. E. Curry and G. D. Tudor from Oxford (both of whom represented Great Britain in the 1948 Olympics in the 3,000-meter steeplechase) and Chris Brasher from Cambridge.

In winter 1947, Thames's M. F. Kensit, although besieged by a cramp, finished seventh after a final sprint with undergraduate Roger Bannister in a match against Oxford University. Right before Christmas in 1948 Bannister's name appeared again, this time with a second-place finish in the Oxford/Cambridge cross-country dual, where Chris Brasher finished fourth, the first Cambridge man to cross the line. On December 3, 1949, Bannister led the Oxford team to victory, running the 12-kilometer course in 41:54.

No explanation of Britain's might during the decade would be complete without the mention of Dr. Frank Aaron from Yorkshire, who was not only the inter-counties champion in the latter years of the 1940s, but was also a three-time English national champion (one shy of the all-time winning record held by Alfred Shrubb and Percy Stenning). Aaron competed for the Leeds St. Mark's Harriers, and represented England four times at the International Cross-Country Championships, finishing in the top 10 three times, with a high of second place in the 1951 event.

THE UNITED STATES REASSERTS ITS DOMINANCE

The United States was spared from the ravages of war and motivated by patriotic fervor. Thus, the popularity of cross-country running expanded rapidly at the high school and collegiate level in the postwar period of the 1940s. Not only was it seen as being essential and beneficial for athletic programs of all sizes following the allied victory—it was more inclusive than other sports. Distance running was about to ignite in America in a big way.

In 1947, Hilmer Lodge was hired at the newly built Mt. San Antonio College as the track and cross-country coach. And despite an enrollment of just over one thousand, Mt. San Antonio College initiated the first major cross-country invitational in Southern California in October 1948. In its first running, the meet attracted ten high schools and nine community colleges with a total of 148 runners competing in two prep divisions (open and novice) and one varsity junior college race. High school runners completed 1.2- to two-mile races, their community college counterparts ran 2.5 to 3.1 miles, while athletes participating for four-year colleges ran up to four miles.

> **Did You Know?**
>
> In 1965, a new three-mile, spectator friendly course was designed for the Mount San Antonio College "Mt. SAC" Cross-Country Invitational with added hills (including the famous "Poop-Out Hill") and some "switchbacks." In 1998 the course was again altered, reconfiguring a portion of the "Valley Loop" as a safety matter to match the meet's growth in popularity. Today the Mt. SAC Invite is host to 570 teams and 20,000 athletes not including the 5,800 junior college runners or the middle and junior high runners. It is the largest cross-country invitational in the United States.

By the start of the 1940s Iowa, New Hampshire, Connecticut, Rhode Island, Oklahoma, Massachusetts, Michigan, Ohio, and Pennsylvania had established sanctioned high school cross-country state championships. This decade also saw the development of the sport in other areas for high schools: New York University continued their Spiked Shoe Invitational, which attracted high school harriers in late October at Van Cortlandt Park. Minnesota, South Dakota, Indiana, Illinois, Florida, Vermont and Virginia sanctioned state championship meets between 1943 and 1948. Idaho State College began to host interscholastic cross-country "state" meets in 1943 as well. Missouri and Oregon followed suit with their first state championships in 1949. And California saw the Los Angeles Section, Sac-Joaquin Section, and San Francisco Section all start their own cross-country championships within the decade.

FRED WILT AND ROBERT BLACK

Fred Wilt, one of America's top distance runners in the '40s, was outstanding at Indiana University before becoming an Olympic competitor while running for the New York Athletic Club. Wilt graduated from Indiana in 1941, a product of Coach Billy Hayes and hot on the heels of legend Don Lash. While at Indiana, Wilt claimed two national collegiate titles (one in cross-country and the other in the two-mile run), and the 1941 Big Ten Conference cross-country title. In the winter of 1949, Wilt won his first US National Cross-Country Championship title at Warren Valley Golf Course in Detroit, and went on to win again in 1952 and 1953.

While Wilt was grabbing headlines as the All-American from Indiana, Robert Black was busy becoming the finest distance runner in Rhode Island history while competing for the University of Rhode Island in the late 1940s. He won seven national championships (two in cross-country in 1946 and 1948), six New England crowns, and each of the Yankee Conference titles in which he competed. Undefeated in cross-country in 1948, Black won the Intercollegiate Association of Amateur Athletics of America (IC4A), National Collegiate Athletic Association (NCAA), and Amateur Athletic Union (AAU) (US) National Championships in succession. He was also NCAA Cross-Country champion in 1949 and won every New England intercollegiate championship he competed in.

With four-successive IC4A championships in addition to his two NCAA crowns, few runners were as dominant as Robert Black during the postwar period in the United States.

SWEDEN GRABS HEADLINES DURING THE EARLY YEARS OF THE DECADE

The United States was not the only nation to avoid the ravages of World War II. With successful communication with both Nazi and Allied forces and a dedicated military buildup, Sweden managed to maintain neutrality throughout the conflict. During this time, Sweden became one of the first nations (if not the first) to include a short-course competition of four kilometers in their National Cross-Country Championship. Traditional long-course events typically ran anywhere from eight to 14 kilometers for men.

The Swedish duo of Gunder Haegg and Arne Andersson made headlines between the years 1941 and 1945 when they lowered the outdoor mile record from 4:06 to 4:01. However, despite Haegg's prowess in setting world records in seven different distance events, from the metric mile to the 5,000 meters, it was the speedy Andersson who won two short-course Swedish National Cross-Country Championships at the four-kilometer distance. Meanwhile, elsewhere in Europe, it would be another distance runner with tremendous range who would begin breaking Haegg's records.

THE CZECH LOCOMOTIVE BEGINS HIS LEGACY

Emil Zátopek, born in Kopřivnice, Czechoslovakia, in 1922, began working at the Bata shoe factory in Ziln when he was sixteen. In 1940 Bata sponsored a 1,500-meter race, and Zátopek was persuaded to enter even though he had no training. And after finishing a surprising second, Zátopek began to take a serious interest in running and joined the local athletic club, where he developed his own training program modeled on what he had read about Finnish Olympian Paavo Nurmi.

Ironically, the first notable observer to recognize Zátopek's talent was Nurmi himself, who had become coach to another flying Finn, Viljo Heino. Heino held the world record in the 10,000 meters (29:22) and was a four-time Finnish National Cross-Country champion. In 1948, Zátopek came within two seconds of Heino's 10K mark, prompting Nurmi to declare that Zátopek was the only athlete who understood what hard training meant, and where it would lead.

As with Nurmi, Zátopek discovered the training benefits of military service. Not only was there time and facilities for training, there were also heavy combat boots to make running more difficult. As such, Zátopek would regularly run eight miles after a hard day of military drilling, tromp through forests, and perform wind sprints. Questioned about the apparent absurdity of training as a fast runner while wearing leaden equipment, Zátopek replied "There's a great advantage in training under unfavorable conditions, for the difference is then a tremendous relief in a race."

Other athletes attempted to emulate Zátopek, but none could do it with the same devotion. Zátopek regularly ran 20×400 meters in his army boots. Before entering the service, his interval work consisted of 10×200 meters in 26–28 seconds, and/or 10×400 meters in 60 seconds flat. Occasionally he would run a workout of 10×100 meters in 13 seconds each. To Zátopek, these workouts were nothing compared to carrying a torch to light the way along his eight-mile post-drill runs.

Zátopek first entered the international athletics arena at the 1948 Summer Olympics in London, winning the 10-kilometer run (his second race ever at that distance) and finishing second behind Gaston Reiff from Belgium in the five-kilometer run. As a closing note for the decade, on June 12, 1949, Zátopek set his first world record. Running for the Czech Army Championships at Ostrava, he clocked 29:28 for 10,000 meters, 7.2 seconds faster than Heino's record. And before the calendar changed to 1950, Zátopek had won eleven 10,000-meter races in a row.

* * *

The decade of the 1940s was a recovery period for cross-country running. With the interruption caused by the Second World War, momentum for training and expansion seen in the early stages of the century were brought to an abrupt halt. Yet, all was not lost. The rise of Belgium was a harbinger of things to come. Neutral Sweden saw investment in sound distance running practice—and the arrival of Emil Zátopek was refreshing, sudden, and unexpected. Meanwhile, nations like France and the United States remained undaunted during this decade. Soon they would be able to display their talents against each other in some of the more competitive cross-country events in the future.

EVENT SPOTLIGHT: THE 1940 JUNIOR INTERNATIONAL CROSS-COUNTRY CHAMPIONSHIP (MARCH 24, 1940)

LOCATION: BOIS DE BOULOGNE, PARIS

The Second World War

During World War II, the Federation Francaise d'Athletisme promoted the first junior international cross-country race. The race was held on March 24, 1940, in the Bois de Boulogne, Paris, and was contested between Belgium, England, and France. France won with a score of 34 points (2, 4, 5, 6, 7, and 10); England, 60 points (1, 3, 8, 9, 17, and 22); and Belgium, 102 points (14, 15, 16, 18, 19, and 20). All athletes were twenty years old or younger.

Frank Aaron of England was the individual winner, defeating the French youth Gaston Cottin. At the time, Aaron was a young medical student at Leeds University who, after obtaining his degree, served with the British Forces in the East. At the conclusion of the war, he took up cross-country running again and became one of England's greatest distance runners, winning the English National Cross-Country Championship in 1949, '50, and '51.

Joe Binks, a well-known sports journalist of the *News of the World*, had the pleasure of accompanying the English team for the event. Nothing unforeseen transpired during the journey to France, as planes and destroyers escorted the ship, but on the return trip plans were delayed in Paris for twenty-four hours—much to the delight of the young members of the team—while the Admiralty "swept" the English Channel. English youngsters spent time sitting on their suitcases outside the station singing, "Roll Out the Barrel."

Binks stated: "Coming back, both train and boat were cancelled. Some of the team and supporters spent the night in Paris, but the majority went on to Calais, which was in an uproar after a raid. We were walking along the main street in Calais that evening when some British soldiers passing in a lorry recognized me. I stopped and found that a number of them came from Leeds. Despite the bombing, we celebrated Aaron's great victory in a cafe. The Secretary-General of the FFA, M. G. Jurgenson, and the President of the Junior Section, M. J. R. Suerin, made our sojourn in Paris very happy considering the world was in a state of war."

Date: Sunday, March 24, 1940
Starters: 27
Finishers: 24
Teams: 3 Teams Completed
Distance: 5 miles/8 kilometers
Location: Bois de Boulogne, Paris

Individual Finishers:

1	Frank Aaron	England	27:51
2	Gaston Cottin	France	28:00
3	Jack Timmins	England	28:09
4	A. Poirot	France	28:19
5	Derrough	France	28:24
6	H. Silvestri	France	28:25
7	J. Boutin	France	28:34
8	Jack Charlesworth	England	28:36
9	Arthur Cole	England	28:37
10	G. Contat	France	28:43
11	M. Mainjollou	France	28:55
12	Henri Leveque	France	29:16
13	A. Kerromes	France	29:22
14	Gaston Reiff	Belgium	29:27
15	Michel Verlinden	Belgium	29:31
16	Louis Dubreucq	Belgium	Time Not Reported*
17	G. Harrison	England	Time Not Reported
18	Andre De Roose	Belgium	Time Not Reported
19	Francois Van- debossche	Belgium	Time Not Reported
20	Laurent Van Dyck	Belgium	Time Not Reported
—	G. B. Shaw	England	Did not finish
—	W. H. Marsh	England	Did not finish

Team Results:

1	France	34	(Cottin, Poirot, Derrough, Silvestri, Boutin, Contat)
2	England	60	(Aaron, Timmins, Charlesworth, Cole, Harrison, Nicholls)
3	Belgium	102	(Reiff, Verlinden, Dubreucq, De Roose, Vandebossche, Van Dyck)

*Archival sources failed to publicly report the finishing times for the sixteenth, seventeenth, eighteenth, nineteenth, and twentieth places.

Chapter 11

In my junior year in 1957, the cross-country runners were issued canvas shoes with thin, hard soles that had no cushioning, no lateral support, and almost no heel—they were what a later generation would call minimalist. Then I heard about a very different kind of running shoe that all the Olympic runners were wearing, made by an exotic German company called Adidas. In contrast to the dull black canvas shoes we'd been given by the high school, these Adidas shoes were bright white with green stripes. They were made of superlight kangaroo skin, and when I put them on I thought I could leap like a kangaroo. They were cushioned and felt weightless. I had a magical cross-country season, breaking the school record. Can a sixteen-year-old be in love? I was in love with my running shoes.

—Ed Ayres

THE 1950s: EXTRAORDINARY GROWTH, UNTAMED ACHIEVEMENT

The 1950s was an era of optimism and naiveté. The war ended long before the decade began, but the dawning of the '50s seemed to offer a fresh start, even while ushering in an era in which people viewed the world in terms of "free" or "communist" values.

The postwar era was highly supportive of "impossible" athletic efforts. Roger Bannister remarked: "It happened at a time when there was much less activity than there is today. We had turned away from World War II— rather a gloomy time—and people felt free to take part in sport, climb mountains and sail boats, and it represented the mood of that particular era." Distance running reached new heights, and outdoor achievements such as the breaking of the four-minute mile and the climbing of Mount Everest helped define the spirit of the decade. And breakthroughs in broadcasting and transportation delivered these achievements to the public ways that were not possible before.

The 1950s also provided the means for cross-country running to reinvent itself. The International Cross-Country Championship celebrated its 50th anniversary. A fleet of talented individuals helped to market the sport by providing meaningful competition: Zátopek from Czechoslovakia, Pirie from England, Kuts from Russia, and others—from as far away as Poland and Canada—all played a role. At the club level, Thames Hare and Hounds was rebounding as well, "rising from the ashes" of the war years. Even in the United States, division of the collegiate national championship into a large "university" level and smaller "college

division" level was a reinvention of sorts. It was time for the sport to find new benchmarks to wipe away the social and political troubles of the Second World War.

THE INTERNATIONAL CROSS-COUNTRY CHAMPIONSHIP TURNS 50

In 1953, the International Cross-Country Championship celebrated its 50th anniversary, commemorating one of the oldest international sporting gatherings on the planet. Spain and Holland complemented the strength of England, France, and Belgium this decade, and numerous years featured 10 competing teams for the first time since 1929. Runners Alain Mimoun of France, Frank Sando of England, and Marcel VandeWattyne of Belgium made headlines. Attention was also drawn to the new venues hosting the sport throughout continental Europe.

The 1950 Championship was held at the Hippodrome de Boitsfort, and for the second time in the history of the Union, 10 nations competed. While France secured a team victory with excellent pack running near the front, a very close contest took place for second between Belgium and England, with only five points separating them at the finish (Belgium finished second with 77 points). Lucien Theys, the Belgian National Cross-Country champion, was challenged the entirety of the run by France's Mimoun and Hamza, but squeaked out the individual victory by eight seconds.

The 1951 International, held at Carleton racecourse, omitted "Heart Break Hill" but included four water jumps on each two-mile lap. Heavy rain had fallen the day before the event, making the whole course a quagmire, so much so that the delegates agreed to remove part of the course that was entirely under water. The heavy going suited the English runners, who not only finished the first two (led by Saunders and Aaron), but were successful in winning the event for the first time since 1938.

The 50th anniversary of the International Cross-Country Union was celebrated in Paris on March 21, 1953. The Federation Francaise d'Athletisme made great efforts to invite as many European countries to participate in the occasion as possible, but Switzerland and Yugoslavia were the only newcomers that accepted. However, Holland, now a member country, was chosen to host the 1959 event. Further business was also impactful.

Communication from the secretary of the International Amateur Athletics Federation (IAAF) stated: "In view of the International Cross-Country Championship having assumed much bigger international dimensions, it was felt that the race should in the future come more within the orbit of the IAAF." While the notes of the meeting suggest that the International Cross-Country Union tabled this decision, it was nonetheless meaningful: within twenty years' time the IAAF would assume control over the event.

More than 20,000 people were present at the 1953 race, and extreme temperatures saw the highest number of non-finishers since the inception of the championship fifty years earlier. Yugoslavia, competing for the first time in this event, finished third as a team and produced a surprise individual champion, Franjo Mihalic, who finished 10 seconds in front of England's Frank Sando. England once again led the way for the team score, with France runner-up.

ZÁTOPEK CONTINUES HIS CHARGE

While Yugoslavia's Franjo Mihalic impressed the International Cross-Country Union in 1953 with his first-place finish, Emil Zátopek was representing Czechoslovakia with equal fervor.

The 1952 Helsinki Olympics constituted the first Cold War Games, and many of cross-country's top names lined up on the track in the distance events. Three-time US National Cross-Country champion Fred Wilt, three-time Belgian National Cross-Country champion Gaston Reiff, Thames Hare and Hounds's own Chris Chataway, three-time English National Cross-Country champion Gordon Pirie, French International Cross-Country champion Alain Mimoun, one-time US National Cross-Country champion Curtis Stone, and the Czech Emil Zátopek were all present and vying for Olympic Gold.

In the 10,000 meters, Zátopek claimed the victory with ease. But in the 5,000 meters Zátopek had to come from far behind for a stunning win, closing the last lap in 57.9 seconds. Then, as a surprise entry in the marathon, Zátopek again stunned the field. Running in the longest event he had ever attempted, Zátopek won in an Olympic record of 2:23:03—more than six minutes faster than the previous best. Zátopek suffered from blisters and a headache and was exhausted by the end (he did not take any water or

food during the marathon). "But it is the most pleasant exhaustion I have ever known," he admitted. No one has duplicated the Olympic distance gold-medal trifecta since.

Zátopek never competed in the International Cross-Country Championship—partially because the event was just beginning to open its doors to outside nations (all of whom had to be sovereign independently, which Czechoslovakia was not), and partially because Zátopek was focused on remaining on top of the world leaderboard for the track distance events. Despite this, he was an extraordinary cross-country runner. In the winter of 1953, mere weeks before winning the Saint Sylvester Road Race in Brazil, Zátopek won two minor cross-country meetings in Europe. On April 25, 1954, he won the Czechoslovakian Cross-Country Championship in Prague, beating a field of 75 runners. His time was recorded as 31:12 for 11 kilometers—which was deemed almost too incredible by British track experts, even for Zátopek at his prime (it was the length of the course, not Zátopek's abilities, that was in question).

Further, in 1954, 1955, and 1956, Zátopek competed in the 10,000-meter Cross de L'Humanité—which he won two of the three times he raced. Then, in January 1958, Zátopek won the Cross de San Donostia in San Sebastián, Spain. Known at that point as the International Lasarte Cross-Country Race, it was the third running of the event, and Zátopek won the 12-kilometer race in 39:45 despite wet conditions. It would be Zátopek's final race.

It was after this event when crowds of fans followed Zátopek through San Sebastian's narrow streets. Noticing Czech flags and memorabilia, Zátopek then stopped in a small-town restaurant. The Spanish owner loved Zátopek—so much so that he offered him his dog, named Pedro. Zátopek, aware that it was illegal to import and export animals, graciously declined.

The next day Zátopek drove just past the French border to catch the train home—and while waiting to depart, an old Spanish lady approached Zátopek with a dog. It was Pedro. "This is a gift from the restaurant owner," she said (having just smuggled the dog into France). An overwhelmed Zátopek accepted. He concealed Pedro in his bag, and at the Czechoslovakian border, nonchalantly snuck Pedro past the border guards. They spent the next ten years together.

Zátopek announced his retirement shortly after. As reported in the press, Zátopek stated: "Better to retire at the top than to have to be told to retire. My whole existence has been in sport. Now I can look at life." He was 35 years old.

GORDON PIRIE PUFFS HIS WAY TO GLORY

Gordon Pirie was one of Emil Zátopek's greatest rivals on the track, but the South London Harrier was better known in Surrey, England, for being a top-notch cross-country runner.

Affectionately nicknamed "Puff-Puff" (for the way his cheeks appeared during competition) Pirie won three English National Cross-Country titles in succession, nearly matching the record of four straight set by Alfred Shrubb and Percy Stenning. As early as 1951, just one week after winning the Southern Junior Cross-Country Championship over six miles by a huge margin of 2:30, Pirie defeated the reigning Senior Southern Cross-Country champion, John Stone, to win the Royal Air Force Championship in Wales. In a three-year span Pirie ran on the winning team in the Southern Youth (three miles), Junior (six miles), and Senior (nine miles) divisions—a feat unequaled in English cross-country running history. In the 1953 International, at the age of 22, Pirie finished 19th overall. It was his only appearance in the International Cross-Country Championship.

> **Did You Know?**
>
> Gordon Pirie wrote of his love for cross-country: "The autumn and winter months were spent in cross-country racing. I was well known during those years for destroying the competition with insanely fast starts. In 1954, I opened the 10-mile Cross-Country National with a 2:03 first half-mile through mud. It was my habit as a cross-country runner to settle the question of who would win as early as possible. In 1955, the late British team manager, Jack Crump, said of my cross-country racing successes: 'Gordon Pirie is the greatest cross-country runner I have seen.'"

While waiting to board his flight home to England at the Helsinki Airport after the 1952 Olympics, Pirie encountered German distance coach Woldemar Gerschler, who was "the first man who ever suggested that [Pirie] could do more than [he] was trying to do." Gerschler took Pirie under his wing—although initially only by mail, because Pirie could not afford to travel to Germany—and taught the English runner his new approach to interval training. As Pirie related: "I simply went about my training and racing with a singleness of purpose and determination that was unfashionable at that time, to the point of being downright un-English . . . I was able to beat such great runners because I trained myself to be able to withstand incredibly hard races and still sprint the last 220 yards," Pirie said. "To achieve this, I ran 10 × 220 yards in 24 seconds—not once, but twice in a single day. I could manage 20 × 440 yards in 59 seconds with only a 30-second jog to recover, or 12 × 440 yards in 55 or 56 seconds, with a one-minute recovery jog."

This was the "new" interval approach into which Gerschler initiated Pirie. Within a year, Pirie set British records for 3,000 meters, two miles, three miles, and five kilometers, as well as a world mark (28:19) for six miles.

VLADIMIR KUTS POSES A THREAT TO BEAT ZÁTOPEK AND PIRIE

Emil Zátopek's long-distance gold medals earned in Helsinki understandably caught the attention of many international distance coaches. Gerschler was one; Leonid Nikiforov of the Soviet Union was another. Gordon Pirie was perhaps the first post-Zátopek athlete to bear fruit from Zátopek's methods, but Vladimir Kuts quickly eclipsed him. Under the tutelage of Coach Nikiforov, Kuts began interval training over distances far longer than anyone else attempted (up to two-kilometer pickups), and possessed extraordinary courage as an athlete. Kuts bettered Pirie's three-mile record in 1953, and beat Zátopek's best 5K time that same year, serving notice that Kuts was a serious threat internationally.

The son of Ukrainian factory workers, Kuts joined the Red Army at sixteen. When the war ended in 1945, he continued his service with the navy and started running. And once his ability was noticed, well-known coach Leonid Khomenkov took him under his wing. Then, after being on the international distance running scene for only a few years, Kuts rose to the top of the leaderboard, although he had one weakness: he could be beaten in the final sprint. Still, he retired with two Olympic golds, a European gold, and five world records. He broke the 5,000-meter world record four times and his 13:35 world-record time stood from 1957 to 1965.

Amidst controversy and strain surrounding his training, Kuts was no slouch when it came to racing across country. Like Pirie and Zátopek, Kuts sharpened his racing skills by competing internationally, joining Zátopek on a few occasions in the Cross de L'Humanité, beating Zátopek for the individual title in 1956, and winning the Soviet Union's National Cross-Country Championship in 1957. But as time went on, Kuts was warned that continuing to train at a top level might negatively impact his health. He announced his retirement in 1959.

THAMES'S CHATAWAY AND BRASHER LEAD BANNISTER TO A NEW WORLD RECORD

Quite some time before Thames Hare and Hounds's most famous triad made history on the track—breaking the proverbial "barrier that could not be broken," the four-minute mile—they were getting their start by defeating the opposition across country.

The winter of 1949 saw Chris Brasher victorious in a Thames Hare and Hounds cross-country meeting against Cambridge. At the Cambridge and Oxford University Cross-Country Match in December a year later, Brasher finished third behind D. H. Gilbert of Cambridge and an Oxford runner named Chris Chataway, who won in a time of 40:59 for 12 kilometers. In 1951, Chris Chataway won his second Oxford/Cambridge cross-country title, beating Gilbert for the second time in as many years. And two years previously, on December 3, 1949, a young student by the name of Roger Bannister had made a name for himself in cross-country by also winning the Oxford/Cambridge cross-country dual meet in a time of 41:54 for the 12-kilometer race over Wimbledon Common.

Brasher went on to represent Great Britain in the 1952 Olympics held in Helsinki, competing in the 3,000-meter steeplechase. By September, he was back at the Thames club, where he won four straight titles for the short-distance cross-country challenge cup. Brasher's fourth victory came in the winter of 1954. And by then Brasher, Roger Bannister, and Chris Chataway were all running for Thames. Chataway won the 10-mile cross-country race on March 27, 1954, merely five weeks before helping Roger Bannister (with Brasher's help) break the four-minute mile on the track for the first time.

As a medical student, Bannister could train for only one hour a day. He had an exceptionally low distance base compared to model standards, especially for a miler, but he dedicated himself to high-quality track workouts. In the weeks before his sub-four effort, Bannister performed seven interval workouts on the track, three of which were time trials (half mile in 1:53.0, three-quarter mile in 3:00, and two three-quarter mile repeats separated by eight minutes rest, the first in 3:14, the second in 3:08.6).

Ten of the days during the final weeks before his sub-four effort were devoted to recovering. Bannister's preparations were consistent both with his schedule and the philosophies of Coach Franz Stampfl, who argued that, "The athlete who believes that all normal social life and entertainment must be abandoned in the interest of training is a man devoid of imagination. A Spartan life in which all other interests are sacrificed to a single ideal is no existence for a man intent on achieving physical and mental fitness." On five of his ten days of "rest," Roger Bannister went rock climbing.

Bannister's sub-four-minute-mile achievement was tantamount to man landing on the moon. For generations it had been taught that running a mile run in less than four minutes was impossible. And the fact that another athlete ran a sub-four-minute mile just months later didn't undermine Bannister's groundbreaking moment. On the contrary, men cheered precisely because the young medical student had shown the strength of human imagination. Roger Bannister had willed himself to do the impossible, and the rest of humankind followed.

THE REEMERGENCE OF THE UNITED STATES

Wes Santee deserved some credit for pushing Bannister through the four-minute barrier. Although the Kansas native never broke four minutes himself, it was not for lack of effort or talent. The Kansas University star had gone undefeated in the mile since high school, and was as dominant over the countryside as he was on the oval. His progress, along with Don Gehrmann, Fred Wilt, and Horace Ashenfelter, captivated the attention of American audiences along the track—but each man made significant strides in cross-country as well.

In 1958, the National Collegiate Athletic Association (NCAA) established a National Cross-Country Championship for its College Division and held this first "small school" championship in Wheaton, Illinois. Prior to 1958, the College Division only held national championships

in basketball, but the cross-country event proved to be a success, and the race grew from 16 schools in 1958 to 84 schools by 1972, necessitating a further split into NCAA Division II and Division III. In 1973, both factions still held their championships in Wheaton but separated to different sites the following year.

The National Association of Intercollegiate Athletics (NAIA), a collegiate governing body alternative to the NCAA, held a cross-country championship that started in 1956. South Dakota State took the first title, but Fort Hayes State and Emporia State would both eventually combine for eight victories and seven runner-ups. In 1963 Emporia won both the NCAA Division II and NAIA, as did individual winner John Camien. In 1965, NAIA runners were put to a true cross-country test when 25-degree temperatures, 14-mile-per-hour winds, and a foot of snow hit the four-mile course in Omaha. Fort Hayes won by 74 points.

Individually, miler Don Gehrmann of the University of Wisconsin emerged as a runner able to push Fred Wilt to his limits. Gehrmann and Wilt were so closely matched, that in their first clash on the track it took the judges eleven months to decide who beat whom. Gehrmann won the Big Ten Conference Cross-Country Championship twice and was the NCAA Cross-Country runner-up in 1948 and '49. He also helped Wisconsin to two team titles in the Big Ten Conference in 1948 and '49.

But with an established legacy both on the track and running cross-country, Fred Wilt entered the decade having won a US National Cross-Country title (Warren Valley Golf Course in Detroit in 1949) and was going for more. In November 1952, Wilt achieved this goal, winning his second national cross-country title in Buffalo. The following year he returned to the same site, Delaware Park, to get two in a row. Three titles in five years ensured Wilt's legacy.

Horace "Nip" Ashenfelter also battled heads-up against Fred Wilt. Foremost a steeplechaser, the nimble Nip had a running repertoire as flexible as his frame. Horace won US National Cross-Country titles in 1955 and 1956, in Buffalo and Philadelphia, respectively. As Horace claimed: "I liked cross-country more than anything. It was more fun."

Did You Know?

While at Penn State, one of his most poignant memories for Horace "Nip" Ashenfelter was finishing second in the NCAA Cross-Country Championship in 1947: "I went the wrong way. I was leading by twenty or thirty yards fairly early in the race at Michigan State. The course wasn't marked very well and with no one in front of me I made a wrong turn and ended up about fifty yards behind the fellow who had been in second. After my mistake I caught up to him too quickly and didn't have anything left at the end and so he ended up winning."

In addition to the aforementioned milers, Wes Santee of Kansas University not only challenged the American mile record, but also performed admirably on the cross-country course. With a lifetime mile-best of 4:00.5 he came close to breaking the elusive four-minute barrier, but complemented his track speed with longer distance success as well. In 1953 he won the individual title in the NCAA Cross-Country Championship, running the four-mile course at Michigan State in 19:43. Santee's performance also resulted in Kansas University's only team title of the 1950s at NCAAs. At the top of the NCAA for distance running in this period, Kansas University (KU) groomed four national champions in five years for cross-country, and produced top finishers in events ranging from the 1,500 meters to the 10K on the track. Remarkably, KU did not send a team in 1952 despite having Herb Semper, the defending champion the previous two runnings.

Junior Allen Frame went on to win the individual title for Kansas in 1954, but Kansas slipped to fourth place in the team scoring, missing second place by 11 points. Frame returned the following year to finish fifth overall as a senior.

This success at Kansas was attributed to the head coach, Bill Easton. A disciple of Indiana's Billy Hayes from 1922 to 1927, Easton produced 32 All-Americans and eight Olympians in three decades of coaching. As coach at Drake University from 1941 through 1947, Easton produced three consecutive NCAA champion cross-country teams (1944–46), and was responsible for developing two-time NCAA Cross-Country champion Fred Feiler. In 1947, Easton moved on to the head coaching position at Kansas.

During his years as head coach at Kansas, Easton's KU men's cross-country team won 16 consecutive Big Eight conference championships, and before his retirement in 1965, his teams had won 39 conference championships in cross-country and track. Easton coached such notable names as Herb Semper (two-time NCAA Cross-Country champion), Wes Santee (NCAA Cross-Country champion), Al Frame (NCAA Cross-Country champion), and Billy Mills (All-American in cross-country in 1958, '59, and '60 and the 1960 Big Eight Conference Cross-Country champion).

One of Easton's star pupils, Mills went on to become America's only Olympic 10,000-meter gold medalist. And during his time at Kansas, Mills was one of the nation's best distance runners, finishing fifth two times and sixth once in a three-year span at the NCAA Cross-Country Championships. Later, Mills even won the famed Cinque Mulini cross-country race in Italy. Orphaned at a young age, Mills went to boarding school at Haskell Indian School in Lawrence, and battled through persecution as a Lakota Sioux Native American in the heart of the Civil Rights movement (Mills was asked to remove himself from the official after-race photo on three separate occasions when he had made All-America in cross-country). But Mills was desperate to communicate a greater point: "It was not the fault of the University of Kansas," Mills said. "It was America."

Michigan State Rekindles the Flame

Along with Kansas, Michigan State University (MSU) also experienced success at the top during the 1950s. This was attributed to the Kennedy brothers, Henry and Crawford, who hailed from Canada, who, along with a supporting cast, led MSU to five team championships at the NCAAs and six team championships at the Intercollegiate Association of Amateur Athletes of America (IC4A) Cross-Country Championship.

Longtime Michigan State coach Lauren Brown was entering a new chapter of his life as the 1950s neared. The war years were difficult for both Coach Brown and his Michigan State program, and in 1947 he stepped away from the team. Nevertheless, Brown remained in close contact through the mid-1960s with new coach Karl Schlademan, the cross-country program, and the NCAA, in his roles with the National Collegiate Cross-Country Coaches Association and the national championship.

Karl Schlademan was fifty-seven years old before he became MSU's track and cross-country coach, an assignment he held for nearly twenty years. In that time, Schlademan led the Spartans to seven Big Ten championships, six NCAA national championships, and five IC4A titles in cross-country. The Spartans also finished as runners-up in 1950 and 1957. In track, he expanded the Michigan State relays, coached 25 individual Big Ten champions, and four NCAA individual champions. He won three IC4A track titles and produced a number of Olympian distance runners.

With Schlademan at the helm, the Spartans welcomed Canadian sophomore transfer Henry Kennedy in 1955. Already with outstanding cross-country credentials, the twenty-three-year-old native of Glasgow, Scotland, helped Michigan State return to the national spotlight in 1955. Although the IC4A team title eluded MSU, Henry Kennedy finished first, and also led the way for the college's fourth Big Ten Conference title in six years one week later.

And after racking up these victories, Kennedy became the favorite at the 1955 NCAA Cross-Country Championship—which saw frigidly cold weather (dropping to 12 degrees) and winds gusting at 23 miles per hour—but it was his teammate Selwyn Jones who led the field through the first three of four miles before Henry took over. When Southern California's Max Truex (a future individual champion in 1957) faded from third to ninth, Kennedy only had one challenger to beat, Charles "Deacon" Jones from Iowa. Kennedy led the race until the closing strides, when Jones surged past to deny him a "triple crown" (individual victories at the Big Ten Conference, IC4A, and NCAA Championship meets). However, Michigan State came through to claim their sixth team championship. The final times: Deacon Jones in 19:57.4, Henry Kennedy in 19:57.5.

After repeating as IC4A and Big Ten cross-country champion in 1956, Henry Kennedy welcomed the arrival of younger brother Crawford in 1957. Crawford proved to be more talented, and both brothers kept Michigan State at the top for the third straight year. At the IC4As, MSU successfully defended their team title, and Crawford Kennedy won the individual championship. In the NCAAs that same year, Michigan State dropped to second place as a team, losing to Notre Dame by a mere six points.

When Henry graduated, Crawford kept the Kennedy tradition alive by successfully defending his IC4A title in 1958 and '59, and continued his momentum into the NCAA Championship, winning the individual title (running a new course record) in 1958, and the Big Ten title in 1959. Both seasons Michigan State repeated as winners of the NCAA team title, winning their fourth crown in five appearances.

LYDIARD, CERUTTY, AND THE TALENTED AUSTRALASIANS

Far from American shores, New Zealanders in the 1950s were inspired by the efforts of countryman John Lovelock, who, in the 1930s, had obtained Olympic success and dominated cross-country running—all while applying scientific principles to his training (he was a doctor). Likewise, Charlie Weller, a member of the Wanganui Harrier Club, led by example when he won four New Zealand National Cross-Country titles consecutively from 1936 to 1939. Further international success proved runners from the South Pacific could also contend with the best from other corners in the world.

After a hiatus for the war, successful cross-country talent emerged with the running of Kerry Williams, who, by the end of the 1950s, had New Zealand National Cross-Country titles of his own. Williams was dominant, receiving early accolades as the New Zealand junior one-mile champion, two-mile champion, and cross-country champion between the fall of 1950 and the spring of 1951. In 1958, when Kerry won his fourth Senior National Cross-Country title in a row, his brother John won the New Zealand National Junior Cross-Country title.

The primary competition for Kerry Williams in cross-country during the 1950s was Pat Sidon from Otago. Sidon dominated the Steeplechase Edmond Cup during the 1950s and 1960s, winning the men's individual title 11 times. He also won the Otago cross-country title 13 times, won the National Junior Cross-Country in 1951, and the Senior title a decade later. He first represented New Zealand in 1957 against Australia and captained New Zealand at the International Cross-Country Championships in 1965. Alex Barr coached Sidon, and a feature of his training was a Monday night track session at Tahuna Park, where Sidon would run 400 meters 24 times at race pace.

Kerry Williams was also a member of the New Zealand National Cross-Country team in 1957 that competed in Australia with Sidon. Williams finished second and third in races behind Murray Halberg and Australian Dave Power.

Born in Maitland, New South Wales, Dave Power developed into one of Australia's great distance runners. Power won the Australian National 10,000-meter cross-country championship in Perth in 1954, relishing the sand-dune terrain, and again in 1955 when it was held in Hobart. In 1957 he was victorious for the third time in Brisbane (the Australian National Cross-Country Championship remained a biennial affair, but ran in back-to-back years in 1954 and 1955). And when Power eventually ran 4.00.2 in 1960 he became the then-sixth-fastest Australian miler of all-time.

Dave Power's training diary from 1956 provided a look into a week of winter and summer training. He was training three times a day in the winter (except for race day) and twice a day in the summer. In the winter week he covered 110 miles, running on roads, beaches, and grass. Training included a 6 × one-mile session and a 36 × 440 session.

Power, a bank clerk by profession, was a disciple of the unorthodox, inspirational Victorian coach Percy Cerutty. And Cerutty spent a lot of time convincing Power he was a world-beater. "Up until then I'd been playing second fiddle to the likes of Al Lawrence and Albie Thomas," Power told Brian Lenton. "Once Perce convinced me I was every bit as good as them, if not better, I started winning races. I'll always owe Percy in that respect." In 1961, Power retained his national three-mile title but lost the six-mile to Bob Vagg and then finished sixth in the national cross-country in Sydney.

Dave Power's personality was summed up well by Herb Elliott: "Dave Power is perhaps the most lion-hearted athlete I've known. Although it was against his nature to be ferocious, his patience and powers of endurance were qualities Percy [Cerutty] felt should be paying higher dividends. And ultimately they did."

Back in New Zealand, Murray Halberg, who was primarily coached by Arthur Lydiard, was dominating the National Cross-Country event. Halberg won his first, and only, New Zealand Cross-Country National title in 1953, two years before Williams won his first of four in a row.

At the age of seventeen, Halberg had injured his left shoulder playing rugby, leaving his left arm paralyzed. He was still able to run, holding his limp left arm "tucked up," he explained, and "pumping myself along with my right." His local running coach saw Halberg's potential, and asked Arthur Lydiard to take over. Lydiard, who had not yet achieved his worldwide reputation, saw "astonishing tenacity" in his new pupil, and Halberg's success came quickly. After winning New Zealand Junior titles in 1952, Halberg was national mile champion in 1954 and earned a place on the Empire Games team. In-between, he was able to run away from the field in the New Zealand Cross-Country Championship, speeding over the Trentham 6.25-mile course in 38:24.

Murray's performances enshrined him into a new category of distance running greats from New Zealand during this period. Capitalized by training theories that were new and at odds with the interval-heavy approach seen in other parts of the world at the time, ripples in the cross-country waves were being seen in the South Pacific.

SOUTH PACIFIC MILERS EXCEL IN CROSS

Dave Power wasn't the only athlete to receive guidance at a particular training camp in Portsea, Australia. Inspired by the 1956 Olympics in his home country, young miler Herb Elliott also relocated to train with running guru Percy Cerutty.

Cerutty had the perfect background. As a youth he had trained with the Malvern Harriers, running a respectable 2:07 for 880 yards. But poor health and self-doubt plagued him. He was too unfit to serve in the First World War, and in 1939 had a nervous breakdown. But during his illness he read philosophy and religion and began endurance tests to build up his self-confidence. Here Cerutty developed his "Stotan" Philosophy, and investigated alternative medicines and natural diets. Returning to the Malvern Harriers in 1942, he began running successfully over road and cross-country, and at the age of fifty-one set a Victorian marathon record of 2:58.11. Also that year he ran 100 kilometers from Portsea to Melbourne in 8 hours, 28 minutes.

After "retiring" in 1946, Percy bought the property at Portsea, which in turn became the famous camp he called "Ceres." Athletes came on weekends to run on the beach and up the sand dunes. While at the camp, Cerutty had the athletes live a Spartan lifestyle and would read philosophy and poetry to them. Cerutty believed that athletes were not only there to run better, but also to get an education in life.

Did You Know?

Herb Elliott reflected on his relationship with Coach Percy Cerutty, forged during his sojourn at Portsea, and Cerutty's idea of athlete-as-Stotan ("Stotan" was coined by Cerutty and was derived from the words "stoic" and "Spartan"). Cerutty attributed his methods to Swedish coach Gosta Holmer, the father of fartlek, whom Cerutty met at the Helsinki Olympics—and on the thinking of Friedrich Nietzsche. Cerutty explained: "The amount of experience, of effort, of pain, and suffering that results in a work of art, or a book that becomes a classic, is stupendous. So it is with track. The weak fall by the wayside, and the strong train on." Cerutty worried that modern conveniences made people weak—the excellent athlete, in Cerutty's theory, was the natural man— the one who trained and raced as nature intended. To train at Portsea meant, in Elliott's words, "to live like an animal." Cerutty emphasized not only running, but weightlifting, swimming in the Australian surf, eating an uncooked vegetarian diet, and sprinting up sand dunes until exhaustion. Reminiscing about Portsea, Elliott recalled: "You couldn't afford once in a training session or in a race to let a guy get past you once the chips were really down, because it just might be too early to let it happen again." That attitude undoubtedly sprang from Coach Percy Cerutty.

With immediate success under Cerutty, Elliott won the Olympic 1,500 meters in 1960 in world-record time, and eventually moved onto a degree course at Cambridge, in England. And during his two years at the university Elliott divided his time between running cross-country, studying, and flying with the University Air Squadron. But his approach was casual and he ran at Cambridge because he was there, it was expected of him, and he was the best of the crop of freshmen that autumn. In fact, he was probably the most gifted natural runner there was at the time.

In his debut cross-country match, a three-way meet between Cambridge, the South London Harriers, and Walton University, Elliott finished eighth after "taking a tumble in the mud" (as reported by the *Tuscaloosa News*). Gordon Pirie, representing South London Harriers, was the winner. Two years later, Elliott reappeared to finish fourth in a cross-country match against the Thames Hare and Hounds. Elliott continued as an individual in the

Eastern Counties' Championships at Ampthill, Bedford-shire, where it was a wicked and typically English nine-mile course of deep mud, hills and plough, riddled with fallen trees that had blown down during a recent gale. Elliott finished second, a minute behind the runaway winner, Norman Clarke. Elliott still ran regularly, but it was the running of a man who loved to do it, not the training of someone who had something to prove. And all the while Elliott remained loyal to the training bestowed upon him by the legendary Percy Cerutty.

In 1957, while Cerutty was helping Herb Elliott become the world's greatest miler, New Zealand coach Arthur Lydiard was working on turning Peter Snell into an equally formidable distance runner. Where Elliott was rangy and tough, Snell was big and strong, preferring the 800 meters (or the 880 yards) to the mile. Lydiard made certain that Snell, as with every other athlete he coached, received enough of a distance running base to complete a marathon if he needed to. Lydiard had Snell run intervals, hills, and cross-country to sharpen his speed, but he still emerged as the first known coach to emphasize a gradual building of strength from a sound distance base. In this regard, Snell was the real modern heir to the training methods of Walter George and Alfred Shrubb, and became the New Zealand National Cross-Country Champion in 1962.

CROSS-COUNTRY BLOOMS IN THE HIGH SCHOOLS ON THE WEST COAST OF THE UNITED STATES

While Lydiard was developing Snell in New Zealand, there emerged a similar coach-pupil arrangement in the United States with outstanding high schooler Ron Larrieu and Northern California's first great high school coach, Forrest Jamieson. Longtime observers of the San Francisco running scene remember Jamieson as the "father" of local high school distance running, having founded the first peninsula cross-country team at Palo Alto High School in 1952. However, his influence cuts a much broader swath throughout the nation's cross-country arc.

As a youth, Jamieson had been a do-everything runner, competing in one of Northern California's first cross-country invitationals (outside Sacramento in 1935), and running everything from a 50-second quarter-mile to a 4:30 mile to a 10-flat two miles while at Sacramento City College. Jamieson's range caught the attention of Franklin "Pitcher" Johnson, head track coach at Drake University who was recruiting in Northern California. Johnson saw Jamieson as the ideal relay specialist: a runner capable of handling 400-meter relay legs while scoring occasional points in the open 880 and mile. With Drake University's interest, Jamieson accepted a track scholarship and went off to Des Moines, Iowa.

Through his participation on Drake's cross-country team, Jamieson became acutely aware of the popularity of the sport of cross-country throughout the Midwest and East Coast. Bill Easton, who became Drake's head coach a year later, hailed from Indiana University (twice Amateur

Athletic Union [AAU] National Cross-Country Champions in the 1930s, and NCAA champions in 1938 and 1940), and Drake later dominated collegiate cross-country during the war years, winning NCAA Championships in 1944, '45, and '46.

After graduating, Jamieson continued his ties to the sport by founding the boys' cross-country program at Chula Vista High School in San Diego in 1947, and sought to increase student participation in the area. Thus was born the "Center Meet," an invitational meet held two or three times each season, every year, offering each runner the opportunity to gauge his progress over the span of his high school running career. In the fall of 1948, Chula Vista hosted its first Center Meet on the grounds of San Diego State College. As the postwar economic boom accelerated, more schools opened and more cross-country teams sprang forth; Jamieson's Center Meets flourished.

Coach Jamieson returned to Northern California in 1950 intent on pursuing his master's degree at Stanford University, and by 1952 he was teaching and coaching track and field at the nearby Palo Alto High School. In autumn of that year, Paly had its first cross-country team. But cross-country teams at the preparatory level on the San Francisco Peninsula were sparse at that time. Only a handful of schools in San Francisco, a few in the San Jose area, and a smattering in the East and North Bays of the region offered the sport following the war. Even Stanford University was without a cross-country team until 1956. But the university did have a beautiful, verdant, oak-studded golf course located midway between San Francisco and San Jose. It was the perfect venue for a Center Meet. With the assistance of Jack Weiershauser, then head track and field coach at Stanford, Jamieson convinced the University's administration to open its golf course each fall to the local high school harriers.

But Jamieson's legacy ultimately became linked to the career of Ron Larrieu, arguably America's first teenage distance running prodigy. While on the track in late March 1956, Larrieu raced two miles in 9:39, breaking the national scholastic mark of 9:44 set thirty-one years earlier, helping to catapult Palo Alto's cross-country team to national prominence. In retrospect, Ron Larrieu and younger sister Francine Larrieu were true pioneers, standard bearers for generations of American distance runners to come.

In 1959, Jamieson—seeking a change and stirred by the phenomenal performances of Australia's elite middle-distance runners, including Herb Elliot, John Landy, and others trained by mercurial coach Percy Cerutty—boarded the Pacific Orient Liner bound for the South Pacific. Jamieson then found himself anchored in New Zealand for two months. While conducting coaching clinics there, Jamieson received word of Arthur Lydiard, an Auckland shoe cobbler and former runner renowned throughout the island nation for his revolutionary coaching methods.

Though their first meeting was a bit icy and restrained, Jamieson's lifelong friendship had begun with Lydiard. Jamieson's fortuitous introduction to the renowned coach, a man now judged to be one of the most influential figures in the history of distance running, would challenge and dramatically alter Jamieson's approach to training American high schoolers, ultimately ushering in a golden new era in the annuals of American distance running beyond the performances of the Larrieu siblings.

NEW YORK OFFICIALLY SANCTIONS STATE CROSS-COUNTRY FOR HIGH SCHOOL

At the other end of the American continent, on November 18, 1950, at an inner-city park in upstate New York, close to 100 runners started off in a race that would forever change the landscape of interscholastic sports. The event, the first annual New York State Public High School Athletic Association (NYSPHSAA) Cross-Country State Championship, had a beginning spun from dreams that literally hung by a shoestring. But the approximately 200 total runners who ran in two races that day blazed the trail for later generations of high school athletes in all sports.

With the 1950 meet, cross-country became the first public high school sport to establish a statewide championship in New York, one that has run annually to the present day. As a result, the schedules of the NYSPHSAA teams transformed to include preparations for the Sectional State Qualifier and the Intersectional Championship meets. Big invitationals, such as the New York University (NYU) Spiked Shoe remained important, but the New York State Meet became the featured finale, characterized by crowded conditions at the Eastern Intersectionals.

Did You Know?

The first New York State Cross-Country Championship was not the first intersectional meet the state had seen. Major cross-country meets had been run in New York since the early 1900s. Then, a boom in scholastic sports in the 1920s led New York public schools to mirror the college regional section setup, with eight sectional athletic conferences formed (a number that would soon grow to 10, and finally 11, with the split of Long Island in 1957). But it was in 1923 that the NYSPHSAA was founded to provide a central management role. At that time, cross-country invitationals took precedence, the biggest being the Manhattan College Invitational (started in 1925). After World War II, it was former Nott Terrace coach Bill Eddy who brought back the New York State Intersectional Championship and hosted it over a Central Park course. From there, with support from all eight sections, the Intersectional Meet Committee put together a structure for the first state meet. A two-tier race system was followed and split the competition between an "A" race for large schools and a "B" race for small schools. With everything finally set, all that was left to do was to find out which teams and runners would be appearing at Central Park on November 18, 1950.

After an eventful inaugural 1950 event in Central Park that saw the Class A race decided by one point (New Rochelle celebrated an upset after two hours in review, beating Mount Pleasant 59 to 60), runners returned to Central Park for the New York State Championship in 1951, and hometown heroes Mount Pleasant would win the Class A title by 11 points over Sewanhaka (Arlington claimed the B title). In 1955, the venue was moved to Bear Mountain State Park, where Vestal won three straight Class A titles. In 1960, the New York State Cross-Country Championships expanded to three classes. And in 1975, following an earlier resumption of interscholastic athletics for students of all genders, the girls ran in their first "States," with Kathy Mills from Fayetteville–Manlius victorious.

FITNESS BECOMES A FOCUS FOR HIGH SCHOOL HARRIERS

Meanwhile, World War II had underscored the low fitness levels among Americans serving in the military (it turned out the armed forces had needed to reject nearly half of all draftees or give them noncombat positions), and the nation's attention refocused on improving physical fitness practices for children. Early in the 1950s, tests were conducted nationwide in American schools to measure muscular strength and flexibility in the trunk and leg muscles. Close to 60 percent of American children failed at least one of the tests, compared to only nine percent of children from European countries. In the competitive climate that marked the Cold War, these startling statistics launched a new campaign among US political leaders to promote health and fitness among the nation's youth.

President Eisenhower responded in June 1956 by holding a White House conference, which led to the formation of the President's Council on Youth Fitness and the appointment of a Citizens' Advisory Committee on the Fitness of American Youth. During this period, educating the public about the consequences of low fitness levels became a goal for several organizations. For the sport of cross-country at the high school level, this meant expansion and a greater emphasis on state-led sanctioning.

By the start of the decade, eighteen states had already sanctioned the sport of cross-country running for boys, with three more states offering "unofficial" state championship competition. Fourteen more added sanctioned competition over the course of the decade.

WOMEN REVIVE THE INTERNATIONAL

New events in the United States were not the only changes being seen. Internationally (after women had a chance to compete in their own cross-country championship in 1931, '32, '35, and '38), it was decided that a women's international should be reinstated, albeit unofficially, in 1954, with the distance extended from 3,000 meters to 4,000.

This international "championship" was really a meeting between England's best and Scotland's best. The event, which was the first postwar women's international meeting, ran at the Bromford Bridge Racecourse—the same site that the men would run the following week. The English team dominated Scotland, securing the first six places overall before the first Scottish female runner crossed the line. English national champion Diane Leather led home the field.

Despite the rout in 1954, the event was again held in 1955, with the English and Scottish female runners again competing a week removed from the men, but this time at a different location. With only 12 women competing in the championship, the result was nearly identical to the year prior. Diane Leather repeated as champion, and the *Glasgow Herald* reported that "Miss Leather's time of 16:08 was 2:20 faster than that in which Miss A. Drummond (Maryhill) won the Scottish title over the same course two weeks ago."

In 1956, England again met Scotland in an unofficial "International Championship," this time held on the same day as the men, but in a different location. The course distance was reduced to 3,000 meters, and this time only the first four runners out of the six were scored. Despite the changes in distance and scoring, the results remained the same. England accumulated a perfect score—led by Roma Ashby, with June Bridgland in second, and Diane Leather in third.

1957 marked the fourth time in succession that England and Scotland met at their own "International," England's Diane Leather exacted her revenge over the 3,000-meter course, reclaiming the individual title in a time of 11:15. Leather, a member of the Birchfield Harriers, was not only notable for winning the International three times in four tries, but was also the first woman to break five minutes in the mile.

WOMEN MAKE STRIDES IN THE 1950s

Spurred by the need to find female competition for the Scottish national team, women competed in their own non-sanctioned "national championship" during the 1950s, open to any willing female participants. The top six finishers were selected to face England for the "International." It wouldn't be until 1958, a year after Scotland decided to focus on their home talent, that they would withdraw and *officially* sanction a women's national championship. Held on March 8, 1958, I. M. Mooney won this first 3.6-kilometer national championship in 12:36.

Germany instituted their first national women's championship in 1954. Marianne Weiss won the 1,200-meter event in Gonsenheim in April 1954. In 1956, '57, and '59 Edith Schiller claimed victory on the frighteningly short courses, which were between 1,000 and 1,200 meters long.

Women from Australia and the United States joined these other nations, when they too offered the opportunity for cross-country competition at the end of the decade. Australia hosted their first women's championship in 1960 over a 1.5-mile course (despite the men's championship

meeting biannually, the women's was contested every year). The United States began to advocate for women's equality in 1957 with the formation of the Road Runners Club of America (RRCA), and the AAU formally ran a women's cross-country national championship in 1964.

THE INTERNATIONAL CONTINUES TO THRIVE

The men's field at the International also continued to expand and featured better competition.

In 1954 at Birmingham, Antonio Amoros, Spain's National Cross-Country Champion, was touted as a formidable opponent for France's champion Alain Mimoun. Mimoun won comfortably, 22 seconds in front of England's Ken Norris—though England kept the team title. Amoros finished a commendable 11th.

In 1955, with the absence of Mimoun, England's Frank Sando crushed the field, leading home English teammates in six of the first eight places. Belgium's champion Lucien Theys (fourth overall), and Spain's Antonio Amoros (fifth overall), prevented a perfect sweep. It was England's best team performance since 1932, and their first individual title since 1951. Belgium narrowly beat Spain for second with a team score of 102 to 109. France dropped from second to fourth with a score of 116. The 1955 race also welcomed Portugal as an International competitor for the first time.

Mimoun returned in 1956, winning the event and leading France to team victory. In 1957 Belgium took the win in front of a home crowd at the Hippodroom Waregem. Led by Denis Jouret in fourth, and reigning National Cross-Country Champion Marcel VandeWattyne in seventh, Belgium scored 67 points, beating France with 80 and England with 84. English champion Frank Sando claimed his second individual International title in three years.

In 1958, Tunisia and Morocco accepted membership to the International Cross-Country Union. Also of note was the decision of the ICCU to affiliate with the International Amateur Athletics Federation (IAAF), having administrators serve on their membership board.

MIMOUN SETS THE STANDARD

Alain Mimoun managed to accomplish most of his success during the decade of the 1950s, with five podium finishes at the International. While he was poor and living in precarious circumstances as a café waiter, he remained diligent in his training. In 1950, despite nearing the age of 30, Mimoun began a streak of five French National Cross-Country titles in the span of seven events. By the 1956 Olympics, Mimoun had been International Cross-Country Champion four times and runner up once. Still, it was something of a surprise when he earned a gold medal in the Olympic marathon event.

As he neared his forties, Mimoun's athletic powers began to decline. Although he continued to compete, he

Did You Know?

At his peak in the 1950s, France's Alain Mimoun was nearly unchallengeable. Mimoun recounted: "I started running just for the heck of it. I got interested in distance running at the age of 25. Before that I had been playing soccer, doing bicycle races and so on. After seven years in the army I was inspired by people whom I had seen running in the forest. I had no training whatsoever, but I had lots of natural endurance and was immediately doing well. I was very sore after the 1954 European Championships. It took me a year to get over my sciatica problems. I got fat, and people were saying Mimoun's great career is finished. I did not believe that. Healthy again, I started gradual training, and after eight months I was as fit as I had ever been in my life. In 1956 I won every major race I entered, including the Olympic Marathon. No matter if I won or lost, I was always happy. It was just sport, but it gave me fantastic joy and enjoyment." Eleven national and international cross-country titles were earned with Mimoun's dedication.

did not win a national title on grass or the track after 1959. Four further outings from 1960 to 1964 at the International saw individual finishes ranging from 18th to 26th place.

FRANK SANDO, ENGLAND'S STAR HARRIER OF THE 1950s

The other international stalwart came from England during this decade. For the entirety of his athletics career, Frank Sando was a fiery competitor and nearly unstoppable toward the end of races when he made his kick. Mick Firth, a competitor who once finished ahead of Sando at the Southern Counties Cross-Country Championship, had this to say: "I still rank Frank Sando as one of the greatest cross-country runners. Admittedly he is from my era, but he first ran in the senior team as a junior. He ran nine consecutive years when he was in the first nine (finishers) in the National [National Cross-Country Championship in England]. He was in the first three in our international team in those years. Imperceptibly he would drift over muddy ground. He was very underrated."

Frank Sando began his amateur career as a member of the Maidstone Harriers, where he won the Kent County Junior Cross-Country Championship in 1948 and the Kent Youth Cross-Country Championship in 1949.

He finished fourth in the English Youth Cross-Country Championship in 1948 and 1949. Then, after joining the army, Sando broke the Army three-mile record in 1951, which had stood for 23 years. Earlier that year he won the Inter-Services Cross-Country Championship. Leaving the army in 1951, he began working for the Reed Paper Group in Aylesford, Kent, and officially resigned from the Maidstone Harriers. Soon after, Sando joined the Paper Group's athletics club, where he juggled work, professional examinations, family commitments, and his athletic career. It was at this time that he gained the nickname the "Maidstone Mudlark".

In 1952, Sando finished fifth in the English National Cross-Country Championships and ninth in the International. And over the next eight years Sando maintained a record of finishing in the top eight positions in the International Cross-Country Championship.

When Sando achieved the double of winning both the National and International Cross-Country Championships in 1957, he described the lead-up training as such: "Up until Christmas I just enjoyed it, quite easy, no real pressures; then the County Championships, and that was relatively easy. The Area (Southern Counties Championship) was where you weighed yourself up, and aim for the National, and finish in the first six in that. Ten miles of running on Sunday, five on Monday, seven miles fartlek on Tuesday, three miles of ordinary running on Wednesday, two miles of fartlek Thursday; rest on Friday, race on Saturday. Average miles a week: 45. I knew what I was prepared to do. If I ran more than 45 minutes I used to get fed up, and that was the amount of time I would spend out training."

Sando retired from racing at the age of 32 with two gold medals, three silvers, and one bronze to his credit—all from the International Cross-Country Championships—and was the English National Cross-Country Champion in 1957.

* * *

By the start of the 1950s, cross-country running was seeing its most stable period yet. With the horrors of war in the past, the sport garnered a wider audience and individual, national, and international rivalries were born. In Europe especially, the rise in awareness of new talent meant that crowds on an unparalleled level were flocking to witness the world's best. Simultaneously, female and younger runners saw a remarkable boom throughout the decade and would have a significant impact on the sport in years to come.

EVENT SPOTLIGHT:
ZÁTOPEK, KUTS, AND CHROMIK IN THE CROSS DE L'HUMANITÉ (MARCH 19, 1954)

LOCATION: BOIS DE VINCENNES, PARIS

Paris, France

In its inaugural year in 1933, an international cross-country championship called the Cross de L'Humanité started inauspiciously with 500 participants, far from the acclaimed sporting spectacle that it would soon become. However, it did prove to be a marginal success with the fans, planting the seeds for what would eventually evolve into one of the largest cross-country invitationals of the 1940s, '50s, and '60s. Funded and hosted by the communist newspaper *L'Humanité* in conjunction with "La Fédération Sportive et Gymnique du Travail" (FSGT), the event soon attracted the best distance running talent in France and became famous throughout Europe.

In time, more than 4,000 participants would take part in a single Saturday, with eager runners from a wide range of abilities competing alongside specially invited talent from leftist (communist) nations. As an example, 1935, '37 and '38 saw the USSR's Seraphim Znamensky victorious. The 10-kilometer cross-country course featured mud, ploughed-land, a steep hill, and steeplechase barriers, all as it looped throughout the Vincennes horseracing track.

At the eighth holding of the event, held in 1945 after a hiatus for World War II, the return of the race was capped with national fervor. France's own Rafael Pujazon won, and the event drew participants ranging from junior men to senior women and elite internationals alike, not to mention tens of thousands spectators. In addition to the "Le Grand Prix cycliste de L'Humanité" (a cycle race in early May that culminated on the streets of Paris), the Cross de L'Humanité quickly exploded as one of the greatest attended, most well-publicized cross-country events on the planet during the postwar period.

The event was typically held the week after the French National Cross-Country Championship, a date that occasionally conflicted with the International Cross-Country Championship. This inevitably dictated who would be eligible to compete. And as the event grew, the *L'Humanité* newspaper began negotiating travel expenses and accommodations in Paris, which further put the amateur status of some athletes in jeopardy. However, despite the programming challenges, the focus in the 1950s turned to celebrating the communist nation's plethora of distance running talent, as the biggest names in running met at the Vincennes cross-country course.

The 1954 race was especially noteworthy. The event included Czech champion Emil Zátopek, Polish national star Jerzy Chromik, and Ukrainian runner Vladimir Kuts in a cross-country championship for the first time. During the week of March 19 (the first week of spring), Zátopek arrived two days before the event to train and practice his form, touring the course the day after, putting in a few intervals (2×200 meters, 10×400 meters and 5×200 meters). The *L'Humanite* paper excitedly previewed the meeting between Zátopek and Kuts, and while the home competition was sparse (France's Alain Mimoun would be in attendance, but not competing—an edict from the French federation which forbade its members to participate), there were even murmurings that the infallible Zátopek might not win.

On the day of the event, 70,000 spectators traveled to the horseracing stadium in Vincennes. Cross-country competitions ran all day, culminating in the international senior men's championship, run over 10 kilometers. As the gun fired, Zátopek and Kuts accelerated to the fore. Through two miles they jostled for the lead, with Kuts covering Zátopek's occasional surges. For the next two miles it was neck and neck, Zátopek in his trademark grimace, Kuts not falling more than a stride behind. Both men crossed the six-kilometer mark shoulder to shoulder. The audience was on their feet—they wanted a fight between the two men—and it was offered in the purest possible form.

Crossing the six-kilometer mark a full minute behind the leaders was Poland's Jerzy Chromik. Yet the battle lay with Zátopek and Kuts—and in the end, experience prevailed over combative youth. Zátopek subtly detected a moment to make his charge, right on the steep incline (sensing just a minor hesitation by Kuts), and the fight was won. By the time the eighth kilometer was crossed, Zátopek had 200 meters to spare. An exhausted Kuts withered and Zátopek's lead grew to 500 meters, crossing the line in a time of 30:34. Chromik managed to beat Kuts for second, clocking 31:26, while Kuts faded from the early punishing pace to finish third in 31:34. All athletes were swarmed at the finish by a flurry of spectators, and Alain Mimoun congratulated Zátopek personally.

The crowd gave all three men an unprecedented standing ovation, but couldn't contain their enthusiasm when Zátopek popped champagne and addressed the crowd in French. Paris newspapers printed feedback about Zátopek's comments: "It was bestowed with a lively intelligence, a sense of humor and a funny irony, with no hard feelings. It is nice and good. All this, together with his victory makes him the most popular athlete in the world!"

The following year, the Czechs and Soviets arrived in Paris on the same Air France aircraft. With Zátopek on the plane came the handsome Kuts, who—each of them having broken each other's records repeatedly—had helped Zátopek set the record for the 5,000 meters on the track before the Czech retired from that event.

The Cross de L'Humanité championship was truly international, and was attended by the ambassadors of the USSR, Czechoslovakia, Hungary, and Poland, among others. The French apparatchiks included a few important heads of state—all of whom faced long-winded speeches the night before. And military marches and national anthems were featured on the day.

The spring of 1955 had been unseasonably warm, which meant heavy rain in the days leading to the event. Yet the dampening conditions did not put a damper on the event itself, as more than 8,000 runners competed throughout the day of the race, and drenched fans huddled under trees to cheer on their athletes. Meanwhile, the course had become a swamp. This did nothing to lessen the enthusiasm for the main event, which, like the year before, brought Zátopek, Kuts, and Chromik together to decide the title of greatest European distance runner.

At the gun, it was Chromik who shot into the lead. Zátopek remained patient, a full 30 meters behind in the main pack—with Kuts shadowing his every move. After the first two-mile loop Zátopek appeared lost, and the crowd wondered if he would move up with six kilometers left to run. On the penultimate loop, Chromik, still in the lead, surged for the home stretch, thinking he had finished the race. With a devastating kick that further separated him from the field, Chromik sprinted for home—but it was too soon.

On the final loop Zátopek urged fellow Czech Ivana Ullspergera to take the lead and track down Chromik, but instead it was Zátopek who ultimately assumed the burden and increased his pace. Zátopek astounded the doubters as he caught Chromik about a kilometer before the finish, battling shoulder to shoulder in ankle-deep water. Fifty meters before the finish the Pole finally broke. Zátopek, exhausting his strength, won for the second year in a row. Chromik, a close second, collapsed at the finish line. Kuts crossed in third. The top three men appeared identical on the medal stand as the year prior, but the race spoke volumes of difference between the two events.

On the podium Zátopek experienced mixed feelings. His performance on the course used to serve as a barometer of his spring form (slow this year in 1955, with the race covered in mud), and Zátopek was well aware that Chromik only lost due to his race tactics. But he also felt pride. To the cheers of the comrades, Zátopek agreed to say a few words at the podium. "I'm happy," he announced, "but a little sorry a young man didn't beat me. Myself, I'm thirty-three now, I don't have the same will to win anymore, I only run these days for the pleasure of running. I thank you." He received an ovation.

Before long, it was 1956, and Zátopek was training hard for the Olympic marathon in Melbourne. At the 1956 Cross de L'Humanité the weather was much nicer, and the three champions—now well-known and respected—returned to the horse track with playful banter. Zátopek with his pleasant smile and knitted cap with pom-pom prepared to defend his title for the third year, while Kuts, preparing for the Olympics himself, returned more set on controlling the pace from the front.

The Ukrainian did just that, following the example set by Chromik a year earlier, setting a devastating pace from the gun and leading as consummate pacesetter. Many in the crowd expected to see a thrilling come-from-behind victory—except this time it was not to be. Chromik, running more intelligently and vainly trying to catch Kuts, finished in second for the third year in a row—while Zátopek, overwhelmed, crossed in third. "Fine," said a gentle Zátopek without making a fuss, "I have to face facts, I've grown old while these kids were coming along. My time has passed, it's my last season. I still have to train some more to wind it up honorably. Well, an honorable finish has only one name: the Melbourne Games." In 1959, Poland's Jerzy Chromik finally tasted victory, winning the Cross de L'Humanité for the first and only time.

Chapter 12

When you put yourself on the line in a race and expose yourself to the unknown,
you learn things about yourself that are very exciting.

—Doris Brown Heritage

THE 1960s: ACHIEVEMENT UNBOUNDED

The 1960s introduced new talent. Kenya and Ethiopia began to participate in athletics regularly, and the Cold War prompted a surge in national fervor, especially in the Eastern Bloc. As a consequence, the United States also encouraged runners to compete internationally, and the collegiate ranks became the proving ground. At the same time, there were increasing opportunities for women to compete. While competition lent an added sense of seriousness to training and racing, it also reintroduced a sinister financial element into the fold. Top athletes were no longer concerned with just competing against the world's best, they saw an opportunity for monetary gain, too. As Kenyan distance runner Eliud Kipchoge famously said: "Treat athletics as a career. Treat athletics as a profession. See sport as life." For East Africans especially, this decade revealed how cross-country might improve their financial situation.

THE ARRIVAL OF EAST AFRICAN TALENT BEGINS WITH A WHIMPER, NOT A BANG

While today it seems that every running event from the 800 meters, to the marathon, to international cross-country is dominated by East Africans, it wasn't until the 1960s that nations such as Kenya and Ethiopia began building their legacies.

As previously discussed, the era of European colonization at the beginning of the twentieth century had a profound effect on the trajectory of both Kenya and Ethiopia as sovereign nations, and the consequences of this European influence were compounded during the Second World War. Thus, the 1960s became the first opportunity for both Ethiopia and Kenya to make an impression internationally in distance running events—primarily in track events and in the marathon. However, a few opportunities

to display cross-country running prowess, even at these early stages, would be a forebearer of great things to come.

THE RISE OF ETHIOPIA

Despite a four-year Italian occupation during World War II, Ethiopia remained largely untouched by European powers and free from the influence of Western nations. As a result, the sporting influences seen from colonization in countries such as Kenya, where football (soccer), cricket, polo, and track and field were introduced via British influence at the turn of the century, did not immediately impact Ethiopia. Ultimately, it was development as a sovereign nation (largely attributed to the world travels and forward-thinking leadership of Emperor Haile Selassie) that brought exposure to sport to Ethiopia. Shortly after the end of World War II, the Ethiopian Olympic Committee (EOC) was established. First constituted in 1948 at the behest of Emperor Selassie, the EOC was formally accepted by the International Olympic Committee in 1954. Ato Assefa Mamo was the organization's first president.

Coincidently, Abebe Bikila and Mamo Wolde, two of Ethiopia's most talented athletes, had a profound effect on Ethiopia's status in distance running. Both were members of Emperor Haile Selassie's Imperial Guard—a unit of the best-trained, most loyal soldiers. Both men gained international prominence running the marathon. However, while Bikila reached international stardom and brought glory via his marathon exploits, it was Wolde who branched out and claimed glory running cross-country.

Abebe Bikila, born into a humble Oromo family (his father was a shepherd), completed the traditional Ethiopian *Qes* schooling, and was an avid *Gena* player (an Ethiopian game played with ball and crooked stick, where athletes traveled the distance of two towns to score goals). In 1952, at the age of twenty, Bikila began working in the Imperial Bodyguard and soon participated in the national armed forces athletics championships. The hero of the time was Wami Biratu, who held the national records in 5,000 and 10,000 meters—but during the marathon, the crowd at the stadium was surprised to see not Wami Biratu, but Abebe Bikila round the corner in the lead. Bikila went on to break the 5,000- and 10,000-meter records held by Wami and qualified for the 1960 Rome Olympics.

A few hours before the 1960 Olympic marathon, Bikila decided to run barefoot, as he had trained. He was also warned about fellow competitor Rhadi Ben Abdesselam of Morocco (a seasoned cross-country veteran who would win the individual title at the International), wearing the number 26. For unknown reasons, Rhadi did not acquire his black marathon bib before the race, and instead wore his regularly assigned track and field bib, number 185.

Bikila passed numerous runners in the race as he searched for Rhadi's number 26. By about 20 kilometers, Bikila and Rhadi had created a gap from the rest of the pack, but Bikila kept looking forward to find the runner with number 26, unaware that Rhadi was running right beside him. They stayed together until the last 500 meters, when Bikila sprinted to the finish in a record time of 2:15:16, becoming the first sub-Saharan African to win an Olympic gold medal. He finished 25 seconds ahead of Rhadi. After the race, when Bikila was asked why he ran barefoot, he replied, "I wanted the whole world to know that my country, Ethiopia, has always won with determination and heroism."

After his Olympic marathon victory, Bikila was proclaimed a national hero, and soon became an international sensation. With numerous marathon victories around the world, Bikila returned to win his second Olympic gold in the marathon in 1964, running a new Olympic record of 2:12:11. But Bikila was not alone. Placing fourth in the 10,000 meters at the 1964 Olympics was Bikila's countryman Mamo Wolde.

Wolde had a nearly identical upbringing to Bikila. Similar success in *Qes* schooling, early athletic promise, and assignment to the Imperial Guard by the age of 19—but Wolde had different aspirations than Olympic marathon glory.

In January 1963, a full twenty years after the inaugural Cross de Elgoibar, international distance runners were finally given an invitation to compete in the Cross Internacional Juan Muguerza, so named in memorial of local runner Juan Muguerza (a multiple national champion who was killed in 1937 during the bombing of Mungia in the Spanish Civil War), and one of Spain's largest running events. Mamo Wolde was Ethiopia's only stalwart on the line and, incredibly, the country's first international cross-country competitor. Despite the grassy, forgiving terrain, Wolde donned shoes to compete in, and went on to easily defeat the field—beating defending Spanish champion José Azpiroz. Jose Miguel Azkoitia, president of the Mintxeta Atletismo Team, commented on the occasion: "In the 1960s, the thinking was quite narrow—seeing the first African runner [Mamo Wolde] beating the others in Elgoibar was a sensation at the time."

Wolde successfully defended his title the following year, and won again in 1967 and 1968. His four victories in the event quickly made him the winningest individual to take part, and certainly the most prolific from Ethiopia. In addition, Wolde won the Cross de San Sebastian in Spain in 1963, '64, and '67. With previous champions such as Emil Zátopek and Alain Mimoun, victories at the San Sebastian brought further prestige to Wolde's name and exposure for Ethiopia. At the 1968 Olympics in Mexico City, Wolde claimed silver in the 10,000 meters and gold in the marathon.

THE INFLUENCE OF SWEDISH TRAINING

While opportunities to run cross-country in East Africa remained scarce (African athletics expert Geoff Fenwick explained, "In a purely informal way, African cross-country tradition was magnificent. The land was criss-crossed with innumerable trackways created by both animals and men. But very few athletic clubs were open to the general public. Thus, responsibility for cross-country running rested with schools, colleges, military, and quasi-military organizations."), competition in Ethiopia was improved with the international exposure gained by Bikila's marathon victories.

This exposure coincided with the arrival of Swedish coach Onni Niskanen. Niskanen was one of around 600 Swedish citizens who were engaged in the development of Ethiopian society: individuals who were equal parts adventurers and humanitarians. It was an idea born from Ethiopian Emperor Haile Selassie—who, proud of being the head of a nation that remained independent—modernized and asked for help from a neutral Sweden following World War II.

Niskanen, along with ten other compatriots, organized sports following the Swedish model, starting with schools and expanding to the police and military levels. "When we arrived there was not a civilian sports federation, no organizations, no sports grounds and no instructors or leaders," said Niskanen. Ethiopians enjoyed competitions but it took some time before they understood the need for regular training. In the absence of sporting grounds, distance running became the logical starting place. As Niskanen observed, "Running is a lifestyle. Ethiopians are used to running all the time since early childhood." With his commitment, Niskanen was soon named national coach.

Niskanen introduced the Swedish "natural school" methods in Ethiopia. Fartlek in the forests was combined with track sessions (with an emphasis on speed) and long road runs up to 32 kilometers. As Niskanen elaborated:

Cross-country running sessions of 1 to 1.5 hours were part of the daily training for the long distance runners (and it wasn't casual jogging). Pace training, pace training and more pace training. Speed running for 4-500 meters at highest speed, up rather steep slopes, varied with a bit slower running in between. The same thing when it came to track training. Pace! Six to eight 1,500-meter intervals, starting with 4:20 to 4:25, then pressing the times downwards. They also ran on the track for 30–40 minutes, with varied pace: sometimes full speed through the bends, sometimes on the straights. Road running was done twice per week and on distances that were increased day by day. Sauna baths twice a week was included in the training, as well as massage after the road running.

Niskanen eventually moved on to become secretary general of the local Red Cross, but still coached Bikila and Wolde. Fluent in six languages, including Amharic (the national language of Ethiopia), Niskanen was able to solve some of Bikila's training inadequacies: "The dedication, the willpower of this man—there is none like him I have ever seen. Abebe was made by Abebe, not by me or anyone. People asked if he was surprised he won in Rome. He had never run out of the country before. They do not know Abebe. He always expects to win. He does not even know who he is racing against. Clarke, Heatley, Vandendriessche, Edelen? They are just names. Only Mamo he fears, and he defeats Mamo. He has no anxieties."

THE RISE OF KENYA

The situation in Kenya was starker. Colonial influence from the English had left the nation badly segregated: Europeans lived in the European quarter in Nairobi, while the native Africans had settlements on the edge of the city. The schools were separated racially and geographically (European students were given access to European-only schools, which were among the best in the commonwealth), and European students had access to European-style athletic clubs, complete with coaching and equipment from Western nations. For Africans there were no clubs; they relied on programs put together by the colony sports officers. Furthermore, to maintain colonial order, the British believed that they should not prepare Africans to compete against Europeans, lest the Africans forget "their place" in society.

Native Kenyans were not without access to sports, they were just separated from European support. And in the 1950s, track and field was already popular in Kenya. The National Olympic Committee of Kenya was founded in 1955, and they entered their track and field runners in the Summer Olympiad in Melbourne in 1956, with the efforts of a few British organizers helping to lay the groundwork.

As one example, the British Government assigned Arthur "Archie" Evans to be a sports officer for the 70th East African Brigade during the colonial period in Kenya. And after a promotion to the post of Kenya Sports Officer at Jeans School in Kabete, he later became a constituent for the University of Nairobi, specifically to train servicemen. His job description read: "To foster and encourage athletics, sports, games and other physical and recreational activities amongst post-school youth and adults of all races. These include the organization of national sporting

events in collaboration with respective associations and running courses at all levels for active athletes, coaches, and officials."

Evans set about establishing athletics opportunities for native Kenyans with enthusiasm. Grass tracks were laid throughout the country and football pitches measured to the inch. Evans had the first cinder track laid at Jeans School (later the Kenya Institute of Education), which was comparable to what was available in England. Athletics competitions for native Africans emerged. Together, with the help of ex-British retail mogul Derek Erskine, the Kenya Amateur Athletics Association (KAAA) was formed in 1951, which enabled athletes to compete in international competitions, including the British Empire and Commonwealth Games. In 1954, Kenya was represented for the first time in the fifth British Empire and Commonwealth Games, held in Vancouver, Canada.

According to Omulo Okoth, the athletics writer for Kenya's *Standard* newspaper, it was in 1950 that Erskine became involved in the Kenya Amateur Athletics Association, with an appointment to president in 1952 (a post he would hold for thirteen years). "Derek started a campaign in Kenya and England to raise funds to start a national sports stadium," claimed Okoth. "With the aid of funds from the Sir Isaac Wolfson Foundation, he was responsible for the purchase of a piece of land on the Nairobi city boundary which was ideally situated within easy reach of all locations. This was transformed into the 35,000-seat Nyayo National Stadium."

Erskine and Evans, with the help of financial contributions, were able to take a few Kenyan athletes abroad for competition in 1954. Lazaro Chepkwony became the first Kenyan distance runner to race in Europe when he competed in the English Amateur Athletics Association six-mile championship in July. Running barefoot and setting an erratic pace, Chepkwony failed to finish the event—but the following day, in the three-mile event, fellow Kenyan Nyandika Maiyoro featured prominently in a race that saw Chris Chataway break the world record. Maiyoro, defying 1950s European preconceptions that Africans could only ever be sprinters, placed third in 13:54—a Kenyan national record. And after competing internationally, Kenyans began to see the appeal of distance running, especially in improving their quality of life back home.

It wasn't long before Kenya gained its independence in December 1963, and a total shift in authority took place. Sports became a means of developing nationalism and increasing national prestige. The first multiracial school (the Delamare Boys School, which became the Upper Hill School) came to Nairobi, and accommodated an equal number of Europeans, Asians, and Kenyans. Archie Evans departed after fifteen years as Kenyan Sports Officer. In his place came John Velzian, who worked in Nairobi University and helped in the construction of stadiums and playing fields. As a coach in 1965, he took Kenyan athletes to the first-ever African Championships in Congo Brazzaville, which were very successful. When the team returned home, President Kenyatta met the athletes at the airport and led a motorcade all the way to Nairobi. One year later, Velzian returned from the Commonwealth Games in Jamaica with the first Kenyan gold medals. It was a breakthrough for Kenyan athletics and came just two years before the Mexico Olympics.

Omulo Okoth shared the status of Kenyan cross-country running during this period: "Cross-country was very popular among secondary school runners in the 1960s. Kenya used to organize traditional cross-country, whose purpose was to keep athletes busy between the track seasons; it was meant to keep athletes active between October and April." Robert Ouko, an Olympic gold medalist and future Kenyan AAA secretary general, recalled those 1960s cross-country runs: "Cross-country was easy to organize and run. There were only two categories: men and women. We could assemble up to 2,000 runners for a race. It would start at the Kenya Posts and Telecommunications Ngong Road Depot, run around the bushes of Jamhuri Park, Kawangware, and back to the post facility."

"We then introduced it in schools and in disciplined forces: armed forces, Kenya prisons and Kenya police. We placed hurdles and trenches along the route to make it tough," shared Ouko. Together with John Velzian, Ouko approached the Kenyan military to persuade them to accommodate civilian runners at training camps, and shortly thereafter the military began staging races at Ngong racecourse. According to Okoth, the role played by the armed forces was crucial for the development of Kenyan athletics, not just in the staging of the training camps, but also in providing a living wage that allowed many of the runners to train full-time. "Apart from Kipsubai Koskei, who was in Kenya prisons, the rest of the athletes who represented Kenya in the World Cross-Country Championships in the formative years were from the Armed Forces," Okoth stated.

John Velzian helped found the Kenyan Schools Athletics Association (KSAA), which became one of the main sources for athletics talent in the country. The man who took over after him as the national head coach and led the team to the Mexico Olympics was Charles Mukora.

Mukora's name was synonymous with sports. He had the rare experience of having trained as a competitor, coach, promoter, and administrator to the International Olympic Committee (IOC) headquarters in Switzerland. Familiar with the Kenyan national track team, it didn't take long to prepare them for the Olympic Games in Mexico City:

> I selected Nyahururu as the training camp because the altitude was more or less the same as in Mexico . . . Previous to this, the team used to train at Kabete. We stayed at Nyahururu for one month. When I was the coach, I traveled quite a lot with the Kenyan athletes overseas. We were invited to many different countries for friendly competitions. It was very important because the athletes got to know the other strong competitors. They started to learn how they run and how they train.

The training at Nyahururu was quite tough, three sessions a day with a lot of endurance and hill-work. We used a hill called agony hill. The team was selected after the trials. They were the best athletes in the country. Nevertheless we had some people who almost collapsed when they got right to the top of agony hill. People like Kip Keino and Taftali Temu were running up the hill many times. We were running as a team. Tactics already played an important role. If you asked me if I was surprised when Temu and Keino won their medals, I would answer: I was sure that not many people had trained as hard as our athletes.

KIP KEINO: THE FACE OF KENYAN DOMINANCE

Although neither Kenya's first international athlete or Olympic medalist, Kipchoge Keino ranks as one of Kenya's most famous and influential runners. Keino inspired a nation with his international success.

Keino was the first East African to run consistently and successfully in America and Europe. And in the late 1960s he became enormously popular with Western track crowds, as he ran with great personality and flair—not to mention great accomplishment.

First seen on the Olympic stage in 1964, Keino finished fifth in the 5,000 meters in Tokyo, but it was at the 1968 Mexico Olympics in the 1,500-meter event that Keino gained true world recognition. Jim Ryun, record holder in the mile and 1,500 meters, was the favorite for the 1,500-meter gold in Mexico. However, going into the 1968 Olympics Ryun felt he was at a disadvantage: "Always in the back of my mind remained the phantom of Kip Keino, born and bred in the Kenyan highlands which gave Keino an edge in Mexico City's thin air." If Ryun wanted an equalizer he had more than one to choose from—Keino went into the Games with a gall bladder infection, and in the span of eight days he would attempt the 1,500-meter, the 5,000-meter, and the 10,000-meter events.

With stomach pains limiting his performance in the 10,000, and an exhausted finish in the 5,000 that resulted in a silver medal, it was believed Keino would not prevail in the 1,500 against the likes of Ryun. And yet, "How could I go home failing?" Keino asked. Maintaining a world-record pace entering the final lap of the 1,500, *Track and Field News* wrote, "He [Keino] was expected to fall flat on his face at any moment." Ryun was now in full flight, but despite a 54-second final lap the American could not catch Keino, who won by 2.9 seconds. It was Keino's first victory over Ryun. His 3:34.9 clocking was a new Olympic record. It was to be the fastest 1,500 of Keino's career.

Cross-country competition internationally was limited for Keino, as it wasn't his primary focus, though his few victories in cross-country undoubtedly inspired the next generation of Kenyan distance runners. One of his major international cross-country achievements came when he won the 1969 Cinque Mulini in a time of 29:50 over the 9.5-kilometer cross-country course in Italy. At home, Keino also competed in cross-country in the off-season, running the annual Maseno cross-country race, an event that crossed the equator during its course.

When questioned about Kenyan dominance in distance running, Keino had the following to offer: "The Kenyan runner is free of pressure. Whether he wins or loses over here [in Kenya] it does not matter. They develop naturally. In Europe the young runners are told 'win, win' all the time. With no forcing, the athlete enjoys the sport much more. If you have no interest then how can you train hard?"

THE STORY OF STEPHEN MACHOOKA

When Kip Keino defeated Jim Ryun in the 1,500-meter run at the 1968 Olympic Games in Mexico City, it spawned an East African revolution seen in every Olympics, World Championship, and major marathon since. Kenyans became enthralled with becoming world champions. But Stephen Machooka didn't follow that revolution, he led it. The distance runners in the Ivy League witnessed a graceful and effortless Kenyan runner—from far behind—long before Keino's rise.

Born in rural Kenya in 1936, Machooka attended a government-sponsored secondary school where he was coached by Nyandika Maiyoro (seventh in the 5,000 meters in the 1956 Olympics). Under Maiyoro's watch, Machooka ran a 4:15 mile in 1959. After passing the Cambridge School Certificate Examination, and with the help of Cornell graduate assistant Nicholas C. Otieno, Machooka wound up in Cornell's agricultural program. And so, in the fall of 1960, Machooka became the first Kenyan distance runner to take on the United States. And he did so in dramatic style, winning the Heptagonal freshman cross-country race—which included the eight Ivy schools as well as Army and Navy—by a wide margin.

Machooka was even better the following fall when he won six straight races—including a Franklin Park collegiate cross-country course record in Boston—heading into the Heptagonal Championships at Van Cortlandt Park in New York. The windy, 50-degree weather did not affect Machooka as he led all the way, finishing the hilly course 100 yards ahead. With that performance he became the first black athlete to earn first-team All-Ivy status in cross-country and helped Cornell claim a surprising team victory. When asked about his pre-race plan, Machooka replied, "I just run."

That strategy worked again at the Intercollegiate Association of Amateur Athletics of America (IC4A) Championships a few weeks later, when Machooka won by about 60 yards in what remain the worst conditions in meet history. Despite freezing sleet and snow, Machooka claimed victory wearing a blue woolen hat with earflaps and socks on his hands.

At one point in the race, Vic Zwolak of Villanova made a move and passed Machooka. Afterward the five-foot-eleven, 128-pound Machooka said, "I wanted to see how fast Zwolak could run." Within a few hundred yards, Machooka reeled in the future National Collegiate Athletic Association (NCAA) champion and 1964 Olympian, reclaiming the lead. He later said, "It was fun passing him, the whole race was a lot of fun." When asked about the socks on his hands, he told reporters, "I didn't have any gloves."

Zwolak remembered the race quite well. "I was running well my sophomore year," he recalled. "I was one of the favorites in the race, but the ground was a sea of slush and mud. I was a power runner and I didn't run very well in that slush and snow, but my friend described Machooka the best. He said, 'He floated on top of everything.' It was like he had snowshoes. I remember that he was very cordial in victory."

But circumstances changed Machooka's running trajectory. Needing to work to pay his expenses and struggling in his studies, he was urged by an academic advisor to spend less time running and more time with his courses. Thus, Machooka gave up competitive running before his senior year, and graduated in 1964. He was married soon after and returned to Kenya, where he grew corn and kept cattle in Kitale.

Still, the arrival of Stephen Machooka was noteworthy, not only for inspiring his home nation, but also in regard to the role of foreigners in US competition—especially in their eligibility relative to the standard practices within the NCAA and Amateur Athletic Union (AAU) at the time. However, it would be years before eligibility rules were revised and put into place. At issue instead was the very amateur ideal that had perpetuated one hundred years of distance running in the United States to that point.

ORGANIZATIONAL PROBLEMS TRANSFORM AMATEURISM IN THE AAU

Avery Brundage, president of the Amateur Athletic Union in 1928 and president of the International Olympic Committee from 1952 to 1972, was viewed as the "apostle of amateurism." In a speech at an AAU convention, Brundage made his thoughts on the topic clear: "The amateur code, coming to us from antiquity, contributed to and strengthened by the noblest aspirations of great men of each generation, embraces the highest moral laws. No philosophy, no religion, preaches higher sentiments." It was these "high sentiments" that came under scrutiny during the 1960s.

Despite calls for public accountability, the AAU continued to operate under the myth—supported in part by a court ruling against former cross-country champion Wes Santee, and by continued government inaction—that as a private voluntary organization the AAU had no public responsibility to anyone, including the athletes. The group told outspoken athletes that they did not have to belong to the AAU if they opposed its policies. Of course, this meant that the athletes would be ineligible for all international and (most) domestic track or cross-country competitions.

Additionally, despite a thriving underground economy for athletes—with evidence that a good middle-distance runner might earn between $100 and $600 a meet during the American indoor track season—most runners were struggling to get by. *Sports Illustrated* put the financial limitations in perspective: "Track and field is a semi-professional sport; there's not enough money in it to support a professional cadre; there's too much money to expect top amateurs to compete year after year solely for the love of the sport." The economics of the sport in the 1950s could not support a large cohort of truly professional athletes, as distance running simply did not generate enough revenue. Former New York University star Jim Herbert recalled that although he received padded expenses, he "didn't make a living out of it. When I retired I didn't have five dollars in the bank."

Furthermore, the AAU had a difficult and contentious relationship with the NCAA. The conflict first appeared once the NCAA increased its interest in track in the 1920s. But by 1946, the NCAA and AAU had signed the *Articles of Alliance*, an agreement that supported the amateur ethos and kept peace between the two groups for the next fifteen years.

The accord masked continued unhappiness among college coaches, which exploded in the 1960s. NCAA coaches and administrators bristled at the level of control that the AAU had in a number of amateur sports, including track and field. They felt slighted by the AAU's greater presence on the United States Olympic Committee (USOC) and their own absence in international amateur sport organizations. NCAA track coaches remained embittered that a large number of elite track athletes trained on college campuses, traveled on college budgets, and benefited from college athletic facilities and coaches—but AAU officials controlled international competition. College track coaches and NCAA administrators argued that AAU control was dictatorial and its authority undeserved. And by 1960, the collegiate track coaches decided the time had come to challenge the AAU's power.

The long-simmering dissatisfaction of college track coaches led to a highly organized and forceful coup. The NCAA canceled the *Articles of Alliance* in April 1960. Meetings between NCAA and AAU leaders failed to resolve NCAA complaints. Coaches witnessed a high level of athlete dissatisfaction, which included an athlete-led boycott of a 1961 America-Soviet dual meet. And after a final meeting with the AAU in September 1961, the National Collegiate Track Coaches Association (NCTCA) moved ahead with its plan to form a competing track and field organization, the United States Track and Field Federation (USTFF).

THE RISE OF THE USTFF

The college coaches' assault on the AAU began with a well-coordinated media attack. Lengthy articles supporting the

new track and field federation appeared in *Sports Illustrated*, *Track and Field News*, and the *New York Times*. Comments from coaches, like Bill Bowerman (University of Oregon), Bill Easton (University of Kansas), and Don Canham (University of Michigan), focused on issues such as the selection process for tours, control of college athletes, and a lack of representation on AAU committees. Similarly, quotes from athletes addressed their treatment by the AAU, such as accommodations on tour and their low allotted per-diem pay.

In retaliation, the AAU criticized NCAA college scholarships as a breach of amateurism and encouraged international sport organizations to investigate and ban them. European amateur sport organizations had been making similar accusations for years. Yet International Olympic Committee president Avery Brundage argued that if the IOC enforced a recent rule prohibiting athletic scholarships in colleges, it would "disqualify about half of the American Olympic Team." The AAU was stuck between a rock and a hard place: they wanted European organizations to crack down but didn't want to compromise American Olympic opportunities.

The AAU had always been willing to make modest compromises, but this time they failed to alter the NCAA's opposition. In July 1962, NCAA college track coaches formed the United States Track and Field Federation (USTFF), which was only nominally independent of the NCAA. This signaled the beginning of a bitter battle for control of track and field—one that left athletes subject to mistreatment from both groups—with the federal government exasperated by the inability of the governing bodies to resolve their differences.

On November 22, 1962, the first US National Cross-Country Championship of the USTFF was held at the Ohio State Golf Course in Columbus. The University of Houston Track Club, the same group that had won the previous three AAU team titles, were victorious at this inaugural event.

The strategies of the two organizations remained clear and steadfast: the AAU would not participate in the creation of a new organization, nor would it voluntarily give up its power that rested in its International Amateur Athletics Federations (IAAF) sanction. Meanwhile, the IAAF strongly supported the AAU, calling the USTFF an "outlaw organization." Between the 1961 and the 1968 Olympic Games, little changed in distribution. The AAU ruled, the USTFF opposed, and the athletes suffered.

THE ROAD RUNNERS CLUB OF AMERICA

In the late 1950s, away from elite distance runners and the administration for control, jogging for health, fitness, and recreation by the public was practically unheard of. Competitive long-distance running was an official Olympic sport and popularized in America by colleges and the AAU, but with the exception of a few races in New England and on the West Coast, there were very few distance racing events in the United States available for the casual runner.

Aware of this void, Olympian and cross-country champion Browning Ross proposed a new development for American distance runners in 1957. In a landmark move, Ross modeled his concept after the Road Runners Club of the United Kingdom (founded 1952), whose members included runners, officials, race sponsors, and coaches. Ross envisioned a group that would encourage running, meet regularly, raise funds, coordinate schedules, recruit sponsors, and promote competition. Response to the concept was positive; meetings were held in December, and by February 22, 1958, the Road Runners Club of America (RRCA) was born.

The beginning saw tough days for the RRCA. Instead of recognizing the good work the RRCA was doing to promote distance running, the AAU refused to admit the RRCA as a member club and took the position that the RRCA was illegal. Meanwhile, the USTFF took the damaging steps of prohibiting several of its affiliate universities from letting RRCA member clubs use their tracks. The RRCA, trying only to promote long-distance running, was caught in the middle. In 1963, the RRCA went on record as favoring the removal of the AAU age requirements for racing, as well as medical requirements and air temperature limits for races. By the end of the RRCA's third year, their members had hosted over 600 races around the country and raised funds for elite athletes to compete abroad. The RRCA also voted to assist track and field committees in sponsoring long-distance races for women.

Further helping the sport independently, by 1964, the RRCA Standards Committee began certifying accurately measured courses, and awarded certificates to runners that met benchmarks. While the program was slow to catch on, it formed the basis for modern day course certification. (The USATF certifies courses today, though the original process was developed and implemented by the RRCA.) And in the fall of 1965, the RRCA held its first National Women's Cross-Country Championship at 2.5 miles, despite significant objection by the AAU.

AMERICAN WOMEN RUN CROSS-COUNTRY

The Road Runners Club of America faced considerable objection by the AAU because female competitors in the United States had just been afforded the opportunity to compete in official cross-country meets, and the AAU wanted control. The AAU, spurred by its recent challenges by the USTFF and others, felt it could appease some of the charges by instituting long-distance competition for women. But the AAU wasn't solely responsible. Outside nations had already implemented female competition in cross-country, with a growing list of nations also sanctioning competition around the same time as the United States (Finland in 1955, Australia in 1960, South Africa and Canada in 1963, Sweden in 1965). And as a result, the United States, feeling the pressure from these outside nations, and boosted from the acceptance of female athletes in the president's national fitness program, saw the number of

female track clubs that offered cross-country rise from a sporadic oddity to well into the hundreds.

Integration was slow, however, as every major regional and national championship for female competitors was contested away from the men's equivalent; it wouldn't be until 1979 that both men and women would compete at the same site on the same day for the National Cross-Country Championship. Yet, at a time when the 800-meter run had been recently reintroduced to female competition (which occurred in 1960, though longer distances were still unavailable to women at the track) the opportunities to race across country proved to be a welcome addition for female competitors. Distances for cross-country races for women typically ranged from just over a mile in length to two miles—although these would expand as time went on.

November 28, 1964, marked a monumental milestone in female distance running with the debut of teenager Marie Mulder. Winner of the inaugural AAU US Women's Cross-Country Championship at the age of fourteen, Mulder went on to be the American record holder in the 800 meters and the AAU champion at 1,500 meters. At this first Women's Cross-Country Championship, held in Seattle, Washington, Mulder won the two-kilometer event in 6:51.

The second annual AAU US Women's Cross-Country Championship saw its first compelling drama when 60 women competed over a 1.5-mile course in Cambridge, Massachusetts. Julia Brand (who had won the South Atlantic AAU Women's Championship the week prior) battled Marie Mulder for the lead early in the race. When Mulder injured her ankle and was forced out of the race at the mile mark, Brand took the lead and held it until the last 500 meters. At that point, Sandra Knott, a twenty-six-year-old registered nurse, sprinted past for the win (Julia Brand eventually finished in fourth, 15 seconds later). Despite the driving rain, mud, and hills, Sandra Knott was not as much a surprise as some expected: she had competed internationally for the United States many times in the 880-yard run to that point, and had won the Ohio Track Club's cross-country championship the week prior.

Marie Mulder would have a chance to exact revenge. The following year in St. Louis, with an expanded field, Mulder was healthy and eyeing her second championship in three years. However, her effort was for naught, as Doris Brown Heritage, an unassuming physical education teacher from Seattle, ran the fastest time for the 1.5-mile course. Heritage, then twenty-four years old, built a lead of 50 yards at the half-mile mark and extended it to 200 yards by the finish. Mulder placed second, while Sandra Knott finished 10th and promptly declared her retirement.

By the end of the decade, *Sports Illustrated* spoke of the AAU women's championship and Doris Brown Heritage in hallowed terms: "Women's cross-country is both crowded and in. Five years ago, at the second AAU championships, there were 40 entrants. Last weekend there were 542." Doris Brown Heritage had won three titles in four years (Seattle Pacific teammate and Canadian National Cross-Country champion Vicki Foltz won in 1967 when

Heritage was suffering from a pulled hamstring). Heritage also claimed the Canadian National Cross-Country title in 1969. "She says she loves the hills, the trees, the grass," *Sport's Illustrated* wrote. "She'd broken an arch, trained right through a case of mononucleosis, smashed a finger running in the dark and won a race while one arm was in a sling because of an injured shoulder. She endures, and she is handsomely feminine." "The femininity issue always comes up," Heritage said, "and I tell people I do not know any girl running who is not feminine."

DORIS BROWN HERITAGE

As a young girl, Doris Severtson liked nothing better than to run freely along the beach in front of her family home in Gig Harbor, Washington, or through the woods nearby. It wasn't training or racing, it was just running for the simple joy of movement and the love of her surroundings. Severtson (who would soon be known by her married name, Doris Brown Heritage) first began competing at the age of fifteen when, as a member of Tacoma's small Mic Mac Club, she set a national 440-yard-dash record for women. And as an undergrad at Seattle Pacific College the school had no women's track team—only a handful in the United States did at the time—so Heritage talked with the men's coach and began training with his runners. "I tried to do their workouts and really didn't run so well during that time," she recalled. It wasn't a case of too many miles but rather that Heritage was running all-out nearly every day. "It never occurred to me," she admitted, "that working two jobs, and being in band and orchestra, and trying to be a student was a little much."

Heritage's approach changed once she teamed up with Dr. Ken Foreman, founder of the Falcon Track Club, a team open to area girls and women. Foreman, however, had no experience with a female athlete of Heritage's caliber: "We were both kind of naïve. My professional training as a sports scientist led me to believe that women just simply wouldn't hold up, but Doris taught me she could do anything the men did."

A broken foot kept Heritage off the 1964 Olympic Team, but that winter she and Foreman continued to fine-tune her training. It was then that Heritage began running daily in the morning: "I heard Jim Ryun was running twice a day," she recalled. "And I thought 'Oh, that sounds good.' Right from the beginning it really worked for me; even my hundred meter time improved." But more than that, the morning runs were spiritually rewarding. "My philosophy became that what you do in the morning is for yourself as a human being, and what you do in the afternoon is as an athlete." Within two years, Heritage would win her first of five national titles in cross-country.

A fortuitous development for Heritage was the staging of the first official Women's International Cross-Country Championship in 1967, which was held on a cold and windy March afternoon outside the coastal Welsh town of Barry. After racing the three-mile course through muddy athletic fields and cow pastures, Heritage entered the quarter-mile homestretch alone. The best European harriers were nearly 200 meters back when Heritage crossed the finish, the first of five consecutive victories in the event. "To win that, because it was the first world championship for women, was a pretty awesome experience," Heritage said. "I remember the feeling—I can see it and taste it and smell it—but I don't know how to put it into words."

More than her victory, Heritage valued the entire experience and what the event held for the future of women's distance running. "I had a feeling," she recalled, "that my winning would make a difference to the AAU, that maybe the US women would get to have a team the next year." Indeed, in 1968 the AAU did send a women's team to the meet. Heritage won again, Falcon teammate Vicki Foltz finished second, and the United States defeated England by a single point. The downside was that everyone had to pay their own way to the competition; but from 1967 onward cross-country was Heritage's training focus. She and Foreman had become an efficient team, and the work Heritage put in dumbfounded most of her contemporaries, male and female alike. "Once," said Foreman, "we were riding in a bus with Gaston Roelants and Mohammed Gammoudi [both world cross-country champions], and they were blown away to hear she had run 125 miles the week before. Even they weren't doing that much." But at this stage, Heritage wasn't the only one making headlines in the Pacific Northwest. A rare opportunity for collegiate fame opened up for an unlikely team and star pupil: the Oregon State Beavers and runner Dale Story.

BAREFOOT DALE STORY CAPTURES THE NCAA CROWN

Dale Story, raised in Orange, California, was an outdoorsman. As a boy, Story loved to run, and he would frolic in the playgrounds of Southern California twelve months of the year, sans shirt, sans shoes. But Story disliked school, and he came from a broken home. In the spring of his sophomore year of high school, not long after running a 4:32 mile, he was ready to give it up. "I had it all figured out," Story said. "Had a thousand rounds of ammunition and a .22. Was going to go up the east side of the Sierras and go to Alaska." A counselor he respected talked him out of it. He stayed, made passing grades and, as a five-foot-eight, 140-pound senior, lowered Dyrol Burleson's national high school mile record, finishing in 4:11.

After a year at Santa Ana Junior College, where he set a world junior record in the two-mile run and won state cross-country and two-mile titles, Story opted for Sam Bell and Oregon State, primarily because the school offered a fishing and wildlife major. Bell, who coached several Olympic distance runners, including Bob Kennedy and Jim Spivey, considered Story "the best physical talent [he] ever coached." At Oregon State, Story established school records at every distance longer than a mile in track and set 13 course or meet records in cross-country. His only national title was at East Lansing, Michigan, on a cold Monday, November 27, 1961. Story beat Billy Mills, Tom

O'Hara, and Australian Olympians Pat Clohessy and Al Lawrence, among others, in 30-degree weather—running barefoot. The Beavers also won the team title. Forty years later, it remains the only national team title in the school's history.

Oregon State entered the national cross-country meet that year on a lark. With no qualifying events, Coach Bell felt he ought to enter his team in the NCAA meet after winning a meet in British Columbia in late October. Athletic Director Spec Keene gave Bell approval with one provision—he could take only five runners.

When the Beavers went for their practice run, Story ran barefoot. Competitors from the far reaches of the country thought he lost his mind. But when the gun went off on the day of the race, Story started fast and took the lead just before the halfway point. "I took a hill about three-quarters of a mile away, and I felt really strong then," Story said. He won by 40 yards, and his teammates followed. Rich Cuddihy was 12th, Bill Boyd 16th, and Cliff Thompson 25th. Then came Jerry Brady, limping home in 51st. "Jerry pulled a muscle at the two-mile point, but he knew he had to finish," Bell said. "If he hadn't, we wouldn't have won."

The Beavers were national champions. And fittingly, at that 1961 NCAA Championship, Oregon State had beaten another unheralded West Coast school, the San Jose State Spartans, for the title.

SAN JOSE STATE'S HISTORIC FEET

San Jose State was in big trouble. The team, unbeaten all season, had come into the 1962 NCAA Cross-Country Championships expecting to win, but 70 runners had breezed by head coach Dean Miller at the mile mark without a Spartan among them. That's when Ron Davis, Danny Murphy, Ben Tucker, Horace Whitehead, and Jeff Fishback looked at each other and said, "We gotta go."

On November 26, 1962, at the 24th annual NCAA Cross-Country Championship, this collection of speedy Spartans became the first integrated team to win the title. As incredible as it was then, the feat may be even more remarkable upon reflection, given the racially charged atmosphere amid a civil rights movement that was dividing the country. For black runners Davis, Tucker, and Whitehead, it was the light at the end of a lengthy and uncomfortable tunnel. "It was always believed that blacks couldn't run anything over 400 meters," Davis said. "What we did was a major surprise to the country."

"The stereotype had to do with sprints being considered a pure burst of speed in which there's no strategy or discipline involved," Tucker said of the prejudiced claim. "It's the same thing that fuels the 'Blacks can't be quarterbacks' kind of thinking. It was based on—incorrectly of course—intellectual inferiority and discipline and being able to hang tough." Davis, who made varsity as a freshman, and Tucker, who excelled in cross-country, finished the 1962 race sixth and 18th, respectively. Whitehead was 30th. The Spartans broke the NCAA record by 39 seconds

and beat perennial power Villanova by 11 points. But the win was far from a foregone conclusion.

"In 1960, we were probably one of the worst cross-country teams in America," Davis said. "We would compete at Stanford—they had a long hill on their golf course—and we would end up walking up that hill." But legendary coaches Bud Winter, who built the San Jose State track dynasty from 1940 through 1970, and Dean Miller, who had plenty of experience and was known for his extraordinary training techniques, knew how to motivate their athletes. After a full summer of workouts, Davis and his teammates weren't walking up the Stanford hill anymore. They finished second at the 1961 NCAA Cross-Country Championship to Oregon State—the first in which San Jose State had ever participated. And by 1962, the Spartans were firing on all cylinders. "We have Mount Hamilton out here in San Jose," Davis said. "We used [to] go to the 19-mile sign and try to run all the way up to the observatory—and the last seven miles were brutal. The first two times we didn't make it, but the third time we told Coach Miller to meet us at the top. And when we got there we all agreed that we were going to win that NCAA championship."

Danny Murphy, a record-breaking two-miler, was the first piece of the puzzle. But despite the 80 or so runners who tried out for the Spartans's track team in 1961, Murphy wasn't impressed with the team's chances until he started noticing guys like Davis, Tucker, and Whitehead, whose strides were smooth and fluid. "We trained for about a week, and these guys are staying with me," said Murphy, who was accustomed to blowing away both high schoolers and collegians. "Where did Bud and Dean find them? I was 11th nationally as a high school junior and now these guys are hanging with me." And Murphy didn't care what color they were. He just wanted the team to win. "There wasn't even a hint of anything racial as far as the guys on the team were concerned," he said. "I mean, you gotta be cool with it when the guy's ahead of you."

Outside the team cocoon, though, it could be nasty. Davis, Tucker, and Whitehead struggled just to find off-campus housing. And long training runs made Tucker especially nervous. Passersby frequently snarled racial slurs from their cars and tossed beer cans at them. "For me, it was startling because I had come from San Francisco, which was a pretty liberal town," Tucker said. "Sometimes you'd get separated on those long runs, so maybe you'd end up by yourself, or maybe two black guys, or one black guy and one white guy. But we often got some kind of blowback. It made me uneasy and I felt vulnerable. Things were boiling up in the South—black folks were getting shot and lynched, and I started thinking, 'Oh my God, I don't want to get shot on one of these lonely roads.'"

The trio persevered as a group. "It was the 1960s; that's just was the way it was," Tucker said. "As long as nobody confronted or physically challenged us, we would just ignore it. We didn't let it bother us—we couldn't let it bother us. We had a goal, and that wasn't going to knock us off course." They hid their fears so well that white teammates Murphy and Fishback weren't really aware there was an issue.

Coach Dean Miller wasn't buying any of the prejudiced jargon, either. When he showed up at San Jose State and started recruiting black athletes, he got some push-back of his own. People would tell him, "Well, you have to be careful not to get too many blacks because you're going to have problems." Miller's response was consistent: "I would always say, 'I don't care if they're black, white, striped, or polka dot. All I'm interested in is how fast they can run, how far they can run, and whether they're willing to commit physically and mentally to being a champion.' I think we set a precedent. Once I got an athlete on the team, we were a team—that's always how I treated it."

East Lansing, Michigan, the city featuring dark-green Spartans, was where the 1962 NCAA Cross-Country Championship was staged. Miller's team had been runners-up in 1961 and weren't keen on repeating that finish. But a number of obstacles had to be overcome. First, the runners didn't plan for the elements. Most of the San Jose State guys just had their singlets to stave off the 30-degree chill. "We were freezing," Tucker said. "We put analgesic balm on just to get warm." To make matters worse, Jeff Fishback had been ill much of the previous week and was in bad shape on race day. He would gallantly finish 17th and score valuable points for the team, but he was unable to stand up for about 90 minutes afterward. Miller said an average runner never would have finished.

Then there was the starting draw: San Jose State ended up on the far right of a starting line that pointed the 300 runners toward the course's first turn—a 90-degree left just a quarter mile away. Miller told his runners to get out in front, but they didn't. Murphy said they couldn't: from where San Jose State was lined up on the far end, the Spartans ended up running about 30 yards farther than most of their competitors to reach the first turn. "I ran a 59 quarter and still ended up second-to-last at that turn, along with my whole team. We were dead at the back of 300 runners," Murphy said. After that came the grueling task of working through the pack, veering sideways at various speeds—expending energy they would later need—to avoid runners the Spartans knew they should have dusted.

Most of the San Jose squad emerged from the pack just after the first mile, and the leaders loomed about 200 yards ahead of them. "I caught Ben Tucker and told him to lock on," Murphy said. Murphy reeled in front-runner Tom O'Hara of Loyola Chicago with about a half mile to go, but O'Hara outlasted him, as did Villanova's Pat Traynor. The *New York Times* wrote: "The trio ran neck and neck for about 440 yards. Then Murphy, a 120-pounder who looks more like a high school sophomore, started to drop back. From there, O'Hara and Traynor put on a stirring duel." Murphy finished third, less than 12 seconds off the winning pace. Davis came in sixth, about 13 seconds behind Murphy. Fishback and Tucker were just a second apart in 17th and 18th, respectively. Whitehead was the other contributor to the Spartans's total. "It turned out to be a remarkable accomplishment," Murphy said. "You

put any other team at the back of the pack at that turn and see how many could rally to win the meet. Nobody could've done that."

"We helped change society's perceptions of black athletes," said Davis, who had posted the fastest time a black runner had ever run on the Michigan State course. Their names were in all the national newspapers and on various television stations. The squad got a hero's welcome upon returning to campus. "Looking back, that experience taught us about life, about getting to know people, and about working hard for accomplishments," Davis said. "We were young athletes who struggled in high school to be good enough to receive a scholarship. We were fortunate that all three of us ended up at San Jose State and were recruited not for our color but for our ability."

REPEATING AFTER A TRAGEDY

If 1962 was special for Ben Tucker, 1963 may have been even more so. Teammates Ron Davis and Horace Whitehead had graduated, but Tucker (along with 1962 runners Danny Murphy and Jeff Fishback) got to experience the repeat, although it came under the most unusual circumstances. The 1963 championship was scheduled for Monday, November 25, but it was delayed. It could have been canceled altogether given what the country was going through.

President John F. Kennedy had been assassinated the Friday before. The NCAA decided to have the championship but rescheduled it to accommodate Kennedy's funeral on Monday. Tucker recalled that the situation was tense. "The country was reeling; all of our parents wanted us to stay home. 'There's no reason to be on the road,' they said; 'We don't know what's going on; the Russians are going to invade.'"

The situation worsened that Sunday. After the Spartans went for a run to familiarize themselves with the course, they returned to the hotel to find everyone crowded around the TV. "Lee Harvey Oswald had just been shot," Tucker said of the historic moment when Jack Ruby walked into the basement of the Dallas Police Headquarters and cut down Kennedy's assassin. "And we were like, 'Oh my God, the world is collapsing.'"

Tucker said that's when Coach Dean Miller huddled the runners and told them: "Up to your rooms, gentlemen." The rooms had no TVs, only radio. "But Dean told us not to turn on the radio," Tucker said. "He said, 'Block all of that out. You've got a mission in two days. After that, you can tune in to what's going on. Tonight is not the time for you to be doing that. America is still here; it will be standing there when you're done. Don't worry about it.'"

It was tough for Tucker not to worry about it. "I was very politically aware," he said. "I was aware of the social conscience of the world at the time; I knew about the Cuban Missile Crisis; I was into political science and history; I knew about the civil rights movement. So for me to shut all of the Kennedy stuff down was a major challenge, but I did." When Tuesday finally came, Tucker finished the championship in eighth place. Fishback and Murphy were third and fifth, respectively. The Spartans beat second-place Oregon by 15 points to complete a remarkable three years of NCAA Championship competition.

THE UNIVERSITY OF KANSAS HOSTS THE NCAA CROSS-COUNTRY CHAMPIONSHIP

Although the National Collegiate Cross-Country Coaches Association (NCCCCA) voted on twenty-four consecutive occasions to award the subsequent year's NCAA Cross-Country Championship to Michigan State, discussion about alternative venues occurred at least eleven times before the decision was made in 1964 to move the meet for the following year. By then, the college championship was truly national in scope and there was widely expressed opinion that regional fairness necessitated the meet be rotated (the vote was seventeen in favor and sixteen opposed to move the 1965 NCAA Championship to the University of Kansas in Lawrence. A subsequent motion also passed, recommending that the Championship "not be held in any NCAA district more than two consecutive years").

The 1965 edition also saw the racing distance increase from four miles to six miles, and Kansas's own John Lawson (the course record holder) had to hold off Doug Brown of Montana (1965 NCAA three- and six-mile champion) in a stirring duel, where both men crossed in 14:14 for three miles, a stunning 4:44 per-mile average. At mile five Brown faltered (and failed to finish). Lawson won in 24:43, and each of the top eight finishers came in under Lawson's former course best.

Less than a week later, Doug Brown had his opportunity for redemption against Lawson. In the fourth annual United States Track and Field Federation (USTFF) Cross-Country Championship, held on November 25 (merely four days after the NCAA Championship), representatives from club teams and colleges from around the nation met to race on a six-mile Echo Hills Golf Course in Wichita. Included were not only Brown and Lawson from the NCAA Championship, but Olympic miler Jim Ryun and Olympic 5,000-meter runner Oscar Moore from New York (running at that time for Southern Illinois University).

In one of the fastest performances of the season, Lawson took the race from the gun, winning in a time of 28:50, a pace of 4:48 per mile; in second came Oscar Moore, more than 30 seconds later; failing to exact revenge was Doug Brown, who came in third; and coming in fourth was Jim Ryun in 30:05—in one of the longest races of his career.

JIM RYUN: WORLD-CLASS CROSS-COUNTRY RUNNER

By 1965 Jim Ryun's name was well known internationally. At the age of eighteen, Ryun had qualified for the Olympic 1,500 meters in Tokyo and had broken four minutes in the mile. But lesser known was Ryun's prowess as a cross-country runner. During his junior year of high school in 1963 he

went undefeated, winning the Kansas State High School Class AA title in 9:22 over two miles in Emporia (a new course record). That same season he competed in a local AAU Junior four-mile cross-country meet, where he finished third behind two college freshmen.

After returning from the 1964 Olympic Games, Ryun again won the Class AA title at the Kansas State Cross-Country Championship as a senior. This time his efforts not only produced another course record—winning with a time of 9:08, which lowered the previous mark by 38 seconds—but also helped his school, Wichita East, to win their fifth state title in cross-country.

And while the 10-kilometer distance at Echo Hills the following autumn was not Ryun's premier event, it spoke volumes about his range as a collegiate freshman. He set world records in the mile and the half-mile on the track that spring, and received *Sports Illustrated's* "Sportsman of the Year" award and the James E. Sullivan Award as the nation's top amateur athlete. Plus, it wasn't the only time Ryun ran cross-country that fall.

The USTFF National Championship saw Ryun finish fourth, while two weeks prior Ryun had finished second overall in the USTFF Midwest qualifier. Ryun's time, a stellar 30:29, saw him finish 150 yards behind winner Pat McMahon, a well-known Irish runner who competed for Oklahoma Baptist University. The weekend of the USTFF National Cross-Country Championship McMahon was in Omaha, Nebraska, winning the 10th annual NAIA Cross-Country Championship—contested in snowy conditions in freezing 32-degree weather.

It was clear that cross-country championships at all levels were beginning to flourish in the United States during the 1960s. In England, however, the adaptation of new governing bodies was making it difficult to keep momentum going for cross-country championships at the college and university level. Oxford and Cambridge were two standouts that upheld the tradition—but they were not alone.

THE BRITISH UNIVERSITIES CHAMPIONSHIP

For college and university men in England during the early years of the twentieth century, most cross-country competition was on an invitational basis. While Oxford and Cambridge maintained their dual-meet rivalry, running a 12-kilometer course annually—save for the war years—most institutions affiliated themselves with the Universities Athletic Union (UAU), established in 1930, which was restricted to English and Welsh Universities (excluding Cambridge and Oxford).

The UAU was the driving force behind all student sport activities in Britain until the 1950s. It controlled student participation in the World University Games (for track and field) until 1952, when the British Universities Sports Board (BUSB) was formed to manage Britain's student representation at an international level. By 1962 however, the British Universities Sports Federation (BUSF) replaced the British Universities Sports Board, and membership exploded: the BUSF was open to all universities in the UK and University Colleges of Wales, as well as the Scottish Universities Sports Federation, the University of Wales Athletic Union, and the Northern Ireland Universities Sports Committee.

In 1964, the first BUSF British Universities Cross-Country Championships were held in Nottingham. It was there that Fergus Murray, a member of the Scottish Dundee Hawkhill Harriers in his second year at Edinburgh University, and Mike Turner, an international cross-country stalwart and president of Cambridge University's cross-country team, both crossed the line in the identical time of 31:19. Each runner alternated victories in the following two years.

And while Mike Turner and Fergus Murray were most famous for their crossing the line together as university students, each went on to also represent their country at the International Cross-Country Championship, the sport's most prestigious proving ground.

THE INTERNATIONAL BECOMES A WORLDWIDE EVENT

The International Cross-Country Championships during the 1960s showcased the world's best distance running talent. Morocco, England, Spain, Belgium, France, and Tunisia all featured individual champions in the men's senior event over the course of the decade, while Wales, Ireland, Scotland, New Zealand, and the United States each had representation on the podium. A junior men's event featuring athletes twenty-one years of age or younger was officially held for the first time in 1961, and women had an opportunity to run in their own official race in 1967. The International Cross-Country Union expanded its membership of official teams by affiliating with the IAAF in 1958, and featured an invitation rota for nations such as Canada, the United States, South Africa, and New Zealand.

In March 1960, Morocco's Rhadi Ben Abdesselam became the 47th winner of the International Cross-Country Championships, beating Belgium's Gaston Roelants by 40 yards. According to the *Glasgow Herald*: "Roelants made the pace almost throughout, with the lanky, long-striding Moroccan close behind him. It was clear after 2-miles that this pair were going to be out on their own and they drew steadily away from the rest of the field." Abdesselam was also the reigning national cross-country champion for both Morocco and France in 1960. Eight countries were represented at the International, with England claiming team honors for the third year in a row.

Belgium rose to the fore in 1961 and '62, with a team title in 1961 and the top two finishers with Gaston Roelants and Marcel VandeWattyne in 1962. An unofficial count saw the participation of 126 athletes from 10 countries for the 1962 championship, including an appearance by South Africa for the first time.

In 1963, the 50th running of the event, the distance of the men's race was reduced from the traditional nine miles (14.5 kilometers) to 7.5 miles (12.1 kilometers). Roy Fowler of England edged out Gaston Roelants for the individual title. Belgium won the team title with 110 points while England and France tied for second place with 113. A total of 125 athletes competed from 11 countries, including Switzerland, which returned for the first time since 1960, and Portugal, in their first appearance since 1959.

In 1964, Francisco Aritmendi became the first Spaniard to win the International, and, in 1965, Algeria, New Zealand, and West Germany appeared for the first time. At the 1966 International, Ben Assou El Ghazi became the second individual champion to represent Morocco. Ireland's Derek Graham crossed the line next, and Tracy Smith from the United States claimed a third-overall finish, beating such greats as Roy Fowler of England, Michel Jazy of France, and Ron Hill. The unheralded Americans placed a respectable fifth as a team, resulting in astonishment among tough Europeans at how well the "soft" Americans performed. A total of 134 athletes participated from 15 countries.

The 1967 International saw the first official women's competition. Doris Brown Heritage covered the 1.9-mile (three-kilometer) course in 14:28. Rita Lincoln of England was second. For the men's senior event, Gaston Roelants of Belgium won his second individual title. The *Glasgow Herald* was able to lend a unique perspective on Roelants's preparation: "Roelants may have appeared casual at the finish of the race, but the nervous energy he consumed during the two days before it was enormous. His face was often drawn. He could not sit still in his hotel. He paced Barry's pebbly beach for hours on end. He trained four times a day. And the cause of it all, he said, was the threat [of] England's Taylor and Scotland's McCafferty. The Belgian need not have troubled: Taylor's light burned all too brightly at the start, and he soon ran out of wick. McCafferty, who led Roelants for the first three miles, chose the wrong spot at the water jump, landed awkwardly, and rolled over in retirement as dozens of pairs of spikes flitted over his body."

After an unremarkable 1968 performance, at the 1969 International, Gaston Roelants joined elite company when he won the event for the third time. The *Glasgow Herald* described the event: "Gaston Roelants, as cocksure a sportsman as you could meet, joined the select band of runners who have won the International Cross-Country title three times when he defeated a field of about 120 on Saturday at Dalmuir Park, Clydebank. Perhaps 'defeated' is less suitable a word than 'demolished' to describe the win." Dave Bedford, John Bednarski, and John Harrison, all representing England, finished one-two-three for the junior men's race, the first time a perfect score had ever been achieved for the event. A total of 193 athletes from 14 countries participated, the largest attendance in the history of the event, and Canada appeared at the International for the first time.

GASTON ROELANTS: PREMIER INTERNATIONAL CROSS-COUNTRY CONTENDER

Throughout the 1960s, no runner stood out more in the International Cross-Country Championships than Belgium's Gaston Roelants. Marc Bloom described him as "the quintessential cross-country runner. Bearded, with longish, flowing hair, his face shows lines of wisdom and experience. He looks the adventurer, the cautious but self-assured explorer. One expects to find him appearing in a late-night movie cresting a mountain ledge, imploring a rash companion to wait for the storm to break before ascending the peak. But Hollywood, he's not. Roelants knows his mission and he reaches it without fanfare." Others gave this description: "Roelants is the swashbuckling adventurer of the track, an impression heightened by the trim goatee beard he sports." Regardless of his appearance, one thing was clear: when Roelants raced across country, he raced to win.

For the ten International Championships of the 1960s, Roelants finished in first place three times and was runner-up twice. Raised near the town of Louvain, Belgium, where his father was a farmer, Roelants was interested in sports from an early age. Initially admonished when he sought to pursue bicycling as a teenager, Roelants turned to running instead.

He began training seriously by the age of seventeen. In his first year as a junior in cross-country in 1955, at the age of eighteen, he finished fifth at the Belgian National in the junior race. The next year he improved to third. In 1958, running in the senior championships for the first time, he finished 11th, but he had been handicapped by a sore throat. He won in 1959, and would claim 11 total titles over the next fourteen years.

Roelants began working with Coach Edmond Van Den Eynde, a teacher at the Catholic University of Louvain, in 1960. While Eynde applied timing intervals and splits, much of the technique with Roelants also consisted of work with hurdles. On a typical weekday, Roelants ran 15 kilometers (9.3 miles) in the morning through the beech and oak forest of Zoete Waters, and would then do a session of repeat 400-meter sprints on the track in the afternoon. His route through the woods covered 1,700 meters a lap, sometimes along dirt roads, sometimes following a narrow path that was once used for motorcycle races, which dipped into deep culverts in places, then climbed steeply out of them. It was a strenuous routine and Roelants continued to get stronger as he gained experience.

To go with his three victories and two runner-up finishes in the International, Roelants won 10 Belgian National Cross-Country titles by 1970; the Cinque Mulini Cross-Country in Italy in 1968; the Cross Hannut seven times by 1972; the Primus Haacht Veldloop in Wespelaar Belgium in 1959, '68, and '69; and the Cross der Vlaanderen in Ronse, Belgium, in 1960, '61, and '62. This consistency in international-caliber fields allowed Roelants to achieve success on the track, the roads, and across country every year he competed, enshrining him as one of the world's best.

BRITISH INDIVIDUAL DOMINANCE

But while the International welcomed a plethora of new nations and individual talent, England remained the most successful, winning the team title eight times in the 1960s. Their dominance was due to their superior teamwork and consistency, along with their primary motivation that it was a cultural expectation that England perform at the highest level on the biggest stage. The strongest distance runners of the time felt it was their duty to excel in the International (an event England founded, after all); and save for two occasions when Belgium narrowly persevered, England was able to follow through with this promise.

National talent was extensive, but in England's National Cross-Country Championship only six different individuals won the title during the 1960s, with three runners—Basil Heatley, Melvyn Batty, and Ron Hill—winning it two times or more, each earning the right to represent England during the International—and each finding themselves on the podium there against the world's best.

BASIL HEATLEY STARTS THE DECADE RIGHT

Born in 1933, and raised on a farm not far from Coventry in the Midlands of England, Basil Heatley was hooked on running by the age of fifteen. At grammar school, he was considered "not brawny enough" to play rugby, but soon found success in cross-country competition: "My first national was the Youths, where I was third. The first time I put on a [Coventry] Godiva vest, I won the Warwickshire. And the next time I put it on I won the Midland. The next year I was third in the English Youths again. So it was a good start. At that time I might have been training more than many other youths. But then came an up-and-down period when it depended on what work I was doing at home on the farm." It is interesting to note how Heatley wound up at the club team Coventry Godiva, which set him on his path to athletic greatness: "I was told I should go down to run in a novices race which I won and no sooner had I got my breath back an official of the club quickly gave me a form to sign on."

As a junior, he continued to excel in cross-country, placing third, 10th, fourth, and ninth in the English Junior Nationals in successive years. And after a stint in the military service, he saw his senior career take off in the cross-country season of 1957. Heatley won the Warwickshire and Midlands titles and then ran brilliantly in the Nationals, where he was up with the leaders for most of the race and finished a surprising fifth, just 24 seconds behind winner Frank Sando. "I was a young man full of go and almost with a one-tracked mind," explained Heatley. This run was no flash in the pan and he ran even better in the International, finishing second, just 11 seconds behind Sando: "The Belgian race suited me because there were a number of obstacles—ditches and fences. I won't go so far as to say I should have won, but I should have been much closer to Frank. I was that overawed at being up there.

I did lead for a considerable time, then Frank came up to me and by me, which I think was due to his greater experience. He was a very intelligent runner."

In 1960 Heatley placed first in the English National, and won again in 1961 before going on to win the International in France—his only win in that prestigious race. "That was probably one of my best runs," he recalled. "Again it was hurdles on a racecourse. The hurdles were quite high, and I was running against Roelants, the steeplechaser. Gaston was hurdling correctly; I wasn't. I put two hands on top and vaulted. I think that hurdling cost him the race: in trying to look good, he expended too much energy. We also had a steep hill in the race. All the Brits called it Heatley's Hill because I was able to break him going up the hill." The *Times* reported that Heatley ran "with courage and perfect judgment" to win by a margin of 24 seconds over Roelants.

Heatley was the heir apparent to Frank Sando in cross-country running and wore his crown with distinction in the early 1960s. But three national titles (Heatley would earn his third in Cambridge mud in 1963) and one International title don't tell half his story. Apart from regular wins in the Midlands, he had seven top-seven finishes in the National and six top-10 finishes in the International. And Heatley achieved all this without a coach.

Basil Heatley's achievements were the products of his own intelligence and fathomless inner strength. He had known hard work from his early years on the farm and he continued live up to that work ethic through his career. Few great runners have done more for themselves.

MELVYN BATTY CARRIES THE MANTLE

Melvyn Batty, England's next great runner of the decade, came to prominence via his older brother Ken Batty, a founding member of the Thurrock Harriers who had experience running against such competition as Emil Zátopek in the 1950s. For the Thurrock Harriers, competition came in the form of interclub cross-country races and, in summer, sports meetings against local factory teams. The club thrived at first, but numbers began to drop away, and by the mid-1950s three founding members—Ken Batty, Fred Seal, and Geoff Edwards—looked out from a committee meeting and saw only two athletes training. One of them was Melvyn Batty. He was running so brilliantly for his age that the committee decided to carry on the work with the club just for the sake of his talent.

As an athlete and coach, Melvyn Batty was a force to be reckoned with—one in which his vibrant personality played a significant role. It was known that Batty was the life and soul of the party, even in his maturity, a reputation somehow at odds with his effervescent behavior—and as he was known to say with glee, "I'm the batty one."

In Leicester in 1964, Batty won his first National Cross-Country title, running 46:34 for 14.5 kilometers. That same year he set the world record for 10 miles on the track. Also in 1964, he managed to win the Cross Der Azen, in Brussels.

In 1965 he successfully defended his English National Cross title, winning at Parliament Hill in North London, a few miles from his Essex home. The judges determined he was edged out by Jean Fayolle of France in the International that year, but Batty always claimed that it should have been a tie at worst. Asked about the subject years later, some of the older members at the French sports daily, *L'Equipe*, agreed. Also in 1965, after winning the 22nd edition of the Juan Muguerza Cross International, Ron Clarke managed to beat Mel Batty's 10-mile record on the track. "I'm going to take a rest with the end of the cross-country season," Batty said after Clarke stole his record, "I've been running somewhere in Britain or Europe nearly every weekend since the season began. But I want that world record back."

He was never able to reclaim the world record, but found success later in life as a coach. Zola Budd was under his guidance, as was Eamonn Martin, who, like Batty, won two National Cross-Country titles. When Martin won the Commonwealth 10,000-meter title in Auckland prior to setting a UK record at that distance in Oslo, it was Batty who helped him get there. Martin later added a win at the London Marathon to his list of accolades.

RON HILL RACES IT IN

While Basil Heatley was victorious in the International in 1961 and Batty placed top-three in 1962 and 1965, Ron Hill was the most consistent throughout the decade in the event. The *Independent* called him "an iconic figure in the distance running world." Yet there was little to indicate that this frail English boy who was "useless" at cricket, and whose exercise was little more than walking to school and back, would evolve into a world-class athlete.

Hill had inauspicious beginnings: he concentrated on his studies and joined the Boy Scouts. When he was fifteen, he connected with the Clayton-le-Moor Harriers and was soon running with the club. He placed 42nd as a youth in the 1955 East Lancashire Cross-Country Championship, 116th in the Northern, and 226th in the National. Hill said, "I was the only person in my school that looked forward to the annual, compulsory cross-country race. In my first year I was 10th on natural ability as none of us trained. In the next 7 years I grew to become team captain and our course record holder. It was a tough hilly course that visiting teams did not enjoy."

His regular training, which soon evolved into a twice-a-day regimen, began to show results in the 1958 cross-country season. He was 14th in the Lancashire Senior, 33rd in the Northern Junior, and 108th in the National Junior. He also became Manchester University cross-country champion. His weekly mileage increased from 40 miles to 70 by the end of 1958. Throughout that winter, one of his "tough" practices was to carry out his training sessions in shorts.

After years of gradual improvement, Hill suddenly had a big breakthrough in 1962 at the age of 23. Married, and with his final exams out of the way and a Courtaulds research fellowship helping to pay the bills, his life became more stable: "One thing that married life brought me was a steady routine . . . Training was regular, thirteen times a week." He had already been training twice a day since 1958, but his new life enabled him to increase his mileage to 90 a week. 1961 saw his most consistent training so far (it should also be noted that in the winter of 1961–62 Hill did interval training with mile specialist John Whetton, which did a lot to improve his basic speed). Hill placed second in the Lancashire, seventh in the Inter-Counties, first in the East Lancashire, first in the British Universities, and seventh in the National. His seventh in the National gained him a place on the England team for the International, where he finished a creditable 11th.

At his best, Hill was hitting 105 miles a week and was finishing fifth or better in every race he entered. The progress was clear. According to Hill, "Cross-country was my first love. I won the English Championship in 1966, which I rank in my top four running experiences, and won it again in 1968. I was second in the International twice; 1964, Dublin and 1968, Tunisia, when Mohammed Gammoudi beat me by 1.4 seconds. I was on five other winning England teams in 1964, 1965, 1966, 1967, and 1968, and was captain of the team on the last four occasions."

Hill, Batty, and Heatley were all members of the English National Cross-Country team that competed in the International in 1964—and it was the only time all three men competed for England at the same time in the International (expectedly, England finished first). With their point total of 38 being the lowest of the decade, England had one of the largest winning margins over the second-place team (France, with 96 points) for the decade as well. Ron Hill finished in second; Basil Heatley was eighth; and Melvyn Batty 14th.

While England had a well-developed program in place to foster young cross-country runners (as evidenced by the success of Hill, Batty, and Heatley), the United States was just beginning to expand theirs. Similar international success in the coming years would be the result.

AMERICAN HIGH SCHOOL EXPANSION

The 1960s were unique for bringing a "great awakening" to the sport at the high school level in the United States. Cold War anxiety had a lot to do with this, but motivation to chase records and compete internationally (the newly inaugurated junior race at the International Cross-Country Championship was but one example of a youth movement globally for distance running) spurred programs and coaches to treat the sport seriously. Coaches like Joe Newton in the Midwest were just beginning to make their mark, and the West Coast was also seeing progress with the continuation of the nation's "phenom" movement.

For the decade, officially sanctioned cross-country championships appeared in a host of new venues. San Diego, Nebraska, New Mexico, Tennessee, the Upper Peninsula in Michigan, North Dakota, Idaho, Maine, Montana, Alaska, and even Hawaii had new titles to strive for by the end of the season.

> **Did You Know?**
>
> It was in the fall of 1960 that Joe Newton, a newly graduated teacher and coach from Northwestern University outside Chicago, accepted the position of York High School cross-country coach in Elmhurst, Illinois. In doing this he inherited a program with little tradition but a bit of talent, and with the right recipe for training, his boys at York quickly found success at the state level. Using principles adapted from Arthur Lydiard, Newton applied methods that were previously unseen, and by the end of the decade York would have three state titles and two runner-up finishes. More than just nomenclature, Newton had the honor of hosting New Zealand coach Arthur Lydiard at his house! At the time, Lydiard was having success with athletes Peter Snell and Murray Halberg, using over-distance training and having his middle-distance athletes run anywhere from 100 to 200 miles a week. According to Newton: "Lydiard taught me that you can do far more than you ever thought you could do. He told me, 'Joe, everybody thinks we're running 100 miles a week, but I don't tell them that in that 100 miles a week I don't count the morning run, I don't count the warm up and I don't count the cool down. So everybody thinks that they can run 100 miles a week and beat us. Hell, Peter's running 200 miles a week.'" By the end of the decade the legacy of the "Long Green Line" at York was well-established.

And in 1966, the Iowa Girls High School Athletic Union officially sanctioned a statewide cross-country championship, the first of its kind for high school female talent in the United States (albeit contested separate from the boys).

THE RISE OF GERRY LINDGREN

Amidst tales of exorbitant mileage and urban legends about his personal motivations and experiences, one thing was for certain: his performances spoke for themselves. The powerful running accomplished by Gerry Lindgren during the 1960s has stood the test of time.

Undersized and soft-spoken growing up, Lindgren was challenged by his abusive, alcoholic father at every turn, and had to overcome an unshakeable feeling of fear in his own home. Among other things, it reinforced a poor self-image of being helpless. Lindgren's Rogers High School coach, Tracy Walters, explained: "Gerry's very humble. Sometimes to a fault. He doesn't think he's really much of anything. He finds happiness in that. He went through some things that maybe we have to work through that we wouldn't want to."

But despite his shyness, Lindgren was inspired to try distance running after watching Rogers High runners Jim Jewel and Barry Robinson battle each other in pursuit of breaking a 4:30 mile. And after the exploits of his freshman cross-country season, Lindgren improved considerably. During his first race his sophomore year, a dual meet with Shadle Park High School, Lindgren took off, taking the lead early on. A teammate from Rogers passed Lindgren, as did four Shadle Park runners. Lindgren never pursued the leaders. As a consequence his coach berated him: "The coach was very disappointed as I had let four guys go by without trying. He said if that is the kind of runner I was going to be that I shouldn't be on the team. It lit a fire under me. I couldn't just try to make our own runners better, but every time I ran I had to try to win. After that I tried to be an example to other people. I never thought about how tired I would get."

Lindgren went on to finish second at the WIAA State Cross-Country Championship at the end of his sophomore season in 1961.

After a summer of high mileage and dominating local competition, Lindgren won the WIAA State Cross-Country Championship as a junior, covering the 2.3-mile Green Lake course in Seattle in a time of 11:06. From there, Lindgren entered the fall of his senior year ready to defend his state cross-country title. That season he would not disappoint: running on legs that saw an average of 25–30 miles a day, Lindgren broke 9:10 on the two-mile Shadle Park course four different times with a best of 8:59, and won the state meet at Green Lake in 10:47, shaving 19 seconds off his junior year time. His state-winning time averaged 4:41 per mile, giving Lindgren the win by 44 seconds over the nearest finisher.

Lindgren went on to Washington State University in Pullman in 1964, where he ran under the tutelage of Coach Jack Mooberry. Lindgren embraced the freedom Mooberry gave him, exploring the miles of roads between wheat fields and rolling hills—well away from the regimented Bowerman program that was coming into place at Oregon.

However, because he ran in the Tokyo Olympics, Lindgren didn't start college at Washington State until after the fall season of 1964. When he did start competing the following spring, athletes were allowed only three years of eligibility—which changed in 1967–68 when freshman eligibility was put in place. Lindgren thus had only three tries at various titles in his sophomore, junior, and senior years, during which he won 11 NCAA championships. He won outdoor three-mile and six-mile doubles on the track in 1966 and '67, and a five-kilometer/10-kilometer double in the '68 Olympic year. He won the indoor two-mile in '66 and '67, then finished second to Jim Ryun in the '68 two-mile (Ryun won a mile/two-mile double). In cross-country, Lindgren won the NCAA Championship in 1966, '67, and '69.

In Lindgren's first season running cross-country at Washington State in 1966 he was able to win the NCAA Championship in dramatic fashion, avenging his early-season loss to Oregon State's Tracy Smith (the first American to medal at the International Cross-Country Championship). The following year, Lindgren defended his NCAA Cross-Country title at over 7,200 feet of altitude in Laramie, Wyoming, with temperatures below freez-ing—finishing 16 seconds ahead of runner-up Arjan Gelling of North Dakota.

Lindgren then redshirted the 1968 cross-country season in anticipation of running the '68 Olympics. However, he didn't make the 1968 Olympic team, finishing fifth in the 10,000 and fourth in the 5,000 at the Olympic Trials at Echo Summit. Thus, in his last collegiate cross-country race, the 1969 cross-country NCAA Championship at Van Cortlandt Park, Lindgren beat Mike Ryan of Air Force (the defending champ who had won in Lindgren's absence), who finished second, and a collegiate freshman by the name of Steve ("Pre") Prefontaine, who finished in third. It was Pre's only defeat in a cross-country championship in his collegiate career.

GO PRE!

At his height, Steve Prefontaine held every American outdoor track record from 2,000 meters to 10,000. In all, he set 14 American records and broke the four-minute-mile barrier nine times. While at the University of Oregon in Eugene, he won three NCAA Cross-Country Championships and four outdoor track titles. But among the other great American distance runners, Prefontaine rests in a special place in the hearts of those who witnessed his exploits. "His talent was his control of his fatigue and his pain," said Walt McClure, his high school coach. "His threshold was different than most of us, whether it was inborn or he developed it himself." For Prefontaine, it was more than just hating to lose.

Growing up in the coastal logging town of Coos Bay, Oregon, Prefontaine was a rambunctious youth, competitive in many sports in junior high. Initially, after viewing high school runners jogging by the junior high during cross-country season, Prefontaine wasn't excited by the idea of running long distances. But during a three-week conditioning period in his PE class, Prefontaine was able to finish second in his group during a mile run around the school. With this newfound success, and some urging by his coach, he fell in love with cross-country.

When Pre entered Marshfield High School in 1965, Coach Walt McClure remembered the reason Prefontaine wanted to run cross-country: "Steve's choice to become a runner stems from his frustrating experience as a too-small junior high football player with few opportunities to play on game days." As a freshman, Prefontaine started out as the seventh man and he progressed to second man by the end of the year, placing 53rd in the State Championship. His sophomore season was similarly unspectacular, save for the district cross-country meet when the diminutive Pre hung with the state mile champion and the state cross-country champion for all but the last 300 yards.

Then, heeding the advice of Coach McClure, Prefontaine took it upon himself to train hard over the summer. Entering his junior year he resolved to be the Oregon state cross-country champion, and the end of the season found him undefeated—reaching his goal without setbacks. That spring track season Pre aimed for goals of a 9:04 two-mile, a 4:08 mile, and a 1:54 half-mile. He recorded personal records of 9:01.3 for two miles (a state record), 4:14 for the mile, and 1:56.2 for the half-mile.

During the summer between his junior and senior years, Pre worked as a lifeguard, a gas station attendant, and as an insurance policy evaluator. McClure recounted, "His summer days were not idle. Pre ran daily distances from four to eight miles." McClure also noted that Pre displayed "a steady growth in maturity and endurance throughout late summer and the fall," capping his senior season with a second state cross-country championship. As quoted by Jack Hall, writer for the *Eugene Register-Guard*, "Prefontaine has a very simple plan for running cross-country. Start with a blistering pace, hold it throughout the race, and make the field pay to stay in contention. Pre ran the 2.5 mile Busch Park course in 11:30.2, shattering the 12:13.8 clocking he made in setting the record last year as a junior by 43.6 seconds."

And after setting a new national high school record in the two-mile at the Corvallis Invitational (running 8:41.5), Pre readied himself for the next level of competition downstream in Eugene as a member of Coach Bill Bowerman's University of Oregon Ducks.

Prefontaine began his collegiate cross-country career impressively, beating Gerry Lindgren on a wet, slippery, and leaf-covered Avery Park (Oregon State course) in Corvallis. Pre's time over six miles (29:13) was good enough to lower the course record held by Tracey Smith by 33 seconds, and to put 150 yards between he and Lindgren. Two weeks later at Stanford, Pre and Lindgren squared off again in one of the most brutal and impressive distance races ever witnessed. "It should have been called a tie," Prefontaine was quoted as saying—as he and Lindgren finished with identical times: 28:32.4 for six miles, though Lindgren was given the win. Lindgren recounted: "We were never more than eight yards apart the whole race. I'd try to shake him, and then he'd try to shake me. Neither of us could." The Oregon Ducks managed to win the team title over Washington State, and both schools geared up for one more showdown at the 1969 NCAA Cross-Country Championship, to be held at Van Cortlandt Park in New York.

For Prefontaine, it would be his third-ever collegiate cross-country race. For Gerry Lindgren, running in his final year of eligibility, it would be his third attempt at a title in four years. Defending NCAA Cross-Country champion Mike Ryan for Air Force was also a contender. Other names included Don Walsh and Ron Bednarski, frontrunners who were competing for the team-favorites, Villanova University and University of Texas–El Paso (UTEP), respectively.

Early footage from the 1969 NCAA Championship shows Lindgren, Prefontaine, Walsh, and Bednarski all out to a fast start, with Pre right on Lindgren's shoulder, and the rest of the pack strung out behind. As Lindgren said:

Before the race started I told Pre that he would have to run the mile of his life. I was in about tenth place

at the mile and I heard 4:08 called out. I ended up in the lead around a mile and a half as we ran through a wooded area of trails. Pre was right behind me on one side and Ryan was right behind on the other side. When we ran around corners we would slow down so I had to pick it up after each corner to get back into my pace. They were right behind me and I would gain a few steps after each corner. When we came out of the woods I had a big lead on Mike Ryan who was also way ahead of Pre. That's the way the race went and we finished in that order. Ryan came on with a really good sprint at the end.

Lindgren ran 28:59.2 for the six-mile course, Ryan came second in 29:01, and Pre came third in 29:12.

After the race, Prefontaine was devastated. "I don't know what happened," he said afterward. "I like a fast pace, but I just wasn't right today." Oregon coach Bill Bowerman knew: "People don't appreciate how much a hard six-mile takes out of you, and that was his third that fall. The young man is eighteen. Mr. Lindgren is 23."

SHIFTING COLLEGIATE POWERS

Coach Bill Bowerman followed an accepted philosophy entering the decade. His Oregon Ducks rarely stressed the cross-country season, as it was great to run over autumnal landscapes, but only insofar as it made runners better on the track. The fall atmosphere was meant to be one of renewal, and for many years Bowerman didn't want to compromise the restorative nature of such training by peaking for major cross-country races. In his first dozen seasons, even though Bill Dellinger (one of Bowerman's first star distance runners) and others had dominated Pacific Conference cross-country meets, Bowerman had never sent a team to the NCAA Cross-Country Championships. But in 1961, under Sam Bell, Oregon State did. Dale Story won the individual race and the Beavers took the team title.

Spurred by Oregon State's success, Bowerman entered his Ducks in the nationals the next three years. But in 1965—the year Lindgren won, Western Michigan took the team title, and Oregon finished eighth—Bowerman was so dismayed and concerned about the damage that repeated six-mile races could do to milers, that he didn't send a team to the nationals again for three years.

That all changed with the arrival of Steve Prefontaine in 1969—and with Bill Dellinger now on board full-time as coach, preparing the squad for cross-country success became a priority. Yet the all-miler cross-country squad for Oregon, which had been so dominant at the Northern Division and Pacific Eight Conference championships, came undone at the championship in Van Cortlandt Park, finishing third behind UTEP and Villanova: "We did as well as we could under the physical condition of the team," said Bill Dellinger. Luckily it wouldn't be the last time Oregon contended for a title at the NCAA Cross-Country Championships.

THE VILLANOVA WILDCATS AND THE UTEP MINERS

The year 1965 marked the first time that the NCAA Championship appeared in Lawrence, Kansas, rather than East Lansing, Michigan. And in the team race, neither Villanova University nor the University of Texas–El Paso were even in contention—in fact neither team even scored at the meet. It wouldn't take long for that to change.

A coach by the name of Jack Pyrah appeared at Villanova in the fall of 1966 and helped turn things around immediately. Known for his sense of humor and encyclopedic knowledge of current and past runners, Pyrah got connected with Villanova after a plane-ride meeting with Coach Jumbo Elliott. Elliott, considered by many to be the best American distance coach of all time, was a staple at Villanova for forty-seven years. From 1966 to 1971, the Villanova Wildcats claimed four of six NCAA Cross-Country titles and six straight IC4A titles in cross-country. These titles weren't without contention or controversy, however—not the least of which came from another dark horse in the form of the University of Texas–El Paso's Miners.

At the University of Texas–El Paso, young assistant track coach Wayne Vandenburg, who started in 1967 at the age of twenty-six, quickly started amassing talented foreign-born athletes to enhance UTEP's distance running pedigree. Vandenburg was billed by the school's athletic department publicist as "The Fastest Mouth in the West," but the results spoke for themselves. Leaning heavily on the legs of John Bednarski, William McKillip, and Matthew Breen, the upstart Miners won the NCAA title over Villanova by 14 points at the 1969 NCAA Cross-Country Championship. Bednarski, a talent from England who had won the South of Thames Cross-Country Championship in 1968, finished fourth at NCAAs. McKillip, a Florida transplant, finished 10th. And Matt Breen, one of three Australians, finished in 18th.

Vandenburg and UTEP had won the championship in their first official season fielding a cross-country team,

a remarkable feat despite the outside success of their athletes coming into the fall of 1969. But it wasn't the first nor the last time that foreign-born talent would stir controversy in the NCAA Cross-Country Championship. In fact, heading into the 1970 cross-country season, with Villanova in a rebuilding phase, and Oregon seen as largely more talented on the track, the UTEP Miners, who were returning all of their athletes from the previous season, became the instant favorites to win the title for a second time in a row.

* * *

The 1960s proved to be a turning point for the sport of cross-country running. Seen previously as a growing market for distance runners, cross-country, which benefitted from the rise of international competition and domestic attention, saw a more serious focus placed on the sport. It became an accepted standard that the value of the sport was greater than or equal to running on the track, as individuals like Roelants, Heatley, and Heritage became "cross-country running specialists" and furthered the cause for a global movement. The East African presence in the sport also helped. Domestically, the rivalries at the college level prompted new appreciation: individuals were spurred by competition, and records were breaking in bunches.

Consequences of this new focus would appear in the coming decades. The treatment of amateurism within distance running and the involvement of sponsorship for athletes would lead to landmark changes within twenty years. Also important were the consequences of importing foreign-born talent to compete at American colleges and universities. In many ways, the level of talent was surpassing the rules in place at the time—and administrators were no more prepared for these changes than the athletes themselves. While the coming decades would be characterized by these issues, it was the individuals themselves—the Kip Keinos, Gerry Lindgrens, and Steve Prefontaines—who were driving the momentum of the sport.

EVENT SPOTLIGHT:
LINDGREN, PRE, AND THE FIRST PAC-8 CROSS-COUNTRY CHAMPIONSHIP (NOVEMBER 14, 1969)

LOCATION: STANFORD UNIVERSITY GOLF COURSE

Palo Alto, California

The inaugural Pac-8 Cross-Country Championship occurred on November 14, 1969, at the Stanford Golf Course. It didn't take long to notice Gerry Lindgren, a fifth-year Washington State senior, twenty-three years old and already considered one of the greatest American distance runners of all time.

Lindgren was a unique amalgam of contradictions. Rumors swirled that in high school he had gotten out of bed in the middle of the night to pee and ended up running 10 miles in the pitch darkness. Other murmurings claimed that he once trained 350 miles a week for six weeks straight. The fact remained that despite an abusive childhood, Lindgren had grown up into a cartoon character with insatiable talent, with an insane willpower to push himself, and with limitations not yet reached. He was an unassuming combatant: pencil-thin, pale, and nerdy—but with ripped thighs that were unable to completely hide his prowess. He was 120 pounds of Clark Kent masking superhero ability.

Then there was Prefontaine, shining bright like the sun. Only the brave had the courage to cast more than two or three glances at the sensational freshman, but Pre was no stranger to celebrity. He was the blue-chip recruit of the nation, a self-glorified rockstar, and before a year would pass he'd find himself on the cover of *Sports Illustrated*, touted as the future of American distance running. University of Oregon coach Bill Dellinger would be quoted in that article as saying, "He's as tough mentally right now as world-class runners who are 10 years older. If the competition is tough or the wind is blowing like crazy or it's awfully hot, hell, that's not going to stop him. There's nothing in running that he doesn't believe he can do."

There was no way that the freshman Prefontaine *should* have thought he could handle a former Olympian five years his senior, but two weeks prior (in his college debut) Prefontaine had surprised the running world by winning the six-mile District 8 Northern Division Championships in a record time—with Lindgren broken in second place—27 seconds back. Word was out that Lindgren had been wounded with an ankle injury and only a fraction of full-strength, so there was no doubt that with time to heal this would be a closer rematch. There was also little doubt that Pre would be looking to win for a second time. The Pac-8 promised to be a heavyweight bout with two contenders

who never thought of losing—except to push themselves to the absolute edge.

In addition to Lindgren and Pre, many big-name rivals were present from the West Coast universities vying for a chance at their first conference title: Cliff West and Bob Waldon from University of California, Berkeley (Cal); top University of Southern California (USC) runners Freddie Ritcherson and Jeff Marsee; University of California, Los Angeles's (UCLA's) Hartzen Alipzar; and Stanford University's Brock, Kardong, and Bob Coe. All of them were prepared for the gladiatorial match that was set to ensue. Stanford's Coe reminisced: "I had never smelled blood before the start of a race, but in the seconds before the gun sounded there was blood in the water, no question about it. I felt as if I wasn't standing on a starting line for a race; I felt as if I was about to jump off a cliff."

Once the gun fired, Pre and Lindgren became guided missiles—sprinting on their toes at breakneck speed on a collision course toward each other. The crowd couldn't believe it: the two were drawn like magnets. The ground shook with thunderous convulsions as the star-athletes became sharks; not hunting helpless prey but grappling with each other with all their might. The race was on. The rest of the field joined in the frenzy, runners already in oxygen debt 100 meters in, hoping that when the dust cleared they would find themselves among the top 10.

At the half-mile mark the pace calmed a little, but far in the distance Pre and Lindgren would cross the mile mark at a near-suicidal 4:18. Lindgren was well-known for this: he went out in 4:14 en route to an American three-mile (12:53) record in 1966. But it wasn't just Lindgren; both runners were courting their own demise in order to destroy the other. Prefontaine was also to blame: "I felt I had to go fast from the start because Gerry is fast," he would later say. Stanford's Coe continued: "As I closed in on the mile mark at least a hundred yards behind the leaders, I realized that I had no clue as to the location of a single teammate. The entire field had become wildly strung out. Coach Clark's imperative at last year's NCAA championship—get together and run as a team—had been completely lost in the mayhem."

When Coe crossed the first mile, Stanford coach Marshall Clark was reading the time aloud: 4:34, and *every* runner had gone out too fast. Stanford hadn't run a single Monday mile-rep in training under 4:45 that season—but Coe had just dropped 10 seconds without a hitch. It was a time-honored strategy that Prefontaine became famous for. Few others could burn his opponents from the start like Pre, and he hated competitors who just sat on their rival's shoulder: "I run a race to see who has the most guts," he would famously say. The first-ever Pac-8 Cross-Country Championship was a "guts race."

Well ahead of an excellent field, Prefontaine and Lindgren were locked together in a duel that *ESPN* would later rank at number 73 among the 100 greatest track and field and cross-country competitions of the twentieth century. The editor of *Track and Field News*, Garry Hill, later said that it was the greatest footrace he ever saw. Trading the lead repeatedly, each man attempted to surge away from the other—yet they were both trapped. Neither could dig deeper than they already had. They averaged a more bearable 4:51 per-mile pace for the remainder of the contest, but Pre and Lindgren stayed glued at the hip.

Going up a small rise 30 seconds before the finish, Pre edged in front of Lindgren, then moved to cut him off completely. Repeatedly, Lindgren later claimed, Pre tried to force him into the crowd to his left, but the wiry Lindgren remained, veering toward Pre, fighting back. They crossed the finish line as one; shoulders together, arms crossed, each man exhausted by the effort—with Lindgren leaning narrowly at the tape, hands half-raised to break it. They had both run Stanford's hilly six-mile course in 28:32.4. A finish so close it was initially called a tie. A myth exists that photographs were examined, but once officials conferred, Lindgren was given the nod on the spot.

Lindgren remembered:

I took off and had a big lead going up the first big hill. Near the top there was Pre going ahead of me and I had to catch him going down the hill. Through the whole race I'd sprint to try to get ahead of him and he would sprint with me every darn time. Approaching the finish I was depleted and there was nothing left. With about 200 yards to go he saw the finish line, and it seemed he was forcing me into the crowd. The last 200 yards was me trying to fight him off. He leaned at the tape and I was straight up. It was an amazing finish to an amazing race.

This Pac-8 Cross-Country Championship of 1969 would fondly be remembered as the last great American distance race of the decade. Nine days later, Lindgren would run scared and conclusively beat Prefontaine at the NCAA Cross-Country Championship.

Stanford's Coe, running the last two miles on fumes, crossed the finish line a minute behind Pre and Lindgren in 29:33, a new personal record for the course by 21 seconds, but buried in 15th place, soundly beaten by teammate Brock (29:08) for the first time all season. Stanford's Greg Brock had finished fifth, just behind University of Oregon's Steve Savage and Washington State University's Rick Riley (an eastern Washington runner who had also competed internationally while still in his teens, and whose interscholastic two-mile record had been broken only the year before by Pre).

As a team, Stanford's 86 points edged USC (90) and avenged a tough early-season loss to UCLA (94), but they were nowhere close to the two Northwest powerhouses University of Oregon and Washington State, who finished one-two, 46 to 63. There would be no return to nationals for that previous year's runner-up. A "force to be reckoned with" early in the season, competing in the toughest cross-country conference in the nation, Stanford would be officially shut down for the year, thanks in part to the two greatest distance runners of the age, Steve Prefontaine and Gerry Lindgren.

Date: Friday, November 14, 1969
Teams: 8
Distance: 6.2 miles/10 kilometers
Location: Stanford Golf Course, Palo Alto, California

Individual Finishers:

1	Gerry Lindgren	Washington State University	28:32.4
2	Steve Prefontaine	University of Oregon	28:32.4
3	Steve Savage	University of Oregon	28:58
4	Rick Riley	Washington State University	29:02
5	Greg Brock	Stanford University	29:08
6	Mark Hillefield	Washington State University	29:10
7	Fred Ritcherson	USC	29:11
8	Jeff Marsee	USC	29:12
9	Roscoe Divine	University of Oregon	29:16
10	Mike McClendon	University of Oregon	29:17
11	Hartzen Alpizar	UCLA	29:19
12	Bob Waldron	California at Berkeley	29:20
13	Cliff West	California at Berkeley	29:22
14	Spencer Lyman	Oregon State University	29:30
15	Robert Coe	Stanford University	29:33
		. . .	
22	Tom Morrow	University of Oregon	29:54
26	Terry Dooley	University of Oregon	29:59
		. . .	
29	Norm Trerise	University of Oregon	30:14
30	Chris Carey	Oregon State University	30:17
		. . .	
34	Steve Squires	Oregon State University	30:40

Team Results:

1	University of Oregon	46
2	Washington State University	63
3	Stanford University	86
4	University of Southern California	90
5	University of California, Los Angeles	94
6	University of California, Berkeley	127
7	Oregon State University	165
8	University of Washington	230

Chapter 13

Cross-country was always my first love in running. It's a wonderful, cathartic experience—a pure feeling being out in the country, especially in the fall when the weather is cool and the leaves change.

—*Craig Virgin*

THE 1970s: THE UNITED STATES EXPLODES ON TO THE SCENE

The 1970s saw American distance talent rise to the fore, most prominently in international cross-country competitions and domestic championships that featured international talent. The amateur ethos was changing globally, and America led the way, with international competition, a strong regional foundation (with a resurgence of competitive club teams), Olympic success, public support, and private funding all contributing. These factors also enabled American talent to face the best in the world to showcase their abilities.

And international competition did not disappoint. From New Zealand to the United Kingdom, Germany to Spain, Belgium to Portugal, France to East Africa—the world standard for distance running was never higher. European cross-country meets experienced an "open door policy" this decade, while the transition from the International Cross-Country Union to the International Amateur Athletics Federations (IAAF) changed the accessibility and talent featured in the newly transformed World Cross-Country Championships. The era was booming and was seen by many as the pinnacle of the sport.

IT STARTS WITH PREFONTAINE

Steve ("Pre") Prefontaine wasted little time becoming a household name. After his debut in cross-country as a college freshman, Pre went on to break four-minutes in the mile and impressed fans with his brash, take-no-prisoners style. After easily defeating the field in the Pac-8 Northern Division Championship—his first sophomore cross-country race of 1970—Prefontaine won again two weeks later, by 50 yards, on a crisp November day at Pullman Golf Course. With this victory, Prefontaine and his University of Oregon teammates qualified for the NCAA Cross-Country Championship.

The 1970 NCAA Cross-Country Championship was held at William & Mary College in Williamsburg, Virginia. Challengers included the University of Texas–El Paso (UTEP), which had won the crown in 1969 and returned all five finishers; Oregon, third in 1969 and led by Prefontaine; and Villanova University, which had won the title in 1966, '67, '68, and finished second in '69. Villanova was rebuilding in 1970 and most observers had UTEP as the favorite.

By the end of the meet, however, Oregon had seemingly pulled an upset: Steve Prefontaine had won the race in 28:00 (a new course record by over one minute and 40 seconds), and Oregon was declared the team champion, beating Villanova 86 to 88. UTEP was third. The championship was awarded to Coach Bill Bowerman and his Ducks. The top teams stood atop the podium; the press conference was held. Oregon departed for the airport, trophy in hand, believing they had won the title.

However, Villanova's fifth man, Les Nagy, noticed that several runners he had beaten were listed ahead of him in the results. Nagy claimed he'd fallen to the ground after crossing the line where several runners passed him in the chute. Villanova filed a protest. Sure enough, Nagy was correct. After reviewing the film, Nagy was awarded 62nd place overall, instead of 67th, and Villanova was declared the champion, 85 to 86 over Oregon. Bowerman had no recourse. Villanova's squad had won its fourth national title in five years.

But after another successful track campaign saw Steve Prefontaine set a new American record in the 5,000 meters, Pre turned his attention to repeating as champion in cross-country in 1971.

At the Pac-8 in '71 at UCLA, Pre ran a distance of six miles and 410 yards in 29:59, shattering the course record.

He won by 300 yards over Dan Murphy of Washington State in a race that saw 10 runners equal or better the former record. Washington State won the meet, placing five in the top 10, and earned their first conference championship in any sport since 1963.

The 33rd annual NCAA Cross-Country Championship, held one week later over a six-mile course at Fox Den Country Club in Tennessee, saw Pre win his second title in three years, beating Garry Bjorklund of Minnesota by seven seconds. Notes from Pre's diary provided a glimpse into the experience: "It seems to get harder every year. It was a very hard race—I had my problems winning. I felt several times like giving into the pain and letting Garry win but I just couldn't." Garry Bjorklund added: "It was a beastly hilly course. We went through the mile in 4:24. There was still a group at 3-miles, so I took off and just started running as hard as I could. At four miles, I started to hurt pretty bad. Pre started to chip at me a little bit. At the top of a big hill, he sneaked away and got about 30 yards. I closed but couldn't catch him." Along with Prefontaine's victory, Oregon won the team title, beating Washington State 83 to 122.

THE ARRIVAL OF JOHN NGENO AT WASHINGTON STATE

After the graduation of Gerry Lindgren in 1969, Washington State University (WSU) coach Jack Mooberry was without a top contender to face Oregon's Steve Prefontaine. And while WSU had taken advantage of the NCAA's relaxed recruitment standards, procuring Don Smith from Australia to compete in 1970 (he would finish 13th at the NCAA Championship as a freshman), WSU had yet to find that one man who could go head-to-head with Pre. It was after trusting the recruitment talents of former athlete and then-Washington State assistant coach John Chaplin that Mooberry finally found what he was looking for—quite by accident.

In the fall of 1971 Chaplin heard talent was available: "Professor Ngeno, an instructor at the University of Puget Sound, contacted the coach at the University of Washington and said he had a brother, Kip, who ran 14-flat for the high hurdles. There was also a 13:16 three-miler. Apparently the coach didn't believe the story. When Professor Ngeno contacted me, I didn't believe it either, but I figured it was worth the price of a stamp. So I wrote a letter and they both came. Can you believe it? A great hurdler and an NCAA champion for the cost of 10 cents." In the summer of 1972, nineteen-year-old John Ngeno arrived in Pullman Washington from Kericho, Kenya.

Ngeno struggled in his initial collegiate season in the fall of 1972. "I did not always like cross-country races with hundreds of runners because I like to start easy," he claimed. In wet, rainy, 43-degree weather, Ngeno finished 43rd at the 1972 NCAA Cross-Country Championship. But Prefontaine wasn't a contender in that race, and with one full year of valuable training under his belt (along with

close races against Pre at the three-mile distance on the track), Ngeno was ready to challenge Prefontaine for the individual cross-country title the following season.

A YEAR AWAY, AND PREFONTAINE'S SENIOR CROSS-COUNTRY SEASON IN 1973

Steve Prefontaine redshirted the 1972 fall season to preserve his eligibility (he was a semester delayed graduating Oregon). In the interim, Pre set more records on the track, competed internationally, and prepared himself for the 1972 Olympics in Munich, Germany. By the end of the summer, Prefontaine had set two collegiate records (the indoor two-mile and outdoor six-mile runs), run 3:56.7 in the mile, set and reset two American records (at 3,000 and 5,000 meters), been the top qualifier in the 5,000 meters at the Olympic Trials, and finished fourth in the Olympic Games.

But despite entering the 1973 cross-country season without a cross-country loss since the 1969 NCAA Championship his freshman year, all of the pressure of training and racing had taken its toll. Pre was suffering from bouts of severe sciatica (pressure on the spine and inflammation of the sciatic nerve). Winning his third title in four years was not going to be a walk in the park.

At the 1973 Pac-8 Districts, Prefontaine nearly lost his first cross-country meet in four years. "At the Northern Division Championships, Pre would match up on a Corvallis golf course with Kenyan John Ngeno of WSU," said former Oregon runner Geoff Hollister. "Pre and Ngeno were locked in a battle of wills up and down the hilly course that was only decided at the end with Pre's driving arm carriage and knee lift, the final uphill finish on a punishing course." The two were separated at the finish by less than a second. Washington State placed three of their five men in the top five finishers to score 27 points, while Oregon finished with 33. Ngeno—who nearly pulled the upset—would have his opportunity for revenge two weeks later in Palo Alto.

At the fifth annual Pac-8 Conference Championship, it was the Pre of old: tough, cagey, indomitable. Through the flat first mile and a half, Ngeno led Pre and teammate Dan Murphy free from the pack. Rain made the going slippery, and at times the Kenyan's gait was close to sprinting as he windmilled around the turns. On the back three miles of cambered hills, Pre closed and caught Ngeno with two miles to go. Pre ran the fourth mile in 4:20 and finished by breaking the record he shared with Gerry Lindgren by a convincing 28 seconds. "He just alternated the pace, and I love that kind of race," Pre exulted. He beat Ngeno by almost 100 yards.

"I ran the last three miles as hard as I could," said Pre. "I was a little conservative for the first three miles because the course was slippery. But then I decided I would go all-out. If I fell on my butt, I fell." With such a close individual race, it was impressive to see a close team battle as well. Oregon exacted revenge on WSU by a score of 32 to 36.

Oregon coach Bill Dellinger said the plan for the race was for Pre to stay with Ngeno if he set a pace: "That was the only chance because he can't stay with Pre in a sprint." While Washington State coach John Chaplin said the Pre-Ngeno battle "was decided by experience. Pre is doing the same thing that Lindgren did to him years ago." Pre looked forward to the NCCA Championship in Spokane: "This race gave me the confidence I need," he said, "My back was hurting and I wasn't even sure if I could run."

THE 1973 NCAA CROSS-COUNTRY CHAMPIONSHIP

The NCAA Cross-Country Championship was contested on a six-mile course at Hangman Valley Golf Course in Spokane, Washington. The weather was 36 degrees with frost on the green, but it was sunny out. A total of 4,300 spectators awaited a stacked field of over 200 participants—one of the deepest fields ever in an NCAA Cross-Country Championship. There was Craig Virgin, a freshman from the University of Illinois who had broken Steve Prefontaine's national outdoor high school two-mile record of 8:41.5 the previous spring (Virgin clocked 8:40.9). There was Neil Cusack from Eastern Tennessee, who had won the cross-country title in 1972, and Doug Brown of Tennessee, the runner-up from 1972 whose team had placed first. Dark horses were also aplenty: Gordon Minty of Eastern Michigan had gone undefeated all cross-country season; Nick Rose of Western Kentucky had finished ninth overall the year prior but had the credentials of being the 1971 World Cross-Country Junior Champion; and there was John Ngeno and Dan Murphy of Washington State—two formidable opponents who were competing in front of a home crowd.

Meanwhile, Prefontaine was hurting. As teammate Dave Taylor recalled: "I'd never seen Pre act like he did before the NCAA meet in Spokane. He'd injured his back and was in a panic. He was just a regular person at that meet. He even locked himself in his room at eight the night before." The course wasn't going to pay any favors for Prefontaine either: a narrow starting area, two 90-degree turns within the first mile, a series of short steep hills, and looping switchbacks—ideal conditions for an upset.

The first mile was tense, as Geoff Hollister explained: "You could see the starter's pistol smoke rise and the mass was off like scampering ants in formation. The sun was reflected brightly off a mane of gold hair in the lead. It was not Pre. With a powerful long stride, an English runner from Western Kentucky was setting the pace—something Pre would normally do. Nick Rose was exacting a punishing pace, intent on running anyone off their legs." Rose ran a 4:20 first mile. Steve Stintzi of Western Michigan and John Ngeno were also at the front.

Mile two was reached quickly, recounted Steve Prefontaine: "It was the farthest anyone had ever been ahead of me in a cross-country race. I thought Rose had gone out too fast—8:57 for the first two miles is something—and I knew that I was coming to the strongest part of my race.

My strong point was between the fourth and sixth miles. Rose was very competitive. He went after it." Daniel Hayes of Indiana University added: "I always ran in front pack early and then hoped to hang on. There was a nearly 180-degree turn around a green, with the bank going the wrong way. I was in second or third at the green, lost my footing, and went down, with 300 long-spiked runners immediately behind me. Spent the rest of the race catching up. Like others, I remember watching the front of the race, particularly Pre and Rose, in the loop-de-loops in the back of the course."

The *Eugene Register-Guard* picked up the story at mile three: "Nick Rose, Steve Stintzi, and John Ngeno were well ahead of the pack at three miles. Ngeno then faded back, as did Stintzi. Pre and Gordon Minty of Eastern Michigan suddenly forged into the scene." Coach Bob Parks added: "At each checkpoint that I see the runners, Gordon is moving up. He is passing everyone. I see him a little later and he's moved up to 10th place. When I finally see him for the last time, he has moved into third place behind Prefontaine and Rose." Rose's lead stretched to 70 yards, but along a series of rolling hills late in the third mile, Pre made a move into second position, slowly closing the gap.

"As the runners came off the hills and circled into a series of switchbacks in the valley, Pre had cut the gap down to 30 yards and was coming," Hollister explained. Mile four was crossed in 19:10. Nick Rose mentioned: "I'd been racing the way I do best. Just hammering for about four miles and then hanging on the last two."

"Rose was still up by 20 yards entering the fifth mile and was on top by 15 yards through mile five. The first five miles were completed in 23:40. With less than a mile to go, Pre made his move," wrote the *Register-Guard*. "According to Pre he was really hurting, so it was either do or die," said teammate Taylor.

"I didn't look around to find out where I passed him. We crossed a bridge with about one-half mile to go; we came to a hill and I charged it, rested it up at the flat and, then, went at him," Prefontaine explained. Rose said, "He caught me and dropped back on my shoulder, just dropped back; I was pretty surprised. I was still with him then and really thought I had a chance. But then we started coming past the people and they started yelling 'Go Pre!' Wow—he went like a shot. He left me there."

Prefontaine's winning time for the six-mile course was 28:14.8. Rose was second in 28:20. Gordon Minty finished an admirable third in 28:22. The University of Oregon team placed number one in team standings, well ahead of runner-up UTEP, winning 89 to 157. As Prefontaine explained afterwards, "It was a great race to end the career on. Of my three wins I'd call this one the toughest, due to the competition, weather and everything put together."

Rose was admirable in defeat: "I was dreaming I had him. I was satisfied with my race, I felt I ran my type of race." His sudden arrival wasn't soon forgotten—in the midst of the championship, it wasn't Minty or Ngeno who put up the strongest fight—the unexpected Rose had challenged Pre to the finish.

THE ADVENT OF NICK ROSE OF ENGLAND

Nick Rose, born in Bristol, England in December 1951, not only exhibited strong natural talent in distance running but also expressed a strong sense of individuality and adventure. Competing for Bristol Athletic Club in his teenage years, Rose received his first big break when he qualified for (and subsequently won) the International Junior Cross-Country Championship in 1971 at the age of nineteen. Rose defeated a talented field that included Eamonn Coghlan and Neil Cusack of Ireland and Léon Schots of Belgium. Rose also led the English team to victory—beating Scotland handily. Rose's victory in the International then attracted the attention of Western Kentucky (WKU) assistant coach Alan Launder, who read about Rose in *Athletics Weekly*. This chance marriage between WKU and Rose blossomed after Launder visited Rose to persuade him to compete and develop his talents in America.

Launder—whose British background explained his Loughborough College degree in physical education and British Amateur Athletic Association tenure—initially arrived at Western Kentucky for a graduate degree, but it wasn't long before his qualifications led to acceptance as an assistant track coach.

For Rose, the location of Western Kentucky meant very little for the boy from Bristol: "WKU to me was the USA. I had no idea where it was, but it was an opportunity to progress as an athlete. On arriving however it was a shock to the system: Bible-Belt, no drinking under 21 and in a bit of a time warp, but I loved it." Unfortunately for Rose, his relationship with Launder was a short one. Launder moved on to the University of South Australia in 1973.

Rose blossomed in America—especially when it came to cross-country—finishing ninth overall and an All-American in his very first season in the NCAA. Out of this experience, Rose developed a strong front-running style (as he would say: "When it gets down to it, everybody's pretty competitive. You see somebody out there pushing and you think well I'm not going to let him beat me."), and it led him to an NCAA title in 1974, two runner-up finishes (in 1973 and '75), a US national title in cross-country, plus other epic battles and a few more appearances at the World Cross-Country Championships. For Rose, it wasn't complicated: "I've always considered myself to be tough. I never drop out of a race, I always try my best. Even if I die I still hang on. A lot of people if they feel pain they back off; if they see a hill they back off. I don't. I try to charge it or run at it and never give in. I think it's something you either have or you don't. You never give in until you see the finish line."

And while Rose's various exploits always challenged the best domestic talent in cross-country (his victory in the 1977 US National Cross-Country Championship was especially noteworthy), one individual stood out among the rest when it came to winning the national during the 1970s. His name was Frank Shorter, and he was the man responsible for the American running boom.

ENTER FRANK SHORTER

"Frank's contributions crossed over—they affected the whole culture," claimed novelist John L. Parker, author of *Once a Runner*. Parker was Shorter's roommate and training partner with the Florida Track Club during the 1970s. "Alongside figures like Prefontaine, Bill Rodgers, and Roger Bannister, Shorter was the quintessential runner," wrote Parker. Shorter's beginnings were inauspicious. Born in 1947, and living in the shadow of an abusive father and a tumultuous homelife, Shorter spent much of his youth in Middletown, New York, going to the public library, playing Little League baseball, and fishing on the lake.

At Middletown Junior High School, Shorter got interested in ski racing. Reading up on the sport, he learned that elite European racers trained by running long distances. So Shorter started running the hilly two-mile route back and forth from school. The miles vanished with a dream-like quality—and as the autumn wore on, Shorter kept running, but he forgot about ski racing. "I was already following my escape route," he said.

Two years later, Shorter enrolled at Northfield Mount Hermon Academy, which boasted one of the top cross-country programs in the Northeast. He then won the New England Prep Cross-Country Championship the following year as a 10th grader. Through his high school years, Shorter continued to excel as a student and athlete. In 1965, he enrolled at Yale, where he ran as a relief from studying. As a senior, when academic pressure eased, Shorter's training intensified.

Despite Shorter's dedication, success was not immediate: he finished a decent 19th overall at the NCAA Cross-Country Championships as a senior in the fall of 1968. Shorter even set a record—as the runner with the most *second-place* finishes at the IC4A and Heptagonal championships—and he was also having trouble winning Harvard-Yale dual meets. Then, in May 1969, with his studies as a psychology major at Yale completed, Shorter began two-a-day workouts for the first time in his life out of "curiosity," he claimed. Three weeks later he clocked himself for six miles and found his time one of the best in the country. He flew to Knoxville and a week later was the NCAA six-mile champion.

In March 1970, Frank Shorter moved to Gainesville, Florida, joined Jack Bacheler (then regarded as America's best distance runner), and became a member of the Florida Track Club (FTC) founded by Jimmy Carnes, head coach at the University of Florida. Shorter then resumed his running career in earnest: "It became a matter of singular concentration, discipline, monomania," Shorter said. "I had to zero in on one thing, I had to make it so nothing else mattered. A distance runner always knows how good he is because he knows the distances he runs, the strength he has. He can't hide anything from himself. He always has the feeling of 'if I worked harder I could have been . . .' I just made up my mind to work and see how good I could be."

The fall of 1970 saw Shorter break through: after running 125 miles a week, Shorter lined up for the US

National Cross-Country Championship, held in Washington Park, Chicago. He had a narrow lead at the mile, was 20 yards ahead at two miles, 100 at three, and it lengthened from there. "Easy, easy," Shorter said later. "I just set my own tempo, and when they let me do that I'm happy. I never like to think I have it won, but I knew no one was going to make up 30 seconds on me in the last mile." As he splashed down the final straight in muddy, cold, and windy conditions, Shorter turned to wave encouragement to teammate Bacheler, in second place. Remarkably, not only did this establish Shorter's cross-country running legacy, it reaffirmed his training: he had also won the United States Track and Field Federation (USTFF) Cross-Country Championship at Penn State three days earlier.

For his second US Amateur Athletic Union (AAU) cross-country title, Shorter won the six-mile 1971 cross-country championship in San Diego, crossing the line in a blazing 29:19. "I was blessed to have outstanding coaches, Samuel Greene at Mount Hermon and, later, Bob Geigengack at Yale—in addition to Carnes in Florida," Shorter said. "All three men believed in laying down a solid fundamental training program, and then letting the runner develop at his own pace. That was perfect for me. By my junior year at Yale, I was essentially coaching myself, which I continued doing post-college." Shorter added that, besides using running to escape his childhood trauma and, later, academic pressure, he used the sport as a means of self-discovery: "I never went into a race focused on winning," he said. "I went in wanting to find out."

Shorter's third attempt at being US National Cross-Country Champion might have been his most memorable, however, not for the manner in which he won but for the manner in which he didn't win it. In the November 1972 race in Chicago, Shorter didn't cross the finish line first. NCAA champion Neil Cusack did, but was eventually placed fourth.

Don Kopriva wrote up the confusing account for *Track and Field News*:

> The trouble started with less than a half-mile remaining in the race—Cusack had about an eighty-yard lead over Shorter. Cusack then missed a loop in the course and shortened his route by roughly 200 yards. Shorter took the same route as Cusack, although he reportedly realized his mistake and backtracked, costing himself 50 yards in the process. The real villain in this drama, however, was the course itself, which was poorly marked with small flags. A white line laid down earlier to mark the route had been essentially demolished by a spate of rain and snow which had preceded the run.

The AAU, in an attempt to placate the involved parties, arbitrarily placed Cusack fourth, which apparently satisfied no one. Cusack refused to accept his placement. Meanwhile, Jack Bacheler, Shorter's FTC teammate, appeared instead to pick up Shorter's gold.

Shorter's fourth straight attempt at victory came in Gainesville, Florida in 1973. Under clear skies, a 29:52 win for the 10-kilometer course immediately cemented his reputation; four straight US National Cross-Country titles were the most earned by an American male in more than thirty-three years. With the 1974 National Championship set to be held on the unforgiving terrain at Crystal Springs Cross-Country Course in Belmont, California, and with Prefontaine's impending graduation making him an immediate threat to Shorter's streak, the stage was set for an epic showdown.

SHORTER AND PREFONTAINE EYE A SHOWDOWN IN '74

After his third NCAA Cross-Country title and graduating from the University of Oregon, Steve Prefontaine prepared to face a harsh reality: extreme poverty. To run his best, he needed freedom to train and travel. A full-time, entry-level job in his major field of communications—lugging equipment at a TV station—wasn't compatible with that. So the bulk of Prefontaine's income came in violation of the amateur code. Pre ran European races (despite his back problems in 1973) where meet promoters paid cash or furnished airline tickets.

Meanwhile, Prefontaine was competing at a level never seen before. In 1974, with his eyes set on the 1976 Summer Olympics, Pre set the American 10,000-meter record in a singlet for the Oregon Track Club, and in the span of a few months, set the American record for three miles (12:51.4), 5,000 meters (13:31.9), 3,000 meters (7:42.6), and two miles (8:18.4).

At the same time, Frank Shorter won his third AAU national title in the 10,000 meters. While his time for the distance was admittedly a full 33 seconds slower than Pre's American record, many believed Shorter was within striking distance should the two meet in a heads-up race in cross-country.

In preparation for the 1974 US National Cross-Country Championship, Prefontaine competed in a European-style 12-kilometer cross-country race hosted by the Oregon Track Club (OTC) on September 28, 1974. Held at Lane Community College, south of Eugene, 200 runners competed across five events. Officially titled the "First Annual Oregon Track Club Invitational International Cross-Country Meet," the event was unlike any other that Pre ran. The European-style course included hurdling steeplechase barriers, water jumps, and rough and rugged terrain. Despite these difficulties Pre won with ease, finishing in a time of 37:37 over OTC teammate Bob Williams in second. While no longer eligible for NCAA-sanctioned cross-country events, Pre was eligible for the AAU National Championship on November 30, and it was after this event that he committed to race.

Shorter had been vigilantly training at altitude in preparation for the championship. In a phone interview leading to the event, he gave insight into his progress: "I'm running at 9,200 feet in northern New Mexico. It's mainly hill running. I've been here for 2½ weeks, and will be flying to Kansas in a couple days for some speed training. I was doing 140-mile weeks before I came up here. Now it has dropped to 120. It's really hard to run up this high. With anybody who trains as much as I do, every two weeks there's a day that really wipes you out. Every day up here is like that."

Joe Henderson, writing for *Runner's World*, gave the tale of the tape: "The AAU race was to have been a classic. Steve Prefontaine against Frank Shorter. Prefontaine—known as a trackman; a two- and three-miler. Shorter: few equals as a road racer. Both, American record holders at 10,000 meters. They'd never raced in cross-country—Prefontaine had three NCAA Cross-Country titles—Shorter had four straight AAUs. Meet director Jack Leydig tried for months to bring the two together—both were reluctant to make a commitment. Leydig finally succeeded in signing up both for this race." But would the brutal course play a part?

THE CRYSTAL SPRINGS INTERNATIONAL CROSS-COUNTRY COURSE

The Stanford Golf Course served as the Bay Area's cross-country venue in the 1950s and early 1960s, hosting collegiate championships, high school center-meets, and invitationals. However, after 1963, runners not affiliated with Stanford University could no longer use the course. Fortunately, through the efforts of local Carlmont High School coach Loren Lansberry and College of San Mateo coach Bob Rush, a permanent home was found. Nestled in the hills of the Bay Area's Peninsula in the town of Belmont, about twenty minutes south of San Francisco, the Crystal Springs International Cross-Country Course was born. Carved into the hillside, this course stands apart from more notable venues such as Franklin Park, Van Cortlandt, and Mount San Antonio College because of its relentless, punishing hills, its lack of shade, and its unique hard dirt surface. And despite the challenges from the terrain, Crystal Springs offers spectators the opportunity to observe more than 75 percent of the action on the course with ease and has remained completely unchanged to the present day.

In November 1974, after a fall that saw a new record for high school participation on the course, the AAU chose Crystal Springs as the venue for the US National Cross-Country Championship. The traditional 2.95-mile course (an odd distance, attributed to a trench being dug where the starting line would have been at three miles) would be looped twice and extended into a 10-kilometer arrangement. More than 300 runners committed to the event. Featured were recognizable names Steve Prefontaine and Frank Shorter; Olympic qualifier Jack Bacheler; NCAA champions Neil Cusack, John Ngeno, Nick Rose, Marty Liquori, and Mike Boit; and even prep standouts like Eric Hulst and Mitch Kingery. It was to be the showdown of the decade.

THE 1974 AAU US NATIONAL CROSS-COUNTRY CHAMPIONSHIP

As is customary in cross-country, the terrain often plays a part in the performance of the athletes—but the rocky, dusty, clay-packed trails of Crystal Springs were particularly unforgiving. "There aren't many places in the country where you can put 400 guys," marathon runner Tom Fleming explained. "There'll be some bitching, but it's a good course." Nick Rose, who had won the NCAA Cross-Country Championship five days earlier, said, "It doesn't seem like cross-country if you don't have grass, does it? That ground is unbelievably hard. It seems better suited for motorcycles, actually." Frank Shorter, who arrived (per his custom) on the day of the race, was examining a course map wryly, and simply said, "I don't get it . . ."

The national championship followed the traditional start for the course. At Crystal Springs this meant all 300+ athletes lined up on a wide start line (wide enough to pack all the athletes in uncomfortably), which began at the highest point of the trail. The start then funneled onto a gravel fire road (which traveled steeply downhill for the first half mile). A turnaround loop at the bottom sent all the runners back the up the same hill, this time on a trail on the west ridge of the mountain, where they crossed the mile mark at the top and saw the spectators once again.

As for the competitors, Prefontaine was nowhere to be seen. Former Oregon runner Kenny Moore had said of Pre in early November: "He's been busy building a sauna now and not running much. I'm all for him taking a length of time off. He's been obsessed too long." Steve Prefontaine shared insight into the matter mere hours before the start: "I'm in the worst shape I've been in for five years, and I don't care to be embarrassed." In his absence, Neil Cusack from Ireland, the Boston Marathon champion and former NCAA Cross-Country champion, seemed the best bet to battle Shorter. "He's gutsy tough," said Nick Rose. "He's a hard driver, better on tough courses." The 4,000 spectators who lined the course (many spilling past the "No Spectator" ropes) were eager to see if Shorter could successfully defend his title for the fourth straight time.

At the sound of the gun, Kenyan half-miler Mike Boit of Eastern New Mexico shot to a 10-yard lead—taking full advantage of his speed down the treacherous initial hill. Ted Castaneda of the Colorado Track Club was near the front, as was Neil Cusack. John Ngeno and Nick Rose were well-placed in the top 20. Shorter was engulfed by the pack. As the field rumbled off, several fallen entrants lay writhing, beating the ground in pain and frustration. After the first mile, Cusack and Rose were in the lead, with Ngeno and Castaneda right behind. Shorter, glassy-eyed and distant, was working his way up from 50th place.

As the trail descended from a ridge that had a misty view of the bay, the relaxed Cusack and the snorting, animated Ngeno moved away from the rest. At halfway, John Ngeno and Neil Cusack were clear of the pack. Shorter and Nick Rose were side by side in 27th place. Shorter was taking a long time to move. At four miles Ngeno surged into the lead, breaking contact with Cusack. It was clear at that point that Shorter had no chance of catching them. At the fifth mile, the Kenyan had a 100-yard lead on the field.

The finish was on the crest of one last cruel hill. Ngeno drove up and over the line in 29:58. Cusack made it 16 seconds later. "That hill took the last bit of momentum," Cusack said later. "It seemed that I ended stock-still on the line, like a crucifixion." Castaneda, the first American finisher, was third, and that performance helped his Colorado Track Club to the team title over the New York Athletic Club. Shorter, ashen and unsteady, finished 11th.

THE INDEPENDENCE MOVEMENT

With the running boom came new qualification standards. Once the IAAF assumed control of the International Cross-Country Championship in 1972, the United States became an official participant in the event. This prompted a new senior men's and junior men's World Trials Cross-Country Championship to be implemented in the spring of 1975 (a senior women's event appeared in 1986 with a junior women's trials appearing in 1989).

This transition also meant that the United States had to pay to send their teams abroad to compete—not easy for the AAU. After 1973 saw the United States represented by a lone women's senior team, it took until 1975 before a squad of senior men made the trip. The vacancies in 1973 and '74 were simply caused by a lack of allocated funds.

The US qualifying system for World Cross was hardly ideal. In 1975, when the AAU's pocketbook was ostensibly empty, the women were not even scheduled to fly to Rabat, Morocco. They were saved by Chuck Debus, UCLA's women's track coach. Apparently with the AAU's approval, Debus formed an 11th-hour setup in which the women could compete in a 2.5-mile track contest at three various sites. The six women who qualified got their money's worth: they won the World Cross-Country Championship.

Quickly the arrangement was revised. The following two years women qualified from the Women's AAU National Cross-Country Championship, run in late November. The men's squads were determined through the new "World Trials Cross-Country Championship," implemented in February 1975. At this first event, held over a 15,000-meter course in Gainesville, Florida, three of the top five finishers were of no surprise: Barry Brown (fifth in 47:47), Scott Bringhurst (second in 46:46), and winner Frank Shorter (46:32), all representing the Florida Track Club. However, the event wasn't without controversy. Due to the race's date and location, it was inaccessible to runners from the Northeast, and overlapped the hectic US indoor track season, causing headaches for runners who did both.

An amicable solution took time, but American talent was so deep the nation was able to absorb these losses and remain dominant.

FURTHER CLUB TEAM DEVELOPMENT

In addition to the Florida Track Club in Gainesville and the Oregon Track Club in Eugene, a few other groups came into prominence in the 1970s.

The 1976 US National Cross-Country team champions were called the Jamul (pronounced HA-mul) Toads. They were led by renowned Southern California coach Bob Larsen. In 1976, the team had only seven members, all victorious in events ranging from the mile to the marathon and all natives of the San Diego area.

Four of the seven ran for Larsen at Grossmont Junior College in El Cajon, California. Larsen's cross-country teams there had won five straight state junior college titles in an area abundant with distance running talent. At that time, California schools were not part of the National Junior College Association, prompting thoughts as to how they would have compared against powerhouse schools from Southwestern Michigan or Allegheny. But Terry Cotton (second in 30:26), Kirk Pfeffer (fourth in 30:33), Ed Mendoza (ninth in 30:41), Dave Harper (15th in 30:47), and Tom Lux (23rd in 30:55) outkicked prominent runners like Steve Flanagan, Gary Cohen, and Don Kardong to win the 1976 US National Cross-Country Championship.

The Colorado Track Club, led by Dave Merkowitz, also dominated the US National. Titles in 1974, '75, and '77 were theirs—featuring names like Ric Rojas (winner of the 1976 event), John Gregorio, Gary Bjorklund, Ted Castaneda, Mike Peterson, Charles Vigil, and Steven Flanagan. Their best performance was arguably in 1975, when they scored the ultra-low point total of 31, beating the New York Athletic Club and Florida Track Club, who came in second and third with 124 and 136 points, respectively.

The final piece of the puzzle came out of the Northeast. Known as the Greater Boston Track Club (GBTC), the team featured Bobby Hodge, Dick Mahoney, and Randy Thomas who lived and breathed the sport twenty-four hours a day. Other members, like Kirk Pfrangle, worked during the day and joined the club at night for hard training sessions. The GBTC coach, the best marathon coach in the world, was a one-of-a-kind man named Bill Squires. He was tall, fifty years old, and had a classic Beantown accent pitched to be heard in the most clamorous Irish barroom. Squires wouldn't use one word if ten would do, and there was no such thing as a straight line or a simple answer. But Squires was whip smart, a Notre Dame grad, and runners underestimated him at their peril. No coach understood the marathon in general, and the Boston Marathon in particular, better than he did. Years later, Bill Rodgers, known as "Boston" Billy, would joke that he started to worry about his mental health when he began to understand what Squires was talking about.

Boston Billy became legendary in 1975 when he won the Boston Marathon. For members of the Boston Track Club, Bill Rogers didn't fit the mold of the stereotypical runner: prior to his arrival he smoked cigarettes, rode a motorcycle, and worked as an orderly at the morgue. His long hair and personal convictions about the draft also belied his serious, competitive side. But he was not only one of the best marathon runners in the world, he was also an established World Cross-Country bronze medalist.

A SWEET SPOT IN TIME

Before he was called Boston Billy, Bill Rodgers was a cross-country runner. And in 1975 Rodgers made an assault on history in Rabat, Morocco, where he finished third—only eight seconds behind Ian Stewart of Scotland and Mariano Hero of Spain—becoming the first American to medal at the World Cross-Country Championship in the process.

The 1975 World Cross-Country Championship featured a stacked field, including Olympic 1,500-meter gold medalist John Walker from New Zealand; Olympic Marathon gold medalist Frank Shorter; Olympic 5,000-meter bronze medalist Ian Stewart of Great Britain; and Olympic 10,000-meter finalist Mariano Haro from Spain. It could be argued the race was loaded with the finest collection of champions from across the globe.

Rodgers shared how it happened:

Held in Morocco it was a perfect 70 degrees, sunny and dry. The race was run on a horse track and I remember we had to jump hurdles. I think it was the best race I ever ran in my life; I never felt tired, I felt great. World Cross was the big deal—to be there with Frank (Shorter)—he was the top distance runner in the world, was a big deal to me. Suddenly I knew and I felt cross-country was very exciting—just to be a part of this team of top notch guys. I remember I forgot my shoes so Gary Tuttle loaned me his spikes and they fit perfectly. For me, to finish third in this race, that moment was a sweet spot in time. Every rare once in a while it comes together—and I've had a few: New York in '76 (2:10.10) and definitely the 1975 World Cross-Country Championships. About once every few years we get one of those. When I left with a bronze medal I thought I could race with anyone.

For Rodgers, there was great significance in representing the United States internationally:

There is a power in cross-country. Being a member of Team USA in 1975, it was huge, I remember getting my uniform in the mail. I remember thinking, we have always done well in the World Championships, and the way the athletes conduct themselves shines brightly for their country. I am patriotic to a certain sense and that is a big part—before money we lived to compete just to run in the race and wear the uniform. Sitting on the plane with Olympians Frank Shorter and Jeff Galloway, I remarked that I was looking for a new pair of shoes for the Boston Marathon. Frank said he knew someone at Nike. I later received a package in the mail with a new pair

of shoes and a letter of congratulations on my third place bronze medal at the World Cross-Country Championships handwritten from Steve Prefontaine. I went on to win my first Boston Marathon in those shoes, he gave me some luck.

> **Did You Know?**
>
> After Bill Rodgers finished third at World Cross in 1975, Steve Prefontaine sent "Boston" Billy some shoes and a letter. "Dear Bill," the letter began, "First of all congratulations on a fine race in Rabat. You have really improved this past year and hopefully will continue until the Olympic Games. The reason I'm writing is because Jeff Galloway told me you were interested in training in our shoes. I'm sending you a pair of Boston '73s and a training shoe. Just feel free to drop me a line and let me know what you think. Wishing you continued success for '75. Sincerely, Steve Prefontaine." The shoes spoke for themselves: one month after finishing third in Morocco, Rodgers won his first Boston Marathon wearing a Greater Boston Track Club singlet, painters' gloves, and a pair of Boston '73s. The time was a new American record of 2:09:55.

While Pre was busy training for the 1976 Olympics during the winter of 1974, he was flourishing as a salesman. Prefontaine had been one of the first athletes to be officially hired by the Blue Ribbon Sports Company—that company, under the new alias of Nike, had reaped a total of $3 million in sales by 1975. Built almost entirely off the backs of the Eugene track and field community—Oregon runners connected with Bill Bowerman and owner Phil Knight—the brand was continuing to eat up market space in what was a newly revitalized running community in the United States.

THE WINGED GODDESS OF VICTORY AND THE SLOW DEATH OF AMATEURISM

By 1972 the Nike Athletic Shoe Company was one of the largest running-shoe manufacturers in America. Based in Beaverton, Oregon, Nike was one of the first manufacturers to understand the commercial value of promoting road races to large fields of hobbyists as well as elite racers. Moreover, Nike and a few similar organizations perceived the importance of "putting back into the sport," that is, of making investments that did not necessarily generate sales but created goodwill. They offered a successful brand because they understood the marketing value of their product being on the feet of athletes like Prefontaine and Rodgers. Nike took care of the athletes who ran well and reinforced their image—and as more success came for the company, so too did they prioritize who they would endorse next. The amateur ethos for distance running was being turned on its head—and cross-country running, the most egalitarian and natural of this form, was quickly being edged out by more lucrative variations on the road and the track, which were more sponsor-friendly and could be represented internationally and in the Olympics.

Later in 1972, the distance running community was rocked hard when businessman Michael O'Hara announced the formation of the International Track Association (ITA). No stranger to sports, O'Hara had previously founded the American Basketball Association and the World Hockey Association. The ITA represented professional track and field. Athletes were going to take money over the table, and payments would be contingent on performance in a given meet—not on negotiations beforehand.

O'Hara's credentials lent plausibility to the ITA, but he was not alone in the venture. Jim Ryun had signed to run the ITA circuit; Lee Evans, 400-meter gold medalist in the 1968 Olympics, had signed; shot-putter Randy Matson, another Mexico City gold medalist, was on board; pole vaulter Bob Seagren, also a Mexico City gold-medalist and world-record holder, was on the ITA team. Later, international stars such as Gerry Lindgren, Jim Hines, and Kip Keino joined. It certainly seemed like a winning proposition; the talent was there.

A number of other professional opportunities such as the made-for-television *Superstars* competitions and open professional road running complemented the professional track circuit. Track athletes embraced these opportunities to apply pressure for change in the governing bodies and amateur rules. The creation of new, open, professional opportunities combined with the escalation in the underground labor-relations system to create chaos in amateur track and a rethinking of the amateur rules throughout the turbulent 1970s.

In America, however, the professional element remained absent from cross-country running. While road races, marathons, and track events drew large numbers of participants, and spectators in the thousands, cross-country running remained blissfully niche and organically operated. The pressures placed on the AAU from the ITA in track and field did not impact the AAU or NCAA National Cross-Country Championships—and local, regional, and national contests grew steadily as they had in the previous thirty years. But larger implications structurally began to damage AAU oversight later in the decade, and these cracks were formed (in part) by the success of professionalized distance running.

THE SLOW DEATH OF AMATEURISM: THE FEDERAL GOVERNMENT STEPS IN

Track athletes routinely called for congressional intervention to protect them from the AAU and the NCAA. But the government opposed a federally mandated solution because it clashed with the amateur sport ideology. By the end of the 1960s this had changed—the fiction of the AAU's amateur sport ethos lay exposed. Only rarely could it be argued that the best American track athletes were still

amateurs or that the AAU did not try to control track athletes' careers.

The reorganization of the United States Olympic Committee (USOC) was also a priority for Congress. In 1972, the NCAA left the committee and it was becoming clear that the United States was not sending its best distance runners abroad to compete internationally.

Other groups also lobbied for change. Organized in 1972, the World Sports Foundation (WSF), which included distance runners Kenny Moore and Kip Keino, argued that the amateur rules were unrealistic and unenforceable. The WSF sought to provide athletes with more power and to liberalize the amateur rules. Suzy Chaffee, head of the foundation, wrote: "The main purpose of WSF is to provide the greatest opportunity for people to participate in sports without misrepresenting themselves."

In response to these vocal cries, the United States Senate proposed a bill called the Amateur Athletic Act in 1973, which would not only create a sports board for every major Olympic sport, but also increase government oversight in amateur athletics, give athletes (including collegiate athletes) more rights to determine their freedom in the sport, and give runners more representation. Unfortunately, after vehement AAU and NCAA lobbying, the bill was redacted—but the result of the measure was the President's Commission on Olympic Sports.

Spurred by President Gerald Ford, the President's Commission on Olympic Sports (PCOS) was surprisingly well funded, organized, motivated, ambitious, and innovative. It conducted a series of lengthy public hearings in a number of major cities that included testimony from leaders in all the important organizations. The hearing also included testimonies from athletes, including cross-country runners Frank Shorter and Kenny Moore. In fact, athlete input was a primary focus of the commission. As Senator Ted Stevens noted, "the role played by athlete members was unique. I think they were crucial to the understanding of the members from business, education, and the government." The PCOS's investigation produced an impressive two-volume report spanning more than six hundred pages in 1977.

This report and subsequent recommendations led to the passage of the Amateur Sports Act in 1978. The AAU's attempts to stave off legislation had failed. In late 1979 the AAU bowed out of track governance and gave its IAAF franchise to The Athletics Congress (TAC), the newly created national governing body for track and field. The ninety-year reign of AAU control of elite track and field governance had ended. The Amateur Sports Act reduced a finally defanged AAU to youth sports. Unfortunately, the newly formed Athletics Congress created more questions than it did answers. The structure of the organization was still unknown, and it remained to be seen how athletic representation would be different from the now-defunct AAU.

AMERICA LOSES A LIVING LEGEND

The pressure put on the Amateur Athletic Union and their monopolizing stranglehold on supposedly "amateur" distance runners was not just conducted by the underground labor-relations system—which paid athletes for travel fare, accommodations, and appearances—but was driven by the athletes themselves. And there was no greater advocate for a more equitable partnership than Steve Prefontaine. Yet before Pre could witness firsthand the fruit of his labors—which would manifest itself in the form of the Amateur Sports Act and the rebuilding of the amateur track and cross-country representation in America—tragedy struck.

In the early hours of May 30, 1975, Prefontaine was killed in a one-car collision on a wooded hillside street in Eugene. The *Track and Field News* obituary read: "He apparently lost control of his small sports car rounding a sharp curve, crossed the center-line, struck a rock wall and flipped over several times. He apparently died instantly, although autopsy reports indicate his injuries (alone) wouldn't have proved fatal. Rather, he was suffocated by the weight of the convertible. Pre's death came as he returned from dropping off friend Frank Shorter at the home of a fellow runner Kenny Moore. All had earlier attended a party following the Oregon Twilight meet to honor visiting Finnish Athletes."

The loss of Prefontaine was a national tragedy. Yet the way he conducted himself—and more importantly, the way he raced, what Prefontaine himself would describe as "a work of art that people can look at and be affected in as many ways they're capable of understanding"—provided the impetus needed to lead the next generation of distance runners.

THE SHOW MUST GO ON: PRE INSPIRES A NATION

As Prefontaine was nearing his prime, athletes in high school and college attempted to emulate his front-running style and brash take-no-prisoners mentality. Runners like Virgin, Salazar, and Chapa idolized the way Pre rose to challenges and never backed down. Not only did Eugene, Oregon, extol Prefontaine, but by 1975 everyone in America recognized him as America's fiercest distance runner.

The bar had been set for this next generation, which included Craig Virgin. Even though his high school didn't have a track, as an Illinois prep, Virgin set 12 age-group world and national class records—a product of Prefontaine's own chase at high school immortality. Virgin's two-mile time of 8:57.4 as a sophomore in 1972 remains the national record for fifteen-year-olds. He also broke Prefontaine's national high school two-mile record, running 8:40.9 in 1973. According to Virgin: "Prefontaine was my role model on the track. His racing style, commitment to training and commitment to developing his gift was what I wanted to emulate."

Virgin broke nine minutes in the two-mile 15 times in high school, a national record he shared with Eric Hulst. Hulst, a high school graduate in 1976, was also a Prefontaine protégé. According to Len Miller, who coached Hulst in his early years at Laguna Beach and later at the

University of California, Irvine: "If you think about Steve Prefontaine, Eric Hulst as a high school distance runner was as great as any of them."

And then there was Alberto Salazar, who was also in the graduating high school class of 1976. "My earliest running heroes were Dave Bedford, the British runner known for his extreme workouts and toughness, and Steve Prefontaine," Salazar said. "This was during the early and mid-1970s, and the cult of Pre was growing nationwide. But I had a personal connection. My brother's coach at Navy was a man named Al Cantello, who would trade workouts with Bill Dellinger at Oregon. Cantello would send Dellinger workouts for throwing events, and Dellinger would send running workouts to Cantello. My brother would say how great the Oregon distance program was. 'If you're serious about the sport,' he told me, 'Eugene's the only place to go.'"

THE HIGH SCHOOL MOVEMENT OF THE 1970s

Not only were American universities developing top athletes during the 1970s—but the entire culture surrounding cross-country at the high school level was changing as well. By the end of the decade, every state in America had legitimized a state cross-country meet at the high school level except for California, which ran section championships for various regions. Forty-two states had also authorized state competitions for female competition.

Media coverage was also changing. In 1973, *New York Times* reporter Marc Bloom saw a lack of comprehensive coverage for high school cross-country and came up with a revolutionary idea: *The Harrier Magazine.* As Bloom described: "I started *The Harrier* in 1974 because at the time there was virtually nothing to be found on cross-country, which I happened to love; it was at the bottom of the running food chain. I covered high schools and colleges more or less equally and started doing national high school team rankings and naming All-American teams. I put out 10 issues a year and acquired a loyal audience." Bloom's rankings of top teams and individuals transformed the sport.

International prestige also played a part in this changing American landscape. In 1974, the AAU used funds allocated by the United States Olympic Committee to hand-pick six junior athletes to travel to Italy to represent the United States at the World Cross-Country Championship. The only condition was that the athletes had to remain nineteen years old or younger during the entire 1974 calendar year. Among those chosen were John Roscoe, Matthew Centrowitz, J. J. Griffin, Pat Davey, Mike Pinocci, and the nation's number one high school distance runner, Rich Kimball from De La Salle High School in California.

The meet in Italy, run on a horse racetrack, covered 7,000 meters (about four and a half miles). Mike Pinocci, an All-American junior college runner for Odessa, Texas, at the time of his selection, had this to say about the experience: "It was completely different from anything I've run before. At the starting line we just walked up and the gun went off. There was no on your marks, get set or anything like that. There were even barriers we had to jump over." The United States team, competing for the first time together overseas, beat runner-up Morocco by a score of 22 to 58. Additionally, up until the final half mile, it was a tight race between John Treacy (Ireland), Venanzio Ortis (Italy), and Rich Kimball, but in the end it was the American who secured the victory by three seconds.

RICH KIMBALL AND MITCH KINGERY: THE BAY SETS THE BAR

At the time of his selection for the 1974 World Cross-Country Championship, Rich Kimball, a seventeen-year-old senior at De La Salle High School in the Bay Area, was the number-one ranked high school distance runner in America. The previous year as a high school junior, Kimball had finished sixth overall in the California state meet two-mile race, running 9:08. A few weeks later he finished sixth again, this time in the AAU Junior six-mile championship, running 29:57, a prep-class best for his grade level.

But Kimball's senior cross-country season saw him make a marked improvement: he won the Artichoke Invitational at Half Moon Bay High School by more than 56 seconds; he defended his California Interscholastic Federation (CIF) North Coast Section title in cross-country; and at the end of November, Kimball flew to Florida where he competed in the AAU Senior US National Cross-Country Championship in Gainesville—where at only seventeen years old he was able to defeat six-mile NCAA champion Charlie Maguire as well as NCAA three-mile runner-up John Gregorio, qualifying for World Cross in the process. Perhaps most amazing was the fact that Kimball had broken his ankle in February and had been in a cast until mid-April.

In a candid interview, Kimball revealed some of his training secrets: "I work out twice a day, every day, all year; usually six miles in the morning and 8–12 in the afternoon. Sundays I do a long run, 15–20 miles. During the summer and cross-country season, I do more distance work and toward the end of cross-country begin adding more speed. I do a lot of interval training, such as 20 quarters at 65 pace with a minute recovery. I try to run in the hills because I enjoy them." And for racing, Kimball stated: "When it comes down to racing, I try to set a quick pace so I won't get caught in the pack. I have no real tactics except maybe on the track where I always let someone else set the pace at the start. I run for the enjoyment of it." But while Kimball may have been enjoying his time at the top—he was being pushed every step.

Only fifty miles away from Kimball, San Carlos's Mitch Kingery was making headlines. As a junior in the fall of 1973, he went undefeated in the six cross-country races he ran, and set and reset the course record at Crystal Springs, running a time of 14:28 on October 25, a mark that still leads the way more than forty years later. Each of his six times for the course were in 14:45 or better, and he won his first Central Coast Section Cross-Country Championship.

In the two-mile, he lowered his personal best to 9:00 flat and again competed at the state meet in California.

Closing out his high school career, Kingery broke 9:00 in the two-mile race at the state meet, running 8:57, and he went on to have a prosperous collegiate career in cross-country at the College of San Mateo and California Polytechnic State University, San Luis Obispo. Kingery's greatest achievement in cross-country, aside from setting the high school course record at Crystal Springs, was finishing second overall at the NCAA Division II Cross-Country Championship in 1978—where as a reward for his effort he was able to run in the NCAA Division I Championship the following week.

BOBBY THOMAS: 1975 JUNIOR MEN'S WORLD CHAMPION

In December 1974, the AAU ran the first junior men's qualifying cross-country championship, which was used to select six runners for the World Cross-Country Championship. Held right on San Francisco Bay in Alameda, California, the event covered an 8,000-meter out-and-back course with four steeplechase barriers. Many of the biggest nineteen-and-under names in the United States participated, including John Roscoe (who had finished sixth the year prior in the World Cross-Country junior race), Roy Kissin, Ralph Serna, Mitch Kingery, Don Moses, Don Clary from Anchorage Alaska, and the phenom from Laguna Beach, Eric Hulst, who had run an unbelievable CIF Prelims at the Mount San Antonio College "Mt. SAC" Invitational in cross-country over the contemporary distance of two miles in the fall of 1974.

Despite these big names, nobody registered Bobby Thomas a threat—then a freshman at Glendale Community College, a school he had led to the state championship in the junior-college division in 1974. He won this World Cross qualifier race, edging John Roscoe at the line—each with identical 24:26 clockings for eight kilometers.

"It was a dream of mine just to compete in a meet like that," Thomas said. "Winning it was something altogether different. I was just praying that no one would catch me." Thomas then won the 4.8-mile World Cross-Country Junior Championship race in 20:59.4, almost 19 seconds ahead of second-place competitor José Luis González of Spain. Incredibly, just two weeks before World Cross, Thomas had won the junior college three-mile championship on the track, setting a national junior college outdoor three-mile record of 13:36.4.

The year Thomas spent at Glendale College in 1974–75 was the best of his life as a runner. Thomas recalled, "I was very fortunate to have great coaches at Glendale High like Jim Jordan and John Barnes that really helped mold me as a runner [Thomas recorded a school-record 9:06 two-mile as a senior in 1974]. But the team at GCC got together the summer before school started in 1974 and coach [Mark Covert] really felt that we had the talent to go all the way to the state meet. Mark Covert and John Tansley were two of the best coaches I ever ran for."

With standout Alaskan prep star Don Clary joining the qualified American junior runners in Morocco (Clary was a two-time Alaska state cross-country champion with a 9:04 two-mile as a senior), and Roy Kissin and Ralph Serna each performing swimmingly, the United States was able to earn its second team gold in addition to Thomas's outstanding individual win. Unfortunately it would be one of his final achievements, as injuries beset Thomas after his magical season and he failed to regain his former standing after 1975.

ERIC HULST AND THE JUNIOR DREAM TEAM

In January 1976, the AAU World Cross junior qualifier was won by Eric Hulst in 22:48 (a pace of 4:39 per mile for 8K). His time was elite—especially considering that the ground was wet from golf-course sprinklers and that steeplechase barriers permeated the course.

Hulst's competition was also superb. Thom Hunt, from Patrick Henry High School in San Diego, finished second; Ralph Serna, a freshman at UC Irvine (and former two-time Southern Section cross-country champion in 1973 and '74) and Don Moses, who ran for Crescenta Valley and was the reigning 1975 Southern Section cross-country "large school" individual champion also competed; as did Tim Holmes, who was the top finisher from Northern California, running for Downey High School. When East Coast champion Alberto Salazar and Texas standout Marty Froelick were added as qualifiers, it was no surprise that the 1976 team was considered the best the United States could provide.

Thom Hunt explained:

We had a super team, Rudy Chapa did not compete, but we were still a super team. That year they had the trials in Irvine, California. We could probably have won Worlds with just SoCal guys . . . then you add Alberto. We had this group, Alberto Salazar, Eric Hulst, Don Moses, Marty Froelick and Ralph Serna. In California, cross-country was 2.0 miles, and that year I beat Eric a few times, but when we ran 8K cross-country he had more strength than I did. We considered Mt. SAC the proving ground of who was the best in the state. At Mt. SAC that year as a senior when Eric and I made the final turn, Eric Hulst, Don Moses, and myself were side by side. I outkicked them and all three of us had broken Terry Williams's previous record. Cross-country was Eric's forte at the time.

In that epic Mt. SAC cross-country showdown in the fall of 1975, Hunt, Hulst, and Don Moses sped past the mile in 4:18. Hunt challenged for the lead in the last 200 yards, setting a course record of 9:45 in the process, while Hulst's time was 9:47. Don Moses was third in 9:51. Prior to the trio, only two people had ever broken 10 minutes on the two-mile course: Terry Williams of Lompoc and Hulst (the previous year as a junior).

Eric Hulst had reason to be proud. As a freshman at Laguna Beach, he decided to go out for cross-country to get in shape for tennis, his first love. But he became a running sensation overnight. Hulst ran 9:04 for the two-mile as a freshman, 8:50 as a sophomore, and 8:44 as a junior—all stand-alone national class records. He won three Southern Section cross-country titles before he was able to compete in the World Cross-Country Junior event in 1976.

His training sometimes brought him as much notoriety as his racing. Hulst ran up to 130 miles a week, sometimes while wearing a lead vest or carrying four-pound hand weights. "Eric had one gear and it was to the wall," said Doug Speck of *Track and Field News*.

The 1976 World Cross-Country Championship Junior Race was a blowout—the most successful team finish until the arrival of Ethiopia in 1982. The United States placed its top five in the first 11 places, with the four scoring members finishing first (Hulst), second (Hunt), fifth (Salazar), and eighth (Moses). Eric Hulst's time of 23:53 for the 7.8-kilometer course was 13 seconds faster than runner-up Hunt and nearly half a minute ahead of the first non-US finisher. Irish athletics reporter Fionnbar Callanan had this to say about the occasion:

It is difficult to imagine a more comprehensive win in such an event than that which American champion Eric Hulst scored. He went to the front right from the gun and ran so powerfully and confidently that I, for one, have no doubt but that he could have doubled his winning margin of 13 seconds had he really wanted to. I yield to no one in admiration of our own John Tracey who had twice been third in this race and was again eligible but unavailable because of exams; I honestly do not think that he could've beaten Hulst but I would dearly like to have seen the pair do battle!

THE ROOKIE

Among the graduating high school class of 1976 was a prep distance star by the name of Rudy Chapa—who set the still-standing national high school record in the 10,000 meters in a time of 28:32 and won the Indiana State mile in 4:04 his senior year. But while Chapa was a two-time Indiana cross-country state champion, neither he nor the other California kings were as decorated or as feared as one other member of that same graduating class: Alberto Salazar from Wayland, Massachusetts. At sixteen, Alberto Salazar was a promising high school runner who had been thrown in with the Greater Boston Track Club and the long-haired, hippie phenomenon Bill Rodgers. The rest, as they say, is history.

According to Salazar:

We lived in Wayland, a Boston suburb, in the 1950s. A man named Fred Brown, president of the North Medford Track Club, instituted a summer series of road races in the area. As a 15-year-old kid competing against grown men, there was no way I could challenge the leaders. I ran in the middle of the small fields of serious athletes; no one showed up at a road race just to finish in those days. I simply focused on notching a PR, on beating my previous best time. Here I am, a freshman in high school, just a kid, and all of this stuff is funneling through me . . . and it began to have an effect. In the fall of that year, I finished 19th in the state cross-country championships.

After finishing undefeated in cross-country as a junior, Salazar went on to finish second overall at the state meet. Then, in 1975, Salazar's magical year began: "My success continued during the first part of the winter indoor season. One day after a meet, a man named Kirk Pfrangle came up to me. He said that he was a member of something called the Greater Boston Track Club, and he invited me to participate in one of the club workouts. I said sure. I was vaguely aware of the GBTC, but I didn't know a lot about it. I didn't realize that Kirk's invitation was the equivalent of a high school shortstop being invited to play with the Boston Red Sox."

Bill Squires, coach of the Greater Boston Track Club, preached long interval training at top speed—a method of thought that went against the long, slow distance being preached elsewhere. Salazar, as a consequence of training with the older, experienced runners, quickly saw results: "In late June, Coach Squires entered me in the USA Junior Outdoor Track and Field Championships, for athletes 19 and under, held in Knoxville, Tennessee. I did not win

the 5,000-meter race—I again finished second—but I competed against athletes significantly older than me, including guys who'd just finished their freshman year in college. Moreover, my 14:14 time tied Craig Virgin's mark as the fastest ever by a 16-year-old. That performance—my first world record—took me to another level. People regarded me differently. More important, my expectations for myself changed."

These moments were the lead-up to Salazar's senior year in cross-country. That fall, Salazar went fully undefeated and made an attempt on the state course record. His time of 14:04.8 for the 5,000-meter course was a brand-new record (Chicopee's Dan Dillon had beaten Salazar the previous season over a 2.85-mile course at Franklin Park). Following his senior cross-country season, Salazar finished an outstanding 24th overall (29:39) in the US National Cross-Country Championships senior race, finishing only 42 seconds behind winner Greg Fredericks and beating such notables as Neil Cusack and Gordon Minty. By the spring, Salazar had crossed the line third in Irvine in the junior qualifier to earn his spot onto the World Cross team—where as a member of the 1976 "Dream Team" Salazar's fifth place finish helped the United States score 16 total points for the win.

RUDY CHAPA MAKES HISTORY

In the spring of 1975, a trio at Hammond High School in Indiana also made history. Three runners, led by their coach, Dan Candiano, broke nine minutes in the two-mile run, the only high school with three runners to accomplish that feat in the same year. Among them was Rudy Chapa, the son of Mexican immigrants, who had legendary toughness—resiliency he would need as he helped set this record at an institution without a track. The secret to Candiano's success was prodigious miles run on a three-quarter-mile dirt loop.

It wasn't planned. It hadn't been a specific goal for any of the trio or their coach; it just happened. Carey Pinkowski did it first, running a solo 8:56 on what was described as a "horrible, cold, windy day." In cross-country, Pinkowski and Chapa had intentionally tied for first in the Indiana State Championships. A few days after Pinkowski broke 9:00, Chapa and Tim Keough rose to the challenge, running 8:52.6 (Chapa) and 8:52.8 (Keough). At that moment the Hammond Trio had the first-, second-, and fourth-fastest times in the country for two miles.

Each of the three students was fiercely competitive and liked nothing better than to demonstrate their deserving to be on top. And charged with directing, disciplining, and developing all this talent was Dan Candiano—a Gary, Indiana, native and recent graduate of DePaul University—who was a rebel in his own way.

Candiano was determined to provide opportunities for his athletes, but it wasn't easy. There was no junior high track or running program, no feeder system, so Candiano had to recruit. As one example, Candiano spotted Pinkowski in his English class. But from his own experience,

Candiano believed that mileage was the secret to improvement. When he had run more, he had run faster, so his team was tasked with a regimen of more than 100 miles a week, training every day, most often two workouts a day. They'd be up at 5:30 a.m., and if they weren't, Candiano would find out why. Alberto Salazar, who counts Chapa as his closest friend, laughs as he recalls Chapa telling him that if he wasn't at practice in the morning, Candiano would come to the house, walk up to Chapa's bedroom, and bang on the door. "Typical Latin family," Salazar said. "Oh, he needs to be at the workout. OK, coach, go get him."

Candiano's training program wasn't a one-size-fits-all, sink-or-swim approach, however. He knew he had to adapt his formula to fit the athletes. Chapa could handle just about anything Candiano threw at him. If his toes hurt, Chapa just cut off the front tops of his running shoes and kept going. Candiano maintained that the key to their success was the strength-building mileage, the emphasis on distance, and the soft ground they ran on in their daily workouts circling Maywood Park. Hammond High had no track, so their track became the three-quarter-mile square park. Instead of a typical program that mixed long runs on the roads with interval training on the track, Candiano's program was similar to how Kenyans trained on the red clay roads of their homeland. Even on the long morning runs the pace always varied, and the intensity of the sessions was dictated by the innate competitiveness of the participants.

"We had some of our hardest races in 'races' in Maywood Park," said Pinkowski. "We did a lot of speed play, fartlek in the morning. Long intervals in the evening–one-lappers, two-lappers. Long run was a 10-lapper hard on Friday afternoon." But Candiano knew that all that hard work had to be supported by other motives. "I knew that to get these guys to do what I was asking them to do, there had to be some recognition," said Candiano. He organized assemblies and pep rallies at the school and hung signs over the locker room and in the school halls touting the accomplishments of the athletes. He made them rock stars at a time when runners often didn't get much attention.

The hard work, high mileage, and fast intervals paid off. In the fall of 1975, Chapa gained his second straight Indiana State Cross-Country title—running 11:46 for 2.5 miles. University of Oregon coach Bill Dillinger recruited Chapa after that. He and fellow freshman Alberto Salazar joined a storied history with the Ducks. While at Oregon, Chapa became a six-time All-American in cross-country and track and won a team title at the NCAA Cross-Country Championship in 1977. Chapa, Salazar, and the others were slowly breaking out of Prefontaine's shadow.

But Prefontaine wasn't the only one giving inspiration. It was Craig Virgin, a farm boy from neighboring Illinois who had broken Steve Prefontaine's national high school record with an 8:40 two-mile in 1973, who served as a hero for the Hammond, Indiana, trio. "It wasn't Prefontaine or Shorter or any of those guys that were as much of an influence," said Keough. "Virgin was one of us. He was our age. He was from the Midwest. Somebody we could relate to."

VIRGIN LIGHTS THE FIRE

Craig Virgin's introduction to cross-country was a chance, serendipitous adventure. Showing up as a high school freshman the day after his fourteenth birthday, Virgin was encouraged to run cross-country by his eighth grade basketball coach. Virgin explained:

> I owed it to my eighth grade basketball coach. I felt the only way I wouldn't get cut from the team was to out-hustle all of my teammates on every running drill. The grade school, junior high and high school were side by side with a big field behind it that was a third of a mile around. My coach timed me and then went to the high school running coach and found out their times and only one or two were faster than me. One day he brought my dad in and said, "Craig should consider running cross-country." He was kind for not saying that I was a pretty lousy basketball player who would just be collecting splinters.

> For my first day of cross-country practice I wore my junior high gym suit and my Chuck Taylor Converse All-Star basketball shoes. I broke away from the team and eventually lapped them all, running 15 laps on the field that was a third of a mile around. As a freshman that day the varsity boys snickered as I shot out front. They thought I would come back to them. I didn't.

In his first cross-country race, he won. In his first sectional, he failed to qualify for the state meet, a setback that lit a fire. Virgin threw himself into year-round training and went unbeaten the next season until finishing sixth in the state meet as a sophomore. He won his next 48 high school cross-country races in a row, setting course records in 46. His final record of 13:50.6 for three miles remains the Illinois state meet course record.

DEERFIELD HIGH SCHOOL AND THE MAGNIFICENT SEVEN

Four years after Virgin's historic high school course record, *The Harrier Magazine* released the first national high school team rankings in 1976. Immediately, a buzz and excitement spread throughout the nation as top programs sought fervently to be crowned national champions. Team rankings were again released in 1977. In that two-year span, the nation's first super program emerged at Deerfield High School in Illinois. They won both years after undefeated cross-country seasons.

Deerfield's most notable feat was a 14:33 three-mile runner average at the 1977 Lake County Championships (72:46 total team time), and it was the Deerfield top-five who made it commonplace to crack the 15-minute barrier. While Virgin and the Hammond trio set the bar, each of the Deerfield athletes were stars of their own, and they did it together. Todd McCallister ran 9:07 for two miles on the track (and 14:15 for three in cross-country); brother Mark McCallister was close behind in 9:10 (14:22); Keith Hampton third in 9:05 (14:33); Tom Stevens, fourth with a 9:12 (14:38); and in fifth came Dane Rutstein, who clocked a 9:16 (14:28). Five sub-9:15 two-milers on one team: simply unbelievable.

Marc Bloom wrote it was a "once-in-a-generation cross-country squad, a team so fine it will inspire awe whenever it competes. The training of Deerfield has been something of cross-country lore . . . training as aggressively as any program in US history. Likened to collegiate workouts, Deerfield's level of accountability at practice was legendary." In the fall *Harrier* preview, Coach Len Kisellus claimed, "Our training program is planned so the athlete experiences a gradual adaptation in stress, and in turn it is our hope that our program develops a greater immunity to fatigue." While Kisellus preached immunity, it was the runners themselves who forged it through hard work and competetiveness.

Varsity standout Dane Rutstein shed light on Deerfield's training:

> Deerfield was a team of thoroughbreds. Twins Todd and Mark McCallister provided us with national caliber speed and mindset: they had been competing under the tutelage of their father and former coach Dick McCallister since elementary school. Their vocabulary was spiced with references to fartlek and cut downs and Igloi training [after the 1950s Hungarian coach who relied exclusively on interval workouts]. To venture out, away from the track, away from the high school course, on a long run of ten miles with the McCallisters was something of an odyssey. To be sure, we would start off slowly, chatting, easing into the mileage. But there would always come a point when the conversation would cease, the pace would quicken, the breathing would become focused and purposeful, and what followed would be a buildup from an unstated start to an undetermined finish that invariably simulated race conditions. The whole thing might go for only three quarters of a mile in the middle of the run and crescendo into a mad sprint to some intersection and then stop, followed by a 4-mile recovery trot home. Or, the buildup might come later in the run and last insanely for a full three miles while you were left to wonder, "Are we pushing like this all the way back home? Should I conserve or kick?" The elements of surprise pace and uncertain distance toughened us all.

TOP HIGH SCHOOL TEAMS IN 1978

In 1978, it was three US teams who fought to be crowned the greatest high school team in the nation. In Indiana, Carmel High School put together an undefeated year for the history books. In Illinois, previous-season runner-up York was going for their seventh state championship under the tutelage of coach Joe Newton—who would go on to say the 1978 harriers were some of the best he had ever coached. And from Eugene Oregon came South Eugene High School, who had been steadily building over the years and was willing to do whatever it took to earn the title of best high school cross-country team in the nation.

Each team did not disappoint: Carmel faced some of the best talent in the Midwest at the Indi-Illini Classic. York attempted to go undefeated, despite being ranked seventh overall in Illinois to start the year. And South Eugene gave one of the best cross-country performances the state of Oregon had ever seen.

Each team possessed thoroughbreds. In Indiana, state-sanctioned courses were traditionally 2.5 miles long (4,000 meters), and at the Pike Cross-Country Sectional Championships in 1978 the Carmel boys made a statement as they placed five in the top 10. Senior Rod Zachowski won in a meet record of 12:14; junior Bill Shuey finished fourth in 12:27; in sixth came senior Scott Beasley who finished in 12:31; behind Beasley was junior Fred Newlin in 12:32; and in ninth was senior Steve Hannah in 12:35. The team average of 12:27 ranked as one of the top team averages in national history over 2.5 miles.

At York, Coach Joe Newton had led the Dukes to six state titles and five runner-up finishes (a percentage of 70 for podium-finishing) in a sixteen-year span, but they were ranked underdogs after losing to Deerfield the year before. At the 1978 Illinois state meet York overcame their ranking to win easily: a team average 14:51 for three miles among their top five. Then-junior Michael Newman knew it was a special year for the Dukes: "Since I ran on the 1978 York team, I have always felt that the *Harrier* rating was a sham. Yes, Carmel was a good team but they would not have beaten us. They did beat Fremd and Maine East at Illiana. Those teams placed fourth and sixth at the Illinois state meet to us, and we beat them pretty convincingly. I wish they would have had Nike Cross Nationals back then—the rankings would have changed. That's not talk . . . it's just a fact."

In Oregon, the South Eugene Axemen, based in Eugene, had won seven straight Oregon state titles. But in 1978, Coach John Gillespie knew he had a talented team on his hands and wanted to impress Marc Bloom in the national rankings for a *Harrier* number one spot.

By the end of the season, South Eugene had run the fastest team average over 5,000 meters en route to the winning the 1978 Oregon State Cross-Country Championship. The team was led by Jeff Hess's individual victory in 14:33; with Pat Allen fourth in 14:54; Mike Tracey 14th in 15:07; Rob Gemmell 19th in 15:14; and Dan Mazo 21st in 15:15—achieving a team time average of 15:01. While this was a special season and unveiled one of the greatest prep teams in US history, South Eugene had made the turning point at the Mount San Antonio College "Mt. SAC" Cross-Country Invitational. To many, the 1978 Mt. SAC Invitational was the greatest ever held. The course length, changed to three miles for the boys, had been around for a few years, and runners were able to really "let it all out" over the new distance.

Notable at this event was the performance given by Jeff Nelson from Burbank High School, which was also considered one of the nation's top distance programs in 1978. Nelson's legacy became a prep two-mile mark of 8:36 set in May 1979. But prior to this race, Nelson had won the state two-mile his junior year in 1978, coming back from injury to win in 8:59. During the summer before his senior cross-country season, Nelson and teammate Lin Whattcott (who ran 9:01 for two miles in 1979) ran upward of 140 miles per week.

The morning of the Mt. SAC cross-country invitational in the autumn of 1978 was cool and slightly foggy. At the sound of the gun, the field flooded up the switchbacks, already chasing the leader Nelson, who was rocketing up the steep hills a 5:00-mile pace, after a mile. South Eugene, in distinctive white and purple uniforms, and Jeff Nelson out in front, continued to pull away from the stacked field. Nelson, who ran on his toes, seemed to be a bit off-balance as he sailed ahead to a staggering 26-second win in the event, finishing in 14:32, with Paul Medvin next at 14:58 (the old course record was 14:56 by John Gerhardt of Costa Mesa that same year).

The team contest was a fierce one, with South Eugene emerging victorious with 91 points (a 15:41 average) to Mission San Jose's 125. Jeff Hess had led South Eugene in fourth overall at 15:15, with Pat Allen 10th at 15:28.

Nelson's 14:32 was absolutely stunning, a time so fast it opened up eyes as to what was possible, while the South Eugene group destroyed anything that had ever been achieved by a team previously with their 15:41 average. Commentators claimed the Oregon runners all looked like they were in their early twenties, shorter and stockier than the California preps at the meet, as if some form of evolution in the mist and trees of the Northwest had created a different type of runner. But it was clear that that 1978 cross-country race raised the bar. In some ways there has never been anything like it since.

LARGO HIGH SCHOOL AND ASTRONAUT HIGH SCHOOL BATTLE IN TITUSVILLE IN 1979

Entering the 1979 season two colossal cross-country programs out of the state of Florida would rewrite the record books. While East Maine and York were battling for the third and fourth spots in the national rankings out of Illinois, two teams in Florida battled for first.

In 1977, Astronaut High School of Titusville, Florida, had completed a magical season, winning every invitational they competed in. They were so powerful that on one occasion Astronaut split their varsity into two teams—supplemented with junior varsity runners—and competed in two major Florida invitationals on the same weekend, winning both. As the team boarded the buses to travel to the 1977 State Championship held in Deland,

Florida, victory seemed inevitable and spirits were high. This was a historic team. They won with record low scores, had 1,500 to 2,000 supporters, and had a marching band for their home invitational. Many in the community of Titusville felt a sense of pride for the success of Coach Nick Gailey's young athletes, and none more than the father of the top girl on the Astronaut team, Steve Flack. Flack brought a sense of passion and support that inspired the young men and women of Astronaut High School to excel.

But tragedy struck on the way to state. As Coach Gailey explained, "We had two buses and Steve was in his own car with his daughter, the top girl on the team, and his son. A drunk driver hit them and there was a big wreck. We were the back bus, so when we got to the wreck Steve's kids were being rushed to the hospital, and we didn't know their status, if they were alive or dead, and Steve was gone. It was incredibly tough for the kids. We didn't know if we should continue." Only hours later, the visibly and emotionally shaken Astronaut boys toed the starting line, and the once unstoppable force was overcome by the emotion of the loss. Offering no excuses, they finished second to crosstown rival Titusville High School, 55 to 59, a four-point defeat to a team they had previously defeated by high double digits on six occasions during the season.

Astronaut had a stable and high-achieving program, and despite the tragic ending to their 1977 season, both they and nearby Largo High School recovered to place in the top 10 nationally in 1978. The only loss Astronaut experienced in 1978 was delivered by Largo, ranked number five nationally. In the initial meet of the season, Largo won 32 to 37.

Entering the 1979 season, all eyes were on Florida. The Astronaut Invitational, the opening event of the year, was greeted by pouring rain and mud. Despite this, over 1,500 spectators showed up. Largo and Astronaut fought for revenge after the previous year's close contest. Largo, led by their top performer Basil Magee, was victorious for the second year in a row, winning the invitational 44 to 57.

Later in September, Largo and Astronaut would clash in a battle of epic proportions at the Winter Haven Classic (a meet that would be a better indicator of national relevance). In hot and humid conditions, Largo's Basil Magee took off at the start, with the following pack comprised of two runners from Largo and five from Astronaut. For three miles Largo and Astronaut ran side by side, runner for runner, until the final quarter mile. At the finish everyone was in shock as the scores tallied to a tie, 35 to 35. On a sixth runner evaluation Largo took 15th in 15:56 and Astronaut 17th in 15:58, with Largo winning by a two-second margin. With Basil Magee of Largo running a course record 14:37, Largo finished with an average team time of 15:28 to Astronaut's 15:35. It was clear both teams had made vast improvements and all eyes turned toward the State Meet in Deland, Florida—the site for a final showdown of the season.

The 1979 State Championship, run over three miles, separated Largo and Astronaut based on divisional school-size.

However, seeing each team perform on the same course on the same day would be the deciding factor as to which team had the stronger program. In the 4A contest (run first), Largo's Basil Magee was finally beaten. Winter Haven's Keith Brantley, who posted the meet record in 14:18 (a 4:46 per-mile average), bested Magee's 14:30. Nonetheless, Largo runners took places two, eight, 13, 14, 21, 23, and 26, scoring 59 points for the win with their top five. Their total team average was 15:09.2.

No team had ever performed so well in the state of Florida, and yet attention quickly turned to the other juggernaut, Astronaut High School. Taking charge from the sound of the gun, senior Ken Correnti led from start to finish, finishing in 14:51, with senior teammate Tony Farris coming in second in 14:52. When senior Mark Zayas came in fifth in 15:02 those in attendance knew something special was happening—lightning had struck twice and history was being made. Junior Guy George came in 12th in 15:20, then sophomore Van Savell in 17th in 15:26. The Astronaut team had scored an amazing 36 points—and more importantly—averaged a team time of 15:06.2 per runner.

Who was the better team? First, there was the mid-season tie. Then, once all attention was placed on the state meet, an evaluation of the top six runners revealed an identical team average of 15:14 to 15:14. These two performances show no differentiating variable. One thing was clear, however; both teams were deserving of being the nation's best in 1979.

The most striking take-away from this meteoric rise for high school running in America was that this spread and development of the sport occurred in a single generation's time. The sport had grown from urban hubs in small pockets of the country to stardom in every national corner in the span of sixty years. To justify cross-country's popularity with high schools and individuals, a new prep-level national cross-country championship was founded in 1979 that provided a consummate proving ground.

THE FIRST FOOT LOCKER (KINNEY SHOES) PREP CROSS-COUNTRY CHAMPIONSHIP IN 1979

During the postwar era, the Kinney Shoe Corporation was one of the largest and strongest distributors of shoes nation-wide—reaching sales of $358 million a year by 1974. Dubbing itself "The Great American Shoe Store," Kinney's expansion into retail branded athletic footwear and accessories with "Foot Locker," opened the market for running, hiking, track and field, basketball, bowling, and golf, as well as roller skates and ice skates. Within five years, seventy Foot Locker stores racked up $20 million in sales annually. Kinney passed the $1 billion mark in 1980, operating 2,115 stores. And in 1979 it launched the "Kinney Shoes Cross-Country Championships," the first national-caliber meet of its kind for high school runners.

On December 8, 1979, Kinney Shoes's first "National Cross-Country Championship" was held in Balboa Park, San Diego. Kinney was interested in promoting their

"Run to Be Fit" program, and the end result was a relatively small group of spectators turning out to watch 35 of the nation's best individual high school cross-country runners. The course, which today loops in a figure-eight fashion through the Morley Field portion of the park, was run on a path near the western edge of Balboa Park in 1979. The top seven finishers for boys and girls qualified through five regional meets: Houston and New York in October, Chicago in November, and San Francisco and Atlanta in December.

While the "Run to Be Fit" program was an intrinsic tie-in to market to a growing consumer base of runners and walkers, Kinney was able to appeal to coaches and meet directors and convey a sense of seriousness with the event that distinguished it from previous attempts (such as those by the AAU) at instituting a "National Championship." Meet Directors like Bob Latham and Vern Gambetta were tasked with managing the qualifying regions, while PR company Rudder and Finn was hired to help market the occasion.

Instead of an offshoot connected with a senior national championship, Kinney made the high schoolers the stars. Accommodations were paid for, and runners were treated to a four-star hotel stay at Mission Bay, while Kinney rented the San Diego Zoo Wildlife Safari Park in 1979 and catered in a special banquet for the athletes, coaches, and dignitaries (future editions would see the high schoolers go to SeaWorld).

The first year, students didn't wear their high school uniforms (as at the regional meets), but each team had different color singlets, shorts, and sweats (East, West, North, South). It helped develop a sense of team camaraderie. And the regional qualifiers posed an additional challenge (unlike the AAU Junior National, which was an open event any individual could participate in). In following iterations of the Kinney event, regional qualifiers would determine regional "teams" on the national stage—and media coverage was paramount.

Once the gun fired at the inaugural event, eventual winners Brent Steiner of Overland Park, Kansas, and Ellon Lyons of Boise, Idaho, took out the race hard. Each were challenged around two miles but both recovered to win, with Steiner beating Barasa Thomas of Santa Barbara 15:05 to 15:10 and Lyons defeating Lynne Strauss of State College Pennsylvania 17:28 to 17:42. Overall, 23 states were represented at this event, and plans were made to continue the Kinney National Cross-Country Championship in subsequent years.

TITLE IX CHANGES THE GAME

As a final chapter in the story of the prep cross-country movement of the 1970s, a portion of the United States Education Amendment of 1972 changed the face of cocurricular sports for good. Commonly known as Title Nine (Title IX), the original intent of the amendment was to offer equal gender opportunity in any school institution that received federal financial assistance. Signed into law by

President Richard Nixon on June 23, 1972, it wasn't until the end of the decade, after a review by the Office of Civil Rights, that a mandate for equal athletic participation was put into action.

While Title IX is best known for its impact on high school and collegiate athletics, the original statute (introduced by Indiana senator Birch Bayh, a women's rights activist) made no explicit mention of sports. The wording of the bill made it difficult to understand at a quick glance, and discussion on the Senate floor included whether the bill would require schools to allow women to play football. Not imagining the potential impact of Title IX once concerns about football were allayed, higher education did not lobby for or against the bill. The elementary and secondary education community remained unaware of the athletic impact because it was seen as being a classroom measure.

Once clarity was sought in June 1975 by the Department of Health, Education, and Welfare, regulations detailing Title IX enforcement were established. Universities receiving federal financial assistance were given three years to comply in all aspects of education, including athletics. And while the NCAA disputed the legality of such a measure, the Office of Civil Rights upheld the title in December 1979. Both colleges and high schools would have to provide equal opportunity, equipment, and facilities to all genders within the three years of the department provisions being passed, or consequences of non-compliance would be issued. In brief, the landscape of opportunity for female participation in cross-country running at the high school and collegiate level changed very quickly during the 1970s.

In 1971 fewer than 295,000 girls participated in high school varsity athletics, accounting for just seven percent of all varsity athletes. Within thirty years that number had grew to 2.8 million, or 41.5 percent of all varsity athletes, according to the National Coalition for Women and Girls in Education. By 1980, forty-two states had officially sanctioned championship cross-country competition for both genders at the high school level (with California designating it at the sectional level for all but two sections prior to their first official state meet in 1987). Today, cross-country running ranks in the top five most frequently offered college sports for women: 90.8 percent of colleges find participation in the sport.

THE ASSOCIATION FOR INTERCOLLEGIATE ATHLETICS FOR WOMEN

Title IX implementation made access of cross-country equal in schools, but the sport had already achieved a significant amount of female participation in the AAU more than a decade before. Consequently, having a younger audience meant faster times outside the school ranks. Faster times led to more interest for the sport, and the Association for Intercollegiate Athletics for Women (AIAW) Cross-Country Championship, held for the first time in November 1975, gave collegiate women their first opportunity for national competition.

The AIAW, founded in 1971, actually had a long history prior to governing collegiate women's athletics. Its predecessor, the Division for Girls' and Women's Sports (DGWS), which operated from 1966 to 1972, was the first nationally recognized collegiate organization for women's athletics and the forerunner of the AIAW, conducting national championships in eight sports for major universities (although cross-country was not one of them). In years when small-college championships (Division II or III) were not contested, and in sports without divisions, there was open competition. By the fall of 1975, however, an official national championship for cross-country running in Division I schools was instituted by the AIAW. Smaller schools—such as those representing Divisions II and III—were unrecognized until 1979. And 1981 finally saw the NCAA conduct their first Women's Cross-Country Championship for all divisions.

IOWA STATE, PEG NEPPEL-DARRAH, AND THE FIRST WOMEN'S COLLEGIATE CROSS-COUNTRY CHAMPIONSHIP

The week leading up to the first Intercollegiate Athletics for Women's Cross-Country Championship was cold and windy with a touch of snow—but by race day, the weather cleared. Iowa State (in Ames) was the site of this first official AIAW championship, as they had a long record hosting an annual end of the year event previously.

In total, 53 teams entered athletes into the championship, which was held over a three-mile course at George Veenker Memorial Golf Course. A total of 169 women took part in the event. Among them was Peg Neppel, the favorite for the individual title and the consummate senior leader of a strong Iowa State team. However, the team was without its traditional number two finisher, Carol Cook, a junior transfer from Southwest Missouri State who was suffering from shin splints and a pulled groin muscle. Relying heavily on freshman Sue Deppe, Annette Klass, and Lisa Hannity to carry the team, there was doubt as to whether Iowa State would go into the record books as the first team champion.

Neppel—who had international experience at the World Cross-Country Championships and had led Iowa State to three USTFF cross-country titles and an unbeaten record in 21 collegiate meets—was not the only contender. Tena Anex, running for the University of California, Davis, was a qualified challenger who had experience running in the 1972 World Cross-Country Championships and had set the US national record for the 3,000 meters, clocking 9:42. Also present was sophomore Kristen Bankes of Penn State, who had finished second in the Pennsylvania state meet in the 880-yard and would eventually go on to finish second in the two-mile race and third in the 1,500 meters at nationals.

Wendy Knudson, one of the most accomplished female track athletes in the history of Colorado State University, was also present. Knudson had been forced to choose between competing on her high school track team or with the Amateur Athletic Union, as high school rules would not allow her to do both. She chose to run for the AAU, competing in and winning her first international meet in 1972. She was profiled in *Sports Illustrated* and later made an Olympic team.

Another runner with Olympic experience was Taiwan's "Kathy" Lee Chiu-Shia, who set the 1,500- and 3,000-meter records at the 1975 Asian Track and Field Championships in Seoul, Korea. Chiu-Shia was training in the United States in New York and was running as a member of the St. John's University team.

Other challengers included Teri Anderson of Leonardville, Kansas, competing for Kansas State, who set an American women's record in the 800-meter run as a freshman in 1972, as well as Kim Merritt of Wisconsin-Parkside, who would go on to be one of the top women finishers at the Boston Marathon in 1976.

But once the gun fired, it was all Peg Neppel. With a fast start in the first quarter mile, the competition was immediately at a disadvantage. Neppel's strategy proved just right, explained Chris Murray, the Iowa State coach: "Our attitude was that we wanted to hit the hills like a cannon and run the whole mile and a half there hard. Peg wanted to 'cool' the first mile. She did it sensibly and controlled the whole race."

Neppel finished the three-mile run in 16:31 and was followed by Tena Anex about 50 yards back. "It's the best field I've run against, but it wasn't my best effort," said Neppel. "I get my best effort when I have someone at my side." Finishing third was Kristen Bankes of Penn State, who clocked 17:12.

Buoyed by the performance of junior Barb Brown (who finished eighth, right behind Wendy Knudson of Colorado State), Iowa State won the team title, scoring 96 points to Penn State's 104.

For the remainder of the decade, Iowa State dominated the AIAW Cross-Country Championship, defending their title successfully in 1976, '77, and '78. In 1979 Iowa State was finally usurped by North Carolina State, who had finished second the year before and provided the individual champion, Julie Shea.

As for Peg Neppel, she went on to set three world records and still holds five Iowa State records. Those records, from the formative years of women's track and cross-country, are a testament to the strength of the first teams at Iowa State: "The cross-country team Peg was on, they'd absolutely annihilate the best teams in the Midwest today," Murray said. "That was back in the '70s. They were hard-nosed kids from the farms."

DORIS BROWN HERITAGE PASSES THE TORCH

As one of the major names in international distance running, Doris Brown Heritage was making the most headway in cross-country. By 1970 she had won the first three International Cross-Country Championship titles offered, and in 1970 and 1971 she added two more victories to that list. Heritage had also claimed five US National Cross-Country

titles from 1966 to 1971. But in 1972, amidst pressure from the AAU to run at either the International Cross-Country Championship or the USSR–USA dual indoor meet, Heritage missed her opportunity to defend her International Cross title.

After 1972, Heritage would go on to run World Cross four times during the '70s. In 1975, Heritage's place of 17th overall (and as the final scorer) helped seal a United States victory for the women's team. But in 1973, after crossing the line in 15th place in Waregem, Belgium, Heritage witnessed Francie Larrieu, the future of American cross-country, finish one spot and five seconds behind. At twenty years old, Larrieu was Doris's junior by ten years but just as fast. Larrieu had claimed her second national cross-country title earlier that spring.

THE NEXT WAVE OF AMERICAN FEMALE TALENT

Francie Larrieu was, in fact, just a continuation of the success that Heritage had started. And Larrieu wasn't alone; Lynn Bjorklund and Julie Brown were not far behind.

Despite being a shy and willowy sixteen-year-old, Larrieu tied an American 1,500-meter record of 4:16.8 and spent the summer of 1969 representing her country in Europe and Japan. "That summer matured me," Larrieu claimed. For the next ten years Larrieu was the United States's dominant female miler. Traveling with the Pacific Coast Club, Larrieu spent the '70s performing in front of raucous crowds in track and field: "The life was abnormal, but I wasn't," she said. "I was happy. I just had this unusual existence in the track and field bubble, and it went on and on, and I won and won, and that was fine."

In cross-country Francie Larrieu was equally dominant, winning national titles in 1972 in Long Beach, California, and in 1973 in Albuquerque, New Mexico. In her 1972 race she beat Doris Brown Heritage handily, running 13:27 for 4K while Brown Heritage ran 13:53.

1974 marked yet another changing of the guard when Larrieu finished in third place on a challenging three-mile course in Bellbrook, Ohio, in 18:03. In second was her UCLA teammate: Julie Brown. The winner was an unheralded champion by the name of Lynn Bjorklund out of New Mexico, who ran a blazing 17:31.

In high school, Bjorklund set the national high school record in the 3,000-meter distance, which led to two straight US National Cross-Country titles in 1974 and '75. She came in seventh overall at the World Cross-Country Championships in 1976—the top finisher for the United States team. And when it came to pointing out a reason for her success at World Cross in '76, Bjorklund claimed it was simple: "I suppose my childhood had all the right factors, including pedestrian play at Los Alamos's altitude. As for that specific race, I had trained more than ever. It made for one exceptional race, but I spiraled into years of chronic overuse injuries that took away my ability to run, as well as the joy of it." At that point, the stage was set yet again for a new leader of the female distance movement.

In 1974, '75, and '76, Julie Brown was the consummate bridesmaid in the US National Cross-Country Championship, finishing second three straight years. Brown's accomplishments as a high school record holder for 800 meters helped her become the first woman to earn an athletic scholarship for cross-country running. Born in Billings, Montana, Brown competed in a variety of distance events winning the Montana State Cross-Country Championship as a senior. Collegiately, Brown won AIAW national championships in the 800 meters, 1,500 meters, 3,000 meters, and a title in cross-country in 1976.

After finishing second in the 1974 US National Cross-Country Championship, however, Brown finally won the 1975 World Cross-Country Championship five seconds ahead of Bronislawa Ludwichowska from Poland, leading a United States team that included Peg Neppel and Doris Brown Heritage. Julie Brown's victory was the first for the United States since Heritage in 1971. Furthermore, despite not running in the US National Cross-Country Championship in 1977, Julie Brown returned in 1978 to claim her first national cross-country title, and won a second in 1981.

But while these increased opportunities led to increasingly strong female competitors in the United States, the most promising male distance runners were forging their reputations at the same time in one of the most challenging divisions in sports: the NCAA.

THE NCAA FACTOR

Even with the absence of Prefontaine, the remaining years of the 1970s were filled with top talent—beginning with Pre's biggest rivals, John Ngeno and Nick Rose, who finished second and first at the 1974 edition of the NCAA Championship, respectively. Relaxed qualifying standards coupled with foreign-born talent made the NCAA Division I Cross-Country Championship one of the most competitive events for cross-country in the world during this period.

Rose upset pre-race favorite Ngeno at the 1974 championship in Bloomington, Indiana, by a full 15 seconds. Both runners broke the previous course record, despite unfavorable conditions. "It was muddy, hilly, demanding," Rose said happily. "Conditions I like. A cross-country race should be tough, not just a track race on grass." Sophomore Craig Virgin made a valiant attempt to chase down Rose, getting as close as the front pack, but as he claimed: "I went to pieces with half a mile left. Everybody and his mother passed me and I went from fourth to 12th."

In 1975, host Penn State created a wide and well-marked course free of tight turns that might slow the pace but with major hills at 2.2, four, and 5.2 miles: a course where race conditions would not be the deciding factor. "I have watched every NCAA championship since 1956," said track coach Harry Groves, "and the only fair course was the one at Kansas in 1965 and '66. This is my masterpiece." Penn coach Jim Tuppeny added, "It's fair. And this is perfect distance running weather—cool and dry. For

twenty-six years the NCAA was at Michigan State, where it snowed every fourth year."

Junior Craig Virgin was primed to take full advantage. Despite suffering a two-year siege of injury and illness, Virgin's competitive instincts and physical ability were unimpaired leading into the fall of 1975—and he set course records in all but one of his seven races during the 1975 season. Despite this, John Ngeno was again a favorite for the individual title, along with teammate Joshua Kimeto, and Nick Rose, running in his senior season.

Within four miles of the 1975 NCAA Cross-Country Championship, Nick Rose and Craig Virgin had separated themselves from the other competitors, including the hard-pressing Kenyans who started the race strongly. The four-mile was marked by the start of a half-mile long hill that rose steadily from the lowest to the highest point on the golf course. Here Rose, the hill specialist, made his first big move in an effort to shake off Virgin. Both Rose and Virgin charged the hill, but when they reappeared Virgin had the lead. Ngeno, still third, and Kimeto, fourth, were falling back. The rest of the field, strung out over half a mile, moved along behind like an undulating multicolored ribbon.

Virgin and Rose continued to battle through the next mile, scratching inches from one another. On the flat leading to the last hill, with three-quarters of a mile to go, Rose lengthened his stride. Virgin's strategy until this point had been defensive. Now, at the final hill, he made a move of his own. The two tore into the rise and, at its top, Virgin had Rose beaten by a step. This time it was Rose's turn to fade; he crossed the finish line 15.5 seconds behind Virgin's 28:23. Ngeno held on to third, and teammate Kimeto finished 14th. But despite all the talent present at the 1975 event, no one captured as much attention as one powerful Kenyan would after his arrival from the Rift Valley.

ENTER HENRY RONO

He came from Kenya and he ran like a god. He was Henry Rono, a man whose love of running came from the demands of his native culture, not from a national spotlight. During an eighty-day period in 1978, he set world records at 3,000 meters (7:32.1), the 3,000-meter steeplechase (8:08.4), 5,000 meters (13:08.4), and 10,000 meters (27:22.4). It was unheralded—a feat no one had come close to achieving—not Zátopek, not Nurmi.

Rono was a member of the Nandi tribe of Kenya's Great Rift Valley, where running was part of the culture: necessary for getting to and from school, tending crops, and herding cattle. Rono was moved to consider competitive running by the example of Kip Keino, who lived in a neighboring village. "At school I played soccer and volleyball," Rono claimed, "and I kept in my mind the idea to run later. One day in 1971 I heard that Keino was coming with other athletes to appear at a place near where I lived. He was from only three miles away, but I had never seen him, so I went. The announcer asked Keino to put up his hand so we would know who he was, and I saw him.

There were many people around him. I stood by myself above in the stadium and watched." Rono paused. "From that time I was a runner."

Rono began running on his own, and though he spoke with other runners about training, he never had a coach. "I began gradually, not doing too much," Rono said. "To build my mind I started with the steeplechase." He was soon winning school races, running an 8:30 steeplechase over barriers (but without a water jump) in 1972. After graduating high school three years later, he laced up army boots instead of racing spikes. In contrast to Nurmi and Zátopek, who flourished as distance runners because of their military careers, Rono quickly decided he hated the service. His military running did result in a berth on the Kenyan Olympic team, an opportunity squelched by the Organization of African Unity (OAU)–led boycott of Montreal. The Olympic disappointment was only a minor problem for Rono; he had already decided his future lay not in the army but at Washington State University in America.

In the fall of 1976, Rono turned up in Pullman after the African boycott forced the Kenya team to depart the Montreal Olympics. "Before the Olympics, these guys from Washington State, like John Ngeno, were training where we were in Kenya. We didn't have as much experience as John. I found out about Washington State because of John Ngeno. These friends of mine, John and Kip Ngeno were there, and they introduced me to Washington State. And well, I had to go."

JOHN CHAPLIN AT WASHINGTON STATE

WSU coach John Chaplin took over the program after the retirement of longtime head coach Jack Mooberry—and his policy was to win track meets for his employer, no matter the cost. Chaplin and several other American coaches had taken the controversial approach of recruiting the best possible talent, regardless of age or national origin. It was then that Henry Rono of Kenya, aged twenty-five years old, became a WSU freshman in the fall of 1976. Almost immediately he won the NCAA Cross-Country Championship.

For Rono, training made a difference: "Before I came to America, I knew nothing about interval training. I learned it is more mental than physiological. The muscles do not change when you do interval work, but the mind changes very drastically to accept pain. If you train to absorb the pain, you are never going to be good, but if you train to break the pain, then you go into a new level. Many runners worry about who is in the race, or they think about the time they must run to win. I only try to run as fast as I am capable—nothing less."

"We can control every race," said Chaplin, who was blunt, sometimes caustic, but passionately devoted to his athletes. "With our ability to surge, anything the opposition [does] is wrong. Go with us and you're in oxygen debt. Stay back, and adiós, we're gone." Thus, Washington State had a long tradition of testing their opponents early with athletes like Gerry Lindgren in the mid-1960s and Ngeno in the 1970s. With Rono, Joshua Kimeto, the two-time

NCAA 5,000-meter champion, Samson Kimobwa, future 10,000-meter world-record holder, and then-freshman Joel Cheruiyot, Chaplin had the strongest team of distance runners in NCAA history by the end of the decade.

Chaplin loved to palm himself off as a hayseed sprint coach. "Distance runners?" he would claim, "I don't know what they do. I just send them off into the wheat fields." He knew exactly what they did. "Everybody graduates," said Chaplin, "and it's hard work. They haven't got time to be killing themselves running." So Rono ran only 80 to 90 miles a week, doing brisk roadwork in the early mornings and intervals on selected afternoons.

In those interval sessions, which usually added up to three miles of hard running, it was Rono who decided how fast they would be. "I run as I feel," he said. "If I feel very good and am fit, I will run twelve 400s in 60 seconds each with a two-minute rest. If I am not good, they will be slower." Sometimes Rono announced he was tired and stopped in the middle of a workout. It was to Chaplin's credit that he trusted and encouraged his runners to make such decisions, because if there was a key to Rono's success, it was his sensitivity to his body's requirements for work and rest. Rono, perhaps better than any other runner, knew when to go hard and when to relax.

In the 1976 NCAA Cross-Country Championship, held in Denton, Texas, defending champion Craig Virgin ran a marvelous race, but it was Henry Rono and Samson Kimombwa who ran away with the title. Rono's winning time was 28:06.6, unheard of for 10,000-meter cross-country. Virgin was 130 yards back in 28:26. Kimombwa, who broke the world's esteemed 10,000-meter track record the next summer, was second in 28:16. Rono raced with imprudent irreverence, hitting three miles in 13:27. He manipulated Virgin, who was both bitter and awestruck: "They don't even know how old they are," said Virgin. "It takes years to develop that much endurance. Their age is too much. I thought they were bluffing, but they showed no sign of weakness. I never dreamed cross-country could be that fast."

"He had a fluid stride but a more muscular build than a distance runner, and he would glide up and down a hill seemingly not touching the ground with his feet," said Geoff Hollister. "When he set the pace for his fellow Kenyans Kimeto and Kimombwa, his surges left Salazar and Chapa hanging back. I had just witnessed Henry Rono for the first time."

At the 1977 NCAA Cross-Country Championship, Rono was untouched for the second year in a row, setting a course record at Hangman Valley Golf Course in Spokane, Washington. Providence's John Treacy was runner-up, nearly 20 seconds behind. The University of Oregon, five point victors over University of Texas–El Paso, had been led by Alberto Salazar, a true freshman, who finished ninth overall.

RONO AND SALAZAR: A MEMORABLE BATTLE IN 1979

After winning the NCAA National Cross-Country Championship in icy conditions in Madison, Wisconsin in 1978, setting a course record in the process, Alberto Salazar knew he could beat the best in the world. Rono, despite toeing the line at the 1978 championship (and holding four world records), had fallen back early, and fans wondered if they had seen the last of the Kenyan talent.

But there was no question the next year would be the true test. Featuring defending national champion Salazar, as well as numerous future distance record holders, Olympic team members, and medal winners, the quality of men's field at the 1979 NCAA Cross-Country Championship was remarkable. The Kenyans running for UTEP, Washington State, and New Mexico were practically the Kenyan Olympic team, as the NCAA still had not issued age restrictions for foreign talent. When the 240 starters lined up at Lehigh University's Saucon Valley Fields in Bethlehem, Pennsylvania, it wasn't just one of the strongest fields for NCAA competition—it was one of the strongest cross-country assemblages, ever.

The conditions on race day, the Monday of Thanksgiving week, were perfect: an Indian summer day of 60 degrees, sunny, with no wind. And the pace from the get-go was brutal. James Rotich of UTEP roared off the starting line, passing the mile mark in 4:20. The chase pack included Salazar, Thom Hunt of Arizona, and Rono. Rotich passed two miles in 8:50. By three miles Salazar and Rono had taken the lead in 13:26, with Salazar now forcing the pace. Rono was quoted afterwards by Gene Beckner in the *Easton Express*: "My plan was just to watch Salazar and not let him ahead of me more than 20 yards. When I try to pull away I lose a lot of energy."

It was a two-person race for the rest of the way. Salazar pushed as hard as possible, but to no avail. An unofficial clocking at the four-mile had them going by in 18:10. "Whenever I felt good on the downhills, I tried to pick it up," said Salazar to the press afterwards. "I knew he was there and I knew I had to break him. He just passed me on the downhill with about a mile left and started to pull away. I'd rather win but I did everything I could. I don't think I could have run much faster and he seemed to have plenty left." This was vintage Salazar—following the tradition of Steve Prefontaine—running to the point of physical breakdown.

Rono broke the tape in 28:19.6, followed by Salazar in 28:28, Kip Koskei in 28:48, Rotich in 29:04, and Hunt in 29:09. In all, 34 runners broke 30:00. Rono's third NCAA Cross-Country title tied him with Pre and Gerry Lindgren for the most wins with three apiece. UTEP won the team title with 86 points to Oregon's 93 with Penn State in third. The Lehigh course has remained unchanged since the championship—and since 1979, no one has broken 29:00.

Although he was never quite as dominant as he was in 1978, Rono continued to run and compete at a high level for the next four years, running one of history's fastest 10,000-meter races in 1980 (27:31.68), and adding another 5,000-meter world record (13:06.20) in 1981. Tragically, Rono would never get to compete at the Olympics, as Kenya boycotted both the 1976 and the 1980 Olympic Games.

THE INFLUENCE OF FOREIGN RECRUITMENT IN THE NCAA

The dominance of runners like Henry Rono, James Rotich, John Ngeno, and Wilson Waigwa, coupled with national championship teams from the University of Texas–El Paso, ushered in an era of the "foreign recruit" within the NCAA. For American-born coaches and athletes, this period felt like a new and frightening takeover—despite a long and storied history within US cross-country running of strong performances from foreign-born talent. East Africans, specifically, prompted Penn State coach Harry Groves, the meet director and coach of the fourth-place team at the 1975 NCAA Cross-Country Championship, to remark: "We won the *American* championship."

And Groves was not alone in his sentiments. Craig Virgin stated: "The issue in the mid-1970s where some coaches brought in foreign Olympians who were in their early to mid-twenties was not fair. I remember Suleiman Nyambui of UTEP having some gray in his beard. I was a World Champion at age 24 and it would not have been fair for me to race in college. When they changed the rule on the overage athletes it became fairer." Rules against overage athletes were in high demand; the 1970s saw them happen.

There was a long history of college recruiting for athletics. Pressure to "produce" a visible sports program led to the practice—and there were few clear-cut guidelines, especially seventy years previously. In 1895 it was asserted that, "men are bought and sold like cattle to play this autumn." Reportedly "no less than seven members of the University of Michigan varsity had never bothered with the formality of matriculating." It was these instances that led to the establishment of intercollegiate governing bodies.

In an effort to attract gate money and boost attendance at events, American college sports from football to basketball were intent on fielding the best teams money could buy. Scholarships for athletes soon followed. By the 1950s, measures known as the "sanity code" (grants-in-aid and jobs) were awarded solely on the basis of the student-athlete's financial need. However, given the pressures to succeed in sports, the sanity code failed to prevent colleges and universities from awarding "full-ride" scholarships, irrespective of need. It was in 1952 that the NCAA repealed the sanity code and allowed the awarding of full scholarships based on athletic ability.

But the 1950s also witnessed the logical extension of the recruiting game—first local, then regional—until it took on an international dimension. By the 1970s the recruitment of student-athletes had become global, with relatively few countries immune (either directly or indirectly) from the encroaching coach.

The number of foreign student-athletes in American schools early in the twentieth century was not large enough to cause any serious concern, and the impact of foreign recruits on NCAA Championships was present but not problematic. However, eyebrows were raised in the late 1950s and early 1960s with the recruitment of foreign athletes in their late twenties—or even thirties—who had several years' experience in their own countries. In 1955, for example, Idaho cross-country coach Joe Glander advertised for runners in a British magazine and ended up with a team of Pacific Coast Conference champions, each member of the team a British import. Idaho was fined $1,000 for what was viewed as "illegal recruiting" but the fine didn't stop the runners from running or winning conference titles, nor did it deter the recruiting of foreigners in track, soccer, tennis, swimming, and other sports.

The Idaho cross-country runners were experienced athletes, and according to the *Chronicle of Higher Education*, "against inexperienced Americans fresh out of high school, the age difference provided a critical advantage." In 1960 the University of Houston cross-country team won the NCAA title with a team made up of foreigners, all over the age of twenty-six, and such perceived abuses were also taking place in tennis, soccer, and, most notoriously, ice hockey. The response of the NCAA was, for the first time, to formally define the status of the foreign student-athlete. This was done in 1961 when an "overage foreigner" rule was imposed, which stated that for every year foreign athletes competed after their twentieth birthday (later changed to nineteenth), they would lose a year of varsity eligibility for NCAA Championship competition. The rule was quickly adopted by most of the major conferences.

Some NCAA institutions flouted the overage rule. In 1971, Howard University in Washington, D.C., a traditionally strong soccer school, won the NCAA title with several mature foreigners on their team. Two years later the NCAA stripped the university of its title because of its infringement of the overage requirement. But Howard took the NCAA to court, challenging the constitutionality of the rule. The federal court ordered the rule suspended because it failed to comply with the equal protection clause of the Fourteenth Amendment (giving all citizens rights without discrimination). This decision contributed to the rapid increase in overseas recruiting during the 1970s.

The increase in foreign recruiting in the 1970s led to more objections, and in 1980 the NCAA rewrote the terms, stating that every year of competition that athletes had after their twentieth birthday would count as one year's eligibility, whether athletes were on college teams or not. Hence, a foreign athlete of twenty-five who had been competing since the age of twenty would be ineligible for collegiate competition. Because this rule included Americans as well as foreigners, it was regarded as non-discriminatory.

But other factors contributed to the number of foreign student-athletes being seen at the collegiate level. In 1974 the NCAA imposed a reduction on Division I schools (from eighty to seventy) in the number of scholarships for all sports except football and basketball. Several sports where foreign recruiting was significant had upper limits placed on the number of scholarships. Fourteen was the upper limit for both soccer and track while the figure for tennis and golf was five. But this had its pitfalls. As Eastern Michigan track coach Robert Parks said, "The rule will stop the recruiting of the marginal foreigner who may develop, but it may increase the recruiting of the big foreign star."

However, these constraints did not apply to NCAA Division II or III schools, nor to NAIA affiliates or junior colleges. Those institutions continued to provide opportunities for foreigners who wished to benefit from subsidized training and coaching in the United States. Furthermore, foreign student-athletes at NCAA Division II and III schools could compete in Division I championships if they had qualified in lower divisional meets—as an example, top finishers at the Division II or III cross-country championship were invited to run in the Division I meet only days later.

Further legislation was passed within four years of Rono's final individual championship, when the military service exemption (which allowed overage foreigners athletic eligibility if they had been in the armed services) was only provided to athletes from the US armed services, thus eliminating many foreign athletes. This especially applied to Africans who were often nominal members of their nations' armies. Other exemptions, such as official church missions and foreign service, were eliminated in legislation enacted by the NCAA in 1984.

Increases in tuition, which meant that (in Texas, for example) the cost of a foreign student became twice that of an American, also curbed foreign recruiting. Budget cuts in many university athletic departments also had the effect of limiting the overall number of athletes on scholarships.

Further, in 1986 the NCAA implemented a rule pertaining to the eligibility of incoming freshman student-athletes. Known as Proposition 48, this rule imposed higher academic standards for freshmen in Division I institutions (extended to Division II in 1988). Essentially, only high school graduates who achieved a cumulative minimum grade point average of 2.00 in a core curriculum could now qualify for athletic scholarships. Furthermore, students entering college under the international standards described for each country by the NCAA, had, under the 1986 rulings, to achieve a combined score of 700 on the SAT test or a composite score of 15 on the ACT test. These tests were normally given only a few times a year and involved the payment of a fee. These requirements further reduced the incentive to recruit internationally.

But while these overage rules were introduced for the entirety of the NCAA, one specific cross-country powerhouse was no stranger to the criticism. Oregon coach Bill Dellinger told the *Riverside Press-Enterprise* in 1995, "The rule was brought on because of what was being done at UTEP." UTEP head coach Ted Banks agreed: "That's the Banks Rule," he laughed. "I never cared how old they were. They weren't youngsters and it was a definite advantage." The new rules may have been aimed at UTEP, but there was no doubt why the juggernaut that Banks built was so strong.

FOREIGN TERRITORY

While the NCAA wrestled with legislation regarding foreign recruitment, the town of El Paso, Texas, provided an unlikely home to the greatest cross-country team ever assembled. By the end of the 1970s, the University of Texas–El Paso had a controversial collection of foreign athletes, much older than most of their competition, who dominated the NCAA like no team before. Ted Banks, the architect of that team, came to El Paso from Long Beach State in the spring of 1973. "I knew I could get kids in, and I knew they had a good budget," Banks says. "I wanted to run with the best, and I knew that UTEP was a place I could do it." Coach Wayne Vandenburg, who had given UTEP their first cross-country championship in 1969, stepped down as coach following the 1972 cross-country season, opening the door for Banks.

"I inherited some good runners when I came, but I knew I would need more to compete," Banks said. When Eastern New Mexico University (Kenyans among them), came to El Paso to train during spring break, Banks talked with their athletes and established contacts in Africa. Soon, Banks received a letter from Wilson Waigwa, a Kenyan runner, saying he'd like to run at UTEP if there was room for him. Banks didn't know what to expect from Waigwa as his team lined up for an early season team time trial in the fall of 1973. Banks led the runners in his golf cart for the trials: "As we got near the finish, I looked back and he was just killing all my best returning runners. I almost turned the golf cart over I got so excited."

Banks's enthusiasm for his foreign athletes wasn't shared by everyone. His teams were referred to as the "Foreign Legion" and coaches argued in the press that the NCAA should ban foreign athletes from the NCAA championship meets. Banks was unfazed by the criticism. "I always said I'm here to build a winning team at UTEP," Banks claimed.

And UTEP was winning—a lot. Despite being NCAA team champions in cross-country in 1969, the UTEP Miners went empty-handed the next five years. The Miners then won the NCAA indoor track and field team title in 1974, and in 1975, UTEP won the indoor, outdoor, and cross-country team titles, the first time a team had won all three in a calendar year. Eighty percent of UTEP's points at the outdoor championships were scored by foreign athletes, prompting runner-up UCLA to stand on the infield waving American flags in protest. Over the next five years, the Miners captured four more indoor titles, four more outdoor titles, and four more cross-country titles. Each team relied heavily, or completely, on foreign athletes—some of them a decade older than their American competition fresh out of high school.

For Banks, all that mattered was putting together a winning team regardless of circumstance or cost. But global circumstance also mattered, and nations began to recognize the drain.

NATIONALISM PLAYS A PART IN THE 1970s

Outside events also impacted the number of foreign student-athletes in the United States during the 1970s. Canada, traditionally a major source of foreign talent in American competition, made attempts to keep skilled athletes at home. The Athletic Assistance Program, initiated in the 1970s and riding on a wave of Canadian nationalism, provided income security for top Canadian athletes with living expenses. The program provided the "necessities" alongside contemporary high-performance sport, offering an alternative to athletes thinking of competing in the United States. The number of recipients of these awards grew steadily. However, under the Athletic Assistance Program, athletes had to sign contracts that made them virtually state employees.

Likewise, in Australia, greater state provisions for athletes and the establishment of a national sports policy reduced the attraction of going to America. Nationally, Australian track and field adopted a more open approach to professionalism in the 1970s and '80s by means of subventions and trust funds. Given such financial rewards, athletes who might have otherwise migrated to an American college remained at home.

Finally, a changing national political regime affected the potential flow of foreign recruits. A prime example was Ethiopia, which, like its African neighbor Kenya, had been a fertile source of distance running talent since the 1960s. American universities would have proved attractive destinations for Ethiopian athletes, but the establishment of a socialist government there led to home-based development of talent instead. Kenya also adopted this model limitedly and within five years of Rono's final cross-country victory, Kenya had established its first national cross-country championship. With new facilities at home, as well as Kenyan initiatives supporting women's track, clear efforts had been made to sway the best athletes from relocating abroad.

NIKE TAKES ON THE INTERNATIONAL THREAT

Following the Montreal Olympics in 1976, Blue Ribbon Sports (soon to become Nike) was motivated to begin an athletic project that would unite the top American-born talent in one place at one time. Unlike East Germany and the Soviet Union, which plucked elite youth athletes and groomed them full-time on the government's dime, young Americans had to finance their own training and travel for competition—a demand that was nearly impossible to meet. With three years until the Moscow Olympics, time was running out if America wanted to avoid total humiliation on the world stage.

In the northwest corner of the country, a decision was made. Oregon, where the state universities had produced the nation's most exciting stars, was the unofficial track capital of the country. Oregon was also home to Nike. Business was booming, and with a little cash to play with, Nike decided to funnel some of their free enterprise profits back into the sport that had inspired their company. They decided to sponsor a small team of professional runners (it was either that or buy a year's worth of advertisements on the back page of a magazine), and if the experiment went well, Nike would get the same publicity. "I believe in this,"

Bill Bowerman declared at the project's outset. "It fills a void, and I'm worried about my sport."

In August 1977, Nike's first move was to hire Harry Johnson, a high school coach legendary for his blunt, warden-like demeanor and rigorous training tactics—and for winning. With twenty-five state titles, Johnson was the winningest coach in Oregon high school history. "Harry Johnson has got the credentials," said Bowerman. "If a fellow really wants to get there, he can get there with Harry Johnson." The coach, for his part, was equally fired up. "This is an enormous challenge for the company, and an enormous challenge for me," Johnson said of the venture.

Nike set up shop in Eugene and started looking for runners—a dozen malleable young athletes with something to learn and something to prove, preferably ones who were dedicated to winning. "The family man has mortgages, a wife who may not understand and other problems and obligations," said Johnson. "We need more of a commitment than that." With the support of business owners in Eugene, the program offered runners a plum arrangement: Nike would take care of travel expenses, provide gear, and find them jobs, but the athletes would have to earn a living wage working five-hour days in flexible local businesses in order to accommodate a full-time training schedule. "We're not going to bring in a bunch of free spirits who want to reach into your pocket book," Johnson vowed to the community.

Steeplechaser George Malley recalled the beginnings well: "Geoff Hollister started recruiting athletes for Athletics West sometime in the summer of 1977, a few of them (Tony Waldrop, Greg Fredericks, and Randy Thomas) turning him down for greener pastures. Others like Craig Virgin and Tiny Kane accepted the offer of a guaranteed minimum income of $1,000 a month and a part-time job. $1,000 a month was good money in 1977, especially in Eugene's awful economy. Up until then, no one was paid openly to run by the shoe companies, and those who were paid under-the-table were few and far between. Against my better judgment, and swayed by the idea that my running career didn't have to end at age 22, I said I'd come out for a year to see if it was for me. We were the first track and field athletes to 'go pro.'"

Under Johnson's guidance, long-distance training began on the rough trails, hills, and bike paths in their own backyard (and occasionally the local track). They ran in the mornings before work and in the evenings afterward—a hard day followed by an easy day, on different terrains, with a long, moderately paced training run once a week. The Athletics West (AW) group could often be spotted bounding up Emerald Street Hill in Eugene in their European-style uniforms, hand-sewn at home by the coach's wife, Jody. ("I don't see any reason to wear the same colors all the time," she said. "We're also working with one which includes the colors lime green, purple and black. It's really pretty.") Expectations for the club were high, and they hadn't even competed yet. As the team geared up for competition, the characteristically outspoken Coach Johnson was careful to control expectations. "We're trying to avoid the 'Dawning of a New Day' overhype syndrome," he cautioned. "We want to produce first."

In coming months, the results verified the training when Jeff Wells won a marathon in Honolulu, George Malley placed first in a 1,500-meter race in Oregon, and Craig Virgin displayed the first Athletics West singlet at the 1977 US National Cross-Country Championship. Within four years Athletics West won their first national team championship in cross-country—six more would follow. In 1977, the team headed to Europe for two months for their first taste of international competition.

In Europe, the team faced a new level of opponent, competing against runners who had benefited from years of state-sponsored training. They followed a grueling schedule, with each athlete averaging ten meets in the brief tour. Though true meet victories were few, every single AW runner clocked personal bests on the trip—a staggering eighty records all told, set by seven runners—including eight apiece by Craig Virgin and Doug Brown.

Though the original nucleus of the team disintegrated after Europe—Craig Virgin had been one of the team's best performers but had tired of butting heads with his coach and left to train elsewhere; George Malley departed for other reasons—the experimental opening season of Athletics West was a runaway success. "Everybody understands and believes in our approach now," said Johnson after the first year. "They realize the discipline and courage involved in taking a long-term approach to training. I think there's a different perspective now."

In the years to come, the Athletics West legacy only grew stronger. During year two, they recruited more athletes, beefed up the regimen with doctors and medical testing, and built a state-of-the-art training facility. Soon they would add women (including superstars like Joan Benoit Samuelson and Mary Decker Slaney) and expand operations to the East Coast, eventually going global. And as it turned out, the United States ended up boycotting the Olympics in Moscow. This wasn't a fairytale, after all, and Athletics West was itself a distance game. But they were more than ready to continue developing the nation's best cross-country runners.

AFRICA PERMEATES INTERNATIONAL COMPETITION

In the 1970s, well-established international cross-country meets—those recognized by the IAAF as boasting large audiences and prize purses—saw domination by new faces in locations where only local talent was victorious before. East African success spilled into places like Italy and Spain, while the International Cross-Country Championship (though still years away from seeing a Kenyan or Ethiopian national team) also began to see a higher multitude of African talent at the top.

The Campaccio Classica del Cross, run in San Giorgio, Italy, witnessed Ethiopia's Wohib Masresha victorious in the spring of 1971—the tip of the iceberg for African proliferation. To that point, the Campaccio had been almost exclusively won by Italians. The Cinque Mulini, Italy's other well-known cross-country race, also saw further African talent after Kenya's Kip Keino won the event in 1969. 1970 saw Ethiopia's Naftali Temu win the race, and countryman Mohamed Yohannes won it in 1977. In-between the Ethiopian victories came Tanzania's Filbert Bayi, who produced back-to-back victories in 1975 and '76.

The Cross de San Donostia in San Sebastián, Spain, was the site of three victories by Ethiopia's Mamo Wolde, which led to four more by countrymen Eshetu Tura, Mohamed Kedir, and Wodajo Bulti (Tunisia's Mohamed Gammoudi won in 1965). Tura added a win at the Cross Zornotza, held in Amorebieta, Spain, in the same period.

African nations in the 1970s also began to impose on the biggest stage of all: the International Cross-Country Championships. Morocco and Algeria represented the African continent in 1971 (where Morocco finished sixth as a team), and Morocco returned the following year to finish second. Along with an appearance by Tunisia in 1973 and 1974, a record *eight* African and Middle-Eastern nations competed at the 1975 World Cross-Country Championships, which were contested in Rabat, Morocco, and featured teams from Saudi Arabia, Sudan, Iran, Libya, and Syria. It was the first time that any Middle-Eastern country was present for international cross-country competition. Despite infrequency in attendance at the World Cross-Country Championships by African nations, the arrival of both Kenyan and Ethiopian national teams in 1981 was seen as a welcome challenge. Few could have foreseen how dominant each team would eventually be, and a lot of that success had to do with the new control of the championship instituted by the IAAF.

THE INTERNATIONAL CROSS-COUNTRY UNION CONCEDES CONTROL TO THE IAAF

On the eve of the 58th edition of the International Cross-Country Championship in 1971, the International Cross-Country Union held their annual congress in San Sebastián, Spain, where members passed a measure to transfer the organization of the championship to the International Amateur Athletics Federation (IAAF). This handing over of control, first proposed in 1953, had been treated more seriously as the International grew in stature. Since the IAAF determined eligibility for all amateur world track and field contests (and had only limited experience governing cross-country events), a committee was formed to make the transition smooth, with the stipulation that once the IAAF took control, the ICCU would dissolve completely. At a meeting in London in March 1972, the IAAF's cross-country committee decided by an overwhelming majority to recommend this move to the federation's full council.

On March 17, 1973, the first IAAF World Cross-Country Championships (known also as *World Cross*) became an annual event replacing the International Cross-Country Championship, and was hosted in Waregem, Belgium. The most striking difference was not the change in authority behind the event, but the acceptance of the IAAF member countries; nations previously labeled as "outside guests" of the International Cross-Country Union were now expected to field a team. IAAF measures in the coming years continued to make the event more accessible.

With newfound cross-country competition from previously unaffiliated IAAF member-countries, England, the originator of the international event, now had a fleet of new competitors to worry about at the World Cross-Country Championships. And while the addition of well-trained runners never threatened British dominance before, the 1970s saw an explosion of talent from places that weren't previously considered. But England wasn't afraid—the home nation was making strides of its own.

DAVE BEDFORD OF ENGLAND

England's David Bedford burst onto the international scene in 1969 when he won the junior men's title by 21 seconds at the International Cross-Country Championship. Wide margins of victory became the norm for Bedford, as did remarkable stamina—and with his high red socks, prominent moustache, long hair, and desire for the extraordinary, Bedford became the poster-child for British running during the 1970s.

Competing for the Shaftesbury Barnet Harriers and Coach Bob Parker, Bedford cemented himself in the lore of English cross-country running in late February 1970, when at the age of twenty, he dominated the Southern Counties Cross-Country Championship senior race. Held on the Parliament Hill course at Hampstead Heath in North London (the base where he trained), Bedford covered three, three-mile loops in deep mud in 45:50 to win by nearly a minute. Then, after his win, word spread that Bedford planned on running the junior championship as well. Unbelievably, there was only 20 minutes between the end of the senior event and the start of the junior.

Bedford won the junior championship, too, this time in 32:12 for two three-mile loops, over a minute better than the runner-up. And in his autobiography, Bedford attributed his victory in the junior race to his fearsome reputation. Had anyone really challenged him, he wrote, he might have buckled. Bedford wasn't in the lead group at the start of the long Parliament Hill, and witnesses claimed he wasn't even in the top 50 for the first mile. But it didn't take long for him to find his rhythm. By the end of the first lap, Bedford was in front and pulling away.

Bedford was the nation's best distance runner by the time he turned twenty. In the 1971 English National, he beat nearly 1,000 of the best cross-country runners in the nation to win by 40 seconds. That same year Bedford went on to win the International by 22 seconds. It wasn't hard to see why. Bedford trained three times a day—eight miles in the morning, six miles during lunch, and a final 16-mile surge at night. Occasionally he would substitute intervals at night. On the weekends he hit up to 25 miles for his long run. While this training produced remarkable success early (victories at the Cinque Mulini, Cross de San Sebastián, twice at the English National, and runner-up once, among others), a host of injury problems beset him, and Bedford was written off, nearly as quickly as he arrived.

Surprisingly, after months away, Bedford turned up at the North of Thames Cross-Country Championships in 1977 and blasted the field to bits to win the individual title. He then went to the National and made the English team once more. He even returned later to win the London Cross-Country Championships before retiring from the scene—and when further injuries brought his career to a permanent end, he remained involved with the sport. Bob Parker commented on Bedford, saying "His qualities were sheer guts and strength," and "There are no sort of flamboyant characters about now, they are just quiet boys. Dave set things alight. A pity we have not got someone like it now—that is why we are not doing so well in all the longer races." While Bedford's style was unorthodox, he wasn't alone at the top of English cross-country prowess. A rival from Surrey named Bernie Ford also saw a meteoric rise to the top.

BERNIE FORD LEADS ENGLAND TO VICTORY

Hailing from Woking, Surrey, Bernie Ford was one of England's fastest and most consistent distance runners for much of the 1970s. A member of the "Aldershot, Farnham, and District Athletic Club," Ford made his first splash in cross-country racing in 1969 at the age of seventeen when he finished third in the youth division at the Surrey County Cross-Country Championships. Within three years, Ford had won not only the youth and junior title for the Surrey County Championship, but the junior title for the Inter-County Cross-Country Championships as well.

In 1973 Ford won the Surrey County senior event, made his first English National team, and helped England finish fifth overall at World Cross. The twenty-one-year-old was following the trend set by Bedford before him—aiming high as young as possible—and the following year he outdid his previous performances, placing first in Surrey County, runner-up at the English National, and 11th at World Cross, where the English team was runner-up.

Ford earned another runner-up title at the English National in 1975, and, crossing 37th at World Cross that year, helped England earn another silver. In 1976, Ford earned his third Surrey County title in four years, his first English National Cross-Country title, and a third-place finish at the World Cross-Country Championships, helping England earn their first team title since 1972. And Ford was just getting started—1977, '78, and '79 saw Ford win the Surrey County title yet again, a second title at the English Cross National, a fifth place overall finish at World Cross, and three English team podium finishes. With Ford's leadership and consistency at the top, England continued their dominance in the sport they helped create.

Meanwhile, in continental Europe, Belgium continued their strong tradition in cross-country. Remarkable victories by Gaston Roelants, national 5,000-meter record holder Emile Puttemans, and World Cross champions Eric DeBeck (1974) and Leon Schots (1977) led the way. In fact, Eddie Declerck, chairman of the IAAF's Cross-Country Committee, was also Belgian.

BELGIUM BELIES THE CRITICS

Victor Goyens, general secretary of the Royal Belgium Athletic League (founded in 1889), stated in 1977 that there were 250 organized cross-country races every season in Belgium—impressive considering it was a country not much larger than the state of Maryland. During the 1970s, eight competition categories existed for men (from *pupilles* at 1,000 meters to seniors at 12,000 meters), and, except for a master's division, women had the same opportunities. The Belgian athletics congress dictated all policy, with club-oriented events the norm for the decade, and prizes given for major races. The season began in November and continued into February and March, when a set of provincial championships were run two weeks before the Nationals and a month before World Cross.

Manfred Steffny, an Olympic marathoner from West Germany, was impressed with a Belgian cross-country race in which he ran in the winter of 1972. George Beinhorn translated the German in a *Runner's World* article where Steffny recounted the event:

> At maximum speed, 150 runners of the main event are off. The snow is melted; the open runners have left behind a deep rut. We sink in almost to our ankles at every step; the mud tries to suck our feet in tight. A fence and stream have been jumped, then there's a gurgling, bubbling marsh where one sinks almost to the knees. At last, there is something like a path. Suddenly a railroad embankment appears. It's no mistake; the flags indicate it's part of the course. Three or four ties at a time? Terrible, inhuman, this race! . . . From the second round on, one looks forward to this section, because there's a trailing wind, and also the filth and water run out of your shoes. Then back to the stadium. I have already fallen in the mud. Shirt and pants are completely filthy; a crust of mud is stuck fast to the cheek, and in my mouth I still have the sweetest taste of earth that just won't be spit out. Yes, it is odd. Man is incredibly adaptable, a creature of habit. War, jail, forced labor, everything can become everyday to him. Just so can he be happy at kilometer six of a cross-country run. The tricks of the ground are more familiar now. Run way over on the left here; jump off at that spot there. Energy is better distributed. A rhythm is discovered. It all becomes just half as bad, no matter if one is overtaken or passes someone else. Finally, the mud bath is over. We go under the showers in full vestments. The most important utensil is not soap but a knife. You can cut open your running shoes—they can't be removed from their feet any

other way—and scrape the mud off arms and legs. And after this preliminary work, the soap has its say. It is a genuine long-distance shower.

Next to England, no team had as many podium finishes as Belgium in the senior men's event at World Cross during the 1970s. First as a team in 1973, '74, and '77; second in '71 and '76; and third in '70 and '75. Cohesive team chemistry and longevity was the key. Within the decade, 10 athletes for the Belgian National team appeared for four years or more. In a sport where Olympic champions were lucky to make only one World Cross event in a single year, runners Frank Grillaert, Paul Thijs, Emile Puttemans, Hendrik Schoofs, and Eddy van Mullen each appeared in at least four different World Cross-Country Championships. Eddy Rombaux appeared five times, his best finish coming in 1976 when he finished 19th overall. Willy Polleunis appeared six separate years, his best performance coming in 1973 when he led the Belgian team to a first-place team finish after crossing the line fifth overall.

Workhorses Eric DeBeck and Karel Lismont, and breadwinner Gaston Roelants, each appeared a total of seven times within the ten-year span of the World Championship in the 1970s. Eric DeBeck won the individual title in 1974, helping Belgium secure first place as a team, and finished 26th or better six times. Karel Lismont finished in third, fourth, seventh, and third in subsequent runnings, all within five years of each other. Roelants was the consummate veteran. In his seven appearances in the decade he crossed the line in second, 12th, first, eighth, 14th, 10th, and 13th. There was not a World Cross-Country Championship contested in the 1970s that DeBeck, Lismont, or Roelants did not score for their team.

CROSS-COUNTRY GROWS IN CONTINENTAL EUROPE

The nations of Germany and France also played a part in the success for the sport during the 1970s. The Federal Republic of Germany didn't have robust cross-country accolades before the start of the decade, but during the '70s the World Cross-Country Championships became a point of emphasis. France, on the other hand, with their long tradition of success at the International, saw their national team finish on the podium five times at World Cross through the decade.

Lothar Hirsh, national coach of the German Athletic Federation described the scene in Germany in 1977: "Races are conducted on weekends throughout the winter, at a range of distances for men and women of all ages. There is individual and team scoring (club participation). There are also separate championship meets just for students and teenagers. The German championship, now held two weeks prior to the IAAF run, consists of 15 separate races over two days (ranging from 11,500 meters for senior men, to 9,600 meters for juniors, and 5,750 meters for women)."

Between 1967 and 1973, the talented Lutz Philipp won six German National Cross-Country titles. Philipp also won the Saint Nikolaus Waldlauf 9.45-kilometer cross-country race (one of Germany's largest distance running events) eight straight years beginning in 1965. For the German women, Ellen (Wessinghage) Tittel won four straight German National Cross-Country titles from 1970 through 1974, and another in 1980. A world leader in the 1,500 meters, Tittel was named the Federal Republic Athlete of the Year in 1975. She was also victorious in the Saint Nikolaus Waldlauf 3.15-kilometer event in 1968, '69, and '78.

France's success had a lot to do with Noël Tijou, who burst onto the scene at the age of nineteen at the 1961 International junior event. Tijou represented France a total of 14 times at the International/World Cross-Country Senior Championship—locking personal-best finishes of fifth place overall in 1969 and 1970, seventh in 1971, eighth in 1974 and 1967, and ninth in 1968. Furthermore, Tijou was the individual winner of the French National Cross-Country Championship seven times in a 10-year span.

Fellow countryman Jacques "Jacky" Boxberger won the Cross du Figaro in Paris a record eight times between 1974 and 1982, earning the nickname "Mr. Figaro." He was also a French National Cross-Country champion two times and represented the French national team at World Cross a total of six times—his best finish coming in 1976 when he crossed ninth overall.

The French also witnessed the profound success of female distance star Joëlle deBrouwer during the '70s. DeBrouwer made her mark in December 1973, winning the Cross du Figaro in Paris, and went on to win the event a total of four times during the decade. In 1975, deBrouwer won her first French National Cross-Country title and won seven more in the next nine years. In addition to her national success she competed at the World Cross-Country Championships 10 times in her life, with her best finish a sixth place in 1976. Away from cross-country she held three separate French female distance running records.

THE HOME NATIONS: DEFINED BY INDIVIDUALS

Scotland, Ireland, and Wales, original members of the International Cross-Country Union, had seen limited success within the sport. However, far-reaching exposure within a competitive decade of racing brought these nations out of the shadows. Much of that success resulted from citizen runners John Treacy, Eamonn Coghlan, and Ian Stewart who found greatness by virtue of the American collegiate running scene and international competition.

Ireland's John Treacy, a resident of Waterford County who attended St. Anne's Post-Primary School in Cappoquin, ran 12 kilometers to school every morning. At the age of sixteen, Treacy made a name for himself when he finished third overall at the World Cross-Country Junior Championship in 1974. Later that year Treacy began training under Bob Amato, coach at Providence College in Rhode Island, and by the end of November, the seventeen-year-old Treacy finished 45th overall at the NCAA Cross-Country Championship.

By the end of his sophomore season, Treacy was showing improvement, repeating his third-place finish in the World Cross Junior race and achieving his first NCAA All-American accolade (21st overall). By winter 1976, Treacy had improved to fifth overall at the NCAA Championship. And by his senior cross-country season Treacy crossed the line in second place overall—claiming his third All-American award—submitting only to the infallible Henry Rono over 10,000 meters of rough country.

After becoming the NCAA indoor three-mile champion in 1978, Treacy applied for a bid to represent Ireland in the World Cross-Country senior event—his first appearance at World Cross in three years. Treacy crossed the line as the individual champion, the youngest ever at twenty years old, defeating the likes of Russia's Alex Antipov (one of Russia's top 5,000-meter runners) and former Marathon Champion Karel Lismont of Belgium. In 1979, Treacy won his second straight individual title in front of 25,000 impassioned Irish fans at Limerick Racecourse in Dublin. Even more surprising was the second-place team finish of Ireland—a nation that hadn't seen the podium in an International Cross-Country Championship since their team finished second in 1925. Bids at the 1980 and 1984 Summer Olympics followed; Treacy claimed silver in the marathon in Los Angeles in 1984. Commentator Jimmy Magee announced him as, "John Treacy from Villierstown in Waterford, the little man with the big heart."

In Scotland, Ian Stewart reinvigorated a nation that already possessed a rich tradition of cross-country involvement with his hard work ethic and natural talent on the track, roads, and cross-country course. Born in Birmingham, Stewart became involved in athletics as a teenager, joining the Birchfield Harriers under the guidance of Geoff Warr and winning the English Midlands Youth cross-country title in 1966 and both the Midlands and National titles as a junior in 1968. By 1970 Stewart had declared that he would henceforth compete for Scotland, his parents' country, in international competition.

In preparation for the 1972 Olympics, Stewart appeared at the International Cross-Country Championship, finishing ninth and recording the highest finish for a Scottish individual in three years. Subsequently, only months before Stewart finished third in the Olympic 5,000-meter run (edging a fading Steve Prefontaine), Stewart finished third at the International—running 38:20 for 12.1 kilometers at Coldhams Common in Cambridge, England.

In 1975, after a brief jaunt as a cyclist, and after winning the European Indoor 3,000-meter title, Stewart won the IAAF World Cross-Country Championship in Rabat, Morocco, running 35:20 for 12 kilometers. Then, despite the speed and grace of this victory, Stewart declined an invitation to return the following year (citing complications from the flu). As a result, his affair with running over cross-country ended with a whimper rather than a bang. In 1978 Stewart ran in the English National for the first and only time and finished second to Bernie Ford. Soon after, Stewart retired.

A GLOBAL MOVEMENT

A handful of individuals from a number of different countries also made a splash in the 1970s. While many nations reported varying degrees of interest in cross-country (frequently building momentum behind well-known meets and champions), a particular subset of individuals left legacies that could not be ignored.

Known as the "Lion of Becerril," Mariano Haro of Spain was unmatched nationally in his versatility, durability, longevity, and success; within the borders of Spain, there was simply no one that could touch him on the track, roads, or cross-country course.

As a young boy, Haro ran almost compulsively, using his gifted legs to run errands and transport him on his daily commute. The key was the 15 kilometers that separated his home from his job in a sugar plantation in Monzón de Campos. In fact, since he lived 16 kilometers from the Spanish capital of Palencia too, Haro would get in a round-trip workout of nearly 20 miles no matter the direction he traveled. Coupled with the mountainous climate of his hometown, Haro lived in an area perfectly suited for training from a young age—but it wouldn't be until he was nineteen that Haro made a name for himself in cross-country. Competing for the Club Educación y Descanso de Palencia ("The Education and Leisure Club of Palencia") Haro became the Spanish Junior Cross-Country champion at the national in March 1960.

After successfully defending his title as Spanish Junior Cross-Country champion the following year, Mariano Haro entered the International Junior Championship, finishing third (five seconds from victory). Haro then went on to amass a streak of 14 consecutive World Cross appearances, with six finishes of 11th or better, in addition to his 11 national cross-country titles between 1962 and 1977.

The 1970s saw Haro's biggest impact. He finished as the Spanish National Cross-Country champion every year from 1971 through 1977. He won back-to-back titles at the Cross de San Sebastian in Spain in 1974 and '75. He won the Cross Zornotza in Amorebieta, Spain, in 1964, '71, and '73–77; the Cross Memorial Juan Muguerza in Elgoibar, Spain, in 1971, '73, and '76–78; and the Cross de Calldetenes in Barcelona, Spain, in 1973 and '74.

Beyond his 22 victories in Spanish cross-country races, Haro was also regarded for his heartbreaking finishes in the World Cross-Country Championships. In the 1972 International, Haro finished second to Gaston Roelants. The following year was a dead-even tie within a hundredth of a second, leading to a second silver in as many years. In 1974 in Monza, Haro again crossed the line within a second of the winner—this time finishing behind Eric de Beck for his third silver in a row. In 1975 in Morocco Haro *again* finished runner-up, within a second of Scotland's Ian Stewart.

Meanwhile, 250 miles from Haro's hometown of Becerril, came Portugal's Carlos Lopes. At sixteen, without prior training and limited experience running, Lopes finished mere seconds behind the top athletes in São Silvestre's cross-country championship. Shortly after, Lopes won the Viseu cross-country and finished third in the juniors' championship at the Portuguese National in 1966. This victory sent him to the International Junior Championship in Rabat, Morocco, where Lopes was the best Portuguese finisher, crossing the line 25th overall.

In 1970, as a member of Sporting Club de Portugal under Coach Moniz Pereira, Lopes began a streak of five straight Portuguese National Cross-Country titles. In 1976, Lopes won on the international stage at World Cross (a victory attributed to training twice a day). Lopes earned three more national cross-country titles in the decade, and finished runner-up at World Cross in 1977, losing to Leon Schots of Belgium by five seconds. After World Cross in '77 Lopes faded into relative obscurity on the international circuit, and, beset by injuries, failed to win another cross-country title during the decade.

Meanwhile, outside of Europe, other nations continued to surge. IAAF governance did not stop at European involvement, and it ushered in performances from faraway countries in the South Pacific.

Brothers Rod and John Dixon out of New Zealand were two athletes to emerge during this period. Voted the "world's most versatile athlete for the last 25 years" by *Runner's World*, Rod Dixon was especially outstanding in the length and versatility of his career as a runner—setting world-class times in events from 1,500 meters to the marathon, and winning World Championship medals in track, cross-country, and road racing. "I have had an extraordinarily varied life as an athlete. When I actually look at what I have done, there have been many singular achievements all around the world. The varied journey defines who I am," he claimed.

It was his unique relationship with his brother that set him on the course to be an all-time great. John Dixon was a remarkable runner himself, helping New Zealand win a team gold medal at the World Cross-Country Championships in 1975. As Rod recalled:

I grew up always chasing him, as he was an excellent runner himself and three years older. So I was always trying to keep up with him as a kid and all his friends. In Nelson, at that time, we were very active, running everywhere. Even some of the jobs I had included running or being active. Everything we did seem to have included running. Later on my brother John, who also had the talent to make the Olympics made the most unselfish move, he decided to forgo his own running career to personally coach me. He even rabbited me in my Olympic 1,500-meter qualifying race, where I did end up qualifying to compete in the 1972 Olympics.

By August 1971, Rod Dixon had won his first senior title in the New Zealand National Cross-Country Championships, and four years later, brother John would win his first title in the same event.

With its strong harrier tradition, New Zealand finished third in the International Cross-Country Championship in 1965 and fared well in the first two editions of the IAAF

World Cross edition. Rod Dixon earned a bronze medal in 1973, running 36:00 to finish seconds behind Mariano Haro and Pekka Päivärinta, leading the New Zealand team to bronze as well.

All things exploded in 1975. Seemingly out of the blue, the New Zealand men's team won the gold medal at the World Cross-Country Championship, beating England by 71 points. With strong finishes by John Sheddan and Bryan Rose in 33rd and 34th, respectively, national champion John Dixon in 26th, David Sirl in 25th, and outstanding running from future national champion Euan Robertson in fifth and Olympian John Walker in fourth, New Zealand surprised everyone with a strong team performance.

New Zealand was perfect for cross-country. As Rod Dixon explained: "On the farm which my grandparents had, I used to love running barefoot along the river banks and through the farm and in the grass and the lovely fresh clover, and it was fantastic. There is the hills and along the forest trails, the river beside you and the birds and the sun coming down. Sometimes I would be running along the lonely road and I would raise my arms in the air and say, 'Isn't this absolutely fantastic,' and I look down at my feet pounding along the road and I become so excited by the whole atmosphere: this is real enjoyment." Dixon won his second national New Zealand cross-country title in August 1977. His brother John, not to be outdone, won his second in 1978. All told, the Dixon brothers scored four gold medals at the national cross in a seven-year span.

FEMALE CHAMPIONS: ENTER GRETE WAITZ

At the team level at the World Cross-Country Championships, New Zealand—led early in the decade by Val Robinson, and later in the decade by runners like Lorraine Moller and Heather Thomson—outperformed nearly every nation during the 1970s in female competition too, scoring podium finishes in 1969, '71, '75, and '77. Of all the IAAF member nations present, only England and the United States earned more accolades through the '70s.

But when it came to individual finishers, one name dominated the international cross-country field: Grete Waitz. Bill Rogers stated: "A lot of us guys—Frank Shorter, myself—we did a lot of things well, but we never dominated. But when it comes to women, there's only one. Grete. She won at every distance. She was dominant. She's the best women's distance runner ever."

Grete Waitz was dominant in records, but not in demeanor. The youngest of three children born to working class parents in Oslo, Norway, those closest to her use words like "reserved," "quiet," and "humble" to describe her style. She enjoyed a Diet Coke and a good mystery novel; lights out by 9:00 p.m., speed work done by 6:30 a.m. Waitz was a talented young runner, but had difficulty getting her parents to take her profession seriously. But Waitz didn't back down. At a time when female athletes were not given the necessary support and funding needed to compete at the top level, she won national junior titles in Norway in the 400 and 800 meters, and in 1972 at the age of eighteen won her first senior women's title in the Norwegian National Cross-Country Championships. She would win the next nine consecutively.

In her first appearance at World Cross in 1978, Waitz was untouchable, taking a commanding lead in the senior women's three mile at the course in Glasgow, Scotland. She went hard from the start and ended up beating her nearest competitor by over half a minute. Two more titles would later come just as effortlessly.

THE YOUTH OF TOMORROW

Exterior European nations also promoted the sport among younger runners. In 1968, the first World Student Cross-Country Championship was held, comprised of amateur youths nineteen years or younger. This inaugural event, held in Ghent, Belgium, saw Great Britain, led by first place finisher Frank Briscoe, run away with the team title, beating Belgium and Italy. A biennial event, the inclusion of female runners occurred in 1976, when Vera Kemper of Germany won by nearly 50 seconds over Moira O'Boyle and Caroline Simpson of England. 1978 marked the first running officially sanctioned by the International University Sports Federation (FISU). Renamed the World University Cross-Country Championships, more than 64 countries have competed over the event's history, but only France, Great Britain, and Spain have been present at all editions of the championship.

Meanwhile, in 1972, a boy named Kirk Dumpleton emerged from the pack to win the Intermediate Boys' Race at the English Schools Cross-Country Championships in Hillingdon, England. Twenty seconds later a sixteen-year-old by the name of Stephen Michael James Ovett, a tall Brightonian with an unkempt mop of hair, crossed the line in second place. Farther back, in 10th, was a fifteen-year-old from Sheffield named Sebastian Newbold Coe.

Aged sixteen, Dumpleton made history by becoming the only British man to defeat Sebastian Coe and Steve Ovett in the same race when he won that event in 1972. "I knew of both Steve Ovett and Seb Coe before the race," Dumpleton shared. "I'd met Steve before and I'd read about Seb in *Athletics Weekly*. Going into the race I knew that I was in great shape. I'd only lost one cross-country race in six months and that was only by a second. The course was quite hilly and I remember feeling fantastic. Even a couple of miles in I realized everyone was blowing quite heavily, so I put a little burst in, kicked away and won by about 20 seconds." His win was an oddity to be sure, and one of the many stories that nearly slipped through the cracks during the decade. And while Ovett and Coe went on to international fame—Dumpleton faded into obscurity.

* * *

The 1970s were particularly special for one reason: in every corner of the globe, at the same time, talent was embracing and participating in the sport at an unmatched fervor. The following decades would perpetuate this momentum. But the updating of archaic policies and traditions wouldn't be the only important measure. The payment and participation of athletes would take center stage at exactly the same time that East Africa rose to challenge the conventional powers in World Cross. The adaptation of the sport would be of paramount importance.

EVENT SPOTLIGHT: IRISH INVOLVEMENT IN THE FIRST IAAF WORLD CROSS-COUNTRY CHAMPIONSHIPS (MARCH 17, 1973)

LOCATION: HIPPODROOM WAREGEM

Ghent, Belgium

The first IAAF World Cross-Country Championship was held in 1973 and was not without controversy, especially from an Irish point of view.

Beginning in the 1930s, an independent Irish athletic council, then called the National Athletic and Cultural Association of Ireland (NACAI), struggled to gain legitimacy within the IAAF. By 1967, after multiple failed attempts to resolve the dispute between governing bodies, two councils, the NACAI and AAUE (the Amateur Athletic Union of Eire, which represented Ireland at the Olympic Games) were both dissolved, and Bord Lúthchleas na hÉireann (BLE) was formed. But it was in 1973 that a group of six "intruders" representing the old NACAI organization decided to make a statement at the inaugural World Cross event in response to the new BLE group. Once three kilometers of the 12-kilometer race had been completed, the six intruders in white vests slipped under a rope and joined the leaders, causing mayhem.

Reporter Fionnbar Callanan for *Marathon* (the only Irish athletics magazine of the time) gave a vivid description on what ensued:

> With almost exactly one quarter of the race over, the field was headed by a tightly grouped 18 or 20 runners. In the forefront, and almost running abreast, were Paivarinta (Finland), Haro (Spain), Cusack (Ireland), Clarke (England) and Dixon (New Zealand). At this point the course was no more than eight yards wide. The group of six intruders ran onto the course in front of the faster-moving field. Neil Cusack told me his first reaction was one of amazement that they could have already lapped some of the runners. But some spectators and officials realized that the intruders had come on and efforts were made to hustle them off. They resisted, and then the field was upon them.

> The awkward arm action of Paivarinta took him through the intruders and sent some of them flying. The diminutive Haro was forced to resort to more belligerent action, and the intruders lifted him off his feet before throwing him into a ditch. Cusack was buffeted but no more. Dixon was given a kidney punch and said later that 'this finished me.'

Eddie Leddy was tripped and fell flat on his face being severely winded in doing so. One Moroccan runner was punched in the face and he was unable to continue. As the race resumed, the Belgian police detained one of the intruders and he was paraded back toward the stands. When the race had concluded, most of the Irish party learned of the intrusion for the first time and there was a great outburst of resentment and anger. Somebody spotted some of the intruders and there was a rush toward them. Some of them were caught and struck before wiser counsel prevailed.

Team manager Billy Coghlan (father of Eamonn) had thoughtfully provided shamrocks for all members of the Irish team and their supporters before the race. "It ended, for me and many others, in anger and shame that the name of Ireland had been dragged in the mud by a thoughtless, irresponsible and undignified performance," he concluded.

The race itself resulted in a remarkable finish. Mariano Haro of Spain and Finland's Pekka Päivärinta eventually crossed the line within one-hundredth of a second of each other. The final time for the 12-kilometer course for Päivärinta was 35:46.4, and for Haro, 35:46.5. New Zealand's Dixon crossed the line in third in 36 minutes even.

Belgium, with Willy Polleunis fifth and Gaston Roelants eighth, won the team gold ahead of the Soviet Union, with bronze going to New Zealand. Despite the intrusion, the rest of the day went off without a hitch, and the IAAF's official governing attempt was taken in stride as they assumed control of the international aspect of the sport.

Date: Saturday, March 17, 1973			
Teams: 19			
Distance: 7.44 miles / 11.98 kilometers			
Location: Hippodroom Waregem, Belgium			
Individual Finishers:			
1	Pekka Päivärinta	Finland	35:46.4
2	Mariano Haro	Spain	35:46.5
3	Rod Dixon	New Zealand	36:00
4	Tapio Kantanen	Finland	36:05
5	Willy Polleunis	Belgium	36:05
6	Roger Clark	England	36:08
7	Juan Hidalgo	Spain	36:12
8	Gaston Roelants	Belgium	36:13
9	Nikolay Sviridov	Soviet Union	36:19
10	Noel Tijou	France	36:21
11	Grenville Tuck	England	36:24
12	Dick Tayler	New Zealand	36:26
13	Norman Morrison	Scotland	36:31

(continued)

14	Bryan Rose	New Zealand	36:38
15	Euan Robertson	New Zealand	36:45
16	Egbert Nijstad	Netherlands	36:46
17	Pavel Andreyev	Soviet Union	36:47
18	Eric de Beck	Belgium	Time Not Reported*
19	Erik Gijselinck	Belgium	Time Not Reported
20	Abdelkader Zaddem	Tunisia	Time Not Reported
21	Nikolay Puklakov	Soviet Union	Time Not Reported
22	Boris Olyanitskiy	Soviet Union	Time Not Reported
23	Valentin Zotov	Soviet Union	Time Not Reported
24	Carlos Lopes	Portugal	Time Not Reported
25	Eddie Leddy	Ireland	36:56

*Archival sources failed to publicly report the finishing times for the eighteenth, nineteenth, twentieth, twenty-first, twenty-second, twenty-third, and twenty-fourth places.

Team Results:

1	Belgium	109
2	Soviet Union	119
3	New Zealand	136
4	Finland	180
5	England	181
6	Spain	260
7	France	273
8	Scotland	291
9	Wales	345
10	Tunisia	392
11	Ireland	393
12	Netherlands	400
13	Italy	474
14	West Germany	508
15	Morocco	544
16	Portugal	602
17	Northern Ireland	657
18	Denmark	847

Switzerland only had two athletes and did not finish a team.

CULTURAL SPOTLIGHT: KIT, EQUIPMENT, AND TECHNOLOGY

As the establishment of amateurism in distance running began to fade, the importance of attire, footwear, timing, and media took on new life. While not new to runners after the 1970s, the inclusiveness of "brand identity" became much more influencial on cross-country running after this decade. In fact, throughout the history of the sport, a variety of identifiable changes in these mediums helped to define it. What follows is a more detailed timeline that explains how attire, footwear, timing, and media presentation all had an impact.

HARE-AND-HOUNDS IN THE NINETEENTH CENTURY

One of the earliest accounts of an identifiable cross-country uniform comes from the Royal Shrewsbury School Hunt record books, where the character of the "Huntsman" appears dressed in a black cap, scarlet jersey, and stockings. Today the Huntsman acts as a race-starter, a club-captain who wears an old-style hunting cap and a bright red sweater that represents the blood of the foxes or hares he has supposedly killed by winning races. He carries a whip to symbolize his captain's role of urging on the slower runners. For the "Huntsman" of yore, the stockings were white, and the "scarlet jersey" a red wool.

Other characters also appeared in time. The "Gentlemen of the Run" followed the first group in the pack, running without a coat but carrying a bludgeon to ward off the stone-throwing town "toughs" who would harass the runners. The second division—older students (ages sixteen to eighteen) recognized as "the field"—wore jackets and mortar-boards ("from which every atom of stiffening material had been removed"). In some cases the boys had hedging gloves sewn into the sleeves of their jerseys to combat the thorny thickets and natural obstacles standing in their way. The "foxes" carried the leather sack filled with shredded paper (the "scent bag") to lay the paper trail.

Author George Melly outlined the uniform of the day when he described Rugby School's "Crick Run" in 1854: "a uniform costume of white trousers supported by a black belt, and white jerseys, with caps of various shape, and wide-awakes of every hue. Coats, jackets, or any outer garment are discarded." In Thomas Hughes's account of the "Barby Hill Run" the character of Tom is described as having "put his belt on, and left all superfluous clothing behind" for the run. These accounts, all featured in the first five decades of the nineteenth century, give some insight into the attire and equipment used by the English schoolboys of the day.

As the formal organization of the sport took hold, the attire changed. When Oxford held its first "College Foot Grind" in 1850 with the fields "swimming" in water, participants wore "cricket shoes and flannels" to race over the ploughed land. The Thames Hare and Hounds standardized dress was "canvas shoes with India-rubber soles, worsted socks, flannel knickerbockers, and white or dark blue watermen's sweaters." The Westchester Hare and Hounds in New York mention their uniform consisted of "black caps with visors, scarlet jackets with black buttons, and black knickerbockers and stockings." The Westchester hares, instead of jackets, wore "tight-fitting black jerseys, with the scarlet figure of a hare on the breast."

NEW CENTURY, NEW ATTIRE

But by the turn of the century, outer attire had changed completely. In 1899, at the inaugural championship held by the Intercollegiate Cross-Country Association, vests made of cotton (which mirrored the style of track singlets today), were common and were coupled with cotton shorts. The Thames Hare and Hounds opted for a large black X to be overlaid on their white jerseys. These were a visible upgrade over the blouse-like upper garments (or undershirts), and the woolen knickerbocker pants of twenty years previously. In colder weather, long-sleeve cotton shirts or wool sweaters were worn. At Yale University and others, large collegiate letters were also sewn into these garments.

Just prior to the Second World War, Michigan State University experimented with wearing dress shirts under their cotton uniform singlets, which had the effect of wicking moisture away and warming the runner's arms.

But by the postwar era, the introduction of synthetic fibers to the marketplace led to the wearing of rayon or nylon tracksuits as opposed to cotton. In 1954, University of Michigan track coach Don Canham explained that cotton-lined shorts and sweats were still the most common items to be worn outside the singlet, but rayon became a new affordable commodity. Leggings and long-sleeved tops featuring lightweight wool were also still being worn.

Within thirty years, synthetics had worked their way into running uniforms and runners opted for singlets that were cotton or nylon (or a hybrid of both). Dri-fit (compression wear) was still years away—and nylon, while designed to be as light as possible—did not wick moisture. Sprinters were more concerned with aerodynamics, which meant a shift to form-fitting speed suits that kept the runner's profile as slim as possible. By keeping the fabric taut, the path of air around the body wasn't obstructed by loose flaps of fabric. Certain clubs, like the Nike-sponsored Athletic West, had variations of color-style and print for their athletes.

FOOTWEAR DEVELOPMENTS COINCIDE WITH THE EXPANSION OF CROSS-COUNTRY

Footwear designed specifically for running appeared in the early nineteenth century, close in proximity to the development of hare-and-hounds—and the ensuing popularity resulted in the development of a lightweight shoe: an all-leather "athletic" variant, which found traction difficult without a rubber-soled bottom. In 1832 this was remedied when Wait Webster patented a process where rubber soles could be glued to leather shoes and boots—the creation of Plimsolls, widely worn by children, soon followed. It wasn't until 1852 when Joseph William Foster—the founder of the company Boulton (now known as Reebok)—had the "eureka moment" and decided to add spikes to the bottom of the plimsolls and created a shoe with a spiked sole.

It would take nearly forty more years before the Spalding Company featured three grades of spiked footwear in their catalog. Low cut and made from kangaroo leather uppers, the soles had six spikes and cost $6.00—a hefty price considering most households survived on only $11.00 a week. Spalding's first "spikes" consisted of little more than nails driven through the sole of the shoe, while the kangaroo leather, touted for its strength and light weight, saw widespread use in the uppers of competition shoes until the 1970s. A specific pair of Spalding leather running spikes, belonging to Earl Spencer of Wimbledon during the 1860s, more closely resembled a traditional dress oxford than a running shoe.

Vulcanization, the process of melting rubber and fabric together, was the next big development. Keds, molded to create a sole for shoes that had a tread design, were the result. First produced by Goodyear in 1892, Keds were lightweight, quiet, and flexible. But it took until 1917 before Goodyear started to advertise Keds as an athletic shoe. By then, Adolf Dassler was tinkering with the design for vulcanized running spikes, which he started in 1920. Each shoe design had a special hand-forged set of running spikes and each design was made especially for a certain running profile (the first-time designs were focused on sprinters or distance runners). By 1936 Adidas were internationally acknowledged as having the best running shoes, and were worn by athletes like Jesse Owens.

In cross-country, improved footwear reflected in faster times during the later twentieth century. From the years 1950 to 2000, the per-mile average of American National Cross-Country champions decreased from 5:14 to 4:40 per mile.

MEDIA ADVANCEMENT LEADS TO GREATER EXPOSURE

Movie newsreels, which debuted in cinemas in Britain and France at the turn of the century, popularized documentaries featuring cross-country running. *Pathé News*, which was founded by Charles Pathé and his brothers, pioneered the broadcast of running competitions in biweekly newsreels as early as 1908. These newsreels were shown exclusively in the cinema and were silent films (accompanied by piano and title-cards) until 1928. Events ranging from inter-county championships to the major International were featured.

The 1908 Summer Olympics in London were the first Olympics to garner media exposure with newspaper reports, photographs, and documentary footage showing the competition in all its public spectacle. All three of the Olympic cross-country contests (1912, 1920, and 1924) were captured this way.

By the Paris Olympics in 1924 (the last time that cross-country running appeared as its own event in the Games), public radio broadcasts were also popular. Radio provided the means for Paris to be the first Games to be broadcast live, and soon it emerged as a mass media technology.

By 1936 in Germany, the opening ceremony of the Games was shown live on closed circuit television in Berlin. According to the official report of the Games "a total of 162,228 people witnessed the XI Olympic games by means of television."

The advent of television also meant that cross-country could now be exposed to a much wider audience—and in the case of the European market that held true. Cross-country championships from Germany to Great Britain appeared on television in the mid-1930s, while in the United States it was decades before events like the NCAA Division I Championship debuted on TV.

Irrespective of location, the greatest difficulty in capturing cross-country for media remained its inaccessibility. John Shrewsbury, senior producer of athletics for the British Broadcasting Company (BBC) (who televised cross-country meets at Gateshead and Crystal Palace), elaborated: "Even with shorter circuits, the terrain can still be a problem. The viewers expect to see the whole race, so in preparing to televise any cross-country event I walk the course well in advance to decide how best to cover it. If a section of it is fairly open, it may need only two cameras to follow the runners for a quarter mile. But in a wooded section, it may need three cameras to cover even a 100 yard stretch."

Shrewsbury went on to say: "You've also got to plan for the ultimate emergency, such as losing a camera at the finishing line through a technical fault, so you have to have another standing by, because twenty or twenty-five other countries may be taking pictures from us."

MEDIA AND SPONSORSHIP

Despite the strict rules of amateurism, shoe companies began to vie for athletes' attention, along with subsequent opportunities for media exposure as athletes set records. The Olympics provided the grandest stage during the modern era and it was there that intense rivalries gained momentum. For example, competing shoe companies Adidas and Puma created a shoe scandal at the 1968 Olympic Games by paying athletes to wear their shoes.

Despite the rules (and the risks), upstart companies like Nike and New Balance circumvented the restrictions by being in the right place at the right time. Geoff Hollister described the scene at the 1972 Olympic Trials: "Under the amateur rules, branding was not allowed on the field of competition. The stripes on the shoes were ruled functional and not touched, but backtabs, the tiny labels on

Hare and Hounds Leaping Wall,
By Stanley Berkeley
Source: *Athletics and Football* by
Montague Sherman (1887)

Thames Hare and Hounds 1868 Team
Photograph
Source: The Thames Hare and Hounds
Collection (1868) with permission from
Simon Molden

A "Paper Chase" of the Westchester Hare
and Hounds Club
Source: *Frank Leslie's Illustrated
Newspaper* (November 1879)

NEW YORK,—A "PAPER CHASE" OF THE WESTCHESTER HARE AND HOUNDS CLUB—THE FLEEING HARES SCATTERING THE SCENT AT THE OPENING OF THE CHASE.

NEW YORK CITY.—THE CROSS-COUNTRY RACE OF APRIL 28TH, UNDER THE AUSPICES OF THE NATIONAL CROSS-COUNTRY ASSOCIATION:
CARTER LEADING, WITH CONNEFF SECOND.

FROM A SKETCH BY A STAFF ARTIST.

The Cross-Country Race of April 28th; E. C. Carter leading, with Conneff second.
Source: *Frank Leslie's Illustrated Newspaper* (April 1888)

Suburban Harriers Team Photo
Source: *Outing* magazine (March 1887)

T. O'DAY. W. F. THOMPSON. E. C. CARTER (Capt). G. Y. GILBERT. E. W. HJERTBERG. P. D. SKILLMAN.
SUBURBAN HARRIERS' CHAMPION TEAM, 1887.

Cornell University Cross-Country Team Photo (1898)
Source: Cornell University Archives

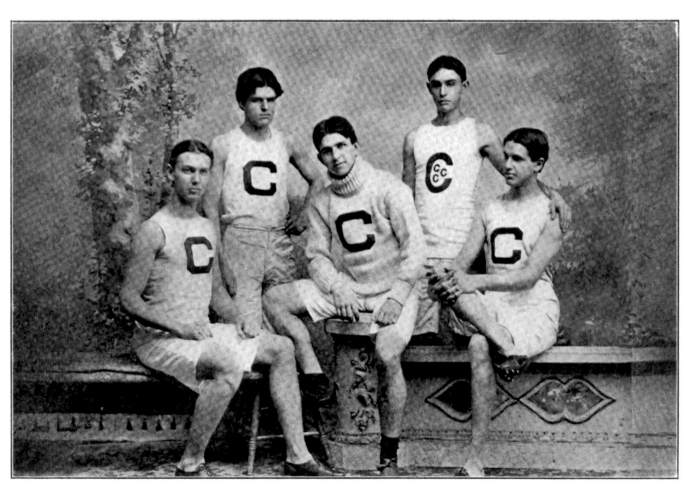

CROSS-COUNTRY TEAM, 1898
Berry   Torrance   Sweet   Coates   Yeatman

The 1929 English National
Source: The Birchfield Harrier Club Collection (1929)

Melvin Shimek Wins for Marquette, Northwestern Dual in 1926
Source: Meet Program (1920s)

Captain Meet Captain with Lauren Brown
Source: Folder 2, Box 1019, Brown Papers,
Michigan State University Archives and
Historical Collections (1928)

The Start of the first NCAA Cross-
Country Championship (1938)
Source: *Michigan Agricultural College: The Evolution of a Land-Grant Philosophy, 1855-1925* by Keith R.
Widder (East Lancing: Michigan
State University Press, 2005), 347

Don Lash Running at Indiana
Source: Creath Smiley, Jr., (Fall 1937), with permission from the Estate of Don Lash.

The Top Three at the Cross de L'Humanitie in 1956
Source: Gérald Bloncourt, Paris, France (1956)

Frank Shorter, Art Dulong, and Steve Stageberg racing at Van Cortlandt Park in the IC4A Cross-Country Championship
Source: Jeff Johnson (1968)

Prefontaine and Lindgren battle to the wire at the 1969 Pac-8 Cross-Country Championship
Source: Laurence D. Mueller, Stanford University (1969)

Doris Brown Heritage leads the AAU Women's Cross-Country National in Saint Louis
Source: Jeff Johnson (1970)

Craig Virgin Wins Big-10 in 1973
Source: Craig Virgin Collection (1973)

Dr. Joe Vigil Speaking at USA
Club Cross in 2015
Source: Andrew Boyd
Hutchinson (2015)

Running barefoot, Jeruto
Kiptum leads the World
Cross-Country junior girls' race
in Morocco in 1998
Source: George Aitkin (1998)

Paul Tergat winning one of his many World Cross-Country titles. Cape Town, 1996
Source: George Aitkin (1996)

Paula Radcliffe wins World Cross-Country in Ostend, Belgium, in 2001
Source: George Aitkin (2001)

The men run out on the 125th holding of the
Oxford v. Cambridge Cross-Country
Source: Andrew Peat (December 5, 2015)

Men's Leaders at USA Club Cross in Golden Gate Park, San Francisco
Source: Andrew Boyd Hutchinson (2015)

Laura Thweatt
Chasing Amy Van
Alstine at USA Club
Cross in Golden Gate
Park, San Francisco
Source: Andrew Boyd
Hutchinson (2015)

Sir Mo Farah close-up at the 2017 Great Edinburgh Cross-Country
Source: Andrew Peat
(January 2017)

Callum Hawkins and Leonard Korir battle to the finish at the 2017 Great Edinburgh Cross-Country
Source: Andrew Peat
(January 2017)

National (NZ) Club Cross-Country Championship 2016
Source: Paul Petch, *GRIT,* Good People Run, New Zealand (June 2017)

the backs of shoes, were taped over, as were logos and brand names on athletic bags. Even branded T-shirts were not allowed. But something curious was happening. The scripted Nike on our new brand looked like 'Mike' and to our delight in the stands, a lot of Mikes were running around on the infield of Hayward Field."

VICTIM OF THEIR OWN SUCCESS

Because the nature of the sport made it unfriendly to spectators, cross-country athletes were immune to high-profile exposure by the media. As a result, major shoe companies were not interested in under-the-table deals: cross-country runners in the 1960s and 1970s were not being chased by Adidas, Puma, or Nike. That is not to say that many top names who ran cross-country went without sponsorship: Roelants, Rono, Rodgers, Shorter, Prefontaine, Francie Larrieu, Doris Brown Heritage (among others) all had well-rounded success outside of cross-country and were endorsed in one way or another. But the amateur ethos of the time, coupled with cross-country running's limited market visibility, meant that the sport did not attract the biggest monetary purse.

Shoe-company funds eventually made waves in distance running. Notably, it created frameworks for affiliation: groups such as Athletics West would never have existed if not for Nike's need to dominate international competition. And performing (and succeeding) in international venues like the World Cross-Country Championships instilled value.

These financial interests eventually spelled the end of amateurism in distance running. This, coupled with the desperate need to see sponsored athletes break world records, resulted in an even more unexpected development: accurate timing systems.

TIMING DEVICES EMERGE AND DEVELOP

Fully automatic timing obtained from a photo finish system is now an integral part of all major running competitions, but hand timing was the norm for most of the sport's history. The first known use of "electric" timing for track and field was in 1891 at a small meeting in Syracuse, New York (and later that same year at the AAU Track and Field Championships), but those contests were started by hand and stopped electronically (the fully automatic system in use today is electronic at both the start and the finish).

At the 1928 Olympic Games in Amsterdam, a Dutch slow-motion film camera, the Löbner camera-timer, recorded the first fully automatic time in the steeplechase. First introduced to the IAAF in 1926, the Löbner camera-timer had the capability of superimposing a chro-

nometer-dial onto cine film (cine film was recorded with a series of rapid-sequence still frames). Not long after, in horse racing, an Italian optical researcher named Lorenzo del Riccio developed a device that kept the camera shutter open with the film moving past the aperture at a regular speed, producing a continuous image.

With the del Riccio advancement came another horse racing invention: the "Gustavus Town Kirby" timing device. The official report for 1932 Olympics in Los Angeles stated: "In addition to hand timing, two auxiliary electrical timing devices were used. Both were started by an attachment to the starters gun. One was stopped by hand at the time the runners hit the tape. The other was provided with a motion picture camera which photographed the runner at the tape and the dial of the time indicator simultaneously."

Throughout the 1950s and '60s, the Omega company (formed out of *British Race Finish and Recording Ltd.* and Olympic timers since 1932), held the honor of being the timing device used most frequently for World Championships. Omega's "Time Recorder" was the first to use a quartz clock and printout results, earning the company a prestigious "Cross of Merit" from the International Olympic Committee. By the 1976 Olympics, it was Omega (with a gun-to-clock attachment) that demanded results be given to the nearest 1/100 second. Thanks to the spread of horse racing, which spurred the development of more cost-effective and less fragile systems, fully automatic timing expanded throughout the running community. By January 1, 1977, fully automatic timing became mandatory for world records ratified by the IAAF.

THE RISE OF THE SWOOSH

Meanwhile, as athletes performed better, the need to market their achievements grew stronger. In 1960 Adidas controlled 80 percent of the running and track shoe market. At the 1972 Munich Olympics, 1,100 of 1,500 athletes were wearing Adidas shoes. But Adidas was a privately held family company, and it missed the moment when Nike was changing the business.

By 1980, Nike had attained a 50-percent market share in the US athletic shoe market, and the company went public in December that year. Most importantly, by 1980 the Amateur Athletic Union had just relinquished control over cross-country running governance, ending a ninety-year stranglehold over the amateur ideal that went against the commercial marketability of distance runners. As such, the role of equipment and technology in the life of a distance runner became more important than ever—not only in where it was coming from, but in who was profiting from it.

Chapter 14

It's my love for a bunch of reasons. The actual team aspect, the close-knit bunch of guys that you work with everyday. It's done in the fall. I love the fall, the leaves on the ground, I love that time of year. There's the hills—the whole non-circularness—of cross-country. You're going places, not just running around an oval. It builds tremendous strength for track. It's an equalizer for kids who might not have the marks on the track. In cross-country other things come into play where they can score and get recognition, and times don't mean anything.

—Pat Porter

THE DECADE OF THE 1980s

Cross-country running in the 1970s changed the world's conception about the sport—and the 1980s celebrated it. Prefontaine, Shorter, Dixon, and others had pushed boundaries, and their heroics brought cross-country running worldwide notoriety. By 1980, seemingly every nation was involved. Distance running became an opportunity for international expression, and Europe, North America, Africa, and Australia all enshrined heroes, with sponsors and media adding to the drama. While Olympic boycotts and performance controversies rocked track and field, cross-country running dodged these hurdles by celebrating multiculturalism, with remarkable performances at every turn.

PORTER ARRIVES

On November 28, 1982, twenty-three-year-old American Pat Porter surprised everyone by beating a world-class field of more than 500 runners to win his first US National Cross-Country title. Held on the inner turf of the thoroughbred racing track at the Meadowlands in New Jersey, the grass track featured an American first: man-made hills. But Porter's victory was noteworthy for two additional reasons—he defeated 1982 National Collegiate Athletic Association (NCAA) cross-country champion Mark Scrutton of Britain by 17 seconds with "Athletics West" emblazoned across his chest; and this title would be the first of eight consecutive titles won by Porter at the US National Cross-Country Championships.

Despite having beaten Scrutton once before in cross-country and defeating a deep field that included Nick Rose of Britain (the 1977 national champion), Por-

ter was still a dark horse. Porter had only been a member of Athletics West for two weeks prior to his victory, and had finished 18th the previous year at the US National. "Usually, I don't do very well on this type of course," Porter claimed later. "I had a lot of trouble at the World Championships—but the pace went out a lot slower than I thought. At three miles I was pretty sure I had it."

With the win, Porter began his legacy of excellence. Prior to the Meadowlands race, Porter had finished sixth overall at the US World Cross qualifying race in Pocatello, Idaho, and had two National Association of Intercollegiate Athletics (NAIA) collegiate national cross-country titles to his name from 1980 and 1981. By the end of the decade—after amassing eight straight national cross-country titles, three titles in the US World Cross-Country trials, eight straight World Cross-Country national teams qualified, and victories at international events such as the "Cross du Figaro" in France (along with two Olympic teams)—Porter was simply legendary. There has been perhaps no greater name in United States cross-country running lore since.

A MAN OF MYSTERY

It was over rough, hilly, sloppy courses that Porter's style set him apart. His first four US National Cross-Country victories were achieved with searing sprints from the start. Then, when close pursuers began to stagger and weave, Porter carried on. "I'm pretty nasty the day of the race," Porter confirmed. "I holler. I get aggressive . . . I like cross-country. Most guys hate it."

Despite his aggression on the course, four years after his first National Cross-Country Championship Pat Porter was still only locally known in his home base of Alamosa,

Colorado. That winter, in 1986, Porter had won the senior men's 12,000-meter US trials for the World Cross-Country Championships, surging away from US National 10,000-meter champion Bruce Bickford and winning by 12 seconds. The fitness Porter had revealed made him the strongest US entry in the World Championships since Craig Virgin had unexpectedly won in 1980 and '81. Porter had no real weaknesses.

Café patrons in Alamosa often sent Porter off with waves and blessings. The town, which lay flat as water between the Sangre de Cristo Mountains in the east and the San Juan Mountains to the west, had more feet in elevation (7,540) than residents (7,000). "The one thing everybody asks," said Porter, "is why am I here? Well, I like it here. It's flat and high. And when you're a runner it's important to isolate yourself, to get away from the crowds. Adds a little mystique." It displayed a little orneriness, too.

Porter grew up in Evergreen, Colorado, a piney community near Denver, and began running in high school. "I wanted the 220 or the 440, but the first guys to volunteer got the sprints. The leftovers got the mile." He ran 4:29 as a senior, and was recruited by no one. He went to Metropolitan State in Denver for a year, and then transferred to Adams State College (ASC) in Alamosa. "We always got beat by them [Alamosa] so terribly, I figured this must be the place to learn. The next year, here I was." He learned. "On the first day, I thought I was a stud. We headed out of town for 10 miles of Indian running, where you take turns sprinting to the front of the pack. I made it there twice." He wobbled back to the campus long after everyone else, near-death, but wiser.

The coach at Adams State since 1965 was Joe Vigil. "He's never had the luxury of recruiting great talent," said Porter, "but if you could measure how far runners come under a coach regardless of where they start, there would be no one better." The coaching world agreed. The Athletics Congress put Vigil in charge of the team in Neuchâtel for the World Cross-Country Championships in 1986 and elected him coach of the distance runners on the 1988 Olympic team. "I have total faith in his knowledge of me," Porter said. "After I got going, I became a work addict. Coach Vigil's job was to slow me down."

Did You Know?

The fall of 1954 Joe Vigil was hired as a high school assistant football coach—and he inherited his first high school track team that spring—only one year after graduating from Adams State. Led by a love of education, Vigil learned why Russian sprinters were forbidden to run a single step in training until they could jump off a twenty-foot ladder with their bare feet (the trauma taught nerves to fire more rapidly, which decreased the odds of training injuries); how sixty-year-old goat-herders in Machu Picchu scaled the Andes on a starvation diet of yogurt and herbs (the high altitude supercharged their metabolism); and how Japanese runners alchemized slow walking into fast marathons (their hallmark was their enormous workloads with weekly mileage over 200 miles and long runs hitting 36 miles). His research paid off sensationally: Vigil took over the dying cross-country program at his alma mater in the middle of the 1960s (after 12 years at the high school level), and from 1967 to 1993, the ASC men won 14 national cross-country titles and 28 Rocky Mountain Athletic Conference titles. The first NAIA title came in 1971. In 1977 and '79 they added two more, along with an individual cross-country champion in Sam Montoya, and Joe Vigil was voted the NAIA Coach of the Year both times.

PORTER'S WILD RIDE

By 1989, Pat Porter was a household name. As Merrell Noden of *Sports Illustrated* profiled in December 1989, "Cross-country runners are connoisseurs of adversity, and Pat Porter sounded positively gleeful as he listed the hazards he would be facing when he sought a record eighth straight US cross-country title in San Francisco's Golden Gate Park. 'This course has got everything,' Porter said. 'Sand, roots, acorns, steep uphills, steep downhills, plus places where you have to run fast.' As it turned out, Porter was able to add wind and rain to this masochist's wish list."

Porter's record spoke for itself. The year prior he had tied Don Lash for the most consecutive American cross-country titles (seven straight). In his wake lay former World Cross-Country Champions Craig Virgin and John Treacy; former world marathon best Steve Jones; US marathon leader Alberto Salazar; and Bruce Bickford, the top-ranked 10,000-meter runner in the world in 1985. Porter's average margin of victory was 12 seconds, but more revealing was the fact that he had not once trailed after passing the 2.5-mile mark. Porter's gasping pursuers often sprawled defeated in the finishing chute.

On November 25, 1989, in San Francisco, an ugly storm blew in from the northwest. Wind tore at the tops of the trees in Golden Gate Park, and rain pelted the runners, leaving ankle-deep mud puddles all over the course. Moments after winning the women's championship, a bedraggled Lynn Jennings gave Porter sensible advice. "It's tough out there," she told him. "So don't go out too fast." "That's when I thought maybe I would go out hard," said Porter later. "You can crush a lot of people that way, on a day like this. You crush their spirit and their will."

No one was surprised when Porter sprinted across the Polo Field into the lead. At the one-mile mark of the 6.6-mile (10.6K) race, which he passed in 4:33, Porter had 10 yards on Norway's John Halvorsen. In the 1989 World Cross-Country Championships Halvorsen finished 10th, 21 places and 46 seconds ahead of Porter. "Right after

I crossed the finish line," recalled Porter, "Halvorsen came up to me, looked me in the eye, and said, 'I'm going to run the national cross-country. I just wanted to let you know.'"

Whatever dreams Halvorsen may have had dissolved in that second mile. Flying down a dirt trail gushing with muddy streams, Porter hit the two-mile mark in 9:22, with Halvorsen 11 seconds behind him. Porter's lead swelled to 18 seconds at 3.5 miles. By that time his leading pursuer was no longer Halvorsen but Tim Hacker, the national outdoor 5,000-meter champion, who had started slowly and worked his way through the pack. "Last year I tried to go with him," Hacker explained. "I paid."

It looked as though Hacker might catch Porter. At five miles, which Porter hit in 24:33, Hacker had closed the gap to nine seconds. But Porter's long, smooth stride never buckled as he reached the finish in 32:08, 11 seconds in front of Hacker. Halvorsen, who spent most of the race paying for the ambitiousness of his first mile, finished sixth, in 32:49. "These are the worst conditions of any of my eight victories," Porter said happily.

"It's unbelievable," said Hacker, shaking his head in wonder. "When Don Lash won seven in a row, that was pretty good. But to do it now, well, that's incredible." Later, Porter enjoyed a standing ovation at the awards banquet.

THE EMERGENCE OF THE ATHLETICS CONGRESS AND PROFESSIONAL RUNNING

The transformation of US distance running had only a little to do with Porter's success. While the Amateur Athletic Union had decreed the "cans" and "cannots" of competition for one hundred years, a transformed national governing body for athletics ushered in a new era of competition in the 1980s. The Amateur Sports Act in 1978 established the United States Olympic Committee and provided national oversight for each Olympic sport. It also created important legal protection for individual athletes: prior to its adoption, only the Amateur Athletic Union (AAU) represented the United States in international competition. After Congress adopted the act and removed the AAU from power, The Athletics Congress (TAC) emerged to govern track and field and cross-country running in America.

The creation of The Athletics Congress in February 1979 gave runners new opportunities, but it wasn't without controversy. Understandably, there was talk that TAC was simply the AAU with a new name. The new organization held its first convention in 1979 in conjunction with the AAU, and a number of AAU leaders held important TAC positions. The financial situation was particularly complicated because the AAU had represented multiple sports that were all now controlled by individual national governing bodies—determining who would get resources was a challenge. The first Athletics Congress president, Jimmy Carnes, explained to the critics, "We don't have desks, we don't have typewriters, we don't have chairs; we have to use what is available at the AAU headquarters. It will take time to move." But The Athletics Congress didn't wait. By the end of 1980 they had ended their

relationship with the AAU. The opening of a separate TAC office confirmed this independent identity.

The Athletics Congress's reliance on AAU resources during its infancy did not stop it from making a sharp and immediate break from old AAU policy. They quickly decided to increase the role of the athletes in governance, a requirement from The Amateur Sports Act, which stated the congress's board be composed of at least 20 percent active athletes. This created a noticeable exhilaration among the elected runners, many of whom, like Don Kardong, had ties with cross-country running. The Athletics Congress also provided the athletes more power through the Athletes Advisory Committee (AAC), which weighed in on issues important to the athletes, such as the creation of development programs, the distribution of money, drug-testing policies, support for athletes seeking reinstatement in the International Amateur Athletics Federation (IAAF), and the liberalization of amateur rules. AAC membership also relied on direct athlete selection, making it a much more democratic and representative body. Perhaps most important, the AAC received an independent budget that allowed it to subsidize athlete travel expenses.

TAC's perspective toward amateurism also represented a remarkable break from the past. A number of athletes who had competed in the defunct ITA (the International Track Association, the professional attempt at US track and field from 1972 to 1976) had lost their amateur status, and appeared at the TAC convention in 1979. At the convention, sprinter John Smith urged the new organization to support the former ITA athletes' petition to the IAAF for reinstatement. Shockingly, the TAC convention overwhelmingly supported the ITA athletes' push for reinstatement. This confirmed that The Athletics Congress was not the same body as the AAU.

In fact, the age-old amateur ethos was about to change for athletes everywhere. Despite the issue not even being on the agenda, following John Smith's appeal, a delegate introduced a resolution from the floor calling for The Athletics Congress to petition the IAAF for the complete and immediate dissolution of all amateur eligibility restrictions. The motion passed quickly and overwhelmingly. *Track and Field News's* Bob Hersh excitedly proclaimed that it was "an absolutely revolutionary proposal . . . After nearly 100 years, one of the leading proponents of international amateurism has defected to the other side." Even Ollan Cassell, longtime defender of amateurism while employed in the AAU offices, agreed, "We've got to be able to stop people from being paid or we have to allow it and control it . . . The problem now is figuring out how we can regulate the payments and endorsements so that the IAAF and its members keep control of the sport." After years of fighting the AAU with little success, athletes found TAC responsive to their needs and desires.

To further the cause, a series of financial decisions late in the 1970s motivated a group of athletes to push even harder against the rules of amateurism. The AAU (and later on TAC), attempted to negotiate with major commercial enterprises, like Hilton Hotels, to sponsor individual athletes for appearance purposes and provide the governing bodies with a percentage of the payments. In 1981 TAC earned $227,500 through commercial deals between runners and a number of companies, including Hilton Hotels, Puma, Adidas, Stanley Tools, ASICS, and Warner Brothers. This exceeded the amount of money TAC earned through television contracts that year by almost $30,000. Bill Rodgers felt the governing bodies were trying to supplant the role of agents, stating, "Now TAC wants to be our agent—they want to be the agent for all their athletes. It's like buying amateurism." The governing bodies thought these accommodations would become a permanent arrangement, but the athletes had other ideas.

Tired of the hypocrisy, American distance runners formed the Association of Road Running Athletes (ARRA) in 1980 to challenge TAC's position of unquestioned authority with the creation of an openly professional road-racing circuit. The blurring of overt and covert financial compensation encouraged athletes to pursue an open and professional running circuit. To separate themselves from the failures of professional track and field, the ARRA did not attempt to generate revenue as a spectator sport, nor did it need to rely on television contracts. Participant fees from recreational runners and sponsorship money from the large, growing athletic equipment companies funded their cause.

It made sense. The corporate sponsors owed their enormous growth and profits to the running boom. The demographics of the road-running phenomenon, overwhelmingly young and well off financially, encouraged large corporations whose businesses had nothing to do with running to also provide substantial funding as they sought access to millions of new participants. If unsuccessful in changing the amateur rules, the road runners could stop competing in amateur competitions and still create a permanent professional road circuit, because corporate supporters like Nike were not likely to abandon potential customers.

With financial support from Nike, ARRA sponsored the Cascade Runoff in Portland, Oregon, on June 29, 1981—the first openly professional running race. The Athletics Congress threatened all participants with suspension. Still, many of the top distance runners in the world, including Bill Rodgers, Greg Meyer, and Herb Lindsay, competed in the race. The athletes' united defiance of the amateur rules surprised and frustrated The Athletics Congress. Don Kardong explained ARRA's uncompromising goals when he announced that the Cascade race "marked the first time in the history of our sport that the athletes, in conjunction with race directors and sponsors, willingly participated in a race, free of under-the-table payments, with a prize money structure available for those who wished to accept it." The Cascade race was a momentous and explicit challenge to the amateur rules and to The Athletics Congress, and was a landmark turn against those who controlled the sport. Greg Meyer, who won $10,000 for his first-place finish, vowed, "If I have to spend the $10,000 to fight The Athletics Congress I will. Maybe I'll never be able to compete

in Europe. Perhaps the Olympics are out of the question now. But I'm gambling that the open circuit begun here will thrive." ARRA planned for five more open professional road races in 1981.

Following the initial Cascade race, Herb Lindsay and a few other ARRA athletes proposed that they put their winnings in a trust fund where they would only withdraw what would cover living expenses and training. In a surprising move, The Athletics Congress supported this, and a number of athletes retained their amateur status. By agreeing to the Lindsay trust fund, TAC and the IAAF acknowledged and accepted over-the-table payments to athletes. Although it was a compromise that some in the ARRA disapproved of, it was a monumental step forward. And although they did not gain the complete, unfettered professionalism they desired, the athletes had clearly won. TAC and the IAAF changed the amateur rules only to keep pace and control the athletes' actions and challenges. This began the transition into open professionalism.

Although athletes recall their participation in the TAC trust-fund operation (labeled TACTRUST) in different ways, they participated in large numbers, and the program expanded rapidly throughout the 1980s. In 1982, 303 track athletes had deposited money into TACTRUST accounts, 129 of them women. And by 1983 more than 700 athletes had deposited upwards of $1 million total in TACTRUST accounts. Further, the TACTRUST system forced the modernization of the TAC national office. By the last year of the decade more than 3,000 athletes had TACTRUST accounts, and The Athletics Congress monitored 10,000 transactions annually.

The athletes and the governing bodies settled comfortably into the trust-fund system throughout the 1980s, and the top athletes capitalized handsomely. The range of acceptable financial opportunities within the TACTRUST system was expansive. Athletes could deposit prize money, commercial sponsorship money, appearance fees, and developmental money provided by the governing body. They still could not, however, accept money directly (except for small amounts through The Athletics Congress's Certificate Program). But the 1980s would soon give way to the forces of open professionalism in the 1990s. As the 1980s ended, the athletes had tired of the TACTRUST system. But the IAAF, on the other hand, remained perfectly happy with the trust-fund arrangement during the decade of the 1980s, which enabled the fiction of amateurism to exist.

LEGISLATION ENABLES ATHLETICS WEST DOMINANCE

The new athlete sponsorship rules granted through The Athletics Congress paid huge dividends to athletic clubs such as Nike's Athletics West team. And after the Olympic boycott in 1980, a renewed vigor was felt throughout the sport of distance running as commercial revenue became available for what formally existed as athlete-to-athletic-club training.

By 1983, along with the emergence of Pat Porter, Athletics West was undergoing its most ambitious expansion to date. Gone was the guidance of Harry Johnson; Bob Sevene was the main Athletics West coach. The Los Angeles Olympics of 1984 and Seoul, Korea, in 1988 were the focus. The training facility in Eugene was state of the art, and legendary distance coach Jack T. Daniels was flown in from Exeter, New Hampshire, to run the operation.

Daniels worked under the guidance of officials Dick Brown and Doug Brown, where his research spanned tests comparing aerobic demand of outdoor running with the same speeds on the treadmill; the effect of wind at different velocities of running; the effect of wearing shoe orthotics; and he discovered, among other notables, that 10K to marathon runners were more economical at slower speeds, compared with 800/1,500 runners, and found the latter to be more economical at faster speeds. He also did a fair bit of swim research with the US Junior and Senior teams, both at altitude and sea level. And all of this produced results, especially in cross-country.

For seven years in the 1980s, Athletics West found themselves the men's team champion for the US National Cross-Country Championships—including six straight titles between 1981 and 1986. Pat Porter, with his unheralded dominance, was an eight straight individual champion from 1982 to 1989. In the men's US World Cross-Country Trials (run separately from the national championship) Athletics West was equally dominant, with member athletes Dan Dillon, Thom Hunt, Dan Heikkinen, Don Clary, Guy Arbogast, Doug Brown, Jeff Drenth, Alan Scharsu, and Steve Plasencia all qualifying for the World Cross-Country Championships (representing the United States). Alberto Salazar, Pat Porter, and John Easker each won the trials event outright in 1982, '83, '84, '86, '87, and '89.

For the women of Athletics West it was nearly an equivalent success rate. For seven years—1981, 1983, and 1985–89—the female contingent won the US National Cross-Country team title for the club. In 1985, 1987–93, and 1996, Lynn Jennings crossed the line as individual champion. Brenda Webb, Mary Decker, Joan Hansen, Marty Cooksey, Joan Benoit, Cathy Easker, Sabrina Dornhoefer, Nan Doak, and Margaret Groos all placed at the women's US World Cross-Country Trials running for Athletics West, while Lynn Jennings and Betty Springs each won titles of their own along the way. For Jennings, the decision wasn't difficult: "If you were a really good runner and were offered the chance to join Athletics West with health benefits, travel money, a monthly stipend and all the kit and shoes you needed, would you have turned that down? The opportunities Athletics West offered to emerging elite were fantastic."

ENTER LYNN JENNINGS

Lynn Jennings did not always have fantastic opportunities—but she did make the most of the opportunities she had. Jennings grew up in Harvard, Massachusetts, fifty

miles west of Boston, and attended Bromfield public high school. Bromfield didn't have a girls' cross-country team, so Jennings ran on the boys' team. As a freshman she came in last in every race.

The following spring, however, she finished second in the high school mile at the girls' state meet and caught Coach John Babington's eye. Babington, a Boston lawyer, recruited Jennings for the Liberty Athletic Club—a women's track club that he coached, which drew its members from all over New England and won five national junior cross-country team titles between 1976 and 1981. That summer, 1975, said Jennings, "I fell in love with the process of running. I just liked going out there and doing it every day." She cut her best for the mile to 5:01, beating, among others, a Bowdoin freshman named Joan Benoit at an open meet in Boston.

As a sophomore Jennings was the top runner on the Bromfield boys' cross-country team. By the end of the year, Jennings, only fifteen, had qualified for the 1976 Olympic trials. She was at or near the top of many all-time high school lists, but what was most impressive was her range. Accomplishments as a high school senior included winning a road 10K in 34:31, the national junior cross-country title by a margin of 12 seconds, 4:18.9 for 1,500 meters indoors (a time that no other high school runner has come within five seconds of), third in the AAU indoor mile in 4:39, and deciding to run the Boston Marathon. At seventeen, Jennings was too young to enter officially, so she started without a number. Running "at what seemed no more than a hard training effort," she crossed the finish line as the third woman, less than two minutes behind winner Gayle Barron, who ran 2:44:52. The marathon soon got its revenge. Leg pains turned out to be symptoms of a torn meniscus, and she had to have arthroscopic surgery on her left knee.

In 1978, Jennings showed up as a freshman at Princeton 12 pounds over her running weight and totally out of place. "I was really a backward little person," Jennings claimed. "I had spent my high school years trying to be a great runner, which didn't mix with growing up as a teenager. I came to college like a fourteen-year-old, socially. I remember my first cross-country party. I sat on the couch reading *Runner's World* and drinking a glass of milk because drinking beer and socializing with people were completely over my head. Poor Peter [Farrell, the Princeton coach]. He got the blue-chip recruit of the country, and she was a mess."

Jennings showed flashes of brilliance in college, but she never approached the level that her early successes had predicted for her. Midway through her junior year, Jennings withdrew from school. She moved back home to Massachusetts and worked as a janitor. She also started to run on her own again. She returned to Princeton after a year; in the spring of her senior year she finished third in the NCAA 3,000. After graduation, Jennings tried to make the 1984 Olympic team in the 3,000. She qualified for the trials but finished last in her heat by 45 seconds. What was worse was being introduced as "former national junior champion." "Definitely the nadir of my career," Jennings said. "There I was at twenty-four, still being remembered for past glories. I felt like I hadn't moved on in life."

After finishing fifth overall at the 1980 Women's US World Cross-Country Trials, Jennings faded from the sport for nearly six years—until she made a striking comeback. "I didn't want to end up thirty and wondering if I could've been a great runner," Jennings said. There was no time for wondering. November 1985 saw her win her first US National Cross-Country title in Raleigh, North Carolina. February 1986 marked the first time she won the Women's US World Cross-Country Trials outright, and she added a runner-up finish at World Cross a month later. Next was a victory at the Cinque Mulini cross-country in Italy, running five kilometers in 17:27. By then, Jennings was also a member of Athletics West: "I got my hunger back and in the fall of '85 I won the first of my nine national cross-country titles in the mud in North Carolina. I loved representing Athletics West," Jennings said.

And for the glory at Worlds, it was an easy fit for Jennings: "I think it was a combination of weather, difficult conditions, tough courses and the fact that everyone in the world showed up for those races. I represented the US at eight straight World Cross-Country Championships and I'm proud of that, because it was an event where there was no prize money. I didn't do it for the money. I did World Cross-Country because I loved representing the US at that event. There was just something incredibly exhilarating about that difficult race and I loved the rough and tumble."

Jennings also never apologized for her intensity: "I have the killer instinct," she explained. "That's how I feel on the starting line. Would you want a surgeon to say, 'Gee, I really hope I do a good job on this heart transplant?' No. You want him to say, 'I'm going to open up that chest, I'm going to take that heart out, I'm going to shove a new one in there, and it's going to work.'" With Babington as her coach, Jennings would go on to become one of the most versatile champions in American history: national titles indoors in the mile, outdoors in the 10,000, on the roads, and in cross-country, where her national-title streak stood at seven straight and nine in 12 years.

THE UNITED STATES: A POWERFUL ENTITY AT WORLD CROSS

In the 1980s, runners from the United States proved to be a dominant force at World Cross. Even with the arrival of Kenya and Ethiopia in the event, American athletes of both genders in the senior and junior ranks had standout performances.

Craig Virgin earned individual gold medals for the senior men in 1980 and 1981, with Alberto Salazar adding a silver in 1982. More than ten men finished in the top 20 or better at some point in the decade for the senior men's division, with many, like Pat Porter, Craig Virgin, Alberto Salazar, and Bruce Bickford doing so multiple times.

The United States's women fared equally well individually with Jan Merrill, Cathy Branta, and Lynn Jennings earning silver medals in 1981, 1985, and 1986, respectively. Furthermore, Merrill, Branta, and Jennings were joined by Margaret Groos, Betty Springs, Joan Benoit, Nan Doak, and Leslie Lehane who each finished in the top 10 at World Cross at least once during the decade (for Groos and Springs it was multiple top 10s).

And with their strong supporting staffs, the men's and women's teams both achieved podium finishes at World Cross throughout the 1980s. The men finished with four silver medals (four in the first five years of the decade, in fact), while the women won one team silver and four team golds in the decade (1983, '84, '85, and '87). To match, the men found themselves on the podium with bronze in 1985 and 1986, while the women earned third in 1980 and '89. Overall, the top US competitors at the senior event won 19 medals—in a decade that saw the largest fields of cross-country competitors to date.

The junior squads both fared just as well. In 1980 it was the junior men who earned team silver, led by the third-place finish of Ed Eyestone. The following year it was team gold, with four top-10 runners in Keith Brantly (third), George Nicholas (fourth), John Butler (sixth), and Chris Hamilton (10th). But with East Africans dominating the top spots, America only earned one more trip to the podium for the remainder of the decade with a third-place medal. The junior women saw their first event in 1989, with the US team placing sixth overall—not bad considering their competition included teams as far-flung as Turkey, Japan, and Chinese-Taipei.

CRAIG VIRGIN COMES FROM BEHIND IN 1980

Craig Virgin won gold at World Cross in 1980, but his journey really began two years earlier. In 1978, in Glasgow, Scotland, Virgin was a member of one of the finest American distance teams to ever compete at the World Cross-Country Championships. As the first American finisher that year at the US National Cross-Country Championships, Virgin made his debut alongside Bill Rodgers, Mike Roche, Jeff Wells, Greg Meyer, Bobby Thomas, and Guy Arbogast—each proficient in cross-country.

Virgin finished sixth overall, helping to lead Team USA to a silver medal (they lost to France by the smallest of margins: 151 to 155). Virgin was hooked: "I used my time in 1978 to pick the brain of Bill Rodgers. I wanted to know how to do well as Rodgers had finished 3rd in the 1975 World Cross-Country Championships. Guy Arbogast got 5th and I got 6th and we were running with Englishman Tony Simmons and the Scot Nat Muir. In that race it rained, sleeted, snowed and hailed. We were separated by five points from France. I left that race thinking we are a country who doesn't take cross-country running seriously and yet we almost won. I said, 'Guys we can do this,' and started recruiting."

The lead-up to 1980 saw Virgin hungrier than ever. The year prior, Virgin slipped and fell in the mud and had to fight through about 100 runners to finish 13th. As Virgin described: "In 1978 I got a good start and was in the top 15 the entire way. In 1979 falling so far back and having to fight my way past 100 runners showed me I could move up if I just waited for openings and surged through them."

Leading to the 1980 event Virgin was more than ready:

In the later part of 1979 in the races leading to World Cross, I ran in the famous Italy cross-country race Cinque Mulini and got 3rd. I ran right with Bronislaw who had finished 2nd in the previous World Championships. I knew I could run with the best when I ran with the best of the world in that Italy race.

I was the team captain in 1980. The gun was up and we were off. I felt we had a great start but in 50 meters they pulled the rope and the race stopped for a restart. I was directing the guys back to the starting line and what happened next I will never forget: I was lining the guys up and the starter shot the gun. My own teammates ran over me, a teammate grabbed me and kept me from falling on my face. By the time everything got sorted I was in 50th and I had a moment of truth. In the first half mile I said to myself, "You've still got seven miles to go—a lot can happen—stay patient and try to work your way up."

During the five-lap race Virgin worked his way up to the back of the lead pack after three laps, finding himself just 100 meters behind leader Nick Rose:

I see 4–5 guys running in the lead pack and about 50 meters in front of them I see Nick Rose running solo and no one was going after him. I had another "moment of truth" decision and had to decide to either stay in the safety of the lead pack, or take off after Nick. Nick Rose and I have history. We had been rivals in college, he had beaten me in the NCAA championships my sophomore year. I beat him my junior year. I knew I would be possibly setting myself up to fail—I knew we couldn't just give him the lead as I didn't think he would die. I thought, 'Did I come 3,000 miles to race for second or to try and win?'

I decided to slingshot around the lead pack and go after him. My goal was to be on Nick's shoulder with a lap to go and to try to out sprint him on the last lap. I got closer and closer but on the home straight with a lap to go he looked back, saw me and took off. I looked over my shoulder and saw two runners coming up and thought I could be in trouble. I worked so hard to catch him and when he took off I was just dead in the water. I was sucking wind and suddenly 3, 4, 5 were coming up on me. In that moment, I had another defining moment of truth and I had to answer the call. Instead of giving

up and saying, "I gave it the old college try," I had to make a decision once again to hang in there and let them push me as they were right behind me. I forced myself to recover on the run. I forced myself to stay with the pack when they caught me.

Over the next 1K I fought through the pain and agony of burning lungs. Then out of nowhere I got a second wind. West German Hans-Jürgen Orthmann and Belgian Leon Schots were on my shoulder and we were chasing Nick Rose with the Russian Aleksandras Antipovis chasing us. The stage was set. Rose paid a price for making a big move at the bell lap. He was fading and we were closing. Orthmann took off with 600 or 700 yards to go. I had practiced the final stretch of the course several times during the two days before the meet and decided the straightaway was too long to start my kick so early. So I held back until under 400 meters to go and made first one move and then a second move with 150 meters to go and got by Rose. I look at the finish line and realize I may be able to catch Orthmann. As I came up behind Orthmann I wanted to use the element of surprise. He looks left and I go right. I didn't want him to see me and by the time he pivots around I have two steps on him and I knew I had it. Then I nailed my last gear with about 100 meters to go and I got past Orthmann. That last 20 meters were the toughest 20 meters of my life. I could smell it but I was starting to run out of gas. I kept pumping my arms and the strength of my weekly hill intervals helped me to hold that drive through the finish. The final 20 meters I put my number one finger up in the air in celebration. I snatched victory from the jaws of defeat in the final 200 meters. In my defining moment of truth I did not give up.

In 1981 Craig Virgin successfully defended his World Cross-Country title in Madrid, Spain, beating Ethiopia's Mohamed Kedir by two seconds and Portugal's Fernando Mamede by four seconds. However, if not for a lap miscount by the Ethiopian team, where the lead Ethiopian runners, including Kedir, thought the penultimate lap was the final lap, the outcome might have ended differently for Virgin. Nonetheless, Virgin called the win the "epoch" of his career and his second victory in as many years set the bar for US distance runners at the World Cross-Country Championships, despite Europe being at its pinnacle of involvement and East African nations such as Kenya and Ethiopia making their debut. It was the American's time, and Virgin wasn't alone in his belief of what was possible.

ALBERTO SALAZAR TAKES THE REINS

November 1979 saw twenty-one-year-old Alberto Salazar finish an exhausted second-place to Henry Rono at the NCAA Cross-Country Championship. Salazar had planned to wear Rono down with a fast early pace, but at the five-mile mark, when he sensed that Salazar was straining, Rono moved effortlessly into the lead and ran away with the race. Salazar never forgot that feeling, despite knocking nearly a minute and a half off the previous course record. And five days after the NCAA showdown, the AAU held the US National Cross-Country Championship on a demanding, newly completed 10,000-meter course bordering North Carolina State's Carter-Finley Stadium in Raleigh.

When Rono decided not to compete in the NCAA-AAU cross-country double, Salazar became the man to beat. Once more Salazar set a fast early pace. He was timed at the mile mark in a startling 4:08.3, a time he later refused to accept as accurate. At the top of a long hill between the one- and two-mile marks, he broke away from the field and ran the rest of the way alone. He finished 20 seconds ahead of the second-place finisher, Herb Lindsay. What's more, Salazar's team, the Greater Boston Track Club, was also an easy winner, with four finishers in the top five. For Salazar, it marked the completion of his amateur cross-country season—he went on to focus his efforts on the marathon, running a 2:09:41 effort in New York less than a year later. And for a significant period cross-country and "the rookie" were apart—until an eventful return in the fall of 1981.

By November of 1981, Salazar had a reputation. He also had a contract with Nike's Athletics West. At the De Bell Golf Course in Burbank, California, more than 300 staunch opponents faced Salazar at the 1981 US National Cross-Country Championship, among them Henry Rono, Herb Lindsay, Nick Rose, and Pat Porter.

At the start came the charge. Quickly the more excitable milers were well up, with Steve Lacy in the lead. As the pack pressed together, many were sealed in. "I just got swallowed," said miler Steve Scott. "There was a lot of kicking and biting there among the anxious." Alberto Salazar ran patiently behind and waited. Henry Rono improved his position by jumping onto a wall of sandbags. Nick Rose worked his way up with sharp bursts as openings presented themselves. Before the race, Rose pronounced himself splendidly fit, saying, "It will be a great race if the others are really ready."

The runners had to lift themselves 320 feet in a wearying two-mile section, and practically none of the course was level, save for the last 160 yards. It wasn't the plowed fields, barnyards, and fences of European cross-country, but it was close. By two miles Salazar led none other than Rose and Rono, though that trio hadn't yet run away from the field. Once those two dropped, it was Salazar and a long-haired runner all in yellow that had pulled to a 50-yard lead. The cries of the crowd were uniform: "Who's that guy with Salazar?"

Searching the program for his number yielded the name of "Adrian Royle." Adrian Royle, twenty-two, from Manchester, England, had won the US Junior-College Cross-Country Championship by a huge margin the year prior while attending Southern Idaho Junior College. "I got run out of Idaho," Royle would say later, mysteriously.

"They don't believe in the 20th century there." So he had moved on, to the University of Nevada at Reno.

Alberto Salazar knew none of this. All he knew was that a guy with a rangy stride and loud breathing was with him and kept pushing the pace. "I thought he'd die," Salazar said later. "He sounded like he was tired. I didn't know who he was so I assumed I could outkick him. I settled down to wait, concentrating on how I would sprint."

At three miles, Royle had a look of elation. "I knew I had him," he said later. "I knew I'd be good on the downhills but I was scared of Salazar." As Royle continued to lead, seeming to grow ever stronger, Salazar understood what was happening. "He was a guy running the race of his life," Salazar said. "He would be willing to pay any price and still be able to kick. And I was trying to avoid having to press hard all the way. I should have realized I couldn't get away with that. I should have tried to kill him on the hills."

Royle was very much alive as they entered the final 160 yards. Salazar moved first, but Royle cut him off before he could pass, then sprinted away to win by two seconds. Royle crossed the line with his face twisted in glee and at once showed himself to be a man quite assertive in victory. "Everybody was here!" he proclaimed. Those he beat, in order, were Salazar, Jan Hagelbrand, Nick Rose, 1977 world junior champion Thom Hunt, and, in sixth, showing amazing stamina for a miler, Steve Scott. Rono finished 37th. Salazar jogged away through the rainy dusk, saying, "It's plain stupidity to underestimate the other guy." Salazar was feeling more sharply what he already knew, that as a world-record holder he was a marked man in every race he entered.

ADRIAN ROYLE OF ENGLAND

When Adrian Royle first started running as an eleven-year-old boy, he never in his wildest dreams imagined going shoulder to shoulder with the some of the best endurance athletes on the planet. But the small Wintringham School pupil always had the kind of single-mindedness that any great success requires.

A raw fitness built up from being an extremely active teenager, coupled with surrounding himself with the right people contributed to his success. Born in Manchester, Royle moved to Grimsby when he was young, and it was there that his passion for competition began. He recalled: "I first started running during my time at Wintringham School. I was in the same class as Tony Ford. He went on to play football for Grimsby Town, I went on to be a runner."

"I was very small as an 11-year-old. I progressed, and by the time I was 16, I was beating the guys who were good at all sports. I was into many outdoor things at that time, not just running. I loved bird watching and cycling." Royale continued: "My teacher, Mike Hobden, kept asking me to do races. Eventually I did a race and won it. In 1976, I joined Grimsby Harriers. I progressed very quickly. I did local and regional races on the track and cross-country. I did okay for a rookie."

Royle then made a decision that would catapult him from a good runner to a world-beating athlete:

I went over to the United States when I was 21. That's where it all happened for me. I started off at a college in Idaho. There were lots of wide-open spaces with national parks and trails. I later went out to Reno in Nevada, which is at high altitude. It was a fantastic training place. It is underrated and relatively unknown. I think it is better than places like Boulder, Colorado. It was perfect for me. It was dry, with sunshine 360 days a year. I used to run twice a day—132 miles a week at my peak. I used to do lots of hill work and cross-country. People talk about experiencing a natural high—I certainly had that. I was up in the mountains, on soft trails, running slightly downhill. I was flying. To be honest, I preferred cross-country in the United States. It suited my style. My first big win was in the National Junior College Cross-Country Championships. I won it by a country mile.

After impressing in his early races in the States, Royle rocked the world of distance running with his sensational victory in the US National Cross-Country Championship: "The big turning point for me was when I won that race against some of the best runners in the world. I travelled to Los Angeles with the sole purpose of winning the race."

Royle's victory over Salazar and his personal bests, such as his 27:47 for the 10,000 meters, would be impressive if set by a runner today, but a mystery illness wiped him out—and although still a formidable athlete, Royle was never quite the same again. He recalled: "I returned to the UK in 1983 after I had been ill for 18 months. I have no idea what it was. But I went from beating the top Africans in the world to not being able to walk around the block." Despite this fade into relative obscurity, Royle's big day pushed Salazar to be even more formidable.

"THE ROOKIE" RETURNS TO WORLDS

Only a few months after his surprising defeat, Salazar emerged again, this time to win the US World Cross-Country Trials in Pocatello, Idaho, on February 15, 1982. This ensured him passage as the leading member of the United States's team to the World Cross-Country Championships, Salazar's first time since attending the event as a junior in 1976. It also meant that the United States was going to send one of its top distance runners to vie for a third straight gold medal, after Craig Virgin had proven it could be done in 1980 and 1981. But for Salazar, a world-record holder in the marathon, the road to Rome for World Cross was wrought with uncertainty after being defeated by the unknown Adrian Royle.

It was clear that Adrian Royle had the race of his life—but Salazar was at his peak. The pace was brutal from the start in the 1982 World Cross-Country Championships, and Salazar remained in striking range for the totality.

Only one opponent could not be overcome: the runner-up from the year prior, Mohammed Kedir of Ethiopia, the man who had let Virgin slip by the smallest of margins. Despite running a tactically sound race, Salazar finished four seconds back of the dominant Ethiopian. But Salazar wasn't making the 1982 World Cross his only focus, as he explained in his autobiography: "I finished second at the world meet at Rome, recalling the third-place performance at World Cross that Bill Rodgers had logged before his first Boston Marathon win in 1975. When I got back to the States, I looked at the calendar and realized that the time had come for me to run Boston, too."

After winning Boston in a remarkable time of 2:08:52 (what was famously dubbed the "Duel in the Sun"), and winning the New York Marathon for the third year in a row, Alberto Salazar emerged on the cross-country circuit again in February 1983 to race the US World Cross-Country Trials, held in Edwardsville, Illinois. Salazar won easily, beating Craig Virgin, his nearest competitor, by 16 seconds, and Pat Porter in third by over half a minute. For the United States's squad at World Cross in Gateshead, England, Salazar was joined by acclaimed runners Thom Hunt, Par Porter, Ed Eyestone, Doug Brown, Mark Anderson, and Craig Virgin. The stage was set.

While Salazar's performance was do-or-die, he missed defending his second-place finish by a mere second, and in fact crossed in an admirable fourth place. The top 10 finishers were all within 25 seconds of each other, a smattering of major names represented with Salazar, including Some Muge of Kenya, Carlos Lopes of Portugal, Dave Clarke of England, and Salazar's teammate Pat Porter. The top five in the race were separated by only four seconds; it was nearly inconceivable for a 12-kilometer cross-country championship to be that close. With concerted efforts given by all the athletes, the United States found themselves back on the podium with a team silver. The champion at the 1983 event hailed from the same East African nation as the year prior, Ethiopia, and it would not be the final time either. For the emergence of Kenyan and Ethiopian distance running talent, the 1980s were pivotal; and it was on the cross-country course that they changed history.

EAST AFRICA ARRIVES AT WORLD CROSS

Kenya and Ethiopia would rewrite the history books at the World Cross-Country Championships. First invited to compete in 1981, both East African nations were welcomed with open arms to the "world's toughest footrace." Each nation possessed a remarkable distance running history, and each too had considerable challenges facing them at home. For Ethiopia, political strife and instability exposed doubt as to the strength of their national team, while for Kenya, a boycott of the 1976 and 1980 Olympics, along with an authoritarian athletics federation, belied similar concerns. No one could have predicted just how dominant both nations would be.

The World Cross-Country Championships were the only athletics event where every elite runner from the

1,500 meters to the marathon was present. Because of this, a gold medal in the event was one of the most prestigious rewards an athlete could receive, and it was coveted by African runners looking for international exposure and a way to garner invitations on the world running circuit.

Great expectations had been billed in 1981, not only because of the debut of the African nations themselves, but who was taking part. Ethiopia had returned to the Olympic Games in Moscow just one year earlier, and the 10,000 meters had been a riveting match against Finnish athletes. Among the members of that memorable one-three-four finish in Moscow were Miruts Yifter and Mohamed Kedir, along with steeplechase bronze medalist Eshetu Tura.

The debut of the Ethiopians at World Cross lived up to the hype. Six of them were well ahead of the field with one lap to go on the course in Madrid, until they slowed to a jog as the bell started ringing, thinking they had already finished. Despite this they managed a team victory—while Kedir had the guts to challenge American Craig Virgin until the bitter end. Yet, the wound remained fresh and Kedir took the win when he returned to World Cross in 1982. A twenty-year-old youngster named Bekele Debele obtained a second individual title for Ethiopia on Gateshead mud in '83, while Some Muge grabbed the bronze for the first Kenyan individual medal ever. Carlos Lopes won the silver. The Portuguese veteran was in his best form ever and no runner could match him, not in the two following editions of the World Cross, nor in the 1984 Olympic Marathon, which he won at age thirty-seven. At the time, it would have been impossible for anyone to imagine that Carlos Lopes was potentially going to be the last man born outside of African shores to win the World Cross-Country Championship.

ETHIOPIA STRIKES FIRST

In Ethiopia, leader Haile Selassie's reign came to an end in September of 1974, when a Soviet-backed Marxist–Leninist military junta, the "Derg" led by Mengistu Haile Mariam, deposed him. The new Provisional Military Administrative Council established a one-party communist state in March 1975 called the People's Democratic Republic of Ethiopia. The ensuing regime suffered several coups, uprisings, wide-scale drought, and a huge refugee problem. Many suffered from forced deportations or from the use of hunger as a weapon. More than 500,000 Africans lost their lives.

Amid the chaos came a few bright spots, most notably in Ethiopian athletics. Ethiopia, having become a communist country in 1975, enjoyed the benefits of being part of the Eastern Bloc. The African nation became a privileged destination for altitude distance training for East German runners such as Olaf Beyer (the man who beat both Sebastian Coe and Steve Ovett in 1978), Jürgen Straub, Utta Pippig, and race walker Ron Weigel. When the German athletes trained in the stadium of Addis Abeba, the Ethiopian coaches were standing by paying close attention.

Later, an exchange developed and Ethiopians travelled to Potsdam, Germany, for training camps and competed in major German track meets. Some Ethiopian coaches even studied in Leipzig at the University for Body Culture (now German Sport University Cologne). Among them was the future national head coach for distance running, Dr. Woldemeskel Kostre.

Despite boycotting the 1984 Olympics in Los Angeles and 1988 Olympics in Seoul, and contending with famine, civil war, and political instability with the Derg, the Ethiopian squad remained competitive internationally—especially in the World Cross-Country Championships. From 1981 through 1985 the senior men's team was the top finisher—an extraordinary achievement for a nation only recently admitted into the fold. From 1985 through 1989 they were just as good, finishing second or third as a team each year.

A *New York Times* article attempted to identify the reasons for such dominating success:

> Ethiopia is a mountainous place where distance running is a passion. It has been so especially since 1960, when the nation's hero, Abebe Bikila, won the Olympic marathon running barefoot through the streets of Rome. Now, says Nigusse Roba, the team's coach, "everybody says that if I can run long distance, I can be a hero in the world." "Sometimes we think they're superhuman," said Ed Eyestone, a member of the United States team. "They do carry a lot of mystique about them." "It's like a movie star that never shows up for a public appearance," said Craig Virgin, the two-time world champion from St. Louis. "They're so unknown and they've done so well."

It was apparent that much of the world was in the dark about what made Ethiopia so dominant.

In the end, the article was able to expose a few insightful anecdotes: "They are often probed for the secrets of their success. 'There are no secrets', says Roba. 'I don't think there is a mystery in the training,' he said. 'We cannot copy American ways or Russian training programs. Everything is different—our weather and living standards.' Still, when he said that his runners trained at altitudes of 4,800 feet, a young man in the audience grabbed his chest and gasped at the thought of the thin air at so high an elevation."

Success also came from a concerted effort of support from the Ethiopian Athletic Federation (EAF). The Shewa Championships, one of the first major track and field events in the Federation's tutelage, was organized in 1966. The first edition of the Ethiopian Athletics Championships was held in 1971. In the late '70s, a new committee, headed by chairman Tesfaye Sheferaw, was formed to administer the federation. Under the guidance of Sheferaw, achievements included the staging of the first Abebe Bikila Marathon and the inaugural Ethiopian National Cross-Country Championships, which occurred in 1983. Construction of the first athletics track, education and hiring of coaches, and major improvement in working procedures were all hallmarks of the early '80s in Ethiopia.

This dichotomy of achievement and struggle enabled Ethiopia to embrace their international "mystique" during their early success at World Cross in the 1980s, but it would be their neighbors to the south who would ultimately impose an even greater legacy at the World Cross-Country Championships.

KENYA'S ARRIVAL AT WORLD CROSS

Kenya's athletics program was not without its own hardships. Kenya's boycott of the 1976 Summer Olympics in Montreal and the 1980 Games in Moscow deprived an entire generation of the chance of chasing their dream. Athletics was languishing on the home front, and in the words of American writer John Manners, "US college scholarships helped keep running from dying altogether in Kenya." It seemed all the young, promising Kenyan runners—such as Samson Kimobwa, Henry Rono, Mike Musyoki, Sosthenes Bitok, and Wilson Waigwa—were in the United States developing their athletics career. Grassroots work in their homeland had come to nothing and Kenyan athletics authorities were not doing their athletes any favors: they controlled their passports, managed their international schedules, cashed any earnings they received, and hassled international federations to allow runners to compete in European meetings. Henry Rono, one of Kenya's most gifted distance runners, had become a moneymaker for agents, promoters, and Kenyan authorities, and his dream of competing in the Olympic Games would never materialize.

Kenya returned to major global competition with their arrival at the 1981 World Cross-Country Championships. Initially, it was German coach Walter Abmayr who led the national team and fostered Kenya's entrance. The first results were commendable, but not dominant: two third-place and two fourth-place collective finishes. And inconsistencies in the following years did not lead to the type of team success some expected. In 1985, a break came from above: the IAAF started subsidizing qualifying nations who could not afford the costs of international competitions. This budget allowed Abmayr and his assistant Mike Kosgei to impart a more rigorous system of regional trials leading to the Kenyan National Cross-Country Championships, as well as a three-week training camp at Nyeri. This time Kenya finished a close second to Ethiopia and Paul Kipkoech grabbed the silver individual medal behind Carlos Lopes.

It was the departure of Walter Abmayr and the appointment of Mike Kosgei as head national coach that ultimately transformed Kenya's fortunes at World Cross. After taking over more leadership duties in 1984, and after seeing the team to a close second-place finish at the 1985 Word Cross-Country Championship, Kenya (under the tutelage of Kosgei) would go on to win the senior men's team title the next 18 years in succession.

KOSGEI MAKES IT A KENYAN EVENT

"Before I took over, the best Kenyan athletes were not based in Kenya; they were all over the place in Europe and the USA. I brought them back to Kenya. Even today most of the athletes are based in Kenya and leave only for the racing season." This is the legacy that Kosgei helped implement.

Educated on scholarship at Washington State University, Mike Kosgei competed in track before an injury ended his career prematurely. Discovering an interest in coaching, Kosgei then studied for a year and a half in Germany before taking on a job as an administrator for the Kenyan Amateur Athletic Association. It was there that he discovered the importance of the national team training camp:

It started in 1985, when I picked the cross-country team for Lisbon. What happened was Kenya used to invite athletes [who were based in] America, and from all over the place. I remember Musyoki was supposed to run in Lisbon, but he came to Madrid and could not make the connection, so he missed the team. He could not run, and I saw a problem. The Ethiopians beat us [in 1985] because they came together as a team. So I said, "I have to train the team together." There is no need for somebody to finish number one, number 50, and 100. That cannot make a team. So they have to be together. That means they have to have almost equal strength. I think [the team camp concept] was successful. That is how the athletes build together. It is a strange thing to call someone from Eldoret, another one from Nakuru, and then you meet at the airport and you say you are going to the championship. That is cheating.

Prior to 1985, the Kenyan team would be selected based on their international performances and brought to a training camp in Nyeri, which was close to home and open to distractions. Kosgei's first move was to relocate the camp to Embu on the Eastern slopes of Mount Kenya, at the St. Mark's Teacher Training College. Here, at considerable elevation and with a more focused program, the Kenyan national athletes would have to earn their spot after three weeks of intense training leading up to the World Cross-Country Championships. Next, Kosgei increased the number of workouts from two to three daily, including both high intensity and high mileage. At the time, this went against tradition in Kenya. A natural talent like Kip Keino showed he could win an Olympic final with almost casual training, but by the 1980s this was no longer possible.

"I traveled around the country and was surprised by the sheer talent among the young generation," Kosgei recalled. "I thought Kenya was going places if only the process of identifying, developing, exposing and professionalizing athletics would be structured." In 1981, the German Walter Abmayr came to Kenya as a national athletics coach. Kosgei was charged with the task of taking him around the country. Their first stop was Kosgei's old school, St Patrick's at Iten. "He got along well with athletes," Abmayr said. "He conducted programs here and we sent him to make presentations abroad." When Abmayr returned to Germany, Kosgei took over as head coach. Accordingly, Kosgei's budget was increased, allowing him to introduce the regional trials races and the training camp, which was modeled on what his neighbors in Ethiopia were doing. Results immediately improved. In Kosgei's first year in charge, Kenya's team came in second, just 11 points behind Ethiopia.

Kosgei was strict. Only runners who had raced at the Nationals were allowed at the training camp, where he would make his team selections. "I wanted people I had seen," Kosgei said, "not people I had heard about." And that was when he moved the camp from Nyeri to Embu. "In Nyeri," Kosgei said, "there were too many distractions—friends, girlfriends, families. I wanted the runners to concentrate. None of them knew anybody in Embu." At Embu, Kosgei forged strong team discipline and loyalty, he also honed the Kenyans' ability to pack tight together as they ran, a vital technique for his tactical approach for taking on the Ethiopians and the rest of the world.

FOLLOWING THE NGUGI TRAIL

Kosgei got his second slice of luck with the emergence of John Ngugi. Here was a young talent that was so determined to succeed that he would do an extra 10 kilometers of training in the dark every morning. The "Ngugi Trail" at Embu is still used today.

This intense, high-volume training was a massive departure from the laid-back, casual approach to preparation that Kenyans had used since the heyday of Keino. Ngugi showed what sort of training was necessary to win, and after he won his first two of five World Cross titles, the whole training camp began to follow his lead. In Auckland in 1988, Ngugi took the title for a third time and led home six teammates in the top seven places.

Training unified the Kenyan mission. High altitude, hills, and dirt roads were the standard at the National Kenyan Training Camp high up in Embu. Meanwhile, talking and living daily with his runners, Kosgei was able to develop a bond few other national coaches could comprehend. The runners would give everything and more for him. "The coach must know and feel his runners. He must understand their emotions," explained Kosgei.

The living accommodations were Spartan: basic school dormitories, metal framed beds, foam mattresses, and a few centrally located taps for water. Cooks prepared wholesome, plentiful, and nourishing food. Attendance at the camp was by invitation only and the costs were covered by the Kenyan Amateur Athletic Association. The hard part of the camp was the training: three sessions per day, six days a week. Sunday was a "rest" day with just one session. The senior men would often log in excess of 240 kilometers (more than 140 miles) of running in the week.

More amazing is the fact that over 30 percent of that distance would be run at a speed comparable to competition pace. "The mentality is so much different when working with Kenyans. A Kenyan is happy if he or his teammate wins. This makes team tactics easier than if you are working with a bunch of individuals," Coach Kosgei explained.

John Ngugi, born in May 1962 to the Kikuyu tribe, migrated to the Nandi district at the age of three. He then decided to join the Armed forces in 1984, where he was employed as a mechanic. When he first started running, he was advised to go home and not waste his time training to become an athlete. Army coach Kiplimo elaborated: "When he walked his feet stuck out, and his style looked even worse when he ran." Ngugi just trained harder. He returned later and showed he could run. After winning both Army and National Cross-Country Championships, he was selected for the training camp in Embu. The rest is history.

Ngugi's lope captured an extraordinary string of five World Cross-Country Championship titles, an Olympic gold medal, and a Commonwealth Games silver. Although tall in stature (compared to other Africans), Ngugi seemed to float effortlessly over any terrain and glide away from his competitors—with huge winning margins. In the mud of Stavanger, Norway, Ngugi ran back in the pack until the orders came from Mike Kosgei. Then he shot ahead and surged to an insurmountable lead. To prove his versatility, Ngugi's last victory was won running in snow, not a surface the Kenyan had prepared for back home. The wintery conditions in Boston did not bother him as he romped to a 15-second victory over teammate William Mutwol.

But John Ngugi's most impactful influence on Kenya's changing fortunes at World Cross was his work ethic. Ngugi believed that the key to success was to build the body with training loads that would scare the average athlete. "Once, we were training together and it was supposed to be an easy day, as we'd trained very hard the day before. Well, Ngugi decides to do a few kilometer repeats—he does twenty!" laughed Richard Chelimo, himself remembered as a formidable trainer. Ngugi also believed in using low-key races as part of training. After finishing 108th in a Kenya AAA cross-country race, he smiled, "This is all part of the ongoing process of training. In Kenya I am always expected to win, but during hard training it is impossible." This reinforced Chelimo's point that when the buildup period took place all else became secondary, even competition.

A MULTITUDE OF EAST AFRICAN STARS DOMINATE INTERNATIONALLY

Ngugi was not the only Kenyan to achieve an unparalleled level of success. Paul Kipkoech also found himself beating many of the world's best over hill and dale. His introduction to the sport was swift: Kipkoech finished 16th overall in 1983 after running 37:32 in the Gateshead mud at the World Cross-Country Championships—his first real taste of international competition.

As a youth Kipkoech ran several miles each day to and from his school in Kapsabet, in the Nandi Hills, in rural west Kenya. In his mid-teens he joined the Kenyan Army, which gave promising runners time off to train and compete. After performing well on the track, Kipkoech would eventually find himself the Kenyan National Cross-Country champion. It would be the first of four Kenyan National Cross-Country titles to his name. At World Cross he would also display bursts of glory: he finished 19th overall in 1984; second in '85; fifth in '86; second again in '87 and '88; and ninth in '90. Having Mike Kosgei as national coach and Embu as the national training camp didn't hurt either.

Kipkoech was at his best in early 1987. In the span of three months—a total of seventy-seven days—Kipkoech went undefeated, winning the Cross Memorial Juan Muguerza (29:37 for 10 kilometers); the Italica Cross in Seville, Spain; the Cross Internacional de San Sebastian (30:35 for 10 kilometers); and the Kenyan National Cross-Country Championships in Kabarak (40:45 for 14 kilometers). He finished as runner-up at the World Cross-Country Championships in Warsaw, Poland (36:07 for 12 kilometers); and finally, won the Cinque Mulini in Italy (30:14 for 9.5 kilometers). His silver-medal performance at World Cross? Run in an identical time to champion John Ngugi—a finish so close that no camera could discern who finished first.

Some Muge was another Kenyan who helped solidify the national effort. After a spirited run for third at the 1983 World Cross event, Muge returned again to finish eighth in '86, fifth in '87, and ninth in '88. Along the way Muge finished sixth overall at the Kenyan National Cross-Country Championships in 1984 and fourth at the same event in 1987. He also competed internationally, fairing well with a 12th place finish at the L'Equipe Cross-Country in Paris in February 1987, and third overall at the Fukuoka International Cross-Country in Japan in March. It was his 35:02 performance over 12 kilometers in Fukuoka that led to his success at World Cross a week later.

Several Ethiopian athletes stood out as well, including Mohamed Kedir. By 1981, Kedir had already competed twice at the Cinque Mulini, had finished seventh in a 12-kilometer cross-country race in Addis Ababa, Ethiopia, and had won an eight-kilometer cross-country meeting at the Crystal Palace in London, just four months before his first World Cross appearance. He would then go on to be victorious at World Cross in 1982 (33:40 for 12 kilometers) and make two more appearances at the Cinque Mulini (finishing first in 1981 and fourth in 1982). Kedir then won the Cross de San Sebastián in 1983 and 1984, and achieved three more top-30 finishes at the World Cross-Country Championships.

Fellow Ethiopian Bekele Debele saw a similar string of success in cross-country. After finishing 10th overall as a junior in the eight-kilometer World Cross event in 1982, Debele would win the senior men's race in 1983. He returned six more times, with top finishes of eighth place in 1984, fourth in '85 and '86, and 13th in '89. He won the Cinque Mulini in 1984 (31:57 for 9.5 kilometers), was runner-up in 1985 (32:46 for 9.5 kilometers), and finished

second at the Cross de San Sebastian in 1988, running 31:46 for 10 kilometers.

And yet, for the decade of the 1980s, it ended with the domination of John Ngugi. With a runner-up performance at the Kenyan Armed Forces Championships (40:34 for 13.4 kilometers) in 1986, followed by his first and only Kenyan National Cross-Country Championship victory (43:22 for 13.5 kilometers), Ngugi started his assault on history. His victories at World Cross were as follows: 35:33 for 12 kilometers in Colombier, Switzerland, in 1986; 36:07 for 12 kilometers in Warsaw, Poland, in 1987 (with a bad ankle); 34:32 for 12 kilometers in Auckland, New Zealand, in 1988; 39:42 for 12 kilometers in Stavanger, Norway, in 1989; and 37:05 for 12.5 kilometers in Boston, United States, in 1992. Beyond his five titles in World Cross, Ngugi was busy competing in other meetings during the decade as well, such as the Cross Memorial Juan Muguerza; the Cross Internacional de San Sebastian; the Kenyan National Cross-Country Championships; the Cinque Mulini; the IAC International Cross-Country in Cardiff, Wales; the Italica Cross-Country; the Cross des As in Vanves, France; and the Cross delle Orobie in Bergamo, Italy.

All told, Kenyan and Ethiopian senior men claimed 16 of the 30 individual medals available in the 1980s at World Cross (and Ethiopia and Kenya were both absent from the 1980 championship), two individual winners of the Cross Memorial Juan Muguerza in Spain, seven individual winners of the Cross de San Sebastian in Spain, and seven individual winners of the Cinque Mulini in Italy. It was more than just team domination, it was an East African statement—a rivalry, and an expectation for victory. And only one man during the decade was able to stand up to the barrage.

THE RETURN OF CARLOS LOPES

Carlos Lopes, one of Portugal's premier distance-running talents, had all but disappeared from the international stage. Entering the spring of 1978, Lopes carried an imposing reputation. He was an eight-time Portuguese National Cross-Country champion, World Cross champion, and an Olympic silver medalist at 10,000 meters. Add those titles to the smattering of other major cross-country victories, including the Cross de San Sebastian in Spain and Amendoeiras em Flor in Portugal, and it was clear Lopes was one of the most dominant European athletes alive. But at the 1978 World Cross-Country Championships, disaster struck. Lopes not only finished out of the medals for the first time in three years, he was witness to a very uncharacteristic abbreviation next to his name in the results: DNF (Did Not Finish).

Furthermore, in the 1978 and 1979 Amendoeiras em Flor he managed only a pedestrian 12th- and ninth-place finish, respectively. Even at the 1979 club cross-country championships, held in Arlon, Belgium, Lopes was merely eighth. Perhaps it was time for other younger athletes to come to the fore. Lopes had a young son to care for, an accumulation of aches and pains, and stiff competition internationally. Perhaps it was time to consider other career options.

Lopes, however, did not concede. Instead he reevaluated his effort, examined his training, revised his schedule, and focused on bettering himself for another run at the Olympics in 1984. His diligence paid off. In 1982 Carlos Lopes won his ninth Portuguese National Cross-Country Championship. He also was victorious at the Juan Muguerza Memorial Cross-Country in Elgoibar, Spain, and by early 1983, reentered the World Cross-Country Championships for the first time since 1980. Lopes finished second overall by a mere stride and ran more than a minute faster than the previous World Cross three years earlier. Twenty days after nearly winning the World Cross-Country Championships, Lopes finished his first marathon, finishing a close second to Rob de Castella from Australia with a time of 02:08:39—only 21 seconds off the world record. Lopes's form and dominance was back.

In early 1984, Lopes was victorious at a few minor cross-country meetings before winning his 10th Portuguese National Cross-Country title, which put him back in World Cross as the man to beat. And as one of the top European finishers from 1983 it was expected Lopes would do well, but with the 1984 Summer Olympic Games looming, he was not seen as a favorite to win the event outright. Lopes began the race with a group of five, covering the initial mile in 4:20 before slowing the pace and putting in a surge later on. Ten kilometers later Lopes crossed the line in front, his second World Cross title, beating Tim Hutchings of England and Steve Jones of Wales by about six seconds.

Published details of Lopes's training methods were scanty. According to Frank Shorter, Lopes trained hard all the time and even when training at medium altitude seldom ran slower than 3:30 per kilometer. Lopes did not change his training substantially before the Olympic Games Marathon either, except that he increased his long runs from 90 to 120 minutes, covering about 35 kilometers.

A year later, in March of 1985, Lopes finished his final 12-kilometer event at the World Cross-Country Championships, a victory in 33:33. This win was Lopes's third—the most earned to that point by any individual since the event came under the auspices of the IAAF, and it proved once again that the Africans were beatable; Lopes defeated Paul Kipkoech of Kenya and Wodajo Bulti of Ethiopia for the title. The event was even more meaningful due to the venue—it was a home affair held at the Sports Complex of Jamor in Lisbon, Portugal. The home crowd went delirious for Lopes's victory, especially after he emerged from the lead pack with only 3,000 meters to go in the race. As Lopes stated: "I always run hard when I am in a race that is important to me. But the most important thing to me is also the most simple—I like to win."

THE BEST OF THE EUROPEANS

From the Mediterranean to the Nordic North, the range of talent on the European continent and in the United Kingdom progressed steadily in line with the talent from the rest of the world.

But if there ever was a shadow cast by the success of Carlos Lopes in Portugal, it fell over the accomplishments of Portuguese compatriot Fernando Mamede. With six national cross-country titles, 11 World Cross-Country appearances, and range on the track that included three Olympic appearances, from the 4 × 400 meters to the 10,000, Mamede was certainly talented—but the reasons for his forgotten legacy swirl in clouds of uncertainty.

Despite growing up as an athletic (and mischievous) youth in the town of Beja, Mamede's first taste of cross-country running came when he stepped in unannounced at the Portuguese Cross-Country District Championship. Held in his hometown, Mamede won the event and was immediately convinced to stick with athletics. His focus on soccer and other sports soon fell by the wayside.

After running 2:36 for the 1,000 meters during a primary school track championship, Mamede eventually caught the attention of the Sporting Club de Portugal and moved to the capital, Lisbon. There, he broke the national 800-meter record in 1970 in Brussels at the age of 19 and was the junior national champion in both track and cross-country, earning the opportunity to participate in the International Cross-Country Championships as a junior (he finished 23rd overall, nearly two minutes behind winner Nick Rose). Yet despite competing in the 1972 Olympics in three events, and earning a second-place finish in the senior-level national cross-country race in Portugal two years later, Mamede never attained a World Championship title or an Olympic medal. In fact, 1979 proved to be the first time that Mamede was able to win the Portuguese National Cross-Country outright. Somehow, he had always succumbed to the pressure of an international championship field.

The 1980 cross-country season proved to be a turning point, and Mamede won the Amendoeiras em Flor and successfully defended his title as Portuguese National Cross-Country champion. But it wouldn't be until 1981 that Mamede placed at World Cross, finishing third overall. What followed were three more Portuguese National Cross-Country titles in five years, and a stellar contribution to help Portugal finish third overall as a team in the 1984 edition of Worlds. Yet only three decades later, Mamede's legacy remains unclear.

With a DNF in the Olympic 10,000-meter final in Los Angeles, and a meager 11th place finish in front of a home crowd at the 1985 edition of World Cross, it was instead the 38-year-old Carlos Lopes (and not Mamede) who was called lion-hearted by the Portuguese press. Mamede faded and was forgotten. Later that year, Lopes would set a world marathon best of 2:07:12 and retire. At the World Cross-Country Championships the following year, Mamede did not finish. For the second time on a big stage, he stepped off the course.

This dichotomy of success and failure haunted Mamede's legacy for the remainder of his days. In perhaps the greatest display of emotion toward the subject, in an interview live on national television, Portuguese national coach Mario Moniz Perreira began crying when asked about Mamede. Among tears and a bit of shame, he mumbled, "He was the best . . ." before trailing off.

Beyond Lopes and Mamede, Portugal had few international stalwarts going into the decade, especially female ones. One runner, Manuela Simões, had won four of the earliest Portuguese National Cross-Country titles, but she hadn't competed at the International Cross-Country Championships. It would be Rosa Mota, with her small stature but fiery determination, who would put Portugal on the map for female distance running during the 1980s.

Hailing from Portugal's downtown neighborhood of Foz Velha, Mota began participating in cross-country while attending secondary school and won her first National Cross-Country Championship when she was only sixteen. From there success came quickly—after winning four National Cross-Country titles she connected with José Pedrosa—the man who would train her for the remainder of her career.

For four of the first six years of the 1980s, Mota won individual cross-country titles for Portugal, with additional victories at the Cross de San Sebastián and the Amendoeiras em Flor. But most remarkable was Mota's consistency in the World Cross-Country Championships from 1981 to '87, where she finished in the top 25 for every event.

To the east, Italy, though one of the earliest European nations to embrace the sport of cross-country running, had not seen much success internationally throughout the postwar era. However, they did have a tradition rich in individual consistency at the top ranks, and that continued into the 1980s with the performances of individuals like Alberto Cova and Francesco Panetta, two runners who won five and six national cross-country titles each, respectively, between 1982 and 1993.

Panetta, especially, had range (with bests at the 3,000-meter steeplechase in 8:08; 10,000 meters in 27:24; and marathon in 2:15:15), and as a nineteen-year-old finished sixth as a junior at World Cross in 1982. Five years later Panetta was receiving coaching from Giorgio Rondelli and had victories in nearly every Italian cross-country event offered. Panetta had also started a streak of cross-country national title victories. After his first national title, and leading his team with a 13th place finish, Italy finished fourth overall at World Cross—behind Kenya, England, and Ethiopia. It was Italy's best finish in the modern era—nearly 200 points better than the United States, who had runners such as Pat Porter, Ed Eyestone, and Steve Plasencia.

Antonio Prieto of Spain was another European champion of note. In February 1982, Prieto won his first Spanish National Cross-Country Championship. From there the floodgates opened: first was the title for the Juan Muguerza Memorial in January 1983, second was a repeat national title in cross-country, and third was a top-five finish at the World Cross-Country Championships—all within a nine-week span. He also competed in every World Cross-Country Championships for the decade but one (missing

1986 with an injury). From 1980 to 1989 he finished in the top 30 five times, with top finishes of eighth in 1980, and fifth in 1981 and 1983. It was a supportive atmosphere in Spain that made it the destination of choice for many top cross-country athletes during the period.

While the 1960s and 1970s saw many European cross-country invitationals opened up to foreigners, it was the egalitarian nature of these internationals that made headlines in the 1980s. In Spain alone, the Cross Zornotza and Cross Memorial Juan Muguerza saw champions from all walks of life.

The Cross Zornotza, which first began in 1954 and opened up to foreigners in 1979, saw winners in the 1980s hail from England (three times), Spain (twice), Ethiopia (twice), Wales, and Portugal. There was not a single repeat champion for the decade. In addition, the meet also attracted top-flight female distance runners, with champions from as far away as England and Switzerland.

The Cross Memorial Juan Muguerza, which started in 1943 and opened to international competition in the 1960s, was equally diverse. Male winners of the event for the decade hailed from England, Portugal, Spain, Wales, and Kenya. Female competition, which had also started in the 1960s, saw champions from Algeria, England, and Spain.

What this reinforced was the legitimacy of the European penchant for cross-country at a time when the United States, Kenya, and Ethiopia were also dominant. Previously strong nations, such as England, were still maintaining a high level of competiveness, and it showed at the Cross Zornotza and Cross Memorial Juan Muguerza. Ideally, the English home nations still felt they had something to prove—they were the originators of the sport, after all.

THE UK MAINTAINS THE CHASE

England displayed a high level of competiveness throughout the twentieth century, and while some would later be critical of their drop in podium appearances internationally during the 1980s, two English runners remained dedicated to staying at the top. Tim Hutchings, two-time silver medalist at the World Cross-Country Championships (in 1984 and 1989), and Dave Clarke, three-time English cross-country national champion (and four-time runner-up) for the decade, kept England committed to excellence.

Tim Hutchings was one of England's premier talents, winning cross-country races in the Sussex countryside as a youth on rugby fitness alone. By the age of fifteen, after a friend began dragging Hutchings out for training runs, Hutchings was able to put in three or four months of dedicated improvement. A member of the Crawley Athletic Club, Hutchings entered Loughborough University after breaking four minutes in the mile in the summer of 1978. Coached by the legendary Frank Horwill, Hutchings related the type of workouts he would subject himself to as a youth:

Kids would come from 150 miles away for long days of training. We'd do these huge, great sessions. We did things like 96 100s and 48 200s and 24 400s. Kids gravitated toward Frank because of his reputation, and he churned out loads and loads of British champions in the age ranks. But he had less experience coaching someone at senior level who was trying to get to world class. Between '84 and '86 I was struggling with shin problems and other things and was getting a little disillusioned with Frank's training. His philosophy was that if you weren't on your hands and knees at the end of a session, you weren't training hard enough.

It would take a chance intervention by another English champion for Hutchings to become world-class.

As Hutchings explained: "In 1986 Dave Bedford starting working with me and helped me for a couple years. He advised me more than coached me, but there were some key moments when he opened my eyes. A few weeks before the European Championships 5,000-meter in '86 he had me run two 1,200s with 15 minutes rest; I did 2:51 and 2:53, and I thought 'Ah, I'm in pretty good shape.' My confidence went through the roof." Hutchings won his first English National Cross-Country title in 1983, and finished second behind Carlos Lopes at the 1984 World Cross-Country Championships.

But it was in the winter of 1986, largely due to Bedford's efforts, that Hutchings won the Cross di Volpiano in Italy and finished third at the L'Equipe Cross-Country in Paris in February. In March, Hutchings won the English National Cross-Country for the second time and capped his spring, after a second appearance at World Cross, with a fifth-place finish at the Cinque Mulini. Hutchings would close the decade with a string of podium finishes in a number of European international cross-country meets (the Cross des As in France, the Cross de Amorebieta in Spain, and the Mallusk Cross-Country in Ireland, to name a few), and won the UK Cross-Country trials in 1989. He then finished second once more at World Cross that same year. As Hutchings stated about his stellar record: "One of the few consolations I have for World Cross: in '84 I came second to Carlos Lopes and he won the Olympic marathon a few months later, and in '89 I came second to Ngugi and he'd won the Olympic 5,000 a few months earlier. So, if you're going to lose, lose to somebody good."

In addition to Hutchings, Dave Clarke also represented well for England. Clarke first qualified for the international junior team for England in 1977, and went on to finish third at the English Junior Cross-Country Championships in the following years.

The decade of the 1980s saw Clarke train with the Hercules Wimbledon Athletic Club and Coach John Sullivan, where he improved from 12th in the senior ranks at the 1980 National to second in 1981. It was in 1982, at the age of twenty-four, that Clarke had his first National win, sprinting away from Mike McLeod on the hill in the latter stages at Roundhay Park, in Leeds. Over the next four years, Clarke would finish second three times, with an additional win in 1987. He won his third title in 1988, though that year's National was not a selection race for the international team.

In his five international appearances in the World Cross-Country Championships during the 1980s, Clarke finished 16th or better, with his best being a seventh-place finish in 1983. All told, Clarke's performances helped the English national team secure a silver medal at World Cross in 1982, 1987, and 1989. The 1989 race, which saw Clarke finish 15th, was led by Hutchings's finish in second overall. By then, it was a collective "Great Britain" team that finished behind Kenya—and if not for the performance of a Welsh runner by the name of Stephen Jones, the UK collective might not have been there at all.

Steve Jones had won nine straight national cross-country titles for Wales by 1986. His first event, set in the picturesque grounds of Bute Park, Cardiff, where he finished seventh in 1976, set the tone for the rest. As an unknown RAF serviceman stationed in the Royal Air Force in Lynham near Swindon, he succumbed to a blistering pace by Cardiff's Bernie Plain that day. For the next installments of the Welsh National, it would be Plain, and everyone else, who would be viewing Jones's backside as he ran hard from the gun during his record streak.

Despite being an expert marathoner and steeplechaser, it was in cross-country that Jones's talents were celebrated. Along with his nine Welsh title wins, he finished second on three further occasions. He was also the finest Welsh performer in the World Cross-Country Championships, finishing third in New York in 1984 behind Carlos Lopes and Tim Hutchings; with two other top-10 finishes (seventh in 1979 and ninth in 1980). He appeared in the World Cross-Country Championships on ten occasions, among the highest number of appearances in World Cross, ever. And without his motivation to set records—"And not just beat them, but annihilate them," he said—his formidable opponents from London and elsewhere would not have been pushed to the limit.

Not a shy character, one of Jones's famous exchanges occurred at the 1984 Chicago Marathon. While en route to a world-record clocking, Jones was oblivious. The lead pack passed through the 10-mile mark in about 48 minutes flat, and Jones turned to Rob de Castella from Australia and asked, "Is that clock right?" Deek shot back, "Why? Is it too slow? You can speed up if you'd like." De Castella wasn't pulling any punches either. As the marathon world-record holder going into that day, he had every right to be confident. De Castella was also a very good cross-country runner.

AUSTRALIAN "DEEKS" WELCOMES THE CHALLENGE

Rob de Castella, widely known as "Deek" or "Deeks," carried on the Oceanic tradition of being a fiery competitor in all that he pursued. However, de Castella saw cross-country running as a particularly essential key to training and an important way to build strength.

Deek was groomed as a runner at a young age. When he was only fourteen, de Castella was brought under the tutelage of Pat Clohessy, a former top Australian middle-distance runner and two-time NCAA Cross-Country champion while at Houston University. With Clohessy's methods, de Castella saw an immediate return for his hard training. Just three months after his eighteenth birthday, de Castella finished fourth overall in the Victorian Cross-Country Championships, running the eight-kilometer course in a blazing 24:19 (a pace of 4:53 per mile). After winning his first title in the Australian Junior National Cross-Country race later that year, succeeding at the senior ranks became de Castella's main priority.

After making his first appearance with the Australian national team at the age of twenty, the inexperienced Australian was overwhelmed at World Cross and finished 37th. A year later, in 1978 at the age of twenty-one, "Deeks" became one of the youngest Australian national champions ever when he won the National Cross-Country senior event in 35:36 for 12 kilometers.

In a 1983 *Runner's World* article, de Castella explained the methods, imparted by Clohessy, which helped him finish in the top-20 five times in World Cross:

> We call it a complex training program and it consists of doing different types of sessions [long runs, hills, and track workouts] each week with basically the same program year-round. My two long runs of a flat 18 miles and a hilly 22 miles are the two most important sessions each week. Pat always says, "If you've got to cut back, try to avoid reducing your long runs, as the strength you get from them is vital." The pace on my long runs is usually 6:15 to 6:30 per mile. I always try to keep relaxed without straining. I think that's one of the secrets. You should concentrate on your form rather than necessarily running fast.

With de Castella's help, the Australian national team had their best finish, fourth overall, just two points away from the podium, in 1983 at World Cross. France, on the other hand saw a fourth place team finish three times during the decade—but for them it was a national tragedy. Thankfully it would not be their best finish in the 1980s.

THE FRENCH CONTENDERS

The 1980s were not particularly kind to the French national cross-country team, and yet, as in many other decades of the twentieth century, they remained near the top of the pecking order. Despite earning fourth to start the decade in the pre–East African World Cross-Country event in 1980, the French team soon found themselves in the middle ranks. In 1981 they finished ninth overall as a team; in 1982, 10th; and in 1983 and 1984, ninth again. It was not the standard they were accustomed to after five podium finishes in the 1970s.

In 1985, after a dismal performance at World Cross with a team finish of 12th place and a total score of 441 points (Ethiopia had won the event with 129 points), the French vulnerability lay exposed: they lacked team cohesion, and they lacked consistency at the top ranks.

It was not for lack of trying. From 1980 to 1985, France had four National Cross-Country champions, and each had been impressive in qualifying. Jacques Boxberger, a two-time National Cross-Country champion and winner of numerous international cross-country meets, won the 1983 National in a pace of just over five minutes per mile. Yet Boxberger struggled for France at the World Cross-Country Championship, finishing 70th (1980), 146th (1981), 50th (1982), 56th (1983) and 110th (1984), before finding himself absent from the event for the remainder of the decade.

Pierre Levisse, another national stalwart, was determined to change France's fortunes. Levisse won France's National Cross-Country Championship in 1979, '81, '84, '85, and '86. Beyond his national prestige (the most titles won by a Frenchman since Noël Tijou a decade before), Levisse was also consistent at the top in World Cross, running nine out of 10 years in the decade, and finishing 15th or better five times. A member of the gold-medal-earning French team in the 1978 World Cross-Country Championships, Levisse was also a proud member of the French national team that earned bronze in 1988—though it was the worst individual showing of his career at a World Cross.

France had finished one spot off of the podium in 1980, 1986, and 1989, but it was one heroic performance by an unlikely cast of runners that earned France third place overall in the 1988 World Cross-Country event. Led by three-time French National Cross-Country champion Paul Arpin, France finished in third—ahead of England, Italy, Spain, and the United States. The cohesive pack running by Steve Tunstall (14th), Jean-Louis Prianon (17th), Joël Lucas (25th), Cyrille Laventure (30th), and Bruno Levant (37th) gave France an edge.

The senior male runners were not the only contenders to make headlines for France during the '80s. So too did the efforts of Annette Sergent. Sergent inherited the title of best French female cross-country runner from Joëlle deBrouwer, who had won eight French National Cross-Country Championships leading into 1984. Sergent herself would win seven in 10 years, and five straight between 1985 and 1989. Born in Chambéry, France, on November 17, 1962, Annette Sergent won the 1987 IAAF World Cross-Country Championships, becoming the first Frenchwoman to win a world title in the sport, and won for a second time in 1989. In addition to these victories, she made 11 appearances at World Cross and placed third in both 1986 and 1988.

Sergent's fifth consecutive French cross-country title came in 1989—and at the 1989 IAAF World Cross-Country Championships Sergent returned to the top, winning a gold medal and leading France to a team runner-up behind the Soviet Union. Yet to start the decade, another female was the most dominant in the sport. Her name: Grete Waitz.

OSLO'S OUTSTANDING CHAMPION

In the 1980s the greatest female cross-country runner in the world came from an athletically underdeveloped country in Scandinavia. Grete Waitz received no sponsorship, worked as a schoolteacher, trained throughout the winter, and still dominated. She did not have success handed to her. She worked for it, and she did so against all odds: the Norwegian Women's Cross-Country Championship field barely reached into double digits, and often Waitz ran against two or three other women. But despite the difficulty in pursuing international success in Norway's bitter winter, Waitz believed it could be done.

Waitz's training was dedicated and aggressive. She ran hard, and when she trained on tour with some of the world's greatest male distance runners, they would politely decline to join her for a pre-breakfast run. Her strength was her determination—and she kept herself close to top physical condition all year round, rather than peaking for a few specific races. In turn, Waitz saw improvement every year while her competitors fell back.

To match her intensity required a special mentality. And there were times that, Waitz admitted, even she was tired of training in the snow and ice and felt like "throwing my running shoes out of the window." But she never did. Instead, she went on piling up a string of national, world championship, and other international victories in cross-country, which included 10 straight Norwegian National Cross-Country titles, and 11 in 12 years; seven straight World Cross-Country podium finishes, with four straight gold medal performances (and five in six years); 19 international cross-country victories in the 1980s, including multiple-time wins at the Cinque Mulini and Carpaccio Cross in Italy. Commenting on the sport, Waitz explained: "There is no pressure of records and lap times, and the scenery is always changing. It's much more fun running cross-country."

According to Waitz, there was no secret to her success:

I get up about 5:30, and start running at 6:00 a.m., but I don't eat until I've run. In the winter it is dark and very, very cold—usually 10 or 15 degrees below freezing. I run for about 50 minutes, covering 13 or 14 kilometers (8-9 miles) and then I go to my work as a schoolteacher. I'm home again about 2:30 in the afternoon, do some shopping and some preparation for the next day, and about five o'clock I do my second training session, which may include shorter or faster runs over 300 or 500 meters, or could be another long run.

In a week I normally cover a total of 120-130 kilometers (75-80 miles), and the worst is between the end of November and late March. I have to train on the roads then, dodging cars, because they clear the roads but not the pavement. On the roads I sometimes fall over, and it is easy to get leg injuries because when you are running on snow and ice, your muscles are always tense. When the snow goes I train much more in the woods and forests, and I think that is what helps me in cross-country competition. I'm primarily a cross-country runner, not a track runner.

I don't do any special hill training, but we now live on hills so I often have to run up them. I have used fartlek sessions in the past too, jogging for 10 minutes, then running 200 or 300 meters very fast. I have also been resting more in recent seasons. To ease down, I train just once a day for five days before the race. I go to bed at 9:00 or 9:30 p.m. in order to be able to get up early. I very rarely miss the morning session, and I make it a good one because, if in the morning the weather is very bad, or I'm very tired, then I have at least one good training session behind me that day.

For an athlete who sought no specific peak, it is easy to see why Waitz would have fatigue produced by very high mileage, especially as she trained for quality all year round. But the results of this training were remarkable. At the World Cross-Country Championships Waitz saw large margins of victory—an average of nearly 25 seconds through five wins—which was stunning, considering that the distance that female competitors were racing was under five kilometers (in most cases between 2.5 and three miles).

Yet if Norway seemed like an unlikely place to harbor a dominating cross-country champion, other corners of the globe were being equally competitive.

THE US WOMEN EARN HARDWARE AT WORLD CROSS

The 1982 American female team at the World Cross-Country Championships did not win a medal. They were not on the podium, and at no point in the Rome Hippodrome in Italy did the US women have a strong pack racing for national glory. Gone were the days of paying their own way for the trip—The Athletics Congress took care of the plane fare—but the women hadn't qualified for the event in a sanctioned trials race the way the senior and junior male teams had. The American women didn't even have their best runners on the line that day. As a consequence, the plan changed. America got serious about sending their best to the World Cross-Country Championships, realizing how essential it was to keep their focus: beating the best in the world, the Soviet Union included, across hill and dale.

The 1980 and 1981 women's teams had done well enough for the podium. Anchored by the infallible Jan Merrill, the US women were making progress: a bronze finish in 1980 and a silver in 1981. But to beat the USSR, who had won those two editions of the championship, the United States needed to send their best. 1982 was the final straw. It would be the next three editions that saw the United States win gold, and four out of the next five. The

Soviets found themselves on their heels, and for once, staring at the backs of the female American distance runners.

So, what changed? The addition of a standalone World Cross-Country qualifier event helped in 1986—that and the arrival of Lynn Jennings, who flew over the sod with incredible ease. But for the championships in 1983, '84, and '85 it was team cohesiveness. In 1983, the top four scoring members (an oddity at World Cross: the men scored the top six at the time, the women, top four) all finished within nine places of each other: fourth, fifth, ninth, and 13th. In 1984 the margin shrunk to eight places between all the scorers: ninth, 10th, 16th and 17th. In 1985, to clinch their third straight, it was a surprise second by Cathy Branta, and a tight triad of Betty Springs in ninth, Shelly Steely in 15th, and Kathryn Hayes in 16th that sealed the deal. And they were winning with different names every year—a testament to sound strategic superiority rather than individual stardom. But one star shone brighter than the rest: Lynn Jennings won the inaugural women's World Cross trials in 1986 and four of the next six. Add that to the nine National Cross-Country Championships she accumulated in that timespan (the most by any American, male or female, ever), and it was clear why she was the undisputed front-runner for the remainder of the decade.

Did You Know?

In the 1970s, the transition from the International Cross-Country Union to the IAAF resulted in the participation of a host of new nations. Despite their long tradition, it wasn't until the end of the 1970s and early 1980s that Canada began training to seriously contend for a world title. For Nancy Rooks, who finished 17th overall in the 1980 World Cross event, Canada became serious with her arrival. A Canadian National Cross-Country champion in 1978, Rooks was motivated to recruit. Thelma Wright, the team manager, was also of note. One of Canada's best runners in the 1970s and a pioneer of women's distance running, Wright had won a bronze medal at World Cross in 1970. Three years later, with Rooks and Wright already successful, Canada's Alison Wiley would challenge for the individual world title. Rooks described: "Wiley's race was astonishing, and behind her the rest of the Canadian team ran solidly excellent performances. Our bronze medal team placing was the chocolate icing on the cake after the excitement of Wiley's finish."

THE NCAA ASSUMES COMMAND OF THE FEMALE CROSS-COUNTRY CHAMPIONSHIP

The Association for Intercollegiate Athletics for Women (AIAW) was founded in 1971 to govern collegiate women's athletics and to administer national championships. And during the 1970s, the association was one of the

biggest advancements for women's athletics at the collegiate level in the United States and grew rapidly, in parallel with national growth in women's sports following Title IX. The AIAW functioned in the equivalent role for college women's programs that the NCAA had been doing for men's programs, but the NCAA sought to govern women's sports, too. Owing to its own success, the AIAW was in a vulnerable position with the NCAA, and cross-country running was in the crosshairs. Following a one-year overlap in which both organizations staged a women's championship in 1981, the AIAW discontinued operation and schools fell under the governance of the NCAA from that point forward.

At its peak, the AIAW had almost one thousand member schools. But by the late 1970s, the NCAA also decided to offer women's championships. The NCAA's Divisions II and III voted to offer championships in 1980; however, Division I members failed to gain a majority vote on this issue until the 1981 national meeting. This decision was quite contentious. During a tense floor debate at the NCAA annual convention in January 1981, AIAW representatives objected to the motion to sponsor Division I championships, but their objections were met with pockets of "ridicule and hissing." Even some of the women who supported the NCAA's sponsorship of women's athletics acknowledged that the debate was "pretty bad." After much discussion, the AIAW seemed to prevail. The first vote on sponsorship of a women's NCAA D1 championship was a tie, 124–124. Then, a recount found the tally to be 128–127 against.

Parliamentary rules permitted "reconsideration" of a vote if someone requested it. Several delegates from the NCAA knew of one institution that had voted against the motion but whose faculty representative favored it. When the influencer of the school's "nay" vote left the room, those delegates prompted a reconsideration. This time it passed, 137–117. "We waited until the person who had influenced that vote left the room, and we asked [the faculty rep] to reconsider, which he did. And the reconsideration passed quite easily," UCLA administrator Judie Holland said. "That, to me, was stunning."

"It was dramatic," said Ruth Berkey, then the NCAA's director of women's championships. "It was pretty euphoric for those people who were excited about the opportunity and pretty devastating for those people who were opposed to it." But for Berkey, the real work began after the convention concluded. The first Division I women's championship, cross-country, would be run that fall in Wichita, Kansas, and would be conducted in conjunction with the men's championship. And Berkey knew the men's committee had already scheduled its next meeting at, of all places, the Playboy Club in Lake Geneva, Wisconsin. The women gamely met with them there.

"It was definitely an interesting meeting," Berkey said. "The men on the cross-country committee were very supportive. They were enthusiastic. The women were excited. I was really nervous, wanting to make sure everything went correctly and everybody was happy. It went extremely well."

The NCAA event in Wichita saw 13 universities participate in their 1981 championship, while the AIAW had 22 schools.

The AIAW, in their final attempt at hosting the event, held theirs on Saturday, November 21, two days before the NCAA, and Iowa State, who had found themselves the winners of the first four editions of the championship in the early 1970s, were pronounced champions for the fifth time in the meet's short history. It was a poetic conclusion, before the NCAA assumed control and merged the participating schools the following year in conjunction with the men's championship.

TRAGEDY STRIKES AFTER THE 1985 NCAA CHAMPIONSHIP

The Iowa State University (ISU) women's cross-country team had been a perennial national contender during the 1970s, earning team titles in the first four runnings of the AIAW National Championship. But heading into the 1985 cross-country season, there were low expectations for the Cyclones. ISU failed to make the national meet for the first time in its ten-year history in 1984, and the Cyclones still had a relatively young team for 1985. Surprisingly, the Cyclones rallied to one of their most successful seasons. ISU finished first or second in all nine meets during the season, led by freshman Jill Slettedahl and junior Bonnie Sons. The duo finished seventh and eighth, respectively, to help the Cyclones place second at the Big Eight Championship, and the pair placed fifth and seventh to pace ISU to the NCAA District V Championship (a precursor to the NCAA regional meet).

At the national championship, ISU exceeded all expectations, with the Cyclones finishing runner-up. Sons and Slettedahl were named All-Americans by finishing 25th and 29th, but ISU received outstanding performances from all its runners: Sue Baxter, a freshman from Brentwood, England, finished 32nd; Julie Rose, a junior from Ashford, England, placed 42nd; Sheryl Maahs, a junior from Spirit Lake, Iowa, placed 45th; and Tami Colby, a freshman from Boone, Iowa, finished 48th.

Iowa State was ecstatic with their finish as the team boarded three ISU-owned planes to take them back to Ames. But icy conditions in central Iowa forced the planes to land in Des Moines rather than Ames. One of the planes, which carried head coach Ron Renko, assistant coach Pat Moynihan, Baxter, Rose, Maahs, student trainer Stephanie Streit, and pilot Burton Watkins, developed problems as it was preparing to land. The plane crashed during an ice storm in a neighborhood two miles from downtown, killing all members on board.

The other two planes landed safely in Des Moines, with fourteen members of the men's and women's teams and coaching staff aboard, but the tragic loss stunned the Iowa State community. ISU president Robert Parks ordered that campus flags, including the flag of Great Britain, be flown at half-mast the following Tuesday, and scholarship funds were established to honor the victims.

On December 4, 1985, more than 5,500 people attended a memorial service at Hilton Coliseum. And ten years later, ISU dedicated a plaque for permanent display at the Iowa State Cross-Country Course to fully honor the crash victims for their dedication.

THE COLLEGIATE COLOSSUS

While the NCAA adapted and perfected the female championship in the early part of the decade, the men's Division I event remained a captivating and compelling drama.

Three programs were more dominant in the 1980s than any other. The first was the University of Texas–El Paso (UTEP) Miners, coached by Ted Banks. The second was an upstart team from the University of Arkansas, the Razorbacks, with Coach John McDonnell at the helm. The third was the University of Wisconsin Badgers, led by Coach Dan McClimon and Coach Martin Smith. Each team earned three team titles at the NCAA Cross-Country Championship, and each also had a single individual champion—but each ultimately went about their business in very different ways.

The aforementioned Ted Banks, head coach of the UTEP Miners, had been successful for nearly a decade before the 1980 cross-country season started. By the time the NCAA enacted rules changes for overage competitors in 1980, however, Banks had already secured a fleet of dominating runners—almost none of them domestic talents. The new rules may have been aimed at UTEP, but the juggernaut Banks built had saved its most impressive achievement for last.

"Banks did a good job coaching them," said Arkansas coach John McDonnell. "They were good, but he kept them in line and ready on the day. People say he had older athletes, but they were available to everyone, and Washington State had them and didn't do anything with them. They'd drop out or find a way to lose. Ted Banks was a very good coach. He got good talent and they performed."

The talent on the 1981 UTEP cross-country team was unprecedented. The anchor was Suleiman Nyambui, a twenty-nine-year-old elementary school teacher from Tanzania. Coming into the 1981 cross-country season, Nyambui was the three-time defending NCAA 10K champion, two-time defending NCAA 5K champion, defending NCAA Cross-Country champion, and Olympic silver medalist in the 5K. "I had a lot of good ones," Banks said, "but he was the best. During workouts, I would get the guys tired and then say, 'OK, Nyambui, put it to them.'"

Nyambui may have been UTEP's best runner in 1981, but he was far from their only weapon. Included on the roster was world-road-10K-record holder Matthews Motshwarateu, future world half marathon record holder and Olympic 10K bronze medalist Michael Musyoki, and two-time Olympic marathoner Gidamis Shahanga. They also had the legacy: the Miners were three-time defending NCAA Cross-Country champions.

At the 1981 WAC Championships their depth was on full display: UTEP posted a team score of 17 points despite not running Nyambui. It was a record-low team score and also marked the largest winning margin in conference history. But with the pedigree of the Miners, the only test that would matter was nationals.

The UTEP men's cross-country team entered the 1981 NCAA Championships as a confident bunch. Before the meet, the runners approached Coach Ted Banks and told him they felt they might be able to get a perfect score. Banks laughed and responded, "Let's just worry about winning." However, the team only narrowly missed their prediction: UTEP set a Division I NCAA Championship record, scoring 17 points (the Miner runners finished in five of the top six spots). Penn State's Alan Scharsu was the only person to keep UTEP from perfection as he finished fourth overall. Providence finished a distant second as a team with 109 points. "We were very fortunate to get 17," Banks said. "It was beyond my wildest dreams. That was the best team I ever had, by far." In the end, it was the first time in NCAA history that a team had seven All-Americans in a single cross-country race.

UTEP remained strong in 1983. With new African runners taking the first, eighth, 28th, 39th, and 61st places in the NCAA Cross-Country Championship—led by Zakaria Barie's individual title—the Miners had done the near unthinkable by winning three of the first four cross-country team titles in the decade of the 1980s, and seven in the previous 10 years. But Barie, a Tanzanian who had won the silver medal at the 1982 Commonwealth Games in the 10,000 meters, was nearing thirty years old when he won—prompting even more controversy—and amidst their exterior dominance, UTEP was in big trouble.

On the interior, UTEP was crumbling. Ted Banks had resigned a few months after the historic 1981 championship in response to the UTEP administration cutting his budget. And the new coach, Larry Heidebrecht, was facing allegations of slush funds and payments to athletes—a clear NCAA violation. In a landmark decision in July of 1986, UTEP's track and cross-country program was placed on three years probation. Money earned illegally, $62,150 in fact, had been held in a bank account by Heidebrecht, and explained how his athletes were being compensated for their international track appearances. The UTEP administration did not protest the decision and the 1983 cross-country title was vacated.

Despite this unfortunate turn, the legacy of Banks and his foreign stars was profound. Bob Braman, the former president of the Division I Cross-Country Coaches Association famously remarked: "It's completely absurd to score only 17 points at the NCAA Cross-Country Championships. The talent on that team was just amazing. I just can't ever see that happening again." Arkansas's McDonnell agreed: "We thought we had a shot going in because Nyambui was hurt and hadn't run. We went down there and they scored 17 points. We ran well but scored over a hundred points. They scored 17. That was the greatest cross-country team I've ever seen. They were out of this world."

John McDonnell was a fiery coach with an old-school approach who hailed from Ireland and inherited a moribund University of Arkansas team in 1972. And it was two years before a rejuvenated Arkansas squad blew out Texas to finally capture the Southwest Conference cross-country title in 1974. The Razorbacks would never lose another conference cross-country championship for the remainder of John McDonnell's thirty-six-year coaching career. Said Steve Baker, an English steeplechase runner and Arkansas standout: "We sprinted out the first mile and had maybe seven of the top ten or twelve places. We made people run our race, and we hurt like crazy, but made other people hurt too. The difference was we hurt every day in training and were used to it."

Three years later, after a 1977 cross-country season that saw a host of young talent barely win the conference title, McDonnell began to accumulate depth through recruiting. The Razorbacks would never fail to crack the top 10 at an NCAA Cross-Country Championships for another thirty years—a streak as remarkable as the conference championship run itself, given how unpredictable it can be at the top.

And after years of trying to attract elite American distance talent, Arkansas's success and McDonnell's developing gravitas suddenly brought in high school seniors Chris Zinn and Joe Falcon from Missouri entering the 1984 season—two runners who were considered among the best preps in the country.

Zinn, who was coached by longtime West Plains High School coach Joe Bill Dixon, had captured three Missouri high school cross-country titles and run 9:05 for two miles. Said Zinn: "I had spoken to Martin Smith [of Wisconsin] and was good friends with Richard Clarke at Missouri State. I just really liked John [McDonnell]. He met Joe and I at the Missouri state cross-country meet and talked to us separately afterwards. He came to my house and met my folks."

And as the number one prep miler in the country with a 4:07 mile to his name, Falcon had been bombarded by coaches from across the country who openly drooled about his upside given his relatively low mileage and the fact that he had only recently given up playing tennis. "You'd have coaches from well-established universities calling and saying come to my university and you'll be the man and you'll do this," said Falcon. "The entire opposite occurred with Coach McDonnell. He said 'You're pretty good, kid. You've done some good things, but I've been working the last twelve years on a system that will win national championships, and I feel like I'm one or two runners away from that. I am confident if you come to Arkansas you can be part of a national championship team before you graduate.' That was very profound to me."

Signing the duo was a major coup and, as it turned out, the foundation for several national championships in cross-country that had eluded the Razorbacks. "Once John got those state champions things really started to move," said Dick Weis, who had been hired at Oklahoma State. "The big one was Falcon. That's when everything changed. He just had an attitude about winning and went right after it."

The Razorbacks later captured their 11th straight Southwest Conference Cross-Country Championship and an equally easy victory at the regional meet. But as it had been all year long, the team's focus was on the 1984 NCAA Cross-Country Championship, set to take place in State College, Pennsylvania. It would turn out to be a battle right to the finish.

After an unremarkable start, Arkansas found itself holding onto a tenuous lead over Arizona and Tennessee with one mile remaining. Although Arkansas's fourth man, Espen Borge, was comfortably in the 30s, fifth man Gary Taylor was 20 seconds back and starting to fall apart as the field closed with a mile to go. "I said to Gary, 'Nobody can pass you! Nobody! Just hold what you've got!'" remembered McDonnell. "There were about fifty guys right on his ass and I said to myself, 'Boy, if they go by him, we're done.'"

Not only did Taylor hold on for 56th, but freshman Joe Falcon passed dozens of runners to catch up to teammate Paul Donovan and place 24th. In what would become an Arkansas tradition of teammates stepping up when others faltered, David Swain made a conscious decision to move up. "I was dying, and I can't understand why but I finally said, 'I'm not going to let this team down,'" remembered Swain. "I passed about twenty people to finish fourteenth."

After the official score took some time to be announced, Arkansas had narrowly edged Arizona 100 to 111 for its first NCAA Cross-Country Championship in school history. "It was just fantastic and a great experience," said Swain. "John [McDonnell] loved cross-country. It was his baby, and it was the harder one to win."

Following a solid 28–60 victory over Texas in the 1985 Southwest Conference Cross-Country Championship, the Razorbacks entered the 1985 NCAA Cross-Country Championships in Milwaukee, Wisconsin, looking to repeat as national champions. They could have hardly expected the conditions that would greet them: "I remember how cold it was and the snow and ice all over the course," said McDonnell. "It had to have snowed two feet, so they cleared off a path for the race. Then the day before the sun came out and melted some of it, and it rolled down the hill and formed ice, and they couldn't get it off. It was really tough because you'd slip, but of course if you wore long spikes, it tore your calves up."

Already slightly favored heading into what was expected to be a tight race, the Wisconsin Badgers had the advantage of not only being acclimatized to the weather but also understanding the terrain. With the course impassible for the most part until race day, few teams had an opportunity to even run a preview of it: "The second half of that race was much tougher, and it definitely would have helped to know that," said one of the Arkansas athletes. "At three miles, I was our seventh man and Wisconsin's fourth man was behind me. We were all running over our heads. I went back like a rock. They just ate us up during the second half of the race."

Wisconsin flipped Arkansas with a strong final two miles to win the meet by a margin of 67–104. With some of his athletes fading during the second half of the race, John McDonnell reflected on his fateful decision to instruct his runners not to wear tights in the blizzard conditions: "It was a mistake not to run in the half tights like Wisconsin did," said McDonnell, "but I tell you cross-country shouldn't even be run in a place like that."

It was in 1986 that Arkansas would have another shot at the title; bolstered by further recruitment and with veteran talent in Falcon and Zinn leading the team. After winning handedly, it was a surprising Dartmouth team that finished second to the Razorbacks, prompting another showdown the following year.

Arkansas entered the 1987 NCAA Cross-Country Championships facing a mature Dartmouth team led by Robert Kempainen and a collection of seniors who knew this was their final shot at glory. Winning would be anything but easy: "They gave us fits I'll tell you," said McDonnell. "I figured Dartmouth would be tough because they had been there the year before and were pretty consistent. They had one star but were really a bunch of hard workers. Vin [Lananna] did a great job with the talent he had there."

Early in the race Arkansas set a hard pace, led by Joe Falcon, Chris Zinn, and Reuben Reina. With Dartmouth right with them at two miles, it was Lananna, the Dartmouth coach, who was looking at his stopwatch to his chagrin: "We wanted to run the way we had all season, which was aggressive without redlining," Lananna said. "I knew that if Arkansas and Dartmouth both redlined, Arkansas would win. Our only possibility was to come in the back door. We both went out aggressively. I looked at my watch (at two miles) and it was 9:20 and for three of our guys that was their PR. That's when I knew we were in trouble."

Toward the midway point of the race, Falcon and the lead pack began to separate themselves from Zinn and Reina. Then at five miles, Falcon attempted to separate himself from the lead pack: "We decided to take it with 1,200 meters to go because there was a turn in it," said McDonnell. "They were all waiting for him to sprint, so at this turn you go up a hill. We were used to running hills, so he surprised them by going hard. It seemed like in fifty meters he put about forty on them."

When he crossed the line first, Falcon was overcome with emotion. "It was the accumulation of everything coach and I tried to do," said Falcon. "That was one of the greatest honors I had in being able to present coach with his first individual NCAA cross-country championship. That meant a lot to me because he was really fired up about it."

About 90 seconds behind Falcon, another drama was unfolding as Arkansas appeared to be in significant trouble holding off a late charge from Dartmouth. Although Zinn and Reina had crossed the line in the top 20, followed by a surprising 47th place from Alex Hallock, Arkansas's fifth-place runner Doug Consiglio was trucking along in the 60s. With Dartmouth's fifth man surging away from a tiring Consiglio, it was anyone's guess who would win: "I went to catch him and was going by him hard," said

Consiglio. "I opened it up and went flying by him and was hurting, but then I saw [Dartmouth's] fourth man, and then I flew by him so we had it sewed up. I turned the corner at 100 meters and was totally dead but held my position. I took out five years of frustration in 600 meters of running."

Arkansas had won its second consecutive NCAA Cross-Country Championship over Dartmouth by a margin of 87–119 on a day when Falcon had won the first individual NCAA Cross-Country title in school history.

As the third strong men's team in the decade for the NCAA, the Wisconsin Badgers put in considerable work and time to remain competitive, but weren't without some drama of their own. Martin Smith took the reigns of the team in 1983 after longtime coach Dan McClimon passed away. "These guys did not want to be coached by anybody but Dan," Smith said. "It was that simple. Nobody else was going to be good enough. He was loved and they were still grieving." A less driven coach might have buckled. "I stayed," Smith said. "For 15 years."

Martin Smith had been a Division III distance runner at Bridgewater College, in Bridgewater, Virginia, and remained local upon graduation, eventually helping the University of Virginia Cavaliers women's cross-country team as an assistant. After Virginia won the NCAA Cross-Country Championship twice in the final two of Smith's three seasons, Wisconsin didn't need to look far to find someone good: "We had the best women's distance program in America," Smith said.

At Wisconsin, Smith's long, detail-intensive practices could eat up an entire Saturday. He would fly into a rage if he thought his athletes were spending too much time fraternizing with the women's team. His temper could boil over into long, hat-throwing, curse-filled diatribes when things didn't go to plan or athletes failed in training or performance. Jerry Schumacher, a future Wisconsin distance coach, was a five-time All-American while running for Smith from 1988 to '93: "One thing I always knew about Coach Smith was he was interested in getting me to perform at my highest level," Schumacher said. "He wanted me to be at my best, and that is what he motivated and pushed me to be. He was not going to let things slip under the carpet. He was hands-on, but I needed that."

In validation of his competition, Smith would channel his rivals: "We'd hear about [Arkansas] when we were working out hard," recalled Schumacher. "Martin [Smith] would talk to us about winning a national title and he'd say, 'Do you think John McDonnell and the Hogs are messing around right now? I guarantee you they are lining up and their toes are in the dirt doing five times a mile!' It created this image [of Smith] as a taskmaster and fiery competitive human being who wasn't going to accept anything less than your best."

Running on a familiar, but icy, Dretzka Park course, Tim Hacker became the University of Wisconsin's second national champion and led the Badgers to the NCAA Cross-Country Championship team title at the 1985 event. The undefeated Badgers, ranked first in the nation throughout the season, placed five runners—Hacker, Joe Stintzi, Scott Jenkins, Kelley Delaney, and Rusty Korhonen—in the first 43 runners to score 67 points and defeat defending champion Arkansas. It turned out to be the fastest NCAA Championships since Texas–El Paso's Suleiman Nyambui in 1980, and Hacker had to sprint away from Iowa State's Yobes Ondieke and Marquette's Keith Hanson in the final 1.5 miles to earn it. In the process, Hacker became the Badgers' first national winner since Walter Mehl in 1939. It capped a perfect season that included titles in the Badger Classic, Big Ten Conference, and NCAA District IV meets.

While four Wisconsin runners—Hacker, Stintzi, Jenkins, and Delaney—earned All-America honors at the 1985 championship, there was no individual in the top 15 when the Badgers won again three years later. "I think this performance is a reflection of everyone this whole season long," said Coach Smith. "We felt if we could get our five men within 20th to 40th, we could win this thing," said Badgers' senior Chris Borsa. Wisconsin's finishing range was from 17th to 44th, which proved more than adequate when the team score was computed. The Badgers finished with 105 points. Northern Arizona was second with 160. Borsa led the way in 17th place. He covered the 10,000-meter course in 29 minutes, 51 seconds—31 seconds slower than the winning time posted by Indiana freshman Bob Kennedy.

Smith's tenure as a coach was getting stronger as the decade came to a close. But young stars throughout the decade (and future ones as well), like Borsa, Falcon, Reina, and Zinn were being spotted and recruited earlier and with better judgment due to two major factors: competitive high school state meets, and the Kinney/Foot Locker Cross-Country Championships. And one state was hotter than the rest during this period: California.

AMERICAN PREP STARS IN 1982 CHANGE THE FUTURE

The 1982 California cross-country season arrived amidst a time of great momentum in prep distance running. In the 1982 season alone, the Golden State provided one of the two Kinney National individual champions and a third place on the other half of the affair—but challenges existed from all corners of the nation.

The 1982 Kinney Nationals course was treacherous—a looping design constructed near the meet headquarters in Orlando, Florida. National Meet Coordinator Max Mayo from Georgia, who had been with the Kinney/Foot Locker series since its start, considered the 1982 winning time of 14:35 by Eric Reynolds (the nation's top prep athlete) from Camarillo, California, as one of the top performances in Kinney/Foot Locker history, with the most impressive feat being Reynolds's 14-second margin of victory despite the uneven footing. Jesus Gutierrez, one of the nations top 10th grade two-milers, was seventh, Mark Junkermann tenth, Jason Flamm 22nd, Jim Ortiz 25th, and George Yuster 29th at the championship—the Western squad finishing second with 49 points to the Northeast's 29 winning total. On the girls' side, it was Christine Curtin (New York), a 4:43.5 miler as a prep later that year, who was the winner at 16:58, with Cory Schubert third at 17:04, Laura Cattivera 6th, Kathy Ebiner 15th, Nanette Garcia 16th, Sandy Blakeslee 17th, and Tania Fischer 22nd, with the West squad again second to the Northeast's 25 with a 57 point total. It was clear, despite these very fast times, that California was not alone in scope of competitive cross-country talent.

On the decade, the West Region had six individual male Kinney National Cross-Country champions, three more than the next two closest regions, the South, and the Midwest—while for the girls, the Northeast had four individual champions, with the Midwest having three on the decade. It was a diverse proving ground in the 1980s, and the Kinney event became the de facto decider for all national discussions of prep cross-country talent.

The Kinney West Regional, which was a late-season cross-country event that enabled individuals to qualify for the national championship, originally had been held at the Crystal Springs Cross-Country Course. That location changed in the early 1980s to Woodward Park in Fresno—a happy coincidence that led to a true California State Cross-Country Meet occurring at that site in late November of 1987. With this meet, California became the final state out of all fifty United States to sanction state-level competition for cross-country running. It has been held at Woodward Park every year since.

* * *

The continuation of strong, experienced, and progressively developed young talent in America continued throughout the 1980s and beyond. As a result, collegiate competition became better, and professional performances both domestically and abroad helped solidify the United States among the distance running elite. It was no accident that the young, talented runners who appeared as prep superstars in the 1970s were the professional heroes of the 1980s. Certainly, it also mattered that this domestic arrival coincided with the affirmation of East African talent in the World Cross-Country Championships along with other notable performers in Europe. The 1980s was a decade filled with surprises, as the sport neared its most accessible pinnacle. Talent was seemingly everywhere, but it was unknown whether this domestic boom would last.

EVENT SPOTLIGHT: EVERY NATION HAS ITS HERO— THE 1983 WORLD CROSS-COUNTRY CHAMPIONSHIPS (MARCH 20, 1983)

LOCATION: GATESHEAD RIVERSIDE PARK

Gateshead, England

The starts are always savage in the World Cross-Country Championships. Hundreds of the world's best runners slash through the turf with half-inch spikes, shoving for position. In the men's race on Sunday, March 20, 1983, in the North of England, Olympic 5,000- and 10,000-meter champion Miruts Yifter of Ethiopia was hurled down and kicked out of the back of the mob like a rugby ball. His teammate, defending champion Mohammed Kedir, lost a shoe and had to go back for it.

For the United States men, Alberto Salazar felt he could help his team most by winning. He hoped for brutal conditions: "The more miserably sloppy and hilly, the better," Salazar said. "Not because I like it but because it bothers everyone else more." For the American men, the assemblage was a dream team of epic proportions: Pat Porter, National Cross-Country champion of The Athletics Congress was there. So was Craig Virgin, two-time World Cross winner from 1980 and '81. Thom Hunt, four time All-American in cross-country and winner of the 1977 World Cross junior event toed the line. Ed Eyestone, a bronze medalist as a junior in World Cross in 1980 was also part of the team.

As Eyestone related, "I was surprised how big World Cross was internationally. As a freshman at BYU I was ecstatic. The enthusiasm was something larger than I had ever experienced."

At the crack of the gun, Pat Porter, then twenty-three years old (and a two-time National Cross-Country champion) got off to a blazing start, and at 550 meters was leading the race. Salazar, wearing black tights against predicted sleet that would never come, began modestly, unworried about catching up. At the end of the first 2,000-meter lap the six Americans were placed well: Porter and teammate Thom Hunt were in the front rank, another US runner, Ed Eyestone, was 21st, and Salazar 25th. Farther back came Americans Craig Virgin and Mark Anderson. Ethiopia's Miruts Yifter, one of the strongest in the field, and Mohammed Kedir, two-time World Cross podium finisher, were out of it, but an unknown Ethiopian ran near the front. This was Bekele Debele, a twenty-year-old army private with a crescent scar under his right eye: "In the middle of the race I wanted to run away," he said, "but I thought if I try, they might stay with me. So I changed my mind and waited."

By the halfway mark of the 12-kilometer affair the race read as a "who's who" of international distance running. England's Dave Clark, Spain's Antonio Prieto, Australia's Rob de Castella, Kenya's Some Muge, Portugal's Carlos Lopes, Italy's Alberto Cova, Ethiopia's Debele, and America's Pat Porter and Alberto Salazar were all near the front.

Debele's patience was acceptable to Salazar, who had joined the leading cluster. Just after halfway, he and Porter were abreast in the lead: "I felt great on the flat," said Salazar, "but on the hills and mud it was tough. The harder I tried, the more I seemed to struggle." So Salazar waited, too. "I'd been running great. I got cocky. I waited for the kick," he said.

At the 7,000-meter mark, Debele made a break for it, stringing out the nine leaders. Later he would remark: "Mud? No, I've never run in it before, but I'm not at all tired." The other champions didn't hesitate for a second. Within a half-mile they reeled in Debele and the pack was uniform once again.

With no one seriously trying to break away, the race remained a nearly unbroken torrent of runners. With a lap to go, Robert de Castella of Australia was leading and seemed to be paying particular attention to Salazar. These two fastest-ever marathoners ended up racing one another a month later in Rotterdam. There, they were isolated elites. Here, they were surrounded. Carlos Lopes of Portugal, the 1976 Olympic 10,000-meter silver medalist, remained, as did Some Muge of Kenya. And Porter, the great revelation of the race, was hanging close.

Porter had miscounted laps. When he expected to turn for the finish, he saw officials ringing the bell for another 2,000-meter circuit. Somehow he steeled himself to keep on. He was in seventh, and he would finish ninth, his remarkably long stride strong to the finish.

Salazar kept waiting. "I thought we had about 800 to go, and I was getting ready, when someone hollered we only had 400 to go, and the other three [Lopes, Some, and Debele] took off," said Salazar. "I was shocked because they seemed tireder than I was." Nonetheless, he put his head down and went after them, and churned past with 100 meters to go. "I thought I'd won it. I thought they'd used their kicks. Then we hit more soft ground. And they had one more spurt."

In the stretch, first Debele shot past, then Lopes and Kenya's Some Muge, a twenty-two-year-old soldier with only two years of running behind him. With 25 meters to go, it seemed anyone's race. Debele, Lopes, and Muge all were given the same time of 36:52, but Debele was the winner. Lopes held off Some for second, and Salazar was fourth in 36:53. De Castella was sixth, seven seconds back. Ethiopia's depth told in the team race—Kedir came back to rally his men to six places in the top 21—and they won with 104 points.

Behind Salazar and Porter, Hunt was 28th, Eyestone 30th, Virgin 42nd, and Anderson 57th, and their 170 points took second, ahead of Kenya's 191, equaling the best placing an American team had ever achieved.

"I screwed up by not pushing the pace," said Salazar, but even in his chagrin he found a positive note. "It was good for me, if only for showing me how I was overconfident. I normally wouldn't think I could outkick those guys. Now I'm hungry. Now I'm down to earth." This had been a grand race, and in a world where victories last only a day, it had sown the seeds of an even grander one.

It was the same in the women's race. Seconds after the gun, the US team had to pick its way through a sea of mud in front of its starting gate. Soon the Americans were boxed behind slowing Spanish and Swedish runners, while the favored Soviets roared past on firmer ground.

"I saw that if someone didn't break through the girls ahead, we'd be stuck," said Jan Merrill later. She had been second to Norway's Grete Waitz in this race in 1981, but this year an injured right hamstring had cut into her training. Yet she wanted to help her team. "I knew if I made myself the point, they'd come through," she said. She wedged a space, and teammates Margaret Groos, Joan Benoit, and Betty Springs followed.

After 800 meters of the 4,072-meter race, Merrill had brought the US women back into contention, but they were still well behind a dense pack of five Soviets, led by 3,000-meter world-record holder Svyetlana Ulmasova. Only Waitz was near the USSR contingent, bleeding from a spike wound in the hand. "Margaret, come on let's go," Merrill said to Groos. "She talked us through the whole thing," Groos would say later. "She practically made me cry about three times. It was the most emotional race I've ever run."

The four, the exact number needed for a full team score, were 11th through 14th at the halfway point. Soon, Ulmasova's pace broke everyone but teammate Tatyana Pozdnyakova and Waitz. The Norwegian, who had won from 1978 through 1981, was running with a right knee sore from tendinitis, which had required a series of cortisone injections.

Merrill had led her crew into striking position, but she was incapable of moving farther up. Benoit surged on, with Springs and Groos following closely. Ahead, the Soviets were coming apart. They had misjudged the severity of the course and begun too hard. Benoit, Springs, and Groos moved to five-six-seven with 600 meters to go. Up front, Waitz was running away from the Soviets to win her fifth World Championship. Alison Wiley, a freckled Stanford freshman from Toronto, Canada, just caught Pozdnyakova in the stretch for second. Benoit and Springs overhauled Ulmasova before the line to get fourth and fifth, and four seconds later Groos was in ninth. The gallant Merrill hung on for 13th. Behind her, the Soviets' Yelena Sipatova, a former 10,000-meter world-record holder, fell to 21st, and the United States were world champions, 31 points to 41 for the USSR.

Merrill almost couldn't get her sweats on due to the hugs from her tearful, grateful teammates. "I've felt more a part of this team than any other," she said. For the United States, it was further proof that they belonged in a field full of international talent: cross-country running truly belonged to America on this day.

Men's Race			
Date: Sunday, March 20, 1983			
Teams: 24			
Distance: 7.45 miles / 12 kilometers			
Location: Gateshead, England			
Individual Finishers:			
1	Bekele Debele	Ethiopia	36:52
2	Carlos Lopes	Portugal	36:52
3	Some Muge	Kenya	36:52
4	Alberto Salazar	United States	36:53
5	Antonio Prieto	Spain	36:56
6	Rob de Castella	Australia	37:00
7	Dave Clark	England	37:05
8	Ezequiel Canario	Portugal	37:10
9	Pat Porter	United States	37:12
10	Alberto Cova	Italy	37:17
11	Nat Muir	Scotland	37:24
12	Mehmet Yürdadön	Turkey	37:24
13	Pierre Levisse	France	37:24
14	Eshetu Tura	Ethiopia	37:28
15	Constantino Esparcia	Spain	37:29
16	Paul Kipkoech	Kenya	37:32
17	Eric de Beck	Belgium	37:34
18	Hans-Jürgen Orthmann	West Germany	37:35
19	Steve Jones	Wales	37:35
20	Wodajo Bulti	Ethiopia	37:35
21	John Andrews	Australia	37:36
22	Mohammed Kedir	Ethiopia	37:37
23	Adugna Lema	Ethiopia	37:38
24	Chala Urgessa	Ethiopia	37:39
25	Jan Hagelbrand	Sweden	37:44

Team Results:		
1	Ethiopia	104
2	United States	170
3	Kenya	191
4	Australia	193
5	Spain	206
6	Portugal	302
7	Italy	306
8	England	318
9	Federal Republic of Germany	322
10	Belgium	373

Women's Race
Date: Sunday, March 20, 1983
Teams: 19
Distance: 2.54 miles/4.1 kilometers
Location: Gateshead, England

Individual Finishers:

1	Grete Waitz	Norway	13:29
2	Alison Wiley	Canada	13:37
3	Tatyana Pozdnyakova	Soviet Union	13:37
4	Joan Benoit	United States	13:57
5	Betty Springs	United States	14:00
6	Svetlana Ulmasova	Soviet Union	14:01
7	Francine Peeters	Belgium	14:03
8	Fita Lovin	Romania	14:04
9	Margaret Groos	United States	14:04
10	Aurora Cunha	Portugal	14:06
11	Alla Yushina	Soviet Union	14:08
12	Nancy Rooks	Canada	14:09
13	Jan Merrill	United States	14:12
14	Agnese Possamai	Italy	14:14
15	Doina Melinte	Romania	14:15
16	Anna-Maria Malone	Canada	14:17
17	Pilar Fernandez	Spain	14:18
18	Christine Benning	England	14:19
19	Christina Boxer	England	14:20
20	Carolyn Schuwalov	Australia	14:20
21	Yelena Sipatova	Soviet Union	14:21
22	Midde Hamrin	Sweden	14:21
23	Lynn Kanuka	Canada	14:22
24	Rosa Mota	Portugal	14:24
25	Nadia Dandolo	Italy	14:24

Team Results:

1	United States	31
2	USSR	41
3	Canada	53
4	England	94
5	Romania	98
6	New Zealand	122
7	Portugal	122
8	Norway	149
9	Australia	156
10	Spain	164

Chapter 15

Cross-country is what I always liked most. It was my world, my passion. Before the IAAF introduced the short course in 1998, all the world class athletes from 1,500 meters to the marathon were in the same race.

—Paul Tergat

THE DECADE OF THE 1990s

With the sudden arrival of dominant East African teams at the World Cross-Country Championships in the early 1980s, it was felt that "Western" hegemony was threatened. As a result, the International Amateur Athletics Federation (IAAF) made a number of format changes which permeated the 1990s. And yet, the level of competition remained high. Kenya and Ethiopia *were* remarkable in their strength and consistency in the upper ranks, and that forced other nations to recognize the bar had been raised. Old practices gave way to better methods in training—which in turn made the runners of the 1990s some of the fastest in history. Additionally, the era of the professional runner was well-established, incentivizing stronger performances.

But these changes brought difficult adjustments. The accessibility and motivation for the sport that boomed in previous decades melted away once the corporate element took hold. Alterations in power structure also affected the popularity of the sport. And yet, this "changing of the guard" separated the wheat from the chaff. New challengers emerged: Morocco rose to prominence internationally to battle the East Africans. The University of Colorado and Stanford University attempted to dethrone the mighty Arkansas Razorbacks in the National Collegiate Athletic Association (NCAA). And new opportunities to compete (as shifts in power created new divisions), prompted athletes to train more ardently in the pursuit of success.

CHANGES TO THE INTERNATIONAL CROSS-COUNTRY FORMAT

In 1987, IAAF President Primo Nebiolo made a major alteration to the voting policy of member nations that impacted "Western" involvement with planning and buy-in. Nebiolo wanted to move away from traditional methods within

the organization and in doing so alienated himself from the British representatives in the IAAF.

For years, the federation had operated under a weighted voting system so that the older members—Northern European and British Commonwealth—held five or six votes per country, while smaller, newer members had one each. When previous proposals to standardize the count to one vote per nation were first put forward in the IAAF Congress the changes were rejected by majority rule, but in 1987 Nebiolo got a measure passed by acclamation, with the protesting voice of a British delegate drowned by the roars of approval.

Additionally, to avoid the danger of a financial takeover by a group of the new members (by the late 1980s the Federation had an annual budget of more than $10 million) Nebiolo created the International Athletic Foundation, a financial trust based in Monte Carlo. And when he changed the timetable for the Seoul Olympic Games because US television wanted it (the price for that move was said to be $10 million itself, most of which went into the IAAF coffers), so too did slices of other athletic sponsorships and television rights become more lucrative, which gave Nebiolo funds to put through many of his plans for growth. In the process, to get away from the severity of English law, Nebiolo relocated the headquarters of the IAAF organization from London to Monte Carlo. Many of these changes, which may not have sat well with the traditional "Western" powers, did two things for the sport: they improved accessibility among nations where distance running was not as popular previously, and they pumped new money, and new lifeblood, into international cross-country running.

In addition to the new voting policy, in 1990 the IAAF introduced the *IAAF World Cross Challenge*, a worldwide circuit of elite cross-country events in which the world's top runners could compete for a total prize purse of $140,000. The 1990 Cross Challenge followed the same basic format as the Grand Prix circuit in track and field, with athletes competing for points in a series of carefully monitored races culminating each year with the World Cross-Country Championships. Athletes could score up to 25 points in each Cross Challenge race—a global tour of sorts, where a runner's four best scores, plus the double points available at World Cross, decided the overall IAAF World Cross Challenge awards for men and women.

The goal of the IAAF was to combat Kenya and Ethiopia's dominance in cross-country. First, the IAAF adjusted the qualifications to run, extending invitations to previously unrecognized nations, and second, they structured cash prizes to draw out better competition. However, the new talent did nothing to supplant the mighty Africans. Despite the IAAF's best efforts, in the ten years of the IAAF Cross Challenge within the decade, only four men finished on the podium who were *not* from Kenya or Ethiopia (out of 30 spots). And none of those four won it outright.

Next, in a further effort to mix up the stagnation at the top ranks, the IAAF introduced a new multi-day format for the World Cross-Country Championships in 1998 that included an additional short-course race to supplement the traditional long-course. Men and women could now run a four-kilometer short race the day before the long race (12K for men/8K for women). Also in 1998, the IAAF implemented a four-scorer system (instead of six) at World Cross to dispel any chance of a numbers game by the East African powerhouses. It was thought that by reducing the number of scorers for each team, the depth featured by Kenya and Ethiopia would not be such a large factor.

Due to these changes, the 1990s saw a drastic increase in international participation at World Cross. Between the 1989 and 1990 editions, attendance jumped from 41 nations to 59. This was partially attributed to a junior women's event, which had inaugurated in 1989 and drew 121 athletes in 1990. In fact, throughout the decade new highs were reached: a total of 760 athletes participated in the 1994 edition of World Cross (only 269 had participated just twenty years prior), while national attendance jumped to 66 countries in 1998 when the short-course was implemented. The year 2000 marked the peak, with 76 nations and 806 total athletes participating in the World Cross-Country Championships.

And yet, the increased participation, changes in format, addition of a challenge series, and added money did nothing to dispel the Kenyan and Ethiopian reign—it was clear that African domination was far-reaching. In 1988 the Kenyan senior men had finished in the first, second, third, fourth, sixth, seventh, eighth, and ninth positions for the championship race. Ten years later, in the inaugural year for the format change (and after scoring two perfect teams in the junior men's and women's races in 1993), the Kenyan team again defied convention, finishing first, second, third, and fourth (a perfect score) in the Men's 4K short-course race. No other team claimed victory in the men's senior event but Kenya during the 1990s.

Fittingly, in a move precipitated by the South American Sports Federation (Confederación Sudamericana de Atletismo) in 1986, and by the Asian Athletics Association in 1991, the European Athletics Association voted to hold a continental "Europeans Only" cross-country championship in Alnwick (Great Britain) on December 10, 1994. Forced separation from the East African nations, it seemed, was the only solution.

TRAIN HARD, WIN EASY—KENYAN DOMINATION

Kenya had proven it was not a one-hit wonder, winning team titles with incredible depth. Bred by training sessions with hundreds of runners, a variety of names kept Kenya at the top—but a few individuals were more notable than others.

One of the strongest was William Sigei, who first stunned Kenyan crowds in the 1992 Kenyan Olympic Trials 5,000 meters, when he ran with (and defeated) five-time World Cross winner John Ngugi—all while competing barefoot. In the spring of 1993, when World Cross was held in Amorebieta, Spain, Sigei used the same tactics that helped him beat Ngugi on the track. Having finished eighth at the World Cross-Country Championships the year before, Sigei allowed teammates Dominic and Ismael Kirui to set a blistering pace until the 10th kilometer, at which point he caught up with them and cruised to victory. At age twenty-three, Sigei looked like a purpose-made successor to Ngugi at the top of the cross-country ranks. It was after his initial surprise 5,000-meter victory at the Olympic Trials that Sigei was recruited by the Kenyan Air Force team and won the Kenyan National Cross-Country title in 1993 and 1994. Each of those years he was also World Cross-Country champion.

Simeon Rono, a neighbor of Sigei's, recalled that Sigei would nearly always train alone. At the pace he churned out his miles, it had to be that way: "Sigei trained very hard; when that man is motivated, he is the best runner in Kenya," said Rono. Sigei's favorite workout was a regulated fartlek advocated by national coach Mike Kosgei—two minutes hard with a minute easy over a 10-kilometer course. Even though the altitude exceeded 6,500 feet above sea level, and the route was quite hilly, Sigei would run this session in about 31 minutes.

But despite breaking the world record in the 10,000 meters on the track in the summer of 1994, running 26:52 in Oslo, Sigei withdrew from the IAAF Cross Challenge in the spring of 1995 with an ankle injury. He would never contend in a national or international cross-country race again.

Sigei's predecessor, John Ngugi, remained a formidable runner in the early 1990s. In 1992, after a two-year hiatus at the top ranks in World Cross, Ngugi won his fifth World Cross-Country title. He also appeared at the Cinque Mulini (finishing fourth), and was first man home at the Cross Ala dei Sardi and Cross dellePradelle in Italy.

Unfortunately, seemingly due to a misunderstanding, Ngugi refused to take an out-of-competition drug test just before the 1993 World Cross-Country Championships and was subsequently banned by the IAAF until May 1995. Following his reinstatement under the "exceptional circumstances" rule, Ngugi returned to competition and made an attempt at a comeback before the 1996 World Cross race in Cape Town. But the two years away from the sport proved too much. In February 1996, in an attempt to make the Kenyan National Cross-Country team to compete at Worlds, Ngugi finished a disappointing 96th place overall. It was the final cross-country race of his career.

To examine that 1996 Kenyan National Cross-Country event is to see a brief but brilliant exposé of what it took to be one of the best cross-country runners in the world. As Olympic silver-medalist Patrick Sang commented: "The nationals are like nothing else. You have over 200 of the best Kenyans fighting like crazy, like a cavalry charge." Already one of the most competitive cross-country races, the 1996 Kenyan National featured a particularly strong field. Among the athletes featured was a long list of World Cross-Country medalists, World Champions, and more than a handful of Olympians. Very few foreigners were entered, and the ones who attempted the event finished nowhere near the top.

The setting for the championships was N'gong Horse Racing Track, twenty kilometers north of Nairobi, and, most remarkably, 6,000 feet above sea level.

Aside from the 1995 winner Paul Tergat (his second title, after winning in 1992 as well), there were a few other Kenyans who had a chance at the podium. Josephat Machuka was one of them. Machuka "could be brilliant or bad," according to runner Joseph Kibor. "He often tries to win the race with front running; he is one of few who has the talent to do it."

For the Kenyan women, other storylines punctuated the occasion. Residing only 12 kilometers apart, Rose Cheruiyot and Sally Barsosio had built an intense rivalry, and in the 1996 senior women's event they went toe to toe once more. Barsosio employed familiar tactics, storming right from the gun. "Sally is tough, very tough. She tries to run people into the ground. Even if they catch her she won't give in; she'll fight all the way," commented Coach Colm O'Connell. Barsosio held on to win. Cheruiyot scratched and clawed at the distance separating them but never managed to reel Barsosio in. Rift Valley Province, with six of the top nine places, captured the team honors. This was unsurprising to Moses Tanui, as he revealed: "Yes. Over 95% of the Kenyan team come from Rift Valley each and every year."

Then it was the moment all had waited for: the senior men's competition. Jogging to the start in a huge mass were the Armed Forces runners, their flag bearer leading the way. They sang in unison, imposing a fierce battle cry. Over 250 of Kenya's best cross-country runners toed the line. No respect was given to celebrity as each runner had to push for a front line spot. Julius Ondieki, sidelined by injury, explained, "Each runner thinks he has a chance at winning, and with the quality of the field if you are left behind at the start then you'll never catch up. They know that."

The first 800 meters, over rough grass and slightly uphill, was covered in 1:56. Then, the white uniforms of the Armed Forces "A" team became prominent at the fore. As predetermined by the Armed Forces coaches, Paul Tergat made his move at eight kilometers. Effortlessly he broke the pack. Joseph Kibor tried grimly to hang onto his shirttails and paid the price. Meanwhile, other established names such as Ismael Kirui, Daniel Komen, and John Ngugi struggled, finishing 42nd, 50th, and 96th, respectively.

Tergat had only himself to challenge as he collected his third National Cross-Country title. With six runners in the top nine positions the team title was a romp, as usual, for the Armed Forces, and the coaches could breathe again. William Kiptum Mugei took runner-up honors, followed by Josephat Machuka. Fourth place was taken by 1,500-meter specialist Stephen Kipkorir Arusei, who later that summer won the Kenyan National 1,500-meter title and an Olympic 1,500-meter bronze medal. "In Kenya you need 1,500 meter speed to run in the distance races," he joked, clearly satisfied with the result. It would be five weeks later when the Kenyan runners would again display their prowess at the World Cross-Country Championships.

Beginning with the Mike Kosgei era and their first World Cross team title in 1986, no other country was able to win the men's 12K team title at the World Cross-Country Championships. Not one. In the years spanning 1986–2000, Kenya's senior-level runners across both genders won 24 of 36 available first-place team medals (including the short course). Adding in the junior-level gold medal teams, the number became 45 first place teams out of a total of 63 for Kenya: a staggering winning percentage of 71 percent covering all divisions during that span. It wasn't just World Cross-Country dominance, it was a national institution.

It came as no surprise then to learn that Kenya also won 12 of 15 possible individual golds for their senior men from 1986 to 2000. John Ngugi (five titles), William Sigei (two titles), and Paul Tergat (five titles) were the only three Kenyan individuals to earn gold. The challenger in the two years between Ngugi's final titles in 1990 and 1991 *was* surprising—as the tiny nation of Morocco usurped the big names and became the welcome challengers to the mighty Kenyan monopoly. And one man was the greatest giant-killer of them all: Khalid Skah.

KHALID SKAH AND THE KADA WAY

The 1990 World Cross-Country Championships was expected to be a Kenyan-dominated event. Thanks to John Ngugi, Kenya had won the previous four events and had also shown tremendous team depth. However, Ngugi was hampered by injuries in the spring of 1990 and placed only 20th at World Cross, but most felt it would make little difference for the winning nation. Just then, a Moroccan challenger rose to start a new rivalry. Khalid Skah had placed 68th in the junior race in 1986 and 56th in the senior event in 1989, but in Aix-les-Bains, France, at the 1990 World Cross-Country Championships, Skah kept with the Kenyan pace throughout, and used his superior kick to defeat Moses Tanui to win the gold medal. It was a massive achievement.

During the 1980s, Said Aouita had been Morocco's distance star. With a junior Moroccan Cross-Country National title (1978) and a senior National Cross-Country title (1980), Aouita had competed at a smattering of cross-country events but was best known for his range on the track, which extended from the 800 (1:43) to the 10,000 meters (27:26). In his shadow trained Skah—and once Aouita went down with a leg injury, it was the younger Moroccan that was able to make a splash. Skah proved he belonged at the top when he successfully defended his World Cross title in 1991 in Antwerp, Belgium, with the Kenyan Tanui again a frustrated second. By 1994, and for the four years following, Kenya wasn't the only threatening African nation. Under the guidance of a motivated coach and an innovative training plan, Morocco had risen to prominence as well.

In 1984, under the direction of President Primo Nebiolo, the IAAF began subsidizing the cost of travel and accommodation for teams participating in the World Cross-Country Championships (50 percent travel and full accommodations). In the early '80s, it was the newly successful World Track and Field Championships (and the subsequent television and endorsement deals) that enabled the IAAF to subsidize these costs for World Cross—but as the international arrangement between amateurism and corporate sponsorship changed in the late 1980s and early 1990s, companies began stepping in to supply funding to not only athletes, but also national athletic associations.

It was at this point that King Hassan II of Morocco set aside funds to rejuvenate Morocco's national sports program, which included designating a training center, procedures for assessing talent, and the hiring of a multitude of coaches to govern the elite athletes centered in Rabat. Of the thirty million citizens who called Morocco home in 1990, 70 percent were under the age of thirty, half lived on less than $50 a month, and an equal number were illiterate. When an organized and well-funded system was put in place (led by motivated coach Abdelkader Kada) young, talented runners fully embraced their opportunity to represent their nation and make a respectable living in the process.

Unlike in Kenya, which was spurred by training camps built to provide hard-working athletes a chance at escaping poverty—and dependent on winning international competitions to pad their coffers—Morocco organized more effectively, and targeted their recruitment on young athletes who passed a gamut of scientific benchmarks. "The success was due to a deliberate selection process," said Aziz Daouda, the technical director of the Moroccan National Athletic Federation. The talent-spotting system sought young men and women between twelve and sixteen years old. The federation used caravans that traveled throughout Morocco with equipment to test the student-applicants in two phases.

The first phase consisted of a sprint test, a longer distance threshold run, and a standing long jump. These three simple tests profiled student's reaction speed, endurance, and explosive strength.

In the second phase, students were subjected to a rigorous medical examination, pushing simultaneous effects from experiments such as running on a treadmill and taking a blood test.

Gifted athletes who finished at the top of these two phases were then sent to "Preparation Local Units" where they were further monitored by athletics coaches until they were sixteen to eighteen years old. These sport centers were sponsored by the phosphate industry, while coaches were paid by the government and the national federation. In 1995–96 alone, 60 percent of the Moroccan territory was covered and inspected, grading available talent.

After developing within the "Preparation Local Unit," finalists were selected for the "*Perfecting* Local Unit" also called the "Training Development Center," which hosted about 60 youngsters between the ages of sixteen and nineteen. The selection for this center was done under a more complex criterion, using test results, biometrical parameters, and physiological factors. Top athletes were then relocated to Ifrane, where at the National Institute of Athletics their training plan was finalized, their running style scientifically analyzed, and their diet corrected. Without the depth of talent or tradition that Kenya could call upon, Morocco took this process very seriously, which explained why so much time and money was invested in the system: "For us, it is the training methods and the atmosphere created around the athletes that is important," Daouda said.

At this level Moroccan athletes worked and trained with the best, were treated as professionals, and did not have any other obligations beyond preparing for major competitions and living at the National Institute of Athletics. The institute thrived due to financial backing from the Moroccan government, and athletes were provided food, housing, and a salary to meet their basic needs. The provisions, while affording valuable security and stability, were not luxurious, and the athletes still had to display an extraordinary level of commitment.

As an example, by the end of the decade, there were 92 athletes (men and women) in Morocco's elite training program, with 17 coaches, three doctors, and five physical therapists. Nutritionists took care of the meals, and the Moroccan Federation acted as business manager, booking international competitions.

It was also a life of austere isolation, even for the nation's biggest stars. Hicham El Guerrouj, world-record holder in the mile (3:43) and international cross-country competitor as a junior-level runner, lived in a well-appointed room at the institute, but was only afforded a curtain to separate his bedroom from the living room. According to Moroccan officials, El Guerrouj made $2 million a year (including corporate endorsements), trained twice a day, and only took three weeks off from training a year.

Frequent visits to altitude were essential. "An accumulation of trips are needed," said national coach Abdelkader Kada. The Moroccan squad visited altitude four to six times a year, with venues including Ifrane in Morocco, Font Romeu in France, and St. Moritz in Switzerland. Each visit lasted three to five weeks. The athletes lived at 8,200 feet above sea level, but came down to 5,000 feet to train. Athletes like El Guerrouj also slept for eight hours a night and a further three during the day. As one coach wryly pointed out, with such an amount of sleep and rest, drugs were not needed. While blood-doping and EPO-use was a trendy and illegal way to speed recovery from heavy training, athletes such as El Guerrouj were encouraging their bodies to recover naturally by imposing an unnatural amount of sleep on themselves.

The Moroccan cross-country teams flourished once these training centers were established; the senior men finished second to Kenya at World Cross in 1994, '95, '96, and '97, and third in '98. The junior men were just as strong, for six straight years beginning in 1993, they finished third to Kenya and Ethiopia. On the short course they also performed well: the senior men finished second to Kenya in 1998 and 1999, third in 2000, and second again in 2001, while the senior women won the short course team title in 1998 and finished third in 1999.

Athletes such as Khalid Skah, Salah Hissou (who consistently finished on the podium at World Cross, the IAAF World Cross Challenge, the Cinque Mulini, and numerous other international cross-country events), Brahim Lahlafi (Juan Muguerza Cross-Country champion and top-five at World Cross), and the brothers Khalid and Brahim Boulami (top-20 finishers both at World Cross) were recruited through the national system in Morocco and were able to develop a more comprehensive distance program because of Coach Kada's methods.

Athletes also had plenty of opportunity to exhibit their speed over training runs. Three to four hard threshold runs a week were the norm, with longer endurance sessions on alternative days. The endurance sessions usually started at a tempo around four minutes per kilometer (about 6:30-mile pace), and gradually picked up to 3:15 per kilometer (just over 5:00 per mile) for an hour of running. This progressive aerobic threshold training was the key to Moroccan endurance.

Power, in the form of hill running, was also emphasized in this group. Khalid Skah ran two sessions of hill work each week, year-round: 20 × 400–meter hills in the morning, and 20 × 400 meters in the afternoon on the track ranging from 58–63 seconds were undertaken. Total mileage was around 200 kilometers a week (120 miles).

With renewed enthusiasm, government-supported training, commercially and internationally backed talent, and impressive workouts, the Moroccans of the 1990s were more dedicated than ever to exposing a chink in the East African armor at the top ranks of international cross-country running. And they had the perfect opportunity after the World Cross-Country Championships of 1995.

KOSGEI: THE LOSS OF KENYA'S NATIONAL COACH

In the spring of 1995, mere weeks after seeing Kenya sweep all four divisions of the World Cross-Country Championships with record-low scores (and after three Kenyans landed on the podium out of six possible spots for both genders in the IAAF World Cross Challenge), Mike Kosgei was dismissed from his position as national coach for the Kenyan team. Or as one Kenyan newspaper wrote, Kosgei was "dispensed with by Kenya's athletics chiefs for expressing dissenting views." The true reason why Kosgei was let go remained shrouded in mystery, which fueled the suspicion that Kenya's cross-country reign was coming to an end.

As the *New York Times* reported, "The firing of progressive national coach Mike Kosgei may have further damaged Kenya's chances." No one wanted to admit that his loss would have been catastrophic to Kenya at World Cross, where the men were undefeated since Kosgei's arrival in 1985. "Kosgei has been the man behind our cross-country successes," said William Tanui, the then 800-meter Olympic champion. "He's the man who's won us gold medals." Despite the shocking news, even more devastating was the reason that Athletics Kenya gave for Kosgei's departure, which, issued by Kenya Amateur Athletics Association (KAAA) Chairman Isaiah Kiplagat, accused Kosgei of fueling a rebellion.

Those closest to the sport saw the situation in Kenya as dire. On the eve of Kosgei's dismissal Kip Keino claimed: "An atmosphere that would make athletes perform well is missing right now." And Kosgei felt his close ties with his athletes put the administration of the sport in danger: "My deep concern remains a threat on the future of this sport that made Kenya a global household name in sports terms," he told *Reuters*. Soon a Finnish running club based in Abo snatched his services up, but Kosgei was able to work long distance, and stayed local to continue training a large number of athletes in the Nandi District. And former athletes were on his side too, with talks of boycotts and organizing against Athletics Kenya. "The athlete is the master, the federation is the servant," Kosgei had said previously. "Not the other way round, as our athletic chiefs would want to portray it."

But while the displays of solidarity were welcome for Kenya's most decorated national coach, opponents to Kenyan domination at World Cross were dismayed to find that it was business as usual in 1996. "Look at the results in South Africa. Kenya won without him and will continue to do so," stated new national coach Joseph Karatu Ngure. And one man more than any other was responsible for Kenya's continued momentum. Training in the N'gong hills was Paul Tergat, the gentleman, who knew only one thing: he who trains hardest, wins. "If somebody beats me, then I am happy for him," said Tergat. "He will have obviously worked harder for the result than I did." Challengers were welcome to try.

PAUL TERGAT: "THE GENTLEMAN"

Tergat's rise to the top took time. After a big breakthrough in early 1992 that saw the twenty-two-year-old finish third in a high-profile military cross-country race in Nanyuki (the Armed Forces Championship), win the Kenyan

National Cross-Country Championship, and repeat at N'gong the following week at the Nairobi International Cross-Country, three years would pass before Tergat was dominant again.

But by 1995, Tergat made winning international cross-country meetings a priority and had his sights set on his first World Championship. He finished third in the Italian Campaccio in early January, came second at the Cross del Calzado two days later, and finished second in the Kenyan Armed Forces at the end of the month. Then, in the span of fourteen days, he won the Kenyan National Cross-Country and the Nairobi International, and finished runner-up at the Cinque Mulini. By the end of March, Tergat was poised to take his first title at World Cross when it returned to England at County Durham.

He won with ease and defended his title successfully four more times after 1995. The following two editions (in 1996 and '97) were battles with Moroccan Salah Hissou, the world 10,000-meter record holder, which came down to the final stages of the race. Amidst it all, Tergat kept his cool and used his superior strength over the countryside to preserve his lead. His final two title defenses ('98 and '99) came as a product of tactical front-running with his Kenyan teammates. "I am a country-man," Tergat stated. "In cross-country I felt at home. These are the kind of races I did when I started running and where I celebrated my first victories. When I was in shape, I knew nobody could beat me regardless of the weather and the surface. It didn't matter if it was muddy or dry, hilly or flat. I am very proud to be a five-time winner."

Despite winning five successive titles at World Cross, Tergat could have added a sixth, had it not been for long-winded meetings with team officials the night before the World Cross event in the year 2000 (held in Vilamoura, Portugal). The debate surrounded the inclusion of Kenyan Charles Kamathi on the team, who was the leader of the IAAF World Cross Challenge standings at the time of the World Championship. And yet, Kamathi had only finished 13th at the Kenyan National Cross-Country Championships and missed qualifying for the national team outright. Kenyan officials decided upon entering Kamathi after long debates the night before World Cross, and as a result, jeopardized the team tactics that had centered around Kenyan Joshua Chelenga, the rightful eighth-place finisher and pacemaker. Without Chelenga, Tergat and the other Kenyans had no one to lead the way, and Tergat's streak of five straight ended with a third-place finish.

"THE EMPEROR"

While Paul Tergat's emotional state may have jeopardized his run at a sixth World Cross-Country title in 2000, not much else had posed a threat to his dominance before then—save but one man. A rivalry had evolved years prior between Tergat and one of Ethiopia's most storied runners, Haile Gebrselassie, who as one of Tergat's greatest adversaries was proficient at the art of cross-country, too.

On January 1, 1994, Haile Gebrselassie won the County Durham International, held in Durham England, in 26:27 (over nine kilometers), and followed in the footsteps of his fellow countryman, Fita Bayesa, who had won the year before. Five days later, Gebrselassie took first-place at the 37th running of the Campaccio in Italy. On January 23, it was a third-place finish at the Cross International de Italica in Seville, Spain—and then Gebrselassie finished out the month the following week by winning the San Sebastian Cross International. In the span of thirty days Gebrselassie had won three international cross-country meetings, and had finished third in his fourth international meet of the month! Gebrselassie capped the season by qualifying and finishing third at World Cross three months later in Budapest, beating Paul Tergat by four seconds.

> **Did You Know?**
>
> **In 1995, the World Cross race was an interesting one, but individual champion Paul Tergat was never challenged. Instead, the Ethiopian team endured a nightmare journey that wrecked the hopes of Haile Gebrselassie. Visa and financial problems saw the Ethiopians lose access to their passports for security reasons, and they were forced to pack several to a room in an Athens hotel on Thursday night. Then, they pooled what they had to pay the bill, but could afford no food. Having been in transit since Wednesday, the team finally arrived in London on Friday. No flights were available to Newcastle, so they made the seven-hour, 300-mile trip by public bus, arriving at midnight, less than twelve hours before the first race. When Gebrselassie finished in fourth, he was in tears: "The [Ethiopian Federation] made two big mistakes. They did not organize our travel properly, and they left out three good men." Ethiopia had withheld three runners after they ran for money in the final IAAF World Cross Challenge race in San Vittore, Italy, three weeks prior—including the winner, Fita Bayesa.**

While Gebrselassie and Tergat would trade victories back and forth both on the track and on the cross-country course, Gebrselassie's introduction to distance running had humble beginnings. In 1988, fifteen-year-old Gebrselassie told his father—who had forbidden him to run—that he was going to Addis Ababa to visit his older brother, Assefa. It was partly true, but the primary reason for going to the Ethiopian capital was to run in the Abebe Bikila Marathon. Gebrselassie finished in two hours and 48 minutes.

It was a chastened teenager who limped back to Arsi Province the following day. "I ran in street shoes with plastic soles," Gebrselassie recalled. "I only finished because there were no cars; there was no other way to get back to the start. The next day, my brother put me on a bus back to Asela, but the bus stopped several kilometers from my village, and I had to walk. I don't know how I did it."

Witnesses to Gebrselassie's victories, medals, and world records since that novice excursion have a pretty clear idea of how he did it: with the same grit, tenacity, and willpower that brought him all that success in the following two decades.

As one of ten children in the hills of Asela, 160 miles south of Addis, Gebrselassie ran six miles to school and back every day (in the dry season) from the age of six. When the rains came and he was no longer able to take a shortcut across a riverbed, it was 7.5 miles. Inspired by the achievements of his countryman Miruts Yifter (who won the Olympic 10,000 meters in 1980), Gebrselassie grew obsessed: he stole his father's transistor radio to listen to commentary of Yifter's Moscow win. After his first marathon at fifteen, Gebrselassie was selected for his regional (then national) team, and at eighteen was discovered by former Dutch distance runner Jos Hermens, who became his coach and agent.

In 1992, under Hermens's tutelage, Gebrselassie announced his presence internationally by winning both the 5,000 and 10,000 meters in the World Junior Championships in Seoul, at age nineteen. Hermens's company, Global Sports Communications, became a surrogate family for Gebrselassie. "I have never asked about competition," Gebrselassie shared. "I say, 'Jos, if you believe the competition is good for me I come.' Always he listens to what I say. We trust each other. The other part is we love each other. Even when I will not be competing, we will be like family."

As a former world-class athlete, Hermens understood the highs and lows of competition. It was his frustration as an athlete that led him into his career as an agent. "I was a teacher originally, and I wanted to stay in the sport. I wanted to coach. But of course it was impossible to become [a] full-time coach at the time. Then I started to work for Nike in Holland around 1979 and then later for Nike Europe [from] 1982 until 1985 and then Nike moved to Switzerland. I worked with a very nice group—Olympic gold medalists from sprinters to Seb Coe."

The experience Hermens gained as an athlete shaped the way he assisted his young athletes. When Gebrselassie raised the question early in his career as to whether he should run the marathon to Ethiopian national coach Dr. Yilma Berta, it was Hermens who guided Gebrselassie to cross-country running first. "You would finish well down the field," Berta noted. "First cross-country, then on the track."

The cross-country terrain of Jan Meda, near the edge of the city, was always included in the training program. This race ground of Addis Ababa, originally belonging to the Emperor, not only provided possibilities for horseracing but also for three to four miles of long cross-country footraces. This was where the national and international championships were held, and also where, especially on Sundays, the city's running and soccer fanatics met.

But with the national records, the international agent and exposure, the world-class rivalry, and the prestige of being one of the world's best distance runners, the 1990s was conspicuously missing one key ingredient: a Western challenger biding to usurp Gebrselassie and the Africans.

WHERE ARE THE AMERICANS?

Compared to the boom in the 1970s and early 1980s, it is easy to see why many experts claimed that American-born runners "under-performed" in the 1990s. There were many factors that justified this drop in international standing, but the situation at-large was more complex. Despite many African and European nations finishing higher in international cross-country competitions, American distance runners remained competitive—oftentimes running faster than at any other point in history—all while reinventing the programs and systems present to give themselves the best opportunity to be successful. They wouldn't stay down for long.

One of these complexities of American standing had to do with their international motivations to compete—with one of their biggest rivalries in athletics fading away. The United States and the USSR national track teams competed in 19 outdoor meets, seven indoor meets, 10 junior meets, and eight multi-event competitions between 1958 and 1985. But while these athletic contests served many purposes for the leaders and participants (one function was as propaganda, another was as a tool for foreign diplomacy), by 1985, attendance had fallen drastically.

The 1982 meet in Indianapolis, Indiana, drew only 8,000 spectators per day (and this decline occurred at a time when track was still relatively popular in the United States). The creation of international championship track meets also contributed to the series' decline. The IAAF organized a legitimate World Championship track meet featuring national teams beginning in 1983. Steve Scott, America's premier miler in the late 1970s and early 1980s recalled that "from every standpoint, the 1983 World Championships were a smashing success." The summer schedule became so crowded that at one point the USA–USSR outdoor meet never took place simply because the Soviet sport leaders and the AAU could not find a mutually agreeable date.

Both nations also stopped sending their best athletes to compete. The list of competitors on the US team once read like a who's who of Olympians and record holders (Alberto Salazar, Gerry Lindgren, Craig Virgin, and Lynn Jennings were a few of the notable cross-country runners who made an appearance), but the appeal of the competition fell away. The United States, especially, faced difficulty fielding a top-tier national team once standards changed for athlete compensation in the late 1970s and early 1980s.

In 1981, almost half of the TAC National Championship winners declined invitations to participate. TV announcer (and cross-country runner) Marty Liquori, who had competed in three of the USA–USSR meets as an athlete, compared competing in the meet with going to a party that your wife makes you attend: "It's OK once you get home." The USSR and the US track teams met one more time in 1985 at a dual scored tri-meet with Japan in Tokyo. The Soviets trounced the United States, 221 to 164. The meet was never held again.

In addition to international motivations, areas within the United States were also seeing a drop. Eugene,

Oregon, traditionally a hotbed for distance running talent, was featured in a news article titled, "Where Have All the Runners Gone?" published by the *Eugene Register-Guard* in 1999. A few reasons for the disappearance were listed: "Distance running has always been Eugene's calling card," reporter Curtis Anderson wrote. "But then Athletics West disbanded, and the city was dealt another blow when Luiz de Oliviera and his talented band of Brazilians—led by ex-Duck Joaquim Cruz, the 1984 gold medalist in the 800—left town for the milder climes of San Diego."

The article cited Boulder, Colorado, as having a large contingent of world-class runners: "Eugene used to be the capital for distance running," Alberto Salazar was quoted as saying. "But now that the benefits of training at altitude have become accepted, Boulder has become the mecca. If I was a distance runner today and I didn't have ties to a specific place, I would go to Boulder. There's no doubt about it. Athletes go to where they think they will get the best training." And the article cited that on the East Coast, the Reebok Enclave team based at Georgetown was receiving guidance from Coach Frank Gagliano and former Oregon Duck Matt Centrowitz in the mid-1990s.

Eugene's Dick Brown, an internationally respected distance coach, echoed these sentiments. "The demise of the club system affected Eugene. Athletics West and ideas like that were a magnet for others to come here," Brown said. "But the fact is that college recruiting also changed, and distance runners stopped coming to school here, and the magnet lost some of its power."

Thankfully, one of the largest contingents of post-collegiate national talent was able to emerge with the Nike Farm Team in Palo Alto, California, which was started by Nike employee Jeff Johnson in 1994 and had a strong relationship with Stanford University. Only partially funded by Nike, more than 50 athletes considered themselves affiliated with the group—and it also provided a training base for Kim McDonald's elite corps of Kenyan runners alongside Bob Kennedy, the best distance runner in the United States at the time. Ironically, when Johnson hatched the idea of starting a post-collegiate program for distance runners, Eugene was the first place he considered. But he vetoed that plan because "there already was a good population of highly regarded coaches."

The fall of 1994 saw the Farm Team plant a partnership between Jeff Johnson (Nike's first-ever hired employee and Stanford grad) and Vin Lananna (former Dartmouth coach who had relocated to Stanford), who provided opportunities for distance runners to continue developing after graduating from college. It was Johnson's intention to form a largely volunteer club comprised of athletes who wanted to pursue Olympic dreams. He intended to return to the days of the volunteer coach and a locally based group of athletes in the hopes of revitalizing the club system. Lananna had the wisdom and long-term plan. Through partnering with Sports Medicine Institute International and its physical therapy services and human performance lab, and with medical expertise from a group of Stanford University physicians and surgeons, the Nike Farm Team provided athletes with an extensive support system.

Originally coached by Johnson, and then on an interim basis by Lananna, the Nike Farm Team also received the guidance of Frank Gagliano. Gagliano stepped in once Johnson left in 2001 and brought with him more than forty years of coaching experience, with NCAA coach of the year honors in 1991 and 1999 (he also produced more than one hundred All-Americans while coaching at Manhattan College, Rutgers University, and Georgetown). "Our team's focus is on track success outdoors, which means qualifying as many members as we can for the 2003 National Championships on our home track in June," Gagliano said at the time. "From there, we're looking to get several members on the team for Paris, with the longer-term goal of placing athletes on the medal stand next summer at the 2004 Athens Olympic Games." The Farm Team won their first cross-country team championship for men and women in 1999 (1996 and 1997 also "counted" when association teams were separated from those deemed "national"), and they would go on to win five more in the subsequent decade.

Along with the Farm Team, one of the first major domestic cross-country events to garner any attention during the '90s was Boston's Mayor's Cup Festival. The Mayor's Cup, with its inaugural running in 1990, always sought the biggest names in distance running. Bill Squires, the founding coach of the Greater Boston Track Club in 1973 and member of the Boston Athletic Association (also the primary organization behind the event), started the first Mayor's Cup to bring open cross-country back to Franklin Park. The first race drew just nine runners, but entrants soon numbered in the thousands—from youth development runners to international caliber harriers. The New York Athletic Club's Brad Schlapak, whose personal best in the 5K was a svelte 13:44, won the race in '92 and '93. Kenyan Silah Misoi, who had range spanning from 3,000 meters to the marathon, also won two titles. For the women, Ethiopian Aziza Aliyli would earn two titles, as would Massachusetts's own Lynn Jennings, who won in '94 and '95. The Mayor's Cup event alone drew in international talent to the park, with winners representing nations as far-ranging as Canada, Kenya, New Zealand, Ireland, and Ethiopia.

And with international talent being a larger feature of domestic competition, The Athletics Congress (TAC), which changed its name to USA Track and Field (USATF) in 1992, began to adjust the format and schedule of national cross-country competitions. In the fall of 1994, the cross-country committee of USATF voted to drop the "Senior and Junior Men's World Cross Trials" cross-country race in February. The women's equivalent was still kept as a selection race for World Cross, while the men's team was chosen based on the December championship.

Dissatisfied with this adjustment, the cross-country committee again voted to change the format, this time in 1997. To accommodate the changes at the World Cross-Country Championships by the IAAF, USA Track and Field implemented a full cross-country championship in February and made the December championship only available for local cross-country clubs. The February event included senior men's and women's long-course events, junior (nineteen years and under) events, and senior men's and women's short-course events. The December event scored only senior men's and women's races, and club team scores and participation were emphasized. Changes to race distance for the February event—adding a four-kilometer short course for men and women, and increasing the junior women's distance from five kilometers to six—had far-reaching consequences.

When the IAAF increased the junior women's distance in 1998, USA Track and Field also changed the national standard. But suddenly, girls who were nineteen and younger were now running a kilometer longer than women in the NCAA for collegiate competition (six kilometers versus five). When the Division I and II subcommittees of the NCAA Men's and Women's Track and Field Committee voted at their 1997 meetings to extend the race to 6,000 meters, responses were mixed: "It's definitely a step in the right direction for women's cross-country," Stanford University's women's coach Beth Alford-Sullivan had said. "Moving the distance provides some separation in terms of making cross-country a separate sport, a sport within itself, which I think is great. Most high schools are running 5,000 meters. The concept of women making the transition to a greater distance is something that should be done. Making the transition is a natural step."

Some coaches expressed concern that the longer race would close the door to middle-distance runners. Two years prior, college coaches who had been surveyed voted against altering the race distance. Tom Henderson, men's and women's cross-country coach at South Dakota State University and a member of the Division II subcommittee, acknowledged that the additional distance would tax middle-distance runners, but contended that they could continue to thrive at the longer distance: "The 800–1,500 runner who is effective at 5,000 meters is still going to be effective at 6,000 meters," he said. "Increasing the distance by 1,000 meters isn't going to prevent those people from competing. It's going to scare some people off, but not a lot."

Ultimately, the measure passed. Alongside the changes in race distance, the fluctuating schedule of how and where members of America's national cross-country team would be selected impacted the United States's chances at being competitive internationally. It simply became harder to peak at multiple times in the year when the selection process adjusted from February (within a month of World Cross), to December (three months from World Cross), and back again.

Additionally, national stalwarts like Pat Porter were getting older. Entering the 1990 cross-country season, Porter had won eight straight national titles, a clear record. But soon, his wins became podium finishes. In 1990 in Van Cortlandt he finished second for the first time since before 1982—then repeated his second-place finish at Franklin Park in 1991. He dropped to third overall in 1992, and

second again in '93 and '94, before a startling and unexpected 20th in 1995. It was his final cross-country race, and the first time Porter had missed out on making the national team. His international World Cross finishes had also been less than competitive, as he mustered only two finishes in the decade: a 68th place run in 1991, and 94th overall in 1993.

The young Americans standing in the way of Porter's crowns were faster and weren't beholden to corporate pressures. And two athletes more than any other defined this period: Bob Kennedy and Todd Williams.

BOB KENNEDY AND TODD WILLIAMS LOOK BACK

On a cold November day in 1991, at the US National Cross-Country Championships in Franklin Park in Boston, a young kid from Tennessee, Todd Williams, all in Adidas green with his baseball cap on backward, stuck with Pat Porter as they traversed the park, lap after lap. Porter was the best cross-country runner in the United States. Williams was a nobody. This day, however, the University of Tennessee grad was sticking Pat Porter pretty hard, pushing the pace, until it came down to the two of them at the very end. Williams won going away. It was a theme that would appear frequently for him: going out hard, sticking it to the other guy, and finding out who had something left.

If the term, "No quarter asked, none given," could be used to describe an athlete, Todd Williams was such an athlete. Williams ran hard, raced hard, laughed hard, and did it with regularity—for nearly fifteen years—before he decided it was time to pursue other interests. He had to: "My first contract was for $8,000 with a few incentives written in," he recalled. In 1991, Williams moved into a self-described "shack" off campus in Knoxville, after wrapping up a good career at the University of Tennessee, living a Spartan lifestyle and training with his former coach.

"In the '90s, really talented guys had to get jobs and never saw their potential fully exposed," claimed Williams. It was only after he defeated Porter at that 1991 National Cross-Country Championship that he was able to cash in on those modest incentives and remain just above the poverty line. As a result, Williams went on to win four US 10K titles; two US cross-country titles; top-10 finishes at the 10,000 meters at the 1992 Olympics, and 1993 and 1995 World Championships; as well as a top-10 finish at the 1995 edition of World Cross. He still holds the US record for the 15K on the roads, but his 27:31 personal record for 10,000 meters has fallen from number four to outside the top 10 on the all-time US list in recent years.

Williams was the domestic leader at World Cross four times in the decade, and knew it was always going to be one of the hardest races of the year: "Pain, pain, pain! The whole race hurt because there was no pacing. It was all out from the gun and you're racing the best in the world from all distances. For example, in 1995 when I finished 9th, I went out close to the lead and we passed the 1k in 2:35 and I thought 'We still have a 11k to go!' I finished (as the top

American) in the top twenty all three senior runs and top 15 both junior runs so the pain was good."

Kennedy, who won four NCAA titles and became the second to win the NCAA and US cross-country titles in the same year, made out better with his first contract from Nike. But his deal was still modest by today's standards, and he too hung around his old campus to train with his old college coach, Sam Bell, and used some of the local resources.

"It was feast or famine for guys coming out of college those days," Kennedy said. "Companies were more invested in sprinters, the high-profile events. I was fortunate to get a feast contract, along with Mark Croghan and a couple of other guys. I think Todd [Williams] barely had enough to live on."

Kennedy eventually left Coach Bell in 1996 and joined Kim McDonald's international training group, with stints in Australia and London. Working with runners like world-record holders Daniel Komen and Moses Kiptanui, as well as miler Steve Holman, Kennedy's mileage shot up 20 miles to 115 miles per week, and he learned how to train like a Kenyan.

Everything was faster. More volume. Shorter rest. "Call it dumb luck or blissful ignorance, but before I knew what I was doing, I was doing it," Kennedy says. And his Kenyan regimen paid off: that year, Kennedy set American records in the 5,000 meters and became the first non-African to break 13:00.

But that didn't mean all American athletes handled those workouts well. "I joined the Kenyans for a workout once," Williams recalled. "It was a downward ladder of 1,600 meters, 1,200 meters, 800 meters and 400 meters. I ran the mile in 4:08. Komen started the workout with a 3:53. I took off my spikes and just threw them. I was like, 'That's it. That's ridiculous.' But, I knew that if Kenyans were in that much pain, then I'd have to find a way to hurt myself in training."

Williams created his own version of masochistic workouts. Two-mile repeats began with a 57-or 58-second first quarter. During repeat miles, he'd run the middle half-mile in two minutes. Williams stuck to the trails in Knoxville, running over 50,000 miles on the well-trod paths. When he needed group support, he trained with the team he helped coach at the University of Tennessee, giving his athletes a sizeable head start before catching them as quickly as possible and trying to hang on. "I forced myself to be in complete agony in every workout," he said. "My coach thought I was nuts."

Meanwhile, Kennedy, who was a Kinney National Cross-Country Champion in high school, an NCAA Cross-Country champion as a freshman in college, and a US National Cross-Country Champion in 1992, finished 14th overall at World Cross in 1995.

LYNN JENNINGS'S PERPETUAL MOTION

While Williams and Kennedy were placing internationally in cross-country for the men, there was no stronger athlete than Lynn Jennings for the American women. Her performances, which had led America in the 1980s, gave the US team a sense of hope internationally at World Cross, and it was continued dominance in the 1990s that sealed her legacy.

"Cross-country provides the basis of excellence for track success," Jennings told *Runner's World*. "And most kids get their start as runners in high school cross-country. I'd like to think that my success with cross-country could serve as a kind of beacon to them." As a beacon, Jennings was well ahead. Starting in the spring of 1990 she easily won the US cross-country trials in February, finished first at the IAAF World Cross in March, added another US National Cross-Country title in November, and started the subsequent winter by winning the Cross Auchan Tourcoing race in France in January.

In 1992, when the World Cross-Country Championships were held in Franklin Park in Boston, it was Jennings who chirped, "I knew everyone. All the technical people and all the officials on the starting line. My neighbors were here with their two children. It was like putting on a race in my own backyard. I wanted to stop and take it all in." By then, Jennings was a more seasoned, confident, and experienced runner. She had won World Cross twice (to that point), run a mile in 4:24, had won numerous national championships in track, cross-country, and on the roads and was being coached by John Babington (her high school mentor). After she crossed the line victorious by only two seconds—thrusting both her arms up in jubilation—Jennings promptly broke down sobbing. "I was crying tears of joy," she said later. "I never did that before."

After falling to third overall at the 1994 and 1995 US National Cross-Country Championship, Jennings rebounded in a big way. In December 1996 she came out to Palo Alto (after placing second to Amy Rudolph in the New England trials the month before) and won the US National Cross-Country Championship, the ninth title of her career. Jennings was one of the winningest individuals at the US National Cross-Country Championships, but in 20th overall that day came the decade's second major female star: Deena Drossin, who, at age twenty-three, was in a prime position to supplant Jennings as the United States's leading lady.

DEENA (DROSSIN) KASTOR, EARNING HER KEEP

It was clear from an early age that Deena Drossin would be a special distance runner. She won two California State high school cross-country titles while running for Agora Hills High School in Southern California (in 1989 and 1990). She made it to the Foot Locker National Cross-Country Championship all four years of her high school career. And in the fall of 1991, she appeared for the first time in the red and white jersey of the University of Arkansas Razorbacks, the nation's strongest Division I collegiate distance running program, under Coach John McDonnell.

Then, after accumulating eight NCAA Division I All-American awards and seven Southeastern Conference

Championship titles in cross-country and track during her career at Arkansas, Drossin was ready for the next step. But injuries had caused her to lose her enthusiasm for running after her sophomore year in college, and she worried that professional running might not be in her future. "Her collegiate career was good but not exceptional," said Joe Vigil, who began to train Drossin when she turned twenty-three. "She earned several All-American recognitions in both cross-country and track and field, but she never won a national championship. The outstanding talent she displayed as a high school runner was never realized in college."

"I knew if I was ever going to run well again, I needed to get into a new environment," Drossin said. Enter Mylon Donley, a former assistant at Arkansas who put Drossin in touch with Vigil. Vigil had guided Adams State College cross-country and track programs to twenty-five National Association of Intercollegiate Athletics (NAIA) and NCAA Division II titles during his tenure from 1965 to 1993 and continued coaching post-college runners after retiring. "Joe [Vigil] was the first coach I talked to," Drossin said. "But after talking to him, I just felt like he was the one to get me going and keep me motivated. He was so passionate about running."

Vigil helped spark Drossin to a slew of career-best performances. She placed sixth in the US trials for the World Cross-Country Championships in February 1997, and was the second American—and 29th finisher overall—at World Cross in Turin, Italy, in March. In track, she lowered her bests to 9:10 in the 3,000 meters, 15:43 in the 5,000, and 32:47 in the 10,000. But cross-country was always where she had her most success: "I love cross-country, that's deep in my bones. There is no purer sport. Running is the foundation of every sport and the embodiment of health and wellness. Cross-country elevates that notion with embodying pure grit and strength. I appreciate a good competition, but add the challenge of weather conditions and terrain to your race strategy, and it becomes so much more exhilarating."

In the 1990s she established herself as the heir to Lynn Jennings's throne, leading the way for the American females in the sport once Jennings stepped away. Drossin had run in the World Cross junior race in 1990 and '91, after she had finished third and fifth, respectively, in the US trials cross-country junior race. She won the Aztec Cross-Country Invitational in college, placed third in the Western Cross-Country Championships in 1996, and won the Arkansas Chile Pepper Invitational as a professional in 1997. She went on to win her first National Cross-Country title in 1997 before improving to 20th overall at World Cross. She finished second in Japan at the 1999 Chiba Cross-Country, then had her best finish ever: a 10th overall showing at World Cross in spring 1999. Within six weeks of the calendars shifting into the 2000s, Drossin went on to win her second National Cross-Country title. It was clear she was on the verge of making history.

But Deena Drossin and the rest of the American runners weren't the only ones trying to claw their way to international prominence. In Europe there were similar murmurings that the sport might have been at its lowest ebb since before the turn of the century. The reason seemed clear on the outset: the entirety of the Western world was attempting to catch the Africans in cross-country. The truth was more complicated.

FIGHT OF THE EUROPEANS

Bruce Tulloh, an English runner known just as much for his barefoot racing tendencies in the 1950s and '60s as his coaching prowess in the 1980s and '90s, offered a unique perspective on the subject of European might at the dawn of the decade:

In 1990 I was coaching a small group of ex-University distance runners, the best of whom was Richard Nerurkar. The previous year he had made the British team for the World Cross-Country Championships, but had finished only 5th in the 10,000-meter trial for the Commonwealth Games. Ahead of him were such people as Tim Hutchings, who had finished second in World Cross, and Eamonn Martin, who went on to beat Moses Tanui for the Commonwealth title. From a national point of view, it is obvious that when you have high standards in the 5K and 10K, more good runners are forced up or out. In 1989, Richard's 13:27 5,000-meter time put him only 9th in Britain, so he naturally chose a longer distance. However, that same time in 2003 would have put him top of the British 5,000-meter rankings.

So what happened? Tulloh continued:

Africa has millions of poor men and they are willing to work hard because they have nothing to lose. By contrast, the young men of the western world look more toward the affluent sports: skiing, sailing, motor racing, biking, rowing, triathlon and snowboarding. The decline in Northern European running has its roots in affluence. In my day, distance running strength came from the clubs in the big cities: Gateshead, Manchester, Liverpool, Portsmouth, Coventry and Derby. It was a sport that cost very little but gave one the chance of success and the glamour of travel. The car workers of Coventry won a stack of international medals thanks to the efforts of guys like Basil Heatley, but these days the glamour of travel is a far less elusive commodity.

The fact that more and more people are running has little connection with success at the international level, because the motivations are not the same. Just as the Ugandans are following the same path as the Kenyans, the British are following the same path as the Swedes and Finns. We have more food, more leisure, more money, more machines and more obesity, but also more diet books, more discos, more gyms, more sports scientists and more leisure clubs. Running is no longer a sport for hard-training introverts; it is part of the consumer society—a leisure activity involving a bit of gentle exercise, a bit of socializing and quite a lot of buying of designer gear. This is not to say that we will never produce any more great distance runners, but they are going to be few and far between.

Tulloh's fears were compounded with the recognition that traditionally strong nations were not reaching the same caliber of success as they had generations previously. Scotland, Ireland, and Wales, for example, did not qualify but two runners between them onto the 1989 United Kingdom World Cross-Country team (men and women combined). Scotland itself had no representatives. IAAF President Primo Nebiolo received the blame for this discrepancy. As the *Glasgow Herald* reported, "Nebiolo, president of the International Amateur Athletic Federation, had pressed for a single UK team and won his point when, for the first time, it was Great Britain who competed in New Zealand last year." The *Herald* went on to state: "[The] British Athletics Federation dominated by English votes controlled by the AAA and WAAA, accuse the Scots of paranoia when they question whether they will get a square deal. This experience will do nothing to calm their fears."

The reality was that while the British (and other European) teams were nowhere near the level that they were at in the 1960s and '70s, they remained competitive in international cross-country competitions sporadically throughout the '90s. Portugal did well among the European powers, finishing third three times for the senior men (in 1993, 1999, and 2000) and fourth-place five times more at World Cross. The Portuguese senior women also fared well, winning gold in 1994 and bronze in 1990 and 1999. Neighboring Spain finished with bronze medals for the senior men in 1990, '91, and '95. France was able to finish a surprise second for the senior men in 1992 at World Cross, while the British teams finished third in '92 for the senior men, and third for the women in 1998.

And while front-running names were for the most part absent from the "traditional" European powers, one runner from England was not afraid to go for it all—although her rise to prominence came from an unexpected place.

GOD SAVE THE QUEEN

In 1984, an eleven-year-old girl traveled from home in Bedford to watch her father run the London Marathon. As she waited, someone else caught her eye: the Norwegian runner Ingrid Kristiansen scything through the field to smash the women's world marathon record in a time of 2 hours, 21 minutes, 6 seconds. "It broke down any barriers I had in my head," said Paula Radcliffe. "I thought: why can't I be in there running and being competitive too?" That day at the marathon changed her, but success did not happen overnight.

Born in December 1973, Radcliffe spent most of her youth in Barnton where she attended Little Leigh Primary School. Despite suffering from asthma and anemia she took up running at the age of seven, and five years later, after the family moved to Bedfordshire, Radcliffe became a member of Bedford and County Athletics Club. Her joining the club coincided with a talented and dedicated coach, Alex Stanton, building the women's and girls' sections into two of the strongest in the country.

"I started coaching Paula when she was 12. But it was my wife Rosemary who first spotted her talent," said Stanton. "I was already working with three very good girls and I needed a fourth. She saw a gleam in Paula's eyes. And Paula came across as being someone who just loved running, both track and cross-country. She was just one of the girls on the team. She wasn't even the best in the group. Her progress was slow but it would come."

Radcliffe's father became club vice-chairman and her mother managed the women's cross-country team. Radcliffe's first race at a national level came as a twelve-year-old in 1986 when she placed 299th out of around 600 in the girls' race of the English Schools Cross-Country Championships. She finished fourth in the same race one year later.

"Paula didn't win a major race until her late teens," said Stanton. "But she was always a very organized girl. Her whole life was organized. And that really helped her in her preparation for progressing up to the top. She just worked incredibly hard. She first won the World Cross-Country Championships [junior title] in 1992 in her last year at school. It was at Boston in America. Our preparation was thorough. We knew what times the opponents would be running. And all we had to do was make sure that Paula could run faster than anybody else!"

Physiotherapist Gerard Hartmann, who had worked with 73 different Olympic medal winners throughout his career, claimed only Keith Wood, an Irish rugby player, could take more pain on the massage table than Radcliffe. Sports scientist Andrew Jones recalled that Radcliffe would prefer to fall off the back in exhaustion during treadmill tests rather than tell him to stop the machine. She was also blessed with something every great endurance athlete required: a huge engine. Tested at the age of seventeen (the same year as her 1992 World Cross junior win) by Jones, her VO_2 max—the maximum volume of oxygen an athlete can use—was seventy, higher than that of any female athlete ever tested.

"For someone who was so young and wasn't doing much training at the time, it suggested a lot of potential," said Jones. "While she shocked many by winning [in 1992], I wasn't surprised." Radcliffe's drive was legendary. She would regularly run 140 to 150 miles a week. Typically, she would run for two or three hours in the morning, followed by two hours of massage or physiotherapy. She would then sleep for up to two hours before a late afternoon run, again followed by massage, strengthening exercises, and ice baths for recovery.

By the time her junior years were behind her, Radcliffe had already made the transition smoothly into the elite ranks. She finished in the top 20 in the 1993 World Cross senior women's event and seventh in the World Championship 3,000 meters later that summer. Missing all of the 1994 season due to injury, Radcliffe made her first Olympic team in 1996 where she finished fifth in the 5,000 at the age of twenty-two. In 1999, Radcliffe won her first of only two World Championship track medals, finishing second in the 10,000 meters. In cross-country, Radcliffe won the European Championship in 1998 and finished third at World Cross in 1999. She would find more success in the early 2000s. "People look at the blonde girl from the outside and think butter wouldn't melt in her mouth," said Hartmann. "But beneath it all she was the hardest, toughest athlete I ever met. Somewhere she got this desire to be better than great."

But while Radcliffe was fighting for her place in the international cross-country pantheon, her biggest rivals weren't conceding an inch.

TULU POSES CHALLENGE TO THE THRONE

Born in the village of Bekoji in the highlands of Arsi Province, Ethiopia, Derartu Tulu got her start in distance running inauspiciously despite a strong farming background and a youth spent at altitude. Unaware of her own genetic prowess, she spent much of her early years horseback riding and tending cattle. Thankfully, Tulu discovered her talent when she started taking part in athletics competitions in her teens—her first significant win coming in a 400-meter race at her primary school where she out-ran the school's star *male* athlete. That performance, along with a win in the 800 meters in her district, convincingly put Tulu on a path to a successful career in distance running. In 1988, Tulu represented the Arsi region and competed in a national 1,500-meter event, winning a bronze medal in the process.

That year, Tulu went to work for the Ethiopian Police Force, and in 1989 she competed in her first international race, the six-kilometer senior women's World Cross-Country Championships in Norway, where she finished 23rd. A year later, she returned to the race and improved to 15th.

From then on, success came quickly. A runner-up finish at World Cross in 1991 was preceded by a win at the Chiba Cross-Country International in Japan and two bronze-medal runs at the Cinque Mulini. Next came wins in the County Durham Cross in England and the Les Mureaux Cross in France in 1993 and 1994. In 1995, she returned to the World Cross-Country Championships to win her first individual gold, an eight-second victory over Ireland's Catherina McKiernan. By the end of the decade Tulu had won the Juan Muguerza Memorial Cross, Cross Zornotza, and Cross International de San Sebastian (all in Spain); the Jan Meda International in Ethiopia; and the Cross Ouest in Le Mans, France; and won the World Cross title twice more.

It was Tulu who beat England's Paula Radcliffe and America's Deena Kastor in 2000 en route to her third title in five years at World Cross, and the runner-up in that event, Ethiopia's Getenesh Wami, was just as much a reason for

Tulu's individual success as she was a contributor to Ethiopia's national domination.

GETE WAMI CONTROLS THE PODIUM

Born and raised in the Ethiopian province of Birhan, Getenesh "Gete" Wami first made her mark in cross-country with a pair of top-10 finishes at the World Cross junior championships, finishing fifth overall in 1991 in Antwerp and ninth overall in 1992 in Boston. From there, a slew of victories and top-five finishes internationally opened the door for Wami and she found herself in prime position to win her first World Cross senior women's title. Starting in November 1995 with the Cross de l'Acier in France (a third-place finish), and culminating with her first senior-level win at the 1996 World Cross-Country Championships that following March in South Africa, Wami paced herself to eight finishes of sixth place or better—all in international cross-country meetings.

The following season Wami won or finished on the podium in cross-country races in the Netherlands, Spain, Belgium, and Northern Ireland. In all, Wami finished third in 1997 at World Cross, third in 1998, and first once again in 1999. In 2000 and 2001 there were back-to-back runner-up finishes at the World Cross-Country Championships. The first came to her countrymate Tulu, and the second came to Paula Radcliffe in a sprint finish under muddy conditions. With seven podium finishes in six years (counting an additional victory in the short-course race), Grete Wami's legacy in the sport was as significant as anyone's in the world.

And as Wami and Tulu led the way for Ethiopia in the 1990s, their women's team found lots of success as well. At World Cross, the Ethiopian senior women finished on the podium every year but one for the decade (1993). They finished first in 1997, '99, and 2000; second in '90, '91, '94, '95, '96 and '98; and third in '92. Following close behind in many cases came a surprise nation that also verified Europe had a few more aces up their sleeve for international cross-country prowess—the nation of Ireland, which finished top five three times in the decade, with their best finish a bronze medal in 1997. Leading the way for Ireland was none other than Sonia O'Sullivan, a hard-working and highly motivated runner who felt it was her national duty to challenge the Africans in cross-country.

SONIA O'SULLIVAN: IRELAND'S MAIDEN

Born in November 1969 in Cobh, County Cork, Sonia O'Sullivan began her running career as a member of Ballymore Running Club (located on the eastern side of Cobh). After doing moderately well in local competitions, and winning the NCAA Cross-Country Championships as a member of Villanova University, O'Sullivan's first major international competition was the 1990 European Track Championships, where she finished 11th in the 3,000 meters. By 1992, she crossed the line seventh overall in the World Cross-Country Championships senior women's race in Boston. And three years later, with another NCAA Cross-Country title under her belt, the twenty-five-year-old O'Sullivan was on top of the world, setting a meet record of 14:46 to win the 5,000 meters at the 1995 World Track Championships in Gothenburg.

O'Sullivan began 1996 as the favorite for gold at the Atlanta Olympics, and though she entered the Olympics unbeaten on the year, she battled an upset stomach on the day of the 5,000 final and failed to finish the race. Three days later, she was 10th in her 1,500 heat and failed to advance to the final. The occasion was a "complete failure," according to O'Sullivan.

However, with a new contract in hand two years later in 1998, O'Sullivan and her coach Alan Storey circled the World Cross-Country Championships on their calendars as the race O'Sullivan would focus on. A win there would prove that the twenty-eight-year-old O'Sullivan could still contend among the world's best.

But first, O'Sullivan had to decide which race she was going to run. In 1998 the IAAF had shifted to a four-race format, with short and long races for each gender (for the women, the distances would be 4K and 8K), and in January, Storey called O'Sullivan to find out which race she would run. O'Sullivan was still debating between the two when Storey told her "everyone knows the real race is the long course." That settled things. "Without any discussion, I wasn't going to argue with that statement: I was running the long race," O'Sullivan said. "So once my mind was made up, then I was focused on the long race."

O'Sullivan's buildup included several weeks of 100+ miles, running as many as 118 during the first week of March (though in reality, that total was probably a little low). O'Sullivan calculated her mileage based on a 7:00-mile pace on her easy days, though Storey estimated that O'Sullivan's easy pace was closer to a 6:30-mile. Her goal in any buildup was always to get to 100 miles per week and then focus on running those miles more efficiently. By the end of the cycle, 100-mile weeks were "routine and became easy to me," claimed O'Sullivan.

As the calendar turned to March, everything was falling into place. O'Sullivan's tune-up races had gone well, and perhaps most importantly, she and Storey had developed the rhythm that they previously had lacked. "Alan Storey started coaching me towards the end of 1996," O'Sullivan said. "In 1997, we were getting used to this coaching arrangement and after an unsuccessful World Championships, I agreed to listen more to Alan and put behind me what I used to do before rather than complicating things by referring back to my earlier training methods."

Back at sea level in Australia, O'Sullivan completed a session of 10 × 800 meters with 30 seconds rest averaging 2:31 and knew afterwards that she was in great shape. "My confidence was pretty high after this session," O'Sullivan said. "I couldn't believe how relaxed I was and how easy the session felt." Even the day before the race, O'Sullivan was still logging mileage, running for 40 minutes in the morning and supplementing it with 20 minutes in the evening for a total of nine miles.

African runners had claimed the last four World Cross titles on the women's side and with hot temperatures on race day, many expected that streak to continue. The conditions didn't faze O'Sullivan, however, as she had spent the Australian summer training in the Southern Hemisphere, so she was accustomed to running in the heat. O'Sullivan recounted:

> In the long race, the main thing for me was to keep up and stay relaxed for as long as possible, and when I felt I was still strong and ready to push hard while others started to drop off I would make my final move and sprint as fast as I could to the finish. When the finish line was in sight, there was just myself, Paula [Radcliffe] and Gete Wami remaining, I was confident of outsprinting both the closer we got to the finish line. As we turned the corner, an official directed us back to run another lap of the course rather than run in to the finishing straight. I started my sprint as I was confident it was the last lap—we heard the bell and I hadn't miscounted—so I sprinted parallel to the finishing straight remembering from my jog on the course the night before that there was a little gap in the fence just before the finish line. I nipped through the gap and everyone followed me.

Just as she had planned, O'Sullivan sprinted away from the competition to win the 8K race in 25:39, three seconds ahead of Radcliffe. The win was clearly special for O'Sullivan: "I had really been through a roller coaster the previous two years, so to be able to get back out and transform the form I knew I had in training to winning a World Championship race was so satisfying and gave me a lot of confidence. I knew I was back."

And that was that. O'Sullivan went back to her hotel and was basking in the glow of victory while lounging around the pool with former coach Kim McDonald and American Bob Kennedy. Both were under the impression that she was running the next day's 4K race and even though O'Sullivan had no plans to do so, but once the thought entered her mind, it became an appealing option. Her name was already on the start list, so she quickly informed Athletics Ireland not to scratch her. The double attempt was on.

There were a few obstacles before she could get to the start line, however. She had to clean her equipment and uniform, which were still muddy from that morning's race, and she had no way of getting in contact with Storey. On the walk to the course the next morning, McDonald let her borrow his phone and she was finally able to call Storey, who voiced his concern. Storey was worried that the confidence O'Sullivan had earned the day before—which had taken two years to rebuild—might be thrown away by a disappointing performance in the 4K race. O'Sullivan assured him that that was not the way she was approaching the race, likening it to a tennis player who wins the singles tournament and enters the doubles competition as a bonus. "I assured him no matter what the result I would accept it and not be disappointed as I felt there was no one in the race I couldn't at least keep up with and I couldn't tell how I would feel until actually back in the race again."

After she was dropped just 800 meters into the race, it looked like O'Sullivan might have made a mistake: "A slight panic set in," O'Sullivan said. "'Did I make the right decision?' Then I realized this was a tactic to scare me. I had to relax and realize this pace could not be maintained by Anita Weyermann (Switzerland) and Kutre Dulecha (Ethiopia)."

Regaining her confidence, O'Sullivan led the chase pack and caught Weyermann and Dulecha at the 3K mark. Sensing that they were tiring, O'Sullivan blew right by them rather than waiting until the end to sprint away and wound up winning the short race by 14 seconds (she ran 12:20 to runner-up Zahra Ouaziz's 12:34). She had become the first person to sweep the long/short races at World Cross; in the nine years of the long and short format, only one other woman (Tirunesh Dibaba) was able to match that feat.

THE MIGHTY VILLANOVA WOMEN

O'Sullivan's strength was not such a mystery after studying her alma mater. For the greater part of the twentieth century, Villanova University in Pennsylvania was known for its great male milers. When women received NCAA eligibility in 1981, Villanova shifted its dynastic ambitions to women's cross-country. With individual stars such as Vicki Huber, Carole Zajac, Jen Rhines, and Carrie Tollefson (along with O'Sullivan), Villanova dominated women's cross-country from 1989 to 1998. The Wildcats won seven NCAA team titles and finished twice more on the podium. To better understand the Wildcats' dominance, consider this: every Villanova women's cross-country runner in the 1990s was a member of at least one NCAA Championship team. And two athletes, Nnenna Lynch and Becky Spies, were also named Rhodes Scholars.

The dynasty began due to the efforts of Coach Marty Stern. Stern took the Villanova reins from Bob Shoudt in 1984 and immediately elevated the Wildcats' women's program into a national collegiate powerhouse, producing thirty-seven All-Americans and eight NCAA individual champions even before the first women's cross-country title. "When I wasn't running [as a youth growing up], I'd be the coach," said Stern. "I just knew that was my God-given talent. I loved to lead people. I was either going to be a general or a coach. They don't shoot at you too often when you're a coach, so that seemed like the safest way to go. It's really fascinating how dreams turn out. I was going to the Penn Relays press conference with Vicki Huber recently, and we're going up the steps and she turns to me and says, 'This is amazing, isn't it? You're really doing this now. You're living it out.'" Prior to Villanova's first team title in 1989, Stern had coached track for twenty-six years at a range of levels—from Interboro Junior High to high school to Division III Delaware Valley College—after having graduated from West Chester University in 1959.

That first team championship win thirty years later in the fall of 1989 came as a culmination of hard work and veteran leadership. Four of the top five scorers for the Lady Wildcats were juniors or seniors—led by the top individual finish of senior Vicki Huber, who won the championship by 27 seconds (running 15:59 for 5K). Four consecutive titles followed. Sonia O'Sullivan, who finished an admirable 26th overall in 1989, came back and led Villanova to their second title in a row in 1990 by winning the individual championship. Then, she and the Lady Wildcats did it again in 1991, with Carole Zajac the second finisher overall. Villanova was slowly inching toward perfection.

Along the way Stern was holding the reigns steady: "Everybody thinks I'm a wild guy who wears funny hats and drinks tequila all day long. Maybe I drink tequila once in a while and I do wear funny hats, and maybe I am crazy. But one thing I do is work hard. What we've accomplished isn't an accident," he claimed. Zajac led the way in 1992 to a fourth straight Villanova individual and team championship. Then it was five in a row in 1993, again with the top two finishers and three in the top seven.

But in a surprise move that stunned friends and fueled conjecture, Marty Stern announced his retirement just four months after securing his fifth straight women's cross-country national title. Citing the demands of travel and a desire to spend more time with his family, Stern said, "I'm tired of packing my suitcase every week. I was starting to lose my enthusiasm, and I don't want to do that. I got to the point where I was tired of missing [my] daughters' school plays and soccer games." Sources familiar with the track program said they believed that Stern, aged fifty-seven, had been forced to resign. They claimed that the Villanova administration failed to back Stern or to extend his contract, which was set to expire on August 1, and that several Villanova athletes had complained to his superiors about his coaching methods.

"There's a lot more to this than a coach tired of the road," said one source. "It was almost like a conspiracy to drive him out." But in Stern's place came Villanova alumnus John Marshall, a 1984 US Olympian and member of the athletic staff. By the fall of 1994, it seemed to be back to business as usual. Jennifer Rhines became the fourth individual Villanova champion in six years, and the Lady Wildcats added their sixth straight team title to the trophy case.

But soon, things changed once again. 1995 and 1996 had seen the Wildcats on the podium, with third- and second-place performances, respectively—but by the spring of 1998, Marshall was also out the door. Marshall told the *Daily News* that Villanova, for reasons he did not know, had attempted "in any way possible" to prevent him from continuing his coaching career. "It's very difficult to find work when an employer does everything possible to prevent someone from carrying on in his pursuits," Marshall said. "Hopefully, this will change all that and I can move on with my life." When Villanova announced in June that Marshall would not return as coach, Villanova portrayed the move as Marshall's decision. Marshall emphatically contradicted the announcement at the time, saying the decision was not his.

Expectedly, many Villanova runners publicly expressed support of Marshall when the news of his dismissal broke. Distance runner Kate Etter led the outcry, calling for the athletic administration to end the "politics" at the school and reinstate Marshall. Marcus O'Sullivan, another Villanova graduate from Ireland, was hired June 22, 1998, to replace Marshall. In spite of the controversy, or perhaps in a move of solidarity, the Villanova Lady Wildcats again won the NCAA Cross-Country Championship, their seventh title in 10 runnings of the event.

Only one other program in NCAA cross-country was as dominant as Villanova during the 1990s, and their supremacy at the top surprised no one. The University of Arkansas Razorbacks won eight national cross-country team championships between 1990 and 2000, and they added two more runner-up finishes. This was a continuation of the seven podium finishes they had amassed in the 1980s. Overall, it was proof that the Razorbacks were nearly unstoppable when it came to having the best male collegiate distance runners in the country.

ARKANSAS CONTINUES THEIR REIGN

Along with South Carolina, the University of Arkansas joined the Southeastern Conference (SEC) for the start of the 1991–92 season. The SEC was a loaded league that included Florida, Tennessee, Louisiana State, Georgia, Alabama, Auburn, Kentucky, Mississippi State, Mississippi, and Vanderbilt.

The departure of Arkansas was the first of many dominoes to fall in what would eventually lead to the complete demise of the Southwest Conference and the formation of the Big 12 Conference four years later. And as the new decade began, Arkansas coach John McDonnell was strategically planning for the future. While his program had won three NCAA Cross-Country Championships and his roster had as many as 60 athletes on it, McDonnell continued to spend days studying his competition to determine their strengths and weaknesses—a necessity in light of the NCAA's decision to limit all major universities to only 12.6 athletic scholarships.

Because of this, Arkansas still maintained strong recruiting classes. In 1990 Louisiana state champion Mike Morin joined the Razorbacks, along with Dan Munz and Dewayne Miner, both 4:10 milers from Missouri. Graham Hood and Niall Burton were also added—two promising young athletes with different attitudes from different parts of the world.

A graduate of St. Aidans College in Dublin, Ireland, Bruton showed range from the 400 meters (48.8) to the two mile (8:42) and even led Ireland at the World Cross-Country Junior Championships. "He liked to sit and kick," said McDonnell. "To outkick Niall you had to be awfully good."

Graham Hood had graduated from Nelson High School in Burlington, Ontario, Canada, and showed similar range

to Bruton's, having run 1:48 for 800 meters and competing at the World Cross-Country Junior Championships. The difference was that he had significantly fewer miles on his legs when he arrived in Fayetteville. "I'd tell each of them how to win so it was very simple," said McDonnell. "Niall had the advantage over Graham because he had more leg speed and a better kick over the last 150 meters but Graham could maintain a long drive from 350 meters out. They both won their share of battles."

That year the Razorbacks put up a perfect score in their final Southwest Conference meet and looked ready to take back the cross-country national title. "Iowa State is a great team but we'll be ready for them," McDonnell confidently told the media. "We've won three national cross-country championships and would like to win another."

But on a tough course with long gradual hills throughout, McDonnell knew the challenge would be tough with such a young team. "To be honest I didn't think we could win it," remembered McDonnell, "but I told our guys it will be thirty minutes of hell for three-hundred and sixty five days of glory. They did exactly what I asked them to do and we turned the tables on Iowa State."

Although Iowa State's Jonah Koech took the individual win (followed by teammate Jon Brown 20 seconds later in fourth), Arkansas won the meet by 28 points, 68 to 96, with four runners in the top 25. And had it not been for the freshman Niall Bruton, hanging on in 44th place, Arkansas would have been empty-handed.

The following year Arkansas had an embarrassment of riches during the 1991 cross-country season. Combined with the additions of David Gurry, an 8:56 high school two-miler from Seattle, as well as Alex Dressell, an 8:14 3,000-meter transfer from the University of Texas, and John Schiefer, a 4:05 mile transfer from the University of Utah, it was hard to see any other team matching the Razorbacks' depth of talent.

The real surprise of the year was Graham Hood—to everyone but himself. After a great summer of training, Hood arrived in Fayetteville determined to prove he belonged in the varsity top-seven. And after opening the season with a personal-best time, the Canadian gained momentum as the season progressed: "I planned on making the team in cross-country that fall," said Hood. "I don't think Coach McDonnell did because I didn't make the travel squad going to Stanford, and there definitely wouldn't have been any guys going to beat for me to travel to Stanford based on what I had done the fall before." After a strong meet at Oklahoma State, Hood continued his astonishing rise by finishing sixth overall at the Chile Pepper Invitational, Arkansas's home meet, on October 19.

"I still remember the look on Coach McDonnell's face when I went by the 5K mark," laughed Hood. "He was pretty shocked. After the race, he was like, 'Yeah, kid, you're on your way on this team.'" For Hood, it all came together at the 1991 NCAA Cross-Country Championships, held at El Conquistador Country Club in Tucson, Arizona. Not only did the redshirt freshman half-miler make the top seven of the Arkansas team, but he finished seventh overall in a race in which Arkansas easily outpaced Iowa State, 52 to 114, for its fifth NCAA Cross-Country Championship, and second in a row. It was an astonishing and eye-opening feat leading into an Olympic year.

For the 1992 NCAA Cross-Country Championship in Bloomington, Indiana, however, the weather and travel experience created more of a nightmare than anything the team had ever experienced. The athletes had a firsthand understanding of the terror of being in a distressed airplane at 30,000 feet.

"There was a tornado and horrible weather in Indiana," remembered McDonnell. "Everywhere flights were cancelled. Then when they tried to land the plane in Chicago, the landing gear wouldn't release, so they had to prepare for a crash landing after they circled for an hour. They were trying to get the landing gear to drop down. Finally a guy opened up a trap door and the landing gear released." The shock of the experience really shook the team up. "Niall said several rosaries," recalled McDonnell. "He said, 'I knew I was going to die.' He was so scared."

When the team finally regrouped to preview the course, Mother Nature had other ideas. "The tornado was still on us, and the siren was on," said McDonnell. "So all of a sudden there was an announcement: 'Everyone off the course!' You're thinking what else is going to go wrong?" But once the meet finally got underway, Arkansas had a nearly flawless performance. The Razorbacks ran aggressively from the gun. They were briefly challenged by Wisconsin midway through the race before surging over the final kilometers to win with a school record of 46 points. "This is the proudest I've ever been of a group of guys after what happened with our plane almost crashing and not having two of our top runners in Baker and Hood," McDonnell told the media afterwards. "Very few teams in any sport could have left two of their best athletes at home and still won a national championship. We ran into trouble midway through the race, but our guys really sucked it up and showed a lot of character at the end."

After an early-season loss at their home meet in 1993 to Lubbock Christian and James Brungei (by a margin of 64–73), Arkansas took the red shirt off Niall Bruton. It proved to be a good decision. At the 1993 NCAA Cross-Country Championship, at a fast course at Lehigh in Bethlehem, Pennsylvania, the Razorbacks were leading by over 100 points midway through the race. Jason Bunston and Niall Bruton finished second and third, and Teddy Mitchell finished eighth. Arkansas outpaced second-place Brigham Young, 31 to 153.

It was one of the more dominating performances in collegiate cross-country history and matched UTEP's record of four consecutive NCAA Cross-Country titles. "People wonder why we were good," said McDonnell. "We were good because we worked our ass off. I worked sixteen-hour days for years. It was just ridiculous when I look back at it. We contacted everyone and shook every tree and got the people in that we wanted." Shaking every tree for talent had resulted in getting runners like Phil Price, who ran a 4:12 mile out of Oklahoma, the fastest

mile by a high schooler in state history, and Ryan Wilson of Westlake, California, who had won the California state cross-country meet and qualified for the Kinney National Cross-Country Championships in 1992.

The 1994 season was a disappointing one for the Razorbacks, who almost lost their first conference cross-country championship in twenty years. The 1994 SEC Cross-Country Championship found Arkansas unexpectedly behind Tennessee with less than 800 meters remaining in the race. "Oh, we had them," remembered Tennessee coach Doug Brown, whose team was ranked number 12 nationally heading into the meet. "We had five or six good runners and nailed it that day. I have to give Arkansas credit. Everyone was hurting coming up that last hill and we had them beat, but they dug down and found a way." The final score was Tennessee 42 points, Arkansas 38. Arkansas failed to win a fifth straight NCAA National Championship that year and slipped to tenth overall.

Though many of the underclassmen on the Arkansas roster would mature and develop significantly during the following year, the addition of Godfrey Siamusiye from Blinn College in January 1995 dramatically changed the Razorbacks' fortune. Siamusiye had won everything at the junior college level, and though he was recruited all over the country, he chose Fayetteville to showcase his talent.

And from the get-go, he had one training gear: fast. "I loved it because he cooked everything, and I finally had someone trying to drop me the first mile of a fourteen mile run," said Jason Bunston. "I had been pining for someone who liked to train hard all the time, and when Godfrey got there, I finally had someone who wanted to burn it every day." The two of them regularly ran the 12-mile airport loop in 1:02 or under. "I had to be careful with both of them," remembered McDonnell. "The one thing Africans do all the time is all-out running. There is no jogging, so I learned something about the hard running and cutting back on the distance. They weren't bitching about somebody setting the pace. They took it. You have to have leaders like that."

That year, bringing a young team short on experience to Iowa State for the 1995 NCAA Cross-Country Championships (where Arkansas sought to upend the defending national champions on their home course), McDonnell knew strategy would play an important role. "Coach looked at me in the eye in the hotel in the morning and said, 'You're going to win, and if you win, we'll win as a team too,'" said Godfrey Siamusiye. After attacking the first mile as McDonnell had instructed, Godfrey threw everything at Mark Carroll, his biggest challenger, to shake him, even setting his watch to beep every two minutes to remind himself to throw in a small surge. "Godfrey was the best cross-country runner I have ever seen," said Ryan Wilson. "Every turn, corner, hill, and dip he cleared time on you. He had an innate ability to run courses better than anyone else. He killed runners on the country that would beat him on the track."

With Siamusiye and Carroll still running stride for stride at four miles, the Zambian made a devastating move to finish the Irishman off. "I had spoken to John [McDon-nell] before, and we reckoned if I took a chance and ran the last two miles quick, maybe at 4:30 to 4:40 for a mile at that point, I would break away," said Godfrey. "So we trained that way. I went as hard as I could for probably four minutes, and I looked back and I had a 100 meter lead, and I realized nobody would catch me. Everyone was getting tired and it was cold too." Godfrey won his first NCAA Cross-Country Championship by an incredible 36 seconds ahead of Carroll. With Ryan Wilson finishing in fifth and the others in the top 50, the Razorbacks unexpect-edly won their fifth NCAA Cross-Country Championship in six years by edging Ron Mann's Northern Arizona team and their early season nemesis from Oklahoma State by 50 points.

VIN LANANNA RELOCATES TO GREENER PASTURES

It was the summer of 1992 when Vin Lananna moved to Palo Alto, California, and inherited the lackluster Stan-ford University Cardinal cross-country program, which had been previously coached by Brooks Johnson. "[Stan-ford head coach] is the only position in the country that I've always been interested in," Lananna said. "This year everybody starts with a clean slate. Working with intelli-gent women and men, there needs to be proof for the ath-letes that they can have the confidence in me to identify reasonable goals. Stanford's results, recently, haven't been all that great, but once it gets rolling, the momentum will be self-perpetuating. My goal is to jump-start the team, to get it moving." With help for recruitment coming from athletic director Ted Leland (who had also been in charge at Dartmouth while Lananna was there), the future looked bright for the Cardinal with Lananna at the helm.

After guiding Dartmouth to runner-up NCAA cross-country finishes out of the Ivy League in 1986 and 1987 from the dreary trenches of cold New Hampshire, it was natural to wonder what Lananna was capable of once he had the reins in sunny Palo Alto. Even John McDon-nell of Arkansas knew Lananna's relocation was a threat to the Razorbacks: "We were checking in when John came up to me and said, 'Congratulations on getting the job,'" remembered Lananna. "I said it's going to be a lot of work because we were really terrible. John said, 'You're going to be a pain in my neck.'"

In 1992, Lananna guided Cardinal senior Gary Stolz to a runner-up finish at the NCAA Cross-Country Cham-pionship, while senior Louise Watson was named Pac-10 Athlete of the Year. The following season, the Stanford women's team won the Pac-10 conference crown for the first time in eight years. And in 1994, just three years into Lananna's tenure at Stanford, the Cardinal made a big splash in the national team races, when both the men's and women's squads managed top-10 finishes at the NCAA meet, finishing sixth and seventh, respectively. Two years later, after stabilizing a new tradition of suc-cess, the Cardinal was on the verge of making NCAA

history, and were set to dethrone the powerful Arkansas legacy.

Having won the pre-national meet on the course that same season, a resurgent Stanford program under Vin Lananna was prepared for the first time to challenge Arkansas in 1996. Unlike ten years earlier at Dartmouth, Lananna now had athletes with more natural talent and leg speed to handle whatever punishing pace Arkansas set during the first few miles of the race. "I loved the way [the Arkansas] teams ran. [They] intimidated everyone," admit-ted Lananna. "We didn't have the talent to run like that at Dartmouth but we did at Stanford. The Hauser Twins [Brad and Brent] had told me their goal was to rebuild Stanford. We had two seniors [Greg Jimmerson and Jeremy White] who were part of my first recruiting class, and I told them they would contend for an NCAA championship by their senior year. So I was running out of time."

After running aggressively alongside Arkansas at the 1996 NCAA Championship, Stanford exceeded expecta-tions and handled the heat better than anyone else. The Cardinal won its first NCAA Cross-Country Champion-ship over Arkansas, 46 to 74, despite another individual win by Godfrey Siamusiye in the final race of his collegiate career. Though Siamusiye appeared to have a bright future in the sport ahead of him, the Zambian was soon felled by a nasty stomach parasite requiring an operation that essentially ended his running career.

When John McDonnell had magnanimously congrat-ulated Vin Lananna in a hotel lobby in 1992 on accepting the Stanford job and commented that he was going to be a "pain in my neck," perhaps even McDonnell might not have realized how true his words would be less than five years later. After winning an incredible 26 out of a pos-sible 38 national championships between January 1984 and June 1996, the Arkansas juggernaut was significantly slowed by the revival of the Stanford program. Whether it was during cross-country season, on the track, or in the recruiting wars, the pain in John McDonnell's neck ema-nating from Palo Alto, California, would only intensify over time.

"Stanford is different than some of the other private schools," said McDonnell. "They have such a name academ-ically, and distance runners have such strong grades that sometimes they can get their school paid for purely academ-ically. I ran up against them all of the time. My gosh, a schol-arship to Stanford? If you had a son yourself, and Stanford or Arkansas kept calling and there was a full scholarship at both, you would probably want him to go to Stanford, and I wouldn't blame you. When Vin got there he really pushed that and was supposedly pretty arrogant about it like, 'I'm here to recruit you.' He had four aces. How could you miss? I'd have done the same thing if I was there."

In 1996, Stanford won both the men's and women's NCAA Cross-Country titles—the first time a team had done so since 1985. Stanford cross-country became a national contender every year thereafter.

The drama continued to unfold the following season. After the surprising loss to the Cardinal at the previous season's NCAA Championship, the Arkansas Razorbacks were focused on taking back their national title at Furman University in South Carolina. It certainly wouldn't be easy. Stanford had registered a perfect score at the Pac-10 Championships.

"I got the impression talking to John that he didn't think we were very good [in 1996]," said Lananna. "I knew in 1997 there was no chance he was going to get surprised again. When John wore his white warm-ups, which I called his medal warm-ups, I was always worried. That's when I knew he was confident they were going to win." The morning of the national meet Lananna saw McDonnell decked out in white. "John loved being at Arkansas and being on top," said Lananna. "He loved that role. He set the bar and went for it every time."

With a fast course for the championship, the Razorbacks pushed the pace faster than ever before and dared everyone to go with them. "Arkansas took that thing out so hard that we were running as fast as we could, and we couldn't catch them," said Lananna. "He had a great team that year. If you asked him the one he was most confident he was going to win, it would have to be that one. I thought he was going to win too." Standing on a green at the second mile, McDonnell watched as every one of his athletes found themselves in the front pack. "Seneca was in the top ten and Ryan Wilson was pushing the pace," said McDonnell. "We had a bunch of guys up there and probably got too excited." That became apparent as the race wore on. Adam Dailey faded to 50th while Seneca Lassiter fell back to 78th. Yet with four runners in the top 20 places, Arkansas still controlled the race with two miles remaining. Of concern was Arkansas's fifth runner, Murray Link, who was running well but beginning to fade while Stanford's fifth runner, Jonathan Riley, was passing runners by the dozen.

"In the last 2,000 meters, the whole face of it changed," said Lananna. "We moved up and they were coming back. Jonathan Riley was in the mid-30s and coming down the hill passing people. McDonnell was there with sweat pouring down his face. He was worried, but so was I. He said to me, 'What do you think?' 'It'll be close,' I said. 'Down to the final straightaway.'"

Ryan Wilson crossed the line in fifth place but was bested by Meb Keflezighi of UCLA to end his perfect season. Sean Kaley and Mike Power finished shortly thereafter in ninth and twelfth, respectively. "We came down the final stretch and I remember Coach was just screaming, 'You gotta keep picking them off!'" said Phil Price. "It was a 600 meter straight shot to the finish, and it came down to the final straightaway. I just remember coming down that hill exhausted, and I saw the Hauser guy in front of me, and Coach was yelling, 'You gotta get him to win the meet!' I don't think I've ever kicked so hard in my life and used so many gears."

By the time Phil Price outkicked Brent Hauser to finish 15th, Arkansas had a five-point lead over Stanford through its first four runners. Yet when Stanford's fifth man, freshman Jonathan Riley, passed six runners on the final straightaway to finish a remarkable 23rd, all eyes turned to Murray Link. A decade after imploring surprise fifth runner Doug Consiglio to finish strong against a Lananna-coached Dartmouth team at the NCAA Championships, McDonnell was once again relying on a Canadian running over his head to pull the team's chestnuts from the fire. "I remember with a kilometer to go he's there yelling at me, 'Come on, kid.'" said Link. "He said I took off like a scalded dog and was picking guys off left and right before dying pretty hard at the end and getting picked off." Though it took some time for the final tally to be announced, Stanford won its second consecutive NCAA Cross-Country Championship by the razor-thin margin of 53 to 56.

"That was my fault," said McDonnell. "Murray Link was running the race of his life, and with six hundred meters to go, I said you have to get those guys. He passed about ten guys and then died. He lost those places and then gave some more back. If I had said nothing, he would have held what he had. Gosh he was devastated, but I said it's not your fault. We had other guys that could have done things."

Quickly McDonnell reloaded his distance squad in an effort to win back the cross-country national championship. Heading to the Rim Rock Farm north of Lawrence, Kansas, for the 1998 NCAA Cross-Country Championships, Arkansas was the decided underdog against a Stanford team that had won the previous two titles. This time it was Stanford who ran more aggressively and assertively early in a race that quickly bottlenecked around a sharp turn one-half mile into the race.

"I'm not sure what [Lananna] told them but the first time up the hill Stanford was pushing it and ended up paying the price," said McDonnell. "They ended up bombing out. It was a tough course at Kansas, and we were used to running hills." With two miles remaining, Arkansas controlled the race. Sean Kaley was locked in a battle for the lead with Adam Goucher of Colorado and Abdi Abdirahman of Arizona, before Goucher blew everyone's doors off by more than 20 seconds. Kaley fell back to fifth, but more concerning was Mike Power, who was unable to finish the race after running in the top 20. Despite the hiccup late in the race, Arkansas beat Stanford, 97 to 114, for the national championship. "It seemed like Stanford changed their strategy, and it backfired on them just as it backfired on us the year before," said McDonnell. "You take chances. They beat us [in 1997] at Furman when they shouldn't have and then [in 1998] they were loaded and we beat them at Kansas. It goes to show you that there is never a sure thing."

To cap the decade, the Razorbacks won the National Cross-Country Championship again in 1999, a slaughtering of 58 to 185 over second-year coach Jerry Schumacher and the University of Wisconsin. The margin of victory was the largest by an Arkansas team at a national meet. "Those were the good days," said McDonnell, rubbing his hands together. "That was the most beautiful race to watch. We had six in the top twenty when they came by at four miles."

THE WETMORE FACTOR

While Villanova had an eight-year podium appearance record for the decade for the women, and the Arkansas men recorded nine podium appearances, teams like Stanford—who split their podium appearances between the women (four times) and men (three times) in the 1990s—were becoming the new model for athletic programs seeking cohesive balance among both genders at the top. Mark Wetmore, the coach of the University of Colorado (CU) program, wasn't interested in streaks—but he knew he could make *all* his runners great with a few key ingredients, and the natural benefits of training in the Boulder, Colorado area.

"We work hard for ourselves, but we also work hard for him because he works so hard for us," said 1998 NCAA Cross-Country champion Adam Goucher. "I don't know any other coaches who would sacrifice like he does. He's in his office every day, even in the summertime. He's always at work. He conveys a work ethic that everyone feeds off of. It's just unspoken."

In 1994, in Wetmore's first fall as the established distance coach for the men, he organized an impromptu meeting. Alan Culpepper was there, coming off a year where he garnered three All-American certificates when Wetmore was coaching as an assistant. The other runners were primarily unestablished junior varsity kids. Wetmore started by giving the team some information about his training methodology before he rather abruptly started talking about his plans for establishing "a new era" in CU distance running. In the process, CU runner Tom Reese said, "He gave us a little insight into his character."

According to Reese, Wetmore shared the following: "Look, this is what I am," Wetmore claimed. "This [coaching] is my main job. I don't play golf. I don't have many hobbies. I don't have a wife. The bottom line is I'm here to make you guys run fast. When I go to sleep at night, my mind's churning, thinking of ways to make you fast. I want you guys to be businesslike in your approach; think like Clint Eastwood. We work every day, and when we go to town, we tie up the horse, spit on the dog, and we leave without a word. We do our talking with our legs." Thus were communicated the principles for success that would be bestowed on an underperforming team without much heritage—a team that would build a legacy lasting decades.

Mark Wetmore moved to Boulder from Bernardsville, New Jersey, and within "24 hours of moving to Boulder" he had discovered Magnolia Road. He was running it "probably the first Sunday I was living in Boulder." This was not by accident. He said, "Knowing where I am going to run is pretty important to me. I take the trouble to get a map, usually a topographical map, and I look for a squiggly wavy road. That usually means it is a little out of the way dirt road."

Few runners knew of Magnolia Road then, and Wetmore said, "The only person I saw up there in the first couple of months was Arturo." (Arturo Barrios was the former 10,000-meter world record-holder from Mexico.) "If I coach here," Wetmore shared with the current CU crop, "you'll be here every Sunday."

Then-CU head coach Jerry Quiller had been searching for a volunteer assistant coach to help with the distance runners, and Wetmore, who had been working at Seton Hall on the East Coast, knew it was time for a change: "It came to a point there when I thought that was as far as I could get in that setting," Wetmore shared. "And so I decided to risk it a little bit and head west."

Wetmore's initial charges were the disgruntled and underachieving middle-distance runners on Quiller's squad, and runner Jason Drake (JD) epitomized the group. A 1989 graduate of Campbell County High School in Gillette, Wyoming, Drake was the first schoolboy in Wyoming state history to run the mile under 4:20 (he ran 4:13). Others in the group included Andy Samuelson, a miler from Colorado who ran 4:11 for 1,600 meters at elevation to win his division at the Colorado state championships, and Mike Sobolik, a miler from Pueblo, Colorado. Alan Culpepper, a 3:50 high school 1,500-meter runner from Texas, also fell under Wetmore's charge.

But despite their top-shelf credentials, neither Andy Samuelson nor JD had qualified for a single conference final in four years. Each also had a full scholarship, along with Culpepper. None of the runners had ever made a varsity cross-country team. They were dispirited and ready to try anything. Clearly, there was a lot of work to be done.

The first change Wetmore made was to add a long run to their program. Said JD, "Every Sunday morning we would do Mags [Magnolia Road]." They started by running 12 miles, and by the end of the fall, they were all running 14 every Sunday. They accordingly upped their volume so that they were all running 70 to 80 miles per week.

But the distance runners remained skeptical. After all, they were interval-trained athletes experiencing moderate success under Coach Quiller's program. Any skepticism about Wetmore's system vanished at the end of the cross-country season when the varsity team left to run the NCAA regionals. The middle-distance runners ran a 3,000-meter time trial while the varsity was gone. JD recalled their performances: "I ran 8:35, a PR [personal record]. Sobolik PR'ed. Samuelson PR'ed. Al [Culpepper] didn't PR, but he ran 8:20 something. The distance guys were blown away. They gave in then [to Wetmore's methods], although they were pretty desperate then [to do well]." Culpepper's performances particularly impressed the distance runners. Said veteran team leader Shawn Found, "He [Wetmore] brought Culpepper back from the dead. By that winter he was running 13:53 for 5K in addition to his mile performances."

The success of Wetmore's runners in the early years sent a message: it did not matter how little talent you had, if you followed his instructions and worked hard, you would succeed. According to Found, "Ever since then, every Sunday run was a rumblefest." Wetmore would tell his guys, "When you live on monster island, someone's breathing fire every day." Now it was clear why.

As head coach, Wetmore's program at Colorado paid great dividends quickly. The men finished second in 1994 at the NCAA Cross-Country Championship, their highest podium finish in program history. In 1997 and 1998 they were again on the podium, this time with third-place finishes behind Arkansas and Stanford. In 2000 they finished second. The women also demonstrated terrific consistency. In 1995 they finished second, in 1997 third, and in 2000, became the first national championship team for the University of Colorado cross-country program. Individual success was also prominent, with championship winners in 1998, 2000, 2002, and 2003. And no other individual epitomized the Colorado program more than Adam Goucher.

GETTING GOUCHERED

"He was talked about widely on a local basis and a national basis," said Mark Wetmore of Goucher. "We weren't coming from a place or a time when we had recruited the very best in the nation on a regular basis. But I think the fact that we were local and things were starting to happen, he noticed I think."

Adam Goucher added:

I remember the first time talking to him and just being fired up. Excited about the future, excited about the possibility of running for CU. My first immediate impression my first week at CU, [was] probably a little bit of fear. Magnolia broke me the first time I was up there. It's a brutal run, especially when you're not used to it and not ready. And my first run there, at the end of our first week at school, that Sunday we went up there and did our long run. People were passing me—other freshman—and I'm going "Oh my god." I was always like, "I could be the best." Even with my teammates. I wanted to be the top freshman if nothing else. And I remember thinking to myself, "Man I don't know. High school is one thing, college is another, and maybe I just don't have it." This run made me do some soul searching—big time. With literally two miles to go this was going through my head: "Maybe I'm not good enough, maybe I just can't do this." I literally cried. It broke me. All of a sudden I realized "Oh this is for real."

Despite winning the City Championship 1,600 meters in 4:42 as a ninth grader, when Goucher started high school he had his eye on football. But Judy Fellhauer (known as Flower), the Doherty High School cross-country coach and an Olympic Trials competitor in the marathon in 1988, had hopes of coaching Goucher since the year before. She spoke to Goucher for the first time after he won the mile title again as a freshman, telling him she would love to coach him. More important, she spoke to Goucher's mother, who explained to Flower that no one in her family had gone to college, and that her only goal for Adam was that he do well enough in a sport to gain a scholarship. Goucher only weighed 125 pounds then, and Flower explained that in order for him to get a football scholarship, he would probably have to gain 50 to 60 pounds and perform really, really well. If Goucher ran, well, she would not promise anything, but she speculated that he may get a scholarship out of it in the end.

Then, Flower watched in disappointment at the beginning of Goucher's sophomore year when she saw him in line to sign up for football. But while in line, Goucher realized he was going to be late for work, so he left for his job in a feed store, figuring he would sign up for football the following day.

That evening, Goucher's mother and sisters persuaded him that Doherty's football team was not that good, and that he was too small to really excel at football, anyway. Goucher called Flower later that evening. "Flower," he said, "this is Adam Goucher. I don't know if you remember me, but is it too late to sign up for cross-country?" "Of course I remembered him," Flower said. "He had no idea everyone [on the cross-country team] was talking about him."

A week and a half later, Goucher ran his first ever cross-country race. He asked Flower beforehand who the best guys in the race were, and she pointed out three or four of the top guys before warning him to pace himself out there. Goucher finished fifth, in 16:50. "Oh my God," Flower thought to herself. "What have I got here?" As the season progressed, Goucher improved dramatically, and at the regional qualifier for the state meet, Goucher finished only five seconds behind the winner. Seeing Goucher's progress, Flower gave Goucher some council before the state meet: "You're the guy," she said. "Go for it, and don't hold back." Goucher won the Colorado state championship in 15:27. It was the first cross-country race he had ever won.

Flower had planned on going to the Kinney (now Foot Locker) regional cross-country championships with only the seniors. But now that Goucher had won, she extended the invitation to him as well. Goucher and his family raised funds for him to make the trip, and he finished fourth in the regionals in Kenosha, Wisconsin, to qualify for the national meet. Only one other sophomore in America, Brian Young from Oklahoma, qualified for Kinney Nationals.

By himself in San Diego for the Kinney Championship, Goucher said, "I was blown away. I was treated like a king." Racing in only the seventh cross-country race of his life, he finished an admirable 13th. But Goucher was less than elated when he called Flower to tell her his result. "When he called," Flower said, "He was like, 'I'm the biggest loser in the world. I got thirteenth.' He was completely mad at himself. But we talked him into it. We explained that it was really a pretty good deal."

That race, said Goucher, "was the turning point. It told me I have the potential to be good." Forced to miss the basketball season because he had "skipped" the tryouts to run Kinney Nationals, Goucher focused his energy on running. That spring, Goucher finished third in the 800-meter at the state meet in 1:57 in his second 800 ever, and he also finished third in the 1,600 meters.

In cross-country, Goucher dominated his junior year. He won every race throughout the season, set course records, and repeated as state champion. At the state championships, he set a state record for 5K, running 15:03. His team had won the championship his sophomore year, and this time they finished sixth, but otherwise, he had thus far met his each of his seasonal objectives.

But at the Kinney Nationals, Goucher finished a disappointing 15th. Flower said, "He felt so good, and quickly ended up in front of the pack. Eventually, the whole pack passed him. He forgot all of our strategies because he was feeling good. I think he learned a lot from that race. He learned more from that than any race he has ever won. He learned about using your head as much as your body."

Goucher's precocity mandated that Flower consider grand ambitions. She said, "We talked about the Olympics right away. Talent-wise, I thought he had it, and I think one of his biggest assets is his pain tolerance and focus. Then there is his competitiveness. He will pay the price. He will train." Her intuition about his physical skills was proven when he was subjected to a battery of tests at the Olympic Training Center in Colorado Springs following his senior year. Flower said, "He excelled in every level. His muscle strength was exceptional. His VO$_2$ Max was exceptional, and his muscle biopsy was exceptional."

In the spring of his junior year, Goucher continued to improve, winning the 1,600- and 3,200-meter runs at the state championships in 4:18 and 9:35. By this time, none of Goucher's teammates could keep up with him, forcing him to train alone. This did not deter him. "Most of the time," said Flower, "He was alone. But he never complained about it. Never."

As a senior in the fall of 1993, Goucher dedicated himself to his goals more than ever. And by midseason he crossed a big one off his list: running a spectacular 14:41 for 5K on the state meet course. And at the state meet, he again covered the course in under 15 minutes despite the fact that it was covered with three inches of snow.

Unfortunately, Goucher was unable to savor his state meet victory for long. Only three hours after the race, Goucher was on a plane to Florida to visit his ailing grandmother. She passed away while he was there. She was originally from Worcester, Massachusetts, so Goucher and his family then went to Massachusetts for the funeral. There was a blizzard in Massachusetts, yet every day, Goucher ran in preparation for the regional meet. "I have to turn this negative energy into positive energy," he told himself. "I have to focus on what I want to do, for the family."

Goucher won the Foot Locker Midwest Regional in 15:13, tying the course record held by former US 10,000-meter champion Todd Williams. It was on to the Foot Locker National Championships for the third and final time. This time, his family accompanied Goucher to San Diego. Throughout the season, Flower had studied the competition by reading results in *XC Express*. "I felt it motivated him to see how he compared to the rest of the guys throughout the year," she said. "We knew that when we got to Foot Locker, we knew everything about everyone."

Once there, they were surprised that Goucher was overlooked as one of the favorites. Instead, all of the pre-race talk was centered around local favorite Mebrahton Keflezighi of San Diego, Matt Davis of Oregon, and Bob Keino of New Jersey. "Adam," said Flower, "was a little miffed at the lack of respect." "This is great," she told him, "because they [the favorites] were not left alone. They couldn't even get lunch. I said, 'Okay, wait till tomorrow.'"

On race day, Flower said, "Adam could hardly wait. He had no fear, just a sheer joy about being there and competing. He had fire in him." There was one major hill on the course, and this is where he envisioned breaking away. Keflezighi had broken from the pack with a mile and half to go, and Goucher plowed up the hill, catching Keflezighi.

On the descent, Goucher rolled away from the field to win the Foot Locker title in 14:41. His widowed grandfather was there to enjoy Goucher's win along with the rest of Goucher's family. "It was," Goucher recalls, "a great moment for the family." His grandfather passed away a week and a half later.

For Flower, Goucher's accomplishment was all the more impressive because of everything he had to overcome. She said: "I love Adam like a son, and he has not had it easy. His dad left when he was in the fifth grade, and his mom struggled to raise him and his two sisters. It was a financial struggle; she was trying to make it a good life for them, and he was the man of the house forever. He worked throughout high school, sometimes closing restaurants at midnight, to pay for his own expenses and fees . . . He struggled with his dad leaving, and his mom made up for it . . . [but] he had it a little hard." Goucher's tough upbringing did not deter him in the least. In fact, Flower said that Goucher was the most coachable athlete she has ever had. "He listened. He was loyal to me as a coach, and he listened to what I said, no questions asked. He never doubted what we were doing. He believed in it. And he always expressed his gratitude."

Goucher appreciated the enormous effort Flower put into her coaching, but after Foot Locker, Goucher said, "I was just fried. For so long I had visualized it, and when it happened, I was ready to be done." After running in the US Junior Cross-Country championships (finishing 11th), and 15th on a trip to Chiba, Japan, for an international 8K race, all that was left for Goucher to do was decide where to attend college.

Flower was "bombarded by college coaches. I got at least a call a night." Goucher listened to Flower's counsel, "but the whole decision was Adam's. I was there to help him." Both were impressed with then Wisconsin coach Martin Smith, but Goucher clicked with Wetmore immediately. "Adam convinced me," Flower said, "more than Mark convinced me, that Mark was a good guy." In spite of being taken aback by Wetmore's ponytail and relaxed appearance, "Mark," Goucher said, "would fire me up." In the end, Goucher decided on Colorado. "I could sense Mark had what it takes to make me the best I can be."

And Wetmore's system paid dividends almost immediately. "I noticed that he was an unusual talent, with an unusual desire to prepare," Wetmore said. "And I noticed that this could be the beginning of something big." As a true freshman in 1994, Goucher finished four seconds behind Arizona's Martin Keino to finish second at the NCAA National Cross-Country Championship. But despite the success, the national title remained elusive: "I think after being second as a freshman—a very close second as a freshman—I just assumed that the following year that I would win. You know I was like, 'I could win this next year.' And then things happened. And then the next year, well things happened. That's just kinda the way it was, I was close but never got it. And going into my senior year I was just like 'This is it.' I could not be denied that cross title."

Goucher had finished second in 1994, but dropped to sixth in 1995 and fourth in 1997. In 1998, Goucher knew it was do or die, and at the NCAA Cross-Country Championship held at Rim Rock Farm in Kansas he took no prisoners. Setting a blistering pace early, Goucher ran neck-and-neck with Arizona's Abdi Abdirahman until the final mile, crossing the line in a new course record of 29:26 for 10K. He had finally achieved his first NCAA Cross-Country individual title.

For Mark Wetmore and the rest of the CU program, Goucher's success was very indicative of what they were looking to accomplish with homegrown talent: "Many of the best people that have come out of our program kind of came to us," Wetmore said. "We are more likely to end up with an agreement with somebody who had interest to begin with than if we just cold call people from the national list." For Colorado, it was the start of a great legacy to come.

BREAKING THE MOLD

The University of Colorado wasn't the only school in the state looking to impart a cross-country tradition. Adams State College (ASC) in far-away Alamosa was on the verge of history—led by the iconic coach Joe Vigil—and with a new competitive home: the NCAA's Division II.

A school of only 3,500 students, Adams State was fortunate to have won seven consecutive NAIA crowns from 1983 to 1989, led by Coach Vigil's attention to detail and sound, progressive methods. But in 1992 they faced a new challenge, the NCAA Division II, which featured smaller, more intimate programs but with higher standards and more available scholarships. Adams State would be running against faster, more determined competition for the first time, and their first NCAA Championship wasn't about to back down.

There were about 1,000 meters to go in the 1992 NCAA Division II Cross-Country Championship, and Adams State's Jason Mohr was hurting. Feeling "pretty crummy," he said. Four teammates—and only them—were ahead of him, but he began to drop back. "Sixteen points, that's still pretty good," he thought to himself. But then came

---

Did You Know?

By 1980, Adams State coach Dr. Joe Vigil had turned ASC's record of success into a legacy. The arrival of Pat Porter added two back-to-back individual cross-country titles while giving the Grizzlies a boost to defend as team champions. 1981 saw the first women's title, with Mary Jaqua the first individual champion. From 1980 to 1989, Adams State lost only one NAIA cross-country men's team title, and had the individual champion seven times during that span. Robbie Hipwood (1985), Rick Robirds (1986, 1987, 1989), and Craig Dickson (1988) followed Porter's two titles. The Adams State women were equally dominant, adding first- or second-place team finishes three times later in the decade. And Vigil became nationally renowned for his impartment of VO$_2$ max (maximal oxygen consumption) on every athlete, a technique he shared while coaching the US World Cross team and in the Olympics in 1988.

---

the stare of a sideline spectator in Missouri Southern State gear—a look Mohr will never forget. The man's expression was clear: *Get up there!* Three minutes later, Mohr responded, gutting out a fifth-place finish behind his four teammates to cap off the one and only perfect score (15 points) in NCAA Cross-Country Championship history. "It was really an honor to be a part of that team," said Mohr. "With all the records that have been set, this is one that can never be broken."

Mohr wasn't the only one hurting before history was made. In the lead during a "sloppy, muddy climb" near the five-mile mark of the 6.2-mile (10K) race, David Brooks also began to feel it, seeing his teammates catch up to him with Phil Spratley of archrival Western State in close pursuit. But as with Mohr, Brooks would have nothing of playing from behind. "At that point, I remember thinking there was no way I was going to let myself fall off the back of that group. I was not going to allow them to get away." Brooks finished third in 32:26, just two seconds off the pace in a race that witnessed Adam State's top five runners all finish in a four-second span, also an NCAA record. Yet if anyone was hurting and had to withstand the pain, if anyone suffered hardship, if anyone willed himself to the finish line on that November day, it wasn't Brooks or Mohr—it was 1992 champion Phil Castillo.

Just one week before the championship race, Castillo received a call from his mother in Acoma Pueblo, New Mexico, saying that his grandmother, with whom Castillo "spent 90 percent of his childhood," had fallen severely ill. He made the four-and-a-half-hour drive from Adams State College in Alamosa to his Native American family's village, where he spent late nights attending to his grandmother before she passed away. With a week of no sleep and his grandmother's burial set for after the team's flight to Pennsylvania, Castillo had no inclination of joining his squad for the finals. At least not until his grandfather gave him an unforgettable look of his own.

"From the moment I arrived home until I left, I didn't run a step because that wasn't my priority," said Castillo. "I had no plans of leaving my grandfather there at home. But he pulled me aside, looked me in the eye, and said, 'Go and win.' That moment still gets me every time I think about it." The drive back to Alamosa took 10 hours. Every 15 minutes, Castillo had to get out and run around the car to keep himself awake. When he finally arrived late the night before the outgoing flight, he told Peter De La Cerda, second-place finisher in the race and Castillo's roommate at the time, to pack his bag for him and wake him up in the morning so he wouldn't miss the plane. "Without Peter, there's no way I would have made the flight. He did everything I asked of him," said Castillo.

In Pennsylvania, the heavens had opened to drop buckets of rain on Cooper's Lake Campground Course, making it a muddy mess. So muddy and so wet, in fact, that two or three miles into the race, Castillo—who calls his vision "anything but legal"—tossed his fog and mud-covered Coke-bottle glasses aside. Half-blind, he began to pass runners one at a time, simply focusing on the blurred jerseys in front of him until the five-mile mark, when all of those jerseys were Adams State green. When the runners came up on a steep downhill slope in the last mile, Castillo shot off "without any regard for falling." "I remember being amazed at how fast Castillo and De La Cerda were going down that wet hill," said Brooks. "I tried to get between them, but they just hit another gear and took off."

Then, in the final 100-meter straightaway, Castillo felt like he was given a slight lift over the grass, running with little to no water splash. He edged out De La Cerda by a stride for the title, fulfilling his grandpa's words. Mohr beat out Spratley by five seconds to secure the top-five sweep for Adams State.

Castillo broke down immediately after the race. "I crossed the line and started crying once again because of the emotions of that race that day. It still gives me the chills because I remember it so well." When Castillo and company finished, they didn't immediately realize what they had done. Of the team's runners, only Paul Stoneham, the fourth-place finisher, had a real mind for running statistics and records. What they did realize was that they had won a team championship in their first year in the NCAA—all of this a part of the philosophy of legendary coach Joe Vigil, who led his ASC men's squads to 14 national titles. "That was the thing with Coach Vigil; he always stressed that when you run, you don't represent just yourself, but all the guys who ran before you, all your teammates who didn't make the trip, and everyone who helped along the way," remarked De La Cerda.

What few know is who Adams State left behind. Not on the seven-man roster for the 1992 championships was Martin Johns, who ran for New Zealand in the 1996 Olympic Games, and Dan Caulfield, Ireland's current national record holder in the 800-meter run (indoor). Another future Olympian, Shane Healy, ran in the 1992 race but didn't finish in the top five. The depth of this particular team was so great that none of the runners were terribly surprised when the perfect score was achieved, or when Castillo, who hadn't won a race all season, came out on top: "There must have been 14 or 15 guys that year who could have been in the top seven," said De La Cerda. "It seems like every time out we had a different top finisher. That's the sign of a great team."

But would Adams State have been able to beat Division I titlist Arkansas that year? Vigil's bunch hints at a yes, and the facts suggest the possibility. ASC had beaten national runner-up Wisconsin handily at the Gopher Invite earlier that year, and Adams State and Arkansas had each defeated Lubbock Christian, the NAIA champ, by the same nine-point margin in separate meets. A head-to-head matchup wasn't to be, but one can't help but wonder. "I like to think we would have given them a run for their money," said Mohr. "But they were studs." Reflecting on the perfect score, it seems the Adams State runners were studs, too.

AN EQUAL OPPORTUNITY CHAMPIONSHIP

Outside of the major teams and names, a final American collegiate anomaly came to a close in the 1990s. At the start of NCAA Divisions (I, II, and III) in 1973, the individual winners of the NCAA III and NCAA II (plus a few additional runners in the early years) were invited to compete in the NCAA Division I meet just two days after winning their own division meet. The NCAA Cross-Country Handbook carried this text: "It has been established for the 1973 Cross-Country Championships that the first five finishers in Divisions II and III will be allowed to compete in the Division I Championships. In 1974 and in subsequent years, the numbers shall be six from Division II and four from Division III. The individual finishers will be able to earn medals, but their finishes won't be counted in team point totals."

This made for some very difficult racing challenges. For example, former SUNY-Cortland coaching legend Jack Daniels related: "We drove to nationals when Marybeth [Crawley] won [in 1989 at Rock Island, Illinois] and drove home all night after the race, arriving at 8:00 a.m. on that Sunday morning. She got some new clothes and we drove to Annapolis for the Monday Division I race. I doubt she was well rested for that one."

From 1982 to 1990, the invitation to run in the Division I meet was then limited to only the Division II and III champions, and then invitations stopped completely before the 1991 season. Division III coaches recalled that the Division I coaches weren't happy with lower division runners taking All-American spots from Division I runners.

An example of this was the final collegiate runner to be a *double* All-American finisher. On Saturday, November 17, 1990, Haverford College's Seamus McElligott, runner-up in 1989, won the NCAA Division III Men's Cross-Country title in Grinnell, Iowa, running 24:46 for the eight-kilometer distance. As the overall winner, McElligott then accepted his invitation to compete two days later at the Division I championship. Historically, those who attempted the double—with few exceptions over the years—finished well back in the pack, tired from the travel and their own championship race two days prior.

McElligott and his coach, the legendary Tom Donnelly, travelled on Sunday to Knoxville, Tennessee, and prepared to square off the next day against the best runners in Division I, all of them fresh and ready for what was widely regarded as the most competitive single collegiate footrace of the year. That next morning, McElligott was not only competitive at the longer 10K distance, he secured the final All-American slot, making him a Division III and Division I All-American over the course of about 48 hours.

The athlete immediately behind McElligott, and thus the first Division I athlete deprived of an All-American finish by McElligott's presence in the race, was none other than Villanova's Terrence Mahon, who had been an All-American the previous year while running for Oregon. Mahon went on to become a prominent distance coach, in charge of such notable Olympians as Deena Kastor, Anna Pierce, Jen Rhines, and Ryan Hall. McElligott also beat the Division II national champion that year, Doug Hanson of North Dakota State, who was one second and two places back, in 30:14.

After that accomplishment, the Division I coaches voted to no longer allow Division II or III athletes to compete in the NCAA Division I meet. Thus, Seamus McElligott was the last runner to ever accomplish this feat.

SETTING RECORDS, AND SETTING RECORDS STRAIGHT

Seamus McElligott's story was indicative of cross-country running in the 1990s. Old patterns and expectations were changing—all while new records were being set.

Internationally, as traditionally strong nations saw a brief decline at the top ranks, new consistent performances from nations such as Kenya, Ethiopia, and Morocco drove the sport to reconsider why cross-country was important and how it fit into the athletic structures from years prior. As prominent names such as John Ngugi and Paul Tergat strung World Championship victories together with a

longer span of success, it was also apparent that world-beating performances could be sustained with more effective training, enabling the biggest names to stay on top longer. These two factors: the place of the sport within athletics and the realization that new standards would not be changing anytime soon, forced the IAAF's hand and the sport modernized more in the decade of the 1990s than any other.

Meanwhile, patterns of championship success also permeated the collegiate ranks. With major programs such as Villanova, Arkansas, Stanford, Colorado, and Adams State pushing the boundaries of what was expected at the top levels, American athletes were beginning to take note again and a few were challenging the mighty East Africans. The US National Cross-Country Championships saw the fastest per-mile pace for champions out of any time in history (nearly 12 seconds faster than the 1970s and 1980s), and a fleet of young names were about to push American distance running back into center stage.

New championship structures were developed as well: longer races for young female distance runners and short-course variations at international competitions were important developments for the sport during this period. More chances to run cross-country meant the sport could expand without restriction, and the most historical races in Europe were now tied in with the global World Cross Challenge series—a meaningful way of ensuring their continued recognition.

* * *

With the fastest times in cross-country running occurring more frequently in the 1990s than any other period in history, an interesting conundrum presented itself: Western powers were no longer finding that their best was good enough. Despite patterns of sustained success domestically, the mighty East African stranglehold on the World Cross-Country Championships created a seemingly insurmountable chasm between those nations willing to sacrifice everything for success and those former powers relying on tried-and-true methods. Thus, a competitive revolution was brewing to challenge the new order. It would remain to be seen whether the onset of a new century would provide these athletes the means to see it to fruition.

EVENT SPOTLIGHT:
JENNINGS, MCKIERNAN, AND DIAS AT WORLD CROSS (MARCH 21, 1992)

LOCATION: FRANKLIN PARK, BOSTON

"The Emerald Necklace"

In New England, the changing of the leaves in autumn is a picturesque pageant of color. Burnt reds, golden yellows, vibrant oranges; each tree a testament to the beauty of nature that borders on the miraculous. But each season is only temporary, every branch of leaves fleeting. By the end of November, only a few steadfast leaves remain. It is in the words of eminent cross-country coach Joe Newton that runners are reminded about the importance of this transition. At the end of the season he urges his harriers to "be the last leaf on the tree—that you aren't going to fall off until you're in the chute."

For every cross-country runner who has battled at Franklin Park, hanging on as the last leaf is easier said than done. Franklin Park is historic. As the largest park in Boston's "Emerald Necklace" of interconnected parks, Franklin Park was designed by Frederick Law Olmsted, a renowned landscape architect and park builder, who in the 1880s made the site his last, significant city park project, and one he considered to be the culmination of years of experimentation. He created a vast country meadow (now the golf course) and nurtured 220 acres of forest in the park. With a professional background as varied as the terrain he sought to protect, Olmsted was driven by the need to create a space, as he claimed, "We want a ground to which people may easily go when the day's work is done, and where they may stroll for an hour, seeing, hearing, and feeling nothing of the bustle and jar of the streets where they shall, in effect, find the city put far away from them . . ."

It was in this environment that Lynn Jennings became the most versatile distance runner in the United States. At the time of the World Cross-Country Championships in 1992, Jennings held national titles indoors in the mile, outdoors in the 10,000, on the roads over eight kilometers, and in her favorite sport of cross-country, where she had won six of the previous seven national titles, including the last five in succession. As Jennings stood in a snow-covered field in Boston's Franklin Park with 126 of the best female runners in the world, she had to tell herself she was going to win again.

Only once before in its 19 runnings had World Cross been held in the United States. That was in 1984, when it was contested over makeshift hills of plywood and dirt at the Meadowlands in New Jersey. The city of Boston, aiming for something a bit more traditional, invested $500,000 in designing and landscaping a course worthy of the event. The 54 countries competing in Franklin Park found a challenging layout. The basic loop was 2,300 meters long, and once in each circuit it climbed over Bear Cage Hill, a wooded mass of rock rising 194 feet over the field below. When someone asked the 31-year-old Jennings if she expected the women's event to become a two-person race between her and world 10,000-meter champion Liz McColgan of Scotland, Jennings grew exasperated: "This is the world cross-country meet," she said. "It's foolish to think that there are only two women in it. There are at least 10 who could win."

But the number of serious contenders in Boston dropped with the temperature. The African women, who were starting to show the same brilliance as their male teammates, had never seen such conditions. Three inches of snow had fallen on the Thursday before the event, leaving the 6,370-meter (3.8-mile) women's course perilously slippery in most places and muddy everywhere else. As the women warmed up, you could see their breath. That was no problem for Jennings, who trained through the winter in Newmarket, New Hampshire: "I would hardly call three inches of snow 'bad' conditions," she said. "I run in snow four months of the year. It doesn't bother me."

Two of Jennings's primary competitors were not local. Albertina Dias was an experienced distance runner who had won international cross-country meetings in France, Italy, Spain, and her native Portugal. And Ireland's Catherina McKiernan, who, running in the event for the third time, was in great form and looking for a good showing or even a surprise victory.

But despite the stiff competition, blustery wind, and cold conditions, nothing seemed to get in the way of Jennings that Saturday. From the gun she charged to the front, pursued by three Kenyans, who, no doubt, had difficulty with the footing. While the rolling parkland course was covered in snow, Jennings, Dias, and McKiernan seemed unperturbed. After staying near the head of the main bunch for the early stages, at the halfway mark it was McKiernan who moved up to join the two leaders, Dias and Jennings.

Along the way the crowd cheered for the spectacle. Park officials put the crowd at 30,000, and at the bottom of Bear Cage Hill the spectators stood 10 deep, screaming themselves hoarse. Many tore back and forth across the snowy fields, hoping to glimpse as much of the race as possible. Among them were Jennings's husband of six months, Dave Hill, and her coach, John Babington. On her first trip up Bear Cage Hill they screamed some significant news to her: McColgan was out of contention. (She finished 41st and complained of a sore throat.)

And one by one the Kenyans fell back, leaving Jennings at the front with Dias, who had finished second to her two years before. With the setting being Boston, some of the spectators might have felt a moment's conflict once Irishwoman Catherina McKiernan caught Jennings and Dias with a mile to go.

As such, in the last kilometer, McKiernan took the initiative (and the lead) but couldn't shake off her two rivals. Suddenly, with a few hundred meters left, Jennings sprang out from behind the Irishwoman and kicked on. Once Jennings pounced, she passed Dias, gained a step on McKiernan, and then slogged through a patch of sand. McKiernan struggled back and inched ahead. "That's where Lynn's willpower comes in—her absolute refusal to be beaten," marveled Babington later. "It was the kick in the butt I needed," said Jennings.

However, for a moment McKiernan fought back, catching and then overtaking Jennings—coming around the final bend with the advantage. Jennings sprinted again, and McKiernan was broken. Thrusting both her arms up in jubilation, Jennings crossed the finish line in 21:16, two seconds ahead of McKiernan. Dias was third, in 21:19.

After the race Jennings found Hill, hugged him, and began sobbing uncontrollably. Twenty minutes later Babington received the same treatment and seemed concerned. "Are you all right?" he asked Jennings a bit nervously. "I was crying tears of joy," she said later. "I never did that before."

There was great Irish delight at McKiernan's achievement: a hard-fought world silver medal in a thrilling race over difficult ground with the prospect of greater things to come. Adding to Ireland's good mood was the seventh-place finish of Sonia O'Sullivan, on the threshold of an even more stunning career that would include a future success in this event.

But the future brought a very peculiar sort of frustration as McKiernan won silver in the next three World Championships and never managed to make the leap to gold. The following year in Spain the same three runners were in the medals again, with Diaz this time relegating Jennings to third. The 1994 race in Budapest saw McKiernan just hang on to silver ahead of another Portuguese runner Conceição Ferreira, and behind Hellen Chepngeno of Kenya. And in the Northern English town of Durham in 1995 she finished second behind Derartu Tulu in a stellar top 10 dominated by Kenya and Ethiopia.

"Of the four silvers, it was the one I should have won," McKiernan later wrote of that 1992 race in *Irish Runner Magazine*, "but I was young and naive and didn't have the experience or confidence to win." McKiernan wasn't wearing any winter gear that day, and there was wonder if that was a factor—after all, Jennings was wearing gloves and a T-shirt.

Meanwhile, the men's race, by contrast, was almost boring, so easily did Olympic 5,000-meter champion John Ngugi collect an unprecedented fifth World Cross title. The 29-year-old Kenyan was dominant with his five-foot-ten frame and pronounced forward lean, his singlet slipping down off his left shoulder. Ngugi finished 12 seconds ahead of teammate William Mutwol, in 37:05 for the 12,530-meter (7.518-mile) course. Kenya packed five of its runners into the first eight places to easily beat France for a seventh straight team title. The highest finishing American was Todd Williams, 19th in 37:51.

As for many of the competitors on the day, Franklin Park provided a suitable challenge as a course for the World Cross-Country event. Along with Bear Cage Hill, there was Schoolmaster Hill, pinched in between the seventh green and a stand of pines, where the poet Ralph Waldo Emerson

once lived. As Emerson wrote, "Each man must think for himself and act on his own instincts." Running on instinct is what cross-country runners know best. Yet, for the challenging terrain amidst the beautiful New England scenery, it was nature that won at World Cross in 1992.

Men's Race			
Date: Saturday, March 21, 1992			
Teams: 22			
Distance: 7.78 miles / 12.53 kilometers			
Location: Franklin Park, Boston, Massachusetts			
Individual Finishers:			
1	John Ngugi	Kenya	37:05
2	William Mutwol	Kenya	37:17
3	Fita Bayissa	Ethiopia	37:18
4	Khalid Skah	Morocco	37:20
5	Richard Chelimo	Kenya	37:21
6	Steve Moneghetti	Australia	37:23
7	Dominic Kirui	Kenya	37:26
8	William Sigei	Kenya	37:27
9	Thierry Pantel	France	37:30
10	Bruno Le Stum	France	37:33
11	Domingos Castro	Portugal	37:35
12	Antonio Martins	France	37:37
13	Mathias Ntawulikura	Rwanda	37:39
14	José Regalo	Portugal	37:41
15	Richard Nerurkar	United Kingdom	37:43
16	Pere Arco	Spain	37:44
17	Eamonn Martin	United Kingdom	37:49
18	Vincent Rousseau	Belgium	37:50
19	Todd Williams	United States	37:51
20	Dave Clarke	United Kingdom	37:52
21	Pascal Thiébaut	France	37:53
22	Hammou Boutayeb	Morocco	37:54
23	Ondoro Osoro	Kenya	37:55
24	Martín Fiz	Spain	37:56
25	António Pinto	Portugal	37:57

Team Results:		
1	Kenya	46
2	France	145
3	United Kingdom	147
4	Spain	171
5	Italy	246
6	Morocco	247
7	Portugal	249
8	United States	263
9	Australia	354

10	Ethiopia		425

24	Zhora Koullou	France	22:05
25	Elena Fidatof	Romania	22:05

Women's Race
Date: Saturday, March 21, 1992
Teams: 19
Distance: 3.95 miles/6.37 kilometers
Location: Franklin Park, Boston, Massachusetts

Individual Finishers:

1	Lynn Jennings	United States	21:16
2	Catherina McKiernan	Ireland	21:18
3	Albertina Dias	Portugal	21:19
4	Vicki Huber	United States	21:34
5	Nadia Dandolo	Italy	21:35
6	Qu Yunxia	China	21:36
7	Sonia O'Sullivan	Ireland	21:37
8	Jill Hunter	United Kingdom	21:39
9	Susan Sirma	Kenya	21:40
10	Luchia Yeshak	Ethiopia	21:42
11	Helen Kimaiyo	Kenya	21:45
12	Jane Ngotho	Kenya	21:47
13	Estela Estévez	Spain	21:48
14	Lième Slegers	Belgium	21:49
15	Hellen Chepngeno	Kenya	21:50
16	Susan Hobson	Australia	21:51
17	Véronique Collard	Belgium	21:51
18	Conceição Ferreira	Portugal	21:52
19	Iulia Negura	Romania	21:54
20	Merima Denboba	Ethiopia	22:02
21	Daria Nauer	Switzerland	22:03
22	Angela Chalmers	Canada	22:03
23	Natalya Sorokivskaya	CIS	22:04

Team Results:

1	Kenya	47
2	United States	77
3	Ethiopia	96
4	Ireland	103
5	Portugal	115
6	Romania	129
7	United Kingdom	129
8	Spain	138
9	France	148
10	Italy	154

Chapter 16

Cross-country has always been my greatest passion. I love winter weather, getting sloppy, using the terrain in my race tactics and also the strength that cross-country builds. My most successful years on the track and in marathons have been when I trained for cross-country in the winter."

—*Deena Kastor*

THE 2000s

This was the resurgence the West was looking for. Talented young runners who were the best from their respective corners of the nation and fearless against homegrown competition, yearning to face the top talent in the world. Spurred by global infrastructure that enabled communication through the Internet, a more organized and comprehensive sponsorship format, and better coaching methods coupled with scientific advancements, it was an ideal zeitgeist for athletes to chase records and challenge convention.

While cross-country had shifted somewhat with the acceptance of East African talent and the role of international stardom within the broader gamut of athletics in the 1990s, the first decade of the 2000s gave the talented rising tide a voice. Athletes were becoming more comfortable with a corporate structure that attempted to reward runners who sought top competition and set records—and there were more opportunities than ever to compete in cross-country competitions. Most importantly, the 2000s saw a grassroots revival of the sport, one that fell in line with previous "booms" in cross-country running. It was led by a definitive youth movement in America.

THE TURNING POINT

Alan Webb was locked on to one thought and one thought only on the morning of the 2000 Foot Locker High School National Cross-Country Championships: *This was it.* Webb already had the makings of an elite runner. As a sixteen-year-old sophomore at South Lakes High School in Virginia he had run a 4:06 mile, breaking an age-record set by Jim Ryun that was nearly forty years old. Then, as a junior, Webb went undefeated in cross-country, earning a spot to his first Foot Locker. But he and others had underestimated another junior, Dathan Ritzenhein, who pushed

to the front in the last half mile as Webb fell to eighth, his spirit broken.

It left Webb hungry. Despite a competitive schedule in cross the following year that included the Virginia State Meet and Foot Locker South Region qualifier, Webb wasn't satisfied: "I was on a personal mission. I was so focused, so motivated. I ran workouts that just about buried me. I prepared for a battle. I was 10 times more ready than the year before." As Webb remained calm on the starting line of the Foot Locker Cross-Country Championship in 2000, he was ready for what he called "a slaughterfest." Everyone knew what Ritzenhein would do: set a searing start at the outset. This time Webb was going to match him.

At the sound of the gun, Webb took off. He was cautious: everything could have vanished in the mayhem of the crowded start. But Webb got out without incident. A runner ahead had his attention: Wesley Keating from Texas, who wasn't a threat. A half-mile passed without change. Keating led; Webb held steady a few yards back. "I felt like we were running slower than five minutes for the mile," Webb claimed.

But where was Ritzenhein? Webb had spent five months visualizing a fierce duel; he even tacked a photo of Ritzenhein on his bedroom door. Webb had pushed all-in with a gamble for a brutal blood-bath. Suddenly, Ritz was nowhere to be found.

"I called it 'The Battle of the Century,'" said Marc Bloom, longtime publisher of *The Harrier*. "In a normal year, you'd be lucky to have one runner performing at such a super-high level. That year there were three." The three were Alan Webb and Dathan Ritzenhein, both seventeen years old, and Ryan Hall, eighteen. Well known nationally, some thought the teen phenomenons would produce extraordinary times and quickly burn out. No one could have predicted how these three would become the face of US distance running for the foreseeable future.

Webb, the miler from Reston, Virginia, was strong and fierce. Nine months before his intended revenge against Ritzenhein he had run a 1,600-meter relay-leg in 3:59.9 at the Penn Relays. In his senior year, he became the first high schooler to ever break 4:00 for the indoor mile. Outdoors as a senior he crushed Jim Ryun's mile record for high school with a staggering 3:53.

Ritzenhein had a gristly build and an aerobic capacity that had no limit. He grew up in Rockford, Michigan, stood a svelte five-foot-six and 112 pounds, and spent all his free time bicycling, swimming, and running. He loved the midweek 20-mile time trials organized by the local bike club. "It was fun to go hard," he said. "Going slow was boring. I liked to improve and break barriers." But Ritz hadn't lost a cross-country race in two years. Eventually he too would have a bountiful future at the University of Colorado (CU), to become the next champion trained under Mark Wetmore.

Ryan Hall, a stoic and powerful thoroughbred, came from Big Bear Lake, California, a small town where the elevation (6,700–9,000 feet) exceeded the population (5,438). He had attended a Jim Ryun running camp and was inspired by Ryun's determination and faith; the year after attending Ryun's camp he ran 1,500 meters in 3:45.12, equivalent to a 4:02 mile. After graduation, Hall attended Stanford University and joined forces with Coach Vin Lananna, where he focused on road races, setting an American record for 20 kilometers and became the fastest American-born marathoner in history.

"For once, the big dogs all came together in one place to go after each other," noted veteran TV commentator Toni Reavis. "And they brought such great stories with them—they all had these amazing running pedigrees but different personalities."

By the fall of 2000, American distance running was at a historical low. The spring of 2000 saw only a single American male and female qualify for the Olympic Marathon, with poor showings in Sydney: Christine Clark placed 19th and Rod DeHaven placed 69th. Americans weren't much better on the track; no American medalled at a distance beyond 400 meters at the 2000 Olympics. Road races were also stark; Kenyans were claiming the top spots in well-known events such as Peachtree, Falmouth, and Bay to Breakers. The same was true in major American marathons: Boston, New York, and Chicago. No American male won any of these in the 1990s.

Cross-country participation was also stagnating. In the 1990s, the number of high school running participants had grown only marginally. At World Cross, despite having some of the fastest times in history domestically, no senior-level team had come even close to the podium since the American women earned silver in 1992.

Thankfully, a high school revival was sparking across the nation. Four things were responsible: the Internet; the 1996 Atlanta Olympics; a training book by Jack Daniels, PhD; and two Hollywood renditions of Steve Prefontaine.

The Internet led the way, particularly sites that had databases where top times could be compared and message

boards where progress could be debated. "The Internet fed a hunger that was already there but completely unserved," claimed Reavis. "It was a new medium for these kids. They had a need, this was their time, and [sites such as] *DyeStat.com* opened the doors to their special community."

The 1996 Atlanta Olympics (despite its share of problems) *had* produced stellar achievements on the track. Ritzenhein remembered the thrill he felt when Bob Kennedy grabbed the lead with two laps to go in the 5,000 meters. Kennedy faded to sixth, but there was no question about his will or the stadium's thunderous response. Webb distinctly remembered US sprinter Michael Johnson, who won two golds, set a world record for 200 meters, and possessed some unique footwear. "Those gold Nike shoes Johnson wore in Atlanta, they were just so cool," Webb said.

Coaching had evolved too. For generations, high school running coaches had been transplants from other sports. They understood how to direct kids, but little else. By the 1990s, more coaches were products of the "running-boom," they knew training, and they could sympathize with their athletes. Plus, in 1998, with the publication of *Daniels' Running Formula*, coaches gained a technical training manual to match their enthusiasm. Jack Daniels, a respected veteran who had been anointed "the world's best running coach" by *Runner's World*, had written a book that explained individualized workouts with pace-specific training plans. "By the late '90s, you began to see a new and wonderful level of coaching across the country," said Bloom. "A lot of the coaches were using Jack's book."

Finally, praised for their artistic merit and historical sourcing, nothing topped the movies *Prefontaine* and *Without Limits*. After seeing the movies, Webb modeled himself after his hero for several years, memorizing and repeating famous Pre quotes like "I run to see who has the most guts." Ritzenhein found a parallel between Prefontaine's working-class roots and his own family, particularly his father's rise from a gas-line grunt to a management position. "Prefontaine worked harder than anyone else, and he put it all on the line every time he raced," Ritzenhein said. "I adopted that as the way I trained and raced."

But at the beginning stages of the 2000 Foot Locker National Cross-Country Championship, Ritzenhein was nowhere to be found. Ryan Hall, the least experienced of the three (running in his first Foot Locker final)—and the most unlikely to win—had also been wary of Ritzenhein. "We knew Dathan was going to go out like a madman," Hall said. But Hall and his fellow West runners had to play it safe: with only seven days rest after their regional qualifier, they couldn't blow out in the first mile. Thus, Hall lagged behind the leaders, trusting that it would prove the right tactic. "My teammates and I got a little bit mired in the middle when the course narrowed," he said. "It was hard finding room to move. And I couldn't figure out what Dathan was doing. Where was he?"

Ryan Hall, as an eighth grader training with his dad, Mickey, survived 15 miles of running at altitude. And his dad was no slouch; Mickey had a marathon best of 3:07

and was prepared to do anything to see Ryan fulfill his potential. Once a resident of Australia in the late 1970s, the elder Hall had met New Zealand's Arthur Lydiard and Australia's Percy Cerutty. Back home, it was Mickey who brought his son to Jim Ryun's Running Camp in Kansas. "It was a huge deal for me to meet Jim Ryun and his family," the young Ryan said. "I didn't feel like just a number at his camp. He was so personal, and such an inspiration." Back home, he covered his bedroom with reminders of his new goal for the mile: 3:59.

Every year Mickey increased his son's training: from 45 miles a week to 85, all at Big Bear's high altitude. With a majority of medium-effort distance runs mixed with steep hill repeats on the local slopes, Mickey's training for Ryan mirrored Lydiard's, which placed little reliance on speed-work. In 1999 Mickey had held Ryan out of the Foot Locker competitions, feeling the long California cross-country season had worn down his son. He related stories of athletes who burned out from too much racing, and of Olympic champions raised on long, moderate distance. Meanwhile, Ryan was impatient. "Coaching Ryan was like working a wild stallion," Mickey said. "He always wanted to run as fast as possible. He always had that fire in his eyes. It was just something he was born with."

Surprisingly, Hall's 2000 season didn't go as planned. He ran several courses slower than the year before, and threw up after a poor effort in the Stanford Invitational. But then the tides changed: Hall broke a twenty-one-year-old record on the Mt. SAC course and became favored to win there a second time when the Foot Locker West Regional returned to the same site. Dehydrated, Hall almost failed to complete the distance. He wobbled to the finish in fourth. "I came close to pulling him off the course on the last hill," said Mickey. "He was white as a ghost. If you want to know the truth about Ryan's senior year in cross-country, it was a disaster. There were so many ups and downs." Hall needed to be his best if he wanted to match the caliber of talent found in Alan Webb and Dathan Ritzenhein.

Webb, an age-group swimmer since the age of six, had always wanted to go fast. "Everyone wants to be a sprinter first," Webb said—but soon he moved up to longer distances. "There's nothing like winning," he claimed. "It gives you a flutter in the gut." And although he set an elementary-school record in the mile run, Webb was still focused on swimming until he began to enter cross-country and track races in ninth grade. Right away, something was different: running was better. "Everything just clicked," he said. "My improvement curve was exponential. I began to wonder: How hard can I push myself? How far can I go? How fast can I run?" Webb knew about tracking statistics from his father, a World Bank economist. And as Webb's passion for running mushroomed—"I went hard core"— he began measuring everything: his miles, his times, his weight lifting. He thought he might analyze the info and detect secret pathways to success. More impressively, while still at a young age, he managed to grasp the big picture: "I remember early on that I realized if you combined a great ambition with a great work ethic, you could produce powerful results," said Webb. And just like his junior season, he ran unbeaten as a senior. All that was left was defeating Ritzenhein.

Moments after the gun went off at Foot Locker, Erik Heinonen settled into the back of the field, right where he intended. Heinonen, from Eugene, Oregon, had placed fifth in the West Regional, passing dozens of runners in the final mile. He hoped for the same in the national championship. "I had a simple plan," he said. "I went straight to the back. That's where I was on the first turn when I looked over and saw another runner beside me. I remember yelling at him, 'Hey, Dathan, what are you doing back here?'"

Dathan Ritzenhein, being at the rear of the mass of runners, was following his coach's advice. In his five years with Rockford coach Brad Prins, Ritz had gotten used to his coach's offbeat comments, enthusiasm for pain, and insane workouts. Still, Ritzenhein had been unprepared for Prins's credence: "Do you know how you're going to beat Alan Webb tomorrow?" Prins had asked. "You're going to go out slow and take it easy. I don't care what the pace is. But as soon as you hit the first mile, you're going to sprint and sprint and keep on sprinting until you break everyone."

Prins was the perfect mix of youth and experience. A thirty-five-year-old Rockford High math teacher, he had started running late in life, lost sixty pounds, and qualified for the Boston Marathon. In his classroom, he delighted in putting nervous students on the spot. At cross-country practice, the torture cut deeper. "Dathan had the drive to push himself to the edge day after day," Prins said. "And I was mean enough to force him out onto that edge."

The two had met when Ritz's father, a triathlete, had brought the seventh-grade Dathan to a workout run by Prins. But at five feet tall, 106 pounds, and a self-described "butterball," Prins took one look at the youngster and declared: "Nope, not going to happen." By the winter of his eighth-grade school year, Ritzenhein had grown six inches, added strength and knowledge, and thrown himself into running. "Suddenly, people were like, 'Who is this kid?'" Ritz recalled. Every morning before school, Ritz ran four miles as fast as he could. Pitch darkness, freezing winds, blizzards; no problem. By early spring, the runs took only 22 minutes. That summer he ran a road 5K in 16:10.

Prins read everything he could about running and experimented on Ritz and his other runners: sprints, stadium steps, ankle weights, plyometrics, tempo runs, and long runs. "We were his guinea pigs, and trained like crazy," said Ritzenhein. "It's amazing I never got hurt. I just kept getting stronger." One day Ritz ran eight miles in the morning and intervals that lasted well into the evening. A final tally showed 32×400 meters in 65 seconds, with enough warm-up and cooldown to give him 22 miles for the day.

Ritz took it all and asked for more. One session Prins brought Ritzenhein to a local ski slope to run hill repeats. However, to avoid running down hill and causing a leg injury (also, Prins wanted to reduce recovery time), Prins met Ritzenhein at the top in his Subaru and drove him back down in 30 seconds, complete with clouds of rising dust. "We pushed hard, but we had fun with it," said Prins.

Ritzenhein agreed. It helped that he was crushing the competition. "I got so much satisfaction getting better," he said. "The longer the distance, the better I did. Others might beat me in speed workouts, but I could kill them in tempos and longer runs. It never bothered me to redline it forever." In the summer and fall of 2000, Ritzenhein hit 100-mile weeks, and averaged 80 throughout the season. He trained through his races and still broke his own course records. "Senior year was a frenzy," he said. "I knew it was my last high school cross-country season, and I knew what was coming at Foot Locker. The tension just kept building. The last couple of weeks, it was almost boiling over."

That's when Prins cut Ritzenhein's mileage and turned up the speed. The week before Foot Locker, Marc Bloom called Ritzenhein for an update. His most recent workout: 9 × 400 meters, with the first three 400s in 66 seconds, the next three in 62, and the last three in 58, 57, and 55. Ritz was already an aerobic monster. Now he was honing his turnover.

It was under these conditions that Ritzenhein found himself at the back of the pack in the most important race of his life. "I know it sounds strange," he said, "but all I remember is that it felt so bizarre to have other runners around me. There hadn't been anyone near me in a race for a long time."

And just before the 32 runners crossed the mile mark, Ritzenhein moved up to the outside of the course and took the lead, pulling ahead of Webb. The mile clock was ticking: 4:42, 4:43, 4:44, and an excited crowd had collected at that threshold, expecting something major. "There was a pulsating energy all along the course," said Bloom. When Ritzenhein scooted passed the mile clock, he saw the numbers hit 4:47. Then he tore loose: lengthening his stride, reaching with his arms, and putting the pedal to the floor. "Basically, I just laid all my cards on the table," he said. "I think maybe the slow first mile threw the guys for a loop, but it was now-or-never."

Webb, idle in second, was prepared for this. He was in a perfect position to counter. The only problem: "I figured no one could run away from me, but the move Dathan made was really huge," Webb said. "He got a few meters right away, so I decided to creep back to him little by little." That was expected. Webb could have sprinted, but he knew there were two miles still to go.

But in a matter of a few quick strides, Ritz had built a gap on Webb and everyone else. And in the second mile, Ritzenhein was in full "Beast Mode," burning any energy in his reserves. "There's a lot of pressure when you commit and go to the front," he said. "Suddenly you become the hunted, and everyone's got you in their sights. I had to make sure Alan never got back on me."

Webb kept waiting to gain on Ritz, and got nervous over the second mile. Over each hill and down the next, across the fairway and around the green, Webb couldn't

catch him. Ritz's lead was constant. "It took everything I had just to stay close," Webb said. "I was so surprised. I expected my breathing to calm down, but I just couldn't get it back. I began to realize, 'Oh my God, it's not happening.'" Ritzenhein covered the second mile in 4:37, 10 seconds faster than the first. He resisted looking back. This was no time to give his competition hope. "I was running out of steam," he said. "Pushing to the limit. I knew I'd have nothing left."

Hall had yet to make a big move. Through much of the second mile he couldn't even see Ritz and Webb up front. Hall's focus was on staying in front of the West runners who had beaten him at regionals. "I missed the critical moment when Dathan and Alan took off, and then they were gone," he said. "I thought they might blow up and come back, but mainly I worked to fend off the other West runners." The strategy worked. Soon Hall was in third place, gaining on Webb. The celebrated trio had raced to the first three positions, although Ritz's lead looked untouchable.

In the last mile, Webb couldn't process the circumstances. Every stride saw Ritzenhein increasing his lead. "I'd never been broken so far from the finish," Webb said. "I couldn't believe what was happening." When he realized Hall was closing near the three-mile mark, Webb kicked hard to maintain his position. He finished second in 14:55; Hall was third in 14:59.

Ritzenhein had caught fire. He burned through the third mile to the biggest lead in the history of Foot Locker. He broke the tape in 14:35, a full 20 seconds ahead of Webb, having destroyed the entire field. Immediately, running fans logged online and declared Ritzenhein the untouchable king of high school distance running. In his three years at Foot Locker Ritz had finished eighth once, and first twice. It was a difficult point to dispute.

Ritzenhein lay on the Disney World grass surrounded. Prins was there, as were his parents and fans. "I was hurting so bad the last two miles," Ritz said. "I kept going by telling myself, 'You only have to hurt another 10 minutes. If you don't keep pushing, you'll regret it the rest of your life.'" Ritzenhein had won with tenacity. He had followed the plan. He won because he understood victory came at a cost, and he was willing to sacrifice: "It was my last high-school cross-country race," he said. "My last Foot Locker. It was so important. It seemed like the biggest thing in the world."

TERRA HAUTE: THE NEW HOME FOR CROSS-COUNTRY

While Ritz, Webb, and Hall raced to put the future of American distance running on the map, the sport was also in the process of receiving a new home for what would become the nation's premier cross-country complex. Terra Haute in Indiana, a sleepy town of 60,000 nestled in the western part of the state, thus became an unlikely location for showcasing cross-country, but was soon a necessary addition to the pantheon of well-known sites.

Some courses were notable for their tradition, or their difficulty, or their scenery. The Lavern Gibson Championship Cross-Country Course became notable for something different: it was spectator-friendly. Originating with LaVern Gibson, a local resident and businessman who owned substantial acreage (240 acres that had first been used as a coal mine, then later as a landfill), a plan was launched to retool the land with cross-country as the centerpiece. In the early 1990s, after the property had undergone complete post-landfill reclamation, Gibson, assisted by his son Max and his grandson Greg, began the transformation.

It wasn't a fast process. Although the landfill had closed in 1987, the site sat vacant for ten years while the Gibsons mapped out plans. LaVern's grandson, Greg Gibson, a successful runner at the Rose-Hulman Institute of Technology in Terre Haute in the 1980s, urged the whole family to get involved and pushed development. As a result, LaVern, who died in 1993, left $300,000 in his will to a local club for the project.

Greg got to work immediately after. He hired an athletic facility design firm to create a course, but the end result wasn't great. Weaving around soccer fields and tennis courts, it felt like a high school course to John McNichols, the Indiana State University men's cross-country coach. ("I think we can do a whole lot better," McNichols had told Gibson.) So, Greg Gibson recruited McNichols—along with his former coach, Bill Welch of Rose Hulman—to retool the course so that it was not only carefully assembled to host championship caliber meets, but also tailored to elevate the fan experience. "To me, the property looked just perfect for what we wanted to lay out," recalled McNichols.

McNichols drew upon his years of coaching experience to address shortcomings he had observed in other courses. "We wanted a long straightaway before the first turn," McNichols said. "So we set that and our final result is an initial straightaway of about 940 meters before we turn. Next, we wanted a wide starting line, so we have 106 meters at the starting line which narrows gradually to the first turn," he added. "It is always a gripe of mine that cross-country typically is not a spectator sport: the runners run away, then you don't see them, you sit there and wait, pretty soon they come back by, and then you walk over to the finish chute and watch them finish," McNichols complained.

"Typically consideration of the spectator experience was never in the planning of a cross-country course. So the way to accomplish that was to narrow the geography. My idea was to have a 3K outside loop with two 1K loops that came in toward the center of the course. With that, you could run any distance from 3,000 meters up to 10,000 meters with that configuration. So we fiddled with the map and got it to work," McNichols said. The design enabled a spectator to stand at the high point near the finish line and see nearly the entire race from that single spot.

In 1997, after donations and a state grant raised $3 million for the course and adjacent Wabash Valley Family Sports Center, the route bearing LaVern Gibson's name opened for its first meet. And as the crown jewel of the Wabash Valley Family Sports Center (a multi-use facility with two gymnasiums, a fitness area, a senior gathering room, a maintenance barn, a concession/restroom facility, a finish line structure, and a finish line building), the purpose-built cross-country course was able to handle every need. "We even have a unique Plexiglas crows' nest structure for media coverage," explained David Patterson, executive director of the Terre Haute Convention and Visitors Bureau.

But perhaps one of the most pivotal accomplishments came two years after the course was officially dedicated. In 1999, the Terre Haute Convention and Visitors Bureau entered into a thirty-year agreement with the Sports Center that ensured the continued sustainability of the facilities. "We have a maintenance agreement in place which is funded by the Vigo County Innkeepers Tax, a 5% tax on all hotel rooms in the county," Patterson explained. "The bond—funded through a portion of the Tax—provides capital to the Terre Haute Convention and Visitors Bureau to maintain the Wabash Valley Family Sports Center going forward."

The executive director was quick to note how efficiently the bonded funding has worked: "We have 20,000 people that come through our town each year just due to cross-country. Essentially, we aren't putting any local money into this maintenance. The Innkeeper's Tax is all money derived from those coming in. So it is kind of a self-fulfilling prophecy in that the better we do, the more funding we have to maintain the facility. The Tax—and consequently the maintenance—is no local burden."

In further years course management made considerable improvements. First came permanent chain-link fencing to mark the various loops that interconnected to create any race distance. Then came the press box, the restrooms, and concessions area—which evolved from basic structures to permanent ones with more comfort and convenience. Then came live scoring, a videoboard, tailgate parties, and an awards stand. At their first NCAA Championships in 2002, meet management even arranged for a fighter jet flyover during the national anthem. In short, cross-country meets at the Gibson course were treated as major collegiate sporting events.

And they hosted a lot of major ones: in the first ten years following the initial NCAA Cross-Country Championship in 2002, nine more followed at Terra Haute (along with the requisite Pre-National Invitational that came with it). NCAA Division III championships, NCAA regional championships, Nike Cross Nationals regional championships, Indiana high school state championships, and other, smaller meets, soon followed.

Luckily, there was little debate among the experts as to the course's legitimacy. Coach Vin Lananna said the Terre Haute course provided a fair competition site for runners, citing the wide starting line and wide-open space. Shalane Flanagan, who won an NCAA title in Terre Haute in 2002, said the course was one of her favorites in college:

"It's not super technical, which is why I like it. It's a very honest course." Flanagan remembered a stark contrast in weather at Terre Haute between pre-nationals in October and nationals in November, however. On race day, athletes could be greeted with dry and warm conditions, she explained, or a chilly mudfest. "You can never win by just having speed," said Sam Chelanga, an NCAA Cross-Country champion over the course in 2009 and 2010 and holder of the 8K and 10K records. "It's an endurance course."

And because the LaVern Gibson site hosted so many championships, runners could easily measure themselves against those who ran before them, Chelanga claimed: "The course has more value now. Everybody dreams of going to Terre Haute." For the local men who created the course, it was incredible validation. "It seems like everywhere I go, I tell them I'm from Terre Haute, and someone will mention the cross-country course," Greg Gibson said. "My grandfather would love this."

THE BIG THREE DISPERSE COLLEGIATELY

While a stable championship venue for the sport was a big reason for its newfound popularity (especially collegiately), the disbursement of "The Big Three," Alan Webb, Dathan Ritzenhein, and Ryan Hall, also kept avid fans interested. The three most exciting young distance runners in a generation knew the stakes were high, and they embraced the profile of their new respective institutions.

All three landed at premier distance running colleges, although Alan Webb found himself a star on a University of Michigan squad that was talented (but not prestigious) in the years leading to his arrival. At Michigan's campus in Ann Arbor, Ron Warhurst, the men's cross-country coach, was forced to embrace a new role once Webb showed up: he had to get his athletes accustomed to reporters, big crowds, autograph hounds, and all sorts of attention. "When we walk out there to run, people are going to look at you," Warhurst told his team before Michigan's first home cross-country meet of 2001. "They'll be looking for Alan. Enjoy the attention. This is what it's like to have a big-time sport."

Webb had run the mile in 3:53 the previous May, breaking Jim Ryun's thirty-six-year-old scholastic record by nearly two seconds, and immediately faced scores of fans, national attention, and television exposure. When Webb ran his first college cross-country race, the Great American Festival in Rock Hill, South Carolina, he won with a sprint finish in 24:06 for eight kilometers after trailing in 25th place through two miles. Afterward, high school competitors, coaches, and parents lined up to meet Webb, take pictures with him, and get his autograph. Webb shrugged off the commotion, saying he was pleased to get a college race under his belt. "I wanted to play it conservatively," he said. "It was my first 8K. I'm just trying to find my zone."

Webb's attachment to Michigan wasn't just about distance running stardom—in fact, he was born there. Webb's father, Steven, had been an economics professor at the university, while his mother, Katherine, a speech therapist, had also been employed by the school. That was a big help when it came to racing and training in a new environment in college.

Meanwhile, Dathan Ritzenhein, perhaps the most prodigal cross-country runner of the group, faced an entirely different environment when he arrived at the University of Colorado in Boulder to train under Coach Mark Wetmore. Following the success of Adam Goucher, the Colorado program had established a legacy of success, but needed to keep it going if they hoped to contend at the top ranks. The addition of top Foot Locker finishers Jorge and Ed Torres, twins from Illinois, kept the Buffaloes ahead of the field. "After Adam Goucher got done with Colorado, those are big shoes to fill. Well how do you fill the shoes of a national champion? Get another national champion," Ryan Fenton, a sports commentator from Massachusetts stated. "And Colorado was able to do that. They were able to get Jorge and Ed Torres, the best duo of high school cross-country runners out there. They get a couple of good athletes in there, Steve Slattery being one of them. But even with the Torres brothers, even with Steve Slattery now on this team, you were still missing the depth of a team that could actually win a national championship." Enter Dathan Ritzenhein in the fall of 2001.

As a senior at Rockford, not only had Ritzenhein added his second Foot Locker title in two years, he had competed at the World Cross-Country Championships that spring, securing a bronze medal. It was the highest finish by an American at the event since Lynn Jennings had finished third in 1993. After surviving nearly five miles of shin-deep mud, Ritz still had the strength to pull away from teammate Matt Tegenkamp, a freshman at Wisconsin, and seventeen-year-old Nicholas Kemboi of Kenya to take bronze. "Mental toughness, guts, whatever you want to call it, he's got it," said Tegenkamp. "He won't give up." For Coach Mark Wetmore at Colorado, receiving the keys to the nation's top distance running recruit meant more responsibility. "It's great to write and read about these young guys now," Wetmore coaxed to *Sports Illustrated* in 2001, "but if you want to read about them in five or six years, my advice would be treat them gently."

Wetmore needn't have worried about gently ushering Ritzenhein into the program. *"Running With The Buffaloes,"* which cataloged the 1998 cross-country season in which Goucher became national champion, "had just come out, and I read it before my recruiting trip, and it just made you want to be a part of that," Ritzenhein claimed. "Dathan, I always joke, was one of the easiest kids I ever recruited in that his coach wouldn't really give me his phone number, and so I just sent Dathan a letter," said Colorado assistant coach Jason Drake. "Basically it said: 'You're probably getting recruited by every school in the country, so here's our number, we wouldn't waste your time otherwise,'" continued Ritzenhein. "So it's funny I ended up going there, they were the ones that played hard to get, but it made me want to go there even more."

And all along, Wetmore saw Ritz's long-term potential. Ritzenhein had chosen Colorado because Wetmore believed in high-mileage training, and Wetmore had faith in Ritzenhein's chances for survival precisely because he didn't seem recklessly passionate: "The kids who come into my office giving the most profound speeches about their dedication are the ones who are done the soonest," Wetmore stated. "Dathan sat down in my office and said, 'Whoa, these mountains are cool!' That was encouraging." "Really, Colorado needed somebody and they hit the jackpot," Fenton proclaimed. "You can't ask for a better fifth person to add to a squad than a national champ; one of the best all time high school runners ever. And instantly they were a force to win the national title."

For Ryan Hall, his declaration to run at Stanford University proved to be an opportunity too good to resist—as it meant he also had a chance at obtaining a world-class education in his home state, a scholarship, and stepping onto a team filled with talent. Entering the fall of 2001, the Stanford men's cross-country team had found themselves on the podium at the NCAA Cross-Country Championship for five consecutive years, including back-to-back titles in 1996 and 1997. In addition, the Stanford men had won five straight West Regional Championships and four of the previous five Pac-10 Conference Championships. They were also returning five All-Americans to the team, including 2000 Olympic semifinalist Gabe Jennings, the 1997 US Junior National Cross-Country champion who had missed the 2000 cross-country season after a late return from the Olympic Games.

Other decorated Stanford runners on the 2001 team included sophomores Grant Robison and Donald Sage (two returning All-American freshman); Louis Luchini, the third-fastest junior 10,000-meter runner in American history; and sophomore Ian Dobson, who finished third at the 2000 US Winter Cross-Country Nationals to earn a spot on the US Junior World Cross-Country team that competed in Ostende, Belgium. "Our returning five All-Americans will undoubtedly be the leaders of this team," Coach Vin Lananna said at the time. "They each have experience competing at the championship level and they understand what it takes to be one of the top finishing teams at the NCAAs. I like our chances to do well with these five young men toeing the starting line for Stanford."

And the 2001 cross-country season paid dividends for the Stanford Cardinal. Ryan Hall impressed in his debut, running 24:00-flat for 8K and winning the 2001 Murray Keatinge Invitational over teammate Louis Luchini (24:03) in early October at the University of Maine, while the varsity squads also swept their home Stanford Invitational at the end of September with individual winners and definitive team performances. While powerful drama was set to unfold later in the season between the major names in the sport, the legacy that the Cardinal was preparing to establish under the tutelage of Coach Vin Lananna was to be the standard-bearer for the decade.

THE CARDINAL AIM FOR GLORY

In many ways, 2001 proved to be the catalyst Stanford needed for one of the greatest cross-country seasons ever

witnessed at the NCAA Division I level. It just so happened that this performance did not occur at the 2001 championship itself—that event, one which was wholly unique for its own reasons—saw the University of Colorado defeat the second-ranked Cardinal by one point. Instead, a core nucleus was developed around a group of very talented young athletes who determined that team success supplanted all. It was the subsequent season, 2002, when it solidified.

"We have established a great niche for ourselves," Coach Vin Lananna began. "That niche is that any middle-distance or distance runner can help make Stanford a contender for the NCAA title year-in and year-out. The strength of the 2002 men's team will be that we have great big meet experience, but the rest of the country is strong as well with perennial national powers such as Arkansas and Colorado returning nearly their entire teams. But with our great group of men returning we will have many options for selecting our lineup: they will play interchangeable parts for most of the season. The important concept is for us to work as a finely tuned machine."

August 2002 saw four All-American Cardinal men return, and they cruised their way to the NCAA Championship with consistency at the top. Junior Grant Robison, one of the four All-American returners, won the Pac-10 individual title for Stanford, his second in a row, before resting at the NCAA regional meet. In his place, Donald Sage, also a junior, won the title at the Regional Championship, which was held at home on Stanford's golf course. In all, the Stanford men swept both the conference and regional qualifying meets easily (their eighth regional title in a row), while securing a winning percentage of nearly 90 going into the national championship.

It was there, at the inaugural NCAA Cross-Country Championship at Terre Haute Indiana in 2002, that Stanford won their first cross-country men's team championship in five years. They laid waste to the competition and bested their nearest competitor by 60 points. Grant Robison's third-place finish in 29:36 led the Cardinal pack, Stanford's highest individual men's finisher since 1992. Louis Luchini (fifth, 29:41), Donald Sage (sixth, 29:44), Ian Dobson (ninth, 29:47), and Adam Tenforde (29th, 30:25) completed the Cardinal scoring, and Ryan Hall (37th, 30:31) joined the five scorers in giving the Cardinal a total of six All-Americans. "This was a fantastic performance by our men's team," declared Lananna. "This NCAA title brought our entire season into focus. We put all the individual stuff aside all year and ran as a team. I haven't seen a team dominate like this at this level in quite a while." "We had high expectations going into the season, but this was amazing for us," added Grant Robison. "Having such a strong team took a lot of individual pressure off me." Surprisingly, the remaining eligibility for many of the All-American finishers indicated that a stronger showing was possible in 2003. Stanford would verify that claim a year later.

If the 2002 season had solidified Stanford's standing at the top, the 2003 season memorialized it. The 2003 Stanford men's roster was a carbon copy of the previous year's squad. In fact, the Cardinal returned every reserve from the 2002 team as well. With an abundance of All-Americans and a highly touted freshman class, the immediate and long-term future of Stanford Cross-Country became apparent, with a successful defense of the 2002 NCAA Cross-Country title on the top of the to-do list.

Six of the most recognized and accomplished runners in collegiate cross-country led the Cardinal in 2003. Along with talent, leadership, and big meet experience, the sextet of Grant Robison, Louis Luchini, Donald Sage, Ian Dobson, Adam Tenforde, and Seth Hejny brought with them a total of 41 All-American awards. With the addition of Hall, who entered his junior cross-country year having overcome injury and inconsistency to bring in another All-American award running in the NCAA Championship in 2002, the Cardinal appeared to have a recipe for one of the most dominant seasons in cross-country history.

Stanford opened the season in early September with a perfect-score victory at the Crystal Springs International Cross-Country Course, defeating their nearest competitor, California Polytechnic State University, San Luis Obispo (Cal Poly), by 30 points. Their top five, anchored by Adam Tenforde, all ran 25:02 or better for 8K. Next came equally easy victories at the Stanford Invitational, where the Cardinal scored a perfect score in the short-course competition and landed five of the first six places in the long-course race. Ian Dobson and Adam Tenforde led the way for the 8K course in 23:46 and 23:57, respectively, with Dobson coming within one second of the course record.

Going into the Pac-10 Conference Championship, the Cardinal men had cruised to more easy victories at the Murray Keatinge Invitational in Maine (scoring 18 points), and the pre-National NCAA meet in Iowa (scoring 25 points), where Ryan Hall had finished second overall, with teammates Dobson and Sage also finishing in the top five. Expectedly, Stanford defeated their nearest opponent (Oregon) 23 points to 91, crushing nine other schools from the Pac-10 in the process. The West Region was won with even better results: 18 total points scored, with four Cardinal in the top five, and another individual victory for Ian Dobson (29:32 for 10K), with Ryan Hall a mere second behind. Cal Poly, the next-closest regional school to qualify for nationals, scored 110 total points.

Thus the stage was set to see just how dominant the Stanford Cardinal men could be leading into the 2003 NCAA National Cross-Country Championship at the Irv Warren Memorial Golf Course in Waterloo, Iowa. But Mother Nature was not without some tricks of her own, and conditions could not have been worse for the Cardinal to defend their title. The 21-degree Fahrenheit temperature felt more like eight degrees with a 25-mile-per-hour wind chill. Unsurprisingly, some prognosticators doubted whether Stanford's harriers would falter in the cold weather: "Everybody has been lobbing comments at us that California guys can't run in the snow and cold," said Coach Andy Gerard. "My guys were excited by it."

Despite the weather, the Stanford juggernaut remained heavily favored and charged to the front at the start of the men's race and controlled the pace for most of the first two-thirds of the 10-kilometer distance. All seven Cardinal runners were within four seconds of the leaders at the three-kilometer mark, with Hall, Robison, Dobson, Luchini, Tenforde, and Sage still together at five kilometers (passed in 14:45) in a tightly bunched lead pack of two-dozen runners that also included Dathan Ritzenhein of Colorado and Eastern Michigan's Gavin Thompson. Ritzenhein was content to run with the pack for the early stages of the race: "I had a side stitch early and was tense from the weather," he said. "I would have liked to get out and help the pace."

Hall and Ritzenhein started to thin out the pack during the eighth kilometer, passing 8K in 23:34. The duo continued to battle over the final two kilometers with Hall leading Ritzenhein by 10 meters with a kilometer to go. The pair engaged in a thrilling stretch battle, with Ritzenhein only gaining his winning advantage in the final 100 meters. "This was something I'll never forget," said Ritzenhein, who covered the 10-kilometer course in 29:15 to win his first NCAA Cross-Country title, just one second in front of Hall. Gavin Thompson claimed third in 29:18, with Stanford's Robison (29:20), Dobson (29:25), and Luchini (29:29) finishing four-five-six. The Cardinal's Tenforde sealed the team title with a 12th place effort in 29:45, while Sage added insurance, finishing 13th in 29:46.

The result? Stanford scored 24 points to win by the largest margin in NCAA history: 150 points under second-place Wisconsin. The Cardinal's low point total was the second best in NCAA Division I history, with only UTEP's mind-boggling 17-point score from 1981 besting it. "Nobody really broke away early, and that was the only thing we were really scared of was that somebody was going to go," Coach Andy Gerard said. "I think the weather really helped us in that regard. But it really didn't force our hand in terms of making a choice between the individual title and the team title. Once things started to break up after about 7K, the instructions they had were to make sure the team title was squared away: look around, communicate—and if it was done then they could go for it. But until the team title was sorted out we weren't chasing individual titles."

For Hall, who finished second overall by a mere tick of the clock, the choice to win an individual title or win as a team was never in question: "I've been running with those guys for three years now, and just to be there is such a pleasure," Hall stated. "Really that's what it's all about. When you're out there running, everything is based on what our team was doing and staying together. There was never any 'I'm going to try and win this thing,' type of thing, it's always like 'Where are my guys at? How can we run this the best so that we can have the best outcome?' 24 points is pretty amazing, so we accomplished our goals."

While the men's team battle was a blowout, the women's side was a nail-biter. Stanford and Brigham Young University (BYU) traded the top position in the rankings all year, with the defending champion BYU Cougars slightly favored the week of the NCAA Championship. But it had been the Stanford women's team that had built a pedigree just as strong as the men's side (and in almost identical fashion). And at the 2003 NCAA Cross-Country Championship, they were finally ready to emerge with a title of their own.

In the years preceding 2003, the Lady Cardinal had frequently found themselves in a prime position to surmount the throne, only to be edged out in the end by Brigham Young University. Every year at the championship meet the story played out the same way: in 1997, following a Stanford women's championship in cross-country in 1996, BYU prevented a repeat national title, relegating the Cardinal to second place by a mere two points. In 1998 it was an almost identical story—BYU second with 110 points, Stanford third with 111. 1999 saw both teams on the podium once again, although BYU managed to win their second title in three years, while the Stanford women again won bronze. In 2000, BYU stayed one step ahead, earning a team silver while the Lady Cardinal finished third. And by 2002 it had been the same two schools in first and second: BYU on top once again.

It wasn't for the Stanford women's lack of trying. The early 2000s saw continual improvement on a team stacked with talent. Veteran All-Americans Lauren Fleshman and Erin Sullivan helped carry the Lady Cardinal through the 2002 season, while emerging younger runners, like future All-American's Alicia Craig and Sara Bei, helped solidify the female squad into the 2003 campaign.

Despite defending champion Shalane Flanagan and top challenger Kim Smith (a New Zealander attending Providence College) quickly separating themselves from the rest of the field in the 2003 NCAA Championship, Stanford finally found themselves victorious thanks to a third-place showing by junior Sara Bei (19:49) and a sixth-place performance by junior Alicia Craig (19:55). The Cardinal were able to dethrone BYU with a final score of 120 points to 128, while Providence was third with 222. The three freshmen completed the scoring for the Cardinal with Katy Trotter placing 21st (20:29), Arianna Lambie 24th (20:31), and Amanda Trotter 92nd (21:12). "The team did a really good job in treating this like any other race," Coach Dena Evans said. "The men's team was a great source of inspiration for us. I think the women's team saw the men's performance and believed it was possible to win if they ran as a team." Four of the five scorers received All-American status and, after winning men's and women's NCAA Cross-Country titles in 1996 and 2003, Stanford became the only school in NCAA Cross-Country history to sweep the men's and women's national titles in the same year two different times. Living in the shadows of BYU was finally over for the ladies from Palo Alto.

Bolstered by the youth of their fantastic freshmen in 2003, the Stanford women went on to claim titles again in 2005, '06, and '07, while the men found themselves on the podium again in 2008. Meanwhile, the University of Colorado Buffaloes were capitalizing on the momentum instilled by their head coach.

NEVER COUNT OUT THE BUFFALOES

In 2000, Kara Grgas-Wheeler (soon to be Kara Goucher) became the first individual NCAA Cross-Country champion for the University of Colorado women's team since the Association for Intercollegiate Athletics for Women (AIAW) era. With her, after running the season undefeated, came the surprising Lady Buffaloes, who up-ended the defending national champion BYU Lady Cougars.

That day, despite wind-chill conditions that brought the late Midwest November temperature to 19 degrees below zero, Colorado methodically worked its way from the back of the pack to the front to win the title. With a program-best 117 points, the Buffaloes finished 50 points ahead of defending national champion Brigham Young.

It was Colorado's first national team title in cross-country and signified history in other ways, too. In the championship sweep, Grgas-Wheeler's win marked the first time since 1994 that the individual national champion was represented on the NCAA Championship team. And although injuries and inconsistencies plagued the Buffaloes in subsequent seasons, four years later it meant they were flying under the radar; exactly where Coach Mark Wetmore wanted them to be.

Four years after their historic team win in 2000, the third-ranked Colorado women followed through with their race strategy to up-end Stanford, BYU, and every other squad at the 2004 NCAA Cross-Country Championship. The women, paced by a runner-up finish by Renee Metivier, placed all five runners in the top 30 to score a program best 63 points, 81 points ahead of runner-up Duke (144), Providence (164), Notre Dame (170), and pre-race favorite Stanford (175). The margin was the fourth largest in championship history.

In 2005 and 2006, the might of the Stanford Cardinal was a bit too much and prevented another first-place performance by the Buffaloes, but they still managed to find the podium in second place. And the Colorado women were not alone at the top. While the under-ranked Buffaloes were beating teams in the women's race, the Colorado men were turning heads just as quickly.

"The 2004 season—it was a rough one—because it was after Dathan [Ritzenhein] decided to go pro, I got injured over the summer, and our number three runner, he actually transferred to Arizona State," said Billy Nelson, a varsity cross-country athlete for Colorado from 2002 through 2006.

Teammate Brent Vaughn added: "I was our [number] four [runner on the team], and Jared Scott was our five at NCAAs in 2003. And we were all in the 120-130 [finishing] range [at NCAAs in 2003]. So if you take that team on paper from 2003 and put them into the 2004 year we don't look very good." Vaughn was one of the rising varsity athletes entering that 2004 season. "We put in a pretty serious summer together: we ran together every day. And almost the entire top eight or nine were there every day at 6:00 a.m. meeting at Potts [Field] doing the training starting July 1st. We were all very close—we were all brothers.

By the end of the summer we would have done anything for each other. And we trained together two or three hours a day. It's not a selfish mentality, it's definitely a team mentality—and a synergistic approach, where the whole is greater than the sum of its parts."

By the 2004 NCAA Cross-Country Championship, the Colorado men were relying on their synergy—but they also had young talent ready to follow the plan that Coach Wetmore had set out for them. "On paper [Wisconsin] annihilated us," explained Vaughn. "They had Chris Solinsky, Matt Tegenkamp, Simon Bairu, Tim Nelson. [Wetmore] was giving us the race plan: you know, be conservative, we're running a team race today, don't go out with the leaders. I think the leaders went through the first kilometer in something around 2:35 or 2:36 that day—and they paid for it." At the halfway mark, 10-plus runners in the lead were all separated by one second, with Arkansas's Josphat Boit in the lead at 15:16 and the 10th place runner at 15:17, with Vaughn (15:25) in 15th and teammate Bret Schoolmeester (15:26) in 19th. Vaughn had taken sole possession of fourth place by the 8K mark, having caught 13 runners in a three-kilometer span, while Schoolmeester chased down 12. At that point, Wisconsin had control of the team race with 80 points to Arkansas's 160, followed by Colorado.

"It was just a race of attrition. It was muddy," continued Vaughn. "We were just moving up through the field, just stalking Wisconsin guys as well as the rest of the field the last three or four kilometers." Vaughn finished in fourth place, crossing the line in 30:48, while teammate Schoolmeester finished eight seconds later in fifth. "I was pumped," said Vaughn. "It was by far the best finish I had ever had. And then I was like 'Oh shoot!' I started thinking we might be able to do this."

Senior Jon Severy, the first men's runner in the program's history to have run on two national title teams, ran the race of his career that afternoon, finishing 21st in 31:26. Severy made up as much ground as anyone, as he was 39th at the halfway mark, 25th at eight kilometers, and ran down most of the competitors in the final stretch. Newcomers Stephen Pifer and James Strang rounded out the scoring for the CU men, with Pifer running 31:56 to finish 44th and Strang running 31:59 to finish 49th. "The front two ran as well as I thought they possibly could and Jon ran way better than I would have expected. All of the five scorers ran better than my most optimistic aspirations. And with Stephen, James and Bradley, all freshmen, the sky is the limit," said Wetmore. And by winning the 2004 championship with the narrow margin of 90 points to Wisconsin's 94, luckily, Wetmore was right. Within two years, the Buffaloes were poised to strike again.

The second-ranked Colorado men headed into the 2006 championship knowing the race was theirs to lose. The muddy conditions were reminiscent of two years before and gave Colorado extra confidence. The temperature neared 50 degrees at race time—the warmest start Terre Haute had seen in three years—and contestants faced slippery conditions after nearly five inches of rain fell during the week

leading to the event. "We did well here a couple of years ago, too, and everyone was telling me that the mud was perfect for us," said Wetmore. "But Boulder is like a desert and isn't very muddy." As was often the case at the NCAA Cross-Country Championship, nothing was guaranteed.

With a fast start that saw eight runners pass the halfway point tied for first, it was the Buffaloes who placed five runners among the top 35 to beat a strong Wisconsin team by 48 points and claim their second men's championship in three years. Junior Brent Vaughn was Colorado's top scorer, finishing eighth among scoring runners and 12th overall. But it may have been junior Stephen Pifer's surge during the second half of the 10-kilometer race that boosted the Buffaloes to victory: at the 5K split he had 52 runners ahead of him, but streaked past 32 of them to nab the 20th spot overall (31:24). "I knew in the second half I had to come back and catch a lot of guys," Pifer said. "So I paid attention to sensory data, which is something that Wetmore has been preaching to us all year, checking your heart rate and breathing and things like that to make sure you are comfortable. The race doesn't really start until the last 3k, so you really have to get going."

CU and Wisconsin were the only schools to have three runners place in the top 15 in the scoring column. Said head coach Mark Wetmore: "I think the race was very fast for us. Every coach has to know their team and how fast they can go. We don't talk a lot about expectations, its aspirations for us. We equaled our aspirations today." "Not only does Colorado beat Wisconsin, but they do it two out of three years," claimed Ryan Fenton. "With those two victories all of a sudden you're thinking: 'Man, if Wetmore's your coach, anything can happen.'"

RITZ GOES PRO

In the spring of 2004, following his victory in the 2003 NCAA Cross-Country Championship, Dathan Ritzenhein found himself as the top American cross-country runner in the nation. And after a winter of strong training under Wetmore, Ritz ran 27:38 for 10,000 meters in April, a new US collegiate record and an Olympic Games "A" qualifier. Ritzenhein felt like this was the breakthrough of his career.

But in June, Ritzenhein went to the Colorado track for an interval workout. "I was in great shape," he said. Ritz ripped off sixteen 400-meter repeats in 62 seconds each, a monster workout, but awoke the next morning with severe pain in his left foot. An MRI showed a stress fracture of the fourth metatarsal. The Olympic trials were three weeks away. Mark Wetmore advised him to skip the trials: "My advice was that he sit it out and get healthy for his college season," Wetmore said. "But he was determined to run."

He had broken the foot so badly that even in a plastic boot, he was limping for two weeks. But after slogging through the Olympic trials race, Ritzenhein's gamble paid off. He was named to the Olympic team, went to Athens, and though he was far too unfit to be competitive (he dropped out of the 10,000 final with four laps left), he experienced the Games from a competitor's perspective.

Upon his return to Boulder, Ritzenhein turned professional, hired agent Peter Stubbs, and signed a five-year contract with Nike worth more than $200,000 a year. Despite having two full years of collegiate eligibility remaining, Ritzenhein was motivated to change. "I needed a new approach to training," Ritzenhein claimed. "I was always rushing back from injuries for the next NCAA season." Despite the urgency in leaving his collegiate opportunity behind, there was never a doubt in Ritzenhein's mind. "I'm sure it's the right decision for me," he said. "I just needed to do a few things differently. My body wasn't strong enough to hold up to the miles." Ritzenhein claimed that it was his bones and tendons that were taking the brunt of the work instead of his muscles.

He turned to former marathoner Brad Hudson for coaching, and began to add different drills and hill repeats to build strength. The foot healed, and on December 31, 2004—one day after his twenty-second birthday—Ritzenhein made his professional racing debut at the Boclassic, an invitational road race in the Alto Adige region of Italy. There, on a twisting 10-kilometer course that included generous sections of cobblestones, he placed third, beaten only by a second by five-time European cross-country champion Serhiy Lebid and Olympic marathon gold-medalist Stefano Baldini. Ten days later Ritzenhein won the Belfast International Cross-Country by surging away from three disbelieving Kenyans on the second of five laps. "They didn't go with me," Ritzenhein said. "It was easy. I shut it down and waved to the crowd." Then, later in February, Ritzenhein toyed with the field at the US National Cross-Country Championships, dropping Alan Webb short of halfway and cruising to a 14-second victory. "I bit off a little more than I could chew, running with Dathan," said Webb. "The guy is on fire right now."

Being on fire and decimating a domestic field at the US Cross-Country Championships was a great return to form, but Ritzenhein had bigger goals: the 7.45-mile senior men's race at the 33rd IAAF World Cross-Country Championships. "I'm not going over to France to concede victory to those guys," Ritzenhein said. "I'm going over there to duke it out and win a medal. I'd be doing an injustice to myself to think that I can't." Joining him was Stanford's Ian Dobson, a three-time NCAA Cross-Country All-American, and Matt Gabrielson, the eventual US Half Marathon Championship runner-up. Paul Kezes, who finished seventh at the US National Cross-Country Championship; Jason Lehmkuhle, a third-place finisher at the US Half Marathon Championship; and University of Wisconsin redshirt freshman and 2003 Foot Locker Cross-Country champion Matthew Withrow were also on the squad. It wasn't a dream team in line with what the United States had put together in previous decades, but it was their strongest team in recent memory. For Ritzenhein, it was his first World Cross in three years, after finishing 24th at the 2002 World Cross-Country Championships in Dublin, and earning the junior men's bronze medal at the 2001 World Cross event.

But unfortunately for Ritzenhein and the men, the race didn't turn out as planned. "I didn't think it would be this hot," Dobson claimed at the time. "I didn't think the heat was the problem, really. It was pretty terrible. After two laps I was ready to be done. The only positive thing I can say about the race is that I didn't drop out. I felt weak and just wasn't competitive. There's nothing I can say."

For Ritzenhein, who began the race aggressively with the leaders, it was blisters on his feet that caused his undoing: "That was probably the main problem. That was the big disaster. Between 2 and 3K, very early on in the race, I started getting bad blisters on the bottom of my feet. My right foot right now doesn't fit in my shoe real well, it's swollen on the bottom," Ritz claimed. "I knew that when they were forming that it was going to be a long race, but it got worse and worse. My foot is really sore on the bottom. It was terrible. I think I could've held on for a respectable finish if it wasn't for this."

Despite finishing in 62nd place (and having the US team come in 13th overall), the seriousness in which Ritzenhein and the others treated the experience led to more American athletes looking at World Cross as a viable racing opportunity later in the decade. As Ritzenhein stated: "I love cross-country more than all other disciplines. From a development standpoint, it is very important. Not so much from a physical standpoint, but emotionally. It helps young athletes fall in love with running. It helps them learn about teamwork, and pushing to get the most out of themselves without thinking about a clock. It really is just about competing." The sport also reinvigorated Ritzenhein and other American runners to start competing in more of the international cross-country meetings around the world, among them the Great Edinburgh Cross-Country in Scotland held in late January. And as the biggest American male names lined up to race the world's best in cross-country, the female contingent also benefitted.

THE US WOMEN FIND THE PODIUM

In the winter of 2000, Deena Kastor (formerly Deena Drossin) was riding a winning streak leading into the World Cross-Country Championships. She had won the Carlsbad Half Marathon, the US Cross-Country Championships (at both the four-kilometer and eight-kilometer distances) and the 15-kilometer Gate River Run in Jacksonville. At the time the United States hadn't seen a podium finish for the women's team event since 1992—while the most recent individual to finish on the podium had been Lynn Jennings with her third-place finish in 1993. But as with the men, the American women knew that with a concerted effort they could challenge the best in the world.

Despite the 2000 Olympics looming that summer, Kastor had been training for World Cross for six months leading up to the event, and she was feeling "confident and fantastic," as they approached. At the starter's gun, she felt a burst of energy and rushed to the lead, surrounded by the best runners in the world—and it felt easy. Things did not work out as planned, however. Early in the race a bee flew into Kastor's mouth—she managed to spit it out, but not before getting stung. Kastor, already at the front of the lead pack for the first two laps, soon felt her throat swelling: "I felt my throat start to close up, and I didn't think I was getting enough oxygen," she said. "I was scared, and I thought about quitting. But you don't want to quit when you've trained so hard and long for one race."

Not long after, Kastor blacked out and fell around the 5,000-meter mark. Scraped and bruised, she was jarred back to her senses and got up to finish 12th and lead the US team to a gratifying third-place finish behind Ethiopia and Kenya. "I was really upset crossing the finish line because I had been unable to accomplish what I set out to do because of something totally beyond my control," Kastor said. "But when I found out that we won the bronze medal, all the disappointment went away." Thankfully, her three US teammates came through with finishing places of 13th (Jen Rhines), 36th (Rachel Sauder), and 37th (Kimberly Fitchen) to beat Ireland by three points and give the United States their best team finish in eight years.

Within two years, after again finishing in 12th at World Cross in '01, Kastor lined up in Dublin at World Cross in 2002. This time she had taken proper rest and recovery into consideration before challenging the world's best. "Good balance is essential in any profession," Kastor said. "You have to love what you're doing. There's also room to be passionate about other things. Fortunately my hobbies and interests are good for my running career. [But while] starting a cafe and writing a book can come at any time, running has a certain window. I want to take advantage of it." Motivated and determined, Kastor and her teammates were ready to engage an all-out effort in Dublin.

It was England's Paula Radcliffe who started the race as a firm favorite, with bookkeepers' odds of 6–4 for her to win, and she started out strongly, moving up into the leaders as the field approached the first kilometer. Once there, Radcliffe encountered Kastor, who was already at the head of the field, a position that she was to maintain through much of the race. And at the end of the second kilometer, the leaders were tightly bunched with around a dozen in the pack, headed by Kastor, and including another two of the favored medal prospects, Ethiopia's Merima Denboba and Kenya's Rose Cheruiyot. Radcliffe was right in the center of the pack at this stage.

With a lap under their belts, the leaders started to spread out a little, with Kastor still in the lead, inseparable from Radcliffe and closely followed by Cheruiyot and Denboba. American Colleen deReuck (who was originally from South Africa but had acquired American nationality just fifteen months prior to the race) trailed a few seconds back in the chase pack. Radcliffe moved into the lead as the bell sounded for the last lap and started to gradually pull in front of Kastor, with Japan's Miwako Yamanaka trailing by 14 seconds alongside deReuck, Cheruiyot, and Denboba. From then on it was a straight run home for Radcliffe as she built up and maintained a lead of 30 meters over Kastor, finishing the race in 26:55 to Kastor's second-place time of 27:04.

With the first two places already assured by halfway through the last lap, the battle for bronze was being fought 100 meters back as deReuck, Yamanaka, and Kuma gradually pulled ahead of Denboba. In the end, it was deReuck who found the resolve necessary to pull ahead of Yamanaka and finish two seconds ahead of the Japanese athlete, who was given fourth in a near photo finish with Eyerusalem Kuma, also timed at 27:19. It was the first time since 1993 that an American woman had stood on the podium at the World Cross-Country Championships (for the long-course race), and on this day there were two. It was also the first time since 1993 that an African-born runner had not featured on the women's podium. It was the highest finish by an American team at World Cross since 1992, as they finished 10 points out of first.

"I never expected to beat Paula as she is so strong and she certainly made this difficult for me," Kastor said afterward. "The course was beautiful, so well manicured and it was not as hard as I imagined it would be." Bronze-medalist deReuck agreed: "The course is just as I imagined green Ireland to be like." DeReuck also could not believe how successful she had been: "My original goal was to be in the top-20 but to get a medal is unbelievable. I think that we were really running as a team and I am delighted that we got the silver team medal."

The following year in 2003, Kastor again found herself second overall at the World Cross-Country Championships, and the American women, buoyed by the performance of Colleen deReuck in seventh and aided by Katie McGregor and Elva Dryer in 13th and 14th, respectively, finished with a bronze medal for back-to-back podium finishes. While the American women no longer featured on the podium for the long-course in the decade (they would finish close, with four top-five placings) the 2005 women also finished third in the short-course championship. It was there, in 2005, that Stanford graduate Lauren Fleshman carried the torch, crossing in 11th place overall and leading the women to a team bronze.

"This group ran with a lot of integrity," Fleshman said at the conclusion of the 2005 race. "We thought we had a chance to win a medal and before the race we all talked about our goals and it's such a mature group of women. Everyone ran with one goal in mind and that speaks volumes about this team. I got some really good advice from some athletes that ran yesterday and got some good advice to stay conservative and stay within myself. I had a really strong kick home and passed some people the last 50 meters to get 11th."

Among the placers for that 2005 squad was a young, up-and-coming runner by the name of Shalane Flanagan, who not only had a bright future in the sport (supplanting Kastor as the premier American female cross-country runner of the decade), but who ran injured in the 2005 championship to help the American women finish third. Flanagan had won the national title for the short-course cross-country championship and finished in 20th overall at Worlds to help the United States. "That's the only reason that I'm here, for the team to get on the stand. I'm so pleased that I could help the team to a top-three finish. The foot is feeling much better [and] I was not hindered by it. If anything it was a lack of fitness and not being able to work out. This meet was one of my goals for this year." For Flanagan, as her national finish indicated, it was just the beginning of her success.

ENTER SHALANE FLANAGAN

Shalane Flanagan, who grew up in Marblehead, Massachusetts, had an unstructured path to distance running success, but was fortunate to have the right genetics: her parents were both World Cross-Country veterans. Her mother, Cheryl Treworgy, was a former marathon world-record holder (as Cheryl Bridges in 1971) and a five-time US World Cross-Country participant. Her father, Steve Flanagan, was also a US World Cross-Country participant and marathon runner (whose personal record was 2:18). And while the young Shalane Flanagan found herself competitive and motivated to run, her high school coach, a former hurdler, had no plan to train the team.

Flanagan related:

My high school coach didn't know much about distance running so we were massively undertrained. I had the desire to get better and I knew that we weren't quite doing enough to get better. I was devouring running books. If I went to a running camp I would take notes at the running clinics. I would bring them back, show my dad and my mom and come up with my own training plans. I made up workouts in high school for myself. It was in a way a method to have personal accountability at a young age. I thrived on not being an innocent bystander and an actual creator of my fitness. I enjoyed that. I had a sounding board with my parents or it probably wouldn't have happened.

As luck would have it, Flanagan's drive and self-motivation led to success at the Massachusetts state level: "I had a really special race at Franklin Park my senior year in a race that was a qualifier to go to the State Championships," Flanagan said. "It was the same exact day as the NCAA Division I Northeast Regional that was on the same course about an hour after my race. I ran a course record of 17:08 and it ended up being faster than what the collegiate women ran an hour later. I remember thinking, 'Oh, I'm in really good shape. I beat all of the collegiate women.' Ray Treacy, coach of Providence came up to me and said, 'Wow! You just beat all of my women!' That was a pretty special performance that day as, not only was I the best high school runner, but I raced faster than a couple hundred collegiate women." After three All-State cross-country performances, a first-place All-State finish in the mile, and a two-mile win whose record still stands, Flanagan decided on the University of North Carolina at Chapel Hill for college.

As a freshman at North Carolina in 2000, Flanagan came out strong in the autumn, placing fourth at the NCAA Cross-Country Championships. And by her sophomore year, the stakes were even higher: "I was in phenomenal shape and actually was predicted to win the race," Flanagan began. "The night before the race I got an award as the national runner of the year. It freaked me out. I literally psyched myself out. I was in the lead and there was a point in the race where my coach told me to run an all-out 800 meters to pull away from everyone. I did. I ran an all-out 800 and it broke me. I basically walked it in to 22nd place. But I was in great shape and had I been able to execute better I probably would have had three NCAA titles in cross-country." Luckily in 2002 and 2003 her aggressive running in cross-country gave her massive margins of victory and she became a two-time individual champion.

Shortly after her second NCAA Cross-Country title, Flanagan entered the US National Cross-Country Championship short race, where she won the four-kilometer event and earned a birth to her first World Cross-Country Championships. Flanagan's performance in the muddy conditions in Belgium led the US women as she finished 14th overall, and it connected her with national teammate Lauren Fleshman (both would return the following year and lead the US women to their bronze medal). Due to the muddy conditions from considerable rainfall, the turns on the course became especially treacherous for the athletes, who were forced to slow down to avoid slipping. As a result, Flanagan finished 27 seconds behind winner Masai Edith from Kenya.

Injuries prompted time away following Flanagan's 20th place performance at the 2005 event, but she reemerged on the cross-country course in the spring of 2007 where she finished second in the US Cross-Country Championship to Deena Kastor. And, after adding a national cross-country title in 2008, and a second in 2010, Flanagan once again decided to race at the World Cross-Country Championships—this time, in the senior women's long race (the IAAF had discontinued the short and long course variations following the 2006 event). Once more, the American women, led by Flanagan's 12th place finish, found themselves on the medal-stand with a bronze. Featured too at World Cross had been a continuation of an American revival, one prompted by Hall, Ritz, and Webb in the years preceding, but carried on now by a new group of three young male stars: the golden trio.

THE GOLDEN TRIO

It was intended to be America's statement to the world at large and the East Africans in particular: three of the fastest and most prolific young distance runners the United States had produced in thirty years, together on one team—what *USA Track and Field* described as "a trio of college freshmen that could lead Team USA to a team medal." It wasn't Webb, Ritz and Hall, either. Three eighteen-year-olds: German Fernandez, Chris Derrick, and Luke Puskedra, were continuing the US legacy and they were bringing America back in the world's toughest footrace.

The stage was the 37th edition of the World Cross-Country Championships in Amman, Jordan. "We have proved ourselves capable of hosting major world championships and we will deliver something special and unique," lead organizer Prince Feisal Al Hussein had promised. The 2009 event would not disappoint.

The "world's toughest footrace" hadn't always been the toughest to win. For the United States, prior to the arrival of Kenya and Ethiopia at the 1981 event, the junior championship had been almost certain victory. First place individual finishes alongside gold-medal team performances were common. Names like Rich Kimball, Eric Hulst, and Thom Hunt helped the United States in their consistent domination of the event. They also managed to earn silver in 1980 and gold in 1981. And the modern revival led by Hall, Webb, and Ritz had shown that America could still contend.

When Ritzenhein finished third in 2001 (along with the fifth-place finish of fellow American Matt Tegenkamp), the hope for America's return to form came to fruition. In 2001 the junior team finished only 47 points away from defeating Kenya, and only three points away from finishing on the podium. It was a kick-start that needed one more push. Eight years later, when Fernandez, Derrick, and Puskedra decided to suit up, hopes were high once again.

Each of the three young athletes entering the event had established reputations well before the World Cross-Country Championships, with top collegiate marks in the NCAA and age-group national records on the track. But Fernandez, Derrick, and Puskedra weren't just going to World Cross to contend—they wanted to win. As Fernandez's collegiate coach Dave Smith said before the 2009 race: "[Skipping NCAAs] was hard for him as a competitor. But he wants to compete against the best in the world. He's going to see that at juniors, get a look again at the guys he's going be facing for the next eight to 10 years. I think it's important for him to see where he is in that field, envision himself winning against that field and having the opportunity to test the waters."

This was because German Fernandez was already a household name by the spring of 2009. After gaining a reputation as one of the strongest runners in California history only two years prior, Fernandez had become the nation's best prep runner, and had built his pedigree by turning faster times and setting some notable course records in cross-country. In fact, as a student-athlete at Riverbank High School, just ninety minutes east of the Bay Area in California, Fernandez hadn't just set new marks—he'd absolutely destroyed them.

A few highlights from his senior high school season in 2007 included running the 36th annual Artichoke Invitational in Half Moon Bay, where Fernandez beat his own previous record, crossing in 11:04 for 2.33 miles. His nearest competitor for the course ran 12:08, a respectable time considering that it was none other than future US junior cross-country champion and NCAA all-region runner Erik Olson.

A week earlier Fernandez had set the course record at the prestigious Stanford Invitational, running 14:42 for

5K in hot conditions. Notable was the fact that his nearest opponent was the state champion in the division above him, a runner by the name of Mohamed Abdalla, who Fernandez beat by more than 40 seconds. Abdalla was one of 1,320 runners Fernandez defeated that day.

By November, Fernandez ran the five-kilometer state-meet course at Woodward Park in Fresno in a mind-numbing time of 14:24, unheard of considering his per-mile average for the course converted to three 4:33 miles back-to-back-to-back. On the day, out of all divisions, Fernandez's nearest opponent was 49 seconds slower. And yet, as columnist Rich Gonzalez reported, Fernandez wasn't the only high school runner making headlines. He shared that distinction with Luke Puskedra, a runner of similar ability from Judge Memorial Catholic High School in Utah: "Most statistical comparisons point to [Fernandez and Puskedra] being nearly even at this point, and the gap between them and all others [in the country] is growing," Gonzalez had said.

Luke Puskedra was a deserving challenger to Fernandez's throne. In fact, Puskedra's favorite experiences in running had been instilled at a young age, when he and his father would travel together to track meets: "In fifth grade I finally convinced my family to let me do summer track. I would finish third or better in every race because it meant I could go to another meet with my dad. Some of my most memorable moments would be those trips with my father."

But winning did not always come easy to Puskedra. As a five-foot-two freshman at Judge Memorial Catholic High School in Utah, he had some lofty goals: "He believed he'd run under four minutes in his freshman year," said Judge coach Dan Quinn. "Every time he went out he tried to do just that. He's been doing it ever since." Following a huge growth spurt between his freshman and sophomore years in which he reached his current height of six-foot-five, Puskedra struggled to find his stride. Despite winning the Utah State cross-country championship as a junior in 2006, he missed competing in the Foot Locker Cross-Country Championships. Puskedra remained vigilant despite his inconsistency.

As a senior, there was no denying him. During the 2007 cross-country season Puskedra set a course record in every race he ran in Utah, including the course record on the state course at Sugar House Park. As the snow fell, Puskedra blew away the field, running 14:54 to repeat as 3A boys' champion. In the process, he shattered the previous state course record held by Josh Rohatinsky (who had won the NCAA Cross-Country Championships), by nearly 13 seconds. 5A champion Stephen Clark ran the next fastest time of the day more than 26 seconds slower. The stage was set for the 2007 Foot Locker West Regional, where Puskedra was eyeing a much-awaited showdown with Fernandez.

Surprisingly, the talk of the town when the athletes arrived at the Mt. SAC regional course wasn't the race for the individual title, but a course change. Due to high amounts of rain that fell the day before the race, course officials decided to use their alternate "rain" course to avoid mud and potential problems on the normal trail. But none of the top athletes let the change affect them. Right from the gun, Puskedra took the early lead, pushing the pace through the first mile in 4:30 (all downhill). By the halfway point it was Puskedra and Fernandez who were pulling away.

With 600 meters to go Fernandez made a strong move to gap Puskedra—and by the finish, Fernandez had pushed hard enough to beat Puskedra by 15 seconds (final time, 14:53). Puskedra finished strong in 15:08 for second—a guarantee he would run nationals and get a second chance at Fernandez. Afterward, Fernandez talked about how the race felt, saying, "My goal was just try and qualify. With 400 meters to go I knew I had to stay focused."

Meanwhile, as Puskedra and Fernandez battled in Southern California, Neuqua Valley senior Chris Derrick was busy setting records of his own in Illinois. Columnist Scott Bush reported on Derrick's 2007 season: "Over the past year, Chris Derrick's transformation from very good runner to great runner has sparked conversation implying Chris could be this year's Foot Locker National Champion. Always a big meet performer, Chris ran 8:54 last year in an amazing 3,200-meter state championship race, where he nearly beat one of the nation's best in Evan Jager. This fall, Chris has stepped up one more level, breaking numerous course records, leading his US ranked squad to an undefeated season, and showing he is perhaps the best harrier in the land." For Derrick the goal was simply to have his team win the Illinois state meet. As the race approached, however, he found he might have a chance to set the course record as well.

Winning the Illinois State Cross-Country Championship as a team, Neuqua Valley scored 86 points to York's 105, denying York coach Joe Newton a 27th state title. Along the way, Derrick ran 13:51, won the boys' individual title, and fell just two seconds short of breaking Craig Virgin's course record. In the process, Derrick became the first runner since Sandburg's Tom Graves in 1977 to break 14 minutes (13:56): "I wanted to kick as hard as I could to get that record," said Derrick. After a national individual and team championship at Nike Cross Nationals, and a relatively easy Foot Locker qualifier, Derrick was also joining the Foot Locker National Championship title conversation.

Any thoughts that the boys would start conservatively were quickly thrown out the window when Luke Puskedra took out the first 800 meters of the 2007 Foot Locker National Championship in 2:10. He hit the mile in 4:28. Coaching guru John Kellogg summed up the sentiment, "If he wins the thing, I'd be shocked." At the mile, Puskedra was closely followed by South champ Colby Lowe, Midwest sixth placer Kevin Williams, Northeast champ Donn Cabral, and pre-race favorite German Fernandez. Midwest starlet Chris Derrick was nowhere to be found, however: "They went out really fast, at about my mile [personal-record] pace," Derrick said. "When I saw at 800 they were at 2:10, I was getting a little bit worried."

Derrick stuck to his guns and the pace slowed dramatically during the second hilly mile. One and a half miles

was hit in roughly 7:00 and two miles was hit in 9:28. By two miles, Midwest regional champ Mike Fout, who had stayed just off the pace at the start, joined the three other regional champs along with Puskedra. Early in the third mile, Fout made a move for glory and quickly gapped everyone else. The other four had no response.

But just when it appeared to be over, Chris Derrick came up hard from the back. Derrick quickly caught up and dispatched the tiring foursome of Fernandez, Lowe, Cabral, and Puskedra—and he was gaining on Fout. Just when it looked like Derrick might do it, there was only 400 meters left and Derrick ran out of real estate. Derrick was second in 14:57, Fernandez third in 15:09. Puskedra, paying for his "suicidal" early pace, crossed in fifth, six seconds after Fernandez. Fout, who had the race of his life, never made the same impact again. But for Fernandez, Puskedra, and Derrick, their legacy was just beginning.

In the months following, German Fernandez, after being sick at the 2007 Foot Locker Cross-Country Championships, managed to win the US Junior Cross-Country title and competed in the 2008 World Cross-Country Junior Championships. But at Worlds he finished a disappointing 25th with a sore Achilles. Rebounding quickly, in June, Fernandez would set a historic double at the California State Championship on the track, running 4:00.29 in the 1,600 meters, and then coming back a few hours later to win the 3,200 in 8:34.23. It was by far the fastest "double" in California state meet history.

In the fall, Fernandez continued his success by winning the Big 12 Conference Cross-Country title as a true freshman for Oklahoma State, clocking 23:47 for eight kilometers. It prompted talks of Fernandez potentially upsetting two heralded seniors in Galen Rupp and Sam Chelanga for the individual NCAA Cross-Country title.

Meanwhile, Luke Puskedra was quickly making a name for himself at the University of Oregon while Chris Derrick was flourishing at Stanford. After briefly leading the nation in the spring by running 8:46 for 3,200 meters, Puskedra trained hard over the summer and appeared as the top freshman finisher at the Pac-10 Cross-Country Championship—beating Chris Derrick over eight kilometers, 23:32 to 23:38. Then, at the West Regional, it was Derrick who got the upper hand, beating Puskedra by a second (28:44 to 28:45) over 10 kilometers. All three runners of the golden trio were once again on a crash course toward greatness at the 2008 NCAA Cross-Country Championship.

However, the NCAA Cross-Country Championship possessed storylines that went well beyond the emergence of the three phenomenal freshmen. Oregon's Galen Rupp, a senior who had been denied an individual victory at the championship the year prior, had only one final opportunity to win. Sam Chelanga, a Kenyan from Liberty University, was vying for an individual title as well. For Fernandez, Puskedra, and Derrick, their team affiliations took higher precedence than their individual titles.

Despite this, each member of the golden trio found themselves in the lead chase pack in pursuit of Rupp and

Chelanga during the start of the race. Oregon's Puskedra was in the best position of the three, part of a front-running cohort of Oregon athletes all chasing teammate Rupp. At 3,000 meters, the Ducks had three runners in the top five, whereas the supposed challengers from Oklahoma State were nowhere to be seen—Oklahoma State had no one in the top 65. Along with Puskedra, Chris Derrick, as the lead runner for Stanford, was staying step for step with the leaders and trailed Puskedra by less than a second until the final 2,000 meters.

Behind Oregon, Oklahoma State, the one team that the experts thought had a chance to win, began moving up. However, any chance they had for a podium finish vanished suddenly when Fernandez stepped off the course. According to an eye-witness: "Fernandez and his teammate Kosgei were running right next to each other in the chase pack for 3rd place. It looked like they were about to make a move to break away from the pack, then all of sudden I saw German's face grimace in pain and he collapsed in the middle of the course. He rolled off the course still writhing in pain on the ground. It was obviously either a sprained ankle or an Achilles injury since he was grabbing his ankle. It looked like Achilles since he was grabbing the back of his ankle, and the reports have proved it to be an Achilles problem."

By the end of the fast 10K championship, the results told the story for the three freshmen: Puskedra finished as the top frosh on the day, crossing the line fifth overall, 24 seconds behind teammate Rupp, who was able to win his first individual title (Puskedra, 29:27; Rupp, 29:03). Derrick crossed the line as the first finisher for Stanford, seventh overall in 29:29. Fernandez was carted off the field without a finishing time, despite running 23:38 through the first eight kilometers. The next time these three would face off over hill and dale, the circumstances would be different: as junior runners all under the age of nineteen (and without team obligations) the pressure would once again be on the shoulders for each runner to make it on the national team for the World Cross-Country Championships.

The 2009 USA Cross-Country Junior Championship, held in early February, told a very different tale than the NCAA Championship. Fernandez, Puskedra, and Derrick, once again toeing the line against each other—this time at Agriculture Farm Park in Maryland over eight kilometers—were seeking to qualify individually for one of six spots on the USA National Cross-Country Team. Fernandez was the defending champion. Fully healed, he had run a world junior record with a 3:56.5 mile only a few weeks before. Derrick too had been on fire, running 13:44 indoors for 5,000 meters. Puskedra wasn't far behind, running a personal best of 13:46 indoors for 5,000 meters. The three of them were well in contention as they followed the course, which was constructed in four 2,000-meter loops.

Runner's World correspondent Amby Burfoot picked up the story: "Last Saturday, when I caught a glimpse of Fernandez for the first time, I was standing at the 1K mark of the 2K loop used for the National XC Championships in Derwood. Fernandez was running up front

with the super talented Chris Derrick and Luke Puskedra. (He buried them in the last mile.) All three are still just 18 years old. People are calling them the future of American distance running, and people might be right. Here's what I saw at that first glimpse: two really good runners, and one who looked completely different. Fernandez looked completely different. I immediately thought, 'He runs like Haile Gebrselassie.' Here's how Fernandez runs like Geb: He's got quick, light feet but they generate an impressive amount of power with each stride. You can't 'see' power, but when someone runs fast with a quick footstrike, it's because his lower legs have that rare ability. No wonder he just ran that surprising 3:56.5 indoor mile with little or no apparent speedwork." Fernandez took the race, winning comfortably in 23:20. Derrick crossed in second 19 seconds later, and Puskedra was third, in 23:53. They were the only three athletes under 24 minutes.

All three runners qualified for the World Cross-Country Championships, and, for the first time in thirty years, spurred talk of the United States claiming the title: "Americans in recent years have yawned at World XC as many of America's top talents have skipped the meet to focus on other events. Not this year," wrote Robert Johnson for LetsRun.com. "The great news is that one of America's best talents is here in German Fernandez and World XC is obviously a huge priority for him, as he just skipped NCAAs to get ready for this race. The better news is he is still a junior so his medal prospects are at least in the realm of theoretical possibilities." All told, there was definitive hype surrounding the event.

The course in Amman was set in a picturesque bowl between tree-lined hills but provided a tough cross-country challenge. The terrain was violently undulating through the countryside; traversing a surface of sand, gravel, and grass. Adding to the permanent features, Mother Nature threw in a strong, chilling westerly wind, especially as runners approached the long agonizing slope of the finishing straight. "I thought it would be rolling hills like an American golf course, but it was nothing like that," said runner Kimberley Smith, "That was the hardest course I've ever run. It was a true cross-country course."

The difficulty of the task went beyond the terrain. Top candidates from Kenya and Ethiopia were also in contention. The junior men's race appeared to have a "clear favorite" according to the IAAF: eighteen-year-old Ethiopian Ayele Abshero, who had run 29:21 for 10,000 meters in 2007 (at altitude). In 2008 Abshero had earned the silver in the junior race at World Cross and then went on to run 13:35 for 5K on the track.

As for the Kenyans, not a lot was known about them. The Kenyan junior trials had been fairly close, as first through fifth place all finished within seven seconds. Experts interpreted this as meaning there wasn't one Kenyan who was better than any other. But after the eight-kilometer Kenyan trials, the qualifiers still carried a mighty reputation: John Kemboi (25:22), Paul Tanui (25:23), Japhet Korir (25:25), John Chekpwony (25:29), and Charles Chepkurui (25:35) seemed difficult to beat. If one runner ran excellently it was impossible to know whether they would come from the front or back—and there was an additional problem. Titus Mbishei, who was fifth in 25:29 at the Kenyan Trials, had run 7:50 for 3,000 meters, 13:27 for 5,000 meters and 27:31 for 10,000 meters in 2008—times that could not be touched by Fernandez, Puskedra, or Derrick even on their best day—and he was Kenya's *fifth* finisher at the trials.

Soon, the time had come. Each of the three Americans toed the line along with 118 others from 29 nations. As expected, the race went out fast. Fernandez and Derrick fell in immediately with the front group, led by Titus Mbishei of Kenya, and they found themselves among such familiar names as Ethiopia's Ayele Abshero and Uganda's Moses Kibet. Puskedra wasn't matching the furious pace and was hanging on for dear life at the rear of the lead group.

The race was driven by the national teams for Kenya and Ethiopia. And despite Fernandez and Derrick's best efforts, the leaders did not crumble during any of the four laps along the 2,000-meter course. To make matters worse, Fernandez was hurting: "The first two laps, my foot felt fine," he said. "But on the last two long loops I thought that the muscle was a little bit tight, and that the same thing that happened to me with my Achilles at NCAA nationals was going to happen, but then it went away. I just blocked out the pain."

By halfway, the outcome was becoming clear: four Kenyans and four Ethiopians were leading and it wasn't close—the leaders had about 40 seconds on Derrick and Fernandez. By the end, despite their best efforts and preparation, victory would not come on this day. Puskedra (24:53) finished an admirable 30th overall, 90 seconds behind the winner and about 40 seconds behind his American teammates. Chris Derrick (24:20) held on gamely to cross the line in 15th. Fernandez (24:13), running as hard as ever, finished 11th overall—the first non-African across the line, and the first American. It was the best finish for an American junior athlete at World Cross in seven years. As Fernandez stated afterward: "I just tried to go out with the front group and stay there as long as possible, and I think I did a pretty good job of it." The US team finished fifth overall behind Kenya, Ethiopia, Uganda, and Eritrea. It was their best team finish since 2001.

As expected, glimmers of cross-country success continued throughout the lives of the golden trio. Beset at times by injuries and low iron, the fragile German Fernandez found only sporadic highs of cross-country glory following his 11th place finish at Worlds. In the Big 12 Conference, Fernandez finished fourth in the fall of 2009, then second, and finally first again in 2011—three years after his initial Big 12 cross-country title. At NCAA Nationals, Fernandez earned All-American honors in 2010 (eighth), and 2011 (11th)—and enjoyed team titles in 2009 and 2010 with Oklahoma State. Professionally, his biggest accomplishment in cross-country was a surprise third-place finish at the 2014 USATF Club Cross-Country Championship.

Luke Puskedra earned All-American honors in cross-country four times, finishing 21st in 2009, third in 2010, and sixth in 2011. A calf injury slowed his training, but eventually Puskedra found success on the roads with times in the elite echelon for the marathon and half-marathon distances.

Chris Derrick's career in cross-country might have been the most notable. He returned in 2009 to win the Pac-10 conference and West Regional cross-country individual titles before finishing third in the NCAA national championship. He also finished fifth in 2010 and second in 2011 to cap four All-American seasons. In addition, Derrick won US National Cross-Country titles in 2013, '14, and '15. His ultimate highlight, however, was helping the United States to a silver-medal finish at 2013 World Cross, a race where he crossed the line in 10th place. It was the United States's first team medal at the World Cross-Country Championships in twenty-nine years. Kenya finished third as a team due to Derrick's effort.

"THE LITTLE PONY"

The United States's youth movement was not confined to the boys. While age-group records were falling by way of names like Ritz, Webb, Fernandez, and Derrick, one female runner had risen to the top in the same period.

At the University of Oregon's iconic Hayward Field, America's biggest distance running names had found their stride: Dellinger, Prefontaine, Chapa, Salazar. Jordan Hasay, born in 1991 and raised in Arroyo Grande, California, became part of that Hayward Field legacy when, as a sixteen-year-old, she knelt before the stadium clock. On it was a new American record in the high school 1,500 meters at the 2008 Olympic trials. In fact, it was just another accolade added to an already long list: two-time Foot Locker Cross-Country champion. Seven-time Junior Olympic champion. Thirteen age-group records. Nine high school class records. There was no doubt why Oregon wanted her.

Hasay's first lesson came on a dirt oval track during a mile run as a nine-year-old. She went out at the gun, following instinct, and held her pace to the end. As she ran, she calmly watched another girl speed up and pass her just before the finish line. Dumbfounded, Hasay asked her coach afterward, "You can sprint at the end?" Armed with this newfound knowledge, Hasay beat the girl the next week. And the week after.

The second lesson had also been at Hayward Field. Hasay looked out at the packed stands of the 2004 USATF National Junior Olympic Track and Field Championships (four years before her record-setting day at the Olympic trials), and she was overwhelmed by the giant crowd. Tears in her eyes, the seventh-grade Hasay turned back from the packet pick-up and told her parents she did not want to run in front of all these people. It was only the second time her parents had had to comfort her since she began running.

Luckily, even as a seventh-grader, the fear didn't stick, and Hasay toed the line at her first Junior Olympics hoping to match the older, more experienced girls. Rather than match them, she ran the fastest times in meet history with a 4:34 in the 1,500 meters and a 9:48 in the 3,000, crossing the line alone in both races. Back home, her running club coach sat her down to tell her she should stop skipping practice to swim. She did. She gave up team sports to forge this new territory alone, keeping pace with the boys on the team or learning to suffer through intervals by herself. Her biggest competition was her own shadow. No one else could keep up.

Originally, Hasay had other motivations: "Once I quit the other sports and began training, my mom would let me join her for four miles of her 6-mile loop," said Hasay. "Eventually, I got up to six. You see, racing was never my favorite part of the sport, this was. I got up early every day and ran that loop." That loop led to the all-time freshman record at the 2005 Mt. SAC Cross-Country Invitational (16:48), a California State cross-country title, and the 2005 Foot Locker Cross-Country Championship regional and national titles. Hasay became only the second freshman to win Foot Locker and did it with the fastest winning time in four years (17:05 over 5K). She also won the 3,200-meter race at the 2006 California State Meet with a time of 10:13 and won the mile race at the 2006 Golden West Invitational with a time of 4:42.21, just 0.21 seconds off the high school freshman mile record of 4:42.0 set by Mary Decker in 1973.

Like Shalane Flanagan, Hasay's parents had athletic backgrounds. Her father was a high school basketball star in Pennsylvania, and her mother was a national-level swimmer in her native England. And Hasay's early recognition of fame was simply an extension of what her youth coach, Jim Barodte of the San Luis Distance Club, already knew: "It's just a thrill to watch her. I knew that she was something special."

As a high school sophomore in cross-country, Hasay dominated the field at the California State Cross-Country Championship and Foot Locker Western Regional, winning both for the second year in a row (before failing to defend her title at the national championship). She then went on to win the USATF Junior Cross-Country Championship in the early spring in a time of 21:44 over six kilometers, leading from the beginning and winning by 14 seconds. She qualified to represent the USA at the 2007 World Cross-Country Championships in Mombasa, Kenya, but she did not participate because of a terrorism warning at the meet. Later in the spring Hasay went on to set the age-fifteen and national high school sophomore class records in the 3,200 meters with a time of 10:04.

As a junior in cross-country, Hasay again dispatched her competitors at the Mt. SAC Invitational, California State Meet, and Foot Locker West Regionals before struggling for the second year at the national championship (finishing third by 11 seconds). She was able to win the USATF Cross-Country Championship Junior Women's 6K in February with a time of 20:32, her second title in a row at that distance.

Hasay's senior cross-country season included her fourth straight California State Meet victory, making her the second athlete after Sara Hall (formerly Sara Bei, of Stanford fame) to win four state cross-country titles.

Hasay then went on to win her fourth straight Foot Locker West Regional title, becoming the first athlete in the history of the Foot Locker National meet to win a regional title four times. Finally, she won the National Foot Locker Cross-Country Championships for the second time, in a time of 17:22. This win made her the sixth runner to win the meet twice, and she became the only athlete to win twice in non-consecutive years.

After graduation, Hasay accepted an offer to run collegiately at the University of Oregon, in front of the very same Hayward Field crowd that had chanted her name only a few years before. Once there, she encountered another prodigal athlete with a similar pedigree: Galen Rupp. By the end of the 2000s, his professional career was just beginning—and he had battled on many a cross-country course to get there.

THE PRODIGAL RUPP

Galen Rupp may have been a well-known runner by the time he encountered Jordan Hasay as a member of the University of Oregon (and later, the Nike Oregon Project), but he didn't start out that way. For most of his youth Rupp had been a talented athlete in a completely different sport: soccer. One of Portland's best young wingers, Rupp played year-round and, in fact, didn't give it up right away after a fortuitous introduction to his high school's new head cross-country coach.

Dave Frank was *not* that coach. However, he was a *good* cross-country coach, and one who was interested in a vacancy at Portland's Central Catholic High School entering the fall of 2000. But his route to the position was full of surprises. After ten years of teaching math and coaching cross-country in the Bay Area (at Saint Francis High School in Mountain View, where he guided the team to a California State Championship in cross-country), Frank was met with some unexpected news.

Prioritizing a move back to Portland (where Frank had grown up), he began conversations with the Athletic Director of Central Catholic about a combination math and coaching position at the school. On the eve of receiving the offer, however, one of those opportunities changed suddenly: an eleventh-hour connection had resulted in the school's hiring of a new cross-country coach—Alberto Salazar. Caught off-guard, Frank unleashed a passionate response: "I told the AD, 'Well, I may not be coaching cross-country, but I am going to every practice and every meet and when we have a meet you'll have to get me a sub,'" explained Frank. "I told him, 'I love cross-country. I'm coaching cross-country. I'll do it for free. I'm going to be out there no matter who's out there.'"

It all worked out. After a beginning laced with apprehension, Salazar and his new assistant coach quickly developed an effective coaching collaboration. "There was no question that Alberto was in charge, the head guy. But we worked together," said Frank. "One of the great things about Alberto is that we would discuss coaching and different approaches. Alberto was really good about that."

With their cooperative partnership now formed, they embarked together on the task of rejuvenating the Central Catholic Ram's lackluster program.

That task became easier right away when cross-country team members brought a skinny, lithe soccer player named Galen Rupp to Frank's attention. "We heard from kids that he was really fast. But we hear that stuff all the time," noted Frank. "But it turned out I knew his mother and we were able to get him to come to a practice. He was by far the best guy on the team from the first minute he ran for us."

Entering the fall of 2000, Rupp's mother Jamie (herself a state mile champion and twice state cross-country titlist at La Salle High) had prodded Rupp to introduce himself to the new cross-country coach at the fall sports school barbecue. That coach was Alberto Salazar. And as luck would have it, Rupp's head soccer coach had trained one of Salazar's sons on his club team, and the two coaches chatted about Rupp's natural running ability. They worked out a system where Rupp trained with the soccer team six days a week and spent the seventh day working out with the cross-country team; but after a few months, Rupp's running talent eclipsed his soccer abilities.

Rupp's mother was aware that her son was fast: "I could tell he had a natural talent for running, but it wasn't something he had much interest in," she said. Despite setting a Catholic Youth Organization record in the 1,500 meters as an eighth-grader, Rupp felt soccer was his love, and he made the Rams' varsity team as a freshman while playing for the state's Olympic development team. Once he stepped foot on the cross-country course, however, everything changed.

Coach Dave Frank recalled Rupp's first high school cross-country race, a freshman 3,000-meter event: "We told him he couldn't take the lead until after the mile. After 800, he asked if he could take the lead. We told him no. We let him go after a mile and he won by 45 seconds." But it was an eventful rise. "He ran a couple of meets but didn't win them, and got sick and didn't run well at the district meet," Salazar said. "I remember thinking, 'Maybe he's not going to want to run now.'"

After soccer season, Salazar convinced Rupp to spend a month focusing on training for the USATF National Junior Cross-Country Championship, held in Reno. Rupp finished second, "with limited background, going against the best age-group kids in the country who were running full-time," said Salazar. "If I had to pick one moment where I realized I had a lot of potential as a runner, that was it," added Rupp.

Rupp stayed with soccer but also ran track that spring. And it was then, after a discussion with his parents, he decided to give up soccer. "I couldn't do both sports and be great," Rupp said. "You have to devote so much time to be really good at any sport. I had to make a decision which way I wanted to go." His parents weren't convinced until that August, when soccer camp was about to start: "I asked Galen if he was planning on going, and he casually told me, 'I'm not playing soccer. I'm running now,'" his mother Jamie said.

Rupp quickly became one of the state's best distance runners, then its best. "I can distinctly remember my sophomore year, really believing it was only a matter of time before I got to this big level," said Rupp. Dave Frank recalled the moment of true awakening: "By the time of Galen's sophomore year in track, Alberto had clearly seen that Galen was much better than I ever could have imagined. In the summer after Galen's sophomore year, we took Galen down to Stanford for the junior nationals to run the 5,000-meter. He finished third in 14:34. After the race, we were walking out and Alberto says, 'I think he's going break the national record.' 'Alberto, you know it's about 13:44,' I replied. With a certain shortness, Alberto crisply responded, 'I know what it is.'" Salazar's foresight proved to be correct. Before entering college, Rupp ran the 5,000 in 13:37.91—setting a new national record and besting Gerry Lindgren's 1964 mark of 13:44.

En route, Rupp captured two Oregon state titles in cross-country (2002 and 2003) and three individual championships in track and field (the 1,500 meters in 2004 and 3,000 meters in 2003 and 2004). He qualified for the Foot Locker National Cross-Country Championship in 2003, finishing third at the West Regional and runner-up for the national title. He finished his high school career with a 10,000-meter race in 29:09 in Brasschaat, Belgium, the fourth-fastest ever for an American high schooler, and became *Track and Field News* "High School Athlete of the Year" in 2004.

Rupp delayed entering college, instead continuing to train and compete while being coached by Salazar. Rupp won the USA Junior Cross-Country title in mid-February 2005, then placed 20th at the 2005 World Junior Cross-Country Championships in France in March. He then enrolled at the University of Oregon in time for the outdoor track season.

Collegiately in cross-country, after setting a new US junior record in the 10,000 meters (28:25), Rupp led the Oregon Ducks at the Willamette Invitational (placing sixth) and Pre-NCAA Invitational (placing 12th). That was until an injury brought Rupp's 2005 cross-country season to an early and abrupt end.

Rupp then came back in 2006 to defeat two-time Pac-10 champion Robert Cheseret of the University of Arizona, becoming Oregon's 10th male runner to win a Pac-10 Conference cross-country title. He also led a young Oregon team to victory over the Stanford Cardinal, who had won the previous six Pac-10 titles. Rupp went on to finish sixth in the 2006 NCAA Men's Cross-Country Championship.

In 2007, Rupp missed defending his Pac-10 cross-country title by four seconds, but went on to claim his first West Regional title—prompting talk of his obtaining a decisive win at the national championship. It was not to be, however, as Rupp finished runner-up (one second behind Liberty's Josh McDougal), though he led the Oregon Ducks to the 2007 team championship.

That race had been a nail-biter. After a slow opening first half, McDougal had increased the pace by the 8K mark and by the ninth kilometer had a 15-meter lead on Rupp. But

Rupp managed to hang within striking distance and closed the gap. As they turned for home and entered the final straightaway (roughly 500 meters from the finish), Rupp pulled back even with McDougal and then went slightly ahead. But McDougal had kept something in reserve. He resurged, battled back at Rupp, and opened up a slim lead that he kept for the win. It was one of the closest finishes in NCAA history. McDougal called Rupp one of his toughest competitors and noted he didn't think he could have responded if the Oregon junior had surged again.

Recovering from the Olympics, Rupp avoided the early 2008 cross-country season, running his first race at the Pac-10 Conference Championships, which he won in a course-record 22:55 over 8K. He then repeated as NCAA West Regional champion by running 27:41 to win the 10K race. In the 2008 NCAA National Cross-Country Championships, Rupp won his first individual NCAA title by outkicking Liberty University's Sam Chelanga in a time of 29:03, a new course record at the Terre Haute site, and leading the Ducks to repeat as NCAA team champions.

But while Rupp had finally set a course record as a senior at the Terre Haute course, he might not have been considered as the strongest individual finisher of the decade at NCAAs. That distinction belonged to a Canadian running at a school in the Midwest, perpetuating a tradition that had been established by the Kennedy brothers decades before.

SIMON BAIRU BOOSTS THE BADGERS

After winning three national collegiate cross-country titles in the 1980s, the Wisconsin Badgers remained somewhat under the radar during the 1990s, with the men's team only reaching the podium at the NCAA Cross-Country Championships three times in the decade. Then, in the late '90s, former Wisconsin alum Jerry Schumacher returned to resuscitate the distance team with the aim of winning a national championship. Among his fleet of new Wisconsin men was Simon Bairu, a Canadian runner born in 1983 to an Ethiopian mother and an Eritrean father.

2002 saw Bairu's debut in Wisconsin, a year in which he finished 38th overall at the NCAA Cross-Country Championship, three seconds behind Ryan Hall. Already a seasoned cross-country athlete in his native Canada, Bairu had qualified for the World Cross-Country Championships twice before (in 2001 and 2002), after pacing the Canadian National Cross-Country Championship junior competition in 1999, 2000, and 2001 (winning outright in December 2001). Five days after helping the Wisconsin Badgers finish second-overall behind Stanford at the 2002 NCAA Cross-Country Championship, Bairu won his second Canadian National Cross-Country title, this time in the senior men's race. This allowed him to travel to Avenches Switzerland in the spring of 2003 to run in the senior men's competition at World Cross, where he finished 52nd overall.

Not many college freshmen had the pedigree of being a two-time national champion or three-time World

Cross-Country survivor by their twentieth birthday, but Simon Bairu was motivated: "I started running for my elementary school when I was about 11 years old," Bairu began. "At first I thought running was really boring and I wanted to continue playing baseball, but my dad paid me to go to a few workouts and after my first month of training I had my first big race. It was an 800-meter against the best runner in the city. I ended up losing the race by less then a second and that was when I got hooked. I knew I couldn't quit because I wanted to beat him. I wanted to be the best runner in the city. Eventually I beat him and then my goals shifted to wanting to be the best runner in the province and so on." It was this drive that led him to compete nationally and to pursue an opportunity at the University of Wisconsin. "Seeing the talent I was going to be working with on that team I thought that winning a team title would be the easiest goal to accomplish. I also wanted to graduate being the best runner in Canada and the NCAA. I knew that if I didn't win at least one NCAA title then I wasted my talent." Bairu would have his chance in the fall of 2003.

With the addition of freshmen Chris Solinsky (a three-time high school state cross-country champion from Wisconsin), and Tim Nelson (a three-time cross-country state champion from California), Bairu paced the Wisconsin Badgers to a second straight runner-up podium finish behind Stanford at the NCAA Cross-Country Championship, improving his performance to a ninth overall finish. Bairu also added his first Big Ten Conference individual cross-country title as well, and Wisconsin easily won conference and regional titles en route to the national championship. Just as in 2002, Bairu again won the Canadian National Cross-Country title a mere five days after his top-10 NCAA placing. In 2004, however, Bairu elected not to run at World Cross, instead running indoor and outdoor track for Wisconsin.

In the fall of 2004, the Wisconsin Badgers looked indomitable. Solinsky and Nelson were joined by Matt Tegenkamp (fifth at the World Junior Cross-Country Championships and a 13:30 5,000-meter runner), and former Missouri high school rivals Tim Keller and Josh Spiker. But Bairu led the way: "Going into [the 2004] NCAA meet I knew that I controlled my own destiny," said Bairu. "The title was mine to lose. I put in the best summer training I had ever put in my life and I stayed healthy throughout the season. What fueled me even more was knowing that there were a lot of doubters out there who didn't think I could pull it off. I also knew that I was going to have a large target on my back. I embraced the challenge and used it to fuel my hunger for success." Bairu won his second conference cross-country title, finished 10th at regionals, and came back to win the NCAA Cross-Country Championship, beating his nearest opponent by only three seconds. In the process, however, the strong Wisconsin cohort lost the team title in a shocking upset to Colorado, finishing runner-up by a mere four points. Following the success of his first NCAA individual victory, Bairu again returned to Ontario and won the Canadian National Cross-Country title, his third in a row.

In 2005, Wisconsin (and Bairu) would not be denied at the NCAA Cross-Country Championships. After storming through his third Big Ten Conference title, and soundly defeating runner-up Richard Kiplagat by six seconds for his second national title in a row, Bairu was finally rewarded with a strong finish from his supporting cast. Chris Solinsky finished third overall, while teammates Matt Withrow (ninth), Anthony Ford (14th), Stuart Eagon (17th), and Tim Nelson (18th) all earned All-American honors for their performances. As a team, Wisconsin finished with an ultra-low score of 37 points (beating their nearest opponent by 68), and Bairu became only the third individual to win back-to-back NCAA Cross-Country titles in the previous thirty years. Speaking of the occasion, Bairu stated: "This was an awesome effort by everybody. This is what we came here for, this is what we trained for all year. It was tough, I'd say [I won it] with about 800 (meters) to go. This was my last cross-country race as a Badger and I wasn't going to lose my last race. I can't even explain it. When I saw Chris behind me and Withrow and these guys coming in, that's what it's about—that's what cross-country's about—it's a team."

Following the tradition he set for himself, Bairu once again returned home and won the Canadian National Cross-Country title, his fourth in succession. Speaking on the occasion Bairu shared, "Winning anything four times in a row is pretty unbelievable. If I had to choose I would probably say winning the two NCAA titles back-to-back [is more special] because of all the international talent that is in the field and knowing that my success at the NCAA level will help me when I move up to racing at the world level." Overall, it was Bairu's dedication to cross-country that gave him the edge. Along for the progression (and more responsible than anybody) was Bairu's mentor and Wisconsin's coach, Jerry Schumacher. Soft-spoken but meticulous in his planning, Schumacher was responsible for the Badgers' rebuilding and had been the architect for all the accolades. Along the way he was poised to keep training Wisconsin's runners post-collegiately too. It was a recipe to bring America back as a distance running powerhouse.

ENTER JERRY SCHUMACHER

For Jerry Schumacher, a coach with a prestigious reputation and meticulous attention to detail, it was a soft-spoken manner and hard-working demeanor that resonated with his team of distance men at the University of Wisconsin. A Badger himself in the early '90s, Schumacher's performance in the 1,500 meters saw him do well enough to train post-collegiately for a brief period, but soon a job opportunity to be an assistant coach at the University of North Carolina allowed him to transition from pupil to mentor. By the end of the decade, the head job at Wisconsin opened up. Schumacher didn't waste a minute coming back home.

Because of his self-prescribed shyness (Schumacher formally told *Running Times Magazine*, "I don't like to do interviews"), his athletes often spoke for him. "One of the best things about Jerry as a coach was that you always knew he was right there with you," said former Badger Ryan Craven. "In many ways, he almost seemed like more of a teammate than a coach. He could hammer out 6:00 miles with you on an easy Tuesday run, and he wasn't shy when it came to locker room antics (he'd laugh as hard as anyone when Chris [Solinsky] would put Simon Bairu into a trash can), and when it came to traveling to meets, his purpose there was as decisively clear as your own. He didn't come to Terre Haute for the social gathering at the hotel: just like his athletes, he came to win a championship."

American record holder and former Badger Matt Tegenkamp added, "Schumacher is a Midwesterner, like most of us. He's a family man, he's conservative, he's blue collar, he's tough. That's why we all chose Wisconsin." "Sure, the winters were hard," Schumacher admitted, "but it prevented us from overtraining. Can you imagine those guys if the weather was 70 degrees and sunny every day? They'd be running around with their shirts off, trying to hammer each other every day."

The success of Schumacher's athletes spoke for itself: Tegenkamp and Solinsky proved they could contend with, and defeat, the East Africans (with times that stood as American records on the track). Simon Bairu ran personal bests in every event from 1,500 meters (3:45) to 10,000 (27:50) his first summer after graduation, a season that culminated with a trip to the World Championships. Schumacher resurrected the career of journeyman Jonathan Riley, a Stanford grad who was runner-up to Tegenkamp at the 2007 US indoor championships (3,000 meters), and ran a personal-best 5,000 meters in 2007 (13:19), just missing a trip to worlds. Even the quiet and unassuming Tim Nelson put together a season that would make many higher-paid athletes envious, running 1,500-meter, 3,000-meter, and 10,000-meter personal bests in 3:42, 7:53, and 28:04, respectively, and would come within an arm's reach of beating Meb Keflezighi at the US National Cross-Country Championships.

It wasn't to last for long. In the summer of 2008, Schumacher was enticed to leave his dream job at Wisconsin to head west and work under the Nike Oregon Project as a successor to Alberto Salazar. In the year before the move, Salazar had experienced serious health problems. A heart attack on June 30, 2007, was nearly fatal, and surgeons implanted a defibrillator in Salazar's chest. But, as Salazar told the *Eugene Register-Guard*, "I'm looking to the future. I have life insurance for my family, and now, with Jerry coming to Portland, I have coach insurance for Galen." Salazar acknowledged that he would need to gradually cut back on his coaching load as he was handling Nike Oregon Project athletes Galen Rupp, Adam Goucher, Kara Goucher, Josh Rohatinsky, and Amy Begley.

But when he arrived at Nike's Beaverton offices, Schumacher also brought several elite distance runners of his own, including Chris Solinsky, Simon Bairu, and Matt Tegenkamp. And once Salazar's health rebounded, a division developed within the Oregon Project. Salazar coached the runners he had recruited, while Schumacher focused on the Wisconsin runners he had lured to Portland.

For several years, the Salazar- and Schumacher-coached Oregon Project was less of a running collective than two training groups operating side by side, athletes said. But this division was a reflection of fissures forming beneath the surface for myriad reasons, not all of them having to do with Salazar and Nike. The Nike Oregon Project was just the latest chapter in a running-club revitalization, and shoe-company money was financing it.

THE NIKE OREGON PROJECT

As previously mentioned, American distance running had reached a new low by the Sydney Olympics in 2000. Thus, the genesis for an upstart running team that could challenge the world's best had come from a feeling of disgust leading into the decade.

It came to a head in April 2001, when Alberto Salazar and Tom Clarke (Nike president of new business development) listened to the conclusion of the Boston Marathon. Korean runner Bong Ju-Lee had beaten an Ecuadorean and a trio of Kenyans to win in a time of 2:09:43. "Then the commentators started gushing about an American taking sixth place," Salazar recalled with incredulity. "We started talking—'How can we be so bad? How can American distance runners be so bad that we're excited about sixth place?'" As Salazar (who once owned the marathon distance world record at 2:08:13) listened to the Boston Marathon commentators heap praise on the first American to finish, he told Tom "I could coach Americans to do better." Tom started writing down some ideas: coaching, talent, sports science.

The Oregon Project was born: "The mission was to develop American marathon and distance runners— Americans who could win marathons and distance races," said Salazar. So, he began recruiting talented runners whose biomechanics he could straighten out, whose training he could improve with Nike technology, and whose workouts he could extend to match that of the international elite. These early recruits were young runners just out of college with impressive résumés. The first few included Dan Browne, Mike Donnelly, Marc Davis, Dave Davis, and Chad Johnson. Salazar's recruitment didn't hinge solely on talent but also on potential. These were runners who were accomplished but that had certain biomechanical weaknesses or other issues that Salazar knew he could fix. It worked, and the momentum built.

Portland native Dan Browne, the first cadet to run the mile under four minutes, was showing a knack for distance races, too, winning the USA Marathon Championships in Minnesota in 2002. In him, Salazar had one of the Oregon Project's first test pieces. Ultimately his coaching got Browne down to a 2:10 marathon—super human by most standards, yet far short of the 2:08 Salazar knew a marathoner would need to compete for a victory. A 2:10 finisher at the Boston Marathon that year would have

placed fifth, hardly gush-worthy under the new project's mission of getting on the podium.

Salazar eventually realized he was hitting a stalling point. The athletes being coached were older, their habits and biomechanics already ingrained after years of running so many miles. He realized that he had to catch them younger, before the bad habits had had a chance to take over.

Galen Rupp—the fifteen-year-old showing raw talent at nearby Central Catholic high school—connected with the coach and Salazar had found his muse. "I explained to Phil [Knight] and Tom [Clarke] that I wanted to start The Oregon Project with the best available professional runners, but ultimately, Galen was going to be the star," said Salazar. Rupp was, after all, what Tom Clarke called "the Project's project."

But despite having the best talent and a seemingly unlimited budget on Nike's bankroll, the Oregon Project (and their athletes) stayed away from running major cross-country championships. "Cross-country is a great training ground for young athletes," Salazar said. "But the reason my athletes like Mo and Galen no longer do it is they have already worked on the strength endurance it gives you and I'm scared of them risking injury." In 2008, as Rupp recuperated after the 2008 Summer Olympics in Beijing, the plan was to begin his senior cross-country season at the small Mike Hodges Invitational at Oregon's Clackamas Community College.

But as *The Oregonian* newspaper recounted, "When Salazar went to inspect the course Friday afternoon, he had concerns about sections that he said were 'rutty.' . . . The course at Clackamas Community College has some footing issues and has been deemed a little too treacherous. Apparently, it's not worth the risk. Rupp isn't going to race tomorrow because he won't have the fast track he was looking for." Decisions such as these prompted critics to question just how serious Rupp, Salazar, and the Oregon Project were treating the sport.

SWOOSH

Salazar's vision wasn't the only Nike-sponsored group to be gaining recognition. The Farm Team in Palo Alto was one of the few post-collegiate running teams in the nation to not shy away from top-level cross-country competition early in the decade. With the arrival of former Georgetown coach Frank Gagliano in 2001, the Farm Team redoubled their efforts to win national championships. In the fall of 2003 (at the USA Fall Cross-Country Championship), Gagliano was quoted as saying, "The Farm Team will have a very, very good team out there. We will definitely be a lot stronger than we were last year in both men and women." It was seen as being on par with Joe Namath prophesying a Super Bowl win over the Colts.

This prophecy didn't come as a surprise. "Gags," as he was known, came to cross-country as a former professional football quarterback. The well-respected coach had molded numerous Olympic runners and coached the

Reebok Enclave team to victory at the Fall Cross-Country Championship in 1998.

However, despite some club cross-country success for the Farm Team in the 1990s, it was in Mobile, Alabama in 2002 that the Indiana Invaders, behind the one-two finish of Priscilla Hein and Collette Liss, plowed over the Farm Team women, 38 points to 47. In the men's race it was closer, the Farm Team and Hansons Running Shop of Michigan wound up tied with 40 points, but the sixth man tie-breaker meant the Farm Team finished second there too. For the Nike-funded cohort, it was nearly a death sentence: "Losing to Hansons on a tiebreaker last year was brutal," said Peter Gilmore, a Cal grad who had finished seventh in the race. Gagliano was brought in to make sure that incidents like that *didn't* happen—but ultimately the men would fall to third in 2003, though the Farm Team women won their division.

Thankfully, the fall of 2004 and spring of 2005 saw the Farm Team men victorious—so Gagliano was still in Nike's good graces. So much so, that when Vin Lananna left Stanford in the middle of the 2000s to become head coach of the University of Oregon in Eugene, Gagliano was brought in with his training group shortly after: "For over four decades, Frank Gagliano has guided athletes to the highest levels of our sport," said Lananna in a press release. "His experience and passion for track and field have positively impacted the college and post-collegiate programs that he has touched. He will be a tremendous benefit to this new club, the athletes, and the entire athletic community in Eugene."

"This new club" referred to the Oregon Track Club Elite, a continuation of the Farm Team model that Nike had employed in Palo Alto. With the resources of Eugene, and with one elite team already on Nike's campus in Beaverton, Gagliano's relocation in mid-2006 came in conjunction with a plan by Nike employees Chris Cook and John Truax to link youth-development distance running (happening with the Bowerman Athletic Club) with a professional element. The Bowerman Athletic Club, an all-ages group independent of the professional coaching of Nike sponsorship, had formed in 2003 under the leadership of Tom Redding. But with oversight from Nike's Cook and Truax, it wouldn't be the only step taken to help the development of youth cross-country in Oregon.

In 1999, Nike hosted BorderClash, one of the first high school interstate cross-country championships, which pitted the top-20 male finishers and top-20 female finishers of the Oregon and Washington state cross-country meets against each other on Nike's campus. The brainchild of Josh Rowe (a Nike Running Manager) and John Truax (who had originally been hired by Nike as a running footwear developer), the meet was designed to create a fun weekend of events that focused on the finest prep harriers from the Pacific Northwest. Runners were treated to tours, free Nike merchandise, and a format for the event that saw the two starting teams face each other (jousting style) with a cannon blast to mark the start of the race.

After the success of BorderClash, Rowe and Truax planned a larger scale event that would lure the nation's top high school harriers to Nike: a true team National Cross-Country Championship. While Foot Locker hosted the top individuals, Rowe and Truax weren't satisfied that students had a fair opportunity to compete nationally with their team. Rowe met with National Scholastic Sports Foundation (NSSF) founder Jim Spier (who had a long history tied in with high school athletics), NSSF Great American XC Festival Associate Meet Director Paul Limmer, and NSSF Director of Business Development A.J. Holzherr to assist in event management—as they had a long history of national championship event success. Additionally, *Harrier Magazine* founder Marc Bloom and *DyeStat* website founder John Dye added to the panel of experts that included *DyeStatCAL* founder Doug Speck, Arcadia Invitational Race Director Rich Gonzalez, and *MileSplit* (website) Chief Operating Officer Don Rich. With Rowe and Truax linking the resources of Nike with this team of experts, Nike Team Nationals was established.

The first Nike Team Nationals Cross-Country Championship in 2004 was a major success, with nationally-ranked high school teams flown in from all corners of the United States to Nike's campus in Beaverton. From there, athletes, coaches, and parents were treated to an exclusive experience, with the main event culminating at Portland Meadows racetrack on Saturday December 4. Fittingly, it was York High School from Elmhurst Illinois (under coach Joe Newton) that pulled off the first team and individual titles, following individual standout Sean McNamara and his winning time of 15:43. Similarly, the girl's champions, Saratoga Springs High School from New York, had dominated *Harrier* national team rankings the previous decade; they were led by four Foot Locker national finalists.

But despite the publicity generated for the new event, and with praiseworthy experiences from all involved, there remained criticism around the selection process. In 2004 and 2005, teams were chosen based on a ranking system determined by the "expert" panel. In 2006, everything changed with the addition of one qualifier in-between the state championship level and the national stage: the Rocky Mountain Region XC Championships.

Twenty-two state champions from five states took part in the Rocky Mountain Regional, an event conceived by Rowe and Truax while attending the 2006 University of Washington Husky Invitational in Seattle. High school runners from Idaho, Montana, Wyoming, Colorado, and Utah met to compete for trophies that were awarded to the top three teams and top three individuals.

Following the Rocky Mountain Regional, Josh Rowe addressed the Nike Board with the intention of bridging a regional system based on a potential Foot Locker/Nike cross-country merge. But Foot Locker management quickly shot down the tournament idea, claiming the team concept was not important. As a result, the Foot Locker/Nike relationship fractured, and Rowe met with Jim Spier and employee AJ Holzherr to find locations for Nike's own regional championships. Holzherr and Spier traversed the country, ultimately deciding upon locations, while Rowe convinced Nike to put up the funding. In coming years these regions were expanded upon, but 2007 marked the first opportunity high school teams across America were given to *earn* their trip to Portland Meadows—a major step in elevating the Nike Team Nationals Championship to the status of a legitimate national proving ground.

Nike spared no expense putting on an international-type event for American high school athletes, and only a year later the standards rose again: 2008 saw Nike Team Nationals become Nike Cross Nationals with opportunities for both individual cross-country standouts to run alongside eligible teams. Hype was building for the sport at a grassroots level like never before, and Nike was at the forefront.

A RUNNING-CLUB REVITALIZATION

While there was a youth running-club renaissance taking place thanks to the Nike Cross Nationals event, post-collegiate training opportunities were also improving in the United States. Hanson brothers Kevin and Keith founded a training group in Michigan in 1999, and the Mammoth Track Club in California, Team USA Minnesota, and ZAP Fitness in North Carolina formed soon after. As Greg McMillan, coach of the eponymous McMillan Elite team (founded in 2007), stated: "Before, there was Todd Williams and Bob Kennedy, then a big gap. We don't see those big gaps anymore. You can look at the top-30 performances in distance events, and they're faster and deeper than they've [ever] been."

For the Hanson brothers, their formula for training an elite team of athletes was different than what Salazar and Nike were using in the Pacific Northwest. The first immediate difference was that none of the Hansons runners were household names. Secondly, they were all American. The Hanson brothers didn't recruit stars, and their runners didn't hail from the nation's big athletic universities, but they believed their special training regimen would make America a dominant force in distance running. "It's actually not a big secret," said Keith Hanson. "It's just about hard work and group training. That's it."

To join the Hansons-Brooks Distance Project meant living, eating, and running together as a team. The brothers owned three houses (two for the men, one for the women) where runners lived in a sort of a post-graduate fraternity setting, with slightly less beer but just as much mess. The accommodations weren't plush, but they were free. To give their runners time to train every day and compete, the Hansons also gave them highly flexible day jobs at their four suburban Detroit shoe stores. "Every morning when I wake up, I know there are 15 other guys out there who expect me to show up, and I expect them to show up, and we motivate each other," said Clint Verran, one of the Hansons' first athletes. "There's no way I could motivate that way if it were just me. Plus, most of the guys are just coming out of college, they're 23, and they're so excited to be here that it makes me excited to be here."

The thing they all shared was a 100-percent Made-in-Michigan belief that with hard work, one could achieve almost anything. The Hansons were the embodiment of solid Midwestern can-do values: competition was good; peer pressure was positive; losing didn't mean whining. And the brothers were fiercely motivated by the Kenyan conundrum. Why couldn't the Americans beat them?

By the early 2000s, after twenty years of distance running hegemony, many in the sport believed that Kenyans were engineered to win, and that the reason Americans weren't beating the Kenyans was because the Kenyans were not only built better but that they spent their formative years running many miles at altitude. Nature plus nurture, in other words. In Michigan the brothers weren't convinced: "We don't buy the genetic argument," said Kevin. "We've spent a lot of time looking at the Kenyans and trying to figure out what they are doing right. And then we looked at the Japanese, and they are also very, very, good at distance running. And one thing the Japanese shared with East African runners was group training." The genesis for the Hansons Distance Project was now crystal clear. "We've also never bought the argument that the East Africans win because they're more talented," Kevin continued. "Forget if they are better physically. They are working harder. They were also forced to pool their resources, meaning they train together."

Unlike many of the training groups funded by grants or supported by major shoe brands, the Hansons had humble beginnings. Keith ran distances from 3–10K as an undergrad at Michigan State, while Kevin was the head coach at nearby Macomb Community College. In 1991, while Kevin was coaching track locally and Keith was working as a purchasing agent at Wyeth Pharmaceuticals, the brothers decided it would be great to own a running store—with $50,000 in stock, they opened Hansons Running Shop in their hometown of Sterling Heights. Kevin worked Monday through Friday, and Keith worked on weekends while continuing his nine-to-five with Wyeth. Within two years they were pulling money out of the business, so they opened a second store in Grosse Pointe, and a third store after that.

By 1998, with some money in the bank, the Hansons began to think about starting their own team—and it wasn't intended to be a half-baked sponsorship deal either. The plan was clear from the start: to beat the Kenyans, the athletes were going to live together, train together, and compete together. In the summer of 1999, they bought a small house and signed Clint Verran, Kyle Baker, and Jim Jurcevich. The next year Verran finished 11th at the Olympic Trials—he had been seeded 59th. By the end of 2000, they'd opened a fourth store, bought a second house, and gone from three athletes to 10.

Athletes received health insurance, agent services—no money skimmed off the top—housing, coaching, gear, and free travel. All of which cost the brothers money. Soon the Hansons were shelling out about $250,000 a year to keep the team going.

In June 2003, a story in the *Wall Street Journal* about the brothers caught the eye of the executives at Brooks Running. Brooks didn't sponsor individual athletes, and sold its shoes only in specialty running shops, so the Hansons seemed like a perfect match for the company. In August 2003, with an infusion of cash and gear and a whole lot of marketing muscle, the team became officially known as the Hansons-Brooks Distance Project. 2001 saw the Hansons' first national cross-country team championship, and by the end of the decade they had six more. Their method was working. Meanwhile, the other professional club teams weren't just looking from the ground up to build their teams and stay competitive—some were looking overseas. It was the next stage of a commercially funded global mindset to find success in cross-country running.

FARAH'S BIG BREAK

Mohamed Muktar Jama (Mo) Farah was a hugely gifted young distance runner. A schoolboy champion and outstanding junior international athlete born in March 1983 in Mogadishu, Somalia, Mo Farah later moved to Britain at the age of eight to join his father, an IT consultant and British citizen. As a result, Farah's pedigree immediately made him the poster-child for a new type of international athlete: one who was fully ingrained and assimilated in Western culture and not just recruited at a competitive age from a faraway homeland.

Farah attended Isleworth and Syon in Isleworth, and Feltham Community College in Feltham. His athletic talent was first identified by physical education teacher Alan Watkinson, who fostered Farah's love for a multitude of sports. As a result, Farah's early ambition included playing as a right-winger for the Arsenal football club, and he later joined the Borough of Hounslow Athletics Club in west London to hone his soccer skills. It was here he got his first taste of athletics.

In 1996, at the age of thirteen, Farah entered the English Schools Cross-Country Championship and finished ninth. The following year he won the first of five English school titles. Recognizing his talent, athletics philanthropist Eddie Kulukundis paid the legal fees to complete Farah's naturalization as a British citizen, allowing Farah to travel to competitions without visa issues. Almost immediately, Farah found success as an international cross-country runner, competing in the European Junior Cross-Country Championships (finishing fifth in 1999, seventh in 2000, and second in 2001), and at the IAAF World Cross-Country Junior Championships.

Farah's first major title was a 5,000-meter track race at the European Athletics Junior Championship in 2001, the same year that he began training at St Mary's University College. That year, Farah became one of the first of two athletes in the newly formed Endurance Performance Centre at St Mary's. He lived and trained at the college, and took some classes before becoming a full-time athlete. In 2004, Farah finished 15th overall in the European Cross-Country Senior Championship (running 9.6 kilometers in 28:26),

and competed in the World Cross Senior Men's Championship in the spring of 2005.

By then, Farah had started working with Coach Alan Storey, who had experience with a number of Olympic medalists, and who had spotted the twenty-one-year-old Farah training at the University of St Mary's track in Teddington that had become a European base for some of Africa's finest athletes.

Watching with interest from America's West Coast was Alberto Salazar, who, as the head of Nike's Oregon Project, was under a bit of pressure. His fiercest rival (and fellow Oregon Project coach) was Jerry Schumacher, and much to Salazar's dismay, Schumacher's athlete Chris Solinsky was flying, particularly over 5,000 and 10,000 meters on the track, where he bettered the best times of both Salazar's golden boy, Rupp, and Dathan Ritzenhein.

A simple solution might have been to simply use Nike's financial muscle to lure a top African to Oregon. But that would have gone against the Nike value system (and Schumacher and the rest of the domestic running community looking to supplant the dominant Kenyans and Ethiopians), and Salazar knew it. To prove his credentials as a coach he had to be more creative, and turning Europe's top distance runner into a world-beater—Farah *against* the Kenyans and Ethiopians—was the challenge Salazar set for himself.

Back in London the situation for Farah was not ideal. Storey had coached Farah between 2004 and 2008, and the relationship had worked well despite Storey's time being split between Farah and the 16 lottery-funded athletes he was tasked with managing for British Athletics. But a problem arose after the Beijing Olympics, with Storey leaving the governing body in acrimonious circumstances.

In the interim, Farah worked with different coaches. There was time with the highly-respected Loughborough University coach George Gandy, then a stint in Australia under Nick Bideau. But Bideau's group, one that boasted the talented Craig Mottram, proved too tough for Farah at the time, and eventually he returned to London with a desire to once again connect with Storey. But in the background things were developing politically, with Salazar now in the shadows and British Athletics keen to sever the link between Farah and his favorite coach.

Nike and Salazar could, of course, offer so much more, including giving British Athletics the incentive of a new kit deal. They replaced Adidas as the official sponsor of British Athletics in 2013 with a multi-million–pound agreement that ran an additional seven years. Meanwhile, Farah's move to Oregon was discussed during a series of secret meetings in Teddington, with former cross-country runner Ian Stewart (an ambassador for UK Athletics), providing the point of contact with Salazar.

Nike could offer Farah a large increase in money, a big house in Oregon, Salazar as a full-time coach, and better training partners in athletes like Galen Rupp. Nike would also pay for Salazar, who would act as a consultant for British Athletics. And Nike would also provide support for Farah and his group to train anywhere in the world, altitude training camps in Kenya and Ethiopia among their favored destinations. Farah's wife, Tania, was certainly encouraging her husband to move, and according to sources even Storey said he should probably go. Therefore, after tying the knot with a new Nike contract, on January 8, 2011, Farah made his debut as a member of the Nike Oregon Project in cross-country. Just under twenty months before Mo Farah and Galen Rupp would cement themselves in Olympic history by finishing first and second overall in the 2012 Olympic 10,000-meter final—the duo battled over icy and snowy terrain at the 2011 Great Edinburgh International Cross-Country Championship in Scotland. Both runners finished identical to their future placing, with Farah winning the 8.22-kilometer race in 25:41 with Rupp second, in 25:50.

The Edinburgh event was a harkening back to the old days of cross-country running. The course featured three short loops (1,234 meters with hay bales) and then three longer loops with a treacherous uphill and downhill that was 400 meters from the finish. The first time up the big hill Rupp went to the lead, but on the second climb Farah struck and started to pull away from the field. With his win, Farah cemented himself as a permanent member of Salazar's Nike Oregon Project camp, and a new type of internationalism was seen professionally in the ranks of cross-country running.

THE CONTROVERSIAL MOHAMMED MOURHIT

Meanwhile, when Serhiy Lebid finished runner-up at the 2001 World Cross-Country Championships in Ostend, Belgium, he was the first non-East African podium finisher for the men since Morocco's Khalid Skah in 1991. Ahead of him had been Belgium's Mohammed Mourhit—an African from Morocco—who was another example of a new breed of athlete. Mourhit was not only training as a full Belgian citizen in Europe, but was assimilating completely.

Born in October 1970 in Khouribga, Morocco, Mourhit gained his Belgian citizenship in 1997 through marriage, and made an impact on the cross-country course from the very start. Nicknamed the "Moro-Belgian," by countrymate Hicham El Guerrouj, Mourhit didn't discover running until the age of eighteen. But inspired by Moroccan champion Said Aouita, he had the opportunity to meet his idol early in his career: "Aouita really inspired me," claimed Mourhit. "I trained with him for four years, we followed the same program. I learned a lot from him, he is a great champion. He always told me that if I continue to train hard, to be as willing and determined as well as nice as I am now, I would break his records and approach the world marks."

Aouita was right. Mourhit showed great potential, rapidly claiming the 1,500- and 5,000-meter national Moroccan titles. Yet, injuries plagued his international career until 1997, when he joined his brother Maurice in Brussels. Taken under the wing of his brother (also his coach and physiotherapist), he placed fifth at the World Cross-Country Championships in Torino. And it wasn't his first appearance internationally.

Mourhit had competed seemingly everywhere, on the East Coast in the United States, in the Japanese Ekiden (distance relay), and all over Europe—winning cross-country titles in Brussels (Belgian National titles), Paris (the Les Mureaux Cross-Country Invitational), and Luxembourg (Reebok Eurocross). But throughout his career, along with nagging setbacks, Mourhit had yet to win the World Cross title outright. To tip the scales, the Mourhit brothers began to spend the winter outside of Belgium, at the national Moroccan training center in Ifrane, high in the Atlas Mountains, before returning to Brussels in the summer. "It's difficult to find a nice winter training center in Europe. In Ifrane, it's 70 degrees and dry," Mourhit admitted. "Ifrane is a heaven for runners."

Entering the 2000 World Cross-Country Championships, after Paul Tergat had won five in succession, the pattern of East African dominance appeared set to continue. And when the gun fired on the 12-kilometer race it looked like business as usual, with the Kenyan team forming a wall at the front of a large leading pack. However, one by one the challengers fell away. When they reached the 10-kilometer mark only three runners—Kenya's Paul Tergat, Ethiopia's Assefa Mezgebu, and Belgium's Mohammed Mourhit—remained.

Biding time, Mourhit launched a devastating kick down the stretch, a huge grin exploding over his face as he realized World Cross victory was his. Mobbed by the Belgian team and old friends from Morocco, he disappeared under a scrum of happy bodies in celebration after crossing the line in 35:00. "This is the happiest day of my life," he said.

The following year saw completely different conditions but much of the same results. The Belgian Federation—aided by organizers of the Ivo van Damme Memorial and Belgian authorities—had stepped in to host the 2001 World Cross event less than three weeks prior to its debut. The original venue, Dublin, had to be changed following outbreaks of foot-and-mouth disease. As predicted by Mourhit, he delivered a masterful performance in front of his home crowd.

Most of the early running at 2001 World Cross was made by the Kenyan trio of Charles Kamathi, Patrick Ivuti, and Paul Kosgei, with Mourhit and France's Driss El Himer running side by side in the second row, and with the leaders pacing themselves gently through the first kilometers. As El Himer and Serhiy Lebid repositioned themselves behind, Mourhit fought forward, running in the center of a tight phalanx of the three Kenyans.

An exultant crowd watched as Mourhit broke away from the Kenyans 27 minutes into the race, on the penultimate lap of the muddy, twisting circuit. Kosgei stayed on Mourhit's heels for a few hundred meters, but as the pair approached the long back straight Mourhit powered slowly away—building up an untouchable lead that would take him across the finish line a good 60 meters ahead of the next finisher.

In the end, it was the battle for second that held the most drama for the final stages. Lebid, who had been hanging on in the rearguard of the leaders, made a final surge in the last 200 meters to cross the line a few strides ahead of Kenya's Charles Kamathi in third.

Speaking after the race, Mourhit, who was grimacing as he left the finish line, confessed that his right ankle, which he had sprained a couple of days before his return to Belgium from altitude training in Ifrane, had been in a great deal of pain: "It was still hurting me on Friday when I arrived, but I didn't really want to say anything about it then," he said. "I was afraid of giving some confidence to my opponents. It was painful in the last stages of the race, but it held up and that was the most important thing. I tried to run the race as easily as possible; with the mud and wind it was not easy, but it was great responsibility for me to defend this title for Belgium and doubly so here in Ostend."

Surprise silver-medalist Lebid, who had been spending time living and training in Verbania in the Piedmont region of Italy, claimed his success was due to his superior training: "People think that I like to run in the mud," he laughed, "but that is not true at all. I made it because I really can finish fast."

Did You Know?

While Paula Radcliffe earned four World Cross medals as the top Western woman for the decade, no European male was as successful at major cross-country competitions in the 2000s as Ukraine's Serhiy Lebid. Lucky, talented, or both—Lebid went from a "who's that?" to a "who's who" of the sport overnight. Lebid won the European Cross-Country Championship numerous times in the 2000s (nine total, between 1998 and 2010) along with a World Cross silver medal. Spotted by the Ukrainian Athletic Association in the early 1990s, and under the guidance of Italian coach Renato Canova, Lebid became stronger every year. Canova commented: "In cross you cannot use high continuous speed, that depends on the level of your anaerobic threshold, especially when it's muddy. You need muscle strength (and Serhiy is stronger than the Kenyans, but not stronger than Bekele), high strength-endurance, and not very high aerobic power. So, a high training volume is very important [lots of miles], as is training for strength [using resistance, such as hills]. Regarding short intervals, they're good for changing pace, and for sprinting during the last part of the race." Using Canova's methods, Lebid won European Cross in 1998, 2001–05, 2007–08, and 2010.

If 2000 and 2001 proved to be the happiest moments for Mohammed Mourhit at the World Cross-Country Championships, then May 2002 would undoubtedly prove to be his unhappiest. After qualifying to run the IAAF World Half Marathon Championships in Brussels, Mourhit was tested for erythropoietin (EPO), a synthetic hormone that stimulated red blood cell production through the kidneys. After failing a blood test first, it was a second test along with a urine sample that confirmed suspicions that he had a higher-than-normal count of hemoglobin. He received a three-year ban from the sport via the Belgian Athletic Association that August.

But this raised more questions than it answered. What other athletes were now suspicious? Where was the source of the blood doping? And why was testing suddenly being conducted? As for athletes like Serhiy Lebid, his coach Renato Canova felt like there was no debate: "Don't speak about EPO or something else. Serhiy is simply the best European in cross-country," Canova claimed. "Every year, he has to reach his top shape early, to win the European Cross-Country Championship—which is not a top event—but can produce good interest for European runners. During last winter, for example, Serhiy was able to win seven races in succession, but by March he was mentally tired." Like with most historical implications, the story about EPO was more complex than it appeared on the surface.

A RAMPANT PROBLEM

For endurance athletes in a number of sports, the need for an oxidative advantage pushed the envelope for legal and illegal methods of transporting oxygen around the body. As early as the 1970s, disciplines such as cross-country skiing and road-cycling saw experiments with blood transfusions, including a case at the 1976 Tour de France where cyclist Joop Zoetemelk admitted to receiving a blood transfusion (despite his claim that he was using it as a treatment for anemia). In distance running, the first known case of blood doping occurred at the 1980 Summer Olympics in Moscow as Kaarlo Maaninka was transfused with two pints of blood before winning medals in the five- and 10-kilometer track races, although it was not against the rules at the time.

A century earlier, two French scientists reported that small amounts of plasma from anemic rabbits injected into normal animals caused an increase in red blood cell production (erythropoiesis) within a few hours. They referred to this activity as "hemopoietine." Over time, as scientists became more convinced that this red-blood-cell stimulating activity was caused by a single protein in the blood plasma, they gave it a variety of names: erythropoietic-stimulating activity, erythropoietic-stimulating factor, and, ultimately, "erythropoietin."

But it wasn't until the 1950s and '60s that several American scientists again took up the potential for a synthetic form of hormone-regulated red cell production. Refining the work of the French scientists, the Americans conclusively showed that the kidneys were the primary source of erythropoietin, and that low oxygen was the main driver of erythropoietin production. Soon, researchers found that patients with anemia responded by increasing their levels of erythropoietin to stimulate increased red blood cell production. Patients who required an increase in red blood cells in order to make up for low oxygen levels in the blood (such as patients with lung disease or patients living at high altitudes) also had elevated erythropoietin levels.

In 1983, scientists discovered a method for mass-producing a synthetic version of the hormone. Experiments were conducted to test the safety and effectiveness of the new drug, EPO, for treating anemia in patients with kidney failure. The results of these early clinical trials were dramatic. Patients who had been dependent on frequent blood transfusions were able to increase their red blood cell levels to near normal within just a few weeks of starting therapy. Patients' appetites returned, and they resumed their active lives. It was the convergence of two technologies: long-term dialysis and molecular biology, which set the stage for anemia management in this group of patients.

After patenting the drug as Epogen in 1984, recombinant erythropoietin became available on the market in 1985—intended to treat patients with impaired EPO production. But shortly after, it was demonstrated that EPO administration to healthy subjects for six to eight weeks resulted in increased VO_2 max and better recovery time after exhaustive workouts. As a result, it wasn't long before EPO was recognized as being a threat to fair competition in endurance sports. It was quickly classified as a doping substance by the FIS (International Ski Federation) in 1988, voted on by the IAAF for running competitions in 1989, and banned by the IOC in 1990. This ban was made (and enforced by all athletics federations aligned with the Olympic program) despite the fact that no methods for precise detection of EPO in the blood or urine had been developed. With no way to enforce the ban, all the sporting organizations could do was measure the drug's impact.

In the first twenty years following EPO's clinical trials, illegal use became rampant among many in the athletics community. Between 1983 and 2003—as sporting agencies scurried to develop a consistent testing method—critics within the distance running community soured at the thought that top-level athletes were gaining an unfair advantage. The method of gaining an advantage from EPO was simple: all it took was an injection into the bloodstream, and the kidneys, thinking the synthetic hormone was the body creating a natural one, would start producing more red blood cells. Tests conducted in Australia by the Australian Institute of Sport revealed that improvements in an athlete's performance over four weeks with the use of EPO matched those expected over several years without it. But by 2003, new methods for detection were put forward from scientists in France touting that detection could be measured more accurately by examining the results of blood sample analysis in addition to urine analysis, further improving the experiments put forward by the Australians.

These techniques, first introduced ahead of the Sydney Olympics in 2000, did not reveal any positive doping results but instead were intended to forecast for an unusual reading of blood cells for athletes using the drug. Then, the subsequent urine test would highlight any difference between the EPO levels produced naturally and synthetically. But skeptics remained critical: Will G. Hopkins, PhD,

a doctor of Physiology and Physical Education at the University of Otago in New Zealand, wrote in 2000: "How good are these tests? My guess—and it is a guess, because no one at the Australian Institute of Sport will comment—is that the urine will test positive only if the last injection of EPO was within a few days of the test. Any earlier and the EPO will have disappeared from the circulation and therefore from the urine. The blood test might detect an injection within the last couple of weeks, because that's about how long it takes the new red cells to mature. If the IOC decides to use either of these tests at the Sydney Olympics, athletes will simply stop injecting a week or so before arriving at the Games village. The ergogenic effect of a course of EPO injections lasts several months, because that's the lifetime of red cells in the circulation of athletes training hard. So the cheats will win again, but hopefully for the last time." There was hope, however, expressed by Dr. Hopkins that, along with the better testing methods ushered in 2003 by WADA (the World Anti-Doping Agency, founded in 1999), *random* blood tests on athletes "out of competition time" (ahead of major championships) would isolate its intended use.

These random screenings (in addition to ones conducted during competition) were both more effective in catching drug cheats after 2003, but also more flawed in their administration. As an example, at the 2003 World Cross-Country Championships, four athletes tested positive for EPO use and were each subsequently banned two years from the sport. Kenya's Pamela Chepchumba, Spain's Alberto García Fernandez, and Morocco's Soumiya Labani and Asmae Leghzaoui were all determined to have elevated levels of concentrated hemoglobin—and this came at only *one* event.

However, as some athletes were tested out of competition, controversy stirred when some medical experts deemed that the methods for comparing blood and urine samples were too inconclusive. In the case of a misread urine sample for distance runner Bernard Lagat in November 2003, Dr. Hans Heid of the Cancer Research Center in Heidelberg, Germany, made it known that the complexity of the testing involved with EPO, combined with transportation and handling shortfalls, could have contributed to an erroneous analysis of Lagat's blood and urine samples.

Lagat's sentiments over the drug tests echoed similar feelings of many distance runners in the sporting community: "I have always been in favor of eliminating drug taking from athletics and strongly endorse drug testing," Lagat said. "But it must be fair and reliable, and seen to be fair and reliable. I don't believe that is the case with testing for EPO at the moment. I wouldn't want any fellow athlete to suffer the way I did during those five weeks [of having one sample suggest a positive test, and then having to wait before the IAAF supported Lagat's eligibility]. The experience was the reverse of natural justice. I appeared to be guilty until I was proven innocent."

Unfortunately, WADA and the IAAF weren't only concerned with EPO use. Furosemide, banned by the World Anti-Doping Agency due to concerns that it may have masked other drugs; Nandrolone, an anabolic steroid that increased red blood cell growth and bone density; and Ephedrine, a blood pressure stimulant that proposed to increase reception by cells within the body—were just a few of the other drugs banned for cross-country athletes.

From 2003 to 2016, more than 150 international cross-country athletes were banned from competition for doping violations, or, in some cases, not consenting to the testing process (synonymous with pleading guilty), by the IAAF. This was across both genders and involved violations including EPO (a majority), but also testosterone, anabolic steroids, Nandolone, Furosemide, and Ephedrine. Many of these athletes heralded from Mediterranean or African states. More than 16 percent of these violations came from Morocco, while Kenya had the next single highest reported at 10 percent. Combining the number of athletes from France, Russia, China, Turkey, Portugal, and Spain accounted for more than a third of all reported cases. Even nations such as Ethiopia and United States had substantial violators—while athletes from more obscure countries such as Algeria, South Africa, and Brazil also found themselves listed.

What was more difficult to ascertain was the extent to which doping affected international cross-country performances *prior* to the 2003 testing procedures. The meteoric rise of specific nations at the World Cross-Country Championships did raise a few eyebrows—but overall it was impossible to know how to account for it all. Preemptive testing was not the norm from 1983 to 2003 (the IAAF admitted that there was no means of detecting EPO use directly in blood until 2009–10, or indirectly, through the Athlete Biological Passport Program, until 2009), and for the official record there was no way to go back and retroactively change results even if there were suspicions. Conclusively, the only certainty was that, of the names of nations listed after testing protocols were put in place in 2003, one nation did not appear on that list: Eritrea—and their top athlete, Zersenay Tadese, was not only the best challenger against the dominant Kenyans and Ethiopians, he was the best example for a clean sport as well.

ERITREA'S ZERSENAY TADESE

Zersenay (*Tadese*, his father's name) was under scrutiny once again. After being born and raised in rural Adi Bana, Eritrea, away from the violence and instability of the Eritrean War of Independence, he had found competitive cycling early in his teens and had worked hard to perfect his craft—Eritrea had been an Italian colony after all: "Cycling was my first love," Zersenay reflected. "I dreamt of being a cycling professional with one of the great teams in Europe. I would've loved to have ridden in a big race like the Tour de France. I won a number of races, mainly over distances of 30 to 50 kilometers. My success at cycling suggested to some local athletics people that I might have good stamina, and they invited me to compete in a local footrace. I won that and I did well in my following races, so I carried on running."

The scrutiny did not concern the split with his cycling team. And it wasn't the confusion concerning his Spanish running coach Jerimo Bravo Rodruez, whose surname and first name aligned shockingly close to a medical doctor's (Jerimo Bravo Sicilia) 222 miles away, a doctor whose research concerned experimental molecular biology and centered around the specialization of EPO/HGH receptors. The scrutiny lay in the fundamental notion that no athlete—especially one who entered the international running circuit so late in life—should have as much immediate success as Zersenay displayed in such a short time.

In 2009 Zersenay became only the second man after Paul Tergat to podium at three World Championships over three different surfaces in the same year—winning World Cross bronze, a 10,000-meter World Championship silver on the track, and gold in road running at the World Half Marathon Championships.

Zersenay also had biological exclusivity: in 2007, *The Science of Sport* studied Zersenay's VO_2 max (83 ml/kg/min), blood hematocrit (44 percent, an average amount—low by endurance athlete standards—and well under the barometer of one who would be on EPO), and running economy (which they determined to be extremely rare and top level—predicting that while running 3:09 per kilometer pace Zersenay was using only 57 percent of his "maximum" VO_2 max).

Finally, Zersenay exhibited local fame: a popular public figure in his home country, 2,500 guests attended his wedding, which was broadcast live on Eritrean television. But even with the achievements and the scrutiny, it was irrefutable that cross-country running was where Zersenay earned his status.

In his first three years as a professional runner, Zersenay seemingly ran every international cross-country competition in Europe. The spring of 2002 saw him on the Eritrean team competing at the World Cross-Country Championships, where he finished 30th (the lowest finish in an international cross-country event for his career), wearing racing spikes several sizes too big for his feet. Later in the 2002 he ran the Cross International Venta de Baños in Spain, finishing second.

In a four-week period in January and February 2003 in Spain, Zersenay finished third at the Cross International de Zornotza, second at the Cross International de Italica, and first at the Cross International de San Sebastián and Cross International Ciudad de Castellón. By March, Zersenay moved onto the Cinque Mulini in Italy, finishing third—and then returned to World Cross in Avenches, Switzerland, to improve to ninth overall (this time with properly fitted shoes).

By the end of 2003, Zersenay returned to the cross-country course once again. November saw him finish fourth at Spain's Soria Cross. In December he competed at the Cross de la Constitución and Cross Venta de Baños, finishing second at each. In January of '04 he ran everywhere from the Great North Cross-Country in Newcastle, England, to the European Club's Cup in Almeirim, Portugal. Zersenay finished no worse than fifth at each of these—and nearing the 2004 World Cross-Country Championship, was poised for further improvement. Zersenay crossed the line in sixth, contended with a devastating pace throughout, and again was the top non-Kenyan or -Ethiopian. Out of 38 international races in all disciplines in his first two years of competition—17 of them were in cross-country for Zersenay.

Naturally, his next goal was finishing on the podium at World Cross. 2005 was the year, and Saint Galmier, France, the locale. Zersenay spent much of the race behind Ethiopia's Kenenisa Bekele and Kenya's Eliud Kipchoge, but put on a masterful surge in the latest stages of the race to finish second overall. It wasn't a passing fancy either, 2006 saw Zersenay finish fourth before his return to World Cross in 2007 in Mombasa, Kenya.

As he built a sizeable lead some 20 minutes into the men's race on Mombasa's picturesque seaside golf course, Ethiopia's Kenenisa Bekele appeared to be kicking into cruise control en route to his sixth straight World Cross-Country title. But the weekend's most unpredictable and daunting variable—the stifling heat and humidity—reared its ugly head. In no time at all, up came a charging Zersenay who not only made up the gap, but went on to pummel past Bekele en route to his first World Cross victory.

Zersenay, who had just accomplished one of the more surprising upsets in World Cross history, had made a career out of chasing Bekele in the three years since his emergence among the world's elite. But left in the Eritrean's wake, an unlikely picture of Bekele emerged: one of a runner broken with simply nothing in reserve. Unable to summon his trademark sprint, Bekele looked drained and confused as he watched Zersenay pull away. Bekele would eventually succumb to the 91-degree temperatures (with 73 percent humidity) and walk off the course 800 meters before the finish. As two medics carried a stretcher in approach, Bekele motioned them away. Later it was confirmed that he struggled with stomach pains in the middle part of the race.

"I feel happy and proud for all Eritreans," said the twenty-five-year-old Zersenay, who had single-handedly led an athletics renaissance in his country. "I'm very happy and have no words to express my feelings." Zersenay went on to claim that preparation in Spain helped him for the conditions in Mombasa: "I trained quite a bit in heat similar to this," he said. Zersenay said he didn't feel surprised when he caught up and passed Bekele, and didn't realize that Bekele had dropped out. "I just didn't see him," Zersenay said.

In all, it wasn't just an Eritrean affirmation that Zersenay had inspired—the entire African continent was cognizant of the difficulty facing Kenya in maintaining their country's strangle-hold on the World Cross-Country Championships, and no runners wanted a gold medal more in the 2000s than the powerful contingent hailing from Ethiopia. At the time of Kenenisa Bekele's withdrawal in the 2007 edition of the championship he had amassed a winning streak of 27 straight cross-country titles. And Bekele was just the tip of the iceberg.

ETHIOPIA RETURNS TO GLORY

Prior to the 2004 World Cross-Country Championships, it was *Kenya* that had won 18 straight men's senior team titles, 16 junior men's team titles, seven senior women's titles, and 10 junior women's titles. They were also the top team in the briefly-held men's short course championship seven of the nine runnings, and once victorious for the short-course women. For a twenty-year period beginning in 1985, there was not a year that a Kenyan men's team was not on the podium for any of the events offered. But while the Kenyan coaches and administration understood that the nation had a legacy to uphold, Ethiopia, Kenya's closest competition—and fiercest rivals—had other ideas.

Ethiopia had seen nearly as much success as a nation as Kenya had at the top of the World Cross-Country rankings leading to the twenty-first century. But a cataclysmic showing at the 2001 World Cross-Country Championships in Ostend, Belgium, provoked the biggest resurgence against their rivals. After five years of podium finishes, the Ethiopian senior men finished a dismal ninth, with their first- and second-place finishers, Yibeltal Admassu (14th), and Habte Jifar (21st), separated from the remaining scorers, Demissie Girma (67th) and Tegenu Abebe (68th), by 46 places. It prompted an immediate change.

The following year Ethiopia returned with a vengeance. Assefa Mezgebu, the bronze-medalist at 10,000 meters in the 2000 Olympic Games (and twice a podium finisher at World Cross) was an immediate help, finishing 12th overall. Fita Bayisa, a bronze medalist over 5,000 meters at the 1992 Summer Olympics was added to the team for veteran leadership: he finished 17th. Habte Jifar, following the guidance of his seasoned teammates, improved to 16th overall, and leading the way for Ethiopia was a runner who had won the men's junior title the previous year by 33 seconds (and added a silver in the senior men's short-course race as well): Kenenisa Bekele. Bekele became Ethiopia's first individual champion of the senior men's race in twenty years, and Ethiopia finished behind Kenya for the team title by only 25 points.

In 2003, Ethiopia returned with a slew of new faces and even better results at World Cross. Bekele again repeated as the individual champion in the senior men's event, and countrymate Gebre Gebremariam joined him on the podium (Gebremariam had won the junior men's event the previous year; in this race he finished third). Sileshi Sihine, a silver-medalist at the 10,000 meters in the Olympic Games in Athens, finished seventh overall for Ethiopia. While Ketema Nigusse, a late-season entrant after doing well at the Ethiopian National Cross-Country Championships, crossed the line in 10th. Ethiopia was quickly rebounding—and in 2003 they inched closer to Kenya, finishing second, 23 points to 17.

The 2004 World Cross-Country Championships was the greatest finish for Ethiopia in their nation's history. While the event was once again in Belgium, it would be a far different result for Ethiopia than what they saw in 2001. On the podium for the senior men stood Sihine (third place, 36:11 for 12K), Gebremariam (second in 36:10), and Bekele (first in 35:52). Ethiopia's fourth and final scorer, Yibeltal Admassu, crossed in eighth. "If I never run cross-country again, I will be happy. I have made history in my own name and with my team," smiled Bekele after the win.

"Kenya had dominated the World Cross for nearly twenty years, so this result could not have been better."

The 2004 Kenyan team had been one of their strongest assembled in championship history and included Eliud Kipchoge (fourth overall), the reigning World 5,000-meter champion; Charles Kamathi (fifth), the 2001 World 10,000-meter gold medalist; Will Talel (10th), the 2002 Commonwealth 10,000-meter champion; and John C. Korir (11th), a former double Kenyan national cross winner. Kenya fell to Ethiopia by a score of 30 points to 14.

That same weekend the Ethiopian men won the short-course competition (17 total points), the Ethiopian women the short- and long-course titles (19 and 26 total points, respectively), and junior women titles (10 points). The Ethiopian junior men narrowly missed the sweep by finishing second to Kenya by five points. And to prove it was not a fluke, the senior men and women repeated their title finishes in both the short and long courses the following year in 2005.

What separated the Ethiopian success from Kenya were not their differences in training—but their similarities. Many of Ethiopia's champions hailed from Bekoji, a small agrarian town one hundred miles outside Ethiopia's capital of Addis Ababa. Rough, rugged roads were the only access between the two cities, and when passing the welcome sign marking this agricultural hinterland, it was very much like stepping into a land completely devoid of technology or modern conveniences.

Bekoji and the neighboring farming districts were some of the most fertile regions in Ethiopia. Farmers toiled for three seasons a year. The main agricultural produce of the area, a grain staple known as teff, was harvested along with wheat, barley, sorghum, and other cereals. Agricultural products, however, were the least known products from this area: "Bekoji is the true production center for Ethiopian long-distance talent," claimed Gebretsadik Tesfaye, the head coach of the Arsi province athletics team, and Haile Gebrselassie's first coach.

Many of Ethiopia's well-known and internationally acclaimed distance stars were born and raised in Bekoji, including Derartu Tulu, Kenenisa Bekele, Fatuma Roba, and the Dibaba sisters, Tirunesh and Ejegayehu. Haile Gebrselassie was born in Assela, twenty miles from Bekoji, and Gezahegne Abera's home village was an hour drive away. The center of Bekoji sat at an altitude of 10,500 feet and had an average temperature of 66 degrees Fahrenheit: "Athletes from this region and other high-altitude parts of Ethiopia are equipped with hemoglobin that has extraordinary levels of oxygen-transporting capability," said Dr. Woldemeskel Kostre, National Athletics team coach, who did his master's thesis on the effects of altitude on long-distance running, and helped introduce the concept of altitude training to the country's runners.

Living at altitude contributed to the high levels of hemoglobin, but the inhabitants' iron-based diet was also a major contributing factor: "Hemoglobin is largely iron-dependent for its normal functioning, and grain staples like teff are excellent sources of iron," confirmed Dr. Kostre. Apart from teff, locals regularly ate wheat, barley,

and sorghum, which provided strength in addition to being excellent sources of iron.

Altitude and the right diet, however, were useless without the right mindset: "The majority of Ethiopian runners will continue to come from the rural parts of the country," said Dr. Kostre. "They have the toughness that many runners from the city do not have." Lifestyles of children in this rural region were much different than that of Westerners or city dwellers. The majority of Bekojians were farmers, and they passed the art of plowing the land on to their children. There were no machines, tractors, graders, or loaders, and all the farm work had to be done manually. For many, the most logical method of escaping the toils of herding cattle and digging earth was education: "I loved math and what I was able to do with numbers," recalled Bekele. "I knew that I did not want to be a farmer. The world was moving on, and I had to work very hard to catch up."

But as Bekele later found out, it was difficult to stay focused on education when there was a proven path to success: "We tell the children stories of how Derartu Tulu and Kenenisa Bekele worked hard to get to the top of distance running," said Sentayehu Eshetu, a sports teacher at the Bekoji Elementary School, one of only two elementary schools in the town. "It inspires them and they work hard in their training to try and make it to the top." Filled with stories of motivation and heroism, hundreds took to the training grounds each morning and late afternoon to fulfill their dreams. "Competition is fierce," explained Eshetu. "You have to be very good to get past the other runners."

The Ethiopian Athletics Federation (EAF), the governing body for athletics in the country, provided the Bekoji town council a small budget to train only 25 to 30 young runners every year, but more than 200 of them typically appeared on selection day for a chance to be included in the youth development project. "It is difficult to drop someone with enthusiasm," claimed Eshetu. "We usually take about 100 or more youngsters, but they must work hard to prove themselves." Eshetu's definition of hard work included training at least three times a week on one of the most punishing hills ever seen, "The Wenz," a double hill, each section 50 feet high, divided by a narrow strip of water. For their cross-country workouts, the runners ran up and down the hill and jumped from one elevation to the next. Typically, they did these repeats 40 or 50 times a day—clearly not for the faint-hearted.

That was only the first half of their weekly training routine, however. The remainder of the week was spent in the Bekoji soccer and track stadium. Here, coaches taught runners basic racing tactics and how to run laps: "At the Wenz, they develop the strength in their bodies," said Eshetu. "But at the stadium, we teach them to think like a runner."

After months of hard work and training, Bekoji's dreamers were pitted against runners from nearby towns: "It always surprises me because kids from Bekoji win the top three or four positions in the Oromiya Regional Championships," said Coach Tesfaye. If they managed to be among the top contenders in the regional championships, opportunities came knocking at their door. The usual next step was selection for the Oromiya team for the Ethiopian Cross-Country Championships.

At this national championship, runners competed against the best from other regions of the country and were scouted by the top clubs: "When we see a potentially good athlete, we tell him or her to come to our trials," said Kassahun Alemayehu, head athletics coach of the Ethiopian Banks Sports Club. "We have trials three times a year upon which we pick the runners and take them on as members of our club." Also during this time, athletes would be contacted by foreign management agencies so that they could have a chance to compete in international meets around the world. Running abroad helped them gain selection for global running events, as the EAF used times from IAAF meets to pick World Championship and Olympic teams.

But the path to glory for an athlete from Bekoji was not guaranteed: "Each year we discover many athletes with potential to reach the top," said Dr. Kostre. "But what we do here [in Addis Ababa] is select the best from the best." An athlete recruited by one of Addis Ababa's clubs or the Ethiopian national team was asked to move to Addis Ababa in order to receive training. However, "moving to the big city is very difficult," recalled Olympic 10,000-meter silver medalist Ejegayehu Dibaba. "Everything is different in Addis Ababa, and life is generally expensive." And until they had the chance to compete in big-money races outside Ethiopia, athletes were forced to get by on a small stipend of less than $50 a month. "We know that it is not enough to live in Addis Ababa," said an anonymous member of Omedla Sports Club. "But we do not have the budget to provide for more."

Despite the need to move and change their lifestyle, athletes of both genders in Ethiopia saw this as a form of livelihood they could use to support their families. Cross-country running internationally became a means of an improved lifestyle that other occupations could not provide. Bekele, for example, bought a house at the heart of Bekoji for his parents and hired laborers to farm the family's land. The Dibaba sisters also built a house for their parents in the city. "Thanks to my daughters, I do not have to worry about farming anymore," claimed their father, Dibaba Keneni.

THE BABY-FACED DESTROYER

Tirunesh Dibaba was a product of Bekoji. Born and raised there as the fourth of six children, it was academics that brought her to Addis Ababa at age fourteen to continue studying. Consequently, this allowed Dibaba to live with her sister, Ejegayehu, who was also a world-class distance runner. Bekelu Dibaba, a cousin, enrolled Tirunesh in the Prison's Sports Club after she proved herself by finishing fifth in a trial cross-country race. Within a year, fifteen-year-old Tirunesh Dibaba placed fifth at the World Junior Cross-Country Championships. But no eyebrows were raised; she returned home to the village of Chefe, where her result did not impress many. A cousin on her father's side of the family had set high standards after winning a couple of

Olympic gold medals. Expectations, even around her own family's dinner table, were going to be difficult to exceed.

The following year in Dublin, Tirunesh Dibaba improved to second in the World Cross junior event, and after winning (and setting a time of 15:13 on the track), returned to Addis Ababa, where she finished second and first at the Siemens International Cross-Country Championship in the long and short races, respectively. This return to the sport after a long season of track races enabled Dibaba to keep her fitness—and she ended up winning the Junior Championship at World Cross outright in 2003. As a result, the Ethiopian Federation kept her in Addis Ababa—and before long consistent training and support translated into more top results.

Remarked Dibaba about her training: "We train two days on the track and one day in the woods with the Federation, while the rest of the time we train on our own. We also train on gravel paths. Most times, we train in the woods [in and around Addis Ababa], in the mornings and in the evenings. In the mornings, we train for about an hour. In the evenings, we train about 40 to 50 minutes." Dibaba also trained in Haile Gebrselassie's gym twice a week and ran a long run of up to 90 minutes. The results spoke for themselves: Dibaba amassed five World Cross-Country Championship victories, including her junior title (Lausanne, 2003), one short course title (Saint-Galmier, 2005), and two long course titles (Saint-Galmier, 2005; and Fukuoka, 2006). When the IAAF reduced the offering to one long course race in 2007, Tirunesh finished with a silver in Mombasa that year and the gold at Edinburgh in 2008.

ANBESSA: THE LION

From 2002 through 2006, Kenenisa Bekele won both the short (four-kilometer) and long (12-kilometer) course titles at the World Cross-Country Championships, a feat no other runner was able to accomplish. In 2004, he broke the world records for the indoor 5,000-meter, outdoor 5,000-meter, and outdoor 10,000-meter races. When he won the 3,000-meter race at the 2006 World Indoor Track Championships in Moscow, Bekele became the first athlete in history to be Olympic champion, world outdoor track champion, world indoor track champion, and World Cross-Country Champion in the same year. And for a period of time from December 2001 to March 2007 Bekele went undefeated in 27 consecutive cross-country races. For many, Kenenisa Bekele was not only the greatest cross-country runner the world had ever seen—he was the best distance runner, ever, period.

Of the many nicknames given to Bekele, *Anbessa*, which translates to lion in Amharic, has perhaps endeared him more to his people than any other. "When I was training up at the Entoto Hills [a popular training venue for Ethiopian runners on the outskirts of the capital Addis Ababa] with my brother Tariku, I swear that I saw a lioness and her cub about 100 meters away," Bekele once said. "We stopped abruptly, let them quietly return to the forest, and then proceeded to turn away. I was scared a bit at the time. I had heard stories that a lioness would get angry if she thought anything would hurt her cub. When we asked shepherds whether lions existed in the area, they said the forests did not have any lions, only cheetahs. I still do not believe it. It was a lioness and her cub just like the ones I saw many times on television." Whether the encounter with the actual lion was legitimate, his times on the track and cross-country course during the decade of the 2000s certainly were.

Although he won the 2001 World Junior Cross-Country Championship, Bekele truly came of age in Dublin in his second appearance in 2002. Many junior champions fade into obscurity, or, at best, struggle to make their national teams once they enter adulthood. Bekele, only nineteen years old when he lined up against the greatest runners in the world in the four-kilometer senior race, stunned them all with a convincing victory over a muddy course. Despite nursing an Achilles tendon strain—which he declined to tell anybody about—Bekele returned to the course the next day to help the Ethiopian team. The result was the same. He destroyed the 12K senior men's field, becoming the only man to ever win both events at the World Cross-Country Championships, and the only man to ever win the World Junior Cross-Country race and then go on to win a senior title. Then he repeated the double in Lausanne in 2003; further testament to his unique talent.

With the prize money from his World Cross victories, Bekele immediately bought himself a house in Addis Ababa and invited his siblings to live with him so they could attend college in the capital. Suddenly the primary breadwinner in his family, Bekele also paid their tuition.

With a meteoric rise matched only by one other runner of Ethiopian heritage, Haile Gebrselassie, comparisons between Bekele and Gebrselassie were inevitable. "I don't mind the comparisons with Haile," Bekele admitted. "Haile did a lot of things while I was a junior and when I started running seriously I noticed this." For the record: both were born in the same region of Arsi province—Gebrselassie from Assela, Bekele from Oromo—where their families toiled as farmers. Both launched their careers as world-class junior athletes. But there the similarities end. Bekele's 5,000-meter/10,000-meter double gold at the World Championships, a year after first achieving the feat at the Beijing Olympics, was something that Gebrselassie, who long hoped to emulate compatriot Miruts Yifter's 1980 Olympic double, failed to achieve. Gebrselassie also never won a Senior World Cross-Country title, while Bekele, the only man to win double gold over 4K/12K, repeated the accomplishment five times, and won the longer event an unprecedented six times. Bekele was also undefeated over 10,000 meters (in 11 races), and wiped Gebrselassie's world track records off the books, from 2,000 meters indoors to 10,000 meters.

To understand the rise of Bekele it is necessary to understand the grand sense of tradition that empowered young Ethiopian runners. Just as Miruts Yifter's victories at the 1980 Moscow Olympics inspired a young Haile Gebrselassie, the success of later Ethiopian Olympians stoked Bekele's enthusiasm: "Derartu Tulu is my hero," Bekele revealed. "She was the first Ethiopian woman to win an Olympic gold medal for Africa and for Ethiopia. I heard all about her when I was starting out."

In 2004, after Ethiopia won the senior men's team championship for the first time in 20 tries (and Bekele was able to win the short and long course titles for the third straight year), the young champion noted, "I will not attempt to run both events again. History is made and I don't believe anyone will come to threaten my record at cross-country. If I never run cross-country again, I will be happy. I have made history in my own name and with my team." Within the year, however, following another undefeated season over the cross-country course, Bekele would toe the line again.

Another "double" victory in 2005 brought Bekele's World Cross medal total to 21 (as an individual: four long-course golds in the senior event, four short-course golds in the senior event, a short-course silver from 2001, a junior championship gold—and as part of a team: podium finishes in all the previous events, plus a junior team silver from 1999 when he made his debut). This made Bekele the most decorated individual in the history of the World Cross-Country Championships. "Life has changed for me," Bekele said. "More people recognize me when I am walking down the street in Addis. They want to shake my hand or they want to say hello. Life is getting better too."

After successfully defending his titles once again in 2006, Bekele had to overcome disaster after World Cross in 2007, when all his hard work came unraveled with stomach pains and oppressive weather in Mombasa, Kenya. It was surprising, then, to see the young Ethiopian on the starting line in 2008—when another near disaster was averted: "Bekele overcame, in turn, a missed flight, overnight stomach troubles, a dislodged shoe early in the 12-kilometer race, and Tadese's determined mid-race surges, to regain the crown he had won in five successive years from 2002 to 2006," wrote IAAF correspondent David Powell. Bekele's win cemented his place in cross-country history. "As far as the sixth long course win is concerned, I tried to accomplish it last year but, because of the weather, I was not able to do it," Bekele said. "This has a very high honor in my life." It was the final time Bekele would contest the World Cross-Country Championships.

* * *

The first decade of the 2000s not only provided a newfound appreciation for top-caliber international competition, but also saw a youth movement rise in the United States. And with this appreciation came attention paid to another unsavory aspect of the sport that was uncharacteristic of distance running: performance-enhancing drugs. How the IAAF would respond to drug cheating would make headlines in not only the years centered on EPO use, but in the coming decade as well. Furthermore, the continued dominance by Kenya, Ethiopia, and Eritrea internationally would have a lasting effect on the Western nations who were fighting to stay relevant at the top of the leaderboard; whether the West could still win or not, remained to be seen.

EVENT SPOTLIGHT: ONE POINT AWAY—THE 2001 NCAA MEN'S DIVISION I CROSS-COUNTRY NATIONAL CHAMPIONSHIP (NOVEMBER 19, 2001)

LOCATION: FURMAN UNIVERSITY, GREENVILLE, SOUTH CAROLINA

Furman University Golf Course

The once indomitable University of Arkansas Razorbacks, winners of 11 National Cross-Country Championships for the men since 1984, had revealed a chink in their armor. In January 2001, head coach John McDonnell suffered a stress-induced heart attack while at his home in Fayetteville. While it was not a major setback for the team and required only a few weeks recovery—it marked a turning point in his life as coach and signaled that previous lifestyle choices would have to be changed.

Arkansas had won the 2000 NCAA Cross-Country National Championship, held in Ames, Iowa, by the skin of their teeth after employing superior strategy given for the conditions of the meet. "I told our guys that I had a sneaking suspicion nobody will want to lead," McDonnell confided. "There'll be a big pack up front so make sure you are at the front of it." When the leaders came through the three-mile mark in a pedestrian time of 15:15 that day, and McDonnell saw his top five runners with the leaders and Colorado well back in the field, he sensed an upset. Arkansas finished with 83 points, edging the formidable Colorado squad by 11 points. "That was an upset for sure because Colorado was a much better team," said McDonnell.

But Colorado, who lacked one essential piece of the puzzle to finalize depth, were able to add freshman Dathan Ritzenhein to the squad entering the 2001 season.

Likewise, Stanford University, which had finished fourth or better as a team since winning the event outright in 1996 and 1997, had the numbers, with freshman standout Ryan Hall joining a young, talented group under the tutelage of head coach Vin Lananna.

Meanwhile, the Razorbacks had added an essential individual during a rebuilding year in which most of their veteran seniors had graduated in the spring of 2001. Alistair Cragg, a talented distance runner from Johannesburg, South Africa, had arrived at Southern Methodist University in Dallas as a freshman in the fall of 2000. After the death of his younger brother, however, Cragg left school until a fortuitous opening landed him at the University of Arkansas: "I saw him at SMU but hadn't paid much attention to him and then of course he went home for a semester and his brother [Duncan] contacted me and told me what had happened," remembered Coach McDonnell.

"I called Alistair and asked him, 'What are your goals?' and he said 'Whatever you want me to do I will do.' So I told him, 'That's easy, but you might regret that!' He was a dream to coach and had a fantastic race head. You could ask him to do anything and he would do it."

Additionally, other schools were enjoying an off-season leading into a 2001 fall campaign rich in individual talent. Alan Webb, after running 3:53 for the mile as a high school senior, promptly joined the University of Michigan and began winning every race in sight. He went undefeated until the Great Lakes regional, where Kenyan athlete Boaz Cheboiywo Kisang from Eastern Michigan demolished Webb and everybody else in the field.

The overwhelming individual favorite heading into the 2001 NCAA Cross-Country National Championship, Boaz Cheboiywo already had a long history of competing internationally before he arrived on campus. Critics were quick to point out that had Cheboiywo made a profit from any winnings from those races, he would be ruled ineligible by the NCAA for breaking amateur rules. The truth was murky. What was known: Boaz had raced substantially—and eyewitnesses confirmed he received payment for competing. But it was unknown whether he simply had his expenses covered, or if he had tried to earn a living. But considering many athletes, including a 2000 Olympian from the United States who competed alongside Cheboiywo that year had lost money in Europe, it was unlikely that Boaz turned a profit. Nonetheless, conspiracy theorists took pride in the fact that Eastern Michigan originally had a different last name for Boaz at the start of the season (Kisang).

The undisputable truth was that Boaz Cheboiywo was crushing the competition and was going to run at the 2001 National Championship. Cheboiywo had finished 12th in the Kenyan National Cross-Country Championships—a race that was notoriously brutal and ranked higher than any competitive domestic distance competition in the United States. And after defeating Webb handily (by 44 seconds over 10 kilometers at the regional), there was seemingly no other competitor in the field that could match him.

Colorado didn't believe that. "We knew that we had the personnel," said Colorado head coach Mark Wetmore. "I remember that everybody was confident that it was within reach."

"I remember Mark sitting down and talking to both me and Jorge [Torres, who finished third overall the year before] and he said, 'I've never had another year where I've had two athletes that could both win the NCAA cross-country title.' But we had to do it in completely different ways," said Dathan Ritzenhein. "He sent out Jorge with the leaders, said, 'Go for it, I just want you to hold on.' And for me he said, 'I want you to sit back and work your way up and just try to close the gap.'"

Stanford too, was optimistic about their chances. "Both [Stanford's men's and women's] teams are well-prepared. We've basically had uneventful seasons. We managed to get through all the rigors of getting to the NCAAs. The athletes are all healthy and prepared to compete well," noted Stanford coach Vin Lananna the night before the big meet. "Our men's team is a very young team. I think that 10,000 meters will be a good challenge for some of them, but the course is set up well." Stanford had swept the West Regional and Pac-10 Conference Championship en route to what was at that point, an undefeated season.

Colorado had come on strong toward the end of the season, having won the Mountain Regional, but the Arkansas Razorbacks were well aware of their own expectations: "I think Coach [McDonnell] thought we could compete for the title," said Arkansas varsity standout Jason Sandfort. "He never went to nationals thinking he was not going for the win, and you have to love that. He was the opposite of [Colorado coach Mark] Wetmore because he believes nothing good happens from the back of the pack."

Once the gun fired on the morning of November 19, 2001, there was no holding back. Hammering hard from the start, Eastern Michigan's Boaz Cheboiywo was pursued by only two individuals—both Kenyan. TCU's Eliud Njubi and Alabama's David Kimani (a 13:10 5k runner and 1999 NCAA champion) followed Cheboiywo in hot pursuit, but neither of them ended up finishing the race. Kimani didn't even make it two miles, dropping out officially because of Achilles tendinitis, but unofficially, at least in part, because of a broken will.

With 6:45 into the race, after a 4:24 opening mile, Boaz and the Kenyans had an amazing 16-second lead on the rest of the field. Ten minutes into the race (well beyond the two-mile mark), the other Kenyans were gone and Boaz's lead was already up to 22 seconds. For all practical purposes, the race for the individual title was over. Boaz would stretch his lead to as much as 26 seconds before Colorado's Jorge Torres cut into it a bit to make things look respectable, and the final margin of victory was 19 seconds. Boaz covered the 10,000 meters in a course record of 28:47, which broke the mark of 28:54 set by Meb Keflezighi (the then-current American record holder at 10,000 meters). To understand just how impressive Boaz's performance was, one needs to understand that Boaz shattered his own eight-kilometer course record en route to the 10K course record.

Amazingly, after the race Boaz revealed that he'd been battling both a hip flexor and Achilles tendon injury since demolishing the field in the Great Lakes Regional. The injuries greatly curtailed Cheboiywo's training and caused him to take six days off completely from running during the final two weeks of the cross-country season. As a result, when he toed the line for the start, Boaz admitted he was "not very confident" about his prospects for the title. Despite the fact that Boaz covered the opening mile in 4:24, he said his strategy for the race was to take it out slowly to see how his injuries felt. "I wanted to go out slow, but when I couldn't feel the injuries at the first instance, I tried to go fast so I could have a clear view of the course," said Boaz. "After a while I said (to myself), 'Let's get going!' as Kimani is very fast compared to me. I've only run 13:30 [for 5K; Kimani's run 13:10]."

With the individual race virtually decided by mile two, all attention quickly turned to the tight team battle. While Stanford and the Arkansas Razorbacks got to the front right away, most of the savvy Colorado Buffaloes were biding their time. The exception was Colorado's top veteran, Jorge Torres: "I knew that we were going to take it out fast," the junior said. "And I took it a little bit more conservative than they did. And I knew I was going to do that. My only thing was I wanted to be as close as I can—in striking distance—toward the last four, three kilometers." The determined Torres narrowed the gap on Boaz in the final two miles, and separated himself from his pursuers, finishing second overall.

"I couldn't tell much what was going on in the race," Dathan Ritzenhein confided. "Just because I started further back. Just being in a battle with [Arkansas's] Alistair Cragg, to see how many places I could get." Ritzenhein had started out of the top 30 in the first mile, crossing in 4:43, about 20 seconds behind the leaders, but coach Wetmore wasn't phased at all. "He was 4:43. Do the math. What's 6.2 4:43 miles? I think that's about third or fourth in the race," said Wetmore of his prodigy. "He has the race experience of a forty-year-old." True to form, Ritzenhein moved up methodically in the middle part of the race, challenging the Razorback Cragg for third until the finish line.

Stanford University had employed nearly the opposite approach, as their top runner, sophomore Grant Robison, found himself the top American at the first mile in 4:31. But while the Buffaloes continued to pass runners all the way to the finishing chute, Robison, who was fourth overall at the mile, ended up as the fourth Cardinal finisher, 21st place overall (in 29:51) by the end. "I think it clearly was a case of Grant's first time of being at the NCAAs," said Stanford coach Lananna. "Even though we talked about not redlining it, he was at the redline at 2.5 miles. And when you do that, you pay the price. But you know what? I'll take it anytime. Those kids ran tough. Don Sage was outstanding—Luis Luchini charging like crazy—and Grant was hurting for a long time in that race, and I give him a lot of credit for hanging on and doing what he did."

Despite expressing complete confidence in Ritzenhein's even-paced start, Wetmore admitted that it was his team's even-paced running style that was tough to handle psychologically: "We're always petrified about being buried at the mile every year. That feeling doesn't change. [The narrowness of the course at the start here] just makes it harder to trust," said Wetmore. "I sincerely believe that living at elevation is an advantage, but training at elevation is a disadvantage. I believe that when our opponents are doing repeat miles in 4:30, we're doing them in 4:42 or 4:45. So we really don't have the choice [to go out hard]," commented Wetmore about his team's strategy. "The leaders today were down around 4:20 at the mile and if I'd sent Jorge and Dathan with them, that would have been suicidal. We would have been fifth today. So we really don't have a choice [but to go out slower]. My job is just to convince [my runners] to trust it and not be nervous at the mile or two mile and blow up out of nerves."

"Cross-country is a wonderful sport," remarked Wetmore, "But one of its weaknesses is that you can sit around for two hours and not know what happened—not know the outcome of the race—and that was one of those years. Videos of the finish line went into the tent, another coach insisted on reviewing place by place every single finish, so it took a long time. And the crowd was gone and the parents were gone when they finally announced it."

After more than one hour of waiting (with the women's race being conducted in the interim) the results were finally announced: Colorado 90, Stanford 91. "We've been right there year in and year out and we've never gotten over that hill," said Jorge Torres. "Today was our day finally." "This was the hardest race, the hardest I've ever run," said Ritzenhein. "It was so fast at the end. This was definitely a step toward my future." "This was a relief," said Wetmore. "I try not to wear my heart on my sleeve, but I was admittedly nervous. We were getting stronger and stronger every meet and felt the pressure of this one."

Despite the fact that their lead in the team battle evaporated in the final stages of the race (literally the last steps as Colorado's Ed Torres passed Dartmouth's Tom McArdle right at the finish to come in 15th overall and as Colorado's third runner), it was great to see Stanford coach Vin Lananna completely unapologetic about his team's strategy and very satisfied with the way his team ran after the race: "I think the guys did a really, really good job. I think it was a difficult way to run the race. But because we knew we didn't have the front fire power [of Colorado], what we needed to do is make sure we got into a position [to win] relatively early, which we did. I think we may have gone out a little harder than we would have liked," commented Lananna despite the agonizingly close one-point loss, "but that's the only way for Stanford to win and we'll always run that way. We will go out and we'll go hard and put ourselves in a position to win the race every time we go out and compete."

Arkansas finished the day with four All-Americans. Not only had Alistair Cragg finished in third place, right where McDonnell predicted, but Silverus Kimeli (13th), Daniel Lincoln (19th), and Jason Sandfort (32nd) were not far behind. With Arkansas's fifth runner Fernando Cabada fading to 70th place overall on the day, the Razorbacks finished third with 118 points. It would be their best finish until they returned to the podium in 2004 and 2005. John McDonnell would eventually step away as coach in 2008.

For Colorado, this men's team victory, after so many attempts, helped them turn the corner to prove they weren't just an institution harboring individuals like Adam Goucher and the Torres brothers; they were committed to winning championships of all kinds. As Colorado coach Mark Wetmore said after the race, "It's a thrill to be here. It's always a thrill to be here. This is the most exciting and dramatic sport in the world for those of us who know it and enjoy it." He then paused for dramatic effect before adding, "And for those of us who go out in the back and move up through the pack [as my teams do], it's the most petrifying sport in the world." The Colorado Buffaloes had captured their first men's team championship and in the process made Wetmore the only coach in NCAA Cross-Country history to have guided a program to team titles and individual titles on both the men's and women's sides.

Men's Race
Date: Monday, November 19, 2001
Teams: 31
Distance: 6.2 miles/10 kilometers
Location: Furman University Golf Course, Greenville, South Carolina

Individual Finishers (Top 25):

1	Boaz Cheboiywo	28:47	East. Michigan
2	Jorge Torres	29:06	Colorado
3	Alistair Cragg	29:10	Arkansas
4	Dathan Ritzenhein	29:11	Colorado
5	Luke Watson	29:19	Notre Dame
6	Ryan Shay	29:23	Notre Dame
7	Donald Sage	29:24	Stanford
8	Matt Tegenkamp	29:26	Wisconsin
9	Josh Spiker	29:29	Wisconsin
10	Travis Laird	29:31	N. Arizona
11	Alan Webb	29:38	Michigan
12	Louis Luchini	29:41	Stanford
13	Silverus Kimeli	29:40	Arkansas
14	Dan Wilson	29:46	Connecticut
15	Ed Torres	29:47	Colorado
16	Tom McArdle	29:47	Dartmouth
17	Josh Horton	29:49	UCSB
18	Mike Wisniewski	29:50	Michigan
19	Daniel Lincoln	29:51	Arkansas
20	Ian Dobson	29:53	Stanford
21	Grant Robison	29:53	Stanford
22	Fasil Bizuneh	29:58	Arizona State
23	Joe Driscoll	29:59	Portland
24	Adam Sutton	30:00	Providence
25	Bruno Mazzotta	30:01	N. Arizona

Team Results:

1 Colorado	90
2 Stanford	91
3 Arkansas	118
4 Northern Arizona	193
5 Wisconsin	245
6 Notre Dame	248
7 Portland	273
8 Villanova	282
9 North Carolina State	293
10 Providence College	294

Chapter 17

One of the last races of Casey's cross-country career took place on a hot, muggy afternoon over a punishing course. He held steady with the front of the pack, but dropped off dramatically in the last half mile and finished in the middle. Then he collapsed and rolled to his side in a deep pain that he had knowingly, willingly put himself in. The paramedics ran through a quick assessment and told us he would be fine and that we were all welcome to stay until he felt better or until they had to use the stretcher for the next kid—whichever came first. Casey smiled and looked around and shook his head. His spikes were covered in mud that ran up both legs into his shorts. His tank top was mashed with sweat and grass and saliva. But he was starting to feel better. 'You get a lot of tennis players in this ambulance?' I asked the paramedics as they began to put away their gear. They chuckled and shook their heads. 'You ever get a basketball player in here who pushed himself so hard he literally couldn't see straight? Or what about soccer players? Do they ever just collapse in pain during the normal course of play?' 'Only the runners do that,' a woman said as she unhooked the monitors from Casey's body and folded the wires into her pockets. Only the runners.

—Marc Parent

THE 2010s

It was a sport on a precipice. Despite a youth resurgence in cross-country running that led to renewed interest and better performances in the 2000s, the Western world was still sorting out the details as to how to better reach audiences, and what to do about the perception that only runners from East African nations could win titles. In an era of media-frenzy, sport stardom, and marketing money being invested into athletics at record highs, the 2010s became a chance to discover where cross-country running fit into the global ethos of the new millennium.

For every major event and new record accomplishment, there was news damaging the sport in major ways. As events such as Nike Cross Nationals motivated prep-school athletes into helping their team become the best high school cross-country squad in the nation, the IAAF was transitioning the World Cross-Country Championships into a biennial event. As high school and college teams broke course records and defied convention in the autumn, professional enterprises were focused on lowering times on the track and shooting for Olympic gold in the spring.

But, with new ambassadors for the sport, there was still legitimate interest in cross-country running, clearly evident in both traditional practices and new enthusiasm. It was a moment of confluence for old and new. Long-striding mudders still thrived in the colder months, and the best coaches still understood that strength was built on the hills and in the grass—away from the stopwatches and synthetic surfaces. Cross-country remained powerful and relevant in those forgotten recesses of distance running for individuals who celebrated the spirit of rebellious fire born all those years ago.

STAY THE COURSE

Coach Al Carius knew about this confluence of changing times. As head coach of North Central College, a private liberal arts university of 3,000 students twenty-eight miles from Chicago, his teams had amassed a cross-country running pedigree that spanned over five decades and was unmatched in the pantheon of larger institutions. The accomplishments of the North Central College men's cross-country program spoke for themselves: 16 NCAA Division III national titles, 15 NCAA Division III national runner-up finishes, 27 NCAA regional championships, 48 College Conference of Illinois and Wisconsin (CCIW) championships, and 111 All-Americans, all within fifty years.

Entering his fiftieth season as the men's cross-country coach at North Central College, it seemed that Al Carius had a formula for success: "The coaching staff and I try to look for every little thing that can be positive or supportive within our culture to help people to do what they choose to do," Carius said. "We try to create the environment and support system to help [the athletes] focus on going out and doing the best they can." But winning was not the most important thing to Carius: "Unquestionably, the relationships that I've made are the most important thing to me," he said. "It's not about developing Olympians; if it's about building Olympians then I'm a total failure as a coach, and if winning national championships is what it's all about then I don't even want to coach."

Thankfully Carius's record, forged out of his mantra that runners "run for fun and personal bests" was no failure, and the nation was taking notice. In 1999 the NCAA named Carius "The Cross-Country Coach of the Century" and in 2008 the US Track and Field and Cross-Country Coaches Association created the Al Carius Program of the Year Award—given annually to the NCAA Division III men's cross-country and track and field program with the highest average finish at the three national championships (cross-country, indoor track, and outdoor track). And Carius's North Central Cardinals had brought the award home three times. But changing times brought doubts that Carius could keep his legacy going. It wasn't always smooth waters—especially as his program transitioned into the twenty-first century.

After a second-place finish at NCAAs in 2004, the leadership from within that had kept the Cardinals on top started to slip. As the season progressed in 2005, Carius sensed a shift in culture, but with decades of success behind the program, he figured the team would rejuvenate itself. Instead, North Central fell to 12th in 2005, 13th in 2006, and 16th in 2007.

Prior to that, the school had finished outside of the top four at nationals only once. Team members and coaches were struggling, while the proud alumni of the program started to wonder whether Carius had lost his touch. "Some guys wanted to be associated with the team, but didn't want to contribute, didn't want to put in the hard work," said Carius, himself a two-time Big Ten cross-country champion as an undergrad at the University of Illinois. "You can't force it on someone. You have to find people that have that passion, and build around that attitude. I allowed it to happen and lowered the standards of what excellence is in our program."

While that might have sent other longtime coaches into retirement, Carius took full responsibility. Prior to the 2008 season, Carius rallied around a core group of young runners and started to see a shift in the team's mindset. Following the strong running of sophomore Mike Spain and junior Kyle Brady, the team started to gel, demonstrating a hunger the program hadn't seen in years. In the end, it was a simple fix: have fun, be true to the sport, run hard, and endure the trials of the miles. It's what Carius had preached for years, but it took a savvy coach to know how to right the program. "You could see them coming together," Carius said. "We were so fragmented the year before, but as the season went on it became clear that they were in it for each other." The Cardinals finished second at the national championships in 2008, then went on to win their first title since 1999 in 2009, scoring one of the lowest point totals in history (51) while having all seven runners earn All-American status.

"Al still hasn't peaked," Washington University coach Jeff Stiles said. "He's not on cruise control. The guy who follows him—in about twenty-five years—has an impossible job." Stiles captained North Central's 10th NCAA Cross-Country Championship in 1997. His Washington College women's team became Division III champions, and his men took third in 2011—the same season that North Central won its second title in three attempts. "It's not like he is some mad scientist or amazing guru. Al is passionate, and people follow passion," Stiles said.

Carius, who grew up in Morton, Illinois, became North Central's track and cross-country head coach in 1966 at the age of twenty-four. Wisconsin tried to lure him away in the early 1970s, but North Central countered by building an outdoor track. Then, in the early '80s, Northwestern tried to recruit him, but Carius was going through a divorce and wanted to stay close to his young child in Naperville.

Carius's road to excellence started long before coming to North Central: "I came from a small high school, and back then I didn't know a lot about running. I had to do a lot of research on my own and learned through trial and error," Carius said. "I had to learn to take responsibility for myself." When he attended the University of Illinois, Carius won five Big Ten Conference Championships: two in cross-country and three in the two-mile event. He also clocked the fifth fastest 3,000-meter steeplechase time at 8:48 at the Kentucky Relays in 1966. "When the Olympic tryouts rolled around, I was going to get married and I wanted to establish a career because back then you didn't get paid a dime for running," Carius said. "I was going to go to the University of Chicago and implement the Foundations of Physical Education Program there when I got a phone call from Bob Wright, who I worked with at the University of Illinois. He said, 'a school by the name of North Central College,' which I've never heard of before, 'called me and said they are looking for a track coach.'"

Coming from a small town, Carius did not like the idea of living in the city, making Naperville a nice fit. "I came up here and loved Naperville because it was a small town and I liked the campus," Carius said. "I began as the track and cross-country coach and didn't think I would stay long, but here I am fifty years later, and I love the place."

"When I first came here, the track here was three or four lanes of cinder with cattails growing and little ponds in it," Carius said. "When I started, we only had six cross-country runners, but I wanted them to experience the joy and love of running I experienced being on the University of Chicago track club under my mentor, Ted Haydon." In its first 32 seasons of Division III competition, just one North Central cross-country team finished lower than fourth in the title meet—a seventh in 1980. That made the 12th in 2005 a shock, especially when followed by a 13th and 16th.

At first, Carius thought the times might have passed him by. Then he realized the problem was elsewhere in a program that had welcomed all-comers from his first year as coach: "I used to think anyone coming out for distance running had to be intrinsically motivated," he said. "But I saw that some people just wanted to be associated with the success and weren't giving their best. It was 100 percent my fault. I had allowed our standards to get lower." The slackers had been pulling down the committed. So, for the first time, Carius split the team—40 runners strong—into varsity, JV, and freshmen. It turned the Cardinals' fortunes around instantly.

"He made a big philosophical adjustment after forty-some years," Stiles said. "That's why he is coach of the century." Carius, father of three and stepfather of his second wife Pam's two children, turned over the head track coaching job to Frank Gramarosso in 2010 but was still teaching, and sought to remain cross-country coach indefinitely. "I will do it until I feel like I have become ineffective or a negative influence," he said. "Hopefully, I would know if that happens."

COLORADO CONTINUES AS PLANNED

The University of Colorado Buffaloes had not strayed far from the podium after winning men's titles in 2001, '04, and '06. While the Oklahoma State Cowboys tasted victory in 2012 and were runners-up in 2011, Colorado also found themselves on the awards stand those years.

The big news for the Buffaloes entering the 2013 cross-country season was the arrival of Jake Hurysz, a junior transfer from North Carolina. "When you look at the 2013 Colorado team, we don't see Jake Hurysz run, so we're wondering what's up," said Ryan Fenton. "And we find out he's injured. And all of a sudden Colorado's without the guy who we think is going to be their number one." "Again, what team doesn't have some interruption?" asked Mark Wetmore. "What team doesn't have their starting running back go out with an ACL? You have to have other people coming."

"They were fired up. They weren't worried at all," said Hurysz. "They handled their business really well. They weren't down, they weren't being negative, they weren't saying, 'Aw, we don't have our number one guy from the 2012 season.' Ben came in and obviously filled that role really quickly." Ben was Ben Saarel, a prodigal Utah prep runner who had finished fourth at Foot Locker and had the second-fastest time ever at the Utah State Cross-Country Championship.

At the 2012 NCAA Men's Cross-Country Championships, Dave Smith's Oklahoma State Cowboys won their third title in four years with four finishers in the top 25 overall. And with four of their top five returning (2012 top Cowboy finisher Girma Mecheso graduated), the Cowboys seemed destined to with the team title again in 2013.

But the Cowboys headed into the national championship ranked second, and it wasn't a top-ranked Colorado squad that stood in their way. In fact, it was a mature Northern Arizona University team that was ranked ahead of both schools. But even as underdogs, the Oklahoma State Cowboys had the chance at becoming the fifth men's NCAA team in history to win four titles over a five-year span, joining the bona fide dynasties of Michigan State, Villanova, UTEP, and Arkansas. It was a powerful motivator:

Did You Know?

The Oklahoma State University Cowboys did not have years full of podium finishes or national cross-country titles. But after four years as assistant, Dave Smith became OSU's fearless leader in 2006 and led the Cowboys back to the top. It was at Michigan State University as an undergraduate that Smith honed his craft: "I probably didn't run as well as I should have [at Michigan State] because I was always exhausted by the end of the season. Our training is much more conservative at OSU. I think we put a high emphasis on getting guys to the starting line feeling fresh and ready to go." When it came to building the team, Ryan Vail from Portland, Oregon was the base—Vail, along with David Chirchir, helped the Cowboys finish third at the NCAA Cross-Country Championship in 2007. Then, Smith and the Cowboys landed one of the top recruiting classes of the decade: Ryan Prentice from Washington (two-mile time of 8:59); Colby Lowe, fourth-place finisher at Foot Locker (two-mile time of 8:47); and the top recruit out of California, German Fernandez (4:00-flat for 1,600 meters and two-mile time of 8:34). With this firepower, the Cowboys won back-to-back titles in 2009 and 2010 (with four All-Americans in 2009 and five in 2010), came in runner-up in 2011, added a third title in 2012, and finished third in 2013. It was a fitting tribute to Coach Smith and the Cowboy runners.

"I know some people thought we were far above everyone else. I never felt that way and still don't. Now people are starting to realize it's going to be battle," said Coach Dave Smith leading to the championship. "We probably aren't the favorites or the best team out there. We are going to have things go really, really well and things not go perfectly for NAU and Colorado if we are going to win." But just as Smith played down the Cowboys chances, he made one key prophecy: "I think the last two times we've had soft muddy courses in Terre Haute, *Colorado* won, so . . ."

Conditions were cold, windy, and muddy the morning of November 23, when the number-three ranked University of Colorado men's cross-country team once again toed the line. Eight days prior, the University of Colorado was soundly defeated by top-ranked Northern Arizona at the regional championship by eight points. Oklahoma State, the reigning NCAA champions and second-ranked team, remained an overwhelming favorite heading into the race. "I like it that people said that we were over-ranked after the conference meet and after regionals," Coach Mark Wetmore said. "That adds a little bit to the enjoyment of winning today."

With a conservative start (Colorado was 10th overall after the first 3,000 meters), the Buffaloes appeared only 19 points behind NAU by the eight-kilometer mark. And over the course of the remaining 2K, they overtook Northern Arizona for the win.

"There's been so many good teams in the past, and we've kind of been living in shadows of those teams," junior Blake Theroux said. "For us to come out and win is to say Colorado isn't just going to be known for those guys that came before us—Jorge [Torres], Dathan [Ritzenhein], Adam Goucher, those guys that won titles in the earlier part of the millennium. Colorado is definitely going to be around for a long time." Theroux, who finished the 10-kilometer race in 23rd place, was one of four Buffaloes to earn the top-40 All-American honor. Colorado was led by true freshman Ben Saarel with an eighth-place finish (30:14), the highest finish for a Buffalo since Richard Medina placed eighth in 2011. With the finish, Saarel became the first true freshman to earn All-American honors since former Buffalo Billy Nelson at the 2002 championship. That year Nelson placed 42nd overall.

"Ben was one of the best high school runners in American just six months ago," Wetmore said. "We knew he was a big talent, but the NCAA Cross-County Championship is a killer race with a lot of mature, developed young men. For him to be eighth overall is indicative of his talent." Colorado claimed their fourth men's team title since 2001 in the process.

The following year, the University of Colorado entered the 2014 NCAA Cross-Country Championship as the top team in the country. The Buffaloes put together a score of 65, placing all five of its scorers in the top 40, three in the top 10, to earn All-American honors and clinch their second consecutive national championship.

The team score was the lowest score since 2005 when Wisconsin won with 37 points. The team runner-up, Stanford, tallied 98 points, and Portland was third with 175. Oregon's Edward Cheserek won his second straight individual title in 30:19. "This is probably our best team ever," Mark Wetmore said. "Again, I had the team that came here with Jorge [Torres] who won and the team that followed it and other great individuals who were followed by good teams but not winners. Certainly, this is the best third, fourth, and fifth we've ever had and certainly I think it's the best team score that we've ever had. So, they are real good and they belong in the pantheon." Colorado's consistency all season was the difference in 2014.

"I'm really proud of those guys," Wetmore went on to say. "It's is hard to be the favorites, it's so hard to have the attention. It's so hard for nine or ten twenty-one-year-old men to keep their egos in check and they really did it. They were talking each other up the whole time. I think any one of them would have sacrificed his day to have a bad day if it would have meant six good days for his teammates. So, that's the biggest feeling I have. Pride, not for me but pride for them."

The Colorado men were not the only ones finding success with Wetmore's formula. The Colorado women, too, after winning a team title in 2004 and two runner-up finishes in 2005 and 2006, returned with top performances in 2010 (sixth), 2011 (11th), and 2013 (seventh). In 2015, their runner-up finish to national champion New Mexico was

a return to form that saw the Lady Buffaloes back on the podium. "They were seventh a year ago, but way, way back," Wetmore said. "New Mexico was a head taller than everyone else but our team did fine. They did everything we asked of them and they're all back but one so we'll be ready to do it again next year."

And while the well-rounded approach to training served Colorado well in the new millennium, a coaching change and deep recruiting also kept another notable team at the top for the men and women: Stanford University.

THE RETURN OF THE CARDINAL

After winning team championships in 2003, '05, '06, and '07, the Stanford Cardinal women, under new coach Chris Miltenberg, returned to the podium in 2012 with a third-place finish. Stanford landed three All-Americans that year with runners Aisling Cuffe, Kathy Kroeger, and Cayla Hatton placing in 14th, 17th, and 21st, respectively. Meanwhile, the Cardinal men were faring equally well. Partly under the leadership of standout Chris Derrick—who became only the sixth individual to finish in the top 10 at the NCAA Cross-Country Championships four years in a row—and partly under a return to team cohesion, the Cardinal men placed in the top five at NCAAs in 2008 (third), 2010 (fourth), 2011 (fifth), 2014 (second), and 2015 (third).

Derrick was the catalyst. With his membership in the "Golden Trio" placing him as one of the top prospects out of the high school graduating class of 2008, he was an outstanding member of Stanford University's cross-country team. In four years of collegiate competition, Derrick finished third or better in the Pac-10 Conference Championship (third, 2008; first, 2009; third, 2010; second, 2011), and seventh or better at the West Regional Championship (fifth, 2008; first, 2009; seventh, 2010; second, 2011). After crossing the line seventh as a freshman at nationals, third as a sophomore, and fifth as a junior, the pressure was on to see if Derrick could secure the individual title at the 2011 NCAA National Cross-Country Championship.

Going into the race, there was no doubt the burden was a big deal. But Derrick was content with allowing others to set the pace, as Oregon's Luke Puskedra took the field through 2,000 meters in 5:39 and Arizona's Lawi Lalang built a 14-second lead by 18:40 into the race. While Derrick crossed the first five-kilometer mark in 14:33, just three seconds back of Lalang, and closed in 14:24, he was unable to reel in the fast Kenyan. He finished second overall, 13 seconds behind. With his effort, however, the Stanford men finished fifth as a team, just out of reach of the podium. While Stanford was orbiting the top podium places as an institution, a smattering of cross-country running specialists were helping matters—as seemingly every runner in the supporting cast would find success in the mud outside of Stanford's confines.

As an example, brothers Garrett and Elliott Heath out of Winona High School in Minnesota overlapped

Chris Derrick's tenure on the team. Garrett, the elder brother by three years, ran at Stanford from 2005 to 2009 before becoming a volunteer assistant coach for the university (before transitioning to Brooks). He earned nine All-American honors in his four years, including one in 2008 for cross-country when the Cardinal finished third overall and Heath 27th for team scoring. "I don't know, I love cross-country," Heath would later famously declare. "I'm starting the campaign to bring cross-country back for the Olympics." Heath made these remarks after winning the US Club Cross-Country title in 2015 and earning three straight victories at various distances at the Great Edinburgh Cross-Country Championship: "I think it's the mud, the cold, and the mud. Growing up in Minnesota, that's just what we grew up with. I prefer a little more snow, but hey, I'll take the mud."

Not to be overlooked, brother Elliott appeared in Cardinal Red from 2008 to 2012, and came into Stanford as a US Junior National Cross-Country champion. He went on to earn 10 All-American honors and suited up next to teammate Chris Derrick at the 2013 edition of the World Cross-Country Championships (finishing 30th overall and helping the United States claim a silver medal). And he had big brother Garrett in his corner: "I'd call [Garrett] the night before a race in cross-country," Elliott claimed. "All the races I was racing, he had raced just a few years prior. I was more talking to him about race strategy for the next day than my coach. He's been my role model in running since I started. He's been there for so much advice, and whether he knows it or not, guidance along the way. There's no person that helps me out more."

With those two came other remarkable cross-country talent out of Stanford. Erik Olson, who ran for the Cardinal from 2010 through 2015, came in as a California State Cross-Country champion and US Junior National Cross-Country champion. Olson scored all four years for the Cardinal at the NCAA National Cross-Country Championship and finished third overall at the 2013 West Regional. Similarly, twins Jim and Joe Rosa out of West Windsor, New Jersey, were dominant out of high school in cross-country, as their team won the 2008 New Jersey state meet and finished fifth overall at Nike Cross Nationals. Both were heralded as top prospects. Jim became a two-time All-American in cross-country, finishing fifth overall at the 2013 NCAA National Cross-Country Championship, and sixth in 2015. Brother Joe received All-American honors at the 2014 NCAA Cross-Country Championship, ironically a year his brother did not run. As the final piece of the puzzle, senior transfer Maksim Korolev joined the Cardinal in 2014 and finished fourth overall at the NCAA Cross-Country Championship. He then finished sixth nationally in cross-country and was chosen to run at the 2015 edition of World Cross in Guiyang, China.

But no runner was more integral to the success of American cross-country running in the decade than Chris Derrick. While Stanford's supporting cast brought the team back into the limelight, Derrick was focused on claiming individual glory and did so in legendary fashion.

DERRICK CHASES HISTORY AT THE US NATIONAL CROSS-COUNTRY CHAMPIONSHIP

"It's good to be aggressive and I really wanted to win. The last two kilometers I wasn't thinking about anything else," said Chris Derrick—a newly minted member of Jerry Schumacher's group, the Nike Oregon Track Club Elite. "It is really good [to beat a deep field]," Derrick stated. "I haven't won a lot of big races. I have won some conference championships. I haven't won any national championships or NCAA championships." But after pulling away from one of the deepest fields in national cross-country history (the field featured ten sub–28-minute 10-kilometer runners), Derrick wasted little time in being crowned for his first national cross-country title in February 2013.

There was a large pack up front for most of the race, held in Forest Park, Saint Louis, over 12 kilometers, as the main contenders were content to run together at a modest pace (just a little over 3:00 a kilometer through eight kilometers) on a cold and windy day. The course featured the essentials of cross-country: grass, elevation changes, a tree root and rock or two to sidestep, plus a biting wind and patches of mud that added to the challenge. At roughly the eight-kilometer mark, the most credentialed cross-country runner in the field, Dathan Ritzenhein, went to the front and broke open the race. Only Matt Tegenkamp and Chris Derrick were able to respond, the three fastest men over 10,000 meters, ready to duel it out to the finish.

The previous year at the Olympic Trials, these three had raced for the final two Olympic spots at 10,000 meters behind winner Galen Rupp, and Derrick came out with the short end of the stick. Here it was different. At around the 10-kilometer mark, Derrick went to the front and pushed for home. Ritzenhein was able to stay close, but soon Derrick broke Ritz, too. Now it was a question of whether Derrick could maintain the lead to the finish. Derrick lengthened it. Coming down the homestretch Derrick looked behind him and saw that the elusive national title was his.

"It went about like I hoped it would," Derrick said. "It feels good. I knew from my training I had a chance. I grow a lot of confidence from my coach's [Schumacher's] confidence. He said I didn't need to do anything special. Jerry told me I was fit and to go for it. I figured Dathan would make a big move and I wanted to go with him. When he first moved I didn't know if he would be able to do that because we were really rolling. One of my favorite tactics has always been to crest the top of a hill then go. That set up perfectly with two kilometers to go." "I tried to push it a little bit and finally things cleared out," Ritzenhein shared. "With two laps to go I really started pushing it. At some point someone had to go."

With the win, Derrick qualified once more for the World Cross-Country Championships. He couldn't have been more excited: "World Cross is one of the greatest races on the planet. I'm looking forward to going there and suffering. [The Africans] really get after it in cross-country. They're so aggressive. It's going to be great." Joining him on the roster in Poland for the US squad was former Stanford teammate Elliott Heath, former Oklahoma State Cowboy Ryan Vail, former Colorado Buffalo James Strang, and Ben True out of New Hampshire, a true cross-country enthusiast who finished fifth overall that day at nationals. But for Derrick, his first win in 2013 wouldn't be the only feather in his cap. He would be back for more.

After winning the Great Edinburgh Cross-Country race in 2014, Derrick prepared to defend his national cross-country title at Flatirons Golf Course in Boulder, Colorado, in 2014. The race wasn't close. Derrick won the 12-kilometer men's senior race in 26:14, beating runner-up Luke Puskedra by 25 seconds.

At 6K, Derrick put in a surge, losing the majority of the pack, and continued to lengthen his lead over the final two miles. As the finish line neared, Derrick took one last look over his shoulder but was not threatened. "I want to be the best cross-country runner in America," Derrick said afterward. "I feel really strong in my training, especially training at altitude at Colorado Springs. I've never done two-hour runs before, and now I'm doing those. I felt the guys were letting me have it, and I felt like I was in a groove, so I went."

One year later, at the same venue, and again after winning the Great Edinburgh Cross-Country to cement himself as one of America's strongest cross-country candidates, Derrick lined up to try for his third straight national cross-country title. Among his challengers were Ben True, Dathan Ritzenhein, Ryan Vail, Garrett Heath, and Luke Puskedra, who once again was prepared to challenge Derrick heads up for the title. Once again, World Cross-Country roster spots were on the line, and once again Derrick was motivated by the chance to return as a member of Team USA.

At the 5K mark, Derrick moved to the lead, with rivals Dathan Ritzenhein and Ben True hanging on his shoulder. Bobby Curtis and Stanford All-American Maksim Korolev ran fourth and fifth. As Derrick continued to set the tone, he picked up the pace tremendously at 6K, gapping the chase pack and ultimately creating a gap his competition could never cover.

"At that point, I felt pretty good, so instead of letting it rest, I decided to go to the front right there," Derrick said. "My coach and I talked about the idea that it doesn't matter when you go, but when it happens I have to be relaxed about it, do it for real, and don't force it. Once I got about 10 meters up, because I did it in a relaxed way, I knew I could run with that rhythm all the way to the finish line."

Derrick ran by himself for the entire second half of the race. The defending national champion looked smooth and at ease leading, and with still over two miles to go, it was clear Derrick was on his game. Derrick crossed the finish line in 36:18, winning his third straight national cross-country title and becoming the first male since Pat Porter to notch three in a row.

Behind Derrick, Ben True led the chase pack for the next two miles, until Ritzenhein took over, along with Bobby Curtis. True faded a bit, while Curtis and Ritzenhein showed great early-season fitness, eventually finishing second and third respectively in 36:48 and 36:51. Rounding out the top six finishers, Ryan Vail ran a strong second half to finish fourth overall in 36:55 while early front runners Smyth and Korolev finished fifth and sixth in 37:01 and 37:03 for the 12-kilometer course.

But it wasn't just the men who were showing improved competition on the course. The US women were fighting harder and more consistently as well, and none displayed the grit and determination necessary for success as much as champion Shalane Flanagan.

FLANAGAN MAINTAINS SUCCESS

In February 2010, Shalane Flanagan returned to the US National Cross-Country Championships for the first time in two years after winning the event outright in 2008. This time, she was set on qualifying for the US team headed to Bydgoszcz, Poland, where the 2010 World Cross-Country Championships would be contested. While Flanagan had finished second overall at the Boston Marathon and third in the Olympic 10K to that point, she knew she hadn't reached her full potential in World Cross, which she saw as an exponentially more difficult event. "I totally love cross-country," Flanagan said after winning the 2010 National Cross-Country title. "It is something that I get super excited about. World Cross-Country is one of my more meaningful ones because both of my parents competed in World Cross-Country and East Africans dominate. When you run cross-country there are a full six from each country. So there are six Kenyans, six Ethiopians and more as opposed to just three on the track from each country." It was an opportunity of a lifetime for her to that point.

The Kenyan women controlled the pace from the start at 2010 World Cross. Within a lap, there was a leading group comprised of Kenyans, Ethiopians, 2004 champion Benita Willis of Australia, Hilda Kibet of the Netherlands, Lebogang Phalula of South Africa, and Shalane Flanagan. But as Kenya's Linet Masai continued to push, the group was gradually whittled down. By the start of the final lap the challengers were 10 seconds off the lead and clearly in need of something special to even get in the medals. Log jumps were the key to ending the challenge on the final circuit as Kenya's Emily Chebet went clear for the title.

Led by Flanagan's 12th, the USA had four in the top 25 places (Molly Huddle 19th, Magdalena Lewy-Boulet 20th, and Amy Hastings 25th) to take the bronze medal—their first since 2003. "It was a lot of fun today," Flanagan later said. "I know that we have to elevate our game in order to be in a medal position. I love the fact that this is a team sport, and there is a great team dynamic going with all of the ladies on the team."

The following year, Flanagan returned to nationals to defend her title and try her hand again at World Cross, this time in Punta Umbria, Spain. The 2011 National Cross-Country Championship went without incident for Flanagan, who had her sights set on racing the best in the world: "As soon as I finished, I looked around to see who was finishing behind me. I think we're going to have an amazing team in Spain. I'm really excited about this squad, and I hope that these ladies will commit to going to Spain. I went out at a fast pace, basically to simulate what I'm going to do in Spain. I was a little more aggressive than I wanted to be, but it all worked out in the end. There's nothing easy about cross-country. It callouses your body for the track."

The women's race at the 2011 edition of World Cross was expectedly difficult. Flanagan was with the lead pack throughout and actually in the front of the group of eight runners at roughly the three-mile mark (15 minutes). Then Kenya's Linet Masai went to the front and started pushing along with teammate Vivian Cheruiyot. With 17 minutes in, the group started to fall apart, and Flanagan was at the back of it.

At the bell with one two-kilometer loop left, the front pack contained four Kenyans in front, two Ethiopians one-second back, and then Flanagan, racing in seventh. But Flanagan was rolling in the right direction. Catching Kenya's Meselech Melkamu for third, Flanagan passed Melkamu going over the log barriers 22 minutes into the race. While up front, Cheruiyot was starting to pull away from Masai. Masai seemed destined to have to settle for silver for the third year in a row. Now, however, Flanagan was closing on Masai fast. Seemingly out of the medals with a lap to go, could she catch Masai and get silver?

No. There wasn't enough distance left. Cheruiyot crossed the line first with the impressive gold, Masai got a well-deserved but bittersweet silver seven seconds back, and Flanagan—three more seconds back—got the bronze. It was the first non-African medal at the event in eight years. "2011 World Cross-Country is up there as something I couldn't believe happened," Flanagan later said. "I think sometimes those moments that you know you have in you that actually come to fruition. I knew I had it in me to do well at cross-country as I have an innate gift as a cross-country runner. Obviously the Olympic stage is what most of the general public recognizes, but I actually think I have a medal that tops that one which is not as recognizable to the masses: the medal of which I am most proud is my bronze medal from World Cross-Country."

For the second straight year, the US women earned World Cross team bronze, finishing third behind Kenya and Ethiopia. American record holder at 5,000 meters, Molly Huddle, was 17th, marathoner Magdalena Boulet was 18th, and marathoner Blake Russell was 19th, giving the United States a repeat bronze medal performance. "It was a tough race. The race seemed really fast, and the heat made it that much harder," said Boulet. "We were shooting for second, and we made some strides. If only we can come out and encourage our top runners to participate in this race."

US WOMEN RETURN TO THE TOP

Did You Know?

Always the bridesmaid, never the bride, Molly Huddle had finished runner-up in 2010 and 2011 at the US National Cross-Country Championship en route to the 2012 event. But Sara Hall was also a prime contender for the throne despite ominous weather, with temperatures low and a steady 18 miles-per-hour wind. At the gun, pre-race favorite Huddle took command of the lead pack, and held a one-step advantage over Hall at three kilometers. But by the final two-kilometer loop, Huddle was having trouble detaching. Sprinting down the home straight, it was the surprising Hall who made one final rally to edge Huddle at the line in a photo finish. "Neither of us knew," Hall said. After deliberating over the finish-line photos, Hall was declared the champion—while both women received identical times (26:50 for 8K). "I really couldn't break away like I normally would like to do," said Huddle. "I've never had a race that close before. I didn't think to lean. You think about a track race coming down to a lean but never a cross-country race."

After finishing third at the 2010 and 2011 World Cross-Country Championships, the United States women's team continued to prepare for a higher podium finish. In 2013, it was a team rife with young talent and a key veteran returnee that was aimed at lowering the 28-point gap seen in the 2011 edition with second-place Ethiopia. Neely Spence, Emily Infeld, Mattie Suver, and Kim Conley—only an average age of twenty-four years old between them—each finished 30th place or better overall in the field. Spence led the way by finishing 13th, while Infield (21st), Suver (26th), and Conley (30th) were within nine places of each other. While the final results indicated the US finished fourth overall as a nation, they were 42 points away from second, and only 17 points away from claiming their third straight bronze medal.

Making a return to the US team for the 10th time at World Cross was Deena Kastor, who had finished third overall in the US National Cross-Country Championships the month before. In Poland at this edition, she crossed the line in 34th place, only seven seconds behind Conley.

In the 2015 edition of World Cross, it was the surprising success of Sara Hall, who finished 20th overall only two weeks removed from running the Los Angeles Marathon, which led the team scoring for the United States. Laura Thweatt (29th), Mattie Suver (34th), and Brianna Felnagle (45th) were the other team finishers. In the race it was Hall who found herself in about 60th place halfway through the first lap, while Thweatt and Suver ran up front in 30th position, before Hall started picking people off over the next three laps, crossing the line in 28:19.

"I'm extremely happy with how I did considering the disappointment coming off the Los Angeles Marathon," Hall said after her top-20 finish. "I was surprised that I kept moving up. The record high temperatures in Boulder and Los Angeles [at the nationals and at the marathon] helped me out with the race today. After LA, I could barely walk, but [US senior women's coach] James Li encouraged me to give it a day or so to see how it feels. I thank him for encouraging me to come out here." The women's score of 128 points dropped them down to fifth place overall, 27 points away from third.

And while the women had finished in the top-five for four straight World Cross events, the men had also been hopeful at re-creating their podium chances after a surprise second-place finish in 2013.

THE US MEN FOLLOW FORWARD

In 2015, it was a highly motivated group of American men that traveled to Guiyang, China, to face one of the largest World Cross-Country fields in recent memory. Among them were Chris Derrick and Ryan Vail, two veterans of the US team that earned silver in 2013. Bobby Curtis, a 2009 and 2010 member of Team USA at World Cross returned to the event after finishing second to Derrick at the 2015 US National Cross-Country Championship, while Patrick Smyth, a Nike athlete and top-10 at the World Mountain Running Championships, and Maksim Korolev, a Stanford alumnus who finished third and fourth overall in successive years at the NCAA Cross-Country Championship, also got to attend.

"A second team medal from successive championships remains the goal," Derrick said at the pre-race press conference. "With team expectations, to simply get a medal is a huge achievement. Ben [True] didn't qualify for the team, which I think hurts our chances. We still have Ryan Vail who was in the top-20 last time and he's very experienced. It's going to be tough to replicate what we did last time simply because so many things went well. I think it's rare for things to go so well two times in a row, but I think the team is still strong."

While Derrick appeared optimistic, privately, he held his own emotions in check: "Realistically, I ran a really good race last time I was here and I think the conditions favored me more than some of the Africans," Derrick said later, from his hotel in China. "I think there are probably six to eight guys that credential-wise are definitely a level above me and then another 10-15 guys that are around my level so I'd like to just go out with the main pack and beat as many of those guys as I can. I think I belong in the front pack. I don't know how long I'll be able to hang in there but I don't want to sell myself short in any regard."

Despite rain that hit the city overnight, the conditions for the championship were fairly mild: overcast with temperatures in the mid to high 50s throughout the day, and with few footing issues on the course. Kenya's Geoffrey Kamworor, a world half marathon titleholder from 2014, and teammate Bedan Karoki, took the pace out hard from the gun. The first two laps of the two-kilometer course (completed in 5:40 and 5:50, respectively) were largely uneventful, but the relentlessly fast pace ensured that the leading pack was whittled down in size by the third lap, completed in 5:43.

Bahrain's Albert Rop was the only non-Kenyan to take the lead with any conviction but the Kenyan duo of Kamworor and Karoki soon re-assumed the pace-making duties midway around the third lap—roughly five kilometers into the race.

Kamworor's attritional tactics soon began to pay dividends. At the start of the fifth lap, a small but noteworthy gap opened up between the leading Kenyans and the chase pack. Running side by side for the most part but unafraid to put in the occasional surge on an especially twisty and rhythm-sapping course, Kamworor and Karoki maintained their pace.

Going into the last lap, with the clock reading 28:50 with the fifth lap completed in 5:52, the chase pack—largely characterized by a strong Ethiopian contingent—remained within striking distance until Kamworor and Karoki gapped them by 20 meters with about a kilometer to go. Even with 400 meters remaining, however, it was still impossible to separate the leading Kenyans. Second and first at the Kenyan Trials last month, the order was reversed after Kamworor unleashed an unexpected but dazzling kick over the last 300 meters to fend off the hard-running Karoki, who was making his debut at the IAAF World Cross-Country Championships. Kamworor crossed the line of the 12-kilometer race in 34:52, Karoki was close behind in 35:00. Despite some palpable competitiveness in the last kilometers, the gold and silver medalists embraced after the finish.

"We are rivals when we are racing, that is competition, but friends when we are not," said Kamworor, with Karoki nodding in agreement at the post-race press conference. "After my world cross-country win as a junior in 2011 and world half marathon victory last year, I was confident I could get a medal but I would not say I was confident I could be the winner," he added. The team standings couldn't have been closer with Ethiopia and Kenya both finishing with 20 points but the Ethiopians secured the title under the tie-breaker rules.

As for Chris Derrick and the savvy Americans, lightning did not strike twice. Bahrain edged onto the podium, while the American men finished 77 points behind them in seventh. Even though Derrick was the first non-African finisher in 24th place overall, the team performance was seen largely as a disappointment. "I started out in the 20s," Derrick said after the race. "There would be a point when I would surge, then I would feel the effects. This was a very tough course. There were points in the race where I thought that I could get four or five guys, but in reality I didn't move. It was very disappointing, but I gave it all I had. It was a really hard race." "I just did the best that I could," Ryan Vail added (34th place overall). "I knew that it was a tough race, and we gave it a shot. This course was really a lot tougher than it looked."

The inconsistencies plaguing the American men and women at the World Cross-Country Championships were not only due to notable competition and tough course conditions—but international support for the event had fallen as well. And it started with the IAAF.

THE IAAF MOVES TO A BIENNIAL FORMAT

The decision to make the World Cross-Country Championship a biennial event was decided ahead of the 2010 edition of the championship—with the continued dominance of two East African rivals cited as the reason why interest in the race was falling in Europe. Quite purely, the dominance of the Kenyan and Ethiopian teams in the event had led to difficulty in securing sponsors to sustain its annual running. Even with adjustments to format and scoring, there was seemingly nothing that the IAAF could do to reinstitute support. Additionally, there were deep divides between those who saw the event as an essential part of the athletics calendar and those who understood that with African nations at the top of the leaderboard, Western interest in the event would fall. What was really happening behind the scenes?

In August 2009, journalist James Waindi wrote an article titled "Future of Cross-Country Threatened." In it he explained the psychology behind the decision: "The future of the World Cross-Country Championship looks bleak after the IAAF announced that lack of sponsorship hinders them from hosting the event annually. Athletics Kenya Chairman Isaiah Kiplagat (who also doubles as an IAAF Council Member) announced this on Monday during a luncheon organized by Kenya Commercial Back (KCB) for the local cross-country team that won the title at the 37th World Cross-Country Championships in Amman, Jordan last month: 'The future of the World Cross-Country Championship is currently not certain because no country is willing to host the event and it is lacking sponsorship. This has prompted IAAF to hold it after every two years instead of annually,' said Kiplagat. 'Next year's event set for Bydgoszcz, Poland, will go on as planned but after that, the event will be held after a span of two years and we will decide the next host during the 12th IAAF World Championships in Athletics in Berlin, Germany, between August 15 and 23,' he said."

Waindi's article wasn't without hope at a local level, however: "Two-time Olympic gold medalist and National Olympics Committee of Kenya (NOCK) chairman Kip Keino said the decision to hold the championship after two years was a blow to local athletes but urged Athletics Kenya to organize more local cross-country events to keep the athletes busy and active. 'It is now a challenge to the local athletics chiefs to organize as many local cross-country events as possible to occupy our athletes. Confederation of African Athletics should also organize continental and regional cross-country competitions to cover up for the global event,' said Keino."

At first, reactions were mixed. *Track and Field News* published an immediate reaction that called the validity of the decision into question, citing: "A Kenyan radio station is quoting Athletics Kenya head Isaiah Kiplagat that the World Cross is about to go every two years instead of being an annual affair. Well-placed sources tell us, however, that this plan has not been reviewed at the requisite IAAF level, so at this point should just be considered speculative." However, after the decision was finalized, then-IAAF president Lamine Diack spoke honestly about the matter.

"Cross-country continues to be a very important part of our life," Diack said. "I think cross-country is a key issue in the development of middle- and long-distance running. We've decided we'll have the World Cross-Country every two years. We will start to develop cross-country more at continental level. I think we will have more countries competing in their continental championships. Each continent will be obliged to have their own cross-country championships." But concern about absences among European nations attending World Cross became an issue that Diack could not avoid. "Despite the dominance of East Africa, we still have countries like Spain and France who are always competing," Diack said. "I'm convinced that in [the] future Europe can compete, Asia can compete, [and] right now we have to learn from them. We have to learn from Kenya, we have to learn from Ethiopia. It's the only way to do it. They run because there is a tradition of running in their country. The world is now a village and everyone has a chance."

Outside journalists also chimed in on the decision, and explanations as to why the East Africans were so dominant reached the mainstream media:

"From the inaugural event in 1973, until 1986, there were 12 British gold medals across all the disciplines. Since then only Paula Radcliffe has stood on top of the podium," wrote Mark Butler, an athletics statistician for the *BBC*. "In recent years the number of European entrants has declined, and only 18 out of 50 eligible European countries competed this year [2010] despite the championships being staged in the heart of the continent. Ironically, the British selectors came under criticism in this country for not sending more athletes, but our team was huge in comparison with Germany, Romania, and Ukraine [no entries] or Belgium, Ireland, and Holland [who sent only four runners between them]."

"So what has brought about the decline of Europe and Britain in this classic test of distance running power?" Butler asked. "The base of the pyramid of talent is smaller and so the pinnacle is lower. Yet the reverse is true for the nations of East Africa. Thanks to better organization, management and coaching in those countries—most of it driven by Europeans—more Kenyans, Ethiopians, Eritreans and Ugandans are able to reach world-class level. It seems that this dominance is now alienating the rest of the world when it comes to entering a championship, but nothing should detract from the quality of the winning performances even if the victorious nations are somewhat predictable."

Butler insisted that great storylines permeated World Cross despite the strength of the African teams: "I would argue that in 2010 it is a wonderful story that a man like Kenya's Joseph Ebuya has risen from poverty to become world champion at the age of 22. This is World Championship competition at its purest, and the sight of masses of Kenyan and Ethiopian vests at the fore of a world-class distance race remains one of the greatest in world sport." Unfortunately, Butler's attitude wasn't universally felt—despite the fact that in coming years the dominance of African nations would become just one explanation for World Cross-Country's fall from grace. In the United States, for example, this explanation was just the tip of the iceberg.

DYSFUNCTION PLAGUES USATF

For background purposes it's important to understand that the administrative structure of USA Track and Field was the life-source of the organization. Led by a fifteen-member volunteer board of directors, a volunteer president (Stephanie Hightower), and a board-appointed CEO (Max Siegel) who governed a small, paid national staff in Indianapolis, the opportunity to be a leader in the organization meant that status was limited and responsibility high for those in charge. The base of the pyramid, USATF's membership, was a legion of more than 126,000 (two-thirds of whom were youth) that included athletes of all skill levels, race officials, and coaches. Local running clubs, such as the New York Road Runners and Nike Oregon Track Club were included (3,475 clubs in total, grouped into 57 regional associations). Organizations such as the NCAA and Running USA were affiliate members, as well. And all of these myriad constituencies chose officers, members, and delegates—about 1,000 total—who had different interests. These bodies organized championship meets, made the rules, and proposed recommendations to the board.

"USATF is the governing body for road racing, [they select the] marathon teams," said cross-country champion Lauren Fleshman. "They are in charge of certifying just about every major and minor race-course you've run. They make the rules. They make the decisions that make our sport cool or not, accessible or not, a viable profession or not." But for years, USATF had been hammered by increasing, and increasingly harsh, criticism. In episode after episode, its leaders bungled the handling of race rulings and ignored the wishes of its members, especially its top athletes. The relationship with some of these athletes had soured to the point that Olympic 800-meter runner Nick Symmonds claimed, "There are days I contemplate boycotting USATF meets for the rest of my career."

David Greifinger, USATF's counsel to the board from 1996 to 2008, blamed the disconnect on the volunteer leadership: "The disease is a board of directors that will not listen to its membership and thinks it knows better." Siegel's

predecessor as CEO, Doug Logan, added that the flaws could be attributed to the organization's power structure: "There is a schizophrenic architecture to USATF that is meant to serve both a volunteer membership and a professional sport," Logan said. "That causes a lot of wacky behavior."

USATF's responsibility to the sport of athletics had evolved dramatically since 1979, when the Amateur Sports Act was passed leading to professionalization. At its inception in 1979, the professional side of the sport was just developing. By 2010, the revenue USATF brought in from sponsorships fueled its very existence. This paradox, and the root of USATF's "schizophrenia," was that the elite and professional sport still only represented a section of the group USATF was chartered to serve (and to determine which athletes qualified as "elite" and which were "professionals"—and thereby entitled to more financial support—was a hotly debated topic in its own right). It wasn't a stretch to say that USATF had a unique governance responsibility, and similarly, no other pro sport was so awkwardly tied to such an amount of bureaucracy. The CEO's job—bringing in sponsorships and expanding USATF business—had become more important than was intended. And with professionalism more *necessary* than ever for the sport, it forced the president and the board to behave in lockstep with the CEO in a way that alienated the membership. The result: a power struggle between USATF's leaders and volunteer base.

It didn't help matters that controversial decisions plagued USATF in competitions and behind the scenes in the early years of the 2010s. As one example, at the 2014 US Indoor Track and Field Championships in Albuquerque, New Mexico, Gabe Grunewald—the female 3,000-meter champion at the event—was victimized by claims that she interfered with Nike Oregon Project's Jordan Hasay during the race. After a video review, the meet referee ruled that she had not. But Nike coach Alberto Salazar argued forcefully with officials and filed an appeal, at which point Grunewald was disqualified. Worse, Salazar could be seen saying something to officials after sticking his head into the area where they were reviewing secondary footage. That, paired with his earlier protests, led some observers to suspect that he was exerting unfair influence as an employee of Nike, USATF's most powerful commercial partner (two days after Grunewald's disqualification, Salazar withdrew his appeal, and Grunewald was reinstated as champion).

But the controversies didn't end there. While Siegel had done exactly what he was hired to do as CEO—bring in more money for USA Track and Field (he'd grown USATF's budget from $19 million to $35 million in 2014, had doubled the prize money at the US outdoor championship, and helped direct a record $11 million toward elite athletes)—he had done it all with a flurry of new sponsorships, some of which caused conflicts of interest. The sponsorships themselves were simple enough: they included a seven-year multi-million dollar deal with Hershey; a six-figure deal with Neustar; a deal with Subway

Sandwiches of unspecified value for support with a youth health initiative; and a twenty-three-year deal with Nike worth $500 million. It was the intent and subjective nature of what the sponsorships entailed that was problematic.

The contract with Nike ensured the USATF would be invested in the relationship through 2040, almost a half-century after the organization entered into its first deal with the corporation to sponsor the national team uniform. And David Greifinger, a longtime legal counsel to USATF's board, found one red flag instantly. Greifinger's critique centered around the "present value" of money—a dollar today being worth more than a dollar tomorrow, because it could be invested—making the case that the deal's ultimate value could be far less due to its extreme length. "In the name of supposed long-term security of the organization, we've mortgaged our future," Greifinger stated. He emphasized the value of the national team uniform. Because most of the world only paid attention to track and field during the Olympics (other team sports received year-round coverage through lucrative leagues) the branding of the sport's national team's uniforms was uniquely valuable. The red, white, and blue laundry had always been USATF's golden goose.

But controversies surrounding the USATF-Nike partnership weren't new or even unique to the Siegel/Hightower administration. One such incident led to threats of legal action by several runners when USATF officials allowed Nike athlete Adam Goucher into the 25-man 10,000-meter field at the 2008 Olympic Trials despite him having the 32nd-fastest qualifying time. USATF explained to seven uninvited athletes, who all had faster times than Goucher, that its bylaws permitted entry of former national champions. Another subjective issue was when Craig Masback, USATF's popular CEO from 1997 to 2008, left the post to take an executive position with Nike, where he was still employed. "If you're not at the table, you're on the menu," claimed Sally Bergesen, founder and CEO of Oiselle, an upstart women's running apparel company that sponsored Fleshman, among others. "Everybody's dealing with the same problem [of feeling] disenfranchised from their sport."

At the very least, the USATF-Nike relationship made some feel uncomfortable. "The main point we were making is that there's a disconnect between the requirements to wear the national team uniform, which happens to be a Nike uniform, and the compensation level to the athletes," Bergesen said. "Other than their travel being paid for, the athletes really aren't compensated for wearing a different brand than the one they are sponsored by the rest of the year." USATF countered this argument with statistics, noting that 60 percent of the elite athletes who received USATF financial support were non-Nike athletes, and that the organization annually directed seven figures of funding into the broadcasting and support of meets sponsored by Nike competitors, including the New Balance Indoor Grand Prix and Adidas Grand Prix.

But the problem was that it was hard to properly identify what USATF's obligation was to its members and to its sponsors. The organization's critics liked to compare USA Track and Field to organizations such as the National Football League, Major League Baseball, or the NBA, but those were independent professional sports leagues, not national governing bodies. LeBron James's $21 million salary was not paid by USA Basketball—the sport's national governing body—it was paid by the Cleveland Cavaliers, a professional team. USATF was chartered to govern, and professional athletes represented only a small fraction of its membership. Compared to USA Swimming, which in 2013 committed less than a tenth of its budget to athletes, the $11 million USATF granted for athletes, athlete programs, and broadcasts of athlete competitions in 2014 (amounting to more than a third of its budget), looked generous. If USATF's business endeavors were critiqued, it had to be understood that the organization worked with much less and had a more complex set of responsibilities than a pro sports league did.

Yet, as the new Nike deal showed, it wasn't as if Siegel's USATF was a small operation. Increasingly, USATF was being run as a business. And parsing out the details between the business decisions, the administration of events, and the obligation the organization had to its members meant that USA Track and Field could no longer rely on the old practices it had used to gain control of athletics in America.

NIKE CROSS NATIONALS LIGHTS THE SPARK

Despite the organizational controversies between Nike and USA Track and Field at the top reaches of the sport, the efforts made by Nike in cross-country at the grassroots level continued to be celebrated. Every year, Nike Cross Nationals (NXN) grew in stature as the definitive format to determine the best high school cross-country team in the nation. At the same time, Foot Locker, who still ran their national championship in Southern California, was losing its hold on persuading the top individuals to run in their championship event. NXN not only featured the best team competition, they were enticing the best individual runners around the country to participate, too, and in 2008 added the opportunity for individual runners to qualify for the championship. It gave American teenagers incentive, and it was paying dividends in the higher levels of the sport.

Nike Cross Nationals featured cross-country's best domestic youth talent. Three-time American cross-country champion Chris Derrick won the individual and team title in 2007. The 2016 National Cross-Country champion Craig Lutz won the individual title in 2009. And in 2010, Lukas Verzbicas, America's fifth high schooler to run under four minutes in the mile, edged out future NCAA Cross-Country champion Edward Cheserek and defending champion Lutz for the victory.

Similarly for the girls, notable winners of the individual event included future NCAA champion Katie Flood in 2009; Sarah Baxter, a two-time winner in 2011 and 2012 who defeated Nike Oregon Project pro Mary Cain; and Alexa Eframison, a record-breaking (future) Nike professional who won in 2013 over Baxter as a senior.

Strong team performances were also notable. In 2008, under the coaching of legend Joe Newton, York High School of Elmhurst, Illinois, became the first boys' team in NXN history to either win the championship or finish runner-up more than two times (they won in 2004 and finished second in 2005 and 2008). Additionally, York became the only team, either boys or girls, to qualify for NXN in each of the first five years of its existence. Adding to the impressive Illinois resume on the boys' side, that year's Class 3A state champion Naperville North (Naperville, Illinois) finished third. Naperville North had beaten York at the Illinois state meet by one point.

Initial girls' champion Saratoga Springs from New York conceded the crown to Hilton High School, another New York State program, in 2005, and then both watched in astonishment as Fayetteville–Manlius High School (also from New York) won it the following *seven* times in a row. Of note was that for five of the first eight championships (2005, 2006, 2009, 2010, and 2011) in NXN history, girls' teams from New York State claimed both the national title and the runner-up team finish in the same year.

In 2012, Arcadia High School became the first boys' team to win more than one national championship when they added their second team title in three years—having won in 2010 with an ultra-low point total of 92 among their five runners, tying York for the lowest winning point total in NXN history. Interestingly enough, the motivation to be the best cross-country team in the nation was strong enough to reach pockets of running that had not received recognition before. And while programs such as Arcadia and York garnered headlines with rosters full of nationally-recognized names, teams from quieter corners in America were also winning state titles with traditions of their own.

One such example was Hopi High School in Keams Canyon, Arizona—a school that was victorious 26 consecutive times in the Arizona State Cross-Country Championship. A streak that was a national record: the longest consecutive in the country for cross-country and the fourth-longest active run for any high school sport, boys or girls. "Hopi have that running blood in them," claimed cross-country coach and Northern Arizona University cross-country All-American Juwan Nuvayokva. "It's up to us to find it and use it."

Hopi High, as modern as any suburban school, had about 400 students in grades nine to twelve. But before it opened in 1986, many Hopi teenagers, like those from other tribes, went to Native American boarding schools in faraway places.

Among them, nearly a century earlier, was Lewis Tewanima. Sent to Carlisle Indian Industrial School in Pennsylvania—where he was a classmate and track teammate of Jim Thorpe of the Sac and Fox Nation—Tewanima became a two-time Olympian. He finished ninth in the marathon at the 1908 London Games and won the silver medal in the

10,000 meters in Stockholm in 1912. He remained a Hopi hero, and an annual race was held on the reservation each year in Tewanima's honor.

Coach Rick Baker grew up in the Hopi village Tewa, and ran cross-country eighty miles away at Winslow High (and then in college in Oklahoma). He was hired in 1987 as a Hopi High physical education teacher and coach and was asked to start a cross-country program. "A lot of schools with Hopi kids had won state championships," Baker said. "And I thought if we could get all the Hopis here, we should have a pretty good team." His first three boys' teams finished in the top 10 in one of Arizona's small-school divisions at State. His fourth, in 1990, won the state title. Hopi High School has won every state title since, through the Fall of 2016.

"A lot of our kids don't have a lot of speed," Baker said. "If you timed them in the 400 meters, they probably wouldn't break 70 seconds. But they have endurance. They can run and run and run." Leigh Kuwanwisiwma, director of the Hopi Cultural Preservation Office, said that the tribe's tradition of running came from its scouts, men who directed tribal migrations and searched for water. (One of roughly three dozen remaining Hopi clans, the Lizard clan, supposedly got its name from such scouts, who were able to survive in the desert with little water, he said.) Running was also the method of sending messages between Hopi villages. It became part of ceremonies, too, which could last for days. Photographs from the early 1900s show Hopi men lined up to run in ceremonial races like the women's basket dance race, most wearing loincloths and no shoes.

"They are for the blessings of the cloud people, for the rain, for the harvest, so we have a good life, a long life," Kuwanwisiwma said. "That's what these ceremonial runners do. They bring this positive energy to the people." Other community members agreed with the feeling that it was for a higher calling. "It might sound a little funny, but running in cultural races is a lot different than running in high school or college," said Devan Lomayaoma, who won two individual state cross-country titles at Hopi High, and also ran at Northern Arizona.

"In cultural races, you never got recognition for it. They have a deeper meaning." Darion Fredericks, a senior on the Hopi team, said he knew that the team was watched, both by opponents around the state and by Hopi on the reservation. "They know what we're capable of," he said. "I definitely feel the eyes on me, even in the community. They say, 'Hey, you're the one that runs.'"

THE ARCADIA APACHES

While some high school programs focused on tradition to guide their success, other schools had to create their own legacies. In Southern California, Arcadia High School, a public high school serving 3,500 students, had a fairly well-known distance running pedigree with the success of Tracy Smith (1968 Olympian and bronze medalist at the International Cross-Country Championship) and the Arcadia Invitational Track Championship, one of the highest-caliber meets in the nation for high school talent, which was started in 1968. In cross-country, Arcadia had long been competitive but had never qualified to the California State Meet. That changed with the addition of Coach Jim O'Brien in 1996.

By 1996 O'Brien was already well known not only as a coach, but also for being one of the most competitive ultra-marathoners in Southern California. In 1989 he had set the course record for the Angeles Crest 100-Miler, had competed at the Leadville Trail 100 and Western States 100, and had run 13 marathons in 12 months (mainly to demystify the marathon process). He was also the head guru of Team Blarney (which became "O'Brien's Army"), a USATF club program that met on Monday and Tuesday nights for legendary track workouts. Runners of all ages would meet up, from 10-kilometer specialists all the way to ultra-marathoners. His students past and present, from Arcadia, Pasadena City College, and CalTech, all took part. "The rationale is kids shouldn't overtrain," said Mike Yamane, a dentist and reserve policeman whose children had run for O'Brien. "Coach has a master's degree in exercise physiology. They have all these macro-cycles and micro-cycles. [O'Brien] teaches the kids all these training things; they become knowledgeable. They're not out there mindlessly running. Do they know what they're supposed to do on Sundays and do it by themselves? They do. Do they know what they're supposed to do during the dead period when the coaches aren't there? They certainly know." Soon the army was training year-round. O'Brien knew it had to be tough, but it also had to be inclusive: depth was his biggest asset in the ultra-competitive market for high school distance running in Southern California.

"We have more races on our schedule, and more high-level races, than just about any team I've ever seen," O'Brien stated. "But not every kid races every race. And so there's this manipulation of the process that is going on throughout the season—and it changes based on the needs of the kid: the stress that they're under, academically; different things. The deeper that you are the more manipulation you can do. The depth of the team has a lot to do with the long-range success. I don't think it's possible for a California team to win nationals unless you have that kind of depth. Because you just can't put that many hard races in a row on your 14 legs of seven guys—and still be standing with a solid opportunity to be successful in that biggest race of the year at Nike Nationals."

For Arcadia and other teams in Southern California, the run to the national championship involved four do-or-die meets before even stepping foot on the starting line at Nike Cross Nationals. League competition occurred two weeks after the Mt. SAC Invitational. Then, Southern Section preliminaries and finals also ran in successive weeks on the Mt. SAC course. Finally, the California State Meet took place at Woodward Park in Fresno and offered an opportunity to qualify as one of the top cross-country teams in the nation. But Arcadia under O'Brien's leadership needed time to develop the depth and talent necessary to win on the biggest stage.

In 2004, the first year Nike ran a national prep cross-country championship in Oregon, the Arcadia Apaches finished a reputable 14th place at the Southern Section Finals Championship, missing their chance at qualifying to state. It was a decent, but not a notable season in the pages of Apache cross-country history. The following year, 2005, saw the team improve to fifth at the Southern Section and their first appearance at the California State Cross-Country Championship, where they finished third overall. Then in 2006, after qualifying for State for the second year in a row (finishing seventh at State and fifth in the Southern Section), Arcadia's cross-country team finished seventh overall in the open race at NXN—a new addition to the program. Arcadia did not have the privilege of earning a spot in the championship race, but by paying their own way, their varsity team got to experience the championship atmosphere of NXN and run on the same course as the national contenders. The seed had been planted.

The year 2007 saw Arcadia qualify for State for the third year in a row and improve to third at NXN in their "Open" championship. Then in 2008, team history was made again when Renaud Poizat finished 57th Overall in the Boy's Championship Race at NXN—the first occasion Arcadia had at competing officially in the "Championship" field. Along the way, the Apaches had finished fourth in the Southern Section Championship, fourth at the State Meet, and second in the NXN "Open," even without Poizat, their best runner, leading the way.

2009 was also historic for Arcadia. The Apaches finished fourth at the Southern Section Finals (merely 13 points out of first with a hotly contested championship) while top runner Ammar Moussa became the Southern Section individual champion. Arcadia then improved to third at State, and for the second straight week saw Moussa as the individual champion. Their season came to an epic close when, in Portland mud, the Apaches finally realized their goal of competing as a team in the Nike Cross Nationals Boys Championship Race.

While the 2009 season provided a new chapter in the annals of Arcadia's cross-country success, 2010 ensured that the Apache program would be remembered as one of the best of all time. The 2010 team stormed through the cross-country season claiming record after record. At the Stanford Invitational, Arcadia averaged 15:16 over 5,000 meters while scoring a meet-low 31 team points and a total team time of 76:17. At the Clovis Invitational held on the State Meet course (Woodward Park), Arcadia again destroyed the meet record and lowered the course team-time set by Mead, Washington, in 1993 (from 77:22 to 77:09). Averaging 15:25 per runner for 5K, Arcadia scored 62 points for the victory. At the Mt. SAC Invitational Arcadia set further records by traversing the course with a new team time of 75:16—bettering the previous record by more than a minute.

In the Southern Section Final Arcadia scored 43 total points and had every varsity runner in 15th place or higher. Ammar Moussa was the section champion for the second straight year. At the California State Championships Arcadia once again broke the Woodward Park 5,000-meter course record en route to a state championship. Averaging 15:14, Arcadia recorded the second fastest team average over 5K in US history behind only the 1980 Bloomington North, Indiana, 15:12 team at the Indiana State Championships. Arcadia capped the season with a perfect record heading into the Nike Cross National Team Championship.

Going into the 2010 NXN Championship, Marc Bloom had Arcadia ranked number one in the nation, while Southwest Regional champions American Fork of Utah and Indiana state champions Columbus North of Indiana had both been featured as the top ranked team in the country at earlier points in the season. York in Illinois was also a potential threat to the Apaches' perfect year after they earned their 27th Illinois State title.

In the mud and cold at Portland Meadows racetrack, the 2010 Boys Championship race got off to a fast start. Up front were individual studs Craig Lutz, Lukas Verzbicas, and Edward Cheserek, with Ammar Moussa in fourth through the first 2K. The rest of the Apaches found themselves in the middle of the pack. After Verzbicas surged at 4K to drop Lutz and win in 16:00 (barely holding off an on-rushing Cheserek, still learning the ropes), he was happy, cracking a smile for the first time all weekend. Standing with a bloody leg caused by a spike wound, Verzbicas, a world-class junior triathlete, said his multi-sport experience helped nurture his victory. "Going through that mud was like riding a bike in heavy gear," he said. "Without my triathlon background, I don't think I would have won today."

Meanwhile, Moussa, who crossed in fourth ("If I was not the winner but my team was, I'd be the happiest man on earth," he later said), grouped the tired Apaches into a huddle under the finishing tent. "We ran our best. We went after it. Whatever the results, we can hold our heads high," Moussa declared. Coach O'Brien broke into Moussa's post-race team huddle to say, "Did anybody not give one-hundred percent?" Silence. "Then I love ya." Once the scores were announced the team broke into cheers: Arcadia 92, Fayetteville–Manlius 135. They had done it; they had gone undefeated all the way to the top. Arcadia's triumph was the first for a California team since NXN began in 2004.

But O'Brien hadn't built his program for a one-and-done season. He was already preparing for the following fall. In September 2011, the Apaches were at it again. With the graduation of Moussa, a senior in 2010, the Southern Section title was guided to Arcadia's Sergio Gonzalez, who had placed fifth overall the year before. It was an unexpected delight to see one Apache pass the torch to another. And for the second year in a row, Arcadia was the top team to finish at the Southern Section—hopes were high heading into state.

After their historic run in 2010, an Apache repeat seemed like a dead certainty. But fate intervened, and Arcadia fell to runner-up at the California State Championship,

despite scoring 87 points and averaging 15:40 among their top five through 5K. Even though Sergio Gonzalez crossed in 15:05 as the individual champion, rival Trabuco Hills eked out the team victory by 16 points with better pack running: a 30-second spread versus Arcadia's 41 seconds between their first and fifth runners. At the California State Championship, the margin of error was really that close. Nonetheless, Arcadia had an automatic bid to the NXN Championship Race for the third straight season.

At Portland Meadows, the story of the 2011 championship was the course conditions: firm ground and temperate climate—which led to faster times. With Verzbicas having graduated, Futsum Zienasellassie of Indiana set the NXN course record in 15:03, bettering Craig Lutz's time by six seconds and running almost a full minute faster than Verzbicas did the previous year to win the individual title. Meanwhile, an astounding 19 of the first 21 runners were individual qualifiers from regions around the nation.

In the team race, it came down to Christian Brothers Academy (New Jersey) and Southlake Carroll (Texas) for the championship. With a four-point margin of victory (91 points to 95), Christian Brothers Academy became the first New Jersey team to claim a national championship. Carroll earned the third podium finish for Texas in NXN history, while Davis (Utah) claimed the first Utah podium spot by taking third place with 157 points. Arcadia, despite their strong finish at State and in the Southern Section, fell to fourth overall with 183 points. "As a team I thought we ran really well," said Coach O'Brien. "As always, Nike Nationals, its tough conditions. For us to come in fourth is really great, I'm not disappointed at all in the team performance, and I know there are a couple individuals on my team that wished they had gone just a little faster. But they didn't go slow for lack of trying. In other words if they went slow toward the end it was only because they were charging out in the beginning, trying to make it stick. You know, we were the defending champions and we wanted to go out and represent. Fourth in the nation is nothing to sneeze at."

The 2012 season was the 16th for O'Brien and the Apaches, and they had found a system of success that was seeing the same high standards with different runners filling the roles. With the graduation of Gonzalez, junior Estevan De La Rosa stepped in as the new leader and promptly led Arcadia to their third successive Southern Section Championship, finishing second overall. At State, De La Rosa finished with an identical time for first (15:05 for the 5,000-meter Woodward Park course), while teammate Mitchell Pratt finished a single second behind De La Rosa for third overall. Their efforts catapulted Arcadia back to the top of the podium with a winning score of 53 points and a team time only 48 seconds slower than their historic 2010 effort.

At NXN in 2012 mud was the name of the game, and after a year off the podium Arcadia was hoping to play the role of spoiler against a Christian Brothers New Jersey squad that was looking to repeat after winning in 2011. Unfortunately for Christian Brothers, a repeat was not to be: in fact, they finished fourth, 21 points out of a podium spot. After eight different team winners in the previous eight years of NXN, Arcadia became the first school in boys NXN history to win a second national title, claiming it twice in three years. Estevan De La Rosa finished second overall by three seconds, while the Apaches crossed the line with their top four all in 29th or better. American Fork finished in second place, scoring 122 points to Arcadia's 108, improving upon Davis High School's third-place finish from the previous year to keep Utah near the top for State bragging rights. The 2008 national champions, North Spokane XC Club from Washington, finished third with 146 points.

However, by the start of the 2013 cross-country season the house of cards built by O'Brien and Arcadia crumbled and almost as quickly as it started—the Arcadia dynasty disappeared. Despite the Apaches returning eight of their top nine in 2013, and with high expectations (bolstered by O'Brien's inclusion of runners from other schools to train with his summer team) the program faced turmoil with news that O'Brien, aged sixty, was let go after 17 seasons. Runners and parents reacted with outrage at the decision; the world of high school running was shocked.

The deciding factor, based on what Superintendent Joel Shawn told O'Brien in a meeting, was that the coach painted yellow Xs on dysfunctional lockers in the locker room. The runners, who were encountering thefts because so many lockers were not functioning correctly, referred to the scandal as Lockergate. O'Brien said he had urged the school to repair the lockers for a long time. When the repairs weren't forthcoming, he emailed school officials that he was going to paint Xs on broken lockers to reduce the incidence of his spring training group losing items to theft and minimize school liability for restitution. As O'Brien acknowledged, Lockergate was merely the latest in a series of conflicts between the coach and school/district administrators and other coaches. "This goes deep," he said. "This isn't about painting lockers."

The coach admitted to being headstrong, impatient, and abrasive. For example, when first-year principal Brent Forsee told O'Brien that he was fired and that the school wanted to go "in another direction," O'Brien replied: "What direction would that be? Down?"

Once the news was delivered, the team rallied in support of O'Brien's reinstatement, but their efforts were futile. Despite organizing letters, personal accounts, speeches, social media campaigns, and record turnout from past teams, parents, and fans, the Arcadia administration wouldn't budge. In the 2013 cross-country season, under an emotional burden put on by the removal of their coach, the Apaches finished first at State once again under the direction of senior De La Rosa and rising sophomore Phillip Rocha. But a third NXN title was not to be. Despite having six of seven seniors on the team from the year before, the Apaches dropped to ninth overall as a team in the championship.

2014 was a continuation of the trend. Without O'Brien as a coach, Arcadia finished ninth in the Southern Section Championship and missed sending a team to State. The poor finish also eliminated their chance at qualifying for NXN, the first time in five seasons the team did not make an appearance in the championship field. Rocha, running well as a junior, was able to win an individual title at the California State Meet and ran as an individual at NXN, finishing 11th overall. But by 2015, Arcadia was without any finishers at all at NXN.

THE FAYETTEVILLE–MANLIUS HORNETS

Coach Bill Aris wandered through the building at Glendoveer Golf Course that housed all of the team cubicles in the final hour before the start of the 2014 NXN championship. The successful coach from Fayetteville–Manlius (in New York) with the tall, lean frame and white beard knew that he had two chances to win that Saturday morning in Portland. His girls had already won seven times in 10 years at this meet and his boys were poised to win for the first time if things fell their way.

As hundreds of athletes and coaches buzzed around the large room, Aris spotted some unused physio tables in the center of everything. He casually walked over to them, sat down, swung his legs up and laid down to rest as if he were prepared to take a nap. He knew that he was in plain sight of everyone, especially his own athletes. "I was thinking to myself, 'How can I set the tone for them to be relaxed and maintain perspective?'" Aris said. "I didn't pace around, or dictate to them. I left them alone and went over to one of those tables, laid down, relaxed and composed."

Aris closed his eyes just a moment before he heard the unmistakable clicks from multiple cameras. The coach turned to face them. "This is my million-dollar photo," one of the photographers said. Aris resumed his Zen-like vibe, unsure if his own athletes had seen him or were perhaps even laughing at him. If they were, so be it.

The record of the Manlius teams at the national championship spoke for itself, but it had been an unorthodox rise to the top for one of the greatest prep programs in American history. In fact, the pairing of Aris with the sport almost never happened at all: "Growing up, I played football, basketball, lacrosse, and pickup games of hockey. I could play schoolyard sports all day and still go running without tiring. I went out for freshman track and ran the 800. But I did not enjoy all the interval training on the track, typical of that era. After that season, I continued running on my own," spoke Aris. "Teammates tried to get me to come out for cross-country, but I didn't want any part of it."

"I got caught up in the 1970s running boom and was inspired by watching Lasse Virén win the 5,000 and 10,000 in the 1972 and 1976 Olympics. I went on to run a dozen marathons. In 1991, I ran my PR of 2:43:12 at Boston," said Aris. "Prior to coaching, my main job from 1980 to 1992 was real-estate manager for a large corporation in the Syracuse area. Dealing with a range of people, honing communication skills, and having to negotiate to satisfy different needs would eventually serve me well in coaching. I think I got to know what made people tick. My company downsized in 1992, and I was let go. We had two children by then, and my wife was a registered nurse. I decided to offer my services at the high school as both a teacher's aide and assistant coach." Fayetteville–Manlius High School, twelve miles east of Syracuse, New York, hired Aris in 1992, and over the years, his duties kept growing. He became the girls' head coach in 1998, and in 2004, the same year the Nike Cross Nationals high school championships began, Aris took over as head coach of the boys' team.

"In the years leading up to 2004, I was looking for fresh ideas. I found what I was looking for in the Stotan concepts of the Australian coach Percy Cerutty, who developed Herb Elliott and many other all-time greats," Aris remarked. "The purity of Cerutty's approach appealed to me. His emphasis on strength-building, running on sand hills, and nutrition and training as a lifestyle all clicked with my own thoughts. I read and studied every book on Cerutty I could find. Cerutty's ideas were so old-school and, considering our culture today, so passé, they felt new and audacious. The pure Stotan philosophy of a 'stoic' and 'spartan' value system was just what high school runners needed."

It was a serendipitous arrangement. Fayetteville–Manlius was a high-achieving public school renowned for its strong academics, art, music, and sports. The Hornets' success in cross-country, while becoming more exceptional every season, fit into a broader context of state championships and recognition in a variety of subjects. As one Manlius resident commented: "The girls tennis team won its 20th consecutive title last season with 308 consecutive wins. The boys tennis team has a 23-year winning streak during the regular season. But it's not all about sports. Their Science Olympiad Team came in first in their region and in the state for the last 10 years. Generally speaking, the athletes are usually also excellent students. So, when F–M kids aren't winning at their sports, they are competing in Math League or traveling for Model UN."

But the turning point was 2004. When Bill Aris became Fayetteville–Manlius's director of both cross-country programs in 2004 and brought his son Jon aboard as the assistant coach, everything started to change. This was the start of the Manlius dynasty and the end for everyone else in New York. Although Fayetteville–Manlius sent "only" two female athletes to the New York Federation Cross-Country Championship in 2004, the boys' team improved by leaps and bounds.

"In August 2004, leading into the cross-country season, I organized a weeklong Stotan camp for our top eight Fayetteville–Manlius boys at the Adirondacks summer home of one of the boy's parents. Our camp was voluntary and free. All the families agreed to it. The only requirement was that the parents purchase the week's food," said Aris. "A typical Stotan day at the camp went like this: three runs, including long trail runs, hills, and tempo hill circuits, totaling 10 miles and up; mind-body discussions;

nutritious meals; jumping in the lake after runs like Cerutty's athletes did in the ocean in Australia. The experiment worked. At the end of the week, I felt the boys had learned many new ideas that they would hold dear to their hearts. They were now different. Our Stotan attributes hit the high school cross-country community with a jolt that fall season of 2004. At the Manhattan Invitational at Van Cortlandt Park in the Bronx, the boys placed first through fifth for a sweep in their varsity race against national power Christian Brothers Academy of New Jersey."

In 2004 the boys finished second in the nation to York High School—by the margin of 35 points—and it was largely felt that if the race had been a kilometer longer, the pairing might have been different on the podium. In 2005 the boys were again on the podium, this time only 23 points out of first. According to Aris, it was the perfect beginning for both genders on the team:

In terms of how we set things up, there are no genders; there are athletes. And we take pride in that. Our athletes, boys and girls, take pride, and are inspired, by what the other gender is doing. In fact, one of our guys, Brendan Farrell, represented it that way. And usually you don't hear a guy saying that they are inspired and take pride in what the girls' successes have been and it motivates them. That, in turn, back in 2006 is a quote from Jessica Hauser, who's at Brigham Young now, along with Tommy Gruenewald. Jessica Hauser said, in our awards dinner, after our first national championship, it was wonderful, and such an inspiration to see what the guys did, in those couple of years, '04 and '05, they inspired the girls.

In 2006 that motivation was apparent late in the season, when, against all odds, the Manlius girls' team rose to the occasion and swept the New York State Meet, the Federation Championship, and the National Championship, all in successive weeks. They capped their season with a 50-point national title victory over defending champions Hilton, 128 to 178. That victory led to six more in succession for the girls who finished first overall every year until the 2013 championship. The crowning achievement for the Fayetteville–Manlius girls was the 2010 squad, which had scored a perfect 15 at the New York state championships, then scored 28 at the NXN New York Regional. They scored one point less at the national finals than they did at regionals. To put their dominance in perspective, Fayetteville–Manlius's 27 points were enough to beat the rest of the nation combined. Once all the individual runners were removed and the rest of the field was scored as one team, Fayetteville–Manlius would have defeated the *rest of the nation* 27 to 30.

Also of note was that the Manlius boys returned to the podium, finishing second overall to the record-setting Arcadia team in 2010. And both teams again appeared at the top of the leaderboard in 2014, when the Fayetteville–Manlius teams each won the national championship at

NXN (the boys defeating Minnesota's Wayzata, 111–159, and the girls defeating California's Great Oak High School 70–149). In winning both championships, Fayetteville–Manlius became the first school in NXN history to win the boys' and girls' title in the same year. "To say we're national champions in both genders, it's humbling. It really is," said Aris. "I don't take it for granted." And it was born out of the Stotan philosophy.

THE STOTAN WAY

"Our Stotan way consists of a comprehensive way to live life, to cultivate and maximize one's personal strengths and virtues, as well as to reinforce one's limitations and areas for improvement," said Aris. "Running is merely a microcosm of how to practice becoming their best in order to apply those lessons to living the rest of their lives to the best of their abilities." The Stotan Philosophy (developed in the 1950s by Australian Percy Cerutty) demanded dedication, commitment to excellence, and a rigorous, challenging existence. Known for thinking outside the box, Cerutty focused on diet, and training methods for the mind, body, and spirit. These principles transcended into running. Most commonly known for coaching seventeen-year-old Herb Elliot to multiple world records and the 1960 Olympic Gold, Cerutty's method encouraged athletes to pursue life to its fullest in a healthy and robust way in order to maximize their potential.

Aris explained his methods in detail:

Our Stotan way is a simple, clean, and pure approach to living. Rather than being captivated and controlled by many of the creature comforts and excesses of present, I preach a more holistic, refreshing, and simpler way for our team members to pursue their lives, both in and out of running. This may sound elementary, but it is the essence of our approach, that being simplicity and clear vision. The kids in our program are normal adolescents, many of whom ascribe to the Stotan way because they like it and it works for them. Plenty of healthy nutritional options, plenty of sleep, sound and balanced physical training geared to the adolescent level are a few of the physical ingredients which comprise their daily lives as athletes. More importantly, however, is what goes on within their minds and souls daily in their approach to daily life.

I can't compare what we do in relation to other program approaches as a means to differentiate us from others because I do not know what other programs do, but I can refer to a few basic tenets which have seemed to work for us. First, we speak of selflessness as a means to team success. When our kids train or race, they do so for each other rather than competing against each other. When one releases themselves from the limiting constraints of individual achievement alone, new worlds open up in

terms of group AND individual potential and its fulfillment. As with the ancient Spartans, ours is a group dynamic interdependent upon each other. Each is capable of standing on their own, but when working together so much more is accomplished both for the group and individual. The whole is greater than the sums of its parts basically, nothing new here.

Next, I would suggest the notion of contribution rather than participation. By this I mean that each kid on our team has an opportunity to contribute to the overall good rather than to merely participate in the process. In this way, regardless of whatever level on the team a kid may be in terms of ability or competitive success, each strives to see themselves as giving something worthwhile of themselves to improve our process, rather than to merely participate or take from the program. Simply put, giving versus taking. All of this is program-wide, inclusive of both the boys and girls I coach.

This selfless approach led the Hornets to consistent program success year after year. "By being selfless, thinking of performing for others—that is, your teammates—you free yourself of the constraints of having to perform only for yourself," said Aris. "Last spring, when we were featured on *Today*, a senior, Olivia Ryan, made the comment on camera that she did not know her PR on any cross-country course. That was a telling remark. We do comprehensive resistance work, including squats, dead lifts, power cleans, and presses, year-round. I do the same work as the athletes. For my sixtieth birthday, I did a 365-pound dead lift. Our program rarely has stars. My whole process is attempting to take average runners and make them above average, and taking above-average runners and trying to make them great. But it's not really making them; it's sharing with the athletes the pursuit of excellence." And the Stotan philosophy was a means to that end that was paying off in spades for the Manlius program.

VERZBICAS, CHESEREK, AND LUTZ

As Manlius and Arcadia were developing team programs that were vying for podium spots at Nike Cross Nationals, three young athletes were developing into the standard-bearers for the next generation. Lukas Verzbicas, Edward Cheserek, and Craig Lutz were the top three finishers at the 2010 Nike Cross Nationals Boys Championship. All three would find illustrious careers running cross-country, but these stars of tomorrow could not have been more different. Verzbicas had a beautiful but brief burst at the top. Cheserek was a foreign talent that had a more gradual progression and quickly became a household name. And Lutz, the only native-born talent of the three, had moments of glory as he built his own pedigree in distance running.

Lithuanian-born Lukas Verzbicas was just nine years old when he and his parents immigrated to the United States, but endurance sports were always part of his life: "I was a full-time triathlete growing up from winter to fall," Verzbicas said. "Taking just the autumn months to fully concentrate on running. I'd do 20,000 yards of swimming per week along with couple hundred miles on the bike. Sometimes I'd end up swimming per week more than running. This gave me an insurmountable base so that when it came time to just run all I needed was to sharpen up my speed and I was set." Once he got settled into the Chicago suburb of Orland Park, Verzbicas found immediate running success at Carl Sandburg High School. As a freshman (age sixteen), Verzbicas set a national high school indoor record in the 5K with a time of 14:18 at the 2009 Nike Indoor Nationals, breaking a twenty-five-year-old record set by Brad Hudson in 1984 by more than 11 seconds. At the Nike meet, Verzbicas also doubled with a win in the two-mile (8:57), shattering the freshman record of 9:16. His freshman cross-country season had been cut short by a back injury, which he attributed to over-training.

Later that fall (and injury-free), Verzbicas became the youngest cross-country national champion in history when he won the Foot Locker National Cross-Country Championship as a sophomore. At the 2009 Foot Locker Championship, Verzbicas defeated 2009 Nike Cross National champion Craig Lutz, solidifying Verzbicas's consensus number one national ranking. After rigorous summer academic work Verzbicas announced that he would be skipping his junior school year academically and would enter the 2010 fall cross-country season classified as a high school senior.

After completing the 2010 cross-country season undefeated, and running the third-fastest course time for the Illinois State Meet (13:54 at Detweiller Park), Verzbicas accomplished a feat never before attained when he claimed both the Nike Cross National and Foot Locker National Championships. At NXN it was deep mud and a strong field (six of the top seven nationally ranked runners were competing) that put up the most resistance for Verzbicas. At Foot Locker, Verzbicas became only the third competitor in the event's thirty-two-year history to win back-to-back races. He improved his time from the previous year by eight seconds, finishing the five-kilometer course in 14:59, more than 10 seconds faster than the second-place finisher.

Along the way, Verzbicas maintained his fitness competing in triathlons: "I think that triathlon was a form of cross-training that helped me become a great runner," Verzbicas said. "I was able to build a very large base off of the swimming and biking. When I was running I would pretty much just do speed work. It also prevented injuries because I wouldn't run long mileage. I got my base in the water and on the bike." And though the balance worked well in high school, Verzbicas recognized that in order to maintain his status as an elite athlete he would need to make a choice. With running and triathlon obli-

gations both anxiously waiting for a decision, Verzbicas mulled over his choices and admitted he was drawn by the mystique of the University of Oregon's track and field program.

"The University of Oregon is the mecca of the sport," Verzbicas said. "It has such a big story and it's every runner's dream. At the time I just wanted to be part of it. There is so much passion about running from the fans and the runners." But after signing a letter of intent to attend Oregon, Verzbicas was hit with shocking news. Kevin McDowell, a close friend who trained with Verzbicas in Chicago, was diagnosed with Hodgkin's lymphoma while he was preparing for the 2011 Triathlon Junior World Championship. Verzbicas temporarily shifted his focus back to multi-sport to fulfill his friend's goal of going for the win in Beijing.

Verzbicas did follow through with his promise to attend Oregon and ran a single cross-country race that fall, but it was not to last. In November 2011, less than a couple of months into the school year, Verzbicas announced that he would be leaving Oregon to pursue a full-time triathlon career. "I was running for Oregon and I wasn't as successful," Verzbicas claimed. "I didn't really fit in and it was just so different than what I expected. The passion of the school was there, but for myself, the training wasn't working. I was used to swimming and biking, and when that got taken away, running became worse. I knew I had a gift and I wanted to continue on and it wasn't happening for me without the swim and the bike." Although he felt he made the right decision for himself, Verzbicas also recognized that he could have handled it differently: "Looking back on it now, it might have been a little immature being that I was just eighteen," he said. "I had all of these things going on and it was the best decision for my athletic career, but I understand that it may not have been the most moral thing."

With his short-lived collegiate career behind him, Verzbicas moved to Colorado Springs, Colorado, to live and train near the US Olympic Training Center. But within a year, disaster struck. While doing intervals on his bike in Colorado Springs, Verzbicas got caught up in wet sand on a descent heading into a turn and lost control of his bike. He crashed into a barrier and was immediately taken to the hospital with severe injuries, including two broken thoracic vertebrae, a broken clavicle, and a partially collapsed lung. Verzbicas underwent several surgeries to insert two rods into his back and several screws in his clavicle. The ordeal became tense when he couldn't move his right leg after his back operation. He eventually regained movement in his leg, but doctors cautioned him that he may never walk—let alone run—again.

"At first I felt like I was being robbed of my gift and my talent," Verzbicas said of his days in the hospital. "I really couldn't live without that in a way. It's my passion and it's all that really matters to me. I decided I would do everything in my power to get back to where I was. It was a scary time. I didn't let anybody else's influence get to me, unless it was a positive one. I took my recovery as training. Each step was a preparation for a race. I used what I learned in athletics as part of the recovery process."

Less than four months after the crash, Verzbicas defied everyone's expectations and returned to racing. He finished third at the 2.5-mile Orland Park Turkey Trot in Illinois on Thanksgiving Day. Less than two months later, he won the four-mile Ringling Bridge Run in Sarasota, Florida. It wasn't the elite competition Verzbicas was used to facing, but it was a sign of his determination and potential for a comeback. Three years later, in December 2015, he finally tied his laces for cross-country once more. Finishing 11th overall for 10K at the USA Track and Field West Regional for Club Cross-Country, Verzbicas had this to say about the experience: "It's been a while since I've last run XC and it was a blast to get out there today, topping off a tough block of training with top-10 finish." His time was 32:24 at the Golden Gate Park course.

For Edward Cheserek, who landed at JFK Airport in the United States in the summer of 2010, the opportunity to run in America was a culture shock. As a freshman in high school in Kenya, the sixteen-year-old frequently missed classes in order to help his struggling family look after their farm. A missionary group called *Stadi za Maisha* identified Cheserek as a candidate for a scholarship to St. Benedict's Prep in New Jersey (a boys-only Catholic school in Newark), having sponsored their first Kenyan student the previous year. For Cheserek, the demanding application process culminated in an epic 60-mile run from his hometown of Kapker to Kapcherop High School in Elgeyo Marakwet County to make it to the screening exam on time. The roads were washed out, driving was impossible; if he hadn't run, Cheserek might have never left Kenya.

St. Benedict's reportedly knew nothing of Cheserek's prowess, even though he'd won Kenyan junior national titles in the steeplechase and the 5,000 and 10,000 meters the previous year and was a member of the Marakwet tribe—a subset of the Kalenjin tribe—the source of arguably the greatest distance runners on the planet. The fourth of seven siblings, Cheserek was the only member of his family to leave Kenya. Back home, one older brother was an engineer, the other in the military, his older sister a teacher, his younger siblings finishing their educations. All of them had given running a shot, but only Cheserek displayed the kind of transcendent talent and resiliency it took to win races in the Great Rift Valley. "My dad was a sportsman, too," Cheserek claimed. "He used to run, a long time ago. You know how people get to this point with running? I think he just had to stop. Everyone in my family tried running. My oldest brother hurt himself and had to stop. My older sister stopped running in college. I could keep going."

A basketball powerhouse—the Cleveland Cavaliers' J. R. Smith was the latest Gray Bee to make a name for himself in the NBA—St. Benedict's had only limited success in distance running until Cheserek arrived. "He's an amazing talent," said Marty Hannon, the head track coach at St. Benedict's. "And it's great to see him have this success after living in poverty in Kenya his whole life. Run-

ning will help Edward get into a college and is a means to a better life for him and his family. It's his dream." For the Kenyan, who had spent the entirety of his life living in a mud hut, the change of locale was dramatic, but not uncomfortable. "It is a boarding school," said former high school teammate Darien Edwards, who ran with Cheserek on many relays. "There are other students going through the same thing you're going through."

Cheserek also found much-needed support in the assistant track coach at St. Benedict's, Chelule Ngetich, who was also Kenyan. "From the beginning," Cheserek said, "Chelule would have me over and his family would feed me Kenyan food. We have a very close relationship." During summer vacations, Cheserek lived with Ngetich. In return, the teenager looked after his coach's young children, helped out with chores, and for all intents and purposes, became part of the family.

Cheserek only returned to Kenya twice. The first visit was after his father, age sixty-one, passed away after a brief illness in the summer of 2011, when Cheserek was about to enter his junior year of high school. "It was so hard to make myself return to the States that first time," he said. "I remember talking to my older brother about it, and he was like, 'This is how life is. Finish your school. Take care of your future.' I was there for only three days." Nonetheless, Cheserek translated his setbacks into success on the cross-country course.

In the fall of 2011, a year after he finished second to Verzbicas in NXN by only two seconds, Cheserek capped an undefeated season (seven course records in seven attempts) by defeating senior Futsum Zeinasellassie by less than a second at the 2011 Foot Locker Cross-Country Championship. Also of note from the 2011 cross-country season was that Cheserek ran 11:55 on the famed Van Cortlandt Park course in the Bronx, New York, marking the first sub-12:00 time ever recorded there.

As the defending champion, Cheserek was the heavy favorite to repeat in the fall of 2012. Although his season was delayed for academic purposes (SAT requirements), he showed no signs of weakness in preparing for a run at the Foot Locker National Championship. He opened his season with a win at the Reebok Manhattan Invitational (11:58 at the Van Cortlandt course, only three seconds slower than 2011 despite not having raced prior that fall season), followed by victories at the Essex County Championships, the NJISAA Prep Championships, and the Foot Locker Northeast Regional. At the 2012 edition of the Foot Locker Championship, Cheserek was content with sitting back and blowing by the competition in the final stretches with his signature kick. He won comfortably by six seconds (14:59 for 5K). "To come and defend my title again is great," said Cheserek, who was undefeated over the 2011 and 2012 seasons. "For me it's really something special to be national champion twice."

Cheserek's success wouldn't stop at the prep level. At the University of Oregon, after only limited action prior to the championship cross-country portion of the season, Cheserek found himself as an underdog against multiple-time winner Kennedy Kithuka, a senior from Texas Tech. Oregon runner Parker Stinson picked up the story: "People are so quick to forget, with all this stuff about how all Edward does is sit and kick, what that cross-country race was like against Kennedy. He got broken, he was gone, but all of a sudden he was back up there. He's just a champion."

There came a point, perhaps three-quarters of the way through that 10,000-meter NCAA Cross-Country Championship race in 2013, when Edward Cheserek was ready to concede defeat. The conditions in Terre Haute were muddy, cold, and windy. Kennedy Kithuka came into the day unbeaten in collegiate competition, and seemed well on his way to capping that with a national title. And just past the halfway point, Kithuka made a strong move. Cheserek wasn't sure he could answer.

"I was like, 'I'm done,'" Cheserek recalled. "'If this guy's gone, I'm done.' I was just going for second." Then, with about 2,500 meters left, the course shifted. The wind Cheserek had been fighting all day—when he wasn't drafting off Kithuka—was suddenly at the Oregon freshman's back. Cheserek saw UO coaches Robert Johnson and Andy Powell jogging alongside the course, exhorting him on. Teammates were doing the same. Cheserek decided to challenge Kithuka one more time. "When I pass somebody, I try to test them," Cheserek said. "If he still has more energy, relax. He didn't come to me, so I knew he was done."

Having made his move, Cheserek wasn't to be caught. He crossed the line 18 seconds ahead of Kithuka, in 29:41, becoming the first Oregon freshman ever to win a National Cross-Country Championship. Johnson called Cheserek's achievement "phenomenal." The previous top finish by a UO freshman was third by the legendary Steve Prefontaine in 1969, something the likes of Alberto Salazar and Galen Rupp couldn't top. Nobody could, until Cheserek. Salazar, in fact, spoke to the Ducks before their trip to nationals. He told them to run strong, have a plan and follow it. Cheserek's was to stick with the lead pack, whatever the pace, and it worked to perfection when he proved to have more left in the tank than Kithuka. "I was like, 'OK, I've got to go, and I might get this thing,'" Cheserek said. He would add two more NCAA Cross-Country Championships in 2014 and 2015.

Craig Lutz was the final member of the three to find outstanding success as a prep-level runner, and who also flourished in cross-country post-collegiately. Lutz, the son of a mother who was an Olympic developmental field hockey player and a father who was a baseball player at Murray State, was in the right household for success. His parents became Chicago cops. Eventually they tired of the life and his father took a job as a restaurant manager in Texas before becoming a personal trainer and starting the Lake Cities XC Club out of Dallas.

Lutz's passion for running started in the second grade with Marathon Kids, a children's health and wellness group that had a goal for kids to walk or run a 26.2 mile marathon after six months of training. Lutz, of course, was at the event and reminisced about his own experience:

"You're standing out here in front of all the [University of Texas] UT athletes and it's just an awesome experience where you get really excited when you kind of see a life that would be really cool to be a part of." This program lit the fire for Lutz, "It got me really excited about running. Granted it was still years away from me actually starting to train for it but I just really enjoyed getting out there."

Lutz eventually competed nationally with his eighth grade cross-country team while running for Lake Cities XC Club. By 2009, Lutz's maturity was clearly there as he reached his junior year at Marcus High School in Flower Mound, Texas. Lutz had a great cross-country year, winning Texas's District and State Championships by 10 and 23 seconds, respectively. He came to NXN and won with a solid, gutsy performance on a difficult course in December and followed that up with a fourth-place finish at Foot Locker, where Lukas Verzbicas from Illinois ran away from the competition.

The next year he was faster (with a personal-best 14:41 at the Texas State Championship for a 26-second victory), but finished third at Nike, behind Verzbicas in first and Edward Cheserek in second. Lutz then finished 29th at World Cross (as a junior) as the first US finisher. In the spring he won his first Texas state track title in 8:52 for 3,200 meters.

That summer he decided on running at the University of Texas at Austin (UT), but running at UT wasn't Lutz's first choice. "Texas was not in my top five," Lutz said. "In fact, Texas wasn't even one of my considerations at all."

John Hayes, who coached Lutz's high school cross-country team at Marcus, convinced Lutz to run at Texas. Lutz said his in-state reputation helped him attract Texas recruiters. Additionally, he won the Texas Gatorade Runner of the Year award in 2010 and 2011.

As a freshman at Texas, Lutz became the 17th Longhorn in school history to earn All-American honors by finishing 33rd at the NCAA Cross-Country Championships in 2011. But despite flourishing in the environment, he was suffering from quad strains throughout track season and ended up with a 5K best of 14:00 at the Stanford Invitational.

Eventually, Lutz finished as an NCAA All-American three more times, and as a senior set personal records in every distance, from 1,500 meters to 10,000 meters. But another national title eluded him. In the 2015 USATF Club Cross-Country Championships, Lutz paced the field for the first mile before fading to 16th overall. His new team, the Northern Arizona Elite, sponsored by the Hoka-One-One shoe brand, finished first as a team, but Lutz was dissatisfied and felt he could have given more on the course. At the 2016 US National Cross-Country Championship in Bend, Oregon, with Chris Derrick absent for the first time in three years, Lutz finally won the individual title.

THE INDOMITABLE SARAH BAXTER

"Greatest High School Performance Ever." So claimed editor Rich Gonzalez, a longtime ambassador for cross-country running in Southern California, after Simi Valley High School's Sarah Baxter ran Mt. SAC in 2012. A quarter-mile in, she was at 71 seconds, leading the pack. 2:31 for the first half-mile with a sizeable lead. First mile in 5:06, all alone. She would stay that way to the finish (her coach, Roger Evans admitted Baxter hated to hear footsteps late during her races). At the crossover point on the course, Baxter was at 8:42. For two-miles, 10:45 (the crowd chanting her name). With a half-mile to go, 13:23, and by the finish line, the clock had crossed the threshold by the slimmest of margins. Total time for the 2.94-mile burn: 16:00-flat.

"She was just so relaxed and smooth," said Evans. "The announcer was making quite a big deal about her times and everything and I have a watch running myself and I'm looking at it and I knew the accuracy of what was occurring, but looking at her, she looked no different than when she is out on a road run during the week. Even as she was coming off Reservoir [Hill] and heading down, the last time I saw her, toward the airstrip, she looked just calm and composed and very, very relaxed." Baxter's poker face belied the gravity of her win. It was a course record by 16 seconds (16:16, set by Amber Trotter of Ukiah in 2001). Seventy-eight seconds was the margin of victory she held over race runner-up Chelsey Totten of Santa Clarita-Golden Valley. And her time was fast enough for her to have scored for the Simi Valley boys' team. The boys placed fourth in their varsity race in 80 minutes even, a 16:00-flat average for their scoring five. Baxter's time would have made her the number four boy on the squad.

Baxter had told the coach earlier that she wanted to break her personal record, "So I told her, run something like 16:30, 16:35," Evans recalled. "I think the weather was just superb and conducive to fast times across the board. Then I think she was just running, and she knew she wanted to PR and she had a memory bank in there when she ran 16:41, and the kind of effort she had put forth at that time, and she was just trying to duplicate that effort." However, duplicating that effort as a junior produced a much faster time than it had as a freshman.

As a freshman in 2010, Baxter was no stranger to breaking records. She won the state Division I Cross-Country title by 31 seconds, the Arcadia Invitational 3,200 meters in 10:14, and the state 3,200 in 10:13. But Evans said that at four-foot-eight and 73 pounds, the freshman star was not ready to be inserted into a pack of varsity boys. And, despite being ranked alongside New York's Aisling Cuffe as the top prep in the nation that year, Baxter cited a desire to end a long season at the state cross-country meet and bypassed the Nike Cross Nationals event, ending the debate.

But by 2012, Baxter was no longer training away from the boys on the team. After sprouting to five-foot-six and 100 pounds in a single season, Baxter would do eight or nine miles with the boys (at 6:30 pace). The Monday prior to her historic Mt. SAC record, Baxter did a Simi Valley staple at practice—6 × 1,000 meters at faster than race pace with the last 185 meters uphill. (Baxter jogged back down the hill and then some for a three-minute recovery). While

she dismissed the session as "not that hard," Evans said that Baxter did the workout a few seconds faster than the boys' team. It was a clear testament to her development.

But what went beyond Baxter's skill, development, and course-record performances was how she handled the pressure. She never lost, so she was never allowed to lose. "It's kind of scary," Baxter said. "I try not to think about it." The expectations became so immense that sometimes, at the starting line, her eyes filled with tears. Baxter said a prayer for strength before every race, and often emitted a sigh of relief afterward. But she remained undefeated because, in her mind, it was never about winning: "When I get really nervous during a race, I just tell myself, 'OK, I don't have to get first place for my team to like me,'" she confided. "When I realize I'm doing this for fun and to be around my friends, it makes it a lot easier to do."

"She's such a grounded kid, she just doesn't get all that's happening around her," said her mother, April. "The most important thing to her is being part of the group." Baxter began her athletic career by playing youth soccer for four years, during which time she failed to score a goal. She also made a brief attempt at baseball, but her younger brother's throws kept hitting her in the face. Her parents, both California Highway Patrol officers and former competitive runners, steered her toward track because she was fast. And while it turned out Baxter did love to run, she didn't really care about winning. So her father, Kevin, began bribing her. He promised to shave his head if she won junior nationals—which Sarah did—and the bribing soon stopped. The victories did not.

Baxter went undefeated in her early high school cross-country career, winning three consecutive state titles and setting a new course record (16:40) in the fall of 2012. She won back-to-back NXN championships and garnered the Gatorade National Girls Cross-Country Runner of the Year award. Her track record was similar: Baxter was undefeated in the 3,200 meters, with three state titles under her belt. And she had the distinction of being the last high schooler to beat Mary Cain (all of this before her senior cross-country season, the projected pinnacle for so many young runners).

But her undefeated streak came to an end in the 2013 Nike Cross Nationals Championship. In the final race of her high school cross-country career, Sarah Baxter's run of perfection was halted. It was the first loss of Baxter's four-year prep career in the sport. Alexa Efraimson of Washington's Camas High won a close race in a time of 16:50 for 5K. Elise Cranny of Colorado's Niwot High was second in 16:53. Baxter came in third in 16:57. Baxter was trying to become the first prep runner—male or female—to win three straight national titles while in high school. But Baxter encountered the unfamiliar sight of runners crossing the finish line ahead of her to snap her remarkable winning streak. "I could barely stand at the end, so I knew I gave my all," Baxter said afterwards.

To add insult to injury, Baxter experienced a stress reaction in her leg after a bout with bronchitis that following spring. After running in the Southern Section 3,200 in May (winning her heat in 10:30), Baxter conceded defeat: "I'm still injured and I'm just not at the place I need to be after taking time off," she said. "This is my last race. My doctor doesn't want me to go any further. I'm done." The injury ended Baxter's quest to win her fourth straight state title in the 3,200. A win at the state meet would have made Baxter only the second runner in California history to win four 3,200 state titles and four straight cross-country crowns, joining Jordan Hasay for that honor.

After redshirting the 2014 cross-country season for the University of Oregon, Baxter climbed her way back into scoring position by finishing 10th at the Bill Dellinger Cross-Country Invitational and 44th overall at the Pac-12 Cross-Country Championships in 2015. But it still remained to be seen what kind of times she would put down to move her way back into the top position in the collegiate ranks and beyond.

THE NEXT COMING OF MARY CAIN

In 2012, while Baxter set cross-country course records in every venue, from the California State Meet to the historic Mt. SAC, only one runner seemed even remotely threatening to Baxter's perfect streak. In the fall of 2012, Mary Cain—a junior in high school from Bronxville, New York—was being coached by Alberto Salazar. And despite setting records herself (notably a US record over 1,500 meters at World Juniors on the track), Cain was simply hoping to improve on her sixth-place NXN finish in 2011. "She's definitely excited to race against Sarah Baxter and the other top-ranked girls running NXN," Salazar said at the time. "And [she's] excited to improve on her finish from last year. But I want her relaxed and not getting fixated on always having to win. She and her parents like the long-term approach that I plan for her like I did for Galen."

Cain had always been fast. In fifth grade, she ran a 6:15 mile. Cain's father, Charlie, an anesthesiologist, knew so little about track then that he had to ask Mary's gym teacher if this was any good. In seventh grade, she ran a mile in 5:03, at which point, recalled Cain—a self-described nerd—"Everybody was like, what?! That wasn't supposed to happen." In ninth grade, Cain won the New York State 1,500-meter championship, breaking the freshman girls' record. The summer after her sophomore year, she flew to the Junior World Championships in Barcelona and ran the 1,500 in 4:11, setting a new American high school record for girls.

Outliers weren't supposed to fit in, and Cain was not accepted by her athletic peers. For Cain's sophomore year, the high school athletic department decided that she would be better off training with the boys' coach. But according to New York State high school sports rules, a girl couldn't compete against girls if she trained exclusively with boys. Not wanting to risk Cain's eligibility, the school switched her back to training under the girls' coach at the start of her junior year. By that point, however, Cain had outgrown her high school program. Her needs departed so wildly from the other runners that the coach,

for reasons that nobody would talk about, didn't even prescribe workouts for her. "She'd show up to practice and do her own thing," her father said. "It was heartbreaking to be a parent of a kid who has all this potential and see her not getting any coaching at all."

Then, one night in October 2012, while Cain was in bed, the house phone rang. Cain's mother answered. A man claiming to be Alberto Salazar, the legendary runner and coach, was on the line. At first she thought the call was a prank. But then Salazar explained that he'd recently reviewed the video of her daughter's Barcelona run. An obsessive about form, Salazar said that Cain's lower-body mechanics were excellent, good enough to make her the best in the world, but that her upper body needed work. In particular, if she wanted to reach her potential, she needed to keep her left elbow closer to her body, swing it straight, front to back, instead of out and across her torso. He referred to the elbow as her "chicken wing." The Cains committed to training with him.

The need for a professional intervention was clear. In 2001 in the United States, only two high school girls had run the 1,600 meters in under 4:50, and only one ran faster than 4:45. By 2014, 46 girls ran faster than 4:50; eight broke 4:45. What changed? Coaches no longer assumed female runners couldn't handle as much training as boys. Gone, too, was the outdated idea that the best way to make a girl run faster was to make her skinnier, so that she carried fewer pounds around the track. The dominant philosophy was that girls, like all other runners, should train to become strong by lifting heavy weights. Running mechanics were fairly simple: speed came from a foot hitting the ground, loading with energy, like a spring, then exploding off with propulsive power. For years, sprinters had trained for strength. But by the 2010s this focus had spread from middle-distance runners to marathoners. All of the Oregon Project runners did squats and dead lifts, some up to twice their body weight.

From the moment Salazar started coaching Cain, he set out to develop her talent slowly over the course of many years, building her up and aiming for her to peak around age twenty-five. And so while Cain was still in high school, Salazar deployed John Henwood, a former Olympic runner from New Zealand (who lived in New York), to monitor her workouts. His job included encouraging Cain to push hard and embrace discomfort, but also to make sure she didn't go too far over the redline by adding too much speed or mileage too quickly. Cain responded well to Salazar's program. In 2013, the first year under his guidance, she broke the American female junior 1,500-meter record, the American junior 800-meter record (becoming the first girl to do it in less than two minutes), and ran a 4:32 indoor mile, breaking the American girls' high school record set forty-one years earlier. Later that same year she broke her own record by four seconds. Cain described that season with considerable understatement as "a lot of fun."

But, with increasing dedication on the track, Cain found herself uncharacteristically absent from the cross-country course. After finishing second to Baxter at NXN in 2012, Cain announced she would forgo her senior cross-campaign that next year. Asked about Cain's plans for that fall, Salazar responded: "Mary will most probably not run any cross-country races. She's doing a remarkable job changing her form, but in order to handle it and not risk injury, she's only up to five miles a day. And the workouts are not very fast as well." Nonetheless, by the fall of 2015, Cain made a late-season run at the Mayor's Cup, held in Boston's Franklin Park, where she finished third overall for 5K. "We went in thinking it would be pretty flat," Cain admitted. "But it was pretty authentic cross-country. I've never been in this good of shape this early before." It was a sign of bigger things to come.

While 2010 and 2011 featured strong cross-country prep talent, the subsequent years also demonstrated that a "boom" or "talent wave" was not going to be a flash in the pan. The graduating class of 2013 continued the trend of featuring talented individuals and teams at the nation's high school cross-country championships and beyond.

THE GRADUATING CLASS OF 2013

As young, developing, collegiate phenoms, the quartet of Edward Cheserek (Oregon), Sean McGorty (Stanford), Ben Saarel (Colorado), and Jake Leingang (Oregon) was good. But watching their performances in cross-country drew parallels to the freshmen class of 2008. That group consisted of German Fernandez (Oklahoma State), Chris Derrick (Stanford), Luke Puskedra (Oregon), and Colby Lowe (Oklahoma State).

The amount of hype behind the golden trio was palpable. At the 2008 NCAA XC Championship, Derrick took seventh and led Stanford to a third-place finish; Puskedra was Oregon's number two on that year's winning squad; Lowe was Oklahoma State's third man in 80th; and, according to Oklahoma State, Fernandez "was in position for a top-three finish at the NCAA Championships with only about 1,500 meters remaining before he crumpled to the ground with an injury to his lower leg that forced him to not finish the race." But when compared to the high school graduating class of 2013, it was more than form that struck a chord. Side by side, comparisons were practically equivalent.

Fernandez versus Cheserek—both were touted as the number one cross-country recruit coming out of high school and were strong favorites to be up near the front at NCAAs throughout their freshmen season. Each also competed close enough to run near identical times at the Pre-National Championship over eight kilometers: 23:34 for Fernandez, and 23:33 for Cheserek.

Chris Derrick and Sean McGorty were also amazingly close. Perhaps overshadowed by some "bigger" names, both Stanford men had a big showing at the Pre-National meet as freshmen and also ran near identical times (23:37 for Derrick and 23:39 for McGorty). In addition to the fact that they both attended Stanford, there was something comparable about Derrick and McGorty when they made the jump from high school to the NCAA—though they

were both atop their class's ranking, neither had that "X factor" to vault them to the number one spot, and neither was regarded as the undisputed number one recruit. Derrick was more distance-orientated (13:55 for 5K at Arcadia), ran 8:48 for 3,200 meters, and took the individual title at NXN. McGorty was more of a miler (4:04.47 for the mile at Penn Relays), ran 8:46 for two miles, and finished second behind Cheserek at Foot Locker. Despite strong credentials, the two didn't have the same pop coming off their senior year as the others. Perhaps that was to their advantage.

Luke Puskedra and Ben Saarel both came from the state of Utah, liked to do their talking with their legs, and possessed limelight similarities too close to be ignored. They were the top freshman finishers at the NCAA Cross-Country Championships (fifth overall for Puskedra; eighth for Saarel), and each helped their team win the title. But predictively, like Puskedra, it was felt Saarel would most likely thrive in longer races. When he made the move up to the half marathon, Puskedra seemed to finally find his niche. Saarel showed excellent talent at shorter distances (with a 1:51 win at the Utah State 800 meters at altitude and a convincing win at the Adidas Dream Mile), but speculation was born from Saarel's own opinion that he'd be a "5 or 10,000-meter guy in the future."

Jake Leingang and Colby Lowe appeared to be the final cornerstone runners who possessed identical prowess. Leingang, 24:03 at Pre-Nationals, and Lowe, 23:57, incredible talents both, were just a step behind the rest of the class. Like Lowe, Leingang could be trusted to come up big when it counted, but not necessarily at the front of the pack. He and Lowe were both guys that their coaches could rely on to run smart when the championship was on the line.

But this parallel universe of graduated classes doesn't just end with individual results—there were similar team implications as well. In 2008, Oklahoma State had their two freshmen (Fernandez and Lowe) in their top five. In 2013, Oregon was calling for their duo to be in nearly the same positions. In both scenarios, a win appeared unlikely at the outset for the eventual champions in their respective years. But ultimately it mattered which team possessed the best depth: a fundamental quality for collegiate teams vying for a title in the NCAA, with or without strong freshmen.

CHALLENGE FOR THE EAST AFRICAN THRONE

While domestic talent was booming in the United States at the high school and collegiate level, young runners from Ethiopia and Kenya were also setting records in the early years of the decade, albeit in international fields and major prize championships.

Imane Merga Jida was one such athlete. Born in October 1988 in the Ethiopian province of Tulu Bolo (not far from Asella, where Haile Gebrselassie was raised), Merga made his mark early and often in cross-country running. In 2007 and 2008, Merga won the Cross Internacional de Oeiras in Portugal (26:34 for nine kilometers), the Cross de l'Acier in France (28:00 for 9.85 kilometers), the Cross du Val de Marne in France (25:56 for 8.6 kilometers), and the Cross de la Constitucion in Spain (28:51 for 9.9 kilometers)—all by the age of twenty years. In his international debut, he finished seventh in the men's junior race at the 2007 IAAF World Cross-Country Championships in Mombasa, Kenya.

As a senior-level athlete he added a victory in the Antrim International Cross in Northern Ireland (24:32 for nine kilometers), and top-five placings at the Cross Internacional Juan Muguerza in Spain (fourth in 32:07 for 10.8 kilometers) and Sendafa Cross in Ethiopia (36:00 for 12 kilometers). At the Jan Meda Cross-Country in February 2011 (the Ethiopian National Cross-Country Championship and qualifier for Worlds) Merga came second, some distance behind winner Hunegnaw Mesfin. However, Merga beat his countryman Mesfin and all other contenders at the 2011 edition of World Cross in Spain, closing the race with a quick sprint finish and crossing the line in 33:50 for the 12-kilometer course. Merga then ended his cross-country season with another win on grass, beating Caleb Ndiku and world runner-up Paul Tanui at the Trofeo Alasport in Alà dei Sardi, Italy.

By November 2011, Merga was back to his winning ways in cross-country, placing first at the Cross de Atapuerca in Spain, and leading the Ethiopian contingent at the 2013 World Cross-Country Championships in Bydgoszcz, Poland. There, it was a runner-up performance in 32:51 for 11.1 kilometers that helped Ethiopia win team gold over the United States.

In Kenya, Bedan Karoki Muchiri, born August 1990, was the most consistent talent out of that region in the early part of the decade. Born in Nyandarua, Muchiri attended Muthiga and Kagondo primary schools in Kenya before studying abroad in Japan. He graduated from high school there and attained a high level of proficiency in Japanese, while spending much of his early career running on the Japanese racing circuit, which included wins at the Chiba International Cross-Country three years in a row, from 2009 to 2011. He also won the Fukuoka International Cross-Country in 2011.

Later in 2011, after Kenya finished third behind the United States and Ethiopia at World Cross, Muchiri was called up to represent Kenya at the 2011 All-African Games, where he finished with a silver medal at the 10,000-meter distance (running 28:18). From there, it was a win at the KCB Nairobi International Cross-Country (35:19 for 12 kilometers), and runner-up finish at the Discovery Kenya Cross-Country in Eldoret (29:00 for 10 kilometers) that put Muchiri in a prime position to qualify for the Kenyan National Team for the 2015 World Cross-Country Championships. In two of three attempts, Muchiri claimed Kenyan National Cross-Country titles, beating some of the strongest fields of distance runners featured anywhere in the world. In 2014 he was victorious in a time of 34:55 for 12 kilometers.

With those two national titles, Muchiri found himself on the Kenyan team headed to Guiyang, China, for the 2015 World Cross-Country Championships, where Muchiri finished second overall to teammate Geoffrey Kipsang Kamworor, who led Kenya to a first-place finish (tying Ethiopia in points), their first such placing since 2011. But while Kenya was enjoying a return to the top of the podium, rumors were swirling as to the legality of some of their athletes, and allegations of EPO use and drug-enforcement cast a dark shadow over Athletics Kenya through the decade.

ATHLETICS KENYA FACES ALLEGATIONS

Red dust swirled around Mathew Kisorio's feet as they struck the ground. Sweat plunged down his face and darkened his shirt. Every day for six years, while based in Nairobi, Kisorio would wake up at 4:30 a.m. and head out to the track with his coach Claudio Berardelli to run 15 miles. That was how Kenya's former World Cross-Country team captain began his mornings—until 2012 when he tested positive for using performance-enhancing drugs. The charges headlined local and international news, and Kisorio became one of the country's most high-profile athletes to test positive for using performance-enhancers. Not only was he banned from competing, but his coach and his agent severed all ties; his fellow competitors wanted nothing to do with him, and he was forced to give back the Kenyan $50 million he had earned over his career. Following the twenty-five-year-old's suspension from competing in 2012, 19 more Kenyan runners were accused of doping, raising a number of questions about the country's most respected sport.

For Kisorio, running was in his blood. His father was Some Muge, the first Kenyan to win a medal at the World Cross-Country Championships in 1983, and Peter Kimeli, winner of the Brighton and Paris Marathons in 2012 and 2013, was his brother. And while his natural-born talent certainly created opportunities, it also carried pressure to perform—which Kisorio did. In his first international race in March 2007, he won the bronze medal in the junior race at World Cross. Several months later, Kisorio won both the 5,000- and 10,000-meter races at the African Junior Championships. But his aspirations vanished when he tested positive for performance-enhancing drugs during the 2012 National Championships. "There was no way I could deny the charges," he said. "I had trained to break the world record for the half marathon and 10,000-meter race, but I didn't get the chance."

Kisorio's pressure to perform wasn't just a product of family legacy: sponsors, managers, and trainers put their hopes in aspiring athletes, and the public scrutiny they faced could be overwhelming. Then, of course, there was the allure of fame. Competitors like Haile Gebrselassie and Paul Tergat were international stars. And for runners who came from poverty, the responsibility to feed their families could be the most compelling reason of all.

As a result, anti-doping officials shifted their focus to drug testing in Kenya and Ethiopia, the two countries that produced most of the best male runners in the world and a good portion of the best female runners. Neither country had an effective national anti-doping agency, and independent agencies couldn't conduct blood tests in either country because there wasn't a World Anti-Doping Agency–accredited lab in the region. For years, neither country had seen many athletes test positive, and in that time it was assumed that Kenyans won distance races simply because they were better runners. After Kisorio tested positive, that assumption began to seem naïve.

Meanwhile, only two years after Kisorio's positive test, a German investigative journalist named Hajo Seppelt released a documentary alleging that Liliya Shobukhova, a 2:18 marathoner from Russia, banned in 2014 under the biological passport, had attempted to cover up a positive test by bribing an official at the IAAF. The two stories hit like one-two punches, prompting many to reconsider a long-simmering question about whether running—like cycling in the mid-2000s—was on the verge of a major, sport-wide doping scandal.

The best information about doping's prevalence in the 2010s came from WADA and the IAAF, which made big scientific efforts to estimate how widespread the practice was. In 2011, Swiss researcher Pierre-Edouard Sottas, a consultant for WADA, analyzed more than seven thousand blood samples from some 2,700 track and field athletes. The samples were anonymous but sorted by region to allow for changes in blood chemistry that were produced by altitude. The sample included athletes from all disciplines, not just distance runners. Sottas used the same analytic tools available to testers under the biological passport, and he found that samples from 14 percent of the athletes he examined showed signs of blood manipulation. But there were huge variations between regions. Sottas found that 48 percent of athletes in one region had suspicious results, and in another only one percent had signs of doping.

Were Kenya and Ethiopia among the high-percentage countries? The results were not made public, but it appeared to be unlikely. Effective doping regimes required a level of medical and technological sophistication that was in short supply in most of East Africa. Kenyan runners needed to travel to Nairobi to find doctors willing to provide them with drugs, or otherwise had to have the expertise to store and inject drugs on their own in training camps, many of which were remote. That said, it wasn't long before a Kenyan TV station filmed an undercover reporter purchasing EPO in Eldoret and Kapsabet, cities where hundreds of runners lived and trained.

"It would probably be hard to have a mass EPO doping program," said David Epstein, an investigative journalist reporting from Kenya. "Do I think it's the prime influence behind the phenomenon we've seen in Kenya? I don't think so. Do I think there is doping going on in Kenya? Absolutely. It's going on everywhere." Still, Athletics Kenya wasn't without problems. As Kenya's national running federation, they suspended Federico Rosa and Gerard Van de Veen, two prominent agents from Italy and the Netherlands, respectively, from working in the country for six months on suspicions that they were doping their runners. A few days before that news broke, Benjamin Limo, a former world champion at 5,000 meters, announced that he had resigned his position at Athletics Kenya because he felt the organization had failed to address cheating. "AK is not ready to fight doping and it happens that the majority of athletes affected by such vices come from almost one camp and AK is doing nothing to curb the vice," Limo said.

But allegations didn't end there. In early 2016, attention was turned to corporate sponsorship, where a Chinese clothing manufacturer, the Li-Ning Company—a Chinese sports empire founded by famous gymnast Li Ning—attempted to buy in to the apparel sponsorship through the Kenyan athletics federation. At the time, Athletics Kenya had a contract with Nike. To persuade them, Li Ning paid upwards of $200,000 to Athletics Kenya. A marketing agent, working as a middleman between the company and the Kenyan federation, then sent nearly all of the $200,000 to employees of Athletics Kenya, money that a top official quickly withdrew.

The sports-marketing agent who made the payment, Papa Massata Diack, had been recently banned for life by the IAAF. Both he and his father, Lamine Diack, the former president of the association, were under investigation by French authorities in connection with several allegations, including blackmail and bribery. And after they received a letter from a Nike lawyer saying there were no legal grounds to terminate the contract, the Kenyan officials abruptly changed course. They negotiated a new contract in which Nike agreed to pay Athletics Kenya an annual sponsorship fee of $1.3 to $1.5 million—plus $100,000 honorariums each year and a one-time $500,000 "commitment bonus."

In the documents, Nike provided detailed instructions on how the $100,000 yearly honorarium was to be used (to cover travel costs and phone bills, among other things). No details were provided for the commitment bonus, even after a former employee, who worked as an administrative assistant and in other jobs at Athletics Kenya for more than ten years, wrote to a Nike executive asking him.

In a sworn statement provided to Kenyan investigators, the former assistant said the $500,000 commitment bonus was "bribe money from Nike" so that the top officials could pay back the $200,000 from the scuttled deal with the Chinese company and then make even more by agreeing to sign up again with Nike. The former administrative assistant requested that his name not be revealed, saying it was extremely dangerous to expose high-level corruption in Kenya—a sentiment shared by others.

Many claimed corruption in the athletics federation was so ingrained and so brazen that officials routinely extorted money from athletes who failed drug tests. It was also noted that the organization's chairman, Isaiah Kiplagat, had asked Nike to wire the bonus directly to his personal account, a request that Nike refused. But Nike did wire the money into the federation's account. And before the transaction was made, the chairman of the federation emailed a Nike executive, Robert Lotwis, with "Invoice" in the subject line. "Urgent!!" the message said. "Dear Robert, US $500,000 being commitment Bonus. Regards, Isaiah Kiplagat, Chairman."

According to investigation documents, the response from Nike came ten hours later. "Got it," Mr. Lotwis responded. "I will submit right away. Thanks." Within days, according to bank records, the $500,000 was withdrawn by Athletics Kenya's top officials. There were no athletics activities going on at the time, and it was discovered that just about all of the money had been concealed from Athletics Kenya's executive committee, including $200,000 sent to a bank account in Hong Kong. It was clear that the chairman's asking for the money to be wired to his personal account and then sending a follow-up email labeled "Urgent!!" should have been a tip-off to Nike that something was amiss. Regardless, the payment went through, and Nike was never charged with any investigation in the United States.

"Whenever I see the words 'commitment fees,' 'commitment bonuses,' 'access fees,' 'access bonuses,' that for me raises a red flag," said Mr. Githongo, a consultant who once headed an anti-corruption unit within the Kenyan government. "It's language used to dress up bribes traditionally." As the foundation of Kenya's athletic federation began to crack beneath the surface amidst investigations, it only gave runners from other places a better opportunity at reaching the top of the cross-country mountain.

EUROPEAN SATISFACTION

In Europe, a few major names came under scrutiny, but for the most part cross-country runners remained wonderfully unaware and under the radar when it came to controversy. In Italy and Spain, especially, distance runners who considered themselves "cross-country specialists" inspired the general public to continue supporting the cause for high-level cross-country running. Furthermore, runners were continuing to adjust their allegiances accordingly. Due to relaxed immigration laws and better avenues for dual-citizenship, some of the world's fastest distance runners were finding new homes of their own where they could establish reputations.

One of the primary examples of this was Spain's Ayad Lamdassem, who won Spanish National Cross-Country titles in 2011 and 2014. Born in Morocco in 1981, Lamdassem first arrived in Spain in 2002 as part of the Moroccan contingent for the World University Cross-Country Championships, which was being held in Santiago de Compostela that year. However, he did not compete and instead deserted the team, using the opportunity to stay on in the country and train with other Moroccans in Valencia. He later moved to Lleida, working with Coach Antonio Cánovas, and received citizenship in 2007 after five years of residency.

A five-time participant at the World Cross-Country Championships (once for Morocco and four times for Spain), Lamdassem was the silver medalist at the European Cross-Country Championships in 2010 and 2011. Lamdassem started his 2010–11 cross-country season with a third place at the Soria Cross-Country in November and a second in the European Cross-Country Championship that winter. Lamdassem led the Spanish men to the bronze in the team competition at Euro Cross, while a third-place finish at the 2011 Great Edinburgh Cross-Country helped the European team to the title.

Lamdassem then took the top honors at the Cinque Mulini in February—a performance that lifted his club, Bikila Toledo, to third for that year's European Cross-Country Club Championships, which was held in conjunction with the race. Lamdassem then became the first European finisher at the 2011 World Cross-Country Championships, taking 16th place. He missed the track season due to injury and returned to cross-country in November, finishing seventh at the Cross de Atapuerca and second at Soria. And at the 2011 European Cross-Country Championships he was again the runner-up, this time to Atelaw Yeshetela. Lamdassem was the top European at the Cross de Venta de Baños later that month, coming second to Kenya's Philemon Kimeli. A third place at the San Silvestre Vallecana closed his 2011 season.

Lamdassem returned to the Edinburgh Cross-Country in 2012 and won the long race, beating European champion Yeshetela. Lamdassem then won the European Club Cross-Country Championship in Castellón, leading his Bikila Toledo team to the title. Further progress came at the European Cross-Country Championships near the end of the year where Lamdassem came in sixth overall. At the start of the 2013 cross-country season he finished in the top two at the Great Edinburgh race and the European Clubs competition.

Lamdassem's teammate on more than one occasion was none other than Spain's Rosa Maria Morato, who won Spanish National Cross-Country titles in 2005 and 2007-2010. Born in Barcelona in 1979, Morato set the Spanish 3,000-meter steeplechase record in 2007 by running 9:26. She also earned a bronze in 2007 in Toro, Spain, and a silver in 2009 in Dublin, Ireland, at the European Cross-Country Championships. In 2010 alone for cross-country, she placed in the top five at the Cross Internacional Zornotza and Cross Internacional de Donostia, and won the Championat de Catalunya de Cross. After finishing runner-up in the Spanish National Cross-Country Championship (running 28:29 for 8K), Morato finished 29th overall at the 2010 World Cross-Country Championships.

In Italy, the name (and face) of cross-country running belonged to Gabriele deNard, who won three Italian National Cross-Country titles in 2006, 2012, and 2013. Born in 1974 and hailing from the Italian town of Sedico, deNard was known for his consistency and range. He helped the Italian team win gold at the European Cross-Country Championship in 1998, and earned podium finishes in events ranging from the Cinque Mulini to the Italian Club

Cross-Country Championships. His most recent finish for Italy at World Cross came in Jordan in 2009.

Meanwhile, the Italian women were buoyed by Silvia Weissteiner, Italian National Cross-Country champion in 2006, '08, '09, and '12. With a pedigree similar in scope to her countrymate deNard, Weissteiner found success on the trails and roads all over Europe in a variety of contexts. Significant performances in the decade included the Cross Valle del Chiese Cross-Country in November 2009 (29:24 for seven kilometers), the Campaccio Cross-Country in January 2012 (20:18 for six kilometers), and the 2012 Campionati Italiani Cross-Country, where Weissteiner took first in 27:47 for 8K. While Weissteiner struggled in the World Cross-Country Championships, she was a two-time Olympian and national supporter of cross-country in Italy. Other European runners were equally strong ambassadors for the sport.

Germany's Ulrich "Uli" Steidl was cross-country's poster child for consistency. Born in March 1972, Steidl was raised in the Bavarian city of Erlenbach, Germany, where his religious parents hoped their first son would be a pious Catholic, marry within the faith, excel in academics, and be a good role model for his younger brothers and sisters. Only one wish came true however—he excelled in academics. When Steidl was seventeen he read about a local race and entered. Powered by "hefelaibchen" (egg bread), he left his competition in the dust, winning that first hilly 9.5K in 37:30.

His parents were neither impressed nor supportive. But two older, more experienced competitors, Hilbert Mueller and Wolfgang Muenzel, noticed Steidl's unusual strength and speed; they became his mentors and training partners and provided rides to the races. Later, when Steidl told his father he placed fifth at junior nationals in cross-country, his father's detached reaction was consistent, if nothing else: "Did you do your homework?"

Young Steidl continued to compete and often placed in the top 10. In 1990, he qualified for the Mountain Running World Trophy in Telfes, Austria, and placed third in the junior competition. In 1991, however, at the World Cross-Country Championships in Antwerp, Belgium, he had a good learning experience: "I got my butt kicked big time," Steidl said. "I placed 113th!" Later that year, in August, he came back strong, placing sixth in the 20K European Junior Championship. In September, he took first place in juniors at the Mountain Running World Trophy in Zermatt, Switzerland. And by 1992, he ran his first marathon, in Frankfurt, Germany, posting a 2:25:14. Later that year Steidl received a letter from the University of Portland offering him a full track scholarship. Shortly thereafter, an excited but quiet young German was on his way to a new life in Oregon.

At the University of Portland, challenging track workouts proved tough for Steidl: "I had a very dedicated coach and teammates, and brutal workouts," he recalled. "The distance running and cross-country program at Portland University was (and is still) excellent. When I came to UP in '92 we had a mix of three foreigners and the rest Americans, mostly from the Pacific Northwest. The University of Portland was pretty unknown as a cross-country team. We changed that. Portland usually doesn't get any of the top recruits in the country. [Coach] Rob (Conner) has been very good in recent years to take runners who were good, but not outstanding—then he coached those runners to be All-Americans and formed a national caliber cross-country team."

The University of Portland offered more than a good coach. "For the first time in my life I had a group of runners to train with," Steidl said. "When I came to the University of Portland, I increased my mileage and the intensity of workouts. Before, I would have done eight or 10 × 400 in 68 (seconds). Now I would do 15 × 400 in 63–64. I had done 5 × 1,000-meters before, now I would do 5 × 1-mile instead."

When he arrived, Steidl was running 5,000 meters at 14:40 and 10,000 at 30:56. The combination of Coach Conner's guidance and Steidl's drive to compete created impressive college personal bests, ranging from 1:56 in the 800 meters to 29:16 for 10,000. In 1994, he placed 10th in the NCAA 10,000, and followed that performance up with ninth- and 12th-place finishes the next two years. He excelled in cross-country as well, notching 35th- and 16th-place finishes at the NCAA national championships, the latter making Steidl an All-American.

Steidl considered 2000 his breakthrough year, when he focused primarily on marathons. The German Track and Field Federation asked him to represent the German team in Pyongyang, North Korea, that year. There, he placed eighth in 2:13:56. "I thought the experience would be an adventure since it was being held in North Korea, and I ran a better marathon than I thought I could," Steidl recalled. "However, if I had run a sub-2:12 I would have qualified for the German Olympic Team." Scott McCoubrey, one of the Northwest running community's most influential and respected members, added his opinion: "Uli is one of the most versatile runners I've ever met. He has very good leg speed out on the trails, and in that arena I don't know anyone who runs faster. He's also a very fast 5K, 50K, trail or 10K cross-country runner—he can win at all those distances. Week in and week out, Uli is more consistent than anyone I know."

Unlike many runners, Steidl never spent time healing his body. He didn't take vitamins, eat a particular diet, stretch, use weights, or get massages. To date, he's only had minor injuries. "Uli has a teeny upper body; no fat with huge quads," said McCoubrey. "His legs are so strong in relationship to his body. He has a natural ability to run 140 to 160 miles a week on a regular basis."

"I really like to compete," Steidl said. "If there were no competitions I couldn't do the training I do, both in volume and intensity. The knowledge that a race is coming up keeps me going when I would otherwise not be motivated to run. That's probably why I run more races in a year than I probably should." Speaking of volume, in 2013 Steidl entered the USA National Club Cross-Country Championship, held in Bend, Oregon.

In the Masters race he finished third, running 34:29 for 10K—but that wasn't all. Less than two hours later he ran the same course *again*, this time in 34:47 as a participant in the Men's Open race! Both scores helped his club team place in the championship. He later repeated the performance, running in both the Masters and Open Championships at USA Club Cross in 2015 in Golden Gate Park (running 32:32, and 33:47, respectively, for 10 kilometers).

Said one fan: "Uli is the man. I once was running the ten-mile loop in Point Defiance and twisted my ankle on a root about as far away from my car as you can get in the park. Luckily Uli came through about five minutes later and after learning the situation he unhesitatingly threw me over his shoulder and ran me the 4+ miles back to my car. I should mention I weigh probably about 30 pounds more than I imagine him weighing. Thank you, Uli!" True or not, it was that kind of do-anything attitude that was alive and well in the European running scene.

ENTER IRELAND'S FIONNUALA BRITTON

If there was one runner prepared to bring Ireland back onto the map for distance running, few would be as qualified as Fionnuala (McCormack) Britton, an Irish steeplechaser who was twice the European Cross-Country Individual champion in 2011 and 2012.

Born in September 1984 and raised in Dublin, Britton got her start in distance running when she placed first in the Irish Inter-Clubs Cross-Country Championship in 2002, running the six-kilometer course in 24:25. From there it was a 33rd place finish at the 2003 World Cross-Country Championships and an Under-23 silver medal at the 2006 European Cross-Country Championships. A lifetime member of Kilcoole Athletic Club, Britton finished 14th in the senior race at the 2007 edition of World Cross—the second-best European performer behind Jessica Augusto—and ended the year with a seventh-place finish at the 2007 European Cross-Country Championships.

After a stint with an injury in 2008, Britton confided: "Despite the fact that the European Cross is where my best moments have come they are also the source of some of my biggest disappointments. Missing European Cross in 2008 through injury when it was held in one of my favorite European cross-country courses in Brussels (was one of them)." After returning, Britton just missed out on a medal at the 2010 European Cross-Country Championships, finishing with the same time as bronze medalist Ana Dulce Félix. In retaliation, Britton took second place at the Lotto Cross Cup Brussels a week later.

In preparation for World Cross, Britton ran at the Almond Blossom Cross-Country in March 2011 and took second. She then finished 16th at the 2011 World Cross-Country Championships in Punta Umbría. Later in November she finished third at the high-level Cross de l'Acier cross-country, and in December 2011, finally won her first gold at the European Cross-Country Championships.

Britton began 2012 with wins at the Great Edinburgh Cross-Country and Antrim Cross, and expressed disappointment that World Cross would not be held that year. Despite the lack of a World Cross-Country Championships, in December Britton became the first woman to defend the continental cross title, claiming victory at the 2012 European Cross-Country Championships. One month later, in January 2013, Britton retained her Great Edinburgh Cross-Country and Antrim Cross-Country titles.

Britton placed 13th at the 2013 World Cross-Country Championships, finishing as Europe's top performer in the race and as one of only two non-Africans in the top 15 (alongside Neely Spence). Britton then competed mainly in European competitions the following two seasons, finishing fourth at the 2013 European Cross-Country Championships, eighth in the 10,000 meters at the 2014 European Athletics Championships, and sixth at the 2014 European Cross-Country Championships (and taking a team bronze).

Britton earned a team bronze at the 2015 European Cross-Country Championships, and she narrowly missed an individual medal in fourth place behind Norway's Karoline Bjerkeli Grøvdal. By 2015, in terms of career cross-country highlights, Britton's outlook on success had only grown more mature: "I always want to do better, to win. When I was 12 or 13 I wanted to beat Maria Slattery and Joanna Cullen in Wicklow and they were my biggest rivals. Then it was girls from Leinster; then all of Ireland; and now it's all of them as well as the rest of the distance running girls in Europe and the world," Britton said. "I wouldn't say no to a third European Cross title. You can never get enough of winning." It would remain to be seen how steadfast she would stick to that goal, but in the meantime, Britton's individual accolades were helping to inspire a nation with a rich distance running tradition.

SURNAME: VERNON, NO RELATION

While Britton and others were finding success over the European cross-country circuit, two male runners—both with the surname Vernon—were helping England rediscover its promise as a cross-country power. Andy Vernon and Steve Vernon, no relation, were national cross-country champions in England three times in five years. Between the two runners there were podium appearances in the Great Edinburgh Cross-Country (Steve earned second in 2009 and 2010, while Andy finished third in 2011 and second in 2014), top-10 finishes at the European Cross-Country Championships (10th in 2012 for Steve, third for Andy in 2013, plus a fifth in 2016), and numerous appearances at World Cross (2008, '09, '10, and '11 for Andy; 1999, 2003, '05, '06, '07, and '13 for Steve)—in addition to the English National Cross-Country title for Andy in 2010, and two for Steve in 2011 and 2014.

But while the two shared a common surname, they were different in nearly every other regard. Steve Vernon, born October 1980 and hailing from Greater Manchester in the Northwest of England, was the older of the two and possessed innate mountain-running speed in addition to his prowess over mucky, dismal cross-country footing. There was good reason for it: a long-term injury problem caused his legs to cramp up when he ran at a sustained pace on even surfaces. This sidelined his track and road racing ambitions, including dreams of racing the Olympic marathon. Even some of his cross-country races had been ruined when the course was flat and firm. As a result, Steve Vernon enjoyed a split-season approach where he targeted the Euro or World Cross Championships in the winter and either the European or World Mountain Running Championships in the summer. "I used to treat it [mountain running] as secondary to cross-country and then Jonathan Wyatt [six-time world mountain running champion] said I could be quite good at it if I stopped messing around with it and took it more seriously," Vernon said. And luckily, it had no detrimental effect on either discipline.

"I've had a great year," Steve said, speaking of 2013. "At the European Mountain Running Champs I was very pleased to finish fifth. Tenth place in the European Cross-Country Championships last December was fantastic. I won my fifth North of England cross-country title and while I was beaten by Keith Gerrard in the National Cross, it was my seventh individual medal at the National, and I'm wondering if that might possibly be a record." Once he added his eighth after winning again in 2014, he was certainly considered one of the best. A runner for the Stockport Athletic Club, the senior Vernon's track bests were not world-class, but his legacy of titles made up for it. With only a track 5K mark of 14:18 at the top of his list, Steve Vernon's reputation hinged on his trail-running exploits: like his fifth overall in the European Mountain Running Championships over 12 kilometers in 2013. The younger Vernon, Andy, definitely possessed pure track speed, however—and lacked none of the cross-country strength at all.

Born in January 1986 in Fareham, in the South of England, Andy Vernon got his first major break in cross-country when he finished 14th overall in the European Cross-Country Championships Under-23 division in 2006. Already an accomplished athlete with an 8:30 3,000 meters to his name, Vernon stunned UK coaches when he ran his Euro Cross debut in 23:34 over eight kilometers. A lifetime member of the Aldershot, Farnham and District Athletic Club, Vernon improved his 2006 Euro Cross performance to third overall in 2007, still in the Under-23 division. From there it was to the English National senior-ranks with a 10th place finish in 2008, and a sixth-place finish at the FISU World University Cross-Country Championships later that spring. Needless to say it was success at an early and often stage for Andy Vernon as he balanced a competitive international cross-country schedule with top performances on the track.

At the turn of the decade, it was finally Andy Vernon's time to earn a cross-country national title. "On the senior level this is the one to get and have your name on the trophy," Vernon said. "It was a good race. On the last lap when we started to go through all the backmarkers I got a few meters on Moumin [Moumin Geele, runner-up], then I thought, maybe he is tiring a little bit so, I was going to wait till we got to the hill then, hopefully, I would have the speed if it came down to the sprint having done the indoors. The first lap seemed really slow then on the second lap I picked it up a little bit. Moumin and I pulled away from a couple of the guys." That made all the difference as Vernon retained his lead to the end.

On the track, it was Vernon's versatility, with a personal best of 13:11 for 5,000 meters and 27:42 for 10,000 meters that separated him from the rising crop of UK runners. It was also his consistency. In 2013 alone Vernon finished third at the Great Edinburgh Cross-Country in Scotland, third at the Antrim International Cross in Ireland, first at the McCain Cardiff Cross Challenge in Wales, and third at the McCain UK Cross Challenge in Birmingham. At the end of the year it was another third-place finish, this time at the European Cross-Country Championships.

While Andy and Steve Vernon both represented some of the strongest cross-country running talent in England, the rest of the competitive pool was without the depth that had been so prominent in previous years. As a result, England was facing challenges when it came to submitting full teams for events such as the World Cross-Country Championships. It was one more strike against the once-powerful pedigree of the sport.

AN ABSENCE OF AN ENGLISH TEAM

By 2015, as British male distance runners dusted off their cross-country spikes ahead of a winter season on the mud, they learned that most of them had virtually no chance of representing their country at the biggest meet of the season: the 2015 World Cross-Country Championships in Guiyang, China. British Athletics (the governing body for the sport in the UK) claimed it would only take senior athletes "who had the ability to be competitive," meaning placing in the top 30. It was a harsh standard that only two British senior men had achieved in the previous decade: Mo Farah and Jon Brown.

If this selection strategy had been operating when Farah was younger, he probably would not have been picked for his first three senior World Cross-Country teams. After placing 59th in the junior men's race in 2001, Farah was 74th and 40th in the short-course senior race, and 37th in the long-course race, before improving to 11th in 2007 and 20th in 2010—followed by world and Olympic track golds galore from 2011 to 2013.

Andy Vernon, the British runner-up to Farah in the 10,000 at the 2014 European Championships, would also have struggled to run in World Cross. His results at the event included finishing 114th, 78th, 43rd, and 57th (and 64th and 48th as a junior). More dramatically, Steve Jones would never have gotten a chance had he been racing in 2015. Thirty years prior, aged twenty-two, he placed a lowly 103rd in the World Cross-Country Championships before going on to break a world marathon record seven years later.

It was in 1988 that the decision was made to create a unified Great Britain team for World Cross. A disputed decision, it was one that some believed contributed to the decline of endurance standards because it removed the carrot of international competition at the highest level.

For the British senior women, the World Cross selection remained equivalent—they had to convince selectors they had the ability to finish in the top 30 in China. Here, however, it was much more achievable: Gemma Steel, as the top example most likely to qualify, finished 31st in 2013; while Charlie Purdue finished 14th and Hatti Dean 21st in 2011, Steph Twell 23rd in 2010, plus many more. Despite this, Paula Radcliffe only narrowly squeezed into the top 20 at her first three World Cross races from 1993 to 1996 before eventually winning senior gold.

Conversely, UK Athletics was committed on sending a junior men's and women's teams to the 2015 edition of World Cross. And Britain was far from alone when it came to running scared from the East Africans. Neither Russia, Germany, nor any of the Baltic or Nordic nations took part in the World Cross-Country Championships in Poland in 2013. In fact, Britain had been one of the strongest supporters of the event until their 2015 standards changed.

Not surprisingly, the IAAF was disappointed by UKA's plan. Liz Lynch-Nuttall (formerly McColgan) was among the ex-international athletes to voice their disapproval. Lynch-Nuttall, winner of world 10,000-meter gold and big-city marathons in New York City and London, finished 71st in her first World Cross-Country Championships in 1982 before going on to win silver and bronze in 1987 and 1991. "We know how important cross-country running is and that it is the backbone to building strong endurance athletes," she said. "The news of only sending an athlete capable of a top 30 placing is ridiculous."

"I'm sure the sponsors (the official Great Britain kit sponsor was Nike) would prefer to see their money invested in full teams competing at major championships," Lynch-Nuttall added. "We have had many medals won from Great British athletes over the country and what a negative message we are sending now to youngsters—you're not good enough in our eyes so no point in trying. Such a joke." Dave Buzza, a 2:11 former Great Britain international marathoner, gave his opinion: "This is ridiculous. We take sprinters to every championships just to act as reserves in case people get injured or to run a heat. Runners would self-fund if it's a monetary issue. It takes away a powerful incentive for distance runners. I would never have been selected using these criteria, having placed seventh in the trial in 1988, but got in as a reserve for Tim Hutchings and finished 34th (fourth Brit out of nine). Athletes need some sort of reason to continue in a very tough sport."

Steve Kenyon, best known for his Great North Run victory in the 1980s, said: "I went to nine World XCs gaining one gold, two silver and one bronze team medals, but I only finished top-30 in three of those nine—a fantastic learning curve for any athlete. A terribly shortsighted decision to say the least." And naturally, the cross-country terrain was ever-changing.

While World Cross used to be a classic clash involving everyone from top milers to marathoners, it was now seen as massively dominated by African runners and held only every two years. The European Cross-Country Championships had evolved into the main focus for the British, offering decent competition, less traveling and the feel-good factor of every athlete on the team often coming home with a medal.

World Cross, though, remained the ultimate test of cross-country running. So it was disappointing that the British senior teams would have such little chance of taking on the world's best at the end of this season. Plus, even if they weren't "competitive," there was nothing wrong with simply earning a spot on the national team while being part of a world championship. Many athletes would have loved the honor and cherished the memory to their grave. But while the upper ranks of the sport debated its legitimacy, the youth of England found no trouble still believing.

JOHN NGUGI VISITS SHREWSBURY

It was the middle of October 2014, and John Ngugi, a five-time World Cross-Country champion and 1988 Seoul Olympic 5,000-meter champion, was inspiring Britain's next generation of athletes at Shrewsbury School in a unique coaching residency. For a week-long visit, Ngugi coached, advised, and assisted the school's cross-country students and staff, interacting with a total of 250 students between the ages of eleven and seventeen.

The highlight was an "Evening with John Ngugi" event where the public, students, staff, and parents had a chance to hear from the Kenyan athletics legend and pose questions to the man who put Kenya firmly on the global cross-country pedestal. The evening also highlighted the work of the John Ngugi Foundation and funds were collected to support development for talents back in Kenya. "There is budding talent here and Kenyans must be wary about the future of cross-country if we are to remain at the top. I was well received here and youths, parents, and coaches are very enthusiastic about the project here," said Ngugi. "I have had a truly wonderful welcome at Shrewsbury School and I am delighted with the coaching residency so far. These students are the future of running in the UK and to play a small part in their development is a great privilege."

Fittingly, Ngugi's trip coincided with the historic race that involved the whole of Shrewsbury School. In 1831, this race, named "The Tucks," was held for the first time—and 183 years later Ngugi presented the prizes to the winners of the 2014 edition. "The Royal Shrewsbury School Hunt is the oldest recorded cross-country running organization in the world. John being here brings him back to the roots of the founding of one of his best disciplines in athletics:

cross-country. We are delighted to have him involved in the life of Shrewsbury School this week," said Peter Middleton, Shrewsbury School cross-country coach and staff member. The trip came together through a partnership that had already existed between Shrewsbury School and Running Across Borders (RAB), a UK-based not-for-profit social enterprise focused on grassroots athletics, education, and sports travel.

Two years prior, RAB founder Malcolm Anderson had brought Ethiopian coach Sentayehu Eshetu—the first coach to teach the Bekele brothers, Dibaba sisters, and Tiki Gelana—to the school. The School Hunt team then embarked on a cross-country tour of a lifetime when they traveled to Iten, Kenya and Bekoji, Ethiopia in October 2013. In 2014 it was Ngugi's turn to relay his expertise and inspire Britain's new talents in athletics. "John is a true legend of running and we are so pleased he could come to Shrewsbury School—the home of cross-country," said Malcolm Anderson, the founder of Running Across Borders. "It has inspired us all."

* * *

While the future of cross-country appeared bright at the dawn of the twenty-first century, the various controversies and dishonor surrounding athletes and their organizations cast a shadow over this once proud staple of distance running. And yet—despite the insistence by the IAAF that the World Cross-Country Championships needed to be moved to a biennial format, the dysfunction of national governing bodies in their administration of the sport, the doping scandals plaguing top distance runners, and the refusal of some nations to send a qualified team to World Cross—there was John Ngugi, still sending off the charges at Shrewsbury. "All hounds who wish to run!" called the Huntsman, "Run hard and run well! And may the devil take the hindmost!" And as the young starter blew a husky blast on his antique bugle, numerous thirteen-year-olds charged off across the grass.

EVENT SPOTLIGHT: THE MIRACLE IN THE MUD—THE UNITED STATES AND KENYA AT WORLD CROSS (MARCH 24, 2013)

LOCATION: BYDGOSZCZ, POLAND

Myslecinek Park

On the final circuit of the 1,820-meter loop in Bydgoszcz, Kenya's Hosea Macharinyang was comfortably in 12th place, 10 meters behind Ethiopia's Feyisa Lelisa and America's Chris Derrick. Macharinyang certainly had the credentials to be near the front: he had competed in seven of the previous eight World Cross-Country Championships and was keen to finally make the podium after six top-10 finishes without earning an individual medal. At the middle stage of the race Macharinyang had been as high as seventh place (about 5.5 kilometers in, which was crossed in 15:15), and cresting the course's final major hill he was poised to make a pass of both Lelisa and Derrick for another top-10 finish. But the conditions were sloppy; mud and snow had been churned up and no runner was graceful coming down.

Derrick was grimacing in tenth, eyes wild and arms outstretched, hardly in control as the mud sucked every foot-strike. Lelisa was mere steps behind—arms flapping bird-like, eyes half shut. Lelisa would catch and pass Derrick by the finish line 300 meters later, crossing one second before the American. Macharinyang would not be as lucky. As he came down the final hill he slipped and lost his balance. He was only able to muster a twelfth-place finish, losing a spot to Algeria's Rabah Aboud in the process. As a result, on Sunday, March 24, 2013, the United States senior men's team defeated Kenya at the World Cross-Country Championships, 52 points to 54. Macharinyang's tumble was the final twist in a fateful day for the Kenyan team, one that led to a legendary outcome for the Americans.

Critics had viewed this particular World Cross-Country Championship with skepticism for the US team. When the 2013 US National Cross-Country Championship had showcased a number of strong distance runners, Team USA was buoyed by the thought of former top finishers, like Dathan Ritzenhein (who placed second at the national) and Matt Tegenkamp (who finished third) being on the squad. However, Ritzenhein stated he wouldn't be running, and Tegenkamp pulled out of World Cross the week before the event. And with these two Olympians missing from the start line, it seemed unlikely that the US team would make the podium. Whatever optimism remained was further stymied when the team landed in Poland, where the course was snow-drenched and race-time temperatures would hover around freezing. Not exactly a runner's paradise, but the American team knew it remained up to them.

Among the chosen members, which included Chris Derrick (who had won the first of three eventual national cross-country titles), Elliott Heath (who placed fourth overall at the US National and seventh in the Olympic Trials 5,000), Ryan Vail (a World Cross veteran), Bobby Mack (the 2012 US National Cross champion), and James Strang (former University of Colorado collegiate cross team champion), was Hanover New Hampshire's Benjamin True. Qualified but lesser-known, True, who finished fifth at the 2013 US National Cross Championship, hadn't been at his best. "At USAs, I finished the race and it was one of those moments of, 'Whoa, I'm definitely out of shape right now.'" True shared. "It was the start of getting back into hard workouts. I don't think my race fitness was there. I was just doing a lot of mileage." Since that qualification, True had been on a mission to gain strength and sharpen his speed. After dealing with Lyme's disease at the Olympic Trials in 2012, True improved from his fifth at the National Cross Championship and was victorious at the USA 15-kilometer Championships two weeks prior to World Cross. His newly found strength would serve him well in Poland, as he looked to improve upon his 35th finish from the 2011 World Cross-Country Championships, where he was the top finisher for the United States.

"Right now I don't really know what expect," said Chris Derrick in the lead-up to the 2013 World Cross-Country Championships. "Except suffering of course. I think top-15 is a decent goal." The other runners from the United States shared similar aspirations. "If we all have good races, I could easily see our top four all being in the top-25, and if that's the case, I think we have a good shot at getting the bronze," said Ben True. "It's definitely the hardest course I've ever seen in my life. There are no straightaways, it's all either mud or ice. And there are nice little mounds that are very interesting, where it's just really short and steep uphill and downhill. And then there's basically a wall that you have to run up six times. I think almost as scary as that uphill is going to be, that downhill off the back side—where it's all in the sun—it's all muddy, and it's very steep with a sharp turn at the end. So I think it'll be surprising if half the field doesn't fall at least one time during the race. Just trying to stay on your feet will be the biggest thing." It was clear the race would be anything but guaranteed. True continued: "I don't think I have a lot of experience. The only thing I can think of is trail running back home in the springtime. It's basically that. Hopefully it'll be strong for the United States. I think it actually helps us, because a lot of the Kenyans and Ethiopians and other nations aren't going to be as used to the cold, as used to the terrible conditions of the course, so hopefully it will bode well for us. I think we're excited. We're not phased by this hard course."

While Derrick had been notable as the fastest American-born runner never to win an NCAA Cross-Country Championship, and the others had established cross-country résumés, Benjamin True's story was a little less publicized. Despite this, True was a big talent. Even from an early age, True was among the top finishers at the 2003 Foot Locker Cross-Country Championship, where he finished fifth—just one second behind eventual NCAA Cross-Country champion Josh McDougal and just five seconds behind eventual Olympic silver medalist Galen Rupp. But unlike Rupp and McDougal, True was barely training. McDougal had been doing more than 100 miles per week in high school and Rupp had been coached by Alberto Salazar. True, hailing from the remote state of Maine, was running low mileage and juggling running with cross-country skiing in the winter. "My relationship with running is complicated," True recounted. "All through high school and college I split my time between running and skiing. I skied because that was my passion, and I ran because people said I was good at it. The coaches were right in pushing me toward track. I did set some Maine State records and I was winning races."

In college, despite being only a part-time runner, True was pretty much unbeatable at the Ivy League level. He was just the fourth runner in history to win three Ivy League cross-country individual titles (2005, 2006, and 2008), and in the 2008 edition he won by 33 seconds over Princeton's All-American Mike Maag, who had run 7:56 earlier that year indoors in the 3K and would run 13:41 the following April in the 5K.

But after graduating, True had to make a decision: invest all in to skiing, or focus on being a long-distance runner. "I really haven't skied at all since I graduated," True said. "I figured that if I really wanted to take a sport to the highest level, I would really have to focus on it. I wanted to try my hand at running. And because of my skiing background, I had a little more bulk on me than some other runners. I've really limited the amount of strength work and gym work that I've done, because I've been trying to lose some of that extra weight. As soon as I get to the gym, I tend to pack on a lot more muscle than I probably should for running, so I have been avoiding that. When I was running in college, I was probably around 170 (pounds) and my skiing was probably around 180. And now I'm probably about 165." It was a complex road that brought True to the sport, but after finishing fifth in the 2013 US National Cross-Country Championship, he was once again set on lacing it up at World Cross.

True and the rest of the world faced formidable talent from the perennial powerhouses Ethiopia and Kenya. Ethiopia was led by Imane Merga, who had won the 2011 World Cross title in surprise fashion. "Last summer (2012) was a disappointment," Merga said. "I had some slight injuries in July and lost my chance to go to the Olympics, but since November I have been steadily improving." Pundits were aware that Merga's best cross-country results had come on dry courses and often in relatively hot weather. His two previous World Cross-Country Championships outings— he had also been seventh as a junior at the 2007 event in Mombasa—had been in warm climate races. But strength in numbers was the key, and joining Merga was teammate and top-class marathon runner Feyisa Lilesa, who showed that he was in shape to contest shorter distances with aplomb when he won the Ethiopian trials the month prior. Kenya, on the other hand, had chosen a team that

appeared competitive but had little experience at the highest level. Only two of their six-man team had competed in the championships before.

For Kenya, seven-time veteran Hosea Macharinyang was a familiar face, and joining him was Japheth Korir— who had raced twice in the championships as a junior in 2009 and 2010, finishing fifth and third, respectively. Eyes were also on the surprise Kenyan trials winner Philemon Rono, who was competing in his first major international championship. Rono, aged twenty-two, could only finish eighth in the Kenyan Police Championships a month before the national trials, and barely made his team for Kenya's top domestic race, but the policeman then completely upset the formbook in Nairobi when he left many of the better-known names in his wake. "Kenya may not have many well-known names in their squad this year, especially in the senior men's team, but they have a lot of talent," said cross-country ambassador Paul Tergat. "It is true that these conditions will prove difficult for some runners, some will find it very cold for them, but others will rise to the occasion."

The start of the men's senior race was frenzied, as was typical of every World Cross-Country event, but it quickly tapered off. The pace was a relatively reserved 5:40 at the end of the first two-kilometer lap, compared to 5:24 for the junior men, but improved a little on the second lap with four kilometers covered in 11:09. A large group of 17 runners were still together a third of the way into the race. Among them were Kenya's Japhet Korir, Tim Kiptoo, and Hosea Macharinyang; Ethiopia's Imane Merga and Feyisa Lilesa; Australia's Collis Birmingham; Canada's Mo Ahmed and Cam Levins; a handful of Ugandans and Eritreans; and Chris Derrick of the United States in 10th place overall.

The pace remained steady up to the halfway point, as the leaders covered the next two kilometers in 5:23, but the group dwindled to nine. Korir and Uganda's Timothy Torotich were the driving forces at the front for the duration and by eight kilometers the group had been reduced to six: Kenya's Korir, Ethiopia's Merga, Uganda's Torotich and his well-known compatriot Moses Kipsiro, Eritrea's Teklemariam Medhin, and Australia's Collis Birmingham. Benjamin True, having the race of his life, joined the group midway through the penultimate lap, while Birmingham started to fade with one lap to go. Ten kilometers was reached in a very fast 27:17.

It was the Eritrean Medhin who reached one lap to go from the front, but he soon ceased to be a factor in the race for the gold (along with the two Ugandans), as Kenya's Korir and Ethiopia's Merga started their own battle for supremacy in the 11th kilometer. Behind them charged the Americans. "It was exciting to hear the team numbers being called out during the race," said Bobby Mack. "On the last lap, I heard people yelling at me that if you get two more people, that we would have a bronze medal. I wasn't going to get passed, and I got those last two guys." "We all had the same game plan and that was to go out conservative," confided Ryan Vail. "And conservative meant going out about 50th place or so. Every lap we worked on picking people off."

After the first of the six laps, Vail and Mack had both been outside the top 50 (Vail was 62nd, Mack 52nd), and at the midway point, neither was in the top 30 (Vail was 34th, Mack 33rd). As a result, by halfway, Kenya was dominating the United States in team scoring: 40 points to 80. But then fate stepped in. Kenya's Jonathan Ndiku, who had been third after the first lap (and had times very similar to Chris Derrick: 13:11 for 5K and 27:37 for 10K), ended up in the hospital, instead of the finish line, with an Achilles injury. His withdrawal was an immediate factor.

Likewise, the Kenyans were losing ground by the final lap, as Vail and Mack were still closing for the Americans. Kenya's Timothy Kiptoo, who had been as high as third early in the race, had dropped to 23rd overall entering the final 2K. Similarly, Geoffrey Kirui, who had been as high as fifth, was in 14th place, and Hosea Macharinyang who had been in seventh, had fallen to 10th. Meanwhile, Vail, who had run World Cross-Country three other times and never finished higher than 33rd—and Mack, who was 66th the last time the race was run in Bydgoszcz—entered the final lap of the course in 21st and 20th place, respectively. "I knew when Vail and I were running number three and four and we were in 30th—we don't go backwards—and Vail and I were just moving up. Then they started yelling that we had two in the top 10, and every point counted," said Mack.

Up front on the final lap the tiring Merga threw in the towel and visibly settled for second place about 200 meters from the finish, letting Korir, who had been sixth in the Kenyan trials the month before (and the last man to be named to the team) cruise to victory. Eritrea's Medhin, three years removed from winning the silver medal in the same city, took the bronze on this occasion in 32:54, closing the gap on Merga in the final few hundred meters. The three medalists were followed home by Uganda's Kipsiro and Torotich as the surprising True finished sixth for the United States.

Japhet Korir, who was blithely unaware that he had become the youngest ever senior men's champion in the history of the IAAF World Cross-Country Championships (he answered "Oh really?" in an underwhelmed response when informed of the fact), waited patiently for his countrymen at the finish line. He would be waiting longer than usual on this day. "Going into this my goal was to get top-25, and the outside shot was get top-15 so I could get the automatic A standard," said Ben True after his sixth-place finish. "Never would have thought I could get top-10, but the course played to my strengths pretty well, I just hung in there, everyone else started dropping off, and I stayed there. I wasn't sure until I crossed the line. That last lap I was hurting. I was just trying to keep the legs moving and still keep going."

Meanwhile, Ryan Vail and Bobby Mack continued to move up in the team scoring. As Derrick crossed in 10th overall behind Ethiopia's Lilesa and Australia's Birmingham, Ryan Vail staggered across the line in 17th, only 19 seconds behind Derrick, and less than a minute behind Korir. Next to him was Bobby Mack, 19th overall—as the top four American scorers all finished in the top 20 places. Kenya's Kiptoo finished as their fourth scorer in 26th position and the nail had been driven in: the USA was victorious over Kenya by two points.

The victory was the best finish by the American men since 1984, and having Derrick and True both in the top 10 was the first time that had occurred since 1986 (when Pat Porter was sixth and John Easker was 10th). In fact, the last time the United States had a single male in the top 10 in the long race at World Cross-Country had been 1995. "It was really hard," said Chris Derrick. "I felt good for the first two laps, and started to push a little bit. It might have been the cold, but I really couldn't see that well over the last few laps. I knew Ben was up there, and that I needed to get in the top ten if we were to have a shot at a medal." "Chris and I were sitting around the low 20s and feeding off each other, and I kept telling myself to hang in there for one more lap, as guys from other teams started to drop back and we started picking them off," added True.

Luckily, the reception by the Kenyan crowd was not reduced because of the performance of their senior men's team. One journalist wrote: "Die-hard athletics fans in Eldoret thronged various social joints to follow Kenya's performance. After attending the Easter Sunday mass service in various churches, many were eager to catch up with the proceedings in the event, given that most athletes on Team Kenya that traveled to Poland come from the region. Hotel attendants had a difficult time stopping patrons from climbing on chairs and tables to catch a good view of their idols on television screens. There was deafening silence as Kenya's Japheth Korir and Hosea Macharinyang started the race against a strong field of Ethiopians and Eritreans. Many watched with joy as Korir broke away from the leading pack to build a gap of 20 meters between himself and the chasing duo of Ethiopia's Imane Merga and Eritrea's Teklomariam Medhin. Korir sprinted to glory, followed by Merga as fans contentedly walked home." Korir's performance had been largely unexpected amongst the success of his competitors from Ethiopia.

While Ethiopia's Merga lost his individual crown, Ethiopia won the team contest for the first time since 2005. Ethiopia put together a total of 38 points, with their other three scorers led by top marathon runner Feyisa Lilesa in ninth place, and Abera Chane and Tesfaye Abera in 13th and 14th.

However, Korir was lucky to be on the starting line in Bydgoszcz at all. Kenyan selectors mulled over whether he was worth bringing to Poland after his sixth place at their own trials. Coming in, it was a resurrection effort: "I was spiked during the Kenyan trials in the 5,000-meter for the IAAF World Junior Championships last year and I had a very bad injury with my Achilles," revealed Korir, who limped home eighth in that race in Nairobi. "Look," he demonstrated, quite happy to pull down his socks and show a nasty scar that still glowed through the Bydgoszcz mud that was caked around his legs. "I had to spend some time in hospital and I was worried about how it was going to affect my running but then I started training again and slowly regained my form. Before coming here, I only had two races since the injury. One was a local race in Kenya and the other was the Kenyan trials. However, once I finished sixth in Nairobi and started training for the World [Cross-Country] Championships, I trained very hard and I think people saw that I was in good shape."

Even if it was naivety, inexperience, youth, or just simply exuberant talent, Korir never seemed to be over-awed by his surroundings despite there being only three younger men among the 102 runners on the start line. "I never feared anybody. I only wanted to finish in a good place," Korir said modestly. "But then I started to feel strong. The weather was cold, and I didn't like that so much, but the course seemed very good and I was running very well."

The Kenyan contingent did very well in all other divisions, with African-born runners taking the top 19 spots in the junior men's championship. For the junior women, Kenya and Ethiopia were essentially flawless equals. They both put all six of their runners before anyone else put in one, as African-born runners took the top 15 spots. For the senior women, African-born runners went 1–12, with Kenya once again on top. The United States women were lucky to finish fourth overall. Said Deena Kastor: "All the girls performed outstanding. Kim [Conley] and Neely [Spence] did an outstanding job, and Emily [Infeld] as well. The future of the sport in the US is very bright."

But the story of the day was undoubtedly the senior men from the United States, and it would not have been possible if not for the top two in Chris Derrick and Benjamin True. "The start of Worlds is a sight to behold," said True. "It's always the same. The gun goes off and everyone sprints all-out. The Africans break away into a lead pack and it's a suffer-fest for everyone behind them after that. I was well back of the African pack. I didn't feel bad. The main thing: I was still on my feet through all the snow and ice." A lot of runners weren't. "The first two laps, Chris and I worked together, and ahead of us you could see guys falling, see guys staggering to keep their feet. We just kept reeling in guys," said True. "Moving like that," said Derrick, "You feel a horde of guys are going to come on up. Like they are going to tear your flesh. I thought I was in serious trouble. The surroundings were taking on a sepia tone." True sensed a similar dimming: "I had mud caked in my eyes. Everything seemed brown. It could certainly have been exhaustion."

Men's Race			
Date: Sunday, March 24, 2013			
Teams: 15			
Distance: 6.9 miles/11.1 kilometers			
Location: Myslecinek Park, Bydgoszcz, Poland			
Individual Finishers (Top 20):			
1	Japhet Korir	Kenya	32:45
2	Imane Merga	Ethiopia	32:51
3	Teklemariam Medhin	Eritrea	32:54
4	Moses Kipsiro	Uganda	33:08
5	Timothy Toroitich	Uganda	33:09
6	Ben True	United States	33:11
7	Goitom Kifle	Eritrea	33:16
8	Collis Birmingham	Australia	33:18
9	Feyisa Lilesa	Ethiopia	33:22
10	Chris Derrick	United States	33:23
11	Rabah Aboud	Algeria	33:28
12	Hosea Macharinyang	Kenya	33:29
13	Abera Chane	Ethiopia	33:31
14	Tesfaye Abera	Ethiopia	33:35
15	Geoffrey Kirui	Kenya	33:38
16	Sergio Sanchez	Spain	33:38
17	Ryan Vail	United States	33:42
18	Abrar Osman	Eritrea	33:42
19	Robert Mack	United States	33:49
20	Elroy Gelant	South Africa	33:53

Team Results:		
1	Ethiopia	38
2	United States	52
3	Kenya	54
4	Eritrea	75
5	Uganda	76
6	Algeria	107
7	Australia	116
8	Spain	127
9	Canada	140
10	Poland	164
11	Great Britain	166
12	South Africa	256
13	Rwanda	298
14	Japan	306
15	Sudan	350

Women's Race			
Date: Sunday, March 24, 2013			
Teams: 15			
Distance: 4.6 miles/7.4 kilometers			
Location: Myslecinek Park, Bydgoszcz, Poland			
Individual Finishers (Top 20):			
1	Emily Chebet	Kenya	24:24
2	Hiwot Ayalew	Ethiopia	24:27
3	Belaynesh Oljira	Ethiopia	24:33
4	Shitaye Eshete	Bahrain	24:34
5	Margaret Muriuki	Kenya	24:39
6	Janet Kisa	Kenya	24:46
7	Viola Kibiwot	Kenya	24:46
8	Tejitu Daba	Bahrain	24:55
9	Juliet Chekwel	Uganda	24:58
10	Irene Cheptai	Kenya	25:01
11	Beatrice Mutai	Kenya	25:05
12	Salima Alami	Morocco	25:05
13	Neely Spence	United States	25:08
14	Fionnuala Britton	Ireland	25:08
15	Genet Yalew	Ethiopia	25:10
16	Sophie Duarte	France	25:17
17	Almensh Belete	Belgium	25:24
18	Kenza Tifahi	Algeria	25:26
19	Nazret Weldu	Eritrea	25:27
20	Kareema Jasim	Bahrain	25:27

Team Results:		
1	Kenya	19
2	Ethiopia	48
3	Bahrain	73
4	United States	90
5	Ireland	115
6	France	122
7	Great Britain	154
8	Canada	167
9	Spain	183
10	Uganda	188
11	Poland	256
12	Japan	278
13	Brazil	298
14	South Africa	305
15	Australia	344

Conclusion

As of this writing, cross-country is as relevant as ever, an important member of the distance running family that includes indoor and outdoor track and field, marathon running, road racing, trail running, and special events such as the Ekiden. Cross-country has a rich, international tradition. For more than two hundred years it has thrilled audiences and participants alike, has provided a natural venue for athletes, and now attracts runners of all ages.

Over the years, some of the biggest names in cross-country have worried about the difficulties in growing the sport. There were multiple reasons why: lack of enthusiasm from professional coaches, the biennial structure of the World Championship, format changes ranging from race distances to monetary compensation, and dominance by specific nations.

Thankfully, others saw it as being vital to protect: "I believe cross-country running is important for *any* long-distance runner, whether you are also running on the track or are moving up to the marathon," Paul Tergat said while in Bydgoszcz in 2013. "If you are a runner and once you start your winter preparation, and you do cross-country, my feeling is that you will do well in the coming seasons."

"European countries need to reassess how they treat the World Cross-Country and get back to supporting this event," added Sonia O'Sullivan. "It's at the perfect time in the year to point winter training towards and test yourself against the best."

O'Sullivan, who was also present in Bydgoszcz in 2013, further identified a frequently overlooked component: "I think the team aspect is really important to encourage athletes who may not believe they can achieve World Championship qualifying standards. It gives them the chance to represent [their] country, run at the World Championships and be inspired to aspire to greater things that you will never do if you don't get to experience this level of competition. It also helps build the depth and quality of distance running standards in each country."

To address the lack of cohesion among the elites about participating in cross-country, O'Sullivan also had a suggestion: "I think the biggest thing we have to do right now is to get into the minds of athletes to show cross-country can lay the foundation for success later on in the year, that it is important and it has a big impact on the rest of the season. You get something out of it, it is a bit of a testing point for you and it is something you can't get in training."

These unique benefits of the sport drove cross-country's historical growth but were also responsible for keeping it relevant in the current day. Even now, professional runners are aware they can engage with cross-country from both the top down (administrative level) and the bottom up (grassroots level). But despite this unique accessibility, cross-country appears to have less appeal. It is bogged down by new challenges that didn't exist before. And as a consequence, new ideas about the sport need to reach the limelight. While it is clear that making cross-country running successful and popular outside of the collegiate and preparatory school ranks in today's world posed a challenge, the goal was closer than many acknowledged.

In 2015 O'Sullivan offered a potential solution: "One way it could be done is if you look at [the] World Cross-Country Championships, we have individuals, you have countries but you could also have continents and make it important for athletes to compete for their continents within the same events," she said. "You would have only one athlete from each country on the continent, you can't have the whole Kenyan team there representing Africa, or the whole American team representing Americas, and it would make it a little bit more interesting, because you would be part of a bigger team."

O'Sullivan's idea made sense in light of the fact that in more recent championships, some countries struggled to send enough professional-caliber runners to complete a full national team. "This would give incentive to athletes from countries not sending full teams to be a part of a team and reason to run their best," O'Sullivan explained. "An athlete can count on their country and continental team if their country sends a team. There should be prize money for these teams also to increase the incentive as often athletes may weigh up financial gains and losses by running World Cross."

O'Sullivan's proposal would reduce the regional dominance of such powerhouse squads as Kenya and Ethiopia, while improving the prospects of teams such as Great Britain, who were concerned about how to remain competitive.

Further debate centered on making World Cross more appealing for the fans and the media. Following the 2017 World Cross-Country event in Kampala, Uganda, Jakob Larsen, director of the Danish Athletic Federation (and next organizer of World Cross in 2019), proclaimed a host of new innovations aimed at "[producing] an event which will reignite a serious discussion about the readmittance of cross-country to the Olympic Program." Among the proposed topics of discussion were "challenge zones" on the course and a relay with two separate loops to help make mass participation possible. "On the subject of the course, we hope for approval for an alternative course layout in order to enable thousands of recreational runners to run with the elite—as is the case in road running," Larsen stated. "At this time, we have several ideas in mind. Which way we will go depends on the discussions with the IAAF, our internal workshops, and discussions with other stakeholders. We propose introduction of challenging course elements located in 'Challenge Zones'; some based on well-known elements of 'Old School' cross-country, others inspired by cyclocross, XC eventing and OCR [Obstacle Course Runs]. All are to be delivered with respect to cross-country as a running event."

The course proposal for Aarhus in Denmark 2019 included approximately 60 meters ascent on each lap—certainly challenging—as well as a series of five "natural" constructed obstacles on each lap, which would have individual names such as *The Kenenisa Climb*, the *Lynn Jennings Log Slope*, or *Muddy Mayhem*. Further "innovations" at the World Cross event included a mixed-gender relay that appeared in Uganda at the 2017 event, and gave athletes the opportunity of running one 2,000-meter loop each.

Beyond official suggestions, other format improvements were also possible. Time-trial segments could be used to qualify for different sections of a specific course. Individuals running for regional or continental pride could "trial" segments in one-kilometer, two-kilometer, or three-kilometer lengths to determine team standing or add to a points system—similar to methods employed by cycling in the Tour de France.

What purpose could these trial segments serve? To handicap participants. From the days of hare-and-hound running and open-ground steeplechasing, setting handicap races "from scratch" was the method used to keep races competitive. If a trials component were added to cross-country, athletes could gain or lose time based on their qualifying performance. This would add a tactical component to the final championship. Handicapping particularly strong runners would encourage greater participation. It would also encourage runners with differing strengths.

Some cross-country races with rich historical traditions, such as the Dipsea, built their reputations on handicapping, which gave older participants a "head start" on younger ones. Meanwhile, other sporting organizations such as basketball's NBA saw men and women and young and old competing side by side during their All-Star Game weekend. There was nothing to prevent a similar "World Cross Through the Ages" event at the World Cross-Country Championship. Creative uses of team and course layout would add excitement.

But creative ideas weren't accepted by everyone—and especially by coaches who knew the difficulties in setting up international championships from firsthand experience. "Anything's possible but I don't love it honestly. It's basically a way to punish Kenya and Ethiopia for being so dominant and that doesn't seem fair to me," noted professional coach Ben Rosario, who oversaw the Northern Arizona Elite team.

"I'd hate to see [the] World Cross-Country Championships turned into something like Tough Mudder or the Spartan race series, but there's a reason those races are popular, and right now there's little to distinguish cross-country from competitive track or road racing," said Peter Vigneron, the senior editor at *Competitor Magazine*.

Presently, it is clear cross-country running has a marketing problem. In fact, distance running historian Roger Robinson summed up the problem succinctly:

> Cross-country seems to be doing better than ever at the high school and college level. Events like the USATF masters champs are strong and competitive. But cross-country is suffering serious decline in its adult base. It's a mixed picture. While traditional cross-country is struggling for numbers, multitudes of runners are crowding eagerly into road races. Even more to the point, they are also in hordes exuberantly putting themselves through the new challenges of mud-runs, color runs, park runs, mountain running, trail running, multi-sports, and other variants of off-road running. The point is not that cross-country is better, but that it still provides something special and valuable, something all those high schoolers and masters want—the challenge of sustained racing over difficult natural surfaces.

How then could cross-country learn from the rapid growth of events like Tough Mudder and Spartan Race?

In her book *Off Course: Inside the Mad, Muddy World of Obstacle Course Racing*, author Erin Beresini explained why these events became so popular: "Athletes burned out on running might have turned to adventure racing instead, while weekend warriors could have made a pilgrimage to Joliet, Illinois, to participate in the world's first Warrior Dash, a 'mud-crawling, fire-leaping, extreme 5K run from hell' that debuted in July 2009 with 2,000 participants."

Beresini's research gave insight into the timeline and limited budget of these events while they grew exponentially, citing how Will Dean organized the first Tough Mudder (seven miles long with over 4,500 in attendance) at a ski resort near Allentown, Pennsylvania, on May 2, 2010. The success of the event, which led to coverage in the *New York Times* and put Dean's Brooklyn-based company of six employees on the map, led to three more events that year and earned Tough Mudder over $2 million in revenue. The first Spartan Race wasn't far behind, beginning in Burlington, Vermont, on May 16, 2010.

Beresini noted that Tough Mudder used little more than $8,000 in Facebook advertising to sell out nearly every event it held, hosting more than 10,000 competitors in a single weekend. The Spartan Race Series also sold out, capping its fields at 6,000 entrants. And as for Warrior Dash, which started with one race in 2009, its events saw more than 20,000 costumed warriors at each one. "In just its third year of existence, obstacle course racing hosted more than 1.5 million competitors," Beresini continued. "That was a 3,558% increase over the estimated 41,000 people who competed in 2010. In that same time period participation in half-marathons, dubbed America's fastest-growing running distance rose 34%, from 1.38 million finishers to 1.85 million."

And while cross-country competitions could probably do without the fire-leaping and costumes, the staggering growth of these specialty events highlighted the problem perfectly: the International Association of Athletics Federations (IAAF), USA Track and Field (USATF), and other national organizations needed a way to reach the masses of people yearning (if only subconsciously) to run cross-country.

Coach Rosario expanded on this point:

> Again, more kids are running cross-country than ever and if you ask them what they like better, cross-country or track, I'll bet you 75% would say cross-country. The marketing problem (or one of them anyway) is not that we aren't getting people involved in cross-country, it's that we're not getting them hooked on the sport at the professional level. Soccer had the exact same problem for many years—huge youth participation numbers but low interest in the sport for adults. The success of MLS [Major League Soccer] and the success of the US at recent World Cups has changed that dramatically. We have to get our stars and our sport on television and in front of potential fans. One more example—the biggest running stars in the US, by far, are our marathoners. Why? Because the New York City Marathon and the Boston Marathon are enormous events, they are televised and they draw millions of viewers across the globe.

USA Track and Field's unique problem was that in its present form, it was a sanctioning organization for both professional and amateur athletes. They had done little to market to the "weekend warriors" of America, and instead of being the go-to destination for post-collegiate and youth athletes interested in an exciting alternative to school races, USATF was content with their limited offering of club cross-country events (both the USATF Pacific Association and USATF New England held a series of grand-prix races). But in order to promote their historic venues (Van Cortlandt Park, Franklin Park, Mt. SAC, Crystal Springs) more broadly they needed to incentivize this audience, and incentives were costly.

Competitor's senior editor Peter Vigneron and Alan Stevens, who served for sixteen years on the IAAF's cross-country committee, also recognized this problem. Cross-country, wrote Vigneron, "doesn't offer a big prize purse and for American runners, it won't trigger a big shoe-company performance bonus. What it needs, I think, is . . . to dial up the elements that make it different from track and road racing. Insert 'arduousness' requirements into host city selections. Make courses more hilly and more slippery, make runners clear ditches, truck in spectators and put them close to the action [much like the epic 2007 US National Cross-Country Championships in Boulder, Colorado]. Make the prize purse outrageously large. Winners [at the 2012 event] would get only $30,000, $10,000 less than they got in 1999, according to David Monti. Change the course type from one year to the next. Snow, then desert, then mountains—reward runners who are versatile, who have different skills, not just the guys with the fastest 10,000-meter PRs."

"Look at recent championships, national and international, and note how many good runners now are not there," said Stevens. "The big money isn't in cross-country, so the best now go straight into the marathon."

Compared to obstacle course racing, cross-country certainly had ample opportunity to attract sponsorship. The first step was to obtain media coverage. As of 2016, The Spartan Racing Series was broadcast on network television with a contract with NBC-Universal, the same affiliate that covered the Diamond League track series with the IAAF, and various track and field meets with USATF, like the Prefontaine Classic, and the US Olympic Trials. Many major cross-country championships, including Nike Cross Nationals, Foot Locker, and the National Collegiate Athletic Association (NCAA) Championships, already had success streaming the event online to hundreds of thousands of viewers. And the only question that remained from a production standpoint was how to adjust to different venues and course layouts, and which events to cover.

But while it could be hard to cover every portion of a cross-country event, a beneficial consequence of the sport was that there was more space on a cross-country course for lucrative advertising deals. Billboards, fences, and sponsored hazards were all possibilities. Furthermore, it would be possible for the teams involved with the sport to also receive sponsorship if USATF and the IAAF changed their rules. NASCAR (auto racing) and FIFA (soccer) offered numerous opportunities for teams to receive commercial backing. Although this element was currently absent from distance running, it could be added—in uniform sponsorship, or club allegiance, for example.

Meanwhile, a marketing opportunity already existed with professional running teams, another area that could be further leveraged (think marketing the Brooks Beasts or Nike Oregon Project as rival enterprises), and there were two other ways USATF and the IAAF could build visibility on big stages: a permanent home for the World Cross-Country Championships and the reinclusion of the sport in the Olympic Games.

In 2013, Rosario was the leader of the organizing committee for the 2013 US National Cross-Country Championships. And at the time, he offered a startling suggestion: hold the World Cross-Country Championships the day before a major marathon. The idea seemed outlandish at first, since many major marathon runners were also good in cross-country. But Rosario highlighted the potential to increase not only participants, but sponsors and spectators as well—three core ingredients that could instantly elevate the status of a World Cross-Country Championship. Combining the two events would put all the action in one place. "I still think the idea has legs, potentially," said Rosario. "But I've also seen how hard it is to put on two world class events on back-to-back days when the United States held their Olympic Trials Marathon the day before the Los Angeles Marathon. The Trials suffered a bit, logistically, because there are just only so many hours in the day. What I have settled on now, and I feel very strongly about it, is that the World Championships would be much better served to have a permanent home, on a permanent course, in a nation with a love for cross-country." This idea seemed much more feasible, given it would provide a stable identity for runners to associate with.

"This is not a crazy idea at all," said Rosario about the idea of a permanent home for World Cross. "Many of the world's greatest sporting events are held in the same place annually (The Masters, all four tennis majors, all five world major marathons, etc.). Having it in the same place allows the local organizers to improve upon the event with each edition, build a regional fan base, and build any number of traditions around the event. As it stands now it seems like it's back to the drawing board with each championship. My suggestions for a country would rather obviously be either the US or Scotland."

Another, more prestigious opportunity would also provide a boost in "off years" for the sport: the Olympic Games. "Cross-country is one of the most challenging aspects of the athletics calendar," Paul Tergat claimed recently. "And six men participate in a team at the World Cross-Country Championships while only three can compete on the track at 5,000-meters and the 10,000-meter at an Olympics; and those other three other men would like to compete in the Olympics. So I think it is high time that cross-country running is included in the Olympics; it's a phenomenal event and it deserves its place on the Olympic stage."

"When you become a runner, I think the Olympics are the epitome of the running world," said athlete Sarah Brown in 2016—an Olympic-qualifying year.

But what made the Olympics so different? "The Olympics are the greatest sporting event because they represent a microcosm of the human condition, inviting us to celebrate human potential and even the nobility of man (beyond one single event)," wrote public relations executive Alistair Nicholas. "The Olympics, with its myriad of events played over two weeks by thousands of athletes from every country able to send a team, celebrates the accomplishments of both individuals and teams and invites all of us to strive to be better (as opposed to one, isolated event, drawing world talent)."

So yes, the Olympics were a bigger deal than World Cross. But a proposal to reinstate cross-country running in the Olympics—which in its most recent measure sought IAAF approval in 2010—wasn't approved by the International Olympic Committee, and wasn't a major priority for then-IAAF president Lamine Diack for the simple fact that the sport had to be run exclusively "on snow or ice."

But, it was time for fresh support. Enter newly-elected IAAF president Sebastian Coe in 2015. Coe, an honored and decorated runner himself, had become a leader and ambassador for the Olympic movement in 2012, when London announced its bid to hold the 2012 Olympic Games. And in 2015, Coe pushed wholeheartedly to include cross-country:

> One of the things that has really worried me in the last few years, is that I don't think enough younger coaches realize how important cross-country is, and I think that in turn has had an impact on the number of people at international level doing the sport. If you look back to all the top track and field athletes: John Walker ran in a World Cross-Country Championship, Steve Ovett did, Steve Cram could run good cross-country, Gebrselassie, Paul Tergat—and they were doing it in the same season. So the coaches [who] are saying you can't do cross-country and track in the same season, are clearly, demonstrably proved wrong. And I do think it's a really important thing. So I would love to see cross-country back in the Olympic program, and maybe even—thinking outside the box for the moment—why not include it in the Winter Olympic program? Because you would then broaden the [Winter] Olympic program to African nations that are not actually feeling a great proprietorial interest.

Finally, after so many years, cross-country had a distance running administrator championing the cause. And he was the popular president of the IAAF, to boot. But what of the athletes? "If cross-country were to be added to the Olympics, I would be thrilled," said American Dathan Ritzenhein. "The only thing I would not like is to have missed the opportunities to run it myself! Really it makes more sense for it to be in the Summer Games I think but either one is better than not having it."

The summer-winter debate was central, as there were not only challenges related to each season, but also in fitting new sports into the program: if cross-country were added (even aside from its necessity to be run on snow or ice), it would mean another qualified Olympic sport might have to be removed.

Plus, the "practicing of [cross-country] on snow or ice" remained central to the Winter Games conundrum. The easiest solution: have the IAAF stage a limited event series where the running of cross-country on snow was the centerpiece. It would give qualifiers an opportunity to participate, and the budget could accommodate it. The IAAF already met all the other criteria for inclusion.

In turn, running long distance with a crowded field on such a surface would also be dangerous—but it isn't impossible. In April 2016, two American record holders, Shannon Rowbury (1,500 meters) and David Torrence (1,000 meters indoors), offered their support for running on snow in a cross-country event for the Winter Olympics. "If cross-country were run on snow, footing would definitely be an issue," said Rowbury. "But if the base surface were something like gravel or cinder (a surface with good grip), and the snow wasn't deep, I would consider running a short-course cross-country event at the Winter Olympics."

"In order to gain support for it, I would reach out to the coaches," added Torrence. "Talk to coaches like Renato Canova, who have a long history with the sport. See what it would take for them to voice their approval."

Coach Rosario also responded. "I would love to see cross-country in the Olympics. I understand the issue of it not being played on ice or snow but if they could make an exception, I think the Winter Games would be the better move. The thing is it's an awesome spectator sport—way better than watching a distance track in my opinion. Go to any high school state meet or go to the NCAA Championships and tell me the atmosphere is not totally crazy. Build a venue specifically for it, with spectators in mind, and you'd be hard-pressed to find a more exciting sport."

In preparing a winter course using snow or ice (the way Rowbury suggested), Rosario also offered a unique perspective: "I don't know. I sort of think we shouldn't have to 'doctor' a course to make it Olympic friendly. The beauty of cross-country is that it's run anywhere and everywhere. Hilly, flat, grass, dirt, hot, cold, snow, rain . . . doesn't matter. So in that sense I would be against changing what I see as a part of the fundamental nature of the sport."

But in terms of running the event, there were more than just format issues: politics at the International Olympic Committee (IOC) were a factor, too.

In order to maintain the Olympics' prestige, and ensure it was still feasible for one city to host all of the events, the IOC would only introduce a new sport if an existing one were removed from the program. "You have a long list of sports trying to get onto the program because it is their one way to showcase their sport to the world," explained former IOC marketing director Michael Payne. "The IOC undertakes a very detailed technical analysis to understand the popularity of the sport, the number of players, infrastructure, TV, media and then finally takes a vote to decide which new sport is welcomed onto the program."

And one man more than any other knew what it took to convince the IOC of a sport's Olympic worth. Mike Lee was the chairman of Verocom, an organization that had successfully campaigned to bring the Games to Rio in 2016, the Winter Olympics to Pyongchang in 2018, and the FIFA World Cup to Qatar in 2022. Lee and his team helped bring Rugby Sevens acceptance into the 2016 Games. It made perfect sense, then, for Verocom to spearhead cross-country's Olympic bid. "You have to look in considerable detail at, not just the sport itself, [but] what it might offer to the Olympic Games, [and] what it brings to the Olympic program," said Lee. "What do you offer to the Olympic experience? What is it your sport will do to enhance the Games, in a way which is also in line with the spirit and the values of the Games?"

Thankfully, cross-country met many of those criteria. To make it onto the Olympic program, a sport first had to be recognized: it had to be administered by an International Federation that ensured the sport's activities followed the Olympic Charter. If it was widely practiced around the world and met established standards, a recognized sport could be added to the Olympic program on the recommendation of the IOC's Olympic Program Commission. According to the Olympic Charter, every edition of the Olympics had to include "core" sports, which were chosen by the session upon proposal by the IOC Executive Board. In the summer, there were twenty-five "core" sports governed by twenty-eight federations, which included athletics events governed by the IAAF. But in the winter, the core included only sports governed by seven federations: the International Biathlon Union, the International Bobsleigh and Tobogganing Federation, the World Curling Federation, the International Ice Hockey Federation, the International Luge Federation, the International Skating Union, and the International Ski Federation.

As a result, there was more leeway in the winter games. The International Olympic Committee could recognize other sports specified by the host city, up to a maximum number of twenty-eight, provided they were in compliance with the World Anti-Doping Code. But the final decision ultimately rested with the Committee, and cross-country would have to take some special measures and receive unanimous support if it were to appear in either session of the Olympic Games.

But regardless of appeal in other formats, at present, the sport was flourishing at the youth level, and the sheer number of young men and women who ran cross-country the world over couldn't be ignored. Each participant was part of a sport two centuries old and part of a tradition of human running that stretched back hundreds of millennia.

With over half a million participants at the high school level alone in the United States in 2016, cross-country's future would be determined by today's teenagers, a group that IAAF president Sebastian Coe has addressed personally on many occasions.

"As far as I'm concerned, there is no greater sport than cross-country," Coe began at an evening at the Foot Locker High School Cross-Country Championships. "It is probably the truest and the fairest judge of human character. And if you're going to judge your athletic career on simply the loss and win tally at the end of your career, I think you'll be poorer people for it. Enjoy what you're doing, and more importantly than that, your tenure is only borrowed. You have [to] ultimately hang onto the sport, or hand off that sport to the next generation of athletes. And all I can ask of you is to make sure that you hand it over in a fairly healthy state, because it is one of the nicest sports, and I think it's up to your generation to make sure that it remains like that."

In the future, cross-country may take new directions, from inclusion in the Olympics to new markets and new venues. There's hope that Coe's call to arms will be heard, and that cross-country running will continue to make history for years to come.

Acknowledgments

My parents Peter and Neva Hutchinson deserve the utmost credit for their unyielding support and love throughout the entirety of this project. From start to finish this book would not have been possible without them. Editor Dustin Jones also deserves an enormous amount of credit—for without his expert abilities this book would not have reached a publishable level, and his dedication over months of time helped me find ways of communicating this story that few others could ever match.

A major _thank you_ to all who follow:

Julie Ganz, Alison Swety, Ronnie Alvarado, Tiffany Edson, and the entire team at Skyhorse Publishing and Carrel Books, for helping shape this masterpiece and reach its intended audience.

Craig Virgin, for his attention to the foreword of this book, and for his friendship. Mike Fanelli, for his contributions to distance running history. Enthusiasts and experts Dr. Joe Vigil, Dr. Jason Karp, Amby Burfoot, Kenny Moore, Gerry Hill of _Track and Field News_, and Andy Waterman and Matt Taylor of _METER_. Andrew Peat of _Sixth Counter_. Coaches Ben Rosario, Dena Dey Evans, and the members of the NorCal Distance Coaches' Collaborative Roundtable. The Keleher Family and the staff at A Runner's Mind in Burlingame. Supporters Hank Lawson, Liam Fayle, Doris Brown Heritage, Thelma Wright, and Trish Porter. Athletes David Torrence, Shannon Rowbury, Max King, Craig Lutz, Ryan Vail, Meb Keflezighi, Brenda Martinez, Nick Symmonds, Grant Robison, Garrett Heath, Alexi Pappas, Sara Hall, Bernard Lagat, Lauren Fleshman, Mina Samuels, and Margaret Schlachter. All members past and present of the Bay Area Running Camp.

Photographers George Aitkin, Jeff Johnson, Paul Petch, and Walt Chadwick. The creative team at Yeah Can!, Anja Merret, Christiaan Pieterse, and Kyra Pieterse. Artist and designer David Stingl, level designer Cristopher Rivas, and animator Jake Goode. Translators and friends, José Alcalá (Spanish) and Sophia Bolte (German).

Albert Caruana, Reese Willis, and all athletes past and present as members of the Crystal Springs Uplands School Cross-Country and Track and Field Program. Ed Riley, Adrian Dilley, Claudia Dilley, Gary and Pam Dilley, Bruce Wernick, David Parkinson, Mike Dailey, and all athletes past and present as members of the Sequoia High School Cross-Country and Track and Field Program.

Gordon Bliss, Ross Headley, Rob Dean, and the members, staff, and trainers of Mobius Fit in Redwood City.

Stanford University, the Cecil H. Green Library, and especially Linda Paulson and the Stanford Master of Liberal Arts Program. Peter Berg and Michigan State University Library.

Lake Forest College Cross-Country athletic department, staff, teammates, and comrades past and present.

The staff and students of Crystal Springs Uplands School in Hillsborough California, with special mention for Amy Richards, Christy Dillon, Andrew Davis, Michael Flynn, Kent Holubar, Peter Kovas, Debra Hunt, Nathan Ladd, Oriana Isaacson, Kara Sargent, Lauren Vargas, Vicky Mann-Hauer, John Hauer, and Julie Daughtry.

The staff and students of Sequoia High School in Redwood City California, with special mention for Lisa Ellerbee Gleaton, Melissa Schmidt Klingenberg, Corey Uhalde, Karin Zarcone, Steve Picchi, and Rob Poulos.

To all who have supported me along this journey: author Jenna Moreci, Cliff Tomlin, Gilbert Tinoco and the Fancy Breed family, Gordon, Lynn, Alex and Alyssa Bliss, the Boyd family, the Johnson family, the Wike family, the Arnout-Smith family, the Hawley family, the Popp family, Travis, Christina, Nick and Chris Gentry (and Silas), the Parvin family, Ulises and Claire, Gary Shoup, Zachary Corbin, Laura Monique Ordonez, the Henson family, and to Natalie Abold and Lana Mae Cortez. I love you all and I've valued, every moment, the support you have given me throughout the previous five years to help this book reach its intended audience.

Now go for a run and be free as nature intended.

Bibliography

Chapter 1: 1800–1850

Castellini, Ottavio. "Grandfathers and Great-Grandfathers of Cross-Country." *IAAF General News*, March 22, 2007.

Crego, Robert. *Sports and Games of the 18th and 19th Centuries.* Westport, CT/London: Greenwood Publishing Group, 2003, 63–64.

Hughes, Thomas. *Tom Brown's School-Days.* 6th ed. London/New York: Harper and Brothers, 1857, c1911, 145.

Melly, George. *School Experiences of a Fag at a Private and a Public School.* London: Smith, Elder and Co., 1854, 141.

Robinson, Roger. "On the Scent of History: Tracing Cross-Country Running's True Origins." *Running Times Magazine,* December 1998, 28.

———. "The Origins of Cross-Country: Hares, Hounds and Hurdles." *Running Times Magazine,* September 13, 2009.

Rouse, William Henry Denham. *A History of Rugby School.* London: Duckworth, 1898, 270.

Ryan, James. *Annals of Thames Hare and Hounds, 1868-1945.* London: Thames Hare and Hounds, December 1968.

Shearman, Montague. *Athletics and Football.* London: Longmans, Green, 1887.

Shrewsbury School Pupils et al. *The Hound Books of the Royal Shrewsbury School Hunt.* Shrewsbury, 1831.

Strutt, Joseph. *The Sports and Pastimes of the People of England: From the Earliest Period, Including the Rural and Domestic Recreations, May Games, Mummeries, Pageants, Processions and Pompous Spectacles.* London: Methuen and Co., 1801, 301.

Thomson, Alice. "Outdoors: Manhunt on the Fells—The Victorians Kept This Savage Sport Secret; Today's Anti-hunting Zealots Might Like to Ban It." *The Daily Telegraph,* June 27, 1998.

Chapter 2: 1850–1870

Burfoot, Amby. "Common Ground: Better Known for Aces than Races, Wimbledon Was the Birthplace of Both Tennis and Cross-Country." *Runner's World Magazine,* July 2006, 92.

Crowther, Samuel, and Arthur Brown Ruhl. *Rowing and Track Athletics.* New York and London: MacMillan Company, 1905, 347.

Radford, Peter. "The Land a Time Forgot." *The Observer,* May 1, 2004.

Ryan, James. *Annals of Thames Hare and Hounds, 1868-1945.* London: Thames Hare and Hounds, December 1968.

Shearman, Montague. *Athletics and Football.* London: Longmans, Green, 1887, 41, 371.

Smith, Ronald A. *Sports and Freedom: The Rise of Big-Time College Athletics.* Oxford University Press, December 27, 1990, 101.

Walsh, John Henry. *British Rural Sports* (originally published as *Manual of British Rural Sports,* by Stonehenge). London, New York: G. Routledge, 1857. 3rd Edition, 1900.

Chapter 3: The 1870s

Baynes, Ernest Harold. "Cross-Country Running." *Outing Magazine,* April 1902, 185.

———. "The History of Cross-Country Running in America." *Outing Magazine,* March 1894.

Griffin, Padraig. *The Politics of Irish Athletics, 1850-1990.* Marathon Publications, 1990.

New York Times. "Cross-Country Running: A Sport Becoming Popular Among Athletes." February 19, 1893.

Rogers, Gareth. *Fleet and Free: A History of Birchfield Harriers Athletic Club.* The History Press Ltd., 2005.

Ryan, James. *Annals of Thames Hare and Hounds, 1868-1945.* London: Thames Hare and Hounds, December 1968.

Smith, Ronald A. *Sports and Freedom: The Rise of Big-Time College Athletics.* Oxford University Press, December 27, 1990.

Telfer, Hamish McDonald. *The Origins, Governance and Social Structure of Club Cross-Country Running in Scotland, 1885–1914.* The University of Stirling, February 2006.

Chapter 4: The 1880s

Baynes, Ernest Harold. "The History of Cross-Country Running in America." *Outing Magazine,* March 1894.

Carter, E. C. "Cross-Country Runners Ahoy! How the Great Sport Has Grown in England and America." *New York Herald,* March 9, 1890, 21.

Donahue, Bill. "Rise of a Running Nation." *Runner's World Magazine,* July 2015.

Griffin, Padraig. *The Politics of Irish Athletics, 1850-1990.* Marathon Publications, 1990.

Hadgraft, Rob. *Beer and Brine: The Making of Walter George, Athletics' First Superstar.* Southend-on-Sea, Essex, UK: Desert Island Books, 2006.

Kidd, Bruce. "Muscular Christianity and Value-Centred Sport: The Legacy of Tom Brown in Canada." *International Journal of the History of Sport* 23 (2006): 701–13.

Korsgaard, Robert. *A History of the Amateur Athletic Union of the United States.* Teachers College, Columbia University, 1952.

Molden, Simon. "Varsity History." *The Oxford University Cross-Country Club.* http://bit.ly/2e3AWJC (accessed 2014).

New York Spirit of the Times. "The Cross-Country Championship," November 7, 1883.

New York Times. "Cross-Country Runners, Athletes Who Chase Through Swamp and Woodland." April 18, 1892.

Nielsen, Erik. *Decentred Britons: Amateurism and Athletics in Australasia and Beyond.* Sydney, Australia: The University of New South Wales, 2011.

Orton, George. *Distance and Cross-Country Running.* New York: American Sports Publishing Company, May 1903, 59.

Outing Magazine. "The New York Athletic Club." September 1884.

Ryan, James. *Annals of Thames Hare and Hounds, 1868-1945.* London: Thames Hare and Hounds, December 1968.

Telfer, Hamish McDonald. *The Origins, Governance and Social Structure of Club Cross-Country Running in Scotland, 1885–1914.* The University of Stirling, February 2006.

World: New York. "The Athletes Great Day. The First American Cross-Country Race Run at Inwood." November 7, 1883.

Chapter 5: The 1890s

American Digest System. "Ruhl v. Ware." *Century Edition of the American Digest: A Complete Digest of All Reported American Cases from the Earliest Times [1658] to 1896.* West Publishing Company, 898.

Association of Road Racing Statisticians. http://www.arrs.net.

Baynes, Ernest Harold. "Cross-Country Running." *Outing Magazine,* April 1902, 185.

Bedichek, Roy. *Educational Competition: The Story of the University Interscholastic League of Texas.* University of Texas Press, January 1, 1956.

Brooklyn Daily Eagle. "Prospect Harriers Win–Champions in the Greatest of Cross-Country Runs." April 26, 1891.

Bushnell, Edward Rogers. *The History of Athletics at the University of Pennsylvania: 1896.* Athletic Association of the University of Pennsylvania, 1909.

Cozens, Frederick W., and Florence Scovil Stumpf. *Sports in American Life.* Chicago: University of Chicago Press, 1953.

Griffin, Padraig. *The Politics of Irish Athletics, 1850-1990.* Marathon Publications, 1990.

Hewett, Waterman Thomas, Frank R. Holmes, Lewis A. Williams, and Lewis A. Williams Jr. *Cornell University: A History.* The University Publishing Society, 1905.

"International Match. England v. France." *Press,* Volume LV, Issue 10037, May 16, 1898.

Korsgaard, Robert. *A History of the Amateur Athletic Union of the United States.* Teachers College, Columbia University, 1952.

Lucas, John A. "George Washington Orton." *Journal of Olympic History*, September 2000, 24.

New York Evening Post. "College of the City of New York." March 7, 1890.

New York Times. "The Cross-Country Run–G. W. Orton an Easy Winner of the Amateur Championship at Morris Park." April 3, 1898.

New York Times. "Cross-Country Running: A Sport Becoming Popular Among Athletes." February 19, 1893.

New York Times. "In the Athletic World, Events of Local and General Interest." April 7, 1889.

New York Times. "Running on Muddy Ground–W. D. Day Wins the Cross-Country Championship." April 27, 1890.

New York Times. "Sports of the Athletes." July 30, 1889.

Orton, George. *Distance and Cross-Country Running.* New York: American Sports Publishing Company, May 1903, 59.

Presbrey, Frank, and James Hugh Moffatt. *Athletics at Princeton: A History.* Frank Presbrey Company, 1901.

Pruter, Robert. "The Beginnings of Cross-Country." *The Illinois High School Association.* http://bit.ly/2emlEwu (accessed 2016).

Richardson, Lawrence N. *Jubilee History of the International Cross-Country Union 1903-1953.* 1st ed. International Cross-Country Union, 1953.

Rogers, Gareth. *Fleet and Free: A History of Birchfield Harriers Athletic Club.* The History Press Ltd., 2005.

Ryan, James. *Annals of Thames Hare and Hounds, 1868-1945.* London: Thames Hare and Hounds, December 1968.

Smith, Ronald A. *Sports and Freedom: The Rise of Big-Time College Athletics.* Oxford University Press, December 27, 1990.

Tarbotton, David, Ron Bendall, Paul Jenes, Trevor Vincent, et al. "A Short History of the Australian Cross-Country Championships." *Athletics NSW*, August 27, 2009. http://bit.ly/2en9tj4.

Telfer, Hamish McDonald. *The Origins, Governance and Social Structure of Club Cross-Country Running in Scotland, 1885–1914.* The University of Stirling, February, 2006.

Thomson, Alice. "Outdoors: Manhunt on the Fells—The Victorians Kept This Savage Sport Secret; Today's Anti-hunting Zealots Might Like to Ban It." *The Daily Telegraph*, June 27, 1998.

Chapter 6: The 1900s

Hadgraft, Rob. *The Little Wonder: The Untold Story of Alfred Shrubb, World Champion Runner.* Southend-on-Sea, Essex, UK: Desert Island Books, 2004.

Hewett, Waterman Thomas, Frank R. Holmes, Lewis A. Williams, and Lewis A. Williams Jr. *Cornell University: A History.* The University Publishing Society, 1905.

Nielsen, Erik. *Decentred Britons: Amateurism and Athletics in Australasia and Beyond.* Sydney, Australia: The University of New South Wales, March 2011.

Pruter, Robert. *The Rise of American High School Sports and the Search for Control, 1880-1930.* Syracuse University Press, 2013, 139.

Richardson, Lawrence N. 1st ed. *Jubilee History of the International Cross-Country Union 1903-1953.* International Cross-Country Union, 1953.

Shrubb, Alfred. *Long Distance Running and Training.* The Imperial News Company, 1909.

Spitz, Barry. *Dipsea, The Greatest Race.* San Anselmo, CA: Potrero Meadow, 1993.

Sullivan, James Edward. *Spalding's Official Athletic Almanac.* American Sports Publishing Company, 1910.

Tarbotton, David, Ron Bendall, Paul Jenes, Trevor Vincent, et al. "A Short History of the Australian Cross-Country Championships." *Athletics NSW*, August 27, 2009. http://bit.ly/2en9tj4.

Cultural Spotlight: The Olympic Movement

Hadgraft, Rob. *The Little Wonder: The Untold Story of Alfred Shrubb, World Champion Runner.* Southend-on-Sea, Essex, UK: Desert Island Books, 2004.

Reineri, Giorgio. "Athletics—Specialties: Cross-Country." *The Italian Encyclopedia of Sports*, 2004.

Richardson, Lawrence N. 1st ed. *Jubilee History of the International Cross-Country Union 1903-1953.* International Cross-Country Union, 1953.

Rogers, Gareth. *Fleet and Free: A History of Birchfield Harriers Athletic Club.* The History Press Ltd., 2005.

Chapter 7: The 1910s

Association of Road Racing Statisticians. http://www.arrs.net.

Bergvall, Erik, and Edward Adams-Ray. *The Official Report of the Olympic Games of Stockholm 1912*. Stockholm: Wahlström and Widstrand, 1913.

Bloom, Marc. "A Century of Testing Runners' Speed and Spirit." *New York Times*, October 12, 2012.

Cross-Country Running. Mountain View, CA: World Publications, 1978.

Hannus, Matti. *Flying Finns: Story of the Great Tradition of Finnish Distance Running and Cross-Country Skiing*. Tietosanoma Publishing, 1990.

Krise, Raymond, and Bill Squires. *Fast Tracks: The History of Distance Running*. S. Greene Press, 1982.

Martin, Chuck. "The History of Massachusetts Cross-Country." *MileSplit Massachusetts*, November 16, 2011. http://bit.ly/2ejDuAX.

Murphy, Michael C. *Athletic Training*. C. Scribner Publishing, 1914.

New York Times. "Gianakopulos Wins From Kolehmainen." January 9, 1916.

New York Tribune. "Morris High Leads Big School Pack–Wins Cross-Country Title Over Stiff Course for Second Year in a Row." December 8, 1912.

Real Federacion Espanola de Atletismo. "Breve Historia Del Campeonato Ds Espana De Campo a Traves" (A Brief History of the Spanish Cross-Country Championship). http://bit.ly/2ectsAq.

Richardson, Lawrence N. 1st ed. *Jubilee History of the International Cross-Country Union 1903-1953*. International Cross-Country Union, 1953.

Seibold, Jack. *Spartan Sports Encyclopedia: A History of the Michigan State Men's Athletic Program*. Skyhorse Publishing, Inc., Nov 18, 2014.

Squire, Jesse. "Great Cross-Country Courses: Van Cortlandt Park." *Track and Field Superfan*, October 21, 2012. http://bit.ly/2f53h0T.

Telfer, Hamish McDonald. *The Origins, Governance and Social Structure of Club Cross-Country Running in Scotland, 1885–1914*. The University of Stirling, February 2006.

Wisnieski, Adam. "Park Watchers at Crossroads Over Trail's History." *Riverdale Press*, October 17, 2012.

Chapter 8: The 1920s

Downes, Steven. "A History of Kenyan Cross-Country Running." *IAAF General News*, March 2007.

Hannus, Matti. *Flying Finns: Story of the Great Tradition of Finnish Distance Running and Cross-Country Skiing*. Tietosanoma Publishing, 1990.

Havitz, Mark E., and Eric D. Zemper. "Worked Out in Infinite Detail: Michigan State College's Lauren P. Brown and the Origins of the NCAA Cross-Country Championships." *Michigan Historical Review* 39 (2013): 1–39.

Havitz, Mark E., Eric D. Zemper, and Ryan Snelgrove. *Detailed Vision: Lauren P. Brown and the NCAA Cross-Country Championships*. North American Society for Sport History, Coronado Springs Resort and Convention Center, Walt Disney World, Florida, May 31, 2010.

Henderson, Jason. "From Paper Chase to Steeplechase: A Short History of Cross-Country Running." *Athletics Weekly* (2001): 18–21.

Krise, Raymond, and Bill Squires. *Fast Tracks: The History of Distance Running*. S. Greene Press, 1982.

New York Times. "British Harriers Conquer Cornell." December 31, 1920.

Ominde, Simeon Hongo, Kenneth Ingham, and Mwenda Ntarangwi. "Kenya: The East Africa Protectorate." *Encyclopedia Britannica*. Encyclopedia Britannica, 2014.

Richardson, Lawrence N. 1st ed. *Jubilee History of the International Cross-Country Union 1903-1953*. International Cross-Country Union, 1953.

Stone, David. *Yank Brown, Cross-Country Runner*. New York: Barse and Company, 1922.

Cultural Spotlight: Women in Cross-Country Running

Bauer, Thomas. *La Sportive dans la littérature française des Années folles* (Sport in French Literature During the Roaring Twenties). Presses Universities Septentrion, 2011, 32.

Leigh, Mary H. and Thérèse M. Bonin. "The Pioneering Role of Madame Alice Milliat and the FSFI in Establishing International Track and Field Competition for Women." *Journal of Sport History* 4 (1977): 72–83.

Robinson, Roger. "Women in Mud, The Rise of Women's Cross-Country." *Running Times*, December 2008, 12.

Rogers, Gareth. *Fleet and Free: A History of Birchfield Harriers Athletic Club*. The History Press Ltd., 2005.

Ward, Gwenda. "Women's Sport—The Foundations." *Women On Track*, April 2013. http://bit.ly/2f68Xrz.

Chapter 9: The 1930s

Association of Road Racing Statisticians. http://www.arrs.net.

Crowley, Joseph N. *In the Arena, the NCAA's First Century*. NCAA Publications, September 2006.

Foster, Brendan, and Cliff Temple. *Brendan Foster*. London: Heinemann Publishing, 1978.

Havitz, Mark E., and Eric D. Zemper. "Worked Out in Infinite Detail: Michigan State College's Lauren P. Brown and the Origins of the NCAA Cross-Country Championships." *Michigan Historical Review* 39 (2013): 1–39.

Havitz, Mark E., Eric D. Zemper, and Ryan Snelgrove. *Detailed Vision: Lauren P. Brown and the NCAA Cross-Country Championships*. North American Society for Sport History, Coronado Springs Resort and Convention Center, Walt Disney World, Florida, May 31, 2010.

"History." Union Sports San Vittore Olona, Italy. http://bit.ly/2vGOZeL.

Lash, Don. *The Iron Man from Indiana: the Don Lash Story*. Paducah, Kentucky, Turner Publications, 1999.

Martin, Chuck. "The History of Massachusetts Cross-Country." *MileSplit Massachusetts*, November 16, 2011. http://bit.ly/2ejDuAX.

O'Neil, Paul. "Duel of the Four Minute Men: Bannister surges to victory in the heart-stirring Vancouver mile." *Sports Illustrated*, August 16, 1954.

Richardson, Lawrence N. 1st ed. *Jubilee History of the International Cross-Country Union 1903-1953*. International Cross-Country Union, 1st edition, 1953.

Rogers, Gareth. *Fleet and Free: A History of Birchfield Harriers Athletic Club*. The History Press Ltd., 2005.

Shippen, Clive. "Arthur Penny 1907-2003." *Belgrave Harriers*, November 2003. http://bit.ly/2v35sue.

Taylor, Simon. "Run of The Mills." *Runner's World UK Event Editorial*, May 28, 2004.

Turnbull, Simon. "Athletics: Magical Memories of Those Olden Holden Golden Days." *Independent*, January 10, 2004.

Chapter 10: The 1940s

Anderson, Bob, and Joe Henderson. *The Varied World of Cross-Country*. Mountain View, CA: Runner's World Publishing, 1971.

Association of Road Racing Statisticians. http://www.arrs.net.

Cobley, John. "Profile: Emil Zatopek." *Racing Past*, May 2012.

Dutch, Taylor. "Mt. SAC XC Invite: 67 Years Strong." *FloTrack*, October 23, 2014.

Mt. San Antonio College. "A History and a Philosophy" and "The Real Story." Excerpts from the *1996 Mt. SAC Cross-Country Invitational Meet Program*. Rhags Nternationale, 1996. http://bit.ly/2eNcabp.

Richardson, Lawrence N. *Jubilee History of the International Cross-Country Union 1903-1953*. 1st ed. International Cross-Country Union, 1953.

Rogers, Gareth. *Fleet and Free: A History of Birchfield Harriers Athletic Club*. The History Press Ltd., 2005.

Ryan, James. *Annals of Thames Hare and Hounds, 1868-1945*. Thames Hare and Hounds, December 1968.

University of Rhode Island. "Robert J. Black (Class of 1950)." *University of Rhode Island Athletic Department Hall of Fame*, 1972.

Chapter 11: The 1950s

Aitken, Alistair. "Frank Sando: One of Britain's Greatest Cross-Country Runners Remembered." *Active Training World UK*, February 18, 2013.

Archives Départementales de la Seine-Saint-Denis. *8eme Cross De L'Humanite (Le)* (The 8th Cross De L'Humanite), 1945. http://bit.ly/2dSIbhe.

Association of Road Racing Statisticians. http://www.arrs.net.

Athletics Australia. "Vale—Dave Power." February 3, 2014. http://bit.ly/2dPQP07.

Ayers, Ed. *The Longest Race: A Lifelong Runner, An Iconic Ultramarathon, and the Case for Human Endurance*. The Experiment Publishing, August 2013.

Bloom, Marc. *Cross-Country Running*. Mountain View, CA: World Publications, 1978.

Cobley, John. "Dave Power: Profile," "Gordon Pirie: Profile," "Murray Halberg: Profile," "Profile: Emil Zatopek," "Profile: Vladimir Kuts." *Racing Past*, May 2012.

Cohen, Gary. "Interview with Don Gehrmann." *Gary Cohen Running*, March 2011. http://bit.ly/2faCZLA.

———. "Interview with Horace Ashenfelter." *Gary Cohen Running*, July 2010. http://bit.ly/2eeDVJU.

Echenoz, Jean. *Running: A Novel*. The New Press, 2013.

Ellick, Adam B. "Emil Zatopek." *Running Times Magazine*, March 1, 2001.

Elsesser, Michael R. *Echoes of Footprints: Racing Through the Years at Crystal Springs*. Athleteka Communications Group, May 2002.

Havitz, Mark E., Eric D. Zemper, and Ryan Snelgrove. *Detailed Vision: Lauren P. Brown and the NCAA Cross-Country Championships*. North American Society for Sport History, Coronado Springs Resort and Convention Center, Walt Disney World, Florida, May 31, 2010.

Heidenstrom, Peter. "Harriers and Cross-Country Running." *An Encyclopedia of New Zealand*. The Ministry of Culture and Heritage, 1966.

King, Perry. "The Starting Line: How One Meeting In Schenectady Changed XC Forever." *MileSplit New York*, July 6, 2015. http://bit.ly/2dQ3xMq.

Krise, Raymond, and Bill Squires. *Fast Tracks: The History of Distance Running*. S. Greene Press, 1982.

Livingstone, Keith. *Healthy Intelligent Training: The Proven Principles of Arthur Lydiard*. Meyer and Meyer Verlag, 2010, 167.

McCollough, J. Brady. "Olympian Billy Mills: A Long Road to Kansas." *Wichita Eagle*, April 18, 2010. http://bit.ly/2dLOJmw.

McMurran, Alistair. "Athletics: Timely Tribute to Otago Running Great." *Otago Daily Times*, June 3, 2009.

Michigan State Cross-Country and Track and Field. "Cross-Country History." *Michigan State University Cross-Country and Track and Field Program*, 2007–2008. http://bit.ly/2e0CCRa.

Nelson Mail. "Glory Days on the Grass Track." March 14, 2009. http://bit.ly/2eA4ZXi.

Panama City News-Herald. "Zatopek Wins Another Race." April 27, 1954, 5.

Sciences Sociales et Sport n° 5. Editions L'Harmattan, 2012.

Pirie, Gordon. *Running Fast and Injury Free*. Dr. John S. Gilbody, 1996.

Richardson, Lawrence N. *Jubilee History of the International Cross-Country Union 1903-1953*. 1st ed. International Cross-Country Union, 1953.

Ryan, James. *Annals of Thames Hare and Hounds, 1868-1945*. London: Thames Hare and Hounds, December 1968.

Schovánek, Dav. "Spring In Paris." *Bezecka Skola*, January 2014.

Williamson, Bill. "Dave Power." *Kembla Joggers Association*, March 2012.

Chapter 12: The 1960s

Aitkin, Alastair. "Basil Heatley The Great Road/CC/Track Runner." *Highgate Harriers, Alastair's Reports*, May 2012.

Anderson, Bob, and Joe Henderson. *The Varied World of Cross-Country*. Mountain View, CA: Runner's World Publishing, 1971.

Bishop, Greg. "The Longest Run: The Story of Gerry Lindgren." *Seattle Times*, November 26, 2005.

Bloom, Marc. *Cross-Country Running*. Mountain View, CA: World Publications, 1978.

Brown, Gary. "San Jose's Historic Feet." *Champion Digital, the NCAA*, October 29, 2012.

Butcher, Pat. "Batty by Name." *Globe Runner*, 2012.

Cobley, John. "Profile: Basil Heatley," "Ron Hill Profile Part 1 and 2." *Racing Past*, May 2012.

Coe, Robert. "Forty-Two Years Ago Tuesday: Pac-8 Cross-Ctry Championship: Pre & Lindgren: A MEMOIR." *LetsRun Message Board*, November 2011. http://bit.ly/2fqetFD.

Cohen, Gary. "Interview with Ron Hill." *Gary Cohen Running*, December 2008. http://bit.ly/2dXerzX.

Downes, Steven. "A History of Kenyan Cross-Country Running." *IAAF General News*, March 2007.

Eggers, Kerry. "Barefoot Champion Heeds Call of the Wild." *Portland Tribune*, July 3, 2006.

Franks, Cliff. "Basil Heatley." *The Birmingham and District Invitation Cross-Country League*, October 22, 2011.

Havitz, Mark E., Eric D. Zemper, and Ryan Snelgrove. *Detailed Vision: Lauren P. Brown and the NCAA Cross-Country Championships*. North American Society for Sport History, Coronado Springs Resort and Convention Center, Walt Disney World, Florida, May 31, 2010.

Hoover, Brett. "Stephen Machooka." *The Ivy League at 50*, October 19, 2006.

Kissane, John A. "A Commitment to Excellence—The Long Run of Doris Brown Heritage." *Running Times Magazine*, November 1, 2002.

Moore, Kenny. *Bowerman and the Men of Oregon: The Story of Oregon's Legendary Coach and Nike's Cofounder*. Rodale Books, September 2007.

Musca, Michael. "In the Beginning: Steve Prefontaine's High School Days." *Running Times Magazine*, October 2006, 42.

Myslenski, Skip. "A PTA Meeting is Tougher." *Sports Illustrated*, December 8, 1969.

Richardson, Lawrence N. *Jubilee History of the International Cross-Country Union 1903-1953*. 1st ed. International Cross-Country Union, 1953.

Road Runners Club of America. "History of Road Runners Club of America." 2009. http://bit.ly/2dWHiV5.

Tanser, Toby. *Train Hard, Win Easy: The Kenyan Way*. Track and Field News Press, June 1, 1997.

Tuluwami, Haile. "Abebe Bikila: The Black African Breakthrough." *First Race I Can Remember*, January 2012. http://bit.ly/2fpDPU2.

Turrini, Joseph M. *The End of Amateurism in American Track and Field*. Urbana: University of Illinois Press, 2010.

Underwood, John. "Chasing Girls Through a Park." *Sports Illustrated*, December 5, 1966.

Wolde, Bezabih, and Benoit Guadin. "The Institutional Organization of Ethiopian Athletics." *Annales d'Ethiopie* 23 (2007–2008): 471–93. http://bit.ly/2eXqjV9.

Your Thurrock News. "Ken Batty: One of founding members of Thurrock Harriers passes away." October 24, 2012.

Chapter 13: The 1970s

Aitkin, Alastair. "Three of Histories Greatest milers—Part 2—John Walker." *Highgate Harriers, Alastair's Reports*, May 2011.

Anderson, Bob, and Joe Henderson. *The Varied World of Cross-Country*. Mountain View, CA: Runner's World Publishing, 1971.

Bale, John. *The Brawn Drain: Foreign Student-Athletes in American Universities*. University of Illinois Press, 1991.

Barbour, John. "Athlete of the Year, Henry Rono." *Track and Field News*, January 1979. http://bit.ly/2foi87D.

Bloom, Marc. "Cross-Country for Grown-Ups: 10 Reasons to Race Cross-Country." *Running Times Magazine*, August 2009.

———. *Cross-Country Running*. Mountain View, CA: World Publications, 1978.

Bosch, Ed. "Remembering the 41st NCAA X-C Championships; Rono vs Salazar at Lehigh." *MileSplit Pennsylvania*, December 22, 2010.

Brant, John. "Frank's Story." *Runner's World Magazine*, October 2011.

———. "The Rookie." *Running Times Magazine*, March 28, 2012.

Burns, Jane. "Peg Neppel Darrah." *Des Moines Register*, accessed September, 2017. http://dmreg.co/2eDERNG.

Cohen, Gary. "Interview with Craig Virgin." *Gary Cohen Running*, August 2010. http://bit.ly/2eIGZRR.

Desmond, John. "Irish 'involvement' in the 1973 World Cross-Country Championships." *Running in Cork*, November 2012.

Eder, Larry. "Considering Eric Hulst." *RunBlogRun*, March 23, 2010.

Ferstle, Jim. "The Magic of Maywood Park." *Running Times Magazine*, July 12, 2011.

Gilmore, Robert. "The World Mile Record Holder, John Walker, Tries to Come Back After a Crippling Leg Injury." *People Magazine*, June 1979.

Glendale Community College Athletic Hall of Fame. "Robert Thomas, Outstanding Athletic Achievement." January 2009. http://bit.ly/2e8xKJI.

Goater, Julian, and Don Melvin. *The Art of Running Faster*. Human Kinetics Press, 2012.

Hendershott, Jon. "Nor-Cal Portrait: Meet Rich Kimball." *Nor-Cal Running Review*, December 1973.

Henderson, Joe. "Shorter Reaches an Impasse." *Runner's World Magazine*, January 1975.

Hollister, Geoff. *Out of Nowhere: The Inside Story of How Nike Marketed the Culture of Running*. Meyer and Meyer Sport, April, 2008.

International Directory of Company Histories, Vol. 14. St. James Press, 1996.

Krise, Raymond, and Bill Squires. *Fast Tracks: The History of Distance Running*. S. Greene Press, 1982.

Leivers, Carl. "Foreign Territory." *Running Times Magazine*, November 5, 2012.

Moore, Kenny. *Bowerman and the Men of Oregon: The Story of Oregon's Legendary Coach and Nike's Cofounder*. Rodale Books, September 2007.

Morrow, Steven. "Athlete Feature 17—Nick Rose." *trackboundUSA*, November 28, 2011.

Newman, Michael. "Put Your Hand On Seven: A Journey to a State Championship." *DyeStat Illinois*, October 07, 2013. http://bit.ly/2e1491E.

O'Reilly, Jean, and Susan K. Cahn. *Women and Sports in the United States: A Documentary Reader*. Boston, MA: Northeastern University, Center for the Study of Sport in Society, UPNE, 2007.

Robbins, William G. "Rudy Chapa (1957-)." *The Oregon Encyclopedia, A Project of the Oregon Historical Society*, August 2014.

Robinson, Roger. "How World Cross Went Off Course." *Running Times Magazine*, March 2012.

Speck, Doug. "Mt. SAC Invitational, A History 25 years ago, 1978—A Magical Year." *DyeStat California*, October 10, 2003.

The Spokesman-Review. "AAU Harriers, Nick Rose Winner." November 26, 1977.

Stephens, Joy. "Rod Dixon." *Wild Tomato Magazine*, 2007. http://bit.ly/2f0PaGO.

Surrey County Athletic Association. "Profile for Bernard Ford." 2016. http://bit.ly/2enpw0J.

Taylor, Aron. "1979 National Team Championship, Largo HS, FL vs. Astronaut HS, FL." *Milesplit USA*, September 30, 2013.

Taylor, Aron. "Team USA, The Journey to Gold—Part 3: Defining the Moment." *MileSplit USA*, March 9, 2011.

———. "Team USA, The Journey to Gold—Part 4: A Sweet Spot in Time." *MileSplit USA*, March 16, 2011.

———. "XC Legacy Special Edition: 1977 Harrier National Rankings." *MileSplit USA*, March 26, 2010.

———. "XC Legacy: 1978 Boys National XC Rankings." *MileSplit USA*, March 01, 2010.

Temple, Cliff. *Cross-Country and Road Running*. Hutchinson Publishing, 1980.

Troy, Marcus. "The Athletics West Club." *Nike Sportswear*, 2012. http://bit.ly/2f9e4EX.

Turrini, Joseph M. *The End of Amateurism in American Track and Field*. Urbana: University of Illinois Press, 2010.

Cultural Spotlight: Kit, Equipment, and Technology

British Pathé. "History of British Pathé." http://bit.ly/2edIlQo.

Bogle, Dustin. "History of Track Spikes." *The Livestrong Foundation*, February 2014.

Canham, Don. *Cross-Country Running*. London: Herbert-Jenkins Limited, 1954.

Hollister, Geoff. *Out of Nowhere: The Inside Story of How Nike Marketed the Culture of Running.* Meyer and Meyer Sport, April, 2008.

Hughes, Thomas. *Tom Brown's School-Days.* 6th ed. London/New York: Harper and Brothers, 1857, c1911, 145.

Kippen, Cameron. *The History of Sport Shoes.* Perth, WA: Dept. of Podiatry, Health Science, Curtin, 1999.

Shearman, Montague. *Athletics and Football.* London: Longmans, Green, 1887.

Temple, Cliff. *Cross-Country and Road Running.* Hutchinson Publishing, 1980.

Turrini, Joseph M. *The End of Amateurism in American Track and Field.* Urbana: University of Illinois Press, 2010.

Chapter 14: The 1980s

Association of Road Racing Statisticians. http://www.arrs.net.

Bedics, Mark. "Not Perfect, But Close Enough, UTEP's Mere 17 Points in 1981 Still NCAA Championship Best." *NCAA Publications*, October 11, 2011.

Castro, Rich. "Track and Field News Interview: Carlos Lopes." *Track and Field News*, November 1984.

Cohen, Gary. "Interview with Craig Virgin." *Gary Cohen Running*, August 2010. http://bit.ly/2eIGZRR.

Daniels, Jack Tupper. "RE: Athletics West." *LetsRun Message Board*, May 10, 2009. http://bit.ly/2f3fY9g.

Green, Trevor. "Former Grimsby Harrier Royle Reigned Over the World's Best." *Grimsby Telegraph*, January 2011.

Hosick, Michelle. "Equal Opportunity Knocks, National Girls and Women in Sports Day Celebrates 25th year." *NCAA Publications*, February 2, 2011.

Kissane, John A. "A Conversation with Tim Hutchings." *Running Times Magazine*, August 2013.

Mable, Dave. "30th Anniversary of the Tragedy of the 1985 Iowa State Women's Cross-Country." *Iowa Momentum Magazine*, October 2015.

Maloney, Andrew. *John McDonnell: The Most Successful Coach in NCAA History.* University of Arkansas Press, April 2013.

Metzler, Brian. "How Steve Jones Ran His Way to Legendary Status." *Competitor Magazine*, October 21, 2014.

Moore, Kenny. "It was a Muddy Good Show of Teamwork." *Sports Illustrated*, March 28, 1983.

———. "Running On A Rocky Mountain High? Colorado's Pat Porter, U.S. Cross-Country Champ Since 1982, is an Athlete Truly in His Element." *Sports Illustrated*, March 17, 1986.

———. "The Battle Went to Royle." *Sports Illustrated*, December 7, 1981.

New York Times. "Porter is Surprise Cross-Country Victor." November 29, 1982.

Noden, Merrell. "Leader of the Pack." *Sports Illustrated*, March 30, 1992.

———. "Return of the Crusher." *Sports Illustrated*, December 4, 1989.

———. "She's the Queen of Hill and Dale." *Sports Illustrated*, November 26, 1990.

Shapiro, Michael. "Focus is on Ethiopia Runners." *The New York Times*, March 25, 1984.

Tanser, Toby. *Train Hard, Win Easy: The Kenyan Way.* Mountain View California: Track and Field News Press, June 1, 1997.

Temple, Cliff. *Cross-Country and Road Running.* Hutchinson Publishing, 1980.

Turrini, Joseph M. *The End of Amateurism in American Track and Field.* Urbana: University of Illinois Press, 2010.

Waldron, Jon. "The Strange Case of Fernando Mamede." *The Runner Eclectic Online*, July 3, 2007. http://bit.ly/2wNSFZ7

Chapter 15: The 1990s

Butcher, Pat. "The Last Gasp." *Running Times Magazine*, August 7, 2012.

Flotrack, FloSports Inc. "Colorado: The Program." November 2014.

Gault, Jonathan. "Sonia O'Sullivan Shares Her Training Log with LetsRun.com—How Did the Villanova Grad Win the World Cross-Country Title (Twice) in 1998?" *LetsRun.com*, May 21, 2015. http://bit.ly/2wK297E

Hovland, Sam. "Perfection with a Look for Adams State." *NCAA Publications*, December 2011.

Lear, Chris. *Running with the Buffaloes: A Season Inside With Mark Wetmore, Adam Goucher, and the University of Colorado Men's Cross-Country Team.* New York: Lyons Press, 2000.

LetsRun Message Board. "25 YEARS AGO TODAY: The last NCAA XC Double All-American." November 2015. http://bit.ly/2fqshNY.

Longman, Jere. "The King of the Mile." *The New York Times*, May 4, 2000.

Maloney, Andrew. *John McDonnell: The Most Successful Coach in NCAA History*. University of Arkansas Press, April 2013.

Mulligan, Kevin. "Villanova Coach Has Life Back on Track." *Philadelphia Daily News*, June 3, 1988.

NCAA. "Women's Cross-Country Races Getting Longer." *NCAA Publications*, September 15, 1997.

Noden, Merrell. "Leader of the Pack." *Sports Illustrated*, March 30, 1992.

Raybould, James. "Nike Farm Team Gearing Up for Oracle U.S. Open, U.S. Outdoor Track & Field Championships." *The Track and Field Foundation*, May 1, 2003.

Rowlerson, Greg. *Moroccan Success; The Kada Way*. Chipmunk Publishing Ltd., June 2011.

Stanton, Alex. "How to Follow in Paula's Footsteps." *BBC Sport: Athletics*, April 2006.

Sturtz, Rachel. "Bob Kennedy and Todd Williams Look Back." *Running Times Magazine*, July 7, 2011.

Tanser, Toby. *Train Hard, Win Easy: The Kenyan Way*. Mountain View, California: Track and Field News Press, June 1, 1997.

Tulloh, Bruce. "Distance Runners: Running Is a Poor Man's Sport." *Peak Performance Online*, October 2007. http://bit.ly/2fuy6gS

Turrini, Joseph M. *The End of Amateurism in American Track and Field*. Urbana: University of Illinois Press, 2010.

Vigil, Joe I. "The Anatomy of a Medal." *Peak Running Performance*, November 2005.

Wirz, Jürg. *Paul Tergat: Running to the Limit: His Life and His Training Secrets, with Many Tips for Runners*. Meyer and Meyer Verlag, 2005.

Chapter 16: The 2000s

Adamson, John W. "The Story of Erythropoietin." *50 Years in Hematology, Research that Revolutionized Patient Care*. The American Society of Hematology, December 2008. http://bit.ly/2fwNfJl.

Big-12 Sports Release. "CU Men Claim NCAA Title." November 5, 2002.

Bloom, Marc. "Running; A Freshman Has Learned to Go the Distance." *The New York Times*, October 27, 2001.

Boylan-Pett, Liam. "Throwback Thursday: Chris Derrick." *Running Times Magazine Web Exclusive*, September 5, 2013.

Burfoot, Amby. "Feb. 10: German Fernandez Is Moving Well And Moving Up." *Runner's World Magazine*, February 10, 2009.

———."The Turning Point." *Runner's World Magazine*, January 2011.

Bush, Scott. "Best of the West: Hasay 3-Peats, Fernandez Shows Strength." *MileSplit USA*, December 1, 2007.

———. "Chris Derrick's MileSplit Journal." *MileSplit USA*, October 10, 2007.

———. "Utah State Champs: Puskedra Breaks Course Record." *MileSplit USA*, October 18, 2007.

Caruana, Albert. "Artichoke Invitational Returns for 36th Year." *Cross-Country Express*, October 7, 2007. http://bit.ly/2f6Bht1.

Clarey, Christopher. "Negotiating a Difficult Course—a Golf Course—in the Hills of Amman." *New York Times*, March 28, 2009.

Cohen, Gary. "Interview with Shalane Flanagan." *Gary Cohen Running*, January 2015. http://bit.ly/2fomvw2.

Craven, Ryan. "Wisconsin Cross-Country: A Study in Pressure." *Flotrack, FloSports Inc*. November 15, 2011.

DeBoard, Will. "He's Just Running the Show." *Modesto Bee*, October 4, 2007.

Estes, Jim. "Team USA Scores Three Top-Five Team Finishes at 37th IAAF World Cross Country Championships." *USA Track and Field*, March 28, 2009.

Flotrack, FloSports Inc. "Colorado: The Program." November 2014.

Gains, Paul. "Kenenisa Bekele, Heir to the Throne." *Running Times Magazine*, September 1, 2003.

Galvin, John. "The Hansons-Brooks Distance Project." *Runner's World Magazine*, June 27, 2007.

Hunter, Dave. "Galen Rupp's Other Coach, Dave Frank Achieves Success, Finds Contentment." *RunBlogRun*, September 21, 2012.

———. "Perched On High Ground, Terre Haute Realizes Aspiration As Cross-Country Mecca." *RunBlogRun*, September 10, 2013.

Johnson, Robert. "An Analysis of German Fernandez's Medal Prospects in the Boys Junior Race." *LetsRun.com*, March 25, 2009.

Lawton, Matt. "How Nike Lured Mo Farah to Work with Coach Alberto Salazar in Oregon." *Daily Mail Online*, June 12, 2015.

Layden, Tim. "Ready to Take On The World." *Sports Illustrated*, March 21, 2005.

LetsRun.com. "2007 Footlocker Quick Boys Recap: Midwest Champ Michael Fout Wins." December 8, 2007.

———. "2008 NCAA Men's Cross-Country Championship Preview." November 20, 2008.

Maloney, Andrew. *John McDonnell: The Most Successful Coach in NCAA History*. University of Arkansas Press, April 2013.

Negash, Elshadai. "Bekele Quietly Confident as Title Defense Approaches." *IAAF General News*, August 23, 2007.

———. "Raising Champion Crops." *Running Times Magazine*, May 1, 2005.

NoBlood Inc. "Erythropoietin (EPO)." 1996. http://bit.ly/2eeRFZh.

Patrick, Dick. "Drossin Maps Road to Success." *USA Today*, October 2, 2002.

Running Times Magazine. "Catching Up with Tirunesh Dibaba." August 15, 2012.

Sproll, Ingrid. "Interview with Simon Bairu." *Trackie Inc. Canada*, November 2006.

Squire, Jesse. "Great Cross-Country Courses: Lavern Gibson." *Track and Field Superfan*, October 22, 2012. http://bit.ly/2f6gTbu.

Stark, Rachel. "Terre Haute's Famous Course Hosts NCAA Cross-Country." *Running Times Magazine*, November 19, 2013.

Sturtz, Rachel. "The Education of Jordan Hasay." *Running Times Magazine*, May 2, 2013.

Sutton, Alan. "Derrick's Fast Finish Nabs 2nd at Nationals." *Chicago Tribune*, December 9, 2007.

Taylor, Aron. "Luke Puskedra: Just Letting it Happen." *LetsRun Message Board*, November 23, 2010. http://bit.ly/2fHPChI.

———. "The Age of Nike Cross Nationals, The Golden Era of Prep XC." *RunnerSpace Media*, November 26, 2013.

Turnbull, Simon. "Tadese is the Wheel Deal." *Independent*, March 29, 2008.

Turner, Chris. "Destination Amman." *IAAF General News*, March 28, 2009.

USA Track and Field via the IAAF. "Fernandez, the Ace in the USA's Junior Pack for Amman." March 18, 2009.

Watts, Daniel. "Fernandez Set to Continue Dominant Campaign." *O'Colly*, March 25, 2009.

Young, Christine. "Runner Leads the Nation, Breaks His Own Record." *Intermountain Catholic*, June 6, 2008.

Chapter 17: The 2010s

Aisi, Anthony, and Eric Akasa. "The Doping Crisis Among Kenyan Athletes." *Destination Magazine*, October 2014.

Binder, Doug. "Bill Aris Reflects on Achievement of 2014 NXN Sweep." *DyeStat*, January 3, 2015.

Branch, John. "Two Hopi Traditions: Running and Winning." *New York Times*, November 4, 2015.

Carlisle, Jim. "Baxter's Record Run at Mt. SAC is a True Crowd Pleaser." *Ventura County Star*, October 23, 2012.

Cohen, Gary. "Interview with Shalane Flanagan." *Gary Cohen Running*, January 2015. http://bit.ly/2fomvw2.

Courage, Jane. "Understanding Uli." *Running Times Magazine*, November 1, 2003.

Flotrack, FloSports Inc. "Colorado: The Program." November 2014.

Gugala, Jon. "Elliott and Garrett Heath's Family Legacy at Stanford." *Running Times Magazine*, March 30, 2011.

Heald, Michael. "Edward Cheserek: Setting the Record Straight." *Running Times Magazine*, September 14, 2015.

Henderson, Jason. "World Cross Set to be No Man's Land for Brits: Policy to Only Take Senior Athletes with Top 30 Potential to the 2015 World Cross is Short-Sighted and Defeatist." *Athletics Weekly*, September 26, 2014.

Hersh, Philip. "Good for the Long Run." *Chicago Tribune*, October 26, 2012.

Horka, Tyler. "Craig Lutz Sets Sights on Making 2016 Olympic Trials." *Daily Texan*, November 2, 2015.

Hutson, Stephanie. "Exclusive Interview with Lukas Verzbicas." *Triathlon Trails of Miles Blog*, January 1, 2013. http://bit.ly/2vGLh4Y

Kastoff, Mitch. "The Fab Four Freshman of 2008 and Cheserek, McGorty, Saarel, and Leingang." *Flotrack, FloSports Inc.*, October 23, 2013.

La Parry, Anthony. "Al Carius Celebrates 50 Years of Coaching." *North Central College Linked*, October 27, 2015.

LetsRun.com. "Chris Derrick Wins 2013 US Cross-Country Title." February 2, 2013.

Merca, Paul. "Sara Hall leads Team USA at the IAAF World Cross Country Championships." *USA Track and Field*, March 28, 2015.

Mills, Steven. "Kamworor Maintains His Perfect Championship Record In Guiyang." *IAAF General News*, March 28, 2015.

Moore, Kenny. "XC: The Greatest Show On Turf." *Competitor Magazine*, February 3, 2015.

Okoth, Omulo. "EXPORTING EXPERTISE: Ngugi Inspiring Britain's Next Generation at Founding Home of Cross-Country." *Standard Digital*, October 18, 2014.

Parent, Marc. "Running Pains Hurt So Good." *Runner's World Magazine*, April 15, 2013.

Patrick, Dick. "Why a Top High School Coach Was Fired." *Runner's World Magazine*, June 27, 2013.

Plaschke, Bill. "Sarah Baxter Doesn't Know How to Lose." *Los Angeles Times*, December 6, 2012.

Robinson, Roger. "Roger on Running: Running Old and New." *Running Times Magazine*, September 21, 2011.

Shryack, Lincoln. "Three-Peat! Garrett Heath Takes Down Farah At Great Edinburgh XCountry." *Flotrack, FloSports Inc.*, January 9, 2016.

Steinberg, Emily. "10,000 Austin Kids Kick Off Marathon Kids Challenge at UT." *Marathon Kids*, August 20, 2014.

Taylor, Aron. "Stotan: The Secret of Fayettville Manlius." *RunnerSpace Media*, September 23, 2013.

USA Track and Field. "Flanagan, Derrick Claim USA Cross-Country Titles." February 2, 2013.

Waindi, James. "Future of Cross-Country Threatened." *Standard Media, Kenya*, April 8, 2009.

Weil, Elizabeth. "Mary Cain Is Growing Up Fast." *New York Times*, March 4, 2015.

Weldon, Nick. "USATF Versus Its Critics: Who's Off Track?" *Runner's World Magazine*, February 7, 2015.

Conclusion

Beresini, Erin. *Off Course: Inside the Muddy World of Obstacle Course Racing*. Mariner Books, January 1, 2014.

GreatRunTV. "Seb Coe—Cross-Country Could Be in Winter Olympic Programme." January 8, 2015. http://bit.ly/2fPlQrd.

New York: Seven Seas Cinema Inc. "Discovery! The Spirit of Cross-Country Running." 1984. http://bit.ly/2fFn8jp.

Robinson, Roger. "Imagining A Future for Cross-Country." *Running Times Magazine*, February 19, 2014.

Rowbottom, Mike. "Exclusive: Innovative Plans Detailed by Aarhus 2019 Organisers to Get Cross Country Back at Olympics." *Inside the Games*, March 24, 2017.

Sammet, Michelle. "IAAF Ambassador Sonia O'Sullivan is a Committed Cross-Country Fan." *IAAF General News*, March 27, 2015.

Vigneron, Peter. "Outkicked: Who Cares About Cross-Country?" *Competitor Magazine*, March 22, 2013.

Index

Stewart, Ian, 115, 135, 136, 223
Story, Dale, 95, 96, 104
Suburban Harriers, The, 21, 24, 28, 29
Swedish National Cross-Country Championship, The, 39, 73
Swiss National Cross-Country Championship, The, 39

TAC/The Athletics Congress (organization), 116, 145–147, 161, 168, 177, 178
Tadese, Zerisenay, 227, 228, 231
Tegenkamp, Matt, 204, 208, 212, 218, 219, 234, 239, 263, 266
Tergat, Paul, 66, 171, 173, 175, 176, 195, 224, 227, 258, 267, 271, 274
Terra Haute, Indiana (location), 202, 203
Thames Hare and Hounds, The, 3, 6, 8–13, 15–17, 19, 20, 33, 44, 59, 72, 75–78, 81, 141
Thomas, Bobby, 118, 119, 149
Tijou, Noël, 135, 139, 160
Timing Systems, 141, 143
Title IX, 124, 125, 162
Tom Brown's Schooldays (book), 2, 3, 9, 19, 44
Torrence, David, 274, 275
Track and Field (sport), xv, 7, 13–15, 20, 21, 23, 28, 37, 54, 60, 63, 65, 90, 93, 94, 115, 116, 126, 131–133, 143, 146, 147, 153, 174, 181, 217, 221, 245, 252, 259, 271, 273, 274
Track Spikes (shoes), 115, 142
Treacy, John, 118, 128, 135, 136, 145
Trevelyan, George Macaulay, 33, 34
True, Ben, 240, 266–269
Tulu, Derartu, 183, 197, 229, 231
Tunisian National Cross-Country Championship, The, 47, 66, 84

University of Arkansas, The, 163–166, 171, 180, 181, 186–191, 194, 195, 205, 208, 232–234, 237
University of Colorado, The, 171, 189–193, 195, 200, 204–208, 218, 232–234, 237, 238, 240, 257, 266
University of Oregon, The, 93, 103, 104, 106–110, 112, 121, 128, 213, 215–217, 221, 252, 253, 256
University of Wisconsin, The, 78, 163–166, 187, 189, 192, 194, 204, 206, 208, 209, 218–220, 234, 236, 238
USATF/USA Track and Field (organization), 94, 178, 179, 211, 215–217, 244, 245, 247, 253, 254, 272, 273
USTFF, The (organization)/The United States Track and Field Federation, 93, 94, 98, 112, 125
UTEP/University of Texas–El Paso, The, 104, 105, 108, 110, 129–131, 163, 164, 187, 206, 237

Vail, Ryan, 237, 240, 242, 266–269
Van Cortlandt Park, 50, 51, 57, 72, 80, 92, 103, 104, 113, 179, 250, 253, 273
VandeWattyne, Marcel, 70, 71, 75, 84, 99
Vasala, Pekka, 66
Vaughn, Brent, 207, 208

Vernon, Andy, 262, 263
Vernon, Steve, 262, 263
Verzbicas, Lukas, 245, 248, 251–254
Vigil, Joe, 145, 181, 193, 194
Villanova University, 80, 92, 96, 97, 104, 105, 108, 183, 185, 186, 190, 195, 234, 237
Viren, Lasse, 66, 249
Virgin, Craig, xi, xii, xiii, 108, 110, 117, 120, 121, 127–129, 132, 145, 149, 150, 152, 153, 166, 168, 177, 213

Waitz, Grete, 66, 137, 138, 160, 161, 169, 170
Walker, John, 66, 115, 137, 274
Wallach, George, 48
Wami, Getenesh "Gete", 183, 184
Webb, Alan, 199–202, 204, 209, 211, 212, 215, 232, 234
Weissteiner, Silvia, 261
Westchester Hare and Hounds, The, 13, 15, 23, 141
Wetmore, Mark, 190–193, 200, 204, 205, 207, 208, 232–234, 237, 238
Wide, Edvin, 56
Williams, Kerry, 80
Williams, Todd, 179, 180, 192, 197, 222
Wilt, Fred, 72, 73, 76, 78
Wimbledon Common, 6–8, 11, 12, 16, 20, 59, 72, 77
Wolde, Mamo, 88–90, 133
Women's Cross-Country Championships, 38, 60, 61, 84, 94, 95, 114, 125, 126, 145, 161, 162, 169, 178, 179, 183, 185, 188, 196, 206, 207, 209–211, 216, 241, 242
World Cross-Country Championships (IAAF), The, 115, 119, 127, 133, 135, 137–140, 149, 150, 152–154, 156–162, 168–170, 172–175, 181–185, 196, 197, 209, 210, 212, 214, 215, 218, 224–227, 229–231, 240–244, 260–264, 266–274
1973, 133, 139, 140
1975, 115, 137
1980, 150, 161
1981, 150, 153, 161
1982, 161
1983, 162, 168–170
1984, 157, 159
1985, 157, 160, 162
1992, 180, 196, 197
1993, 172, 197
2000, 224
2001, 224, 225, 228
2004, 228, 229
2011, 241, 262
2013, 241, 262, 266–270
2015, 241, 242
World University Cross-Country Championships (FISU), The, 138, 263

York High School, 102, 221, 246, 250

Zátopek, Emil, 70, 73, 75–77, 86, 87, 89, 101, 127, 128
Zienasellassie, Futsum, 248